REPORTING VIETNAM

AMERICAN JOURNALISM 1959–1975

Introduction by Ward Just

THE LIBRARY OF AMERICA

The material in this volume is reprinted with permission of
the holders of copyright and publication rights.
Acknowledgments are on pages 808–12.

Distributed to the trade in the United States
by Penguin Putnam Inc.
and in Canada by Penguin Books Canada Ltd.

Library of Congress Catalog Number: 99–059744
For cataloging information, see end of Index.

ISBN 1–883011–90–6

Text design by Bruce Campbell.
Cover design by R. D. Scudellari.
Calligraphy by Gun Larson.

Cover photo: Neil Sheehan, by François Sully; courtesy Archives and
Special Collections, Healey Library, University of Massachusetts/Boston.

This one-volume selection is drawn from *Reporting Vietnam*,
a two-volume hardcover set published by
The Library of America in 1998.

Manufactured in the United States of America

Advisory board for *Reporting Vietnam*

Contents

Foreword

FOR many Americans, the Vietnam War can be summed up in a handful of images: GIs setting thatched roofs on fire with Zippo lighters, a police general executing a Viet Cong suspect on a street in Saigon, a tank evacuating wounded marines from Hue, a naked Vietnamese girl fleeing her village after a napalm strike, American helicopters dropping from the deck of a ship into the South China Sea. A quarter of a century after the war, we can almost persuade ourselves that we witnessed these events at first hand, unmediated by the camera. Their authenticity, hence their authority, appears beyond question. The first two, in particular, helped to change the course of the war by contradicting the official news briefings held each afternoon in Saigon. How could the Five O'Clock Follies contend with pictures worth a thousand words apiece? Or newsreel footage worth over a million words per minute?

Yet, for all their eloquence, these images are ultimately inscrutable. "We will show you everything," they seem to say. "We will show you more than you can bear to see. But don't ask us what we mean."

Meaning depends on relation, the relation of one event to another in a sequential or causal chain. This kind of meaning has traditionally been the province of the story, a term broad enough to embrace myth, history, fiction, and yes, war journalism. Although Vietnam was a technologically advanced war, in the pressroom as well as in the field, its depths had to be sounded with an ancient medium. Whether they regarded themselves as traditional or "new" journalists, the men and women who reported Vietnam used storytelling techniques that were familiar to Homer and Herodotus.

Like all storytellers, war journalists must decide where to open and close their stories, which characters and events to emphasize, which details of setting to describe, and—most important—what to make of it all. Each of the 61 selections in this volume has its own narrative integrity. Yet the collection is more than the sum of its parts, for the separate stories coalesce into subplots of a larger narrative. One subplot reports the fighting at ground level, the old story of men killing men because they were ordered to do so. Another tells a tale of mutual seduction and betrayal, the diplomatic romance between the world's most powerful nation and a small Asian country. Another recounts the struggle of the other side, the North Vietnamese civilian population and the enemy soldiers whom we knew as the North Vietnamese Army and as the Viet Cong. Yet another follows the domestic conflicts we took to Vietnam, with battle lines drawn according to race, class, generation, and moral conviction.

Taken together, the selections in this volume trace the rising action of the big story from July 1959 to its climax in the Tet Offensive of late January 1968, then follow its decline until the last helicopter lifted off the roof of the U.S. Embassy in April 1975. The story's beginning and ending are of course arbitrary. What we call the Vietnam War—what the Vietnamese just as logically call the American War—began long before the first American advisers were killed in 1959, and for many participants it has yet to end. *Reporting Vietnam* nevertheless provides a coherent and compelling account of 16 crucial years. Borrowing a phrase from Norman Mailer's *The Armies of the Night*, we might call the result a "collective novel" of history.

The collective novel, like the camera, converts the raw material of history into another medium. Both convey the slaughter and mayhem of war in ways that may haunt us for the rest of our lives. The more deeply events are embedded in story, however, the more they can tell us about past mistakes and future challenges. If we are to understand events and not merely react to them viscerally, we will continue to need the narrative skills of writers like the men and women who reported the Vietnam War. What they covered then, often at great personal risk, they help us to recover today.

MILTON J. BATES

Introduction

by Ward Just

THESE 61 pieces are selected from the 106 originally published in two volumes in 1998 by The Library of America as *Reporting Vietnam: American Journalism 1959–1975*. It would be misleading to describe this anthology as "The Best Of . . ." The quality was so high in the original volumes that the most that can be hoped for here is a good-faith effort at a representative sample, the shape and trajectory of things over 16 years of war as seen in American newspapers and magazines. So why do it? The objective is to put a moderately priced paperback within reach of the widest possible audience, particularly students. The war ended 25 years ago but it is not done with, and anyone seeking answers to why, and why so long, could do much, much worse than begin right here.

The war, like any important corporate activity, was widely diversified, even multinational. So the datelines include countries like Laos and Cambodia, and cities like Washington, Miami, and Kent in Ohio, along with Khe Sanh, Dak To, Hue, Saigon, and Hanoi. There are pieces on politics and protest, profiles of notables, and glimpses into the world of the enemy, together with more traditional battlefield reportage—and there was much that was traditional about the war, including the reporting of it. Vietnam was the last war in which American military authorities willingly transported reporters into battle. All you had to do was show up on the flight line at Tan Son Nhut, hail a C-130 or a Caribou, and climb aboard. When you arrived at the command post you were briefed, pointed in the direction of the gunfire, and then left alone to do your work. In the field you often filed over military telephone lines. There was never any censorship except self-censorship, an ethical matter that varied with the reporter.

The contributors are—or were, many have passed away—professional writers, mainly journalists, historians, and novelists. Connoisseurs of style will find it worthwhile to compare the work of Norman Mailer and Mary McCarthy, Mailer at the Pentagon and McCarthy in Hanoi, and then to set both alongside career war correspondents like Homer Bigart and Jonathan Randal. The novelists work in leisure, the reporters in haste. For the novelists, facts are elastic; for the reporters, they are graven in stone. Think of them as circus performers, the free flight of the acrobat on the high wire opposed to the scrupulous authority of the lion tamer in the cage. Two non-writers are Air Force Captain Jerry Shank and Lieutenant Commander (now United States Senator) John S. McCain III. What their prose lacks in craft, it more than makes up for in the raw emotion of eyewitness.

I am tempted to suggest that the reader open this book at random and begin, a tourist wandering through the ruins of a defunct civilization. But since one thing always leads to another, the reader might want to begin at the beginning—two pages from *Time* magazine, "First U.S. Advisers Killed In South Vietnam: July 1959." This report would not have been composed the same way in a later year. It's a period piece: the evening movie, stealthy Viet Cong sappers, sudden gunfire, American troopers dying, and the South Vietnamese infantry arriving late. The story became so commonplace later on that it virtually defined the war. The attentive reader will discover a number of these pieces—new-minted at the moment, and then suddenly worn with use. There's an awful poignance to these dispatches and a foreboding, too, because we know the outcome.

Journalism is not prophecy. It is strongest when it arrives at the unexpected and modestly sticks to the facts. At its best, war correspondence resembles description of an artist's erratic progress, his destination only dimly seen. Too bad for you if you happen upon the master in his conflicted middle age, and alarming because you knew him in his uncomplicated youth. What precisely does this picture mean? The war in Vietnam unfolded in this way, a perverse logic of its own, apprentice-ship followed by a blue period followed by Cubism followed by—I believe the word is derangement. Much of the battle-field reportage belongs to the early and middle periods. Alter the language, make the necessary transpositions, and you could be reading a dispatch from Antietam or First Marne.

Then, in 1968, the canvas turns anarchic, lawless in a physical sense. Read Michael Herr. Read the accounts of the last days of Saigon. Read in sequence or read helter-skelter, the effect is something like coming upon "Guernica" for the first time.

West Tisbury, Massachusetts
November, 1999

Death at Intermission Time

IT WAS a quiet evening in the sleepy little town of Bien Hoa 20 miles north of Saigon, base camp for the South Vietnamese crack 7th Infantry Division and its eight-man U.S. Military Assistance Advisory Group. The presence of the Americans symbolized one of the main reasons why South Viet Nam, five years ago a new nation with little life expectancy, is still independent and free and getting stronger all the time—to the growing chagrin of Communists in neighboring North Viet Nam. Since the beginning of 1959, Communist infiltrators have stepped up their campaign of terrorism, assassinating an average of one South Vietnamese a day, frequently hammering lonely victims to death and then hanging their battered bodies in trees under a red flag. But not since 1957 had the Communists dared attack any Americans.

In the residential compound where the eight Americans lived in Bien Hoa, Master Sergeant Chester Ovnand finished a letter to his wife in Copperas Cove, Texas and dropped it in the mess-hall mailbox. Major Dale Buis of Imperial Beach, Calif. had arrived in Bien Hoa only two days before and was showing his new friends pictures of his three young sons. Two of the officers drifted off to play tennis; the other six men decided to watch a Jeanne Crain movie, *The Tattered Dress*, on their home projector in the grey stucco mess hall. While they were absorbed in the first reel, six Communist terrorists (who obviously had cased the place well) crept out of the darkness and surrounded the mess hall. Two positioned a French MAT submachine gun in the rear window, two pushed gun muzzles through the pantry screen, the other two went to the front of the building to cover the Vietnamese guard. When Sergeant Ovnand snapped on the lights to change the first reel, the Communists opened fire.

In the first murderous hail of bullets, Ovnand and Major Buis fell and died within minutes. Captain Howard Boston of Blairsburg, Iowa was seriously wounded, and two Vietnamese guards were killed. Trapped in a crossfire, all six might have died had not Major Jack Hellet of Baton Rouge leaped across the room to turn out the lights—and had not one of the terrorists who tried to throw a homemade bomb into the room miscalculated and blown himself up instead. Within minutes Vietnamese troops arrived, but the rest of the assassins had already fled.

Time, July 20, 1959

Paddy War

by Malcolm W. Browne

A DRENCHING, predawn dew had settled over the sloping steel deck of the landing craft, and I slipped several times climbing aboard in the inky darkness.

Soldiers cursed sleepily as they heaved heavy mortar base plates and machine guns from the pier onto their field packs on the deck.

The night was still and moonless, and the air would have been warm except for that unpleasant dew, sometimes laced with raindrops. The French used to call it "spitting rain."

This was December, 1961, and I was going out for my first look at an operation against the Viet Cong. There were no American field advisors in those days (and no helicopters and almost no communications), and I tried to stay close to soldiers or officers who could speak French. Most of them could.

The place was a town called Ben Tre in the heart of the flat, fertile Mekong River Delta, about fifty miles south of Saigon. Ben Tre, the capital of Kien Hoa Province, still takes pride in the fact that it has produced some of Viet Nam's top Communists. Ung Van Khiem, former Foreign Minister of the Hanoi government, came from here. Kien Hoa is also famous for its pretty girls.

It was about 4 A.M., and I was dead tired. I had been up late with the province chief, Colonel Pham Ngoc Thao, a cat-like man with short-cropped hair and a disconcerting walleye.

Thao had been an intelligence officer in the Viet Minh during the Indochina War, and had gone over to Diem after independence in 1954.

The night before, Thao had invited me to the opening of a theater he had had built in Ben Tre, and the curious town residents had turned out in their holiday best. The bill of fare was a traditional Vietnamese drama and some comedians, jugglers and singers. It lacked the glamour of a Broadway opening night, but it was about the fanciest thing Ben Tre had ever seen.

Two masked actors in ornate classical costume were intoning verses about a murder they were planning and the audience was murmuring expectantly when Thao leaned toward me.

"My troops are going out in the morning. We have intelligence that a battalion of Viet Cong is moving through one of my districts. I'm not going, but would you be interested?"

Just then, the action on stage reached a high point. Several actors in stilted, oriental poses were supposed to portray violence, their brilliantly colored robes swishing. Applause rushed through the theater, and children put down their pop bottles to chatter. Thao, obviously pleased, warmly joined the applause.

He always liked the theater. A year or so later, when Diem sent him on a special mission to the States, he made a special point of visiting Hollywood, where he was photographed with actress Sandra Dee. The picture was sent back to Viet Nam by news agencies, but Diem's censors prohibited its publication, presumably because they felt it would be detrimental to fighting spirit.

The 300 or so troops on the pier that morning were an odd-looking bunch, a mixture of civil guards and self-defense corpsmen. Some were in neat fatigue uniforms with helmets, others in the loose, black garb of the Vietnamese peasant, topped with old French bush hats. There were no troops from the regular army on this operation. The commander was a crusty, French-trained captain with several rows of combat ribbons on his faded olive drab uniform.

The diesel engines of the three landing craft carrying our makeshift task force belched oily smoke and we were moving, the black silhouettes of palm trees sliding past along the edges of the narrow canal. Here and there a dot of light glimmered through the trees from some concealed cluster of huts.

For a few minutes, the commander studied a map with a neat plastic overlay, making marks with red and black grease pencils, under the light of a pocket flashlight.

One of the few things Western military men have taught

Vietnamese officers to do really well is mark up maps. The Vietnamese officer studies his sector map like a chessboard. Even if he has only a squad or two of men under his command, he uses all the ornate symbols of the field commander in marking his deployment on maps. This love of maps has often infuriated American advisors, who feel more time should be spent acting and less on planning.

After a while the light flicked out. A few of the troops were smoking silently, but most had arranged their field packs as pillows and had gone to sleep amid the clutter of weapons. We were not scheduled to reach our objective until several hours after sunrise.

I finally dropped off to sleep, and must have been asleep about an hour when a grinding lurch and the sound of splintering wood roused me.

It was still pitch dark, but people were screaming, and on the deck of the landing craft, troops were rushing around. In the darkness, we had somehow collided with and sunk a large, crowded sampan. Twenty or thirty sleeping occupants had been thrown into the canal, with all their worldly possessions. A few of them apparently were hurt.

The two other landing craft were chugging on down the canal, but we had stopped. Troops holding ropes were helping swing the people in the water over to the shore. When everyone had reached safety, we started up again, people still yelling at us in the distance. We must have destituted several large families at a blow, but there was no thought of getting their names so that they could be compensated by the government. I couldn't help feeling that their feelings for the government must be less than cordial.

The sky began to turn gray, and at last we left the maze of narrow canals and turned into a branch of the great Mekong itself.

The sun rose hot and red, its reflection glaring from the sluggish expanse of muddy water. We were moving slowly ("We don't want to make too much engine noise or the Viet Cong will hear us coming," the commander told me), and the dense wall of palm trees on both banks scarcely seemed to move at all.

It was nearly 9 A.M. when our little flotilla abruptly turned at right angles to the left, each vessel gunning its engines. We had reached the objective and were charging in for the beach. As we neared the shore we could see that the beach actually was a mud flat leading back about fifty yards to the palm trees, and it would be arduous hiking getting ashore.

The other two landing craft were going ashore about one mile farther up the river. The idea of this exercise, it was explained to me, was to seize two sets of hamlets running back from the river front, trapping the reported Viet Cong battalion in the wide expanse of rice fields in between.

We slammed into the mud, and the prow of our clumsy ship clanked down to form a ramp. We leapt into waist-deep water and mud and began the charge toward higher ground.

If the Viet Cong had even one machine gun somewhere in the tree line, they certainly could have killed most of us with no danger of encountering serious fire from us. Each step in that smelly ooze was agonizingly slow, and at times both feet would get mired. Little soldiers carrying heavy mortars and machine guns sank nearly to their necks. It happened that no one was shooting at us that day.

The first squads clambered up to high ground and began firing. Two light machine guns began thumping tracers across the open rice field, and mortars began lobbing shells at random. Individual soldiers with Tommy guns (I was surprised how many of our group were equipped with submachine guns) were emptying their magazines into a string of huts or into the field. Off a mile or so to our right, noises told us that our companion party was similarly employed. It really sounded like a war.

I was standing on a high path running parallel to the river near a machine-gun position, looking out over the field where our Viet Cong battalion was supposed to be trapped. The green rice was nearly waist high, and there might easily be a battalion concealed in this field for all anyone knew.

Suddenly, a man leapt up about fifty yards away and began to run. This was it!

Every machine gun, Tommy gun, rifle and pistol in our sector poured fire at that man, and I was amazed at how long he continued to run. But finally he went down, silently, without a scream.

Our little army continued to pour intense fire into the field and several huts until it occurred to someone that no one was shooting back, and it might be safe to move forward a little.

Some of the troops began to move into the huts, shooting as they went.

Near me was a cluster of five Dan Ve (local Self-Defense Corpsmen) dressed in ragged black uniforms with American pistol belts and rusty French rifles. The group was detailed to go into the field to look for the man we had seen go down, and I went with them.

We found him on his back in the mud, four bullet holes stitched across the top of his naked chest. He was wearing only black shorts. He was alive and conscious, moving his legs and arms, his head lolling back and forth. There was blood on his lips.

The Dan Ve squad, all young peasant boys, looked down at the man and laughed, perhaps in embarrassment. Laughter in Viet Nam does not always signify amusement.

Perhaps as an act of mercy, perhaps as sheer cruelty, one of the men picked up a heavy stake lying in the mud and rammed one end of it into the ground next to the wounded man's throat. Then he forced the stake down over the throat, trying to throttle the man. The man continued to move. Someone stamped on the free end of the stake to break the wounded man's neck, but the stake broke instead. Then another man tried stamping on the man's throat, but somehow the spark of life still was too strong. Finally, the whole group laughed, and walked back to the path.

The firing had stopped altogether, and several old peasant men were talking to the officers of our party. Two of the old men had a pole and a large fish net.

The peasants—I think they were hamlet elders—walked out to the wounded man, rolled him into the fish net, and with the net slung between them on the pole, carried him back to the path. As they laid him out on the ground, two women, both dressed in baggy black trousers and blouses, ran up from one of the huts. One of them put a hand to her mouth as she saw the wounded man, whom she recognized as her husband.

She dashed back to her hut and returned in a moment carrying a bucket, which she filled with black water from the rice field. Sitting down with her husband's head cradled in her lap, she poured paddy water over his wounds to clean off the clotting blood. Occasionally she would stroke his forehead, muttering something.

He died about ten minutes later. The woman remained seated, one hand over her husband's eyes. Slowly, she looked around at the troops, and then she spotted me. Her eyes fixed on me in an expression that still haunts me sometimes. She was not weeping, and her face showed neither grief nor fury; it was unfathomably blank.

I moved away some distance to where the operation commander was jabbering into a field telephone. When his conversation ended, I handed him a 500-piastre note (worth about $5.00), asking him to give it to the widow as some small compensation.

"Monsieur Browne, please do not be sentimental. That man undoubtedly was a Viet Cong agent, since these hamlets have been Viet Cong strongholds for years. This is war. However, I will give her the money, if you like."

I don't know what happened to that money, and I didn't go near the place where the woman was sitting, but I walked into the hut I had seen her leave.

It was typical of thousands of Mekong Delta huts I have seen. The framework was bamboo, and the sides and roof were made of dried, interlaced palm fronds with a layer of rice straw thatch on top. The floor was hardened earth. A large, highly polished wooden table stood near the door. Peasants eat their meals on these tables, sleep on them and work on them. There were four austerely simple chairs. In a corner were several knee-high earthen crocks filled with drinking water. Just inside the door was the family altar, extending all the way to the ceiling. Pinned to it were yellowed photographs and some fancy Chinese calligraphy. On a little shelf a sand pot containing incense sticks smoldered fragrant fumes.

To the right, from behind a woven bamboo curtain, two children were peering with wide eyes. The eyes were the only expressive elements in their blank, silent little faces. Incongruously, one of them was standing next to a gaily painted yellow rocking horse, one rocker of which was freshly splintered by a bullet hole.

I walked out of the hut and down the path. By now, troops were strung all along the path between the two hamlets about a mile apart, and were stringing telephone wire and performing other military chores.

Snaking through the palm trees, a water-filled ditch about twenty feet across obstructed my progress. But a few yards away, a soldier had commandeered a small sampan from an old woman and was ferrying troops back and forth. I went across with him. As I continued down the path, scores of mud walls about five feet high obstructed progress. All were obviously freshly built, and most had gun slots. It was strange that no one had decided to defend these good emplacements against us.

I came to a small hut straddling the path, consisting only of upright bamboo spars and a roof. The little building was festooned with painted banners, the largest of which read *"Da Dao My-Diem"* ("Down with U.S.-Diem"). A group of young women were dismantling the hut as soldiers trained rifles at them. I was told that this was a Viet Cong "information center."

Finally, the troops began moving out from the tree line into the field itself, converging from three sides: the two hamlets and the path itself. The battle would come now, if ever.

We moved single file along the tops of the dykes that divided the field into an immense checkerboard. The thought struck me that if there were guerrillas hiding in the tall rice we would make fine targets as we moved along, but no one seemed worried.

Progress was slow. The mud dykes were slippery as grease, and every time a soldier toppled into the muddy paddy, the whole column halted as he was pulled out. I was reminded somehow of the White Knight in Lewis Carroll's *Through the Looking Glass.* Superficially, we combed the field from one end to the other, our various forces finally meeting in the middle.

A little L19 spotter plane droned overhead, radioing what was no doubt useful information to the ground commander.

It would be difficult to search that field more completely than we did, and we found not the slightest trace of a human being. Of course, the rice could easily have concealed a thousand or even ten thousand guerrillas, without our knowing.

Viet Cong guerrillas have developed the art of camouflage to an incredible degree. In rice fields, they often remain completely submerged under the muddy water for hours, breathing through straws.

But by now the sun stood like a blast furnace in the sky, and the troops were tired. A few had tied to their packs live ducks and chickens they had pilfered from the hamlets, and were looking around for level ground on which to prepare lunch.

"It looks as though the Viet Cong got away again," the commander told me. "It's time to go. It's not a good idea to be moving around out here when the sun starts going down."

By noon, 300 mud-drenched, tired troops were boarding the landing craft, and silence had settled over the hamlets again. We had suffered one wounded—a Civil Guard who had stepped on a spike trap, which had pierced his foot.

The three landing craft churned their way out into deep water, and the tension disappeared. Soldiers lighted cigarettes, talked and laughed, and spread their sopping clothing on the deck to dry.

All of them had a warm feeling of accomplishment, of having done a hard day's work under the cruel sun. The irregularity in the palm-lined shore that marked our hamlet receded into the distance.

And I couldn't help thinking of the old travelogues that end, "And so we leave the picturesque Mekong River Delta, palm trees glimmering under a tropic sun, and happy natives on the shore bidding us 'aloha.'"

from *The New Face of War*, 1965

A *"Very Real War"* in Vietnam—
and the Deep U.S. Commitment

by Homer Bigart

SAIGON, Feb. 24—The United States is involved in a war in Vietnam. American troops will stay until victory.

That is what Attorney General Robert Kennedy said here last week. He called it "war . . . in a very real sense of the word." He said that President Kennedy had pledged that the United States would stand by South Vietnam's President Ngo Dinh Diem "until we win."

At the moment the war isn't going badly for "our" side. There is a lull in Viet Cong activities, and the South Vietnamese forces are both expanding and shaping up better as a fighting force. But all that is needed to precipitate a major war is for the Chinese Communists and Communist North Vietnam to react to a build-up of American forces.

American support to Vietnam has always been based on the fear that Communist control of this country would jeopardize all Southeast Asia. And it continues despite the fact that Diem's American critics—especially liberals repelled by the dictatorial aspects of his regime—have been predicting his imminent downfall.

Diem remains firmly in charge and Washington's support for his regime today seems more passionate and inflexible than ever.

Actually the United States has been deeply involved in the fate of Vietnam since 1949 when the decision was made to subsidize the continuation of French rule against the Communist Viet Minh rebellion. The first United States Military Assistance Advisory Group (M.A.A.G.) arrived in 1951 to supervise the distribution of supplies. Thereafter the United States played an increasingly important role. To use a favorite

Washington term, aid was "escalated" until today $2 billion has been sunk into Vietnam with no end to the outlay in sight.

This may sound more reckless than the best brinkmanship of John Foster Dulles' days, and perhaps it is. But the United States is on this particular faraway brink because the Kennedy Administration seems convinced that the Communists won't rise to the challenge of the American presence and assistance.

The battle in Vietnam currently involves some 300,000 armed South Vietnamese and 3,000 American servicemen on one side, against 18,000 to 25,000 Viet Cong Communist regulars operating as guerrillas.

The battle that is being fought is complex—in the nature of the fighting, in the internal political background and in its international implications.

The United States does not have any combat infantry troops in Vietnam as of now, but we are getting ready for that possibility. Marine Corps officers have completed ground reconnaissance in the central Vietnam highlands, a potential theater of large-scale action between American troops and Communist forces coming down from the north.

American combat troops are not likely to be thrown into Vietnam unless Communist North Vietnam moves across the seventeenth parallel or pushes large forces down through Laos into South Vietnam.

In that case the United States would have to move in fast. Forty miles below the frontier with North Vietnam and parallel to it is Highway 9. This road has high strategic importance. Not only is it one of the few adequate roads open across the mountains to the Laotian border but it extends across Laos to Savannakhet on the Mekong River frontier with Thailand. If Highway 9 could be held from the Mekong to the sea by American, Vietnamese, Laotian and Thai forces, South Vietnam might be saved.

The situation right now is far more stable than it was last September, when the Communists were attacking in battalion strength and were even able to seize and hold a provincial capital, Phuoc Vinh, for a few hours. The September action seemed a prelude to an all-out Communist drive to overturn the Diem Government. It precipitated the present flood of American military advisors and service troops.

Today American warships are helping the embryonic Vietnamese Navy to guard the sea frontier against infiltration from North Vietnam and U.S. Navy servicemen presently will arrive to help clean out guerrillas from the maze of tidal waterways in the Mekong River delta. The U.S. Army helicopter crews have come under fire taking Vietnamese combat troops into guerrilla zones or carrying pigs and other livestock to hungry outposts surrounded by hostile country. U.S. Air Force pilots have flown with Vietnamese pilots on bombing missions against reported enemy concentrations and against two frontier forts recently evacuated by the Vietnamese Army.

So far our contribution in blood has been small. One American sergeant has been killed by enemy action and another is missing and presumed captured. Inevitably our casualties will grow.

It has not been easy to change from conventional warfare, in which the Vietnamese were trained so many years by M.A.A.G., to unconventional counter-guerrilla warfare. Under French influence, the Vietnamese had developed two tendencies difficult to erase: first, the habit of staying inside forts designed for the troops' protection rather than for the security of the populace; second, the habit of good living—a leisurely lunch followed by a siesta.

But counter-guerilla warfare demands hard living. Troops must live in the jungle just as the guerrillas do and eschew the comforts of barracks life.

There are some minor difficulties: most Vietnamese recruits are from the densely populated lowlands—rice paddy boys who have a fear of the jungles, not merely fear of snakes and tigers but fear of getting lost. They move fearfully, with the instinct of a herd, tending to bunch up and thus present fat targets for a Viet Cong ambush.

The Viet Cong guerrillas also were former rice paddy boys, but they became inured to hardship by on-the-job training in the jungle. Further, the Vietnamese are somewhat smaller than Americans, so they get weary toting eleven-pound M1 rifles and pine for the lighter French weapons they were formerly equipped with.

At a higher level, United States advisors, besides trying to eliminate political manipulation of troops, are attempting to dissuade the Vietnamese from launching large-scale operations based on sketchy intelligence. They see no justification for such operations until a more adequate intelligence system is developed and greater tactical mobility achieved.

Intelligence will improve only when the Government is able to break the grip of fear with which the Viet Cong muzzles the rural population. Greater mobility is being provided by American helicopter companies, but this is a costly and dangerous way to move troops.

The man who is at the center of the Vietnamese effort and who is also a center of controversy—President Diem—is something of an enigma. He is a mandarin (an aristocrat) and a devout Catholic. So there are two strikes against him at the start, for mandarins were regarded by the masses as greedy and corrupt, and Catholics as an unpopular minority.

Diem, however, has proved incorruptible. Rumors of personal enrichment of members of his family have never been proved. And Diem has been careful not to arouse Buddhist hostility. He is a man of great personal courage, but he is suspicious and mistrustful. The creation of a central intelligence agency here was delayed for months until Diem found a director he could trust.

Diem, a 66-year-old bachelor, often has been accused of withdrawing inside his narrow family clique and divorcing himself from reality. Critics say he distrusts everyone except the family and takes advice only from his brothers, particularly Ngo Dinh Nhu, his political advisor. His brother Nhu and his attractive, influential wife, are leaders, according to critics, of a palace camarilla which tries to isolate the President from the people.

As commander-in-chief of the armed forces, Diem keeps close tabs on military operations. His personal representative on the General Staff is Brig. Gen. Nguyen Khanh who has appalled Americans by taking general reserve troops on quick one-shot operations without coordinating with the area commander. Khanh is young, vigorous and driving but, according to his critics, lacking balance and experience.

Lieut. Gen. Le Ven Ty is Chief of the General Staff but he is in his sixties and lacks vigor. Consequently much of the military direction comes from the President through Khanh.

It is well to remember that Diem has been right and the United States wrong on some crucial issues. In 1955, for example, Diem wanted to crush the powerful Binh Xuyen gangster sect that controlled both the police and the gambling dens and brothels and made a mockery of government authority. President Eisenhower's special ambassador, Gen. Lawton Collins, opposed Diem's plan fearing civil war. Diem coolly proceeded to assert his power and used loyal troops to crush the Binh Xuyen in sharp fighting in Saigon's streets.

More recently the United States resisted Diem's urgent requests for aid in the creation of the civil guard and self-defense corps. The United States insisted that a 190,000-man regular army was all Diem needed for national defense. Diem went ahead and organized the two forces, arming them with antiquated French rifles. Finally, after alarm bells were ringing to the widespread revival of Communist guerrilla activity and vast sections of the countryside were lost to the Viet Cong, the Americans conceded Diem's point. Last year the United States started training and equipping the civil guard.

It is now generally agreed that the civil guard and the self-defense corps are absolutely vital. For until these reserve forces are ready to take over the defense of villages, railroads, harbors, airports, provincial capitals and so on, the army will be so tied down to static defense duties that it will not have the manpower to chase guerrillas.

Last week, in another apparent concession to Diem's wisdom, the United States agreed that any relaxation of tight political controls would be dangerous now. In a speech cleared with the State Department, Ambassador Frederick E. Nolting Jr. urged Diem's critics to cease carping and try to improve the government from within.

Just how serious the criticism is is not clear and there seems to be no agreement among observers whether the President's popularity is rising or falling. One former Diem advisor said he was shocked by the loss of support among the people in the past two years. He blamed this on the fact that Government seemed to grope from crisis to crisis without a clear policy: "It's just anti-Communist and not pro anything."

But another qualified observer, perhaps less biased, cautioned against underrating Diem. Increased guerrilla activity had not been matched, he said, by a corresponding rise in popular discontent and this failure to respond must have depressed the Communists.

Most villages, he added, were like a leaf in the wind: "When the Viet Cong enters, the population turns pro-Communist; when the Government troops arrive, sentiment shifts to the Government." But generally the village people would settle for the Government side, he said, not because they admired the Government but because they wanted peace.

Consequently the Government has a great advantage. He estimated that of the 30 per cent tending to the Viet Cong, only a third were hard-core, another third would adhere to the Communists under adversity, while the remaining third would break off under pressure.

Freedom from dictatorship and freedom from foreign domination are major propaganda lines for the Viet Cong. Americans in uniform have now been seen by the peasants in virtually all sections of the country. This has given the Communists a chance to raise the bogey of foreign military domination.

The lack of trained troops to keep the Viet Cong under relentless pressure probably will continue to handicap the military command throughout 1962, because at least a year must elapse before the self-defense units will be really capable of defending their villages.

Whether because the Army is beginning to take the initiative and is penetrating secret areas of Viet Cong concentrations or because the Viet Cong has abated its activities in order to recruit and train, the fact remains that security seems better in most parts of Vietnam.

In peaceful, booming Saigon there is much speculation on how the Viet Cong will react to an American build-up. Senior American officers have been studying an enemy guide book to guerrilla warfare searching avidly for clues, as though this modest work were the Viet Cong's "Mein Kampf."

There will never be enough troops to seal off the frontiers. There aren't even enough troops to ring Viet Cong enclaves near Saigon. Not before summer, when the civil guard and self-defense units are slated to take over the burden of defending their villages will enough troops be freed for a counter-guerrilla offensive. Then, instead of a conventional setpiece offensive of limited duration, a counter-guerrilla drive will seek to keep Viet Cong units on the run at all times, tire them out by constant pressure and force them into less hospitable country where food supplies are scarce.

The offensive cannot succeed unless the Government is able to mobilize positive popular support. This will be difficult, for the Government is just beginning to develop grass roots political cadres.

Meanwhile something more than narrowly anti-Communist goals must be offered Saigon intellectuals, who are now scorned by both Diem and the Americans. This group may be permanently alienated unless there is promise of democratic reforms. Without pressure from Washington, there is not likely to be any relaxation of Diem's personal dictatorship. The struggle will go on at least ten years, in the opinion of some observers, and severely test American patience.

The United States seems inextricably committed to a long, inconclusive war. The Communists can prolong it for years. Even without large-scale intervention from the north, which would lead to "another Korea," what may be achieved at best is only restoration of a tolerable security similar to that achieved in Malaya after years of fighting. But it is too late to disengage; our prestige has been committed. Washington says we will stay until the finish.

The New York Times, February 25, 1962

INTERVIEW WITH HO CHI MINH:
JULY 1962

Master of the Red Jab

by Bernard B. Fall

"It took us eight years of bitter fighting to defeat you French in Indochina . . ." said the slightly built, grandfatherly man with the wispy goatee. "Now the South Vietnamese regime of Ngo Dinh Diem is well armed and helped by ten thousand Americans. The Americans are much stronger than the French, though they know us less well. It may perhaps take ten years to do it, but our heroic compatriots in the South will defeat them in the end."

After a pause he continued, speaking slowly in flawless French and looking thoughtfully out the high French window onto the manicured formal garden of his palace in Hanoi.

"I think the Americans greatly underestimate the determination of the Vietnamese people. The Vietnamese people always have shown great determination when they were faced with a foreign invader."

The speaker, looking very spry in a tropical uniform, was Ho Chi Minh, the 72-year-old president of Communist North Vietnam, who directs the guerrillas that the United States is fighting in South Vietnam. Every time an American dies somewhere in the swamps of the Mekong Delta it will be because North Vietnam hungers to extend its rule into South Vietnam, into Laos and Cambodia, into all of the fertile crescent that was once French Indochina.

No American has been to this enemy land since the last U.S. consulate was closed down in 1955 after a yearlong blockade. And the only sign of America that I saw in the whole country was, oddly enough, a copy of Doctor Spock. It remains a mystery why the suspicious North Vietnamese should have admitted me, a Frenchman now teaching at Howard University in Washington, D.C., and why they should have allowed me to spend two weeks there, touring more than 500 miles around the country, including some areas that no outsider has seen in more than a decade. Conceivably it was my criticisms in previous books on Vietnam which prompted the Communists to try to convince me of their claimed achievements.

Flying northward in a Boeing Stratoliner of World War II vintage—operated by the Canadian-Polish-Indian International Control Commission that is supposed to supervise the 1954 truce—I thought for a while that the land looked much as it had when I had known it in the days of French rule. In the Red River Delta I could see dark green patches where tree-lined villages nestle between the rice fields of lush light green. But something had changed even here. Some fields no longer are small, handkerchieflike squares but are far larger than before, with no dikes to interrupt their expanse. They belong to the new collective farms. Communism already has left its mark on the landscape. And as we came in for a landing I noticed the brutal reds of new tile roofs and the glaring whites of factory walls where there once had been nothing but farmland or French forts. Here the industrialization drive of Communism had left its imprint.

Hanoi looked about as it must have looked the day after the French pulled out—no cars in the streets, the city in a state of "brown-out," a few passersby walking in an eerie atmosphere of silence, as if every noise were filtered through cotton stoppers in one's ears. In the once-fashionable "French" section of town, the stuccoed villas were in disrepair, the shops boarded up, the broad avenues empty. Not a street seemed to have been paved, nor a house repainted since the French evacuated the city.

The car assigned to me, a rickety Soviet Pobieda (Victory), took me to the hotel I had known as the Metropole. Now it was the Hotel Thong-Nhat (Unity). By coincidence I was assigned to a dining table I had occupied nine years ago, No. 2, and the waiter brought me an example of what a North Vietnamese chef thought French cooking should taste like. It was edible, but I kept thinking of French officers I had known here, one shot down over Langson, another blown up by land mines, and others long dead in the battle against Ho Chi Minh's guerrillas—the battle that Ho had won.

The only people now eating in the 75-table dining room

were a Chinese technician, silently manipulating chopsticks, and a Laotian couple. The husband, a colonel, had attended the U.S. Command and General Staff College at Fort Leavenworth, Kansas; he had also fought with the neutralist forces against the Western-backed government during the Laotian civil war. As we ate, the public-address system—perhaps in my honor—switched from a propaganda speech to a scratched record of Glenn Miller's "In the Mood."

This is official Hanoi. There is another Hanoi, full of the bustle of any Asian city, with children swarming around, street merchants peddling duck eggs, and lines forming in front of movie houses. I saw one food queue too—people lined up to buy the Vietnamese equivalent of Popsicles. Here one can see that the average citizen of Hanoi is neither well fed nor starving (in the immediate postwar period of 1945–46, nearly one million did starve to death). The basic food staples, rice and fats and sometimes meat, are rationed but at bearable levels. Adult rice rations vary between 28 and 40 pounds a month. Clothing is rationed, too, at three yards per person per year, and it lacks the gay colors that brighten many Asian street scenes. There are only two basic colors of clothes: black cotton trousers and white cotton shirts. Recently a new color has been added to the output—faded blue. As for more luxurious goods, the shopwindows of Hanoi hold out little more than a promise. They contain such items as Czech tape recorders and Russian cameras—at prices of $600 and more. Even a pair of poorly made shoes costs $8.50, two weeks' pay for an average worker, and Chinese T-shirts cost $1.25.

I was not restricted in moving around Hanoi. I was escorted on official visits by a member of the Foreign Office, but otherwise I was left on my own to go to the local markets or the movies or to visit the few Western missions still sticking it out under virtual quarantine. And although my Vietnamese is awful I found many people in markets and stores who were willing and able to talk French.

The reasons for Hanoi's general shabbiness became more clear when I got outside the city. The cement that does not go into Hanoi pavements apparently goes into five-story apartment buildings and huge factories in places where I had seen only open rice fields nine years ago. There are an electrochemical complex at Viet-Tri, a fertilizer plant at Lam-Thao, a ceramics factory at Hai-Duong, a blast furnace at Thai-Nguyen and a tungsten mine and ore refinery at Pia-Ouac which also produce uranium for Communist China's future atomic bombs. The whole Communist bloc has pitched in with close to $1,000,000,000 in aid to make the industrialization of North Vietnam a Communist success in an area where America is deeply involved. In contrast to China, the industrialization of North Vietnam is relatively easy, for it is a nation a little smaller than Missouri with a population of 17 million. A few modern machine-tool plants, for example, can change it from a machine-importing to a machine-exporting country. Its turret lathes already have made an impressive debut at the New Delhi Industrial Fair. North Vietnam is not becoming a Japan, but it is acquiring an industrial backbone stronger than that of any non-Communist country on the Southeast Asian mainland. This country is functioning, and developing at a very rapid rate.

The people working in these factories are an extraordinary collection. At the Hanoi machine-tool plant, which produces turret lathes, carpenters' planes, irrigation pumps and drills, I was surprised to meet a foreman who addressed me in purest French factory slang.

"You're damn right I talk like a Frenchman," he said. "Worked for sixteen years at the Renault plant outside Paris."

Nearby I saw an old Tonkinese woman wearing brown peasant garb, her teeth lacquered black in the traditional fashion, standing at a turret lathe with a caliper in her hand. And next to her, as at most machines, was a younger woman. "There are two workers at each machine," I was told, "because the first teaches the second. This way we won't have any trouble when we build the next machine-tool factory."

Glaring errors are still made. A senior official at the all-powerful State Planning Board, which directs the whole North Vietnamese economic machinery, filled me with complaints—including complaints about Red Chinese aid. In the case of the 400-acre Thai-Nguyen steel complex the Chinese had delivered turbines which were so huge that they could not be fitted on any available trains or trucks. Several months went by until the Red River rose high enough for the turbines to be brought upstream on barges. In many plants young engineers freshly graduated from Chinese, Russian, or East German training schools—or, as of this year, from Hanoi's own school of engineering—must step directly into top engineering jobs involving responsibility of thousands of workers.

"It often looks as if a midshipman had been given the command of a cruiser as his first post," said one of the few Western economists in Hanoi. "And it often works out the same way."

The huge Hon-Gay mining complex, which the French ran with 140 technicians and engineers, continued operating for almost seven years under the direction of two Communist cadres. Neither director had an engineering degree. People's Army colonels were in fact the directors of many of the plants I visited. That kind of militarization of industry makes for great labor discipline, but discipline alone cannot replace technical knowledge. This explains the stretch-out of the targets set for the 1958–61 economic plan and the constant lowering of targets set for 1965.

"When we first drew up our plans we just didn't know enough about statistics," said Vo Quang Anh, a leading member of the State Planning Board. "Even for the five-year plan now under way we are still sending our target figures to the individual ministries for evaluation and finding that they are set too high. And now that we know that our population increases by a fantastic half million a year . . ."

That population increase is an obstacle to all economic growth, as it is in all underdeveloped nations, and it means that even a constant increase in food supplies will not end the people's hunger. Yet partition cut off North Vietnam from its normal supplies in the South, which used to provide 225,000 tons of rice a year. Today as I saw in trips around the countryside, every available inch is under cultivation. In areas where rice won't grow, the peasants have planted corn and yams. In the long run, however, North Vietnam's hope of success depends on its being able to export industrial goods to such agricultural nations as Burma, Cambodia and Thailand.

The struggle for economic development requires an almost military discipline, and Ho Chi Minh has succeeded in imposing it on the whole country. At the basic level, six-year-old Young Pioneers are taught to "help" their parents "correct their backwardness in economic thinking." Many a small-time black marketeer or would-be political opponent is turned in by his own family or his neighbor's children. On the next level is the Street Committee, theoretically a non-political organization of "mutual help." In actual fact the Street Committee is an unofficial police force which plays on a man's desire to keep the Joneses down with him if he cannot keep up with them. To buy a suitcase, for example, you need an authorization signed by your Street Committee. In other words, you must explain to your neighbors why you might be planning a trip and how you can afford it.

The Street Committee not only keeps a check on every one of the inhabitants within its area but it also sees to it that everyone turns out every day for early-morning gymnastics classes directed by a voice from a loudspeaker. These loud-speakers are everywhere, as are huge posters exhorting people to further achievements on the "production front"; to greater solidarity with the "heroic struggle" of the Cubans, Congo-lese, Angolans; to continuing hatred of the United States. In fact, Hate America Month was officially proclaimed during my stay in Hanoi. All of this establishes an atmosphere like that of George Orwell's *1984*—a feeling that Big Brother is every-where and knows everything.

Aside from the Street Committees for every home, there is the production cell for farms and factories. The production cell sees to it not only that work quotas are met but also that its members are properly indoctrinated. Returning to my hotel at midnight I could often see the night shift at a printing shop, which formerly housed the French newspaper *L'Entente*, sitting together around a dim light bulb while a production-cell member read aloud from the speeches of Comrade *Ko-Rut-Sop* (Khrushchev).

Above all these low-level organizations there is the party itself, an elite of faithful believers. North Vietnam's Com-munist *Dang Lao-Dong* (Labor Party) is 800,000 strong, and its membership has gradually shifted from the unsophisticated peasantry to the students and factory workers who constitute the political backbone of the regime. Its leadership, forged over thirty years of bitter struggle against overwhelming odds, is tough and resourceful.

And finally, beyond the party, there is the fearsome Vietnam People's Army. The French—who have good reasons to know it well—estimate it to be one of the best combat-infantry forces in the world today. It is at the same time a thoroughly political army. Its creator and commander-in-chief, Gen. Vo Nguyen Giap, declared in his book, *People's War, People's Army*: "The People's Army is the instrument of the (Communist) Party and the revolutionary state, for the accomplishment, in armed form, of the tasks of the revolution."

From a 24-man platoon in 1944, the army has grown into a force of 400,000 men, lavishly armed with Soviet automatic weapons. Yet in spite of this modern armament the army has lost none of its incredible agility in cross-country maneuvering. Whatever training I could see in North Vietnam—none of it was shown to me deliberately—seemed to confirm that the North Vietnamese were as ready as ever to fight in the swamps and jungles of their country. I saw infantrymen dog-trotting along the roads with full field kits in the blazing tropical sun. I saw officers instructing militiamen—there are an estimated 2,000,000 of them—in how to attack concrete bunkers. They were not training to fight against an imaginary enemy but against South Vietnamese—and Americans.

As to the loyalty of those troops there is little doubt. The People's Army is better housed and fed than most civilians, and its discharged veterans have high preference for good jobs in the administration and industry. This loyalty was tested on the one occasion when a large group of Vietnamese attempted a rebellion. In November, 1956, at just the time when the Hungarians rose in revolt, 6,000 farmers in Ho Chi Minh's own native province rebelled against the collectivization of their land. Soldiers of the 325th Division unhesitatingly shot down their compatriots and restored order.

In the face of such an awesome control apparatus, reaching from the family to the armed forces, the individual discontented North Vietnamese has almost no chance of rebellion. And any guerrilla movement sponsored by South Vietnam would have little chance of surviving in Ho Chi Minh's land.

All this, and more, was in my mind as I faced Ho Chi Minh, the grandfatherly man who still holds Vietnam's fate in his hands, and his prime minister, Pham Van Dong, 56, who looks

exactly like the aristocrat he was by birth. Both men had led
Vietnam's Communist movement since its inception. Ho Chi
Minh, though all too little known in the outside world, is the
last of the Old Bolsheviks still in power. He was a senior Comintern agent at a time when Khrushchev was still on a farm in
the Ukraine. Unlike many other Communist leaders, Ho has
traveled widely. He has been to the United States (he wrote
a pamphlet on the shocking conditions in Harlem in 1918).
He even served as a pastry-cook's apprentice under the great
Escoffier at the Carlton in London. As a member of the
French Socialist Party, he was one of the founders of the
French Communist Party in 1920. As a Comintern agent,
living in Thailand in the disguise of a Buddhist monk, he organized violent dock strikes in Singapore, later turned up in
Berlin during the last days of the Weimar Republic, finally
began organizing the Vietnamese underground in 1941—with
the help of the American O.S.S.

Ho himself is reluctant to speak of his own past. "You
know, I am an old man, and an old man likes to hold on to
his little mysteries," he said to me. When I objected to this
he said with a humorous twinkle in his eye, "Wait until I'm
dead. Then you can write about me all you want." Nevertheless, before I left Hanoi I received at my hotel an unsigned
five-page typescript which contained some hitherto unknown
details about Ho's life, obviously delivered on the old man's
instructions.

Ho has, too, a kind of human vanity and gallantry that one
scarcely expects in an old revolutionary. I had brought him a
book of mine which contained a portrait of him by my wife.
"Where? Where?" he cried. "Let me see it. Providing that
she's got my goatee right . . . providing the goatee looks all
right." After thumbing through the pages and inspecting the
portrait he was pleased. "Yes, that is very good. That looks
very much like me." He looked around him for a moment,
then took a small bouquet of flowers from a vase on the table
and handed it to me. "Tell her for me that the drawing is very
good and give her the bouquet and kiss her on both cheeks
for me."

Most of my political questions, however, were answered by
Premier Pham Van Dong. He sounded almost contemptuous

of South Vietnam's President Ngo Dinh Diem, whose regime
the United States is trying to uphold. "Monsieur Diem's position is quite difficult," said Dong. "He is unpopular, and
the more unpopular he is the more American aid he will require to stay in power. And the more American aid he receives, the more he will look like a puppet of the Americans
and the less likely he is to win popular support for his side."

"That sounds pretty much like a vicious circle," I said.

The premier's eyes showed a humorous gleam as he said
that it was more than "vicious." "It is really more like a descending spiral."

There is, I fear, some justification for the Communist
leader's optimism. The French lost Indochina to Ho's guerrilla armies because they had no political program that could
win the support of the peasantry. In South Vietnam today,
Diem's regime remains a family autocracy in Saigon, with few
reforms in sight, and there is no indication that it has attracted
any real support from the majority of the people. Without that
support, American helicopters and modern weapons cannot
do very much. And although American officials speak of fighting for years against Ho's guerrillas, I doubt that most Americans realize what such a protracted war really means.

Despite huge sums in American aid, guerrilla depredations have changed South Vietnam from an area which once ex-
ported as much as 1,000,000 tons of rice to one which has
had to import 100,000 tons in 1961–62. Its exports covered
only 27 percent of its imports in 1961, and that figure fell to
18 percent by mid-1962. South Vietnam is becoming, in the
words of one American economist, a "nation of mendicants."
For Americans, this war means not only an economic drain
but a political drain. "Americans do not like long, inconclusive wars—and this is going to be a long, inconclusive war,"
remarked Premier Pham Van Dong. "Thus we are sure to win
in the end."

Could we negotiate a settlement? Ho Chi Minh told me he
was ready to negotiate with "any" South Vietnamese regime
that was "willing to sit down with us at the same table and
talk." Premier Pham Van Dong spoke in more detail. "We are
willing to give all the guarantees necessary for the South to
get fair treatment. . . . We do not envisage an immediate re-

unification and are willing to accept the verdict of the South Vietnamese people with regard to the institutions and policies of their part of the country." What this means, in effect, is a neutralized South Vietnam, deprived of large-scale American support and vulnerable to Communist subversion. The South Vietnamese and Americans naturally oppose this. One of Diem's chief officials even stated publicly that the American willingness to neutralize Laos meant that "the American government . . . has fallen entirely within the scope of Communist strategy."

But part of the Western reluctance to negotiate is based on a feeling that the West is on the defensive in South Vietnam, that it would be bargaining from a position of weakness. This is true if we continue limiting ourselves to anti-guerrilla warfare in the South. One of the most ominous things about North Vietnam, as I look back on it, is the air of massive tranquillity—no guards in watchtowers, no airplane patrols. The Hanoi traffic police don't even carry pistols. But the U.S. doesn't necessarily have to let the North Vietnamese remain so placidly confident.

It is one of the paradoxes of the Vietnamese war that the huge American military commitment to South Vietnam is not well suited for waging a guerrilla war but provides a strong political bargaining position. For it enables us at least to threaten direct retaliation against North Vietnam itself. While Ho's guerrillas in South Vietnam can elude American air power, his factories in North Vietnam are extremely vulnerable to it.

The North Vietnamese are very conscious of this. When I spoke to Premier Pham Van Dong I reminded him of the risk of American retaliation against North Vietnamese territory. I reminded him that he had been to North Korea and said, "You saw what American bombers can do." The premier showed he was aware of the danger. "We fully realize that the American imperialists wish to provoke a situation in the course of which they could use the heroic struggle of the South Vietnamese people as a pretext for the destruction of our economic and cultural achievements. We shall offer them no pretext which could give rise to an American military intervention against North Vietnam."

The North Vietnamese genuinely fear American retaliation. They fear it not only because it would wreck their country but because it would raise the specter of Communist Chinese intervention and occupation. Until now, North Vietnam's rulers have followed Russian rather than Chinese leadership, and they are aware of China's ambitions for expansion. If we took into account these North Vietnamese fears of outside intervention, I believe we could press more effectively for some kind of truce settlement on terms that would definitely not be a "surrender." We could demand the immediate end of guerrilla fighting in the South and a far more effective international inspection system to police the truce. We may not achieve such a settlement, but I feel very strongly that we have no reason to fear it. And we must clearly realize that the alternative means the bloodshed and misery of a long and probably inconclusive guerrilla war—a war which Ho Chi Minh is well prepared to fight.

The Saturday Evening Post, November 24, 1962

SUICIDE IN SAIGON: JUNE 1963

"He Was Sitting in the Center of a Column of Flame"

by Malcolm W. Browne

THE LONG, brown joss sticks that burn at Buddhist holy places and homes throughout South Viet Nam generate a pleasing fragrance said to find favor with ghosts. But the smell of joss sticks is one that I shall never be able to dissociate from the ghastly smell of burning human flesh.

The two odors mingled June 11, 1963, at the intersection of two busy Saigon streets, to create a political explosion, the effects of which are still felt in Washington and elsewhere. I was there, and it happened like this:

On Monday, June 10, I got a telephone call at my office from a young Buddhist monk named Thich Duc Nghiep whom I had known some time. Duc Nghiep became well known to Western newsmen later as official press spokesman for the Buddhist rebels, by virtue of his fairly fluent English. At this writing, he is in the United States studying for a master's degree in comparative religion.

"We shall hold a meeting tomorrow morning at eight A.M.," Duc Nghiep said. "I would advise you to come. Something very important may happen."

For nearly a month, top Buddhist monks had been holding marching street demonstrations and hunger strikes in Saigon, all aimed at wringing concessions from the authoritarian Ngo Dinh Diem regime. Demands included one for government permission to fly the five-colored Buddhist flag in public. The Buddhists also wanted an end of alleged government favoritism to Catholics, an end to arbitrary police arrests, and "social justice for the nation."

The whole thing had been touched off on Tuesday, May 8, 1963, when Buddhists observing the birthday of Buddha were forbidden to fly their flag in the streets. A pagoda protest

29

meeting organized by the powerful young monk Thich Tri Quang had been tape recorded, and the Buddhists demanded permission to broadcast their recording on the local government radio station. Permission was denied, and several thousand Buddhist marchers led by monks headed from Hue's Tu Dam Pagoda for the radio station in the center of town.

As the marchers approached the radio station and surged around its entrance, the local military commander, a major named Dang Sy, had a bad case of jitters. He ordered troops and armored cars to move in.

Several grenades, apparently thrown by trigger-happy soldiers, exploded in the midst of the crowd. A few of the marchers (including children) were crushed under the tracks of the armored vehicles. Eight persons were killed on the spot, and, of the scores wounded, several died later.

The people who died in the Hue incident became the first of the Buddhist martyrs in what was to become a fierce struggle to destroy Ngo Dinh Diem and his family.

The Diem government, rather than back down, applied increasingly harsh measures against the Hue Buddhists, and the pleasant little city on the banks of the Perfume River became an armed camp. In another incident later in the summer, marchers with arms folded were blocked at a street barricade, and staged a sit-in on the pavement. Troops dispersed them by hurling glass containers of acid, which splashed over demonstrators and sent more than seventy of them to the hospital.

The masses of the nation were stirring, and the showdown was nearing.

In Saigon, demonstrations by monks during the first month after the Hue incident were orderly and staged with military precision. Monks would converge at key parks around the city in taxicabs and bicycle taxis with such perfect timing that formations of three or four hundred saffron-robed Buddhists appeared to materialize from thin air, under the noses of security police.

Street marches, especially on Tuesdays, became so frequent they appeared to be losing their impact. Tuesday was the day of choice, because the ascension of the spirits of the dead from the Hue incident was said to be marked by seven-day intervals, and the victims had died on a Tuesday.

Some time in late May, one of the English-speaking monks at the cluster of concrete buildings known as An Quang Pagoda had given a visitor a piece of blood-chilling intelligence. He said that two monks were planning to commit suicide publicly in support of Buddhist demands—one by disembowelment and the other by burning. The Buddhist high command (consisting of about ten top monks, including Tri Quang) had not yet authorized the suicides but was considering them, the informant said. Nothing further was said about this plan, and many people wrote it off as an idle threat, on grounds that the nonviolent Buddhist faith would never condone suicide.

But something special was in the air the morning of June 11.

I arrived about a quarter to eight at the small pagoda off Phan Dinh Phung Street where I had been advised to go. The concrete pagoda building was set in about thirty yards from the street with a muddy alleyway as an entrance. In the rear was a small courtyard, jammed with yellow-robed monks and gray-robed nuns. Loudspeakers nailed to trees and corners of the pagoda building were blaring in rapid Vietnamese.

More monks and nuns, all of them standing, were jammed in the main pagoda room, where another loudspeaker was howling.

I was shown to an alcove in which a large, gilded Buddha statue stood, and asked to sit down at a low table. Six or eight women wearing the white dress of mourning were busy preparing tea. One of them brought me a steaming glass cup of tea, and tried to smile politely, although tears were coursing down her face.

My monk informant, Thich Duc Nghiep, spotted me and came over. He whispered in my ear, "I advise you to stay until the very end of this, because I think something very important will happen."

At exactly eight o'clock, the jabber of Vietnamese from the loudspeakers stopped and the chanting of prayer began. One monk led the chanting with a microphone and another one next to him kept time, beating rhythmically on a gourd.

"*Na Mo A Di Da Phat*," the ancient prayer begins, each word equally accented on the same monotonous note.

It is the most hypnotic kind of chant I have ever heard, and on that hot June morning, clouds of incense in the air, I found even myself affected. All the monks and nuns joined that chant, quietly at first, then with rising, hammering volume, as the verses were repeated over and over, the tempo speeding up slightly.

Eyes all around me were fixed straight ahead, almost glazed in the absorption of fervor. But at exactly 9 A.M. it stopped.

Monks and nuns, who apparently had drilled their procedure many times, lined up in the alleyway, moving out into the street in two ranks. Some unfurled banners in Vietnamese and English calling on the government to answer the Buddhist demands. In a minute or two, the procession of 350 or so monks and nuns was formed and moving. At its head was an innovation in the street marches—a gray sedan with four or five monks riding inside. It seemed strange to me at the time that monks were now riding instead of walking.

Police ahead of the procession cleared the streets as usual, keeping clear of the marchers, and not interfering, except to shunt traffic and crowds away from the line of march. Preceding the Buddhist car by about a half-block, a white police jeep kept pace. At that time, the main crackdown on Buddhists by government officials was in Central Viet Nam, not the Saigon area.

People leaned from shopwindows along Phan Dinh Phung, and children stared at the passing procession.

The marchers reached the intersection of Le Van Duyet Street, one of the most important boulevards in Saigon, always jammed with heavy traffic. On one corner of the intersection stood the massive, gray Cambodian consulate building, with its stone lion statue. On two other corners were apartment buildings, and on the fourth corner, an Esso service station. At precisely the center of the intersection, the Buddhist car stopped, apparently stalled. The police jeep was already halfway down the next block.

The marchers began to move past the car, and then abruptly turned left into Le Van Duyet, quickly forming a circle about thirty feet in diameter, of which the car formed a link. It was now nearly 9:20 A.M.

The monks in the car had gotten out, and one of them had

opened its hood. From inside, he pulled a five-gallon gasoline can made of translucent plastic, filled to the brim with pink gasoline. Three other monks were walking from the car side by side to the center of the circle. One of them placed a small brown cushion on the pavement, and the monk in the center sat down on it, crossing his legs in the traditional position of Buddhist meditation known as the "lotus posture." This monk was the Venerable Thich Quang Duc, destined to be known throughout the world as the primary saint of modern Vietnamese Buddhism.

The three monks exchanged a few quiet words. The two who had flanked Quang Duc brought the gasoline container quickly to the center of the circle, and poured most of it over the bowed head and shoulders of the seated monk.

The monks stepped back, leaving the gasoline can next to the seated man. From about twenty feet away, I could see Quang Duc move his hands slightly in his lap striking a match. In a flash, he was sitting in the center of a column of flame, which engulfed his entire body. A wail of horror rose from the monks and nuns, many of whom prostrated themselves in the direction of the flames.

From time to time, a light breeze pulled the flames away from Quang Duc's face. His eyes were closed, but his features were twisted in apparent pain. He remained upright, his hands folded in his lap, for nearly ten minutes as the flesh burned from his head and body. The reek of gasoline smoke and burning flesh hung over the intersection like a pall.

Finally, Quang Duc fell backward, his blackened legs kicking convulsively for a minute or so. Then he was still, and the flames gradually subsided.

While the monk burned, other monks stood in positions at all four entrances to the intersection, holding banners reading: A Buddhist Priest Burns for Buddhist Demands.

City police at first watched in stunned horror, and then began running around aimlessly outside the circle of Buddhists. One of them radioed headquarters, and three or four fire trucks arrived with a platoon of helmeted riot police carrying fixed bayonets. The riot police charged down the street in a wave, but stopped short in confusion a few yards from the circle. As the fire trucks moved down the street, several monks leaped in front of their wheels, and other monks chocked themselves behind the rear wheels, making movement impossible without crushing someone.

All the while, leading monks with portable electric loudspeakers harangued onlookers, both in Vietnamese and English, with a highly emotional explanation as to why the suicide had taken place.

A black delivery truck with large Buddhist flags painted on its sides arrived, and monks unloaded a wooden coffin. The flames by now were completely out, and monks tried to transfer the charred body to the coffin. But its splayed arms and legs were rigid, and could not be forced into the box.

Seven monks shed their saffron robes (wearing brown robes underneath) and made a kind of sling to carry the body. The circle broke and formed into a procession once again, the body at its head. Marching a few blocks more, the group arrived at Xa Loi Pagoda, the main Buddhist pagoda in South Viet Nam, where a bell was tolling mournfully from the concrete tower. It was 10 A.M. sharp, and the demonstration was finished.

Quang Duc was the first of the Buddhist monks to die by fiery suicide the summer of 1963. He also was the only one to die with such elaborate public trappings. The other suicides all were sprung by surprise without processions. In Saigon, one young monk arrived in a taxi at Saigon's central market place, walked to the center of the traffic circle, and set himself afire. Three American newsmen attempting to photograph the incident were badly beaten by police. Another young monk, his clothing apparently impregnated with gasoline in advance, died on a street corner facing Saigon Cathedral one bright Sunday morning, as Catholic worshipers were arriving for mass. A policeman tried to beat out the flames, but without success.

Two monks in Hue burned themselves to death inside their barricaded pagoda, with no outsiders as witnesses. Another monk burned to death in front of a soldier's memorial, completely alone, in the coastal town of Phan Thiet. And a thirty-three-year-old nun died in flames near her pagoda outside another coastal town, the seaside resort of Nha Trang. In all, seven died, all with the blessings of the Buddhist high command.

Thich Quang Duc's body was taken for cremation at the Buddhist cemetery just outside Saigon, and monks in charge of burning the body claimed that Quang Duc's heart would not burn. A singed piece of meat purporting to be the heart was preserved in a glass chalice, becoming an object of worship.

Quang Duc's ashes were distributed to pagodas throughout the country. The yellow robes in which his body had been carried were cut into tiny swatches and distributed to Buddhist followers everywhere. Pinned to shirts and dresses, these bits of cloth were thought to have miraculous healing properties, and also were symbols of the Buddhist uprising against the government. At one point, police tried to crack down on wearers of the yellow cloth, but there were too many of them.

Tidings of miracles spread throughout the land. In the evening sky over Saigon, thousands said they could see the weeping face of the Buddha in the clouds. Traffic was jammed everywhere as crowds of people stood gazing into the sky.

Tens of thousands of followers poured through Xa Loi Pagoda each day to worship before the heart in the glass chalice.

from *The New Face of War*, 1965

The Fall of the House of Ngo Dinh

by Stanley Karnow

AT THE French mission church of St. Francis Xavier in Cholon, Saigon's shabby Chinatown, the early-morning Mass had celebrated All Souls' Day, the day of the dead. A few minutes after the congregation had gone, two men in dark-gray suits walked quickly through the shaded courtyard and entered the church. South Vietnam's President Ngo Dinh Diem and his brother Nhu, both haggard after a sleepless night, were fugitives in the capital they once commanded. In the remote church they prayed and took Communion, and it was their ultimate sacrament. Within less than an hour their bloody, crumpled corpses lay ignominiously on the deck of an armored car rumbling through the Saigon streets.

Thus ended the fragile reign of the Ngo Dinh family—a stubborn, self-righteous oligarchy that, in its eight years of rule over South Vietnam, had degenerated from clumsy paternalism into almost insane tyranny. When, after careful plotting, a host of Vietnamese officers rose against it, Diem's rotted regime fell apart with surprising ease.

Not long after the smoke of rebellion had cleared away, the chief of South Vietnam's new military junta invited me into his spacious, map-lined office. Gen. Duong Van Minh, known among Americans in Saigon as Big Minh, is a heavy, fierce-looking soldier whose single tooth is a proud badge of the Japanese torture he suffered during World War II. He is a deceptively gentle man, and when he spoke of the *coup d'état* that lifted him into office, there was a discernible tone of apology in his voice.

"We sincerely wanted to work with Diem," he said. "But the guerrilla war we are waging must be fought with the hearts of the people. Diem had lost the people. Army discipline was disintegrating, morale was low. If we had been winning the war, we wouldn't have staged the *coup d'état*. We overthrew Diem in order to restore unity to the country and give a new spirit to the army—so we can beat the Communists."

Whatever future problems the new junta faces—and they will be considerable—their *coup d'état* was the only alternative to the Diem regime. For Diem's government had, in effect, ceased to function long before it completely collapsed.

An austere, inflexible autocrat, Diem could not cope with the double threat of a Communist guerrilla enemy and a growing internal opposition. Like the flawed hero of a Shakespearean tragedy, he succumbed to his own worst instincts. He withdrew from reality and, more and more, abdicated power to his neurotic, conspiratorial brother Nhu and his beautiful, arrogant sister-in-law, Madame Nhu. In the process, he gradually alienated his country's army, its intelligentsia and a significant mass of its common people.

At the same time, he estranged himself from his main foreign supporters. Mindful of its own image, Diem's own Roman Catholic Church strove to disassociate itself from a regime described by a high Vatican official as "medieval and reactionary." More important, in giving free rein to his brother's repressive policies, Diem provoked the hostility of the United States, which had dedicated men and money to help save his nation. "We wanted a change in the way this country was being run," says a top U.S. diplomat in Saigon. "If those in power couldn't change their ways, then we favored changing those in power. Don't misunderstand me. We didn't plot Diem's downfall. But we certainly created the climate and state of mind that inspired his opponents to overthrow him."

Diem had been living on borrowed time since November, 1960, when his crack paratrooper battalions surrounded his palace and then naïvely let themselves be double-crossed by his promise to reform. Again, in February, 1962, two fighter pilots attacked his palace and reduced it to rubble. The assaults against him reinforced Diem's distrust of all but his family and a handful of flunkies.

Nowhere did Diem's paranoid suspicions have a more debilitating effect than in his armed forces, where officers were judged more by their fidelity than their ability. Even imaginary

misgivings about a man were enough to tarnish his career. A
general who helped to save Diem in the 1960 revolt, for example, was thereafter suspect because he had too easily passed
through the rebel lines. Constantly worried that his leading
generals might overthrow him, Diem deprived them of
troops. Experienced men like General Minh, the country's
highest ranking field officer, were made presidential aides or
given innocuous staff positions.

In recent months, military men were also disenchanted by
widespread reports that Diem and Nhu were putting out
serious feelers for a deal with Communist North Vietnam.
Several times Nhu or his representatives indirectly contacted
delegates from Hanoi to discuss prospects for a reunified, neutral Vietnam. Despite his professions of anti-Communism,
Diem himself was thinking along similar lines: "Why do the
Communists attack us so ferociously? After all, our two systems are not so much different. We're both for the welfare of
the people."

Nothing so profoundly undermined Vietnamese military
morale, however, as Diem's repressive measures against the
Buddhists, by far the largest religious group in the country.
Throughout the summer, as the Buddhist crisis developed
into a broad political protest against Diem's regime, some
strategically placed officers finally started to organize a revolt.
There were some odd and unlikely figures among them. The
military security chief Col. Do Mau, for example, was so distrusted by Diem for alleged pro-Buddhist sympathies that he
felt forced to join the conspiracy. Brilliant Lt. Col. Pham Ngoc
Thao, an ex-member of the Communist Vietminh and later
one of Diem's close confidants, reluctantly went into opposition, convinced that only the regime's downfall could save
the country.

These conspirators worked cautiously. Sometimes they met
in their homes; often they talked out in the countryside; and
occasionally their conversations took place in noisy Saigon
nightclubs. By early autumn they controlled a powerful force
of about 2,500 paratroopers, marines, infantry and armor.

While these junior officers were planning rebellion, however, a more prestigious group of Vietnamese generals, headed
by Big Minh, was also considering ways of overthrowing the

government. While both factions maneuvered for position, the generals sent agents out into the provinces to line up units they might use. Last August, at the height of the Buddhist crisis, they suggested to Diem and Nhu that martial law be declared and soldiers be moved into Saigon. Secretly they planned to order these legions to rebel.

Constantly suspicious, Ngo Dinh Nhu shrewdly thwarted this plan. He accepted the generals' counsel to declare martial law. But instead of letting them call in provincial troops, he turned the military control of Saigon over to a more trusted general, the yeasty little Ton That Dinh. It was under Dinh's tactical command that Nhu's Special Forces and secret police raided the city's Buddhist temples on August 21. And after that, Dinh considered himself a national hero. "I have defeated Henry Cabot Lodge," he proclaimed. "He came here to pull a *coup d'état*, but I, Dinh, have conquered him and saved the country."

In the week that followed the violent anti-Buddhist raids, the plotting insurgents in Vietnam were greatly heartened by strong signs of U.S. distaste for the Diem regime. President Kennedy had made it clear that he disapproved of the Ngo Dinh family. The U.S. aid to Vietnam was curtailed, and Ambassador Lodge bravely told Diem that his brother Nhu was undesirable. And the CIA chief in Saigon, John Richardson, the man in the American mission closest to brother Nhu, was summarily called home.

But none of these encouraging gestures made the mechanics of revolt any easier, and the insurgent generals began to work out another design. This time they concentrated on winning over the loyal General Dinh. A courageous but not very bright soldier, Dinh's fidelity to Diem was exceeded only by his monumental egocentricity. The generals played on this fatal weakness.

They softened Dinh up with flattery, telling him that he was a personage of historic proportions, and they even bribed an astrologer to depict an important political future for him. Finally, when Dinh was inflated with ambition, they urged that he ask President Diem to appoint him Minister of Interior.

The trick worked as they had expected. Diem flatly refused him. Dinh, suffering from a loss of face, went off to sulk in a mountain resort for a few days. His faith in Diem and Nhu was clearly shaken. But Dinh did not immediately swing into the insurgent ranks. Instead he returned to Saigon and, as he told me, "I decided to give Diem another chance."

General Dinh now claims that he remained loyal to Diem in the hope of reforming him. But many knowledgeable Vietnamese insist that Dinh really stayed with the ruling family in order to participate in a fantastic machination then being devised by Ngo Dinh Nhu. His network of agents had kept him informed of impending revolts, and Nhu worked out a plan to put an end to all conspiracies. It was to be a fake *coup d'état*, which Nhu called "Operation Bravo." "Coups are like eggs and must be smashed before they're hatched," he said.

On an appointed date in early November, according to the scheme, Nhu's faithful Special Forces commander, Col. Le Quang Tung, would stage a "revolt" in Saigon with the aid of hand-picked police elements. Diem, Nhu and selected members of the palace household would flee to a prepared refuge at Cap St. Jacques, a seaside resort east of the capital. General Dinh and loyal army troops would remain on the outskirts of the capital. Inside Saigon, mob violence would "spontaneously" erupt. Gangs would loot and pillage—particularly the homes of Americans. A number of Buddhist and student leaders would be somehow killed. During all this confusion, the "rebel" Colonel Tung would announce the formation of a "revolutionary government" composed of well-known political opponents of Diem. Madame Nhu's father, Tran Van Chuong, former Vietnamese ambassador to Washington but now an outspoken critic of Diem's regime, was to be named president of the new government—without his consent. Saigon radio would blare anti-American, pro-neutralist propaganda and an appeal to end the war against the Communists.

This charade was scheduled to last 24 hours. Then, from their positions around Saigon, the loyal troops would march into the city and easily crush the uprising. Diem would return triumphantly to his capital, reaffirm his legitimate right to power, and Nhu would have a field day. For the fake coup would have plainly "proved" that:

• Opponents to Diem were neutralists, anti-Americans and

pro-Communists. Therefore the U.S. should give up any hope for his downfall.

• Adversaries of the Diem regime could not control the plundering mobs, which directed their pillage against Americans. Only Diem could assure law and order.

• The army really supported the Diem government, since it declined to join the revolutionaries and crushed them instead.

In addition to all these important propaganda points, Nhu expected that his phony "revolt" would bring to the surface a vast number of his enemies, making them easy to mark and cut down in the future.

Hardly had Nhu conceived his bizarre plan, however, than details of it filtered back to the various men plotting against the regime. Some of them considered the fake revolt an opportunity; they advocated letting it start, then taking it over. Others disagreed on the grounds that such a complex operation would result in too much confusion and bloodshed. The junior conspirators decided to beat Nhu by staging a real coup beforehand. D day was fixed: Thursday, October 24.

The generals, however, contended that any move without the cooperation of General Dinh and his Saigon garrison was doomed. Unable to persuade the young soldiers to alter their plan, the generals sabotaged it. They sent a key rebel regiment off on a minor operation against the Communists, and the junior conspirators had no choice but to postpone their project. When one of the plotters went home on October 24, he found a CIA man waiting to ask him, "Why didn't it start this morning?"

By now the generals realized that they had to act fast, both to keep up with the impulsive junior officers and to circumvent Nhu's crazy Operation Bravo. They focused on finally signing up Gen. Ton That Dinh. It is obvious from subsequent events that they promised Dinh almost everything, including the cherished Ministry of Interior Diem had refused him. It is still far from clear, however, whether Dinh was wholeheartedly for the revolt or was playing along with both sides, ending up with whichever was victorious.

By October 29 Dinh was apparently in the rebel fold. The rebels then set a trap for Nhu by deliberately letting him learn of the coup. General Dinh dispatched one of his deputies to the 7th Division headquarters at the town of Mytho, about 40 miles southwest of Saigon. The deputy gathered a group of division officers and declared that a *coup d'état* was being organized in Saigon. He cited some of the men involved, pointedly revealing that General Dinh was "not yet involved." Just as Dinh and the plotters expected, there was an informer among the divisional officers at Mytho. Within hours, Diem and Nhu heard of the budding conspiracy. Next day, General Dinh was summoned to the presidential palace and advised that one of his deputies was a traitor. A magnificent actor, Dinh put on a noisy performance. Weeping and gesticulating, he vowed death to the renegade.

But it was beyond Nhu's understanding to consider anything so simple. Instead, he suggested that Dinh infiltrate the plot and turn it into a countercoup against the insurgents. Moreover, he ordered Dinh to prepare for action on November 1—All Saints' Day—when Saigon offices would be closed, streets uncrowded and the movement of troops relatively easy. With the air of a master conspirator, Nhu announced that this new plan superseded his earlier scheme. Ever consistent, Nhu dubbed his latest project "Operation Bravo II."

General Dinh's first problem was to evacuate Diem's four loyal Special Forces companies from the capital. He explained to Diem's faithful Special Forces commander, Col. Le Quang Tung, that fresh troops would have to be brought into Saigon for Operation Bravo II. "But if we move reserves into the city," Dinh went on, "the Americans will be angry. They'll complain that we're not fighting the war. So we must camouflage our plan by sending the Special Forces out to the country. That will deceive them."

Next day, with Diem's approval, the Special Forces left Saigon. A major obstacle to the *coup d'état* was thus removed. Now Dinh's job was to deploy his forces for the revolt.

With Diem and Nhu under the illusion that he was preparing for their protection, Dinh rapidly shifted troops in and out of Saigon. D day was Friday, November 1; H hour was 1:30 P.M. Throughout the preceding night and following morning the insurgent legions rushed to take up their position. Two battalions of marines accompanied by armored cars were readied to attack the capital's radio stations and police headquarters. A battalion of paratroopers, resting at a seaside resort 70 miles away, was ordered to rendezvous with tank and artillery units and race to the city for an assault on the presidential-guard barracks. Infantry was called in from the north and southwest.

As the troops converged on Saigon, only senior officers knew the purpose of their mission. "I told my company commanders what we were up to beforehand," a marine colonel said later, "but I lied to my platoon leaders. I told them that the police were plotting to overthrow Diem and we were going to save him." Said a paratrooper lieutenant, "When we started out, I guessed it was the coup but I really didn't know. We reached a command post in the suburbs, and a colonel said the presidential-guard barracks was our objective. 'Who is the enemy and who our friend?' I asked, and he said, 'Anyone who opposes us is the enemy.' "

By midmorning of November 1, the whole area around Saigon was in stealthy movement, and no single person knew precisely what was happening everywhere. At about nine A.M., for example, Diem's loyal navy commander, Capt. Ho Tan Quyen, was met by two subordinates who came to give him birthday greetings. Instead, they asked him to join the revolt, and when he refused, they drove him outside town and shot him.

American military advisers, who live with the Vietnamese army, were well aware that a revolt was in the making, and those attached to General Dinh's staff knew the exact time it would begin. They reported the information to their headquarters, but the U.S. commander, Gen. Paul Harkins, apparently did not believe the news. Ambassador Henry Cabot Lodge was probably less skeptical, however. At 10 A.M. he took visiting Adm. Harry Felt, commander in chief of the U.S. Pacific forces, to see Diem for an hour. It was an odd confrontation. Both Lodge and Diem knew that a major event was in the offing, and they discussed "rumors" of a revolt. But if Lodge expected the real thing, Diem awaited Operation Bravo II, his brother's complex countercoup.

As the insurgent units wheeled into striking position, the rebel generals were arranging another astute scheme. Friday was the day for their regular weekly luncheon to discuss assorted military problems. At a dining room in the Joint General Staff headquarters, they laid extra places at the table and invited a few special guests, such as Special Forces Commander Colonel Tung and other officers loyal to Diem.

At 1:30 P.M. the revolt began. Spearheading the attack, two marine battalions sped into the city. They quickly captured the police and radio stations, and a rebel officer immediately went on the air to broadcast that the revolt was on. Meanwhile, at their luncheon, the generals announced to the assembled officers that the coup had begun and invited them all to join. Almost everyone signed up. Diem's faithful Colonel Tung flatly refused. As he was taken out to be shot, he shouted at the generals, "Remember who gave you the stars you're wearing."

In the presidential palace Diem and Nhu at first figured that their own countercoup was unfolding. They fully believed that General Dinh was loyal to them and would, as calculated, turn on the plotters and take the situation in hand. Soon after the action started, for example, a police official telephoned Nhu and frantically cried that his headquarters was under attack. "It's all right," Nhu reassured him. "I know all about it."

As the afternoon wore on, however, Diem and his brother slowly began to sense that something was going wrong. They had received the expected telephone calls from the insurgent generals demanding their surrender, and they rejected them. But time and again they tried to reach General Dinh to ask when his counterattack would start. Each time they were disappointed. Dinh was not at his office, but at the Joint General Staff headquarters. "Dinh must have been arrested," Diem was heard to say, still unable to imagine that the general had betrayed him.

A bit past four P.M. insurgent artillery opened fire on his presidential-guard barracks, and Diem knew he was in trouble. He telephoned Ambassador Lodge to tell him that the army was rebelling. Coolly acknowledging that he had heard some shooting, Lodge expressed his concern for Diem's welfare and reminded him that the rebels had offered him a safe conduct out of the country. "I shall try to restore order," snapped Diem. Replied Lodge, "If there's anything I can do to assure your personal safety, let me know."

Recalling his siege in 1960, when he had stubbornly turned almost certain defeat into victory, Diem held fast. From a special transmitter inside his yellow stucco palace, he broadcast radio appeals to his provincial commanders for help. Not a single reply came back. Only five blocks from the palace Diem's praetorian guards were besieged, and the palace itself was surrounded by rebel troops and armor.

Diem had carefully prepared for every variety of attack. Under the palace, for example, he recently completed construction of a $200,000 air-conditioned shelter against aerial bombing. He had built three tunnels leading far from the palace, and he had several plans for retreat.

About eight P.M., with the palace surrounded, Diem and Nhu fled through a tunnel that took them to a wooded area near the Cercle Sportif, Saigon's sporting club. They carried nothing but a briefcase crammed with U.S. greenbacks. At the tunnel exit, a confederate was waiting to drive them to the home of a Chinese merchant, Ma Tuyen. The house had a direct link with the palace telephone. Neither the insurgent forces attacking it nor the troops defending it ever knew that night that they were fighting for an empty palace.

In their new hideout in the Chinese district of Cholon, Diem and Nhu still hoped that General Dinh would rescue them, and they doggedly continued to telephone him. It was past midnight when, for the first time that day, they reached him directly at the Joint General Staff headquarters. With the other insurgents beside him, Dinh was apparently anxious to dispel any doubts about his allegiance to the rebel cause. Using a choice lexicon of Vietnamese obscenities, he barked at Diem: "Dinh saved you m——rs many times, but not now, you b——s. You s——s are finished. It's all over."

Obstinately Diem still refused to surrender. Through his palace radio transmitter, he went on issuing appeals for help. He called on his hand-picked province chiefs to send him irregulars, and he begged for his brother's Republican Youth Corps to rise up. He even implored Madame Nhu's paramilitary women's committee to mobilize in his defense. None of them responded. Instead, messages of loyalty to the rebels were pouring in from all over the country.

At dawn Diem's palace defenders ran up a white flag. A

horde of troops and civilians, almost incredulous at the rebel victory, stormed the building. They found its ornate chambers a shambles, and they poked curiously through the rooms, stealing Madame Nhu's negligees and her husband's whiskey. Diem's bedroom was littered with American adventure magazines, and on Nhu's desk were copies of a book entitled *Shoot to Kill.* But nobody could find Diem and his brother.

By about 8:30 A.M. Cholon was fully awake and bustling. Diem and Nhu decided to seek sanctuary in the church of St. Francis Xavier. From there Diem telephoned the Joint General Staff headquarters. He offered to yield on condition that: (1) he be permitted to surrender honorably, (2) members of his family be allowed to leave the country, (3) he be maintained as president of the republic for a decent interval in order to retire gracefully. A rebel representative granted the first two points. As for the third, he said: "We'll discuss that later." Diem agreed and disclosed his whereabouts.

Within minutes, three armored cars were dashing across the city. At about 9:45 they pulled into the narrow, dead-end street facing the church. Personally commanding them was Gen. Mai Huu Xuan. A high police official in the French colonial administration, Xuan had been shunted into a minor job by Diem, and he detested the president. He was a poor choice for this delicate mission. But he was the only man who dared accept it. Asked to accompany Xuan, another general declined, saying, "Diem doesn't deserve two generals."

Despite the bitterness of their fight against him, the insurgents could not shake off their respect for Diem. When the armored cars arrived at the church, the rebels hesitated to arrest the president and his brother immediately. Instead, they sent in a once-loyal officer to lure them out. At the sight of the faithful subordinate, Diem and Nhu emerged. The rebel troops promptly seized them. They tied the brothers' hands behind their backs and unceremoniously pushed them into one of the armored cars.

For some inexplicable reason, General Xuan did not ride with Diem and Nhu. The vehicle that carried them was commanded by a tall, swarthy tank-corps major once connected with the Dai Viet party, a dissident movement that opposed both Diem and the Communists. According to some insiders, the major burned with desire to avenge a close friend whom Nhu had executed.

"As we rode back to the Joint General Staff headquarters," an eyewitness told me, "Diem sat silently, but Nhu and the major began to insult each other. I don't know who started it. The name-calling grew passionate. The major had hated Nhu before. Now he was charged with emotion. Suddenly he lunged at Nhu with a bayonet and stabbed him again and again, maybe fifteen or twenty times. Still in a rage, he turned to Diem, took out his revolver and shot him in the head. Then he looked back at Nhu, who was lying on the floor, twitching. He put a bullet into his head too. Neither Diem nor Nhu ever defended themselves. Their hands were tied."

When the armored car reached staff headquarters with the two bodies, the generals were aghast. They had not the slightest sympathy for Nhu. But for all their impatience with his policies, they had always been awed by Diem's courage and stature. Besides, they had promised him safety and now their own honor was betrayed. One of them wept openly, and General Dinh said later, "I couldn't sleep that night."

To cover their obvious sense of guilt, the generals first claimed that Diem and Nhu had committed suicide, a tale that was later amended to "accidental suicide." Privately they admitted that Diem and his brother had been murdered. Adding to the mystery, they refused to state publicly where the bodies were buried. They are believed to lie in a prison cemetery near Saigon airport.

In the days following the coup, a few well-organized gangs smashed up pro-Diem newspaper offices, including the American-owned *Times of Vietnam* (whose proprietor, Mrs. Ann Gregory, after long berating U.S. "plans" for Diem's downfall, fled to the American Embassy). On the whole, however, Saigon's citizens behaved with restrained pleasure. Girls shyly presented flowers and food to rebel heroes, and youth delegations visited army camps to make solemn speeches of gratitude to insurgent officers. Forgetting Madame Nhu's senseless ban on dancing, nightclubs went into paroxysms of twisting.

And political prisoners slowly emerged, some with horrendous tales of brutality. A slim, pretty girl of 21, arrested in a pro-Buddhist demonstration last September and held for more than a month, told me how policemen had attached electric wires to her wrists, earlobes and breasts, shocking her into senselessness during their interrogations. Harvard-educated Dr. Phan Quang Dan, one of Diem's most prominent political opponents, was held for two years in a 27-square-foot dungeon under Saigon's Botanical Gardens. One day in early 1961, Dan recounted, Nhu personally visited him to demand his allegiance to the regime. Dan refused. Nhu enumerated the tortures he would suffer, and they were applied. The doctor was shocked with electricity and gagged with water. Last September he was transferred to Poulo Condore, a kind of Devil's Island. "After the dungeon, it was luxury," Doctor Dan said. "I was able to see the sunlight and hear sounds other than the cries of people being tortured."

As dictatorships go, the Diem regime was far from the worst. Yet, during those days after its downfall, enough evidence of its tyranny flowed forth to disturb and embarrass many Americans. For this was the government U.S. reporters had been cautioned not to disparage. Looking back on that era, a veteran American official in Saigon could not conceal his disgust. "For the sake of so-called 'realism,' we abandoned our own principles," he said. "We expected the Vietnamese people to endure a regime that we ourselves wouldn't have tolerated for five minutes back home. Maybe morality has a certain place in foreign affairs."

The new military junta's alternative to Diem is not going to be town-hall democracy. But most certainly, the new administration in Vietnam will have to strive for efficiency and public support. These are not ambiguous clichés but immediate political necessities, for a significant mass of the Vietnamese public has undergone a profound transformation.

Apathetic and apolitical as recently as six months ago, the students of Saigon quite suddenly and spontaneously burst out as a fresh force in the country. The Buddhists themselves, for years fragmented and subdued, have grown into a strong, solid organization. Most important, Vietnam's young captains, majors and colonels—the men whose units gave the revolt its muscle—have taken measure of their strength and, almost to their own surprise, have found it impressive.

One evening not long ago I dined with a group of junior officers, and they talked openly of their problems. It was a refreshing change from the covert conversations during the days of Diem rule. "It's good to speak freely," one of them said to me as the meal ended. And smiling, he added, "Let's hope that we haven't just been attending the first meeting of the next revolt."

The Saturday Evening Post, December 21, 1963

PROFILE OF JOHN PAUL VANN:
1962–1964

"They Can Win a War If Someone Shows Them How"

by David Halberstam

For Lieutenant Colonel John Vann, the battle of Ap Bac and the subsequent Vietnamese and American reaction to it were a bitter disappointment. Many Americans considered him one of the two or three best advisers in the country. In September 1962, when General Maxwell Taylor had come to Vietnam on one of his frequent trips, he had lunched with four advisers of different rank who were generally considered outstanding; Vann had represented the division advisers.

Vann was a man of curious contrasts. Thirty-seven years old, one of the younger lieutenant colonels in the Army, he was clearly on his way to becoming a full colonel, with a very good chance of eventual promotion to general. (His recognizable superiority is the reason that some of the high people in the Pentagon wish that Vann had never happened, for his case documented and symbolized so many embarrassments that might otherwise have been swept under the rug.) He was clearly about to take off in his career—one of those men who reaches his mid-thirties and suddenly begins to pull away from his contemporaries.

Yet most Army officers of this type tend to be sophisticated and polished, usually with a West Point background, often from second- or third-generation Army families—in contrast to some of their colleagues who excel as combat officers, but who find other aspects of the Army a bit baffling. Vann, however, could hardly have been more different from the traditional gentleman-soldier. There was little polish to him: he was a poor boy from Virginia, who always reminded me of a good old Appalachian South redneck—and it was literally true that on operations his neck and arms always turned an angry red.

50

Vann had risen by sheer drive, vitality and curiosity. After one year of college he had enlisted at the age of eighteen, and became a B-29 navigator at the end of World War II. In 1950 and 1951 he commanded the first air-borne Ranger company to be sent to Korea, specializing in actions behind enemy lines and against North Korean guerrillas who were trying to harass UN forces behind our lines. After Korea the Army sent him to Rutgers to teach the ROTC units there; he learned as well as taught, going to night school and receiving his B.S. degree. Then he was assigned to the University of Syracuse (the Army is very good about encouraging its people to pick up extra degrees), where he got an M.A. in business administration and all the credits necessary for a Ph.D. in public administration. (He has written one thesis, which is all he lacks for the degree, but is not satisfied with it.) He also attended the Army's Command and General Staff College.

Vann is a blunt, essentially conservative, at times almost re-actionary man. One of the ironies of Vietnam was that at a time when the Pentagon and other elements unhappy with our reporting were claiming privately that the foreign corre-spondents in the country were a bunch of liberals who op-posed Diem on ideological grounds, much of our information came from men like Vann.

Vann had volunteered for duty in Vietnam. Once there, he had shaken a desk job; then, knowing that he was to replace Colonel Frank Clay in the Seventh Division, he had gone on as many helicopter missions in the Delta as possible while preparing to take over; by the time he left Vietnam he had participated in more than two hundred helicopter assault landings. As a result, he knew as much or more about his area of Vietnam than any other adviser—or indeed than any Viet-namese officer—that I ever met. He also *walked* through one operation every week, and even ordered his Air Force liaison officer, Major Herb Prevost, to walk with the field soldiers regularly. Hence, Prevost became that rarity in Vietnam: an Air Force man who knew something about the effect of his weapons and about the political complexities of the war.

Once a week Vann also visited the three regiments and seven provincial capitals within his bailiwick, driving to some, going by light plane to others. His Vietnamese counterparts,

Cao and Dam, who hated traveling by light plane and frequently became airsick, were delighted to have him take over these inspection tours. He frequently stayed in these local headquarters as a guest of the province chief; invariably the chief would send a girl up to the room—an attempt, Vann suspected, to get something on him and thus give the chief some leverage if there should ever be any conflict.

Vann endlessly interrogated the missionaries and priests in his area, and any time a reporter saw him, he was likely to be questioned closely about what he had seen in other parts of Vietnam.

Vann also tried to set an example by his personal courage, and his walking in the field on major operations had a considerable effect on the Vietnamese troops, who had never seen any of their own officers above the rank of captain in the field. But the walks had another purpose: they were a futile attempt to shame Vietnamese officers into walking in the paddies too. What Vann, and many others like him who tried similar tactics, failed to realize was the power of the mandarin legacy: the whole point of being a major or colonel was that you *didn't* have to go into the field, and therefore the distinction and class separation of such officers from their juniors was much sharper than in a Western army, and the prerogatives of a high rank were more fondly cherished.

What the Americans were attempting to do, by setting examples like this, epitomized our entire problem in Vietnam. They were trying to persuade an inflexible military ally, who had very little social or political sense about its own people, to do what the Americans knew must be done, but this would force the Vietnamese officers to give up the very things that really mattered to them and that motivated them in the first place. How could anyone make the Vietnamese officers see, almost overnight, that the purpose of promotion was not primarily to separate them from the misery whence they came, but to get them to inspire or lead others?

Vann also insisted on driving his own jeep unescorted after dark in an attempt to change the Vietnamese belief that the night belonged to the Vietcong. Moreover, he ordered all his advisers to go out on at least one night operation or patrol each week; this well-intentioned directive failed, simply because many of the advisers could not persuade any troops to go with them. Eventually, at Cao's request, the colonel rescinded the order.

If Vann had any shortcoming, it was one typical of the best of the American advisers in Vietnam: the belief that the adviser's enthusiasm, dedication and effort could, through diplomatic guidance of his Vietnamese counterpart, successfully buck the system. This naïveté was the result of favorable encounters with other systems, and an overly optimistic view that in time of war common sense will prevail and allies will be inclined to agree on basic goals. This hope was doomed in Vietnam; the system was stronger than the men bucking it, particularly in the pressure of the fighting in the Delta. Tantalizingly, there was always just enough of a glimmer of success, or a transitory victory or just plain luck, to make the advisers keep trying.

We reporters admired Vann greatly, not because he gave us scoops—there are no scoops in a rice paddy—but because he cared so desperately about Vietnam, because he knew so much about his area, and because whenever we were with him we had a sense that a very real war was being fought—and not fought on a peacetime footing with peacetime hours and peacetime arrogance toward an Asian enemy. The remarkable thing about Vann, and a few others of his caliber who were fully aware of the shortcomings of the war, was that they still believed that under certain circumstances the war could be pursued successfully. This was the best kind of optimism; it was not the automatic we-are-winning push-button chant of Saigon, but a careful analysis of all the problems on both sides, and a hope that there were still time and human resources enough to change the tide.

In part, the reporters believed this too; though we were frequently criticized for being too pessimistic, I believe that a more valid criticism would have been that we were too optimistic. This is debatable, of course, but I think that anyone watching so much bravery squandered during those months could not have helped wondering what would happen if that talent were properly employed.

In the days before Ap Bac, Vann was something of a celebrity and reporters were quickly channeled to his area by the

PIO's. Later, after the atmosphere began to sour in the Delta, visiting reporters and officials were sent to the montagnard region, inhabited by primitive mountain people, where they were often initiated into a tribe, watched a buffalo being slaughtered, drank rice wine (or pretended to drink the raw liquid), received a genuine montagnard tribal bracelet, and were told, with varying degrees of accuracy, that the war was going well in that region.

The first time I ever met Vann he shook hands, told me that I was lucky because there would be an operation the next day that I could go out on, and then said, "Well, Halberstam, the first thing you'll learn is that these people may be the world's greatest lovers, but they're not the world's greatest fighters." He paused, and then added, "But they're good people, and they can win a war if someone shows them how."

Over a period of time Vann and a few officers like him taught most of the foreign correspondents the essentials of guerrilla war: why the outposts were a detriment ("They know where we are, but we never know where they are"); the danger of using the wrong weapon ("This is a political war and it calls for discrimination in killing. The best weapon for killing would be a knife, but I'm afraid we can't do it that way. The worst is an airplane. The next worst is artillery. Barring a knife, the best is a rifle—you know who you're killing"); the dangers of the American material commitment ("By giving them too much gear—airplanes and helicopters—we may be helping them to pick up bad habits instead of teaching them to spend more time in the swamps than the enemy"); the importance of the weapons exchange ("I don't think the Vietcong have any problems of recruiting; I think for varying reasons they can get all the people they want. Their problem right now is getting weapons; that's the only thing limiting the size of their units and the nature of their attacks, so unless we stop arming them we'll be in a very serious situation").

There was nothing ideological in Vann's make-up; he was simply a man of consuming curiosity and drive. He ran all the time, and he forced the young American officers around him to run just as hard, whether it was in the field or playing volleyball at the old seminary, where the Seventh Division advisers were housed. It was hard for him to compromise; he once told me that the trouble with compromise was that often it meant taking a position between something that was right and something that was wrong, with the result that you ended up with something that was neither right nor wrong. In war, Vann said, that's not good enough. It was this sense of commitment, and this unwillingness to compromise and blend in with the system—the American system, which was fast becoming a parallel of the Vietnamese—that finally brought Vann to a showdown with his superiors.

In February 1963, in the midst of the dry season, the Seventh Division was still virtually inactive. It had refused to fight at Ap Bac, and now it was refusing countless other opportunities to engage the enemy at a time of year that favored the hunter rather than the guerrilla. Our intelligence had improved, and knowledge of the enemy's whereabouts vastly exceeded the Government's willingness to act on it. For weeks the officers in the advisory group waited and fumed about the sham operations that the division was launching. Finally, in the first week of February, Vann sent a long and detailed message to American headquarters. In it he noted that there were now ten points where the Vietcong were known to be located in company strength or more; about thirty-five areas where they were known to be located in platoon strength or more; and that despite this intelligence the Vietnamese refused to act. It was a very strong and fully documented indictment.

When it reached Saigon, the message created a major controversy. President Diem was already angry with Vann because of the press coverage of Ap Bac and had urged General Harkins to remove him. Consequently, Harkins was less than enchanted with Vann; in addition, he held Vann partly responsible for the press coverage of Ap Bac. The general felt that somehow Vann should have been able to manage the outflow of news better. He was so angered by Vann's latest message that he called a meeting and designated a staff officer to investigate the report. If there were any mistakes in it, he wanted Vann relieved.

The officer spent eight hours checking the intelligence reports at My Tho. On his return to Saigon another staff meeting was held, and the officer announced that the only thing wrong with Vann's paper was that all of it was true. Harkins still wanted to relieve Vann, claiming that his relationship with Colonel Dam must be unsatisfactory. After the meeting, however, several other generals on the staff persuaded Harkins that if Vann were relieved it might seriously damage the morale of the advisory group, and that when the reporters found out about Vann's dismissal it might create a major scandal. (As a matter of fact, Vann never told any of the reporters about this; I only learned of it weeks later from another staff officer who was still angry about the incident.)

Thus began the quiet struggle between the field advisers and Harkins. Gradually others became involved, but throughout this showdown Harkins was aided immensely by the traditional pressure an army places on its younger officers not to contradict a superior.

The task before General Paul Donal Harkins could hardly have been more difficult; he was a diplomat without leverage, a commander without true command authority. (For example, on Thanksgiving Day in 1962, after the largest helicopter operation of its kind had turned into a major flop—fifty-six aircraft had been used in an assault which resulted in the death of seventeen water buffaloes—Sheehan had written that the operation had taken place with the cooperation of MACV under the command of General Paul Harkins. Lieutenant Colonel Jim Smith, the PIO at the time, called Sheehan to complain about the use of Harkins' name. "Uncle Paul doesn't want his name used. We're only here as advisers," he said. Sheehan answered, "Tell Uncle Paul that he's in charge of the American Military Command here, that he's the man who released those helicopters, that those are American helicopters flown by American pilots and that his name goes in my stories.") Although Harkins was a general, his job was not so much to command fellow soldiers, but to get along with Diem and Nhu, extraordinarily difficult and suspicious allies with most unmilitary minds.

Harkins is a West Point man who served with distinction as a staff officer to General George Patton during World War II. He had been chosen for this post in Vietnam by General Maxwell Taylor, who had written the victory plan for Vietnam. Harkins was also known in Army circles as a good diplomat, a man who could be counted on to get along with a difficult man like Diem. His boiling point was relatively high and he was not likely to pound the table, speak indiscreetly to reporters or veer from the policy line. His appointment was, in fact, a substantive *part* of the policy; the hard line against Diem had been abandoned and the soft line, the tactic of smothering Diem with kindness and keeping our own people in line, was put into effect with Harkins' appointment.

The private instructions that Harkins received from Taylor are a matter of conjecture, but almost certainly they must have included the suggestion that Harkins turn his cheek to a great deal of Vietnamese mendacity. Thus, when Vann challenged the direction of the war in his area—the Seventh Division— he was raising doubts about the effectiveness of our whole policy and questioning the role of the man who had been specifically chosen because he would go along with the policy. If the Kennedy Administration, knowing that it was a tenuous policy at best, had selected as its instrument someone more likely to draw a line, there is a chance that the story of Vietnam might have been slightly different—but of course this is pure conjecture.

Even today when Washington admits to the great discrepancy between its prolonged optimism and the obviously serious existing situation, it talks in the most superficial terms about increases in terrorism and post-coup command changes, rather than facing squarely the substantive factors which, step by step, determined the pattern and rhythm of defeat.

Harkins had other problems. He had spent a lifetime in conventional-war situations and had no particular preparation for a complex and delicate political war, where the most important voices often spoke in the softest whispers. He was probably more willing to settle for the straight "kill" statistics characteristic of traditional military situations than for the circumstances which produced those statistics. One's impression was always that MACV's figures reflected what MACV wanted to hear. There was no differentiation, for instance, between Government forces killed on offensive operations and those killed in static, defensive points, though this would have been one of the truest indicators of how successfully the war was being conducted. An estimated 70 percent of the total casu-

alties—and this remained a constant, according to American
advisers—were inflicted at static points, thus proving that the
attempt to mobilize the Government forces had failed.

Another factor was against Harkins: his age. He was born
in 1904 and was in his late fifties during his years in Vietnam.
The problems which existed in Vietnam in those days—the
legacy of a colonial war, racial tension, poverty, anti-Western
feeling—were alien to the experience of a military man whose
formative years had been spent in far less complex situations
than those created by nationalism emerging from vast colonial
empires. (In this connection, I believe that part of the truly
remarkable admiration for President Kennedy in much of the
underdeveloped world came from the feeling of these peoples
that because he was young, he *understood*.) In contrast,
Lodge, though virtually the same age as Harkins, had been in
politics all his life and immediately sensed the turbulence of
the situation on his arrival.

The middle-aged Western military man, regardless of his
nationality, has been trained in military orthodoxy and has
little feel for a war practiced by guerrillas; in such a situation
he clings to whatever traditional evaluations he can—such as
statistics. In reality, however, statistics mean next to nothing
in this kind of war and inevitably give an erroneous impression
by favoring the side with the most equipment. (I remember
a sharp argument between Sheehan and an American senior
officer. The latter cited the high rate of Vietcong casualties
and claimed that this proved that the war was being won.
Sheehan insisted, however—and most guerrilla war authorities
support him—that this was simply a sign that the war was
being lost and that the Government was losing control of the
war and the population. In a successful insurgency, he insisted,
when you are doing well the casualties do not rise; they drop,
and the war simply goes away.)

Consciously or subconsciously, the Army staff system tends
to reflect the thinking of the senior officer. If the commander
wants to see an aspect of a war a certain way, the staff will
find facts to confirm their superior's thesis. "I am an optimist,
and I am not going to allow my staff to be pessimistic,"
Harkins was quoted by *Time* in a cover story in May 1962. I
remember with chilling clarity an interview I had with Harkins

about the outpost problem in October 1963. Colonel Basil Lee Baker, at that time the chief PIO, was present, and he spent much of the interview interjecting bits of what he considered positive news about some place in the mountains where "hundreds of montagnards had come in," or about another place where there had been "lots of Vietcong killed, and even our own people think it's pretty good." I was convinced that he was talking not to me but to Harkins, and I had a terrible feeling that the scene resembled those taking place at Gia Long Palace, where Diem had surrounded himself with carefully chosen assistants and where bad news was softened, strained, diluted and rewritten.

For such reasons MACV headquarters decided not to listen to Vann's warnings in those crucial months early in 1963. Whether by then the situation was already beyond recall is difficult to tell; the impression of some Americans then was that there was still time. But Westerners have always underestimated the Vietcong, and it may be that even early in 1963 the guerrillas' capability was already far greater than was imagined and that they were simply not exploiting their full capacity.

Ignoring Vann's warnings meant two things: first, that the situation in the Delta would deteriorate even more rapidly as the Vietcong was permitted to move virtually unchallenged; second, that the split within the American ranks would grow sharper as more people realized that Vann was right. Some of these people included Ralph Harwood, head of the strategic hamlet program in the Delta; Vann's eventual successor, Colonel Larry Brady; and Lieutenant Colonel Elzie Hickerson, the military representative on a joint civilian-military investigative team in the Delta, who received sharp criticism from Major General Richard Stilwell, Harkins' young deputy chief of staff, because of Hickerson's pessimistic view of the Delta hamlet program. Finally, in September 1963, Rufus Phillips, who was in charge of the strategic hamlet program for the whole country, went to Washington to warn officials there of the critical situation in the Delta and of the rotten state of the hamlet program, thereby setting off a bitter reaction at MACV.

Throughout all this MACV insisted that the war was going well—though by mid-1963 it qualified this by stating that the war was being won more slowly in the Delta than in other parts of the country. By the fall of 1963 the line had been revised again: the war was still being won in the Delta, but—in the words of one of the PIO's—"the guerrillas had been pushed down south by successful operations in northern areas."

Shortly after Vann filed his report, pointing out the ARVN's failure to follow intelligence in the Delta, MACV and Harkins were to receive one more thoroughly documented warning. Once more it was from an impeccable source: Colonel Daniel Boone Porter, Vann's immediate superior and the corps adviser who was responsible for the entire Delta. Porter is a mild, professorial sort; there was always a briefcase under his arm, and he looks as if he was on his way to give a lecture on the use of the English language. But people who knew him said that he had been a fire-eater in the past; moreover, he was reputed to know as much about basic small-unit infantry tactics as any man in the Army. He was a dedicated, hard-working soldier, and those who knew him, Vietnamese and American alike, swore by him. Charged with the responsibility for the entire Delta, Porter had seen the vast disparity between Vietnamese potential and accomplishment; similarly, the optimism of his superiors conflicted with the danger signs he saw in the field.

In February 1963, Colonel Porter submitted his final report before going home. Friends who read advance copies warned him that it was unusually strong and suggested that perhaps he sweeten it by noting some of the progressive steps taken: the increased number of operations, better communications, better care of equipment, and so on. Porter declined; he had already noted some of the improvements in an earlier report, he was deeply concerned over current trends and he was going to write what he felt.

Before writing his report Porter consulted his two immediate subordinates: Vann in the Seventh Division and Lieutenant Colonel Fred Ladd in the Twenty-first. Though the report included ideas of both Vann and Ladd (who was as pessimistic as Vann, but whose division commander was more aggressive), it was, according to one officer who saw it, fully "Porterized" in its final form. Officers who read it considered it the most acute study of the situation ever made by an American. It analyzed the character of the enemy, the character of the Vietnamese peasants and the character of the Government officials.

According to one officer, Porter's final recommendation particularly angered Saigon. He suggested that responsible high American officers confront top Vietnamese officials and that they discuss their mutual problems. It should be done tactfully, the report said, but it must be done. "We would tell them our problems and they would tell us theirs. It was also quite detailed on the failings of some of their senior officers. I think what angered the American command was that it would be a terrible thing if the Vietnamese knew we felt like this—and of course we did feel like this, and of course they knew it," one staff officer said who read Porter's report.

Harkins was so upset by the report that he ordered all copies of it collected. At a meeting of senior advisers, according to one officer who attended, the general said that Colonel Porter's report would be "sanitized," and that if there was anything of interest in it afterward, it would be made available to them. The report was never seen again. This was highly unusual; most senior officers' reports were immediately made available in Saigon for other officers to read.

Unfortunately for us reporters, Porter was extremely close-mouthed about this whole affair; none of us learned of the incident until long after he had left Vietnam.

At about this time Harkins received still another report on the Delta, this time from a general on his staff. A friend of mine who saw it after it left MACV headquarters said that all along the margins of it were notes in Harkins' handwriting which said simply, "Vann," "Porter," "Vann again."

Meanwhile, in April 1963, an angry Vann was on his way home from Vietnam, his tour completed. Unlike most Americans who were unhappy with our role in Vietnam, he was not just a dissenter, but a dissenter armed. A business statistician by education, Vann had spent long hours documenting the failures and errors of the war in terms of meaningful statistics. He could point out that during his tour in the Delta the number of small outposts had not only not decreased, but that

despite their vulnerability and the fact that they sharply reduced mobility, there were actually more outposts than on his
arrival. He could prove that as everyone had suspected, the
province chief's political relationship with Diem had a direct
bearing on the number of troops he received. Long An, for
instance, a heavily populated province immediately south of
Saigon, in which the majority of the Vietcong incidents in
Vann's zone had taken place, had fewer troops than Kien
Phong, a thinly populated province in the Plain of Reeds,
which had less than 10 percent as many incidents. As a result,
by the end of October 1963 the Vietcong were virtually in
complete rural control of Long An.

Vann could also offer unique documentation of the charge
that Government commanders were unwilling to risk casualties with their ARVN troops; in his year as senior adviser fewer
than fifty of over fourteen hundred friendly troops killed were
of the ARVN, the best-equipped and best-armed soldiers the
Government had. This did not show, as Saigon liked to think,
that these troops were fighting well; it simply proved that they
were doing very little fighting at all. The casualties were being
suffered by the Civil Guard and the Self-Defense Corps, and
they were being inflicted in defensive positions at night.

After spending a month with his family, Vann showed up
for duty in the Pentagon in mid-May 1963. There he found
that no one seemed to be interested in Vietnam or in his
opinions on it, though he had just returned from perhaps the
most critical and certainly the most controversial area in this
country's only war. Although men of division-adviser rank
were normally de-briefed in Washington, the three ranking
Delta experts, Colonels Porter, Ladd and Vann, were not
asked to give their views. When Vann began a search for the
de-briefing officer, he was told that it was "Saigon's wish"
that he not be interrogated.

So at first the Colonel gave informal talks to a few friends,
but as word spread he slowly found himself in increasing demand among higher officers. Finally General Barksdale
Hamlett, the Deputy Chief of Staff of the Army, heard Vann's
briefing, and at the general's request the item was placed on
the agenda of the Joint Chiefs of Staff for July 8. Vann was
advised by some of the generals who had already heard him

talk that he must be more moderate, and that in particular he must be careful not to be critical of General Harkins, the personal choice of Maxwell Taylor, the Chairman of the Joint Chiefs of Staff.

By a curious coincidence the Chiefs had just heard another briefing on Vietnam by McNamara's special adviser on guerrilla warfare, Marine Major General Victor Krulak. Krulak was to play an important role in Vietnamese affairs as a special investigator, and according to him the war was going well. At this point Krulak had just returned from a brief trip to Vietnam and had written an extensive report, which was extremely sanguine about the strategic hamlet program. According to one member of Harkins' staff, the report had been prepared with the close collaboration of the MACV; in any case, Krulak was simply telling the Pentagon what it wanted to hear. Vann's feelings were well known, and when his appearance before the Joint Chiefs was scheduled, Krulak's office began to telephone Vann's superiors for a copy of his report. Vann was warned by several high officers to stall and not to let the report be seen by others until the last possible minute. His briefing was set for 2 P.M. on a Monday; at about 9:45 A.M. on the morning of the briefing he sent a copy of the report to Krulak's office.

Vann arrived very early for the briefing and waited outside the office of General Earle Wheeler, the Army Chief of Staff, in case there were any late developments or questions for him to answer. According to his wife, "He was as shined and polished as a man can get—John was really prepared that morning. There wasn't a wrinkle near him."

What follows is Vann's report of the incident, but it has since been confirmed by a member of Wheeler's staff.

At 10:45 A.M. there was a telephone call to one of Wheeler's aides in the waiting room outside the general's office. The conversation went like this:

"*Who* wants the item removed from the agenda?" asked the aide.

After a silence the aide said, "Is it the Secretary of Defense or the Chairman's office?"

There was more talk at the other end. "Is that an order or a request?" Wheeler's aide asked. Then, after listening to the reply, the aide said, "Let me get this right. The Chairman *requests* that the item be removed." He then added that he would check with General Wheeler and call back. Hanging up the phone, he turned to Vann and said, "Looks like you don't brief today, buddy."

In a few minutes the aide returned, dialed a number on the phone and said, "The Chief agrees to remove the item from the agenda."

And so the Joint Chiefs did not have to hear Vann's briefing, nor did anyone else during the brief period that he remained in the Army while waiting for his papers to be processed. On applying for retirement he was immediately placed under the strictest orders not to talk to anyone about Vietnam. After hearing the news in Saigon I cabled our Washington bureau and suggested that Rick Smith, the *Times* man covering the State Department, meet Vann and try to get the expert knowledge I knew was impossible to secure in Washington. Smith tried his damndest, and then cabled back that nothing "can persuade your friend Vann to unclam."

For whatever reasons—perhaps because he was not a general, perhaps because he lacked expert advice in how to handle and exploit a protest of this sort, perhaps because it was not an election year, or perhaps because no one was that concerned over the state of the war in Vietnam in those days— Vann's retirement caused little stir at the time. There were a few stories and interviews—one in the *Times*, an excellent story in the New York *Journal-American* and a good interview in *U.S. News and World Report*—but they were sparse, so the Pentagon was really never forced to explain why Vann had left the Army.

Colonel John Vann retired from the Army so that he could speak out on Vietnam. He took a job with an aircraft company in Denver—at a considerable increase in pay—and spent his spare time and weekends speaking publicly to all kinds of audiences about where we had gone wrong in Vietnam. Even today it is obvious that he misses the Army with all his heart. "You know you miss it, John," his wife said at the airport in Denver when I visited them in the spring of 1964. "You know you've never really been happy since you left."

Vann had done, however, what no other American official has done in defense of his convictions about our role in Viet-

nam: he thought that the lies and failures were serious enough
for him to retire from a service that he loved. In temperament
he is not the kind of man who protests or who rebels against
the system—but he had become personally involved. He had
tried desperately to warn his own country of what was happening in Vietnam, and he had failed. Everything that he had
predicted would happen in the Delta had happened—and
happened even more quickly than he had imagined.

When I left Vann in Denver last March, I remembered another airport scene—in Saigon, when Vann was going home,
another frustrated and disappointed American whose tour had
ended. A group of correspondents had accompanied some
other officers and pilots to the airport to say goodbye to him,
and in recognition of his remarkable courage and integrity, as
well as for many happy hours together in the field, we reporters presented him with a silver cigarette case, signed by
us and inscribed, "Good soldier, good friend." As Vann was
about to board the plane, I told him that we had always been
worried about writing about him and about his area of the
Delta for fear of making life more difficult for him with his
superiors. He looked at me with a very small, tight smile and
replied, "You never hurt me any more than I wanted to be
hurt."

from *The Making of a Quagmire*, 1965

"We Are Losing, Morale Is Bad . . . If They'd Give Us Good Planes . . ."

Air Force Capt. "Jerry" Shank is dead—a combat casualty of the war in Vietnam.

While he lived and fought Jerry Shank wrote to his wife and family in Indiana every chance he got—sometimes twice a day. Those letters make up a moving "battle diary" of a war in which more than 15,000 Americans are fighting and dying in combat against the Communists.

Excerpts from his letters are presented here with the permission of his widow. All references, by name, to his Air Force companions have been eliminated to spare them any possible embarrassment.

Nov. 14, 1963

. . . We're using equipment and bombs from WW2 [meaning World War II] and it's not too reliable. This is an interesting place here. Everybody works together, officers and enlisted. We're out there lifting bombs and such. Every possible time, we give the men a chance to ride. On a test hop or something like that—it gives them a little motivation. We can't take them on missions, 'cause we have to have our VNAF [Vietnamese Air Force] student pilot along. . . .

We 23 Air Force run the whole T-28 war in the Mekong Delta. This will give you some idea of Uncle Sam's part in the war. . . .

Nov. 22, 1963

Been real busy with the armament job—really makes a day go fast. Got all kinds of problems—can't get parts or books or charts describing the different bombs and systems. The Air Force hasn't used any of this equipment since Korea, and everybody seems to have lost the books. The main problem is personnel—no good officers or NCO's over here that really

66

know their business. Most of them are out of SAC [Strategic Air Command] and have dealt only with nuclear weapons. This doesn't apply over here; what we need is someone from World War II. Some days it's like beating your head against a brick wall. . . .

Nov. 27, 1963

. . . Sunday all hell broke loose with the VC [Communist Viet Cong guerrillas]. We had a big airborne operation against them—both choppers and parachutes. I woke up at 4:30 to fly my first night attack—darker than hell. . . . By 9 o'clock in the morning we had launched 12 sorties, which is a lot for our little operation. The Viet Congs got one chopper and one B-26 that day, but we (T-28s) hurt them bad. There is far more detail to this, but I don't want to put it in a letter. . . .

I'm up to 20 missions now and am real confident in myself. I do good work, I feel like a veteran and I feel like a different man. I think I am older. . . .

I have changed my opinion about the VC. They are not ornery little fellows. They are mean, vicious, well-trained veterans. They are killers and are out to win. Although this is called a "dirty little war" and it is far from the shores of old U.S.A., it's a big, mean war. We are getting beat. We are undermanned and undergunned. The U.S. may say they are in this, but they don't know we need help over here. . . .

If the U.S. would really put combat people in here we could win and win fast. It seems to be the old story of a halfhearted effort. . . .

Dec. 4, 1963

. . . I have debated for a week and a half now over telling you of Black Sunday—Nov. 24, 1963. I'm going to tell you and, if you don't want to hear about these things again, well, say so. You do have a right to know. . . .

. . . This was not a typical day. We flew 20 sorties. But the VC hurt us bad. All in all that day, 23 airplanes were hit, one B-26 crew lost their lives, three choppers crashed. The VC won.

What they had done was pull into the little village and commit their usual atrocities, then pull out. But all they had were

small arms and rifles on them. So headquarters thought they
would teach this little group of VC's a lesson and sent this
operation I spoke of in after them.

But the crafty little b——s withdrew from the town into
foxholes and bunkers and hiding places they had been secretly
building for a week. Also, they had many friends in there plus
large antiaircraft guns and all sorts of machine guns. So when
the first wave of troops went in, they thought it was just a
routine chase of VC's. But they soon ran against the VC wall
and we pilots soon discovered that they had more weapons
than pistols and homemade guns. Shrewd plan—and they
won.

. . . We could have won but I could write a chapter on
that. I hope you were able to follow that, Connie. A lot happened that day and it happened fast and furious. It's not a
good thing to tell a wife, but she has to know—no one else
will say it—no one else can or will, I guess. There are no
heroes over here but there are a lot of fine men—America
better not let us down. We can use help. We can win, but
America must come over, for the Vietnamese will never hack
it alone. We've either got to get in all the way, or get out. If
we get out the VC will be in Saigon the next day.

Dec. 14, 1963

. . . I do get a kick out of the Vietnamese people. They're
poor, dirty and unsanitary according to our standards, but
they're happy and some are hardworking. . . .

Dec. 16, 1963

. . . The VC's [Communist guerrillas] sure gave them a
rough time.

The VC are kind of a Mafia. They terrorize and then they
sell "insurance" so that the people will not be harmed again.
They strike especially villages where Americans have been
seen. They terrorize these villages and then blame it on Americans by saying, "If Americans hadn't come to your village,
we would not have plundered and killed, so if you don't want
it to happen again, pay us money and don't let Americans into
your village."

So you see, they gain from this. First of all, they get money or food; secondly, they instill a dislike for Americans—dirty b——s! But I do like the Vietnamese I've met and talked to. They are friendly, happy, and childlike—good people. . . .

Dec. 21, 1963

. . . We got a briefing today of the total result of that operation on 24 November. I'll repeat it briefly.

The air power got credit for 150 to 200 killed. No one can be sure of the amount, for the VC carry off all their dead and wounded. They never let you know for sure how bad you hurt them. . . .

Anyway, there were approximately 700 VC's dug in with three 50-caliber antiaircraft guns and three 30-caliber antiaircraft guns, plus many hundreds other machine guns. They were waiting for us, but we hurt them even though we lost. We lost because we had them trapped and they got away.

It's so mixed up over here—there are over 3,000 Air Force in Vietnam, yet there are only 50 combat crews (B-26 and T-28). What a ridiculous ratio. Also, the Army tried to show the Air Force is no good and vice versa. Ridiculous. Down at Soc Trang, Army and Air Force will die for each other, but up with the colonels and generals it's a big fight for power. And most of these idiots don't even have any idea of what it's like out in combat. . . . They're trying now to find out why we pick up so many hits. The dumb b——s. We get hit more now because the VC have very fine weapons. There are Chinese over here now. . . .

I think the next few months will tell. Either the VC will quit or this will turn into another Korea. I hope it doesn't take the U.S. too long to realize this. . . .

Dec. 22, 1963

. . . Flew another mission today. We escorted three trains across no-man's land and then struck some VC's. Our FAC (the guy in the L-19 who tells us where to hit) received three hits, but we got them. I'm credited with destroying a 50-caliber antiaircraft gun. Bombed him out of this world. I guess I'm a true killer. I have no sympathy and I'm good. I don't try to rationalize why I do it. No excuses. It's a target and I hit it with the best of my skill. It's a duel; only (I repeat) only the best man wins. You can't afford to be second. . . .

Dec. 30, 1963

. . . Well, here goes. I got shot down yesterday. We were escorting a C-123 and I picked up three slugs in my airplane. One went into my fuel strainer and I lost all my fuel. I made it to a field called Pan Tho and landed safely. Me and the airplane are both okay, not a scratch except the three bullet holes. No sweat. . . .

Jan. 3, 1964

Down at Soc Trang, one of the airmen came up with the idea of putting chunks of charcoal in our napalm tanks. Napalm is a gasoline which is jelled into a mass about the consistency of honey. We carry two tanks of it, each weighing 500 pounds. When you drop it, it ignites and spreads fire about 200 to 300 feet. With charcoal in it, the charcoal is thrown about another 200 feet farther, like a burning baseball, and does further damage to VC houses. We've had it at Soc Trang and it works real well.

Tomorrow three birds are going out with one half of their load of straight napalm and the other half with charcoal napalm (Madame Nhu cocktails). A photo ship is going along to take pictures. If higher headquarters thinks it's all right, then they'll buy us the charcoal. So far we've been buying it ourselves or else "borrowing" it from the kitchen.

Jan. 7, 1964

. . . Morale's at a big low over here, especially among the combat crews. It's the same old stuff we got in MATS. No consideration for the crew.

Lost two guys today. One was a pretty good friend of mine. The only guess is—the airplane just came apart. B-26—third or fourth that have done that now. . . . Pretty bad day—just hard to find any good news to write. Can't even talk to anybody—nobody has anything to say. Just a blue day. . . .

. . . I don't know what the U.S. is doing. They tell you people we're just in a training situation and they try to run us as a training base. But we're at war. We are doing the flying and fighting. We are losing. Morale is very bad.

We asked if we couldn't fly an American flag over here. The answer was "No." They say the VC will get pictures of it and make bad propaganda. Let them. Let them know America is in it.

If they'd only give us good American airplanes with the U.S. insignias on them and really tackle this war, we could possibly win. If we keep up like we are going, we will definitely lose. I'm not being pessimistic. It's so obvious. How our Government can lie to its own people—it's something you wouldn't think a democratic government could do. I wish I were a prominent citizen or knew someone who could bring this before the U.S. public. However, if it were brought before the average U.S. family, I'm sure all they'd do is shake their heads and say tch-tch and tune in another channel on the TV. . . .

Jan. 9, 1964

. . . Had a good target today finally. Felt like I really dealt a blow to the VC. On my second bomb I got a secondary explosion. This means after my bomb exploded there was another explosion. It was either an ammo dump or a fuel-storage area. Made a huge burning fireball. You really can't tell when you roll in on a pass what is in the huts and trees you are aiming at. Just lucky today, but I paid them back for shooting me down. . . .

Jan. 15, 1964

. . . Another B-26 went in yesterday. Nobody made it out. A couple of guys I knew pretty well "bought the farm." . . .

One of the new guys busted up a 28 (T-28) also yesterday. He thought he had napalm on but he had bombs. So at 50 feet above the ground he dropped a bomb. It almost blew him out of the sky. But he limped back to Bien Hoa and crash landed. The airplane burned up, but he got out all right. . . .

. . . That news commentary you heard is absolutely correct—if we don't get in big, we will be pushed out. I am a little ashamed of my country. We can no longer save face over here, for we have no face to save.

We are more than ever fighting this war. The Vietnamese
T-28s used to come down here to Soc Trang and fly missions.
But lately, since we've been getting shot so much, they moved
up north. I kid you not. First they didn't want to come to
Soc Trang because their families couldn't come. Second, because they didn't get enough per diem [additional pay].
Third, because they didn't want to get shot at. There were a
couple of more reasons, but I can't remember them. These
are the people we're supposed to be helping. I don't understand it. . . .

Jan. 20, 1964

. . . I have never been so lonely, unhappy, disappointed,
frustrated in my whole life. None of these feelings are prevalent above the other. I guess I should say loneliness over-
shadows the others, but that's really not true.

I am over here to do the best job possible for my country—yet my country will do nothing for me or any of my
buddies or even for itself. I love America. My country is the
best, but it is soft and has no guts about it at all.

I'm sure nothing will be done over here until after the elections. Why? Because votes are more important than my life or
any of my buddies' lives. What gets me the most is that they
won't tell you people what we do over here. I'll bet you that
anyone you talk to does not know that American pilots fight
this war. We—me and my buddies—do everything. The Vietnamese "students" we have on board are airmen basics. The
only reason they are on board is in case we crash there is one
American "adviser" and one Vietnamese "student." They're
stupid, ignorant sacrificial lambs, and I have no use for them.
In fact, I have been tempted to whip them within an inch
of their life a few times. They're a menace to have on
board. . . .

Jan. 26, 1964

. . . I've done almost nothing all week. I needed the rest
very badly. I actually think I was getting battle fatigue or
whatever you call it. I've got 50 missions, almost all without
any kind of a break, and it was telling on my nerves and temper. I feel real good today after all that sleep. I kinda hate to

go to work tomorrow, for we start two weeks of combat again. But I'm rested for it now and am ready. . . .

Jan. 31, 1964

. . . All you read in the paper is the poor leadership of the Vietnamese, but we are just as bad. Everyone over here seems to be unqualified for his job. Like me—I'm a multi pilot, but I'm flying TAC fighters. We have no fighter pilots in our outfit. I'm not complaining, but, if the Air Force was serious, they would have sent over experienced fighter people. The same on up the line.

Feb. 2, 1964

. . . I'm getting to like Vietnam. Maybe I didn't say that right. I think it is a pretty country. These little villages in the Delta are about as picturesque as you'll find. Tall palm trees, fields of rice, and all kinds of flowers. The people seem happy enough, if it wasn't for the terror of VC raids. . . .

Feb. 6, 1964

. . . We scrambled after a fort under attack. We hit and hit good, but it got dark so we headed up here for Bien Hoa. Pretty hot target and we both were hit. Coming in here to Bien Hoa they warned us that VC were shooting at airplanes on final approach. Well, we made a tight, fast approach and held our lights (it was pitch black) until almost over the end of the runway. I forgot my landing gear and went skidding in a shower of sparks down the runway. Airplane's not hurt too bad. I'm not even scratched. My pride is terribly wounded. That was my 62nd mission. I thought I had it "wired" after that much combat experience. Then I go and goof so badly. . . .

Feb. 17, 1964

All B-26s are grounded, so we are the only strike force left. . . . A B-26 crashed at Hurlburt last week. Another came with the wing just coming off. Finally the Air Force is worried about the airplanes—finally, after six of my friends have "augered in."

Feb. 21, 1964

. . . Tuesday evening —— —— got shot down. He fell in his airplane next to a Special Forces camp and got out without a scratch. The airplane burned completely up, though. [Another airman] was going in on his seventh strafing pass and never came out of it. Don't know what happened—whether he got shot or his controls shot out. That was two airplanes in two days. Kind of shook us up.

Not only that, the B-26s have been grounded since Monday because the wings came off one again at Hurlburt. So after the last crash the whole USAF fighter force is down to six airplanes. This should set an example of how much Uncle Sam cares. Six airplanes. Might as well be none.

. . . Rumor now is that B-26s will fly again only with greater restrictions. . . . I'm pretty well fed up. Poor B-26 jocks are really shook. That airplane is a killer.

Feb. 24, 1964

. . . We're down to five airplanes now, all of them at Soc Trang. We have actually got nine total, but four are out of commission because of damage. The B-26s aren't flying yet, but they've been more or less released. I don't know what U.S. is going to do, but whatever it is I'm sure it's wrong. Five airplanes can fight the war—that's just ridiculous. Tell this to my dad. Let him know, too, how much the country is letting everyone down. . . . We fight and we die but no one cares. They've lied to my country about us.

Feb. 29, 1964

. . . We've got a new general in command now and he really sounds good. Sounds like a man who is out to fight and win. He's grounded the B-26s except for a few flights. But they have to level bomb, not dive bomb—no strain for the aircraft that way. He has ordered B-57s (bombers—jets) to replace them, and has asked for immediate delivery. He has also demanded they replace the T-28s with the AD-6. The AD-6 is a much more powerful single-engine dive bomber. It was designed for this type of work and has armor plating. We are pretty excited about all the new airplanes. We can really do good work with that kind of equipment. . . .

March 13, 1964

McNamara [Secretary of Defense] was here, spent his usual line, and has gone back home to run the war with his screwed-up bunch of people. We call them "McNamara's Band." I hope and pray that somehow this man does something right pretty soon.

Just one thing right will help immensely. He did send a representative over here. All he did was make the troops sore.

One of our complaints was that we can't understand the air controller, so he suggested that we learn Vietnamese. We said we didn't have that much time, so he suggested we stay here for two years. A brilliant man. He's lucky to be alive. Some of the guys honestly had to be held back from beating this idiot up. This man McNamara and his whole idiot band will cause me not to vote for Johnson no matter how much I like his policies.

McNamara is actually second in power to Johnson. But, as a military man, he finishes a definite and decided last—all the way last. . . .

Rumors are fast and furious. Nothing yet on B-57s. Rumors that B-26s are all rigged up with extra fuel tanks for long overwater flights. B-26 should never fly again, even if rejuvenated. Also a rumor that B-26 pilots will get instruction in the A-1H—another single-engine dive bomber. All is still in the air—all rumors. . . .

March 22, 1964

. . . Been flying pretty heavy again. We've only got 20 pilots now and 11 airplanes. It keeps us pretty busy. Also got two more airplanes they're putting together in Saigon, so we'll soon be back up to 13 airplanes again. Hope these last for a while. . . .

That was Captain Shank's last letter. He was killed in combat two days later.

U.S. *News & World Report*, May 4, 1964

After the Washington Teach-In

by Meg Greenfield

I. The Arrangers

A FEW weeks ago, Richard Mann, who teaches psychology at the University of Michigan and who is executive secretary of the Inter-University Committee for a Public Hearing on Vietnam, wrote a letter inviting Presidential Assistant McGeorge Bundy to participate in a national teach-in that the group planned to hold in Washington. Somewhat to Mann's surprise, Bundy telephoned him the next day in Ann Arbor and accepted the bid "in principle." Thereupon negotiations began between Bundy, the committee, Bundy's deputies, William J. Jorden and his assistants from the State Department's Bureau of Public Affairs, and a number of pro- and anti-administration professors, with a view to working out a suitable format for debating the government's policies and its aims in Vietnam.

In the course of three personal meetings and by way of innumerable phone calls and letters, it was agreed to by both sides that there would be no placards present in the hall that had been hired for the occasion in the Sheraton Park Hotel and also that there would be no demonstrations. The committee's negotiators assumed direct responsibility for seeing to it that no one would stamp, chant, march, or immolate himself in response to Bundy's presence. For what the committee understood to be "personal reasons" Bundy was not disposed to debate with Professor Hans Morgenthau of the University of Chicago, and he also was cool to Senator Wayne Morse. He accepted the political scientist and Asian specialist George Kahin of Cornell.

Another of Bundy's conditions was that his side be fairly represented on the panels. Thus it was that Bundy was permitted to provide a list of congenial—or relatively congenial—persons not in government from whom the committee was to choose one to speak at the morning meeting. When his first choice, the columnist Max Lerner, demurred, Bundy submitted the names of Wesley Fishel of Michigan State, John P. Roche of Brandeis, and Arthur M. Schlesinger, Jr., formerly of Harvard. Of these, the committee selected Schlesinger.

While Washington has experienced just about every other conceivable kind of protest in the past, it was clear to those in charge for the government side that the new technique required new and rather elaborate responses. Accordingly, the government's spokesmen were chosen with great care for their academic credentials. Many of them attended strategy sessions in the office of William Jorden, who among other duties runs a sort of State Department speakers' bureau. The bureau attempts to counter the charge of governmental unwillingness to discuss Vietnam by sending government representatives to campuses around the country, where they are then denounced as "truth squads" and "propagandists." Between them, the State Department and the White House are said to have requested (and been granted) more than three hundred tickets out of the several thousand available for the affair, and reporters did believe they discerned a pronounced and atypical enthusiasm for the government's position in the first four rows of the cavernous hall. The department had also rented the hotel's Franklin Room for the day, in the privacy of which a number of edgy-looking persons stood about waiting to meet any research emergencies.

The arrangers for the other side—chiefly teachers from the University of Michigan—were spread through a suite of stencil-littered rooms elsewhere in the hotel. There, by midweek before the Saturday event, a reporter could wander pretty much at will and observe them making such snap decisions as whether or not to continue a crucial telephone conversation with a television representative at the risk of failing to meet the plane of the Sovietologist Isaac Deutscher, who was flying in from London for the occasion. Unlike the government side, the teach-in leadership had taken its support where it could find it, and whether by reason of an excess of democracy or as a result of other pressures, it had done little or no co-ordinating or even previewing of its speeches. Thus, there was considerable surprise in the hall when Deutscher rose at the opening meeting and delivered a classical attack from the Left on Stalin for failure of revolutionary zeal. Press accounts of this remarkable episode tended to dwell upon Deutscher's physical appearance—his gestures, his beard, his resemblance to Lenin. And while such observations may have been superficial, it is nonetheless true that within minutes of embarking on his Trotskyite discourse, Deutscher had so utterly transformed the ballroom into some remoter hall in time and space and had worked such tricks upon the imagination that one expected him to be interrupted in mid-sentence by a bearded figure rushing onto the stage with an ax.

For all its more careful planning, the government side is said to have undergone a few surprises of its own, among them the speech of Arthur Schlesinger, who in turn seemed somewhat taken aback by the crowd's reaction to him. In establishing his independence of the administration, he dealt what many considered to be a superabundance of blows at Dean Rusk, the White Paper, the Dominican action, and the decision to become involved in Vietnam after the signing of the Geneva accords. Not that any of this seemed to make more palatable to the audience his arguments against a U.S. withdrawal from Vietnam or his declaration that the intellectuals of South Vietnam were not allied with the Vietcong and that withdrawal would mean "betraying people like ourselves" there. When Schlesinger had finished his remarks, members of the audience, bursting with impatience, lined up six deep at various microphones to present him with their many-parted questions of rebuttal. "When I hear questions like that, I begin to wonder whether Mac Bundy might not be right," he growled at one point to a full accompaniment of boos and hisses. "What kind of audience is this?" he murmured when he came down off the stage.

II. The Participants

The audience of course was preponderantly academic, both by profession and in style. Everyone on both sides seemed to have a favorite historical analogy at the ready, excessively courteous titles were dispensed ("Mr. Ho Chi Minh"); the grim and sidewise joke, particularly as it was offered up by Morgenthau ("the noble war we are fighting," the "poor victim of aggression"), rarely failed to get a laugh. And, not surprisingly, people who had traveled hundreds and even thousands of miles to register a protest were overwhelmingly inclined to the view that (1) the government was acting out of unexampled malignity and (2) it had caused us to be hated with renewed fervor around the world. Indeed, the mere expression of either of these sentiments tended to produce an outpouring of cheers and applause that went beyond agreement to something like exultation and which was reminiscent of nothing so much as the happy automatic shout with which New York's Democratic party workers in the election of 1960 used to greet Carmine De Sapio's every dark announcement that the nation's economy was on the verge of collapse.

Among the sponsors and supporters of the teach-in were veterans of the peace movement, which has primarily concerned itself with disarmament in the past decade and which has focused rather suddenly and late on the problem of Vietnam—A. J. Muste, Seymour Melman, Arthur Waskow, Kenneth Boulding, Herbert Kelman, Staughton Lynd. Some, such as the economist Paul Sweezy, who in 1949 was arguing the perniciousness and futility of the Marshall Plan at the Waldorf-Astoria world peace conference, have been making their dire predictions at these conventions for almost twenty years. Others who were present in large numbers probably weren't twenty years old—students from high schools and universities in the Washington area. The meeting was notable for the dearth of big names from the world of arts and letters and even more notable for its heavy weighting of sociologists, physical scientists, and, above all, psychologists. There were, for instance, 181 professors of psychology as compared with seventy-eight political scientists in the roster of teach-in sponsors.

Despite the emphasis that the teach-in's leaders placed on facts and expertise, it remained essentially an apolitical—or even an anti-political—affair. Speaker after speaker professed not to understand why, if the government was engaged in negotiations, it could not tell the people all about them. Much

of the argument seemed to be based on a psychiatric explanation of the behavior of Communist countries coupled with
a kind of mote-and-beam moral logic by which the United
States was disqualified from making even the simplest political
judgments. As one of the organizers of the teach-in, Professor
Anatol Rapoport, put it in the course of an interview, "Is it
up to us to say who is a Communist and who is not?" The
world whose outline had emerged by the end of the day's
discussions was one without people or politics but only the
reality of "social and economic forces." One of the heartiest
laughs the audience enjoyed, in fact, was at the expense of a
pro-administration panelist who went so far as to suggest that
revolutions were fomented by revolutionaries. Revolutions,
the counterargument ran, were fomented by "forces" which
were regularly exacerbated by us. "Terror on our side," said
Professor Stanley Millet of Briarcliff, "accounts for all that has
happened in Vietnam."

On the occasions when speakers for the government side
attempted to question the moral character of some of the protesters' positions, however, the protesters took shelter in a
sudden hardheaded practicality. To the observation of Professor Wesley Fishel of Michigan State University that he could
not see why they were so eager to hand sixteen million people
over to Communism, Kahin quickly replied that no one was
"eager" to do that, but one had to be "realistic." Professor
Mary Wright of Yale even found evidence of some sort of
superior life adjustment on the part of the government's critics, who were "more able" than the government spokesmen
"to accept the fact" of Communism's inroads. As the day
wore into night and a kind of combined exhaustion and stupefaction overtook the assemblage, the statements seemed to
become ever more extreme and improbable, ending with a
post-symposium outpouring from the floor. "We in the West
are irrelevant," one man sternly announced. And a young
woman associated with the American Friends Service Committee related the impression that she and Seymour Melman
had gained after a recent interview with Secretary of Defense
McNamara. There was "no question in our minds," she said,
"that the President is advised by men of unparalleled arrogance, stupidity, and incompetence." There was applause.

III. Teaching In

In an appeal for public support, the organizers of the national teach-in were at pains to point out that sponsorship of their effort implied "only a deep concern with the present situation in Southeast Asia and a conviction that questions related to peace and war should be open to responsible debate." The description could probably fit the position of any number of government supporters, and it surely was broad enough to include almost all the participants in the teach-in—from those at one end who seemed genuinely curious and troubled to those at the other who were raising money for medical supplies for the victims of "U.S. aggression." One of the built-in problems of the new movement, however, seems to be its indiscriminate generosity in granting critics of every persuasion of the government's activities in Vietnam a home within its ample tent. The dangers of the practice—diffusiveness, pointlessness, and the final lack of any coherent and identifiable argument—all seemed to be realized at the end of fifteen hours at the Sheraton Park. Nor did the combination of protest and analysis develop as a particularly happy one. The sleepless, marathon aspects of the meeting only served to blur any hoped-for sharpness of argument; selectivity and purpose were sacrificed to a public display of endurance. To whom were the participants addressing their arguments? The public? The administration? Each other? Was the teach-in a protest or was it, as announced, a chance for a great and informative debate? The question is nowhere resolved in the literature of the movement, and the participants spent a good amount of their time extolling the event as a major contribution to the process of debate in a free society. Still, it appeared unlikely that many of the teachers-in had come to Washington with a view to being taught anything at all. When I asked Dr. Rapoport on the eve of the meeting whether he entertained the possibility of changing—even ever so slightly —any of his opinions as a result of the pending exchange, he replied: "I do not feel the government has any case whatsoever."

Within the huge audience and even among the teach-in leadership, there was a fairly wide range of attitudes toward the function—particularly the future function—of the teach-in. And such differences of opinion and of degree of militancy as existed in the group seemed to be reflected in their different responses to the sudden cancellation of Bundy's appearance. Shortly after ten on Saturday morning, Richard Mann and Professor Ernest Nagel of Columbia had been called out of a meeting in the hotel and told that Jorden would take them to the White House, where Bromley Smith of Bundy's office wished to see them. Word of the cancellation started to spread around the hotel shortly after noon; and it soon was evident that there was anything but unanimity on the part of the leadership on what it meant and how to deal with it. Mann, who accepted the legitimacy of the explanation, attempted to soften the attacks Bundy's absence quite naturally provoked. A professor from Hofstra explained it all as evidence that Bundy had felt "personally threatened" by the criticism of his former colleagues. Arthur Waskow, in an impromptu press conference, averred that he had been told by a State Department official that Bundy's action was intended as an insult. "I suggest that individual press conferences take place somewhere else," another teach-in leader remarked when he came upon Waskow and the reporters outside the press lounge. Waskow finally drafted the telegram of challenge to Bundy that the group dispatched the next day, and it was somewhat milder in tone than a "minority report" version that was voted down in a sponsors' meeting that Sunday morning.

What by then had come to be known as "the question of Bundy" consumed almost as much time as the group's efforts to arrive at a conclusion on how to organize itself for political action in the future. But a good deal of time and argument was devoted to the latter problem. There were some who wanted to work through existing peace and political organizations. Others wanted to institutionalize the loose teach-in organization that had been set up. There were motions and motions to reconsider motions to set up a variety of guiding boards and committees. There were short tempers also. "I have never seen a more self-destructive act in my life," said Barry Commoner, a Washington University botanist, when a Michigan woman moved to reconsider some motion or other.

How could Commoner say that, another man rose to ask, at a meeting on *Vietnam* policy of all places?

Little was settled as to future plans before the group dispersed and went back to their campuses. But it was clear that they had some decisions to make on how to bring their influence to bear on Washington, and that their problem was not unlike some of Washington's own—particularly the one the group had theoretically assembled to consider. "The administration won't talk to us," as one professor solemnly warned his colleagues, "unless we have some strength."

The Reporter, June 3, 1965

Eight Dedicated Men
Marked for Death

by Don Moser

LOC DIEN, VIETNAM
EARLY on Monday morning, while the haze still blurs the dark bulk of Truoi Mountain off to the east, the old men walk through the village of Loc Dien. Like a line of ravens in their black formal robes, and holding their black umbrellas, they walk slowly, almost in lock step, through the pale green fields of young rice toward the house of the father of the vice chief. Behind them trudges Ngo Truy, the village policeman, looking out of place in his khakis and white sun helmet, and carrying his carbine over his shoulder. Truy is burly for a Vietnamese, but with large, dark eyes and a gentle manner that seems incongruous for a cop. He looks tired and he is, for he has been awake ever since he heard the shots at midnight. At first light he found the two bodies on a jungle path: one, the father of the vice chief; the other, a Buddhist leader. Pinned to their chests were statements accusing them of using their influence to turn the villagers against the National Liberation Front—the Vietcong. The V.C. had shot the vice chief's father through the chest, and treated the Buddhist leader with sacrilegious contempt—the whole front of his head was crushed in, and between his eyes was a bullet hole you could stick your thumb in. The head is very sacred to the Buddhists.

The delegation of old men finally reaches a clearing around the house of the father of the vice chief. It is a neat building of cement painted sky blue. Inside are a few wooden tables and benches where other old men sit, looking very formal and sage in their black robes as they sip pale tea. As Truy and the visitors enter, Chuong, the vice chief, comes out from behind a curtain at the back of the room. Chuong is not a pretty

84

man—one of his eyes has a wandering cast—and now his face is drawn with grief, but he politely greets Truy and the others, offers them tea, and draws back the curtains.

The body of the old man, his father, lies on a wooden bed. It is wrapped in a sheet and the face is covered by a piece of paper. To the right, incense smolders; to the left, an oil lamp burns. The old men in black move forward to look.

As they do, someone from outside begins to scream. Chuong's sister, who lives in a nearby hamlet, has heard the news. Now she bursts out of the jungle, running, her mouth wide open as she shrieks, the noise rising in pitch and volume. Dashing across the clearing she stumbles, then comes on staggering, tearing off her conical hat and flinging it aside. She lurches through the door to throw herself on the body on the bed.

"Cha oi, cha di mo? Cha di mo?" she moans. "My father, where have you gone?" As she clutches at the body, the sheet slips aside, exposing one of the old man's hands. It is the hand of a farmer, brown, with dirt under the cracked nails, strong-looking even in death.

"Why have you left me?" the girl screams harshly. "You were innocent. Why did the Vietcong kill you?"

The country village of Loc Dien lies some 400 miles north of Saigon, near the old Imperial capital of Hue. Ten thousand people live in Loc Dien. The village consists of 13 hamlets or neighborhoods, sprawling for six kilometers along the River Truoi. Loc Dien lies in lush, tropical country, and its little hamlets are tucked away among thickets of bamboo and trees that hang with bananas, coconuts and breadfruit bigger than a man's head. Loc Dien is prosperous by Vietnamese standards, and lovely by any standard. Along with the peasant huts of lath and buffalo dung are many houses made of cement, again painted a distinctive blue; here and there throughout the village are little one-room elementary schools, and an occasional small Buddhist pagoda. Most peasants have some land of their own, and around the houses the jungle is checkered with small fields of rice, tea, corn, potatoes, and garden truck. On Loc Dien's few dusty streets, and on the jungle trails that connect the hamlets, pretty schoolgirls ride their bicycles, the

long skirts of their white *ao dais* flowing gracefully behind. In
the hamlet by the Bay of the Two Bridges small boys wade in
the waist-deep water, beating rhythmically with bamboo poles
as they drive tiny fish into the nets held by their parents. The
farmers plow their fields behind hump-shouldered water buffalo, or sit for hours pedaling crude pumps which lift water
from the irrigation ditches up over small dikes into the rice
paddies. The wives heap their produce, in top-heavy piles that
defy gravity, on the tops of rattletrap buses that run to the big
markets in Hue; or they carry their goods in baskets to the
market in the village, where they squat all day, amicably chat-
ting among themselves and chewing cuds of mildly narcotic
betel nut.

But Loc Dien is not so tranquil as it seems. Beneath the
peaceful surface, the struggle between the government and
the Vietcong goes on night and day. By day most of the village
belongs to the government. But the night is a different matter.
Eight times this year alone, small bands of Vietcong have
come down from Truoi Mountain after dark, dragged a vil-
lager from his bed and shot him dead. Scores of other villagers
have been kidnaped and taken away into the forest for political
"education." The highway that bisects the village has been
mined. Grenades have been thrown into the market place.
Almost every day people find leaflets which the Vietcong have
strewn the night before. Or they hear rumors from woodcut-
ters who have encountered Vietcong in the jungle. Both leaflets and rumors promise future violence. Not long ago the
Vietcong left a leaflet that named eight influential villagers
they promised to execute—eight shown at the top of these
pages. For these men, and for the villagers as a whole, fear is
something one gets up with in the morning and goes to bed
with at night.

The hub of the village of Loc Dien is the great steel bridge
on which Highway One and the Vietnam Railway—the only
lines of ground transportation between Hue, to the north,
and the American military stronghold of Da Nang, to the
south—cross the slow-rolling River Truoi. Just to the north
of the bridge is the barbed-wire enclosure of an old French
fort which now serves as the garrison for a Vietnamese army

battalion. Just south of the bridge, in Loc Dien proper, is the railroad station, a small dispensary, and a cluster of metal-roofed open-front shops. Off the highway, on Loc Dien's dirt main street, is the village office. And there, on the Monday morning following the two assassinations, the chief of the village works at his battered desk. In the evening Nguyen Dong likes to go about barefoot and clad in floppy trousers and an undershirt, but now he wears sandals and a shirt neatly pressed in accordance with his high station. A limp, home-rolled cigaret dangles from his lower lip, dribbling ash on his papers as he works.

At 55, Dong is, in effect, the mayor of Loc Dien. He is a civilian. The chiefs of Vietnam's larger political units—the districts (equivalent to our counties) and provinces (equivalent to our states)—are army officers, military governors with enormous authority. Dong must answer to his district chief whose headquarters are 14 kilometers to the south, but Loc Dien itself, like all Vietnamese villages, is a little democracy. The chief, his vice chief, and the chiefs of the 13 hamlets are elected every other year by all the adults of the village. With his small staff—a policeman, a tax collector, an information officer, and a few clerks—Dong worries about everything from issuing marriage licenses to protecting his people from the V.C.

Nguyen Dong is tired. He has had a lifetime of war and public service. Between his inheritance from his father, a prosperous farmer, and the canny investment of his own salary in land, Dong has acquired two good cement-block houses, four water buffalo and six hectares (about 15 acres) of rice land. But he must find someone else to work his rice fields, since he dares not work in such an exposed situation himself. He has not slept in either of his fine houses for more than two years. Dong's name heads the Vietcong assassination list and he must sleep each night on a cot in the railway station, where all the hamlet chiefs and village officials gather. There a handful of village soldiers can guard them all. Sometimes Dong wishes he could quit his job as chief, but in the last election 90% of the villagers voted for him, and now he cannot resign. "I would lose their respect," he says simply.

NO. 1	NO. 2	NO. 3	NO. 4
VILLAGE CHIEF	VICE CHIEF	PROPAGANDIST	NATIONAL
DONG	CHUONG	CAO	POLICEMAN
			TRUONG

Dong can hardly remember a time of serenity in Loc Dien. When he was a young man, the country was run by the French, through a puppet emperor. Late in World War II came the Japanese, harsh and unpredictable, and then Ho Chi Minh's Communist Vietminh. In 1947 the French began their attempt to push the Vietminh out of the Loc Dien area and there followed seven years of being in the middle of a guerrilla war. It was not very much different from today, with the villagers fearing and despising the French and Vietminh almost equally. Then, too, there were assassinations, night raids and reprisals. Dong's father was kidnaped by the Vietminh one night and never seen again. Six months after that, the Vietminh returned and burned Dong's house to the ground.

For a while, after the country was partitioned in 1954, the village had a taste of peace and growing prosperity. But by the late '50s, President Diem—and his detested brother and sister-in-law, the Nhus—had lost touch with the countryside. The Communists, who called themselves the National Liberation Front, became active again. The succession of coups and governmental overthrows since Diem's death have bewildered Dong and his villagers. They wonder cynically whether the Saigon government will ever be stabilized. Meanwhile, the amount of Vietcong influence in the village has grown steadily.

Dong maintains that only 5% of the villagers sympathize with the Vietcong. Only a few young men have gone off to the mountain to join them. But at night Loc Dien is so insecure that people tremble with fear every time a dog barks.

NO. 5
VILLAGE
POLICEMAN
TRUY

NO. 6
HAMLET CHIEF
CACH

NO. 7
EX-HAMLET
CHIEF HACH

NO. 8
EX-VILLAGE
CHIEF VAN

Recently the Vietcong have attempted to drop mortar shells onto the Vietnamese battalion garrisoned at the old French fort—something they could do only by setting up their weapons within the borders of the village. But some of the rounds have been short and the villagers who live near the fort have had to dig fox holes and tunnels beneath their houses. On the 80-kilometer stretch between Hue and Da Nang the V.C. blow or mine the road and railway every night, so that rice and other goods imported from the south have almost doubled in price over the last few months. Now people can hardly afford to buy the food they need. The railroad-highway bridge over the River Truoi, just 50 yards from Dong's office, is a prime military target, and in the propaganda leaflets left by the V.C. they have promised to attack it. They have also promised to attack the railway station where Dong and the others sleep at night. They have promised to get an old friend of Dong's named Hach and cut him in half. And just yesterday the boy who herds Dong's water buffalo heard a rumor that the V.C. plan to throw a grenade into Dong's house to kill his wife and his children.

Dong rarely sees an American, for none is stationed in the village. But once in a while, when the battalion garrisoned across the river is home from the field, its American and Australian advisers come to Loc Dien for a glass of beer, or an American medic holds sick call for the villagers. When the Americans first came, the people feared they would be like the French. But the Americans played with the children, who soon followed them in droves, shouting "Hello, OK," and they were off-handedly friendly to everyone, not offending the villagers' pride, as did the French, by treating them like inferior beings. Now, when the V.C. leaflets say that the Americans rob the people of food and leave the hamlets with their pockets bulging with stolen bananas, Dong and the villagers laugh.

The summer heat in Loc Dien is a vicious thing. The humidity is like that in a greenhouse and the sun blasts straight down out of the sky. But despite the intense heat, Policeman Truy—whose name is fifth on the V.C. assassination list—still tramps the jungle trails, a growing splotch of sweat darkening the back of his khaki shirt as he tries to learn more about the killing of the Buddhist leader and the vice chief's father. Truy is a solid, gentle little man of 38 who is not only the village policeman but also the leader of the security platoon that guards Loc Dien against the Vietcong. His men belong to the Popular Forces—full-time soldiers who are paid very poorly by the government, and who serve in their own villages as a kind of self-defense corps.

As the morning goes on and Truy talks to the peasants, he puts together the pieces of what happened during the night. The pattern was familiar. At around 11 o'clock an unknown number of V.C. crept into the village, dressed in shorts and odds and ends of military clothing. In the space of an hour, groups of four or five of them appeared at houses, each of which belonged to a farmer of status in the village. They woke the inhabitants, tied the arms of the man of each family, tersely told wives and children to go back to their beds, and took the men out into the darkness at gunpoint. Two of the men were shot on the path outside, the others, presumably, were kidnaped.

The V.C. may, or may not, have been under the command of a V.C. leader known as Le Nang (Dung is another of his many aliases) who is reputed to be the V.C. cadre chief for Loc Dien. His job is to recruit men, to distribute propaganda and to carry out acts of sabotage and terrorism. Truy saw Le Nang just once, years ago, and knows that he is a big man, powerfully muscled, in his early 50s. But beyond that he is a shadowy, unknown figure. Truy knows about Le Nang's activities only from rumors passed among the peasants. In the past, they say, Le Nang was twice imprisoned as a V.C. suspect, but each time he managed to wriggle out and now he has government identity papers which enable him to live in a sampan and masquerade as a fisherman. He is supposed to keep weapons hidden on his boat, and to have cached many guns in a swamp nearby for a future attack on Truoi Bridge. There is a rumor, too, that he will soon attempt to recruit two more platoons for his guerrilla force from those living in the hamlets of Loc Dien, and that it may have been he who drew up the murder list of eight names.

The fact that the V.C. have promised to kill him does not bother Ngo Truy, for he has been fighting guerrillas half his life. As a partisan under the French he fought the Vietminh near Hanoi, and became a red beret—a paratrooper. He is a mild-mannered man, but he was in continual trouble with the French. Once he struck a French soldier who kept ordering him to do menial tasks. On another occasion he and a friend drove off a French soldier who was raping a village girl. In 1949 the French arrested Truy's brother as a Vietminh suspect and later executed him. His brother, Truy knows, was innocent.

There are two things in this world Truy desires and he can find no way of getting either. One is an education for his six children. But his salary from the government is only about 2,000 piasters a month—say, $20—and he cannot afford anything better than the Loc Dien's one-room elementary schools. The other thing Truy wants is a Browning Automatic Rifle. On paper, Truy has some 40 men in the village's Popular Force, but most of them are on permanent guard duty at the bridges on Highway One, and so Truy has only nine soldiers to protect the 13 hamlets. Truy can rarely count on help from the garrison across the river, for the battalion is usually on operations elsewhere in the province. Truy's own men are armed only with carbines and one Thompson submachine gun. When the V.C. do attack the railway station, Truy knows that they will come with many automatic weapons. A B.A.R. would be useful against them. That the V.C. will come when they are ready, he has no doubts.

*

On Tuesday morning, Nguyen Truong is happy. Truong, No. 4 on the assassination list, is an agent of the national police. He is stationed in Loc Dien, the village where he was born, to gather intelligence about V.C. activities and to ferret out V.C. suspects. He finds his job enormously frustrating. "How can I operate when everyone knows who I am?" he asks irritably. "And what will happen if I learn that one of my friends is a Vietcong?"

Today, though, one of the village's Popular Force members has picked up three strangers. They are children—two young girls in *ao dais* and a barefoot, ragged boy, all of perhaps 15. Though children do not need to carry identity cards—as Vietnamese adults do—when they leave their home village they are supposed to carry a paper from the chief vouching for their identity. These youngsters had nothing.

As Truong looks them over, his vulpine face is lit with pleasure. He is a small, thin man of 29. He wears his fingernails long to signify that he does no manual labor. His left arm bears a long white scar from wrist to elbow. The scar is the work of a Vietminh, who slashed him with a sharpened bamboo stake in hand-to-hand combat when Truong was a soldier with the French in 1954. Truong likes to show off the scar. He killed the Vietminh, and has never stopped hating them.

Now he begins barking questions at the children: What is your name? Where are you from? I have never heard of that place. Where is it? Why did you come to Loc Dien? Why do you say you do not know each other when all three of you were found together?

Big-eyed with fright, the children mumble confused answers and dig their bare toes into the dirty cement floor of the office.

"You are lying!" Truong snaps at them. Standing before them, he waves a long bony finger beneath their noses and shouts, "You came here to try to gather information for the Vietcong!"

The children are too terrified to respond. Truong sits down and looks them over slowly, his eyes glittering. He will send them off to the district headquarters to be put in jail until their identities can be established. Perhaps they are innocent, but the V.C. have often used children as agents and Truong intends to take no chances.

Nguyen Truong would like to get the war over and done with. He wishes that the Americans would bomb Hanoi and kill Ho Chi Minh. And perhaps even take on China. "China," he likes to say, "is like a tiger lying ill in the forest. If we give her time to rest, she will become very dangerous."

Truong is also personally irritated by the war. He has been married for only a year, and he is afraid to stay at home with his wife at night. He does not even think it is safe to stay in the railway station with the other officials, and so he sleeps in the homes of friends, moving each night to a different house so the V.C. won't know where to find him.

Just across the highway from where Truong questions the children, a boy of 6 is being treated at the village dispensary. The V.C. dropped a mortar round on his house and each morning he comes to the little building to have the deep wound in his foot cleaned and dressed by Nguyen Ba, the medical officer. Now, grim-faced as the boy screams in pain, Ba hacks his way through a roll of bandage with a dull, rusted pair of scissors. They are the only scissors he possesses, and he must also use them to cut the umbilical cord when he delivers a baby. "They will hardly cut paper," he says angrily.

Nguyen Ba had only two years of medical school in Hue, but for all practical purposes he is the doctor to the people of Loc Dien. As such, though he is not on the V.C. assassination list, he can never feel entirely secure. On occasion the V.C. will direct their terror against any influential member of the community; schoolteachers and medical officers are especially vulnerable. Already one of Ba's assistants has been kidnaped and another, working in a village across the river, was assassinated.

For instruments, Ba has the scissors, an equally dull and pitted scalpel, a single pair of forceps and two syringes. He repeatedly requests new instruments from his superiors at the province capital in Hue, but nothing appears and in order to give injections he sometimes must buy new syringes out of his own meager salary. With medicines it is the same.

Ba has lived in Loc Dien for eight years. Dedicated to the

villagers, he works hard all day, and frequently gets up to handle emergencies in the small hours of the night. He knows that he can never become a real doctor, but he passionately wants to go to the big hospital in Hue for more study. "How can I do it?" he asks sadly. "There is no one to replace me."

On Friday morning, the village holds a funeral for Vo Van Diem, the man the V.C. shot through the head. Diem, a well-to-do farmer, headed the Buddhist political party in the village, and although this is a country funeral it is accomplished with all the pomp appropriate to Diem's high station. In a serpentine line that winds along the dikes by the rice paddies comes a procession of some 300 mourners: first the Buddhist youth club—the boys in gray shirts and broad-brimmed hats, then the small children carrying religious banners, a man strewing symbolic money along the coffin's path so the dead man will have wealth in the afterlife, men carrying a small shrine filled with burning incense, then the monks, stately in their orange robes, chanting mournfully and ringing small gongs, and at last the coffin, moving forward on the shoulders of the men and trailed by the wailing, sobbing sisters and aunts and nieces of the deceased, all in white robes of mourning.

The ceremony itself is a long drawn-out affair in the searing sun, with much chanting and ringing of gongs, but at last the friends of Vo Van Diem carry his coffin to the grave and begin to lower it on ropes. At this precise moment there is a loud *whump* off to the east. The children and the Buddhist youth, who have been behaving solemnly up till now, rush to the top of a nearby burial mound and stand there giggling and yelling as they watch four fighter bombers of the Vietnamese air force loose their sticks of bombs on the lower slopes of Truoi Mountain. For a minute or two the sounds are all mixed up together: the crumping of the bombs, the excited giggling of the children, the chanting of the monks, and the banshee wail of the women as the coffin of Vo Van Diem is lowered slowly into the grave.

On the afternoon of the day of the funeral, Ton That Cao holds a public meeting at a little cement-block schoolhouse about half a mile down Highway One from the Truoi Bridge. Cao is the village information officer, and it is his job to distribute government leaflets, put up patriotic posters and

banners, hold anti-Communist rallies and otherwise dissemi-
nate government information and propaganda to the people.
He is as much of a contact as the people of Loc Dien have
with the Saigon government. Today he has planned everything carefully. He has set up the battery-powered sound system on the porch of the school, and the triple-striped,
butter-yellow flags of the Republic of South Vietnam whip in
the breeze coming off Truoi Mountain. This morning Cao
had the hamlet chiefs spread word of the meeting, and now
down the road and through the rice paddies come the villagers. Most of them are from the hamlet where the two assassinations took place, and they still wear their black robes and
carry the black umbrellas they took to Diem's funeral.

A quick, intelligent man of 36, Cao has a little drygoods
shop in the market which earns him a good living. He accepted the job as Information Officer, which places him No.
3 on the V.C. murder list, not so much because he needed the
money as because his friend Chief Dong wanted him. Also,
one suspects, because he fancies himself as something of an
orator. Now, as he tells the villagers that there will be a minute
of silent meditation in honor of the two dead men, the black
umbrellas fold, the hats come off and the people stand bare-
headed and silent in the hot sun.

The meditation finished, Cao introduces his speakers: the
chief of the hamlet in which the assassination victims lived, a
representative of the old men, and finally a young boy who
represents the village youth. Each reads a short speech affirm-
ing his willingness to fight the V.C. They are inspiring and
patriotic speeches, but, of course, they should be. Cao and
the district information officer wrote them for the speakers.

When the last speaker has finished, Cao looks himself up
and down, buttons an open button on his shirt, steps to the
microphone, thrusts his fist into the air and shrieks, "Why do
the V.C. kill innocent people? Down with the Vietcong!"

"Down with the Vietcong!" the people shout back.

"Da dao Vietcong!" Cao shouts again and again, and each
time the people echo his cry. But looking down from his place
on the porch, among the shouting people here and there, Cao
sees a mouth set firm, a sneer.

*

There is one man from the hamlet where the two assassinations took place who has not bothered to attend Cao's meeting. He is Ngo Quan, a stooped little peasant of 59 with a face like a shriveled apple. While Cao and the villagers shout their slogans against the Vietcong, Quan is working in his fields a kilometer away. On the night the Buddhist leader was shot, Quan himself was dragged from his house by five Vietcong and taken off into the jungle. There the V.C. bragged to him about their recent military victories and scoffed at the Americans. Quan kept his mouth shut and listened, and in the morning the V.C. let him go, admonishing him to mind his own business, work in his paddy and forget about the government. That's all right with Quan. He never intended doing anything else.

Quan served with the French army during World War II, saw Toulouse and Marseilles and acquired a love for French carrots, but the experience did not add much to his sophistication. He cannot read or write and he does not listen to the radio. He knows the name of Ho Chi Minh and remembers Ngo Dinh Diem, but he has never heard of General Ky, the newest premier. He has never heard of Mao Tse-tung, or Lyndon Johnson. Just as he didn't care who won between the French and the Vietminh, he now does not care who wins between the government and the Vietcong. He doesn't care whether the Americans stay or leave. He needs no help from anybody. He has a little patch of land for himself, and when he needs more money he works by the day for the bigger landowners. All he wants to do is work his fields—just as the V.C. on the mountain told him.

That evening Bui Van Cach, the young chief of Su Lo Dong hamlet, loads a round into the chamber of his carbine, hooks a couple of fragmentation grenades to his belt, says goodnight to his wife and children and goes out into the jungle. Cach is No. 6 on the V.C. assassination list—for the best of reasons. He likes to fight. A handsome, dynamic fellow of 33, he was in a Vietnamese commando outfit that fought against the Vietminh, and since returning to civilian life he has lost none of his aggressiveness. Come nightfall, when the other 12 hamlet chiefs sleep in the comparatively secure railroad station, Cach and an odd little band of warriors lie in ambush for the Vietcong.

At dusk they assemble—as motley a group of irregular soldiers as can be imagined. Nine of the men are peasants, wearing shorts and sandals and conical peasant hats. And Nguyen Che, who in the daytime is custodian of the village elementary schools, has completed his nightly metamorphosis into a squad leader. Festooned with grenades and flares that he has scrounged from friends in the army, with a carbine in one hand, a swagger stick in the other and a cocked .45 in his belt, he cuts a figure that is simultaneously fearsome and absurd. But the Vietcong find nothing funny about him, and they have spread the word that for the death of Nguyen Che, or for any of the men in his squad, they will pay a bounty of 5,000 piasters.

Bui Van Cach is intensely proud of his little group. "The V.C. are afraid to come here," he says with a grin all across his round brown face. "The people in this hamlet believe this hamlet will never be attacked. The people say we are *their* men, not government men. They do not have to be afraid when dogs bark at night."

Now, in the gathering dusk, Cach and the grenade-laden Che move through the hamlet, informing trusted peasants where they will spend the night in case there is any trouble. Then, with their squad, they set out trip flares along the jungle trails to tip them off to any V.C. movements, and disappear into a patch of jungle near the hamlet border to lie in wait for whatever may come.

Later this same Friday night, as Cach and his men wait in the jungle, policeman Truy is also awake, standing beneath the banana trees near the railroad station and peering out into the darkness. Truy and his Popular Forces squad also lay ambushes for the V.C., but they have the additional responsibility of guarding the officials who sleep in the railroad station. So Truy never has enough men available to pose a serious problem for the V.C.

At midnight, after checking on his guards, Truy goes on into the railway station and stretches out on a mat on the concrete floor, his arm for a pillow. An hour and a half later he is shaken awake. One of the men from the patrol tells him excitedly that they have just spotted a strong V.C. unit moving up the highway toward the railroad station. Quickly Truy wakes the sleeping men. His nine soldiers and all the hamlet chiefs who possess weapons are posted at windows and among the trees just outside the station. He has 17 guns in all, and hopes it will be enough. The battalion from the fort across the river is away on an operation and Truy knows he can expect no help. If only he had a B.A.R., it would make a difference.

At 2 o'clock the night is shattered by the fire of automatic weapons as the V.C. attack suddenly from three sides. Bullets spit and whine off the concrete facing of the building. Truy grabs his carbine and starts firing rapidly at the points of muzzle flashes out in the darkness. Screaming, "We will cut off your heads!" the V.C. press forward three times and try to throw grenades through the windows, but each time the grenades fall short. Then Nguyen Lach, one of Truy's soldiers, falls to the ground, his skull creased by a ricochet. A few minutes later, by the light of a flare, Truy sees the Vietcong dragging a wounded comrade away and the attack ends as abruptly as it began.

Next night, the V.C. attack again. Once more they try to grenade the railway station; once more Truy and his men beat them off. But this time the attack is just a diversion. Half an hour later another band of V.C. attacks a highway bridge near the school where Cao held his meeting. But they, too, are driven off by the bridge guards.

On Monday morning, just one week after Truy found the bodies of the vice chief's father and the Buddhist leader, the hamlet chiefs and village officials hold their weekly meeting at the village office. Six of the eight men on the assassination list are there. Presiding, Chief Dong sits behind the stamp pad and bronze seal that are his badges of office. The policeman Truy is there, and Truong the agent of the national police, and Cao the information officer, and the brave young hamlet chief Cach, and even vice chief Nguyen Chuong, still in mourning with a piece of black cloth pinned to his shirt. When the Vietcong shot his father and the Buddhist leader, the act was, of course, intended as a warning to Chuong himself. As vice chief, Chuong is No. 2 on the assassination list. But since he sleeps in the railroad station and the V.C. cannot easily get to him to kill him, they killed his father instead. Unless Chuong quits his job next time the attack might be directed against a brother or an uncle. But no one in the family has asked Chuong to resign his post. It would no more occur to them to ask him to resign than it would occur to Chuong actually to do so. "I cannot refuse my duty," he says. Now Chuong hates the V.C. as never before, and at night he lies awake and thinks bitterly of vengeance.

As the village office begins to fill for the meeting, Do Cho arrives and takes his seat on one of the wooden benches set aside for the hamlet chiefs. Cho, a handsome, shock-haired man of 32, is the chief of the hamlet by the bay, the poorest of the 13 hamlets of Loc Dien. All of the people in the hamlet by the bay are fishermen who live in their sampans and own no land. Indeed, the songs the men sing as they drag in their nets often refer to the fact that the young girls all want to marry a farmer and have security, and none wishes to marry the poor fishermen.

Since the hamlet by the bay is so remote from the village center, V.C. come there frequently, even in the daytime, to take fish from the fishermen, paying them with worthless V.C. money. This year the V.C. have assassinated two men from the hamlet. The place is so insecure that teachers will not come there as they do to the other hamlets, and many of the children are illiterate.

The fishermen have almost as much trouble with the government as with the Vietcong. Elsewhere in the village, the people like the A.R.V.N. soldiers from the battalion and invite them into their houses. The men are well-disciplined, and if they steal or cause trouble, Captain Tung, the battalion commander, will put them in jail. But there are other government soldiers who patrol the bay in motor boats. When they visit Do Cho's hamlet, they beat up the teen-age boys, accusing them of being V.C., and two months ago they killed a respected fisherman merely on suspicion. The hamlet people are still bitter at his death.

Before long, all the hamlet chiefs have arrived and taken

their seats beside Do Cho on the wooden benches in the office. The room is stifling and overcrowded. A couple of years ago, a spacious new cement-block office building with several rooms was built with American aid money and cement. But the building was erected a kilometer down the highway from Truoi Bridge, and after the V.C. threw a hand grenade into it one day, everyone decided that it was too far from the village hub to be safe. Dong and the others thereupon abandoned the new building and moved back into their cramped old office near the bridge.

After Chief Dong calls the meeting to order, Truy speaks proudly of the performance of the hamlet chiefs and his soldiers when the V.C. attacked the railroad station. "The Vietcong thought we were just administrators," he says, his gold teeth gleaming. But then he tells the chiefs that they must improve the security of the village. The first project will be to cut down brush and trees around the railway station and at other key points in the village, so the V.C. will not be able to find cover for their attacks. All men in the village are expected to help, and work will begin immediately.

Then Chief Dong takes up the weekly business. From now on, he says, anyone who goes to Truoi Mountain to cut firewood will be arrested—there is too much chance of V.C. finding them there and getting information from them. And beginning this week the hamlet chiefs will collect from their people lists of friends and relatives who have gone to join the V.C., so that the District Chief will have more information about the local guerrillas. Also, the V.C. have been using young people as spies, and so from now on the young men of 16 are required to have identity cards.

Then Dong explains that he has received 13 radios from District Headquarters. The government cannot give these radios away, but the people can buy them for a very special price of 800 piasters—about $8. Those who purchase radios at this special price must tell the truth about the war to those who cannot afford radios. There are 13 radios and 13 hamlets, Dong says, but he has decided that only the secure hamlets will be allowed to buy them. Certain hamlets cannot buy radios because he fears that the people may listen to the Communist stations from Hanoi.

Dong's statement unleashes an uproar. "It is not fair!" the hamlet chiefs shout. Each hamlet must get a radio. For 15 minutes the chiefs argue violently—Do Cho, from the hamlet by the bay, most passionately of all. "Why do you do this?" he asks Dong. It is not legal. His people *must* have one of the radios.

Dong says nothing. He sits behind his stamp pad and bronze seal, sipping tea, impassive as a stone Buddha. At last he cuts off the argument sharply. "Each hamlet can have one radio," he says. "But if I learn that any person is listening to the Communist radio, I will hold his hamlet chief responsible." Dong's words carry an obvious warning. As chief, he not only has personal authority, but he has the ear of the all-powerful District Chief, and it is not wise to incur his wrath.

Immediately Do Cho is on his feet. He cannot accept responsibility for the people in his hamlet listening to the Communist radio. Under those circumstances he does not want a radio. Several other hamlet chiefs respond identically—now that they must accept the responsibility, they would rather not have the radios.

As Dong listens, his face remains expressionless. But he has won. One suspects that he never doubted for a moment that he would.

That afternoon, Policeman Truy journeys to the military hospital in Hue to see Lach, the soldier who was wounded when the V.C. attacked the railroad station. The man sprawls listlessly on a dirty sheet, his left arm and leg oddly akimbo. His wife, there to tend him, explains that the bullet which apparently only grazed his scalp has paralyzed the whole left side of his body. The doctors say he may be all right in a few months, but she does not know. Truy mumbles a few words of thanks and encouragement to the man. Then he fishes in his pocket and pulls out some crumpled piaster notes and puts them on the bed. He has collected this money from the grateful people, he explains. He picks up the money again and counts it, bill by bill. It comes to 500 piasters—about $5. He gives it to Lach's wife. Then he just stands there, his dark eyes sad. Lach is a good man and has served him well, but Truy knows nothing more to say.

*

Next morning, Tuesday, a peasant comes to the village office and tells Truy excitedly that Nguyen Da and his brother
Thuan, two of the men who were kidnaped on the night of
the assassinations, have just come limping out of the jungle.
Truy gets his carbine and goes about a kilometer down Highway One. He meets the men just as they are crossing the road.
Da hobbles painfully, supporting himself with a stick. He and
his brother have been walking for two days and two nights,
coming down from the vastness of Truoi Mountain, and Da's
bare, brown feet are so cramped with pain that he can hardly
stand. Truy accompanies the brothers home, and as their
wives bring them tea and their children clamber onto their
laps, they tell about their experiences.

They had been wakened by the V.C., told to get 10 days'
supply of rice and hurried so much that Da had no chance to
put on his sandals. Then, with their arms behind their backs,
they were led into the jungle. For two days and two nights
they walked, stopping to rest only for 10 minutes at a time.
At last, deep in the jungle, they reached a "mind-clearing"
camp—a big nylon tent where a dozen other kidnaped peasants from different villages were waiting. As the indoctrination
began, the brothers were told curtly to name their crimes
against the National Liberation Front. When the men failed
to condemn themselves, they were harshly accused of spying
and providing information to the government—in fact, Da
and Thuan had never done so. "You deserve to be killed on
the spot," they were told. They were paralyzed with fright.
But then everything suddenly changed. "You deserve to be
killed," said the V.C., "but since we are men of good will,
you will simply be educated."

Now the brothers were treated with respect and courtesy
by their captors. Each day a different instructor came to the
camp and held class. The instructors were urbane men who
wore military clothing, but they had the soft hands and the
pale skin of men who do no hard work out-of-doors. None
of them was from this part of the country—one sounded as
if he might be from the north—but all were educated. Pleasantly, they informed the brothers that they would not be heavily guarded, but of course the Front must protect itself from
government troops, and so there were many mines around

the camp. It would be most unwise for the brothers to try to leave.

Never during the instruction was there any mention of Communism or collectivist ideology, but some telling blows were struck at the Americans. The Americans, one instructor sneered, change the Saigon government more often than a man changes his buffalo boy—you keep a boy to herd your buffalo for at least a year or two, but the Americans change the Saigon government every couple of months.

If the Americans are such great friends of the Vietnamese, the brothers were asked, why do their planes and helicopters destroy whole villages and kill many innocent people when there are only a couple of V.C. there?

In the end, the instructors told the brothers that they had better withdraw their support from the Americans, because soon the Americans will give up and go home—and the villagers won't be able to go with them.

After five days of class, Da and Thuan were released. "Go home now and tend to your rice paddies and do not work against the Front," the last instructor told them. "If you fail to do as we say, we will come to visit you again."

That evening, Tuesday, 10 days after the assassinations, the last two men on the murder list walk to the houses of friends to spend the night. Neither Bach Duc Hach nor Bach Thanh Van has slept at home in years. Hach, a vigorous man of 45 who can open beer bottles with his teeth, is a former chief of the strongly anti-Communist Su Lo Dong hamlet; Van, who at 53 is so crippled with rheumatism that he can barely walk, worked hard to build up the strategic hamlet program when he was Dong's predecessor as village chief. Neither man has held office in the past couple of years, but the Vietcong have long memories. If the V.C. do come, Hach at least wants to go down fighting. If only he had a gun, he would fight and die on the spot before he would let the V.C. capture him, and he tells his wife and children, "I want to die here in this hamlet so that you can bury me . . . and not be carried away by the Vietcong."

Every night the people of Loc Dien sleep uneasily as the artillery officer at District Headquarters, 14 kilometers to the south, fires air bursts from his two howitzers over Highway

One, hoping to catch some roving band of V.C. All night the shell bursts flicker like lightning off to the south. Tonight the attack does not come until 2 a.m., when the V.C. strike at a bridge near the south edge of the village.

Next day Truy hitches a ride down to the area to see what happened. The V.C. attacked in force, driving off the guards and demolishing the bridge with explosives. For good measure they kidnaped 10 peasants from the neighboring hamlet and laid three mines in the road. Early this morning a civilian truck hit one of the mines and its whole front end was blown away. The driver and his wife were killed.

Late in the day, Truy stops in at the little cafe near the village office to wash the dust from his throat with a beer—a refreshment he enjoys but can rarely afford.

Truy is tired, his sad eyes bloodshot. In the last 10 days he has had little sleep, and things have never been more dispiriting: the vice chief's father dead, the Buddhist leader dead, 15 kidnaped, two more dead from the mine, the railroad station attacked twice, a highway bridge blown, and his friend Lach in the hospital, paralyzed perhaps for life.

There must be something he can do, Truy says glumly to a friend, but he does not know what it is. Each time he develops a plan, the V.C. have a new plan. The people do not like the V.C. and more than anything else they want to be protected. But he cannot protect the village with his nine men, and except in the anti-Communist Su Lo Dong hamlet he cannot get anyone to create a militia.

He cannot dare to think of what will happen if the Americans leave. He is quiet for a moment and then he says, "The Americans do everything for Vietnam. They even die for Vietnam."

There is one thing he knows for sure. He will never leave Loc Dien. He could go to Hue to join the National Police and live securely and make much more money, but there he would be only a civil servant. Here the people respect him, not because he is a policeman but because they like him. They all say hello to him on the street, and when he lost his job for a while after the overthrow of President Diem, the people took in his family and housed them and fed them for a month.

This is his village and he will stay in it and try to protect the people from the V.C. He does not know about other villages, but in this village the people have borne war for 20 years, and 10 more years is nothing. If they have to, they can bear that too.

Truy is talking quickly now, his brown eyes flashing. The important thing is to keep the minds of the people—not to let them become defeatist in spirit. He must tell this to the leaders and to the militia and to his men. The people of the village want peace. But if the leaders fight, the people will follow. They will fight on until the Vietcong are defeated.

Outside the cafe, evening has come. The village is peaceful. The smell of incense is in the air. Small bats arc above the River Truoi, and in the houses the chichas, Vietnam's omnipresent little lizards, chirp as they stalk mosquitoes beneath the thatch. It has cooled somewhat after the blistering day, but the houses still hold the heat, and the people sit on their steps, old men sipping the raw homemade rice whisky they like to nip before bed. The children, restless in that hour before dark, run and play in the dusty streets, the boys shooting at each other with toy guns they have made out of bamboo and rubber bands. Most of the guns are remarkably detailed replicas of the much-admired Browning Automatic Rifle, complete right down to bipod and sights, and they will shoot their wooden bullets clear across the street.

Around dark, the streets begin to empty for curfew, and across from the cafe old Nguyen Dong comes to the door of the village office wearing his floppy pajama trousers and undershirt, a cigaret pasted on his lower lip. He stands there looking out. Pretty soon Truy goes over to join him and then, one by one, coming in from various parts of the village, the men turn up—the hamlet chiefs, and Chuong the vice chief, and Cao the information officer, and the others. They stand around for a while talking softly, their cigarets glowing in the twilight, and then they move out, a motley little band, walking up the darkening street to spend another night at the railroad station.

Life, September 3, 1965

Vietnam Blitz:
A Report on the Impersonal War

by Bernard B. Fall

"Bernard Fall . . . is now convinced that American air- and fire-power will carry the field." *Newsweek*, September 27

"They have made a desert, and have called it peace."
Tacitus, *Life of Agricola*

IT WAS during one of the quieter periods of his stormy tenure as Ambassador to Vietnam that General Maxwell D. Taylor developed the theme that there was not *one* Vietnam war, but 44: one for each of the provinces of the country. It was a good public relations line, and it lived at least through one or two stateside TV shows before dropping out of sight. The fact remains that there are many kinds of war that are being fought in Vietnam, often in one and the same place—from the Dr. Strangelove missions flown by B-52 superbombers designed to carry H-weapons, to the *punji* stakes covered with human excrement, one planted by the Viet Cong in the middle of a path in the hope that they will pierce a GI's boot and give him a festering wound.

But there are not 44 wars in Vietnam and there never were. There are vast areas where ricepaddy-and-swamp wars are fought; other areas where ridge-running prevails, as it did in the Appalachians during the French and Indian Wars; and, finally, there are even a few areas where one can engage in the kind of jungle-fighting familiar from Late Late Show films dealing with Guadalcanal. All this gets fairly abundantly reported in the American press, particularly when it involves US troops and thus allows the citation (with nickname, age, and hometown) of as many men as space and local interest permit. Of course, there are also the Vietnamese, on whose territory—the hard-nose term is "real estate"—the war is fought.

The Vietnamese fall into two categories; the Viet Cong (also known as VC, Victor Charlie, Charlie, or "the Congs"), and "our" Vietnamese, for whom there are no particular nicknames, except perhaps "our allies" or "the friendlies"; both terms followed by a guffaw.

As human beings, neither type of Vietnamese appears to be any longer of great importance. The VC is almost never seen close up; he leads a shadowy existence in deep forests and grottoes, displays no unit insignia even when he wears a uniform, carries no dogtags by which to identify him, manages to bury his weapon before he is found dead on the battlefield; and pushes his uncooperativeness with our side to the point where he—contrary to more normal armies, including the North Vietnamese when they were fighting the French—constantly changes unit numbers. This hopelessly fouls up Intelligence estimates, order-of-battle reports and other EEI's (estimates of enemy intentions). The "off-again-on-again" Northern 325th Division may well be an example of such totally unorthodox and highly unfair camouflage tactics. For all anyone knows, only a few small segments of that ten-battalion force may have been "in-country," as one says in Saigon. As of the time I left a few days ago, no Intelligence officer was ready to swear that the 325th as a unit had joined the battle in South Vietnam.

The VC, in contrast to the old rule that knowing your enemy is a good step forward to defeating him, have to most Americans (even those who fight them) remained faceless and often nameless. There are no "Wanted" posters in Vietnam offering rewards for the capture of a Communist leader. There are such posters, however—now in tatters but still quite prominent—offering rewards for the capture of various non-Communist losers of Saigon military coups. This impersonality (or depersonalization) of the enemy merely reflects how this war is being fought. When one expects to destroy the opposition through massive use of firepower from afar, regardless of whether it is from aircraft, artillery or naval turret guns, it becomes totally irrelevant to know who the leaders of the "Liberation Front" are, or whether a given VC unit commander is a local boy or from a North Vietnamese cadre. For all one cares, the chairman of the Liberation Front could work as a cleanup boy in a US mess hall in Bien Hoa, and nobody would recognize him.

In the same sense, the "friendlies" have become irrelevant. What happens (or who happens to be in power) in Saigon has largely become unimportant. Thanks to the sheer enormity and multifariousness of the American commitment, it is now possible to just about do anything without the approval or the cooperation of the Vietnamese. A few months ago, as long as "Arvin" (shorthand for ARVN, the Army of the Republic of Vietnam) troops were required to mount an operation, American advisers had to plead with often reluctant local commanders. Now, if need be, a whole operation can be mounted from stem to stern without involving a single Vietnamese. The Chulai operation was typical of this: It was American-planned and executed, and the plan was kept a secret from the Vietnamese to prevent the notorious "leaks" for which Saigon is famous. American power also has become great enough to stave off just about any kind of military disaster. When a helicopter-borne outfit of the 101st Airborne was erroneously put down in the midst of a VC assembly area a few days ago, the result should, under normal circumstances, have been unmitigated disaster. During the French Indochina War that happened several times to misdropped paratroop battalions, who invariably made a futile but heroic last stand and got wiped out because there were no reserves available and, above all, insufficient airborne firepower to make the area around the cut-off unit unlivable.

Today in Vietnam, there is *so much* of everything available that almost any kind of military error, no matter how stupid, can be retrieved on the rebound. In the case of the recent battle near Ankhé the misdropped unit was reinforced by other helicopter outfits and progressively surrounded by a protective wall of American firepower until the enemy, unable to maintain his position, broke off contact. At Bongson, on September 24, the VC overran a government outpost, but in the "reaction" operation they allegedly lost 600 men—500 of whom were killed by American aircraft. Against that kind of slaughter, the teachings of Mao Tse-tung, superior tactics, popular support for the VC, or, conversely, poor motivation among the Arvins and patent ineptness among many of their officers, and even the "mess in Saigon" are totally irrelevant. If tomorrow morning Mickey Mouse became prime minister of South Vietnam it would have precious little influence on the men of US Army Task Force Alfa (in fact, a full US Army Corps in everything but name) or on the fighting ability of the 3d US Marine Division.

Much has been said about the use of B-52's in a counter-insurgency operation or, as it should properly be called, a revolutionary war. Joseph Alsop, always willing to swallow uncritically every official handout on Vietnam, has again assured us in a recent column that the B-52's are necessary to destroy "deeply dug-in" VC installations, thus making a few underground bunkers covered with sandbags and bamboo look like the Siegfried Line.

His words had hardly appeared in print when the Air Force switched targets on Alsop and flew three raids into the Mekong Delta, followed by several raids along the Central Vietnam shore. The trouble with the Mekong Delta is that it is so flat, and the water table so high that one cannot dig a pit privy in the place without hitting water. It is well-nigh impossible to build underground positions in it. And, as official population density maps of Vietnam clearly show, the Delta has (with the exception of one single district out of perhaps thirty) an average population density of about 250 people per square mile, with one belt of districts across the whole Delta reaching the fantastic density of *one thousand people* per square mile! With an average bomb load of 500 tons per thirty-plane raid and a known bomb dispersion pattern of about 2,000 yards by 1,000 yards for such a raid, the effects of such a bombardment on a heavily-populated area can be readily guessed.

The point is that this consideration, too, has become irrelevant because it presupposes that hate or love for Saigon or the acquiescence of the Vietnamese population in its own fate, is important. In the view of many of the *realpolitiker* in Saigon and Washington, this is no longer true. Even the old-fashioned military view that a given target must be attained or destroyed before the operation can be called a success no longer holds. The B-52 raids (or "in-country" raids by smaller aircraft) do one thing regardless of whether they hit a VC

installation or a totally innocent and even pro-government village—they keep the Viet Cong on the move, day and night,
in constant fear of being hit. Gone are the days of large and
even comfortable jungle hospitals above ground; of the VC
rest camp with warm food, clean clothes and a good swimming hole; of the large ammunition depot and weapons repair
plant with electric generators chugging away peacefully. The
heavy bombers have changed all that. The VC is hunted down
like an animal. His wounded die unattended. A VC combat
unit returns from an operation only to find its camp area destroyed and its painfully-amassed rice and ammunition reserve
shattered.

And now there are research figures (for this is the most
operations-researched conflict in human history) to back up
the allegations of success through firepower. Before February
1965—that is, before the United States began to use jets inside
South Vietnam—only about two percent of VC deserters cited
air action as a reason for leaving their side. Since then the rate
has risen to 17 percent. Indeed, as many an informed observer
in Saigon will concede, what changed the character of the
Vietnam war was *not* the decision to bomb North Vietnam;
not the decision to use American ground troops in South Vietnam; but the decision to wage unlimited aerial warfare inside
the country at the price of literally pounding the place to bits.

There are hundreds of perfectly well-substantiated stories
to the effect that this merciless bombing hurt thousands of
innocent bystanders and that one of the reasons why few
weapons are found in many cases is that the heaps of dead in
the battle zone include many local villagers who didn't get
away in time. And every observer in Vietnam meets several
American officers who will curse loudly every time they hear
a jet overhead, because it again means an invisible objective
hit blindly—for an F-105 travels far too fast to see what he hits
and must be guided on his target by a "FAC"—a Forward
Air Controller in a spotter plane. The same goes for the incredible wastage of artillery ammunition. "In my area," said
an American provincial adviser to me, "we shot a half-million
dollars' worth of howitzer ammunition last month on un-
observed targets. Yet the whole provincial budget for in-
formation- and intelligence-gathering is $300."

In another instance known personally to me, a plantation hospital had been pilfered by the VC. When informed of that fact by a plantation official, the immediate reaction of the local command was *not* to pursue the retreating VC with troops—always a tiresome and risky affair—but to propose the laying-down of an artillery barrage on the plantation area. "I had the devil's own time dissuading them from it," said the plantation official later. "After all, we have 9,000 workers and 22,000 women and children here."

Here again, operations research comes to our rescue. Thus far, interrogations seem to show that there is no *positively* hostile association between the devastation wrought upon the countryside, and the United States or the Saigon government. In the words of one of the experts, the aerial attacks on the villages "of course cause unhappiness, no doubt on the part of the villagers, [but] do not cause them automatically to become VC's. In fact we have never met one who has become a VC as a result of this." But perhaps the answer should have read: ". . . who has been willing to admit that he has become a VC as a result of this." Be that as it may, and punchcard stacks to the contrary, a high-level mission was sent to Vietnam a few days ago to investigate the effects of that massive firepower on the Vietnamese. It will probably split along service lines.

The usual reply to all this is that the Communists, too, kill civilians. They murder local officials (over 400 since January, 1965), bombed the US Embassy, hit a Saigon restaurant with a mine which killed and maimed over 20 people, and so on. That is perfectly true. But their ability to do harm is immeasurably smaller than that of the other side, and there is no doubt in anyone's mind, and that includes the Intelligence specialists in Saigon, that the VC are deliberately keeping terrorism at a low level because of its psychologically adverse effects. If the VC set its mind to it, it could go on a rampage that would leave most Vietnamese urban centers a shambles (and it may yet do so if pushed back into the terrorism phase of guerrilla war as its field operations fail), but it has not thus far.

Another aspect of the progressive irrelevance of the human aspects of the Vietnam war is the universally callous attitude taken by almost everybody toward the crass and constant violations of the rules of war that have been taking place. The long-suffering (and far too long silent) International Red Cross finally addressed an appeal in July 1965 to both sides, exhorting them to live up to the Red Cross and Geneva agreements; and it was hardly an accident that Secretary of State Dean Rusk chose August 12, 1965, the sixteenth anniversary of the Geneva Convention on War Victims, to reaffirm America's adherence to the treaty, which was fully ratified by the United States Senate. Both North and South Vietnam also have ratified it.

As personal questions to both American and Vietnamese unit commanders have shown (and I made a point of touching on the subject with most of them), there is only the vaguest idea among them as to what exactly is covered by the 1949 Convention; in the few cases where the terms "rules of war" meant anything at all, the officer concerned very often confused the rules of land warfare of The Hague with the Geneva Convention on Prisoners of War of 1929, the 1949 Convention, the Red Cross Convention, and the American Code of the Fighting Man. Several officers would argue that the VC were all "traitors" and thus could be shot out of hand, in yet another misinterpretation of the laws covering treason. But in that case, following the logic of the State Department's assertion that the North Vietnamese were "foreign aggressors," North Vietnamese regulars caught inside South Vietnam would have to be treated as regular POW's, as were American pilots until now if shot down over North Vietnam. Needless to say, no such distinction was made between North Vietnamese regulars and VC regulars, nor between both of them and the VC guerrillas: they are all being treated under the same appalling conditions. The attitude of "this isn't *our* war; it's a Vietnamese war" could hold as long as US combat troops were not operating on their own and taking prisoners all by themselves. Now, this is no longer possible and the Viet Cong are in the position of virtually bulldozing the United States into accepting responsibility for what happens to prisoners; they can shoot in reprisal American POW's whom they hold whenever America's Vietnamese ally executes VC prisoners, as just happened in Danang. Two American servicemen had to pay with their lives for that gratuitous gesture. The September 29 announcement by Hanoi that henceforth American pilots caught in the North will be treated as "war criminals" is a direct consequence of Washington's lack of foresight on the POW problem.

If total disregard of signed treaties is allowed to continue, then the Vietnam war will degenerate to an ignominious level of savagery far below that experienced in other guerrilla wars since World War II. During the French Indochina war neither the Viet Minh nor the French were exactly models of knightly behavior, but one-armed Monsieur Durand, the Swiss IRC representative in Saigon, could be seen visiting the camps where the French held their POW's. And while virtually 70 percent of all Frenchmen in Communist camps died from the brutal climate and disease alone, only a very few ever complained of deliberate inhumanity. Indeed, in such savage fighting areas as the Vietnamese Mountain Plateau, the 803d People's Army Regiment was often known to leave French wounded on a jungle trail, with their wounds attended, to be picked up by their own side; and the same happened in the no-holds-barred Battle of Dien Bien Phu.

To me, the real moral problem which arises in Vietnam is that of torture and needless brutality to combatants and civilians alike. The issue has been sidestepped in the United States; or worse, simply ignored as not being an "American" problem. When the famous newsreel was shot showing Marines burning down houses with lighters, the reaction among officialdom in Saigon was not so much one of distress that the incident had happened as one of furor at the reporters for seeing and reporting it. And then to see the Secretary of the Navy trying to explain the act by dubbing the village of Camné a "facility developed by the Viet Cong" hardly raises the moral stature of the whole operation. Yet, since then, charges of unnecessary brutality have again come out of Vietnam. On September 11, 1965, the *Saigon Daily News*, a newspaper published entirely for the English-speaking Western community of Vietnam, showed on its front page a large photograph of American servicemen standing with drawn weapons over a heap of what the caption describes as "dead VC"—all lying face down on the ground, *and with their hands tied behind their backs.* If, contrary to the caption, the dead were not Viet Cong but, instead, helpless villagers shot by the Communists, I'd be only too happy if some of my friends in Saigon corrected the record, or if the Pentagon would issue a detailed denial of the event and a believable explanation of what actually happened.

For the real problem of what such methods of warfare finally do, to the men who practice them or who tolerate them in their surroundings, will have to be faced up to by the United States, just as the problem of torture in Algeria finally had to be faced up to by the French: not just by their government but by every citizen, every educator and every clergyman all the way up to the Cardinal Primate of Gaul. Even the French Army was split down the middle on the subject, with some Intelligence officers (just as some of their American counterparts in Vietnam now) protesting against torture on the practical grounds that it drove the enemy to a "no-surrender" attitude, while an even smaller minority protested on strictly moral grounds. The best-known case was that of Brigadier General de la Bollardière, a much-decorated combat veteran, who resigned from his command in Algeria because, in his words, he was a paratrooper and not a Gestapo torturer. The uproar in France compelled the Paris government to appoint a Commission of Safeguard to investigate the situation; and books by survivors of such tortures, such as Miss Djamila Boupacha or Henri Alleg (*The Question*) became known the world over.

Before I went on a napalm-bombing mission in Vietnam aboard a US Air Force "Skyraider," I was given a full briefing on "E-and-E" (evasion and escape) procedures. I noted that among the items of the E-and-E kit there was a card with a copy of the Geneva Convention of 1929, informing the American pilot of his rights as a possible prisoner and of the obligations of the enemy toward him. It should not be impossible to provide every American serviceman in Vietnam (not just the pilots) with a handy resumé of *his* obligations under the existing laws and treaties toward the hapless civilian population as well as toward the enemy combatant. And while we're at it, a half-million copies in Vietnamese could be printed up for the Arvins to read at their leisure.

There is one central factor in the Vietnam situation which becomes apparent in the field, although it is not yet recognized on the campuses in the United States and, to a certain extent, in Hanoi and Peking: the immense influx of American manpower and firepower, and the ruthless use of the latter, have made the South Vietnam war, in the *short run, militarily* "unlosable." The italicized qualifiers are of great importance—and I am sure that, as in *Newsweek* of September 27, I will be misquoted by their omission—but the core proposition is essentially correct.

Early last spring, it was militarily almost feasible for the Viet Cong to destroy, in a series of brutal frontal attacks, one or two Arvin divisions; cause the defection of thousands of dis-spirited South Vietnamese troops; and present the United States with the *fait accompli* of a non-existing anti-Communist South Vietnam. Similar counterinsurgent nadirs have existed in other such wars: in Algeria and Cyprus, in Aden and Madagascar, in Palestine and Angola. The power of the insurgent is usually underestimated at the outset. Insurgency is at first left to the totally inadequate local police or security forces, and things go radically downhill until the Queen's Own Fusiliers or *les Paras* appear on the scene in great numbers and are promptly backed up by jet fighters roaring overhead.

The fact that the British were soundly beaten at Khartoum by the Sudanese Mahdi and at Mafeking by the Boers of Paul Kruger did not stop them from stumbling on to victory. In the battles of Hoa-Binh and Cao-Bang in North Vietnam, the French lost more troops than at Dien Bien Phu two years later, but fought on. What broke at Dien Bien Phu was France's will to resist—not her ability. And there, it seems, lies the greatest difference between Vietnam in 1954 and Vietnam now; and there perhaps also lies the secret of what may yet become Peking's and Hanoi's greatest policy error with regard to Southeast Asia. In all likelihood both Asian Communist countries (and, for that matter, a great many Europeans, and notably Frenchmen) simply thought of the American effort as being, of course, somewhat larger and more modern than what the French had been doing; but essentially of the same kind. Well, the truth is that the sheer magnitude of the American effort in Vietnam renders all such comparisons futile. The most striking example is of course the air war. Before Dien Bien Phu, the French Air Force had for *all* of Indochina (i.e., Cambodia, Laos, and North and South Vietnam) a total of 112 fighters and 68 bombers. On September 24, 1965, the United States flew 167 bombers against North Vietnamese targets alone, dropping 235 tons of bombs and *simultaneously* flew 317 bomber sorties "in-country," dropping 270 tons of bombs. In addition, a number of B-52's slammed a Viet Cong stronghold north of Saigon, known as the "iron triangle." In that single day, *even without the B-52 raids*, the US delivered more bomb tonnage than the French Air Force did during the whole 56 days of the Battle of Dien Bien Phu.

Confidence in total material superiority now pervades all of the governmental machinery dealing with Vietnam. The whole problem has in one sense become completely controllable; the build-up now can forego crash programs and emergency troop lifts. In Vietnam itself, leases and construction contracts are being let for a three-year period. From a situation full of uncertainties, Vietnam has become a perfectly manageable situation, whose difficulties can seemingly be quantified. It takes a known number of B-52 raids to liquidate the VC redoubt of "Zone D"; it took a known number of weedkiller flights to eliminate 3,000 acres of rubber forest near Bencat; it will take some 300,000 tons of imported rice (South Vietnam used to export 1.5 million tons, but that was long ago, in 1939) to keep the country from starving this year.

The one unknown quantity is the Communists. Now that the fortunes of war have turned against them, they may find it to their long-range tactical advantage to let the war die rather than to openly admit defeat at the conference table. Or they may, as they did in 1951 against France's Marshal de Lattre de Tassigny, lick their wounds for a season and revert to small-scale warfare; and simply stay alive in the hope that a Stalinist coup in the Soviet Union might bring about an American-Soviet confrontation which might provide them with the sophisticated weapons they now need to stay in business. Or they may simply conclude, on the basis of America's newfound willingness to intervene almost anywhere with troops, that "liberation war" was just another tactic that failed (just as "counterinsurgency" has failed on our side) and revert to the nuts and bolts of political agitation.

A few months ago, William J. Pomeroy, who had fought with the Huks against the Filipino government until he was captured, published a small book on *Guerrilla and Counter-Guerrilla Warfare: Liberation and Suppression in the Present Period*, in which he presents an interesting left-wing viewpoint on the causes of a Communist guerrilla failure. According to him, the Huks failed because "phases of legal struggle that were still possible and the creation of a broad united front of a nationalist character were neglected in favor of a rapid build-up of Huk armed forces."

The same may have happened to the Viet Cong in the face of the huge American military build-up, which has largely reduced the whole war to a slugging match between two military forces, the more so as the present Communist leadership in both Hanoi and the jungles of South Vietnam is so quagmired in the war and in its own rigid posture as to have no political leeway whatever. It is now Washington's turn to show whether it can come up with more statesmanship than Hanoi or the VC, or whether it will fall prey to the attractiveness of its own deployed firepower. In the latter case, a prostrate South Vietnam, plowed under by bombers and artillery and still in the hands of a politically irrelevant regime, may become the victim of aroused social and political forces for which no aircraft carrier and eight-jet bomber can provide a ready answer in the long run.

The New Republic, October 9, 1965

Death in the Ia Drang Valley

by Specialist 4/C Jack P. Smith

THE 1ST BATTALION had been fighting continuously for three or four days, and I had never seen such filthy troops. Some of them had blood on their faces from scratches and from other guys' wounds. Some had long rips in their clothing where shrapnel and bullets had missed them. They all had that look of shock. They said little, just looked around with darting, nervous eyes.

Whenever I heard a shell coming close, I'd duck, but they'd keep standing. After three days of constant bombardment you get so you can tell from the sound how close a shell is going to land within 50 to 75 feet. There were some wounded lying around, bandaged up with filthy shirts and bandages, smoking cigarettes or lying in a coma with plasma bottles hanging above their stretchers.

Late that morning the Cong made a charge. About 100 of them jumped up and made for our lines, and all hell broke loose. The people in that sector opened up with everything they had. Then a couple of our Skyraiders came in. One of them dropped a lot of stuff that shimmered in the sun like green confetti. It looked like a ticker-tape parade, but when the things hit the ground, the little pieces exploded. They were antipersonnel charges. Every one of the gooks was killed. Another group on the other side almost made it to the lines. There weren't enough GI's there, and they couldn't shoot them down fast enough. A plane dropped some napalm bombs just in front of the line. I couldn't see the gooks, but I could hear them scream as they burned. A hundred men dead, just like that.

My company, Charlie Company, took over its sector of the battalion perimeter and started to dig in. At three o'clock another attack came, but it never amounted to anything. I didn't get any sleep that night. There was continuous firing from one until four, and it was as bright as day with the flares lighting up the sky.

The next morning the order came for us to move out. I guess our commanders felt the battle was over. The three battalions of PAVN (People's Army of Vietnam—the North Vietnamese) were destroyed. There must have been about 1,000 rotting bodies out there, starting about 20 feet from us and surrounding the giant circle of foxholes. As we left the perimeter, we walked by them. Some of them had been lying out there for four days. There are more ants in Vietnam than in any place I have ever seen.

We were being withdrawn to Landing Zone Albany, some six miles away, where we were to be picked up by helicopter. About noon the column stopped and everybody flopped on the ground. It turned out that our reconnaissance platoon had come upon four sleeping PAVN who had claimed they were deserters. They said that there were three or four snipers in the trees up ahead—friends of theirs who did not want to surrender.

The head of the column formed by our battalion was already in the landing zone, which was actually only 30 yards to our left. But our company was still in the woods and elephant grass. I dropped my gear and my ax, which was standard equipment for supply clerks like me. We used them to cut down trees to help make landing zones for our helicopters. The day had grown very hot. I was about one quarter through a smoke when a few shots cracked at the front of the column.

I flipped my cigarette butt, lay down and grabbed my M-16. The fire in front was still growing. Then a few shots were fired right behind me. They seemed to come from the trees. There was firing all over the place now, and I was getting scared. A bullet hit the dirt a foot to my side, and some started whistling over my head.

This wasn't the three or four snipers we had been warned about. There were over 100 North Vietnamese snipers tied in the trees above us—so we learned later—way above us, in the top branches. The firing kept increasing.

Our executive officer (XO) jumped up and said, "Follow me, and let's get the hell out of here." I followed him, along with the rest of the headquarters section and the 1st Platoon. We crouched and ran to the right toward what we thought was the landing zone. But it was only a small clearing—the L.Z. was to our left. We were running deeper into the ambush.

The fire was still increasing. We were all crouched as low as possible, but still keeping up a steady trot, looking from side to side. I glanced back at Richards, one of the company's radio operators. Just as I looked back, he moaned softly and fell to the ground. I knelt down and looked at him, and he shuddered and started to gurgle deep in his stomach. His eyes and tongue popped out, and he died. He had a hole straight through his heart.

I had been screaming for a medic. I stopped. I looked up. Everyone had stopped. All of a sudden all the snipers opened up with automatic weapons. There were PAVN with machine guns hidden behind every anthill. The noise was deafening.

Then the men started dropping. It was unbelievable. I knelt there staring as at least 20 men dropped within a few seconds. I still had not recovered from the shock of seeing Richards killed, but the jolt of seeing men die so quickly brought me back to life. I hit the dirt fast. The XO was to my left, and Wallace was to my right, with Burroughs to his right. We were touching each other lying there in the tall elephant grass.

Men all around me were screaming. The fire was now a continuous roar. We were even being fired at by our own guys. No one knew where the fire was coming from, and so the men were shooting everywhere. Some were in shock and were blazing away at everything they saw or imagined they saw.

The XO let out a low moan, and his head sank. I felt a flash of panic. I had been assuming that he would get us out of this. Enlisted men may scoff at officers back in the billets, but when the fighting begins, the men automatically become very dependent upon them. Now I felt terribly alone.

The XO had been hit in the small of the back. I ripped off his shirt and there it was: a groove to the right of his spine. The bullet was still in there. He was in a great deal of pain, so a rifleman named Wilson and I removed his gear as best we could, and I bandaged his wound. It was not bleeding much on the outside, but he was very close to passing out.

Just then Wallace let out a "Huh!" A bullet had creased his upper arm and entered his side. He was bleeding in spurts. I ripped away his shirt with my knife and did him up. Then the XO screamed: A bullet had gone through his boot, taking all his toes with it. He was in agony and crying. Wallace was swearing and in shock. I was crying and holding on to the XO's hand to keep from going crazy.

The grass in front of Wallace's head began to fall as if a lawnmower were passing. It was a machine gun, and I could see the vague outline of the Cong's head behind the foot or so of elephant grass. The noise of firing from all directions was so great that I couldn't even hear a machine gun being fired three feet in front of me and one foot above my head.

As if in a dream, I picked up my rifle, put it on automatic, pushed the barrel into the Cong's face and pulled the trigger. I saw his face disappear. I guess I blew his head off, but I never saw his body and did not look for it.

Wallace screamed. I had fired the burst pretty close to his ear, but I didn't hit him. Bullets by the thousands were coming from the trees, from the L.Z., from the very ground, it seemed. There was a huge thump nearby. Burroughs rolled over and started a scream, though it sounded more like a growl. He had been lying on his side when a grenade went off about three or four feet from him. He looked as though someone had poured red paint over him from head to toe.

After that everything began getting hazy. I lay there for several minutes, and I think I was beginning to go into shock. I don't remember much.

The amazing thing about all this was that from the time Richards was killed to the time Burroughs was hit, only a minute or two had elapsed. Hundreds of men had been hit all around us, and the sound of men screaming was almost as loud as the firing.

The XO was going fast. He told me his wife's name was Carol. He told me that if he didn't make it, I was to write her and tell her that he loved her. Then he somehow managed to crawl away, saying that he was going to organize the troops. It was his positive decision to do something that reinforced my own will to go on.

Then our artillery and air strikes started to come in. They

saved our lives. Just before they started, I could hear North Vietnamese voices on our right. The PAVN battalion was moving in on us, into the woods. The Skyraiders were dropping napalm bombs a hundred feet in front of me on a PAVN machine-gun complex. I felt the hot blast and saw the elephant grass curling ahead of me. The victims were screaming—some of them were our own men who were trapped outside the wood line.

At an altitude of 200 feet it's difficult to distinguish one soldier from another. It's unfortunate and horrible, but most of the battalion's casualties in the first hour or so were from our own men, firing at everything in sight.

No matter what you did, you got hit. The snipers in the trees just waited for someone to move, then shot him. I could hear the North Vietnamese entering the woods from our right. They were creeping along, babbling and arguing among themselves, calling to each other when they found a live GI. Then they shot him.

I decided that it was time to move. I crawled off to my left a few feet, to where Sgt. Moore and Thompson were lying. Sgt. Moore had been hit in the chest three times. He was in pain and sinking fast. Thompson was hit only lightly in the leg. I asked the sergeant to hold my hand. He must have known then that he was dying, but he managed to assure me that everything would be all right.

I knew there wasn't much chance of that. This was a massacre, and I was one of a handful not yet wounded. All around me, those who were not already dead were dying or severely wounded, most of them hit several times. I must have been talking a lot, but I have no idea what I was saying. I think it was, "Oh God, Oh God, Oh God," over and over. Then I would cry. To get closer to the ground, I had dumped my gear, including the ax I had been carrying, and I had lost my rifle, but that was no problem. There were weapons of every kind lying everywhere.

Sgt. Moore asked me if I thought he would make it. I squeezed his hand and told him sure. He said that he was in a lot of pain, and every now and then he would scream. He was obviously bleeding internally quite a bit. I was sure that he would die before the night. I had seen his wife and four kids at Fort Benning. He had made it through World War II and Korea, but this little war had got him.

I found a hand grenade and put it next to me. Then I pulled out my first-aid pack and opened it. I still was not wounded, but I knew I would be soon.

At that instant I heard a babble of Vietnamese voices close by. They sounded like little children, cruel children. The sound of those voices, of the enemy that close, was the most frightening thing I have ever experienced. Combat creates a mindless fear, but this was worse, naked panic.

A small group of PAVN was rapidly approaching. There was a heavy rustling of elephant grass and a constant babbling of high-pitched voices. I told Sgt. Moore to shut up and play dead. I was thinking of using my grenade, but I was scared that it wouldn't get them all, and that they were so close that I would blow myself up too.

My mind was made up for me, because all of a sudden they were there. I stuck the grenade under my belly so that even if I was hit the grenade would not go off too easily, and if it did go off I would not feel pain. I willed myself to stop shaking, and I stopped breathing. There were about 10 or 12 of them, I figure. They took me for dead, thank God. They lay down all around me, still babbling.

One of them lay down on top of me and started to set up his machine gun. He dropped his canister next to my side. His feet were by my head, and his head was between my feet. He was about six feet tall and pretty bony. He probably couldn't feel me shaking because he was shaking so much himself. I thought I was gone. I was trying like hell to act dead, however the hell one does that.

The Cong opened up on our mortar platoon, which was set up around a big tree nearby. The platoon returned the fire, killing about half of the Cong, and miraculously not hitting me. All of a sudden a dozen loud "crumph" sounds went off all around me. Assuming that all the GI's in front of them were dead, our mortar platoon had opened up with M-79 grenade launchers. The Cong jumped up off me, moaning with fear, and the other PAVN began to move around. They apparently knew the M-79. Then a second series of explosions went off, killing all the Cong as they got up to run. One grenade landed between Thompson's head and Sgt. Moore's chest. Sgt. Moore saved my life; he took most of the shrapnel in his side. A piece got me in the head.

It felt as if a white-hot sledge hammer had hit the right side of my face. Then something hot and stinging hit my left leg. I lost consciousness for a few seconds. I came out of it feeling intense pain in my leg and a numbness in my head. I didn't dare feel my face: I thought the whole side of it had gone. Blood was pouring down my forehead and filling the hollow of my eyeglasses. It was also pouring out of my mouth. I slapped a bandage on the side of my face and tied it around my head. I was numbed, but I suddenly felt better. It had happened, and I was still alive.

I decided it was time to get out. None of my buddies appeared able to move. The Cong obviously had the mortar platoon pegged, and they would try to overrun it again. I was going to be right in their path. I crawled over Sgt. Moore, who had half his chest gone, and Thompson, who had no head left. Wilson, who had helped me with the XO, had been hit badly, but I couldn't tell where. All that moved was his eyes. He asked me for some water. I gave him one of the two canteens I had scrounged. I still had the hand grenade.

I crawled over many bodies, all still. The 1st Platoon just didn't exist anymore. One guy had his arm blown off. There was only some shredded skin and a piece of bone sticking out of his sleeve. The sight didn't bother me anymore. The artillery was still keeping up a steady barrage, as were the planes, and the noise was as loud as ever, but I didn't hear it anymore. It was a miracle I didn't get shot by the snipers in the trees while I was moving.

As I was crawling around looking for someone alive, I came across Sgt. Barker, who stuck a .45 in my face. He thought I was a Cong and almost shot me. Apparently I was now close to the mortar platoon. Many other wounded men had crawled over there, including the medic Novak, who had run out of supplies after five minutes. Barker was hit in the legs. Caine was hurt badly too. There were many others, all in bad shape. I lay there with the hand grenade under me, praying. The

Cong made several more attacks, which the mortar platoon fought off with 79's.

The Cong figured out that the mortar platoon was right by that tree, and three of their machine-gun crews crawled up and started to blaze away. It had taken them only a minute or so to find exactly where the platoon was; it took them half a minute to wipe it out. When they opened up, I heard a guy close by scream, then another, and another. Every few seconds someone would scream. Some got hit several times. In 30 seconds the platoon was virtually nonexistent. I heard Lt. Sheldon scream three times, but he lived. I think only five or six guys from the platoon were alive the next day.

It also seemed that most of them were hit in the belly. I don't know why, but when a man is hit in the belly, he screams an unearthly scream. Something you cannot imagine; you actually have to hear it. When a man is hit in the chest or the belly, he keeps on screaming, sometimes until he dies. I just lay there, numb, listening to the bullets whining over me and the 15 or 20 men close to me screaming and screaming and screaming. They didn't ever stop for breath. They kept on until they were hoarse, then they would bleed through their mouths and pass out. They would wake up and start screaming again. Then they would die.

I started crying. Sgt. Gale was lying near me. He had been hit badly in the stomach and was in great pain. He would lie very still for a while and then scream. He would scream for a doctor, then he would scream for a medic. He pleaded with anyone he saw to help him, for the love of God, to stop his pain or kill him. He would thrash around and scream some more, and then lie still for a while. He was bleeding a lot. Everyone was. No matter where you put your hand, the ground was sticky.

Sgt. Gale lay there for over six hours before he died. No one had any medical supplies, no one could move, and no one would shoot him.

Several guys shot themselves that day. Schiff, although he was not wounded, completely lost his head and killed himself with his own grenade. Two other men, both wounded, shot themselves with .45's rather than let themselves be captured alive by the gooks. No one will ever know how many chose that way out, since all the dead had been hit over and over again.

All afternoon we could hear the PAVN, a whole battalion, running through the grass and trees. Hundreds of GI's were scattered on the ground like salt. Sprinkled among them like pepper were the wounded and dead Cong. The GI's who were wounded badly were screaming for medics. The Cong soon found them and killed them.

All afternoon there was smoke, artillery, screaming, moaning, fear, bullets, blood, and little yellow men running around screeching with glee when they found one of us alive, or screaming and moaning with fear when they ran into a grenade or a bullet. I suppose that all massacres in wars are a bloody mess, but this one seemed bloodier to me because I was caught in it.

About dusk a few helicopters tried landing in the L.Z., about 40 yards over to the left, but whenever one came within 100 feet of the ground, so many machine guns would open up on him that it sounded like a training company at a machine gun range.

At dusk the North Vietnamese started to mortar us. Some of the mortars they used were ours that they had captured. Suddenly the ground behind me lifted up, and there was a tremendous noise. I knew something big had gone off right behind me. At the same time I felt something white-hot go into my right thigh. I started screaming and screaming. The pain was terrible. Then I said, "My legs. God, my legs," over and over.

Still screaming, I ripped the bandage off my face and tied it around my thigh. It didn't fit, so I held it as tight as I could with my fingers. I could feel the blood pouring out of the hole. I cried and moaned. It was hurting unbelievably. The realization came to me now, for the first time, that I was not going to live.

With hardly any light left, the Cong decided to infiltrate the woods thoroughly. They were running everywhere. There were no groupings of Americans left in the woods, just a GI here and there. The planes had left, but the artillery kept up the barrage.

Then the flares started up. As long as there was some light, the Cong wouldn't try an all-out attack. I was lying there in a stupor, thirsty. God, I was thirsty. I had been all afternoon with no water, sweating like hell.

I decided to chance a cigarette. All my original equipment and weapons were gone, but somehow my cigarettes were still with me. The ends were bloody. I tore off the ends and lit the middle part of a cigarette.

Cupping it and blowing away the smoke, I managed to escape detection. I knew I was a fool. But at this stage I didn't really give a damn. By now the small-arms fire had stopped almost entirely. The woods were left to the dead, the wounded, and the artillery barrage.

At nightfall I had crawled across to where Barker, Caine and a few others were lying. I didn't say a word. I just lay there on my back, listening to the swishing of grass, the sporadic fire and the constant artillery, which was coming pretty close. For over six hours now shells had been landing within a hundred yards of me.

I didn't move, because I couldn't. Reaching around, I found a canteen of water. The guy who had taken the last drink from it must have been hit in the face, because the water was about one third blood. I didn't mind. I passed it around.

About an hour after dark there was a heavy concentration of small-arms fire all around us. It lasted about five minutes. It was repeated at intervals all night long. Battalion Hq. was firing a protective fire, and we were right in the path of the bullets. Some of our men were getting hit by the rounds ricocheting through the woods.

I lay there shivering. At night in the highlands the temperature goes down to 50 or so. About midnight I heard the grass swishing. It was men, and a lot of them too. I took my hand grenade and straightened out the pin. I thought to myself that now at last they were going to come and kill all the wounded that were left. I was sure I was going to die, and I really did not care anymore. I did not want them to take me alive. The others around me were either unconscious or didn't care. They were just lying there. I think most of them had quietly died in the last few hours. I know one—I did not recognize him—wanted to be alone to die. When he felt himself going, he crawled over me (I don't know how), and a few minutes later I heard him gurgle, and, I guess, die.

Then suddenly I realized that the men were making little whistling noises. Maybe these weren't the Cong. A few seconds later a patrol of GI's came into view, about 15 guys in line, looking for wounded.

Everyone started pawing toward them and crying. It turned me into a babbling idiot. I grabbed one of the guys and wouldn't let go. They had four stretchers with them, and they took the four worst wounded and all the walking wounded, about 10 or so, from the company. I was desperate, and I told the leader I could walk, but when Peters helped me to my feet, I passed out cold.

When I regained consciousness, they had gone, but their medic was left behind, a few feet from me, by a tree. He hadn't seen me, and had already used his meager supply of bandages on those guys who had crawled up around the tree. His patrol said they would be back in a few hours.

I clung to the hope, but I knew damn well they weren't coming back. Novak, who was one of the walking wounded, had left me his .45. I lost one of the magazines, and the only other one had only three bullets in it. I still had the hand grenade.

I crawled up to the tree. There were about eight guys there, all badly wounded. Lt. Sheldon was there, and he had the only operational radio left in the company. I couldn't hear him, but he was talking to the company commander, who had gotten separated from us. Lt. Sheldon had been wounded in the thighbone, the kneecap and the ankle.

Some time after midnight, in my half-conscious stupor, I heard a lot of rustling on both sides of the tree. I nudged the lieutenant, and then he heard it too. Slowly, everyone who could move started to arm himself. I don't know who it was—it might even have been me—but someone made a noise with a weapon.

The swishing noise stopped immediately. Ten yards or so from us an excited babbling started. The gooks must have thought they had run into a pocket of resistance around the tree. Thank God they didn't dare rush us, because we wouldn't have lasted a second. Half of us were too weak to even cock our weapons. As a matter of fact, there were a couple who did not have fingers to cock with.

Then a clanking noise started: They were setting up a machine gun right next to us. I noticed that some artillery shells were landing close now, and every few seconds they seemed to creep closer to us, until one of the Cong screamed. Then the babbling grew louder. I heard the lieutenant on the radio; he was requesting a salvo to bracket us. A few seconds later there was a loud whistling in the air and shells were landing all around us, again and again. I heard the Cong run away. They left some of their wounded a couple of yards from us, moaning and screaming, but they died within a few minutes.

Every half hour or so the artillery would start all over again. It was a long night. Every time, the shells came so close to our position that we could hear the shrapnel striking the tree a foot or so above our heads, and could hear other pieces humming by just inches over us.

All night long the Cong had been moving around killing the wounded. Every few minutes I heard some guy start screaming, "No no no please," and then a burst of bullets. When they found a guy who was wounded, they'd make an awful racket. They'd yell for their buddies and babble awhile, then turn the poor devil over and listen to him while they stuck a barrel in his face and squeezed.

About an hour before dawn the artillery stopped, except for an occasional shell. But the small-arms firing started up again, just as heavy as it had been the previous afternoon. The GI's about a mile away were advancing and clearing the ground and trees of Cong (and a few Americans too). The snipers, all around the trees and in them, started firing back.

When a bullet is fired at you, it makes a distinctive, sharp, cracking sound. The firing by the GI's was all cracks. I could hear thuds all around me from the bullets. I thought I was all dried out from bleeding and sweating, but now I started sweating all over again. I thought, How futile it would be to die now from an American bullet. I just barely managed to keep myself from screaming out loud. I think some guy near me got hit. He let out a long sigh and gurgled.

Soon the sky began to turn red and orange. There was complete silence everywhere now. Not even the birds started their usual singing. As the sun was coming up, everyone expected a human-wave charge by the PAVN, and then a total massacre. We didn't know that the few Cong left from the battle had pulled out just before dawn, leaving only their wounded and a few suicide squads behind.

When the light grew stronger, I could see all around me. The scene might have been the devil's butcher shop. There were dead men all around the tree. I found that the dead body I had been resting my head on was that of Burgess, one of my buddies. I could hardly recognize him. He was a professional saxophone player with only two weeks left in the Army.

Right in front of me was Sgt. Delaney with both his legs blown off. I had been staring at him all night without knowing who he was. His eyes were open and covered with dirt. Sgt. Gale was dead too. Most of the dead were unrecognizable and were beginning to stink. There was blood and mess all over the place.

Half a dozen of the wounded were alive. Lord, who was full of shrapnel; Lt. Sheldon, with several bullet wounds; Morris, shot in the legs and arm; Sloan, with his fingers shot off; Olson, with his leg shot up and hands mutilated; and some guy from another company who was holding his guts from falling out.

Dead Cong were hanging out of the trees everywhere. The Americans had fired bursts that had blown some snipers right out of the trees. But these guys, they were just hanging and dangling there in silence.

We were all sprawled out in various stages of unconsciousness. My wounds had started bleeding again, and the heat was getting bad. The ants were getting to my legs.

Lt. Sheldon passed out, so I took over the radio. That whole morning is rather blurred in my memory. I remember talking for a long time with someone from Battalion Hq. He kept telling me to keep calm, that they would have the medics and helicopters in there in no time. He asked me about the condition of the wounded. I told him that the few who were still alive wouldn't last long. I listened for a long time on the radio to chit-chat between MedEvac pilots, Air Force jet pilots and Battalion Hq. Every now and then I would call up and ask when they were going to pick us up. I'm sure I said a lot of other things, but I don't remember much about it.

I just couldn't understand at first why the MedEvacs didn't come in and get us. Finally I heard on the radio that they wouldn't land because no one knew whether or not the area was secure. Some of the wounded guys were beginning to babble. It seemed like hours before anything happened.

Then a small Air Force spotter plane was buzzing overhead. It dropped a couple of flares in the L.Z. nearby, marking the spot for an airstrike. I thought, My God, the strike is going to land on top of us. I got through to the old man—the company commander—who was up ahead, and he said that it wouldn't come near us and for us not to worry. But I worried, and it landed pretty damn close.

There was silence for a while, then they started hitting the L.Z. with artillery, a lot of it. This lasted for a half hour or so, and then the small arms started again, whistling and buzzing through the woods. I was terrified. I thought, My Lord, is this never going to end? If we're going to die, let's get it over with.

Finally the firing stopped, and there was a ghastly silence. Then the old man got on the radio again and talked to me. He called in a helicopter and told me to guide it over our area. I talked to the pilot, directing him, until he said he could see me. Some of the wounded saw the chopper and started yelling, "Medic, Medic." Others were moaning feebly and struggling to wave at the chopper.

The old man saw the helicopter circling and said he was coming to help us. He asked me to throw a smoke grenade, which I pulled off Lt. Sheldon's gear. It went off, and the old man saw it, because soon after that I heard the guys coming. They were shooting as they walked along. I screamed into the radio, "Don't shoot, don't shoot," but they called back and said they were just shooting PAVN.

Then I saw them: The 1st sergeant, our captain and the two radio operators. The captain came up to me and asked me how I was. I said to him: "Sorry, Sir, I lost my —— ax." He said, "Don't worry, Smitty, we'll get you another one."

The medics at the L.Z. cut off my boots and put bandages

on me. My wounds were in pretty bad shape. You know what happens when you take raw meat and throw it on the ground on a sunny day. We were out there for 24 hours, and Vietnam is nothing but one big anthill.

I was put in a MedEvac chopper and flown to Pleiku, where they changed dressings and stuck all sorts of tubes in my arms. At Pleiku I saw Gruber briefly. He was a clerk in the battalion, and my Army buddy. We talked until they put me in the plane. I learned that Stern and Deschamps, close friends, had been found dead together, shot in the backs of their heads, executed by the Cong. Gruber had identified their bodies. Everyone was crying. Like most of the men in our battalion, I had lost all my Army friends.

I heard the casualty figures a few days later. The North Vietnamese unit had been wiped out—over 500 dead. Out of some 500 men in our battalion alone, about 150 had been killed, and only 84 returned to base camp a few days later. In my company, which was right in the middle of the ambush, we had 93-percent casualties—one half dead, one half wounded. Almost all the wounded were crippled for life. The company, in fact, was very nearly annihilated.

Our unit is part of the 7th Cavalry—Custer's old unit. That day in the Ia Drang Valley, history repeated itself.

After a week in and out of field hospitals I ended up at Camp Zama in Japan. They have operated on me twice. They tell me that I'll walk again, and that my legs are going to be fine. But no one can tell me when I will stop having nightmares.

The Saturday Evening Post, January 28, 1967

THE ADMINISTRATION DEFENDS ITS POLICIES:
FEBRUARY 1966

Teach-In on Vietnam By . . .

. . . The President, the Secretary of State, the Secretary of Defense and the Under Secretary of State

by Henry F. Graff

WASHINGTON.
HOWEVER future historians may write about Vietnam, contemporaries know that the war has entered a new phase in the
past few weeks. The fulfillment of the promises made at Honolulu by President Johnson and in Asia by Vice President
Humphrey and other members of the Administration depends
not only on the national purse but even more heavily on military success in the field. Plans are being made in conformity
with this fact. The plans, as always, reflect the temper, the
mood and the assumptions of the principal policy-makers.

In the third week of February, I had the opportunity to
assay these elements of decision-making in conversations with
President Johnson and some of the men around him. I had
talked to some of the same men last June, just before the big
build-up of ground forces in Vietnam. Among those I talked
to this time, in addition to the President, were Secretaries
Rusk and McNamara and Under Secretary of State George W.
Ball. Once again, I was looking for responses to the kinds of
questions which historians know ought to be answered in the
heat of crisis.

The round of conversations began early on the morning of
Washington's Birthday. It was a brisk, clear day and the public
buildings were almost deserted. The flags were at half-staff in
mourning for Admiral of the Fleet Chester W. Nimitz. I remember thinking, as I walked toward the Department of
State, that the city had an air of melancholy appropriate to
the subject I had come to discuss.

133

I called first on George W. Ball, Under Secretary of State, a lawyer by profession, who has been in and out of Government service for 30 years. I wanted especially to talk to him because, in the aviary of Vietnam policy-making, he is sometimes labeled a "dove."

My first question was: What lay behind the peace offensive of last December and January.

It was, he said, an effort to break the deadlock with Hanoi. Several East European countries "had indicated that their efforts at seeking to end the war were foreclosed by the air offensive against the North." This, he said, had been implied by the Soviet Union, too, "but mostly by the East Europeans."

I asked Ball if the cessation of the bombing in the North had taken place with an eye to the possible favorable political effect it could have in some places here at home. Ball replied that politics can never be excluded—"nor should you or could you." But he went on to point out that the holiday season had advantages, because Christmas and the Vietnamese festival of Tet coincided. The "general stand-down over Christmas" set things in motion, he said.

We turned to the matter of the resumption of the bombing. Ball said—neither apologetically nor defiantly—that he had argued the case against resumption. Out of personal conviction and at the request of the President, he often plays the role of "devil's advocate."

As we talked, he proceeded to give me what he described as "the balance of elements" for and against the resumption. There had been, he said with impressive precision, four arguments in favor of resumption, and he ticked them off. First, it was necessary in order to maintain the morale of the South Vietnamese Government and of our own men—by denying the enemy immunity from the cost of aggression. Second, it was necessary in order to provide a partial interdiction of military goods from the North to the South—"to make the flow of supplies more costly to North Vietnam." Third, it was necessary in order ultimately to convince North Vietnam that the war is not worth the economic price. Fourth, it was necessary because, with no response to the cessation coming from Hanoi, to continue the pause "empty-handed" might have been understood mistakenly as a sign of weak intent.

Next, Ball stated the arguments he had offered against resumption. First, with the increased American presence, beginning in February, 1965, the morale of South Vietnam has no longer been at issue.

Second, although bombing to interdict supplies could make them more costly, it had not been shown that bombing could ever stop those supplies altogether—or even limit them to the point of creating hardships for the Communists in the South. Ball said the effect of bombing, especially in a police state, could be "to dig people in further." He had learned this, he said, from his experience as a director of the United States Strategic Bombing Survey at the end of the Second World War.

The third point bore on the question of China. There are, Ball said, really two wars in Vietnam, one in the North and one in the South. China could be expected to respond one way when a "war of national liberation" was at stake and another way when "the survival of a sister Communist republic was at stake." If air attacks on the North caused Hanoi to become "less free to make decisions without reference to Peking," the attacks could become an "impediment to peace."

When the points on both sides were carefully weighed, the controlling one, he thought, was the one relating to interdiction. He called that argument "very impressive." It is necessary, he said firmly, "to do everything possible to minimize our losses."

Ball concluded this part of our conversation by saying that President Johnson had designated him to write the brief opposing resumption. (I afterward was told that this document of 18 pages, and of "rare brilliance and lucidity," reached the President one midnight and that he read and pondered it immediately for three hours, calling a meeting on it later the same day. Out of the discussion of the pros and cons came the President's insistence that the bombing be strictly controlled and directly related to military targets that sustain Communist efforts in the South.)

What, I asked next, is the position of China with respect to our presence in Vietnam? Ball's answer was that of a man who has lived with the question a long time. He was sure that the Vietnam conflict increases the pressure on China because it affects the competition within the Communist world.

China, Ball went on, probably doubts that we intend ever to get out of Vietnam. They just "don't know how anxious we are to get out of there," Ball said. The Chinese, he continued, hope the United States will regard itself as "stuck in a glue pot, and will tire and quit." While waiting, the Chinese will fight to "the last Vietnamese."

At this point, I asked Ball to do some predicting: What is an informed guess as to how things will go from now on? One outcome to be looked for, he said, is a disintegration or unraveling of the Communist ground forces. Hanoi, he felt certain, will decide what to do only *after* the Vietcong fall apart. He stated his opinion that the Vietcong are now finding it harder and harder to retrain and regroup. They are losing their sanctuaries and must keep moving, a "demoralizing and debilitating experience." The Vietcong are becoming increasingly aware, he said, that they are not going to win.

In his opinion, the war will not end on a single day. It will, he said, paraphrasing T. S. Eliot, probably end "with a whimper not a bang." Peking, Ball thinks, can accept the defeat of the Vietcong—unless the war takes a course more directly involving China's vital interest. However, he added quickly, "I think you can do a great deal in the South with relative impunity."

After lunch, I went to the Pentagon to see Secretary McNamara. He motioned me in warmly and I sat down in the armchair next to his huge desk. I put to him as my first question one which has come to fascinate me: What has happened in the country that the internationalism of a few years ago seems now far less attractive to so many thoughtful Americans?

"You mean neoisolation," McNamara said. "I should by now have given more thought to this question." He proceeded to deal with it.

One explanation, he said, is that "Communism has evolved —it has changed—in the Soviet Union. It has become less violently aggressive." This development, he went on, "is a product of two things. First, the rising standard of living, and, second, the increase of personal freedom." As the Soviet Union has become "less monolithic" and as nuclear weapons have become more frightening, the West has become less united. "I think," he said, "it's the military action we are forced to take which is the reason for so much dissatisfaction among intellectuals."

Of course, McNamara said, neoisolationist ideas are being fueled by misinformed people. He reached behind him to pick up that morning's Washington Post, and read to me from Walter Lippmann's column. In it, Lippmann quoted Hanson Baldwin of The New York Times to the effect that the United States does not have the ready strength to fulfill its foreign policy commitments. McNamara said Baldwin's argument is not supported by fact, but is the "viewpoint of the lobbyists for the militarists in the country."

McNamara now went on to say how strong the United States is. Imagine, he said, we have 300,000 men in combat without having imposed economic controls and without calling up reservists. He called the accomplishment "unbelievable."

He said that General Westmoreland can plan to drop in Vietnam this month two and a half times the average monthly tonnage of explosives dropped in Korea. And he commenced to read to me from a paper in his pocket the specific figures for bombs, rockets, small-arms ammunition, grenades, and mortar and artillery shells. He took care to say that Westmoreland would not need to use all this power: "I can't imagine he's going to find targets to fire all this stuff at."

We turned now to another theoretical subject. How, I asked, do we confront the Red Chinese? Clearly, *this* question McNamara had already put his mind to. We must, he said, obtain multilateral recognition of the threat China poses to Asia and surrounding areas. "Multilateral action must be brought about by the nations threatened," he insisted.

He told of how he and Rusk had attempted within NATO to "get a dialogue started" with the European nations on the question of dealing with Chinese expansion. "It is debatable whether one nation alone can do this," he declared, explaining that he doubted that such a policy would be "politically acceptable."

He added that he thought one of the elements in neo-isolationism has been the unilateral action taken of necessity by the United States. Latterly, more allies have come in and there is a growing concert of response.

Is there a danger of a belligerent riposte by the Chinese to the steps we are taking in Vietnam, I asked. "You are always running risks when dealing with a belligerent power," he replied. He commented quickly that we ran the same risk by our actions in Korea and in behalf of Taiwan. He also added the point that Ball had made, that the Chinese response was not likely to involve war "so long as we do not appear to be striking to overthrow the regime of North Vietnam but only to support the people of South Vietnam in shaping their own destiny." He concluded, "The risk of unlimited war is not very great."

I now reminded McNamara that when we talked last June he had said that we were not moving in the direction of a "land war" in Asia. Did he still have that opinion? Yes, he said, there is no "overt land war" in process. He defined such a war as one in which substantial units of Chinese or North Vietnamese were to enter the fighting "under their own flags."

Can you tell me, Mr. Secretary, I asked bluntly, how large a commitment of men the United States is prepared to make in Vietnam? "I can't answer that," he said—and quickly amended it to: "I don't answer that." He discoursed on the enormous mobility and firepower of the American soldier. "The thing we prize most deeply," he said, "is not money but men. We have multiplied the capability of our men. It's expensive in materials but cheaper in life."

Now I asked McNamara what the word victory, as many —including Vice President Humphrey—are now using it, means. He answered that he tries to avoid such words as "victory" or "win"—which he called "color words." He prefers the phrase "favorable settlement," he said.

And how, I inquired, did he think a "favorable settlement" would be brought about? He said the North could cease "feeding the fires of subversion and aggression in South Vietnam and the N.L.F. [the National Liberation Front] could reduce its activity against the South and withdraw to live in peace. The people could then shape the outcome."

Could China abide such a result, I asked. Yes, McNamara answered. He thought China might charge the defeat of the Vietcong to the other Communist states, which could be blamed for not having sent in sufficient material.

As I prepared to leave, I asked McNamara if there was anything he had done in his five years as Secretary of Defense which he wished he had done differently. I was thinking of Vietnam but he quickly adverted to the Bay of Pigs. *That*, he said, was "a serious error." President Kennedy had taken full responsibility, he commented sadly, "but I was in the room." He added: "We're not likely to make that kind of mistake again—of being so uncertain of our estimates."

And what about the course of the decisions respecting Vietnam? There should, he said, be a critique of the whole episode, but it will be years before we reach it. The lessons, he said, are not completely clear. But some are worth talking about.

My next stop was Dean Rusk's office. I began by mentioning his presentation of the Administration's position before the Senate Foreign Relations Committee the previous week. He quickly shifted the conversation to a by-product, the suggestion by James Reston of The New York Times that the Secretary had enunciated a "Rusk Doctrine," committing the nation militarily to protect some 40 countries. Rusk commented tartly: "I didn't vote for a single one of those commitments. They did"—meaning the members of the Senate. And, he added, "when you go into an alliance you have to mean it."

Rusk, talking of his critics, stressed that "one thing really hasn't gotten through"—that this country means what it says it means. He stayed on the subject: "I saw Chairman Khrushchev threaten President Kennedy with war over Berlin. And President Kennedy responded: 'If that's what you want, O.K., but it'll be a very cold winter.'" The Soviets, Rusk said, had to believe that war would be the result of their belligerence. The same thing, he went on, had occurred at the time of the Cuban missile crisis: "They had to believe our President meant what he said."

It is most important, he declared, that "when President Johnson says, 'You're not going to have Vietnam,' " he must be believed. "If ever the other side concludes that a President does not mean what he says, we're finished."

Then, in a pensive tone, he said: "Most totalitarian countries make a mistake about what a democracy will do at the end of the day." They regard us "as sloppy people with our hands in our pockets." Hitler, he said, made the same wrong judgment.

I switched the discussion to the question of what had happened to the internationalists of only a few years ago who now were saying we ought not to be so heavily committed in the world. Rusk responded by saying that liberal intellectuals had always made a distinction between Fascism on the one hand and Marxism on the other with respect to the intensity of their feeling. "They are more concerned with the Hitler kind of problem" was the way he put it.

Then he said with fervor: "A certain kind of liberalism is jaded and cynical." And he added: "Don't ask me to call a man a liberal who wants to turn over to a totalitarian regime more than 14 million South Vietnamese."

Rusk thought also that some people pinned too much hope on the idea of *détente* with the Soviet Union—"when the Soviets won't push the idea until it fits their needs." People's hopes, "which went far beyond realities," were built exclusively on the nuclear test-ban treaty. "It was a great step, but it did not signal a change of heart in the Communist world." Many came to regard Khrushchev as "an affable old grandfather." But, Rusk clinched his point, "he was 68½ when he put missiles in Cuba."

Rusk, in a matter-of-fact tone now, said that because there was so much hope for a general peace, the war in Vietnam had come as "a rude shock." Some people wanted to put the problem out of sight. Their feelings of frustration, he said, have come in part because "the problem itself arose ambiguously." The aggressors "sneaked" into the area rather than marching across the border.

Rusk turned again to the critics. Many of those who oppose Administration policies, he said, "are not disclosing their premises." At least, he commented, Senator Morse says openly: "South Vietnam is not worth the life of a single American soldier." Others, he maintained, do not state the basis of their position. Yet, he said, "the 'buts' add up to withdrawal."

We moved the conversation to the subject of China. The American people are worried, Rusk said. "They ought to be," he added, "because China is capable of grossly irrational decisions." Since 1945 there has been a possibility of a bigger war in every crisis—and he listed Greece, Berlin, Korea and Cuba. "If we leave the impression with the other side that we can't face the risks, then we'll never settle these questions."

I asked Rusk to talk to me about the peace offensive. How hopeful of good results were the participants? There were, he replied, only marginal hopes. But they were substantial enough to keep it from being "a phony propaganda play." Then he pointed out that since June, 1961, the United States has not been idle in seeking peace in Southeast Asia. In the past year alone, he remarked, more than 125 efforts were made.

In 1961, he said, President Kennedy had suggested to Khrushchev in Vienna that "we all get out of Laos." Khrushchev agreed, but he would not include Vietnam in the agreement. This, Rusk said, "could have been a contribution to peace." Hanoi, in violation of the agreement, left its forces in Laos and later infiltrated them into South Vietnam. Rusk said he thinks the Soviet Union acted in good faith, but that the split between Moscow and Peking was already having an effect on the chances for peace in that part of the world.

He talked of the bombing pause of last May. "By the third day," he said, "we had the answers." Peking said "no" on the radio and Hanoi refused to receive our message. Gromyko told him in Vienna, he said, that the pause and message were an "insult."

But, thereafter, several countries in Eastern Europe were saying the United States could not get talks started unless the bombing stopped. "We tried to find out what would happen if we did," he said. But we received no answer.

The longer bombing pause, Rusk said without anger, was "harshly and negatively" received. The other side simply said:

"Recognize the N.L.F. as the sole bargaining representative of South Vietnam, accept the Four Points, and get out." He commented that it is a mystery, though, as to why Hanoi did not make it difficult for us—by an ambiguous response of one kind or another—to resume the bombing.

The resumption of bombing was a unanimous decision of the President and his senior advisers, Rusk said. He observed: "No President has spent more time than President Johnson gnawing into difficult questions." "The impression he sometimes gives of being impetuous on major issues is false," Rusk wanted to make clear.

China, however, was the lodestone and we were drawn back to it. Rusk said he is sure that there is a "flash point" and "both sides are being very careful." "We don't want blind events to take over." At the moment, we "don't see a movement of forces suggesting a substantial deployment of men to the South," he stated solemnly as he knocked wood on the edge of his desk. "We will be watchful."

I asked Rusk, as I had asked McNamara, if there were some things in respect to Vietnam in the last five years that he wished had been done differently. Rusk answered that he thinks that after the Vienna meeting in June 1961, we should have put down "a lot of blue chips immediately" to head off "the other side" and to say, "You can't have South Vietnam." (Secretary McNamara had earlier suggested to me that he wished we had examined our objectives more profoundly and completely five years ago.)

Rusk said he believed that such action would have prevented misunderstanding with the Communist world. In this regard, he said that during 1964 the Communists had concluded that all the U.S. wanted was to save face. They misunderstood: "We were not interested in saving face but in saving Vietnam."

Now I asked Rusk how he thought the war would end. He said: "They won't come to the table so long as they think they can get South Vietnam by force. If they decide they can't win they may come to the conference table to see what they can get there." They may, he said further, "just let things peter out the way the Greek guerrillas did." This may involve, he thought, a decision on their part to stop for a while and wait for another day. (McNamara had also implied the same possibility.)

Rusk also suggested that the denouement could come suddenly. He recalled for me how cryptically and unexpectedly word reached the United States in 1949 that the Soviet Union was ready to lift the blockade of Berlin.

"The other side is hurting," Rusk observed. The signs are increasing. He listed some of them: The Vietcong and the North Vietnamese lost more men last year than the total United States loss in the Korean war; prisoners report that Ho Chi Minh's statement about being ready to fight a 10-to-20-year war has had a depressing effect on morale; the other side cannot sustain a battalion in combat more than 24 hours because of the intense firepower to which they are exposed; there is no rest for their soldiers, who are always on the move;

'The Steaming Jungle'

Among the Presidential advisers to whom I talked was McGeorge Bundy, then still Special Assistant for National Security Affairs, now departed from Washington to be president of the Ford Foundation. To him, too, I put the question: What has happened to the liberals, who only recently were earnest supporters of America's involvement in the world?

Bundy seized on it. "It's the part of the world we're in," he began, "and it's the steaming jungle."

The liberals, he said, "never learned internationalism with respect to Asia." "If Kennedy were doing it [that is, waging war in Vietnam], they'd be less distressed. They are a prejudiced lot who don't distinguish between style and substance; they don't realize the President has his fist in the dike—he's not MacArthur; he's not Goldwater."

Bundy completed his point: "The aggression in Vietnam is less clear-cut than in Korea, and so it does not force a moral judgment as it did then. This helps our liberal friends cover their shame."

—H.F.G.

defections are up fourfold. Rusk concluded: "On the present basis, they are not going to come out of it like they had hoped."

Of course, he said, a question is: "What are the big brothers going to do?" The evidence is that they are "more cautious in action than in words." "It's a tough game we're playing and we could be wrong," he warned. And he added quickly: "The President cannot rely on a guess on this subject." "Everybody can say, 'Sorry, boss, I was wrong,'" except him.

Those who make policy, Rusk continued, can "draw no doctrinal conclusion about what the other side will *not* do. Decisions have to be based on all contingencies and all consequences of various alternatives." "If the other side is as concerned as they ought to be in similar fashion, maybe we'll get some peace out of it at some point."

In response to a question of mine, Rusk switched back to the subject of the hearings held by the Senate Committee on Foreign Relations. He stated with some heat that Senator Fulbright declares we ought to offer "the other side" something. Yet, Rusk said, "nobody is offering us anything."

As our talk on Vietnam was drawing to a close, Rusk seemed to sum up his feelings on the critics. He said plaintively: "We're caught between the hawks and the doves."

The next morning, I had an appointment at the White House to see the President. He greeted me in his oval office, and immediately led the way into what he had called, the last time I saw him, his "little office," a place he can retreat to just off the main room. Mr. Johnson asked me if he could get me a soft drink; he was having one. I accepted. I sat on a small sofa. The President sat in an easy chair facing me. Press Secretary Bill Moyers, who had joined us, sat across from us.

The President turned to me, his mind plainly on the American soldiers in Vietnam and began to talk.

He was proud, he said, that we had moved between 150,000 and 200,000 men into Vietnam with "the greatest efficiency in the history of the world." He spoke of the medical facilities which had been built and of the care which is waiting for our wounded when they arrive from the field. General Westmoreland, he said, has called our Army "the most mobile under any flag, the best-equipped and the one with the most firepower per man." He said he had asked Westmoreland if he was short of anything and he had replied that he was short of nothing that affects the effectiveness or morale of our men.

The President returned to thoughts of the casualties. "We have," he said, "the lowest ratio of dead to wounded we've ever had," and he attributed that to the mobility of our forces. He marveled at how, through the use of helicopters, it is possible to move a man from the battlefield to a hospital in 30 minutes to an hour. He had praise not only for the medical people but also for the search-and-rescue units.

Then Mr. Johnson alluded to the Vietcong losses. He said they had suffered close to 30,000 killed, wounded, missing and captured in two months. "We don't think Hanoi has yet realized how serious it is," he observed gravely. "They are looking at things through rose-colored glasses, intoxicated perhaps by the debate back here." He said it will take awhile for "their own casualties to catch up with them."

The President shared with me the weekly cable to him from Ambassador Henry Cabot Lodge in Saigon, which had just arrived. It was labeled "Secret Nodis" ("Nodis" is Government language for "not for distribution"). It summarized for the President the important events of the week. It contained the information, for instance, that in one battle Vietcong machine-gunners had been found dead manacled to their weapons. Lodge also reported that he had had lunch with some elements of the First Cavalry Division and that one soldier had told him he found it easier to understand the draft-card burners than the prominent men who seemed willing to carry on the debate at home interminably.

The cable also expressed the concern of the American community in Saigon that this is "the only war we've fought in this century where important men kept flailing policy after it has been debated and decided."

Mr. Johnson spoke sadly about some of the opposition. Senator Fulbright and the others, some of the strongest critics, he noted, had voted for the SEATO treaty—under the provisions of which the United States defends the legality of its presence in Vietnam. Mr. Johnson and John F. Kennedy had been ill at the time the treaty was before the Senate, although the President remarked that he would have voted for it. "I didn't make this contract," he said, "but I intend to keep it."

He told me how he had gone to Congress for the resolution of support in August, 1964, informing the lawmakers that "he wanted them in on the take-off as well as the landing." He explained how he had helped give President Eisenhower a similar resolution to protect Taiwan. He continued calmly: "We inherited this involvement, this commitment, and we are there. I want Congress to go with us." The Communists need to know where we stand.

I asked: Mr. President, how do you account for the opposition to the fighting—Senatorial and otherwise? He replied that there is a strong strain of "cultural alienation" in it, by which he means a feeling that the Vietnamese "are not our kind of people, that they're an ancient people unconcerned with change and reform, that they are so different from us that it would be impossible for us to help them.

"You may think this is begging your question, but I have heard this from the most pronounced critics of our policy. They write off Asia and say: 'Concentrate on Europe. Our destinies are inseparable. Our customs are common.'

"These people may be sincere, but I believe they are wrong. They ignore the fact that the desire to be independent is as color-blind as aggression. They think the hope of catching up with the times is American—or European—exclusively. What we're fighting for is not European or Asian or American—it's basic to man's nature everywhere. We want to give peaceful change a chance to work in Asia as it has in Europe." (At one point, the President said to me, in obvious sorrow, that India may lose as many people by starvation this year as the entire population of Vietnam.)

Mr. Johnson reverted to the subject of the Senate hearings. The Senators came up with "no alternative plan, no alternative program." They could have recommended that we withdraw, that we accept the enclave idea, that we bomb North Vietnam harder, or that we strike China with nuclear weapons. But their main point was, "We're going to get into a war with China." As if they were the only ones who had given any thought to the difficulties we face out there!

The President anticipated the question I had next in

mind—What are the chances that China will come in?—for he spoke it and answered it: "I don't think anybody knows. I'm no expert. Of course, if we spit in her face, that's one thing; but if we don't, most experts don't believe she will want to get involved that way. In the meantime, though, what are we supposed to do—lie paralyzed in fear? That is what they [the Communists] would like us to do."

Now the President referred to what the public-opinion polls show. A solid 10 per cent, he explained, "are hotheads—Goldwater types"; 10 per cent "are ready to run." "We can never change their minds—and it's a mistake to think we can. Every concession we have made to the critics has been met with another demand and—they will never be satisfied. I have listened to them patiently: now I have to prosecute our policies to the best of my ability, hoping they will realize what is at stake."

This led him again to pose a question and to answer it: When is it going to be over?

"When Churchill said we shall fight on the beaches, and in the streets, he did not say when it would be over. When the aggressor changes his mind, it will be over—but not before—not unless the American people succumb to the temptation to take the easy way out. I can't say when this will be over—I would have to take the Fifth Amendment if asked to answer that one precisely," he quipped.

But the President tried to answer the question for me, anyway. He said General Westmoreland is more optimistic. The North Vietnamese casualties are very heavy. The defections are doubling—"averaging 1,700 a month, with 2,000 this month." "After the Alamo, no one thought Sam Houston would wind up so quick," he said in an aside. And then he mused, "Who knows how long, how much?" The important thing is: Are we right or wrong? "I believe we are right."

I broke in to ask him to tell me about the new phase of the war. His face lit up spontaneously. The war is two-pronged, he said. He made two fists. He thrust one forward signifying the military side and then the other signifying the economic and social side. This was the side he plainly *wanted* to talk about. He said proudly: "I want to leave the footprints of America there. I want them to say, 'This is what the Americans left—schools and hospitals and dams.' " Shortly afterward, he said: "We can turn the Mekong into a Tennessee Valley."

The President talked of the income of the Vietnamese as "$65 a year," and of how they need schools, health measures and agricultural assistance. "We can teach them to read and write," he said with elation. He explained that we are trying to introduce television in Vietnam. He said the domestic help at Lodge's quarters were wide-eyed in amazement when they first saw TV, beamed from a plane. He rose out of his chair, his own eyes wide and with his arms raised to illustrate how amazed they probably had looked. Then he said softly: "I remember the first time I heard radio."

The President continued. He said he was asking Ambassador William Porter to be in the economic and social field a counterpart to General Westmoreland. The work of uplifting South Vietnam, he said, is "tough." "You build schools and hospitals and the Communists tear them down. That is just one more reason I get so frustrated when people charge that we should be more sympathetic to the Vietcong. What has happened to American liberalism that it would ignore such tactics? There are times when it seems the Vietcong have more negotiators in their behalf than our soldiers do."

As to the Vietcong in negotiations, Mr. Johnson said soberly: "We'll work out a way for them to be heard—if Hanoi will let them—or if they want to. But history makes it clear that when you bring the Communists in, they can chew you up if you are not as smart or as prepared as they are."

Mr. Johnson shifted now to his impressions of Premier Ky. Ky, the President said with delight, "sounded like Rex Tugwell."* I asked him what he meant, and he recalled that Tugwell in the early days of the New Deal had said that we must "roll up our sleeves and remake America." Ky, in the President's opinion, "is talking like Tugwell—we're hoping he can perform like Tugwell."

As for the South Vietnamese people: "They have 700,000 men fighting. We're not giving them up." He insisted: "We're fighting for a special objective. We don't want to destroy

---

*Rexford G. Tugwell, one of Franklin D. Roosevelt's Brain Trusters and later Governor of Puerto Rico, helped to frame the Agricultural Adjustment Act.

China or North Vietnam. We just want to have them leave these people alone."

To illustrate, he reminded himself of how, years ago, Huey Long had gone into Arkansas to campaign for Hattie Caraway for the Senate.* He told the story with zest and in lively detail, reminding us that the only thing Long wanted to do was "just to protect this poor little helpless woman from those powerful interests arrayed against her."

Mr. Johnson returned to the matter of our strategy. Our aim in bombing, he said, is "not to destroy or kill civilians but simply to stop Hanoi from bringing the stuff down into the South." He said he had been advised by General Eisenhower to let the Communists know there are no sanctuaries from which aggression can be directed.

And, again, Mr. Johnson repeated his main idea: "They" must stop their aggression. "If they'll go home tomorrow, we'll come home."

---

*Hattie Caraway, the first woman U.S. Senator, was appointed to her late husband's seat in 1931. She won her first full term in 1933 by defeating six male opponents in the Democratic primary, with the support of both F.D.R., then Presidential candidate, and Senator Huey Long, the Louisiana Kingfish, father of Senator Russell Long. She was defeated in the 1944 primary by Senator J. W. Fulbright.

The New York Times Magazine, March 20, 1966

Reconnaissance

by Ward S. Just

IN THE SUMMER of 1966 yet another monsoon offensive was predicted in Pleiku and Kontum provinces in the Central Highlands. American intelligence said the North Vietnamese were infiltrating from Laos into Pleiku and Kontum in battalion- and regimental-sized units, well fed, well trained and well and heavily armed. The theory of the enemy objective, which had been expounded in one form or another for two years, was that Giap's regulars would "cut the country in half," driving east from the Laotian border to the South China Sea. It was an implausible theory, owing as it did practically nothing to logic: the North Vietnamese did not have the men to hold a line across the waist of South Vietnam, neither did they have the weapons to ward off attacking American aircraft. Much more plausible was the theory that the North Vietnamese were invading to make the highlands so hazardous that the Americans would be forced to concentrate large numbers of troops there.

But everybody believed the scissors theory, probably because it made rich newspaper copy. An American general once admitted that what the command had in mind was that if the North Vietnamese cut the country in half they would have a marvelous propaganda victory. The reverse was also true, and therein lay the *raison d'être* for the theory. The operative line was given at a Westmoreland press briefing in 1966: "They tried to cut the country in half but we stopped them."

There were a few amateur strategists who insisted that the country was already cut in half, obviously so by the inability of an ordinary citizen to drive from Saigon to the Demilitarized Zone. But these objections were swept aside as the work of cranks. As far as the American command was concerned, the North Vietnamese went on trying to cut the country in half and the American Army went on stopping them. Thus was the territorial integrity of South Vietnam preserved.

No one knew what the strategy really was. Some of the military thinkers believed that all Ho and Giap had in mind was sending as many troops as they could afford, punishing the Americans to the limit of endurance, and assaulting air-fields and base camps until the allies quit from exhaustion. It was, as Westmoreland often said in 1967, a war of attrition; grand strategy did not as a practical matter exist. It was tactics that counted, and what was meant by tactics were the thousands of small-unit engagements from the Camau pen-insula to the DMZ. The sum of these equaled the whole, or should have.

I flew from Saigon to Pleiku and then to the Special Forces camp at Dak To early in June, 1966. I had been told in Saigon that American intelligence officers had identified new North Vietnamese units prowling the highlands. The 1st Brigade of the 101st Airborne Division was to move out into the jungles to find the enemy. It was regarded in Saigon as an important campaign: whatever the argument on whether or not the enemy objective was to cut the country in half, there was no doubt that the highlands themselves were imperiled.

It was the North Vietnamese who drew first blood: on the night of June 6, a battalion hit an American artillery base just north of Dak To and nearly overran it. Firing at point-blank range, the Americans had managed to beat back the attack. Following normal procedure, enemy troops had carried their dead from the battlefield. Only two bodies were left behind, but the artillerymen were confident many, many more had died. No one knew how many. What was surprising was the closeness of the engagement. "You could see the enemy," said one young artillery captain, in wonder. "They saw us and we saw them." It didn't happen that way very often, which lent an interesting and appealing tone to the opening engagement of the operation which would be called Hawthorne, or the campaign for the control of the Central Highlands.

The commander of the 1st Battalion, 327th Infantry of the 101st Airborne Brigade, Major David Hackworth, was stand-ing amid the ruins of the camp when I alighted from a helicopter in the company of one of the ubiquitous public

relations men of the American Army. We had been flying for
nearly an hour, trying to find the base which was neatly hidden in the crotch of two hills. It had been an unnerving ride,
since the hills were nominally, or more than nominally, enemy
territory. Hackworth briefly explained the situation, then said
with a grin that he was sending one of the reconnaissance
units ("recondo," in Airborne argot, meaning commando/
reconnaissance) deep into the mountains to find the enemy
base camp, and to try in the process to round up enemy stragglers. Hackworth was so cheerful about the prospect of heading into the mountains that I instantly asked to go along. He
said fine, then introduced me to Captain Lewis Higinbotham,
the commander of the 42-man Tiger Force, as the recondo
platoon was known. "You'll like Higinbotham," Hackworth
said. "He's a good killer."

Hackworth had words for the men of the Tiger Force, who
were now assembling their weapons and gear, and the words
went like this: "Goddamnit I want forty hard-charging fuckin'
dicks. And if anybody ain't a hard-charging fuckin' dick I want
him out."

"Fuckin'," muttered one of the men.

"Right," said Hackworth.

"Fuckin'," the trooper muttered again.

The English language, like everything else in Vietnam, became unreal after a time. Hackworth's words were—words.
He might have appealed for forty soft-bellied capons, or forty
fine, aggressive young American soldiers, or forty draft-
dodgers, or forty journalists, or forty fat congressmen from
Texas. As it was, he appealed for forty hard-charging fuckin'
dicks. It didn't matter. I unconsciously wrote the words in my
notebook.

Then Hackworth turned to me, banging the palms of his
hands together. Matters were looking up. "My God, we
chased them for five days over every flipping hill in Vietnam.
Five days! And they hit us back here. They kept one hill ahead
of us. One hill all along the way. Well, now they've had it."

The Airborne had that reputation.

A unit assembles its reputation from many sources, but
mainly from its commanders. These were the commanding
general, Brigadier General Willard Pearson, and the two bat-

talion commanders, Lt. Colonel Henry Emerson, and Major Hackworth. There were others, but these were the principal ones. They were professional soldiers, none more so than Pearson, who was the architect of the Brigade's bold and successful jungle tactics. Briefly, these were to probe as far into enemy territory as possible, make contact, then reinforce by helicopter. It required using small units as bait, which you could do only if your men were anxious to fight, and had proved it by signing on as paratroopers, for more money and prestige in the services. Pearson's reputation as a soldier was excellent, but he had strange lapses when dealing with men. Once, approaching a particularly difficult mission, he promised a company of infantry a case of beer if the mission were successful. In those circles, a case of beer was regarded as barely adequate for one man, let alone 200. Pearson, the strategist who wanted to carry the war to the enemy on the enemy's terms, was regarded with a mixture of respect and astonishment.

Not so Hackworth and Emerson. They were quite simply admired, as men and as soldiers. Personal courage is a very attractive quality in men. It is the one quality, as someone said, which guarantees all the others. Hackworth had it, and so did Emerson. They were brave men, without being excessively reckless or self-conscious about it. Hackworth was especially appealing. He seemed to be amused at the whole apparatus of the war in Vietnam; he knew that things were never what they seemed, and that you kept your sanity only by admitting a whole range of possibilities. That day, in the center of the artillery fire base, he strode around with a tiny riding crop, disheveled, unshaven and profane, and after a bit took Higinbotham aside to brief him on the mission.

Lew Higinbotham looked an unlikely killer. Slim, bony-faced, Texas-accented, he was polite and grim, and the dirt deliberately smeared over his cheeks and chin did not conceal youth. He was in his middle twenties, unmarried, a career soldier. Higinbotham had been in Vietnam more than two years, most of it spent in the Delta south of Saigon as an adviser to Vietnamese troops. This was his first mission with the Tiger Force. It was an elite unit and Higinbotham was anxious to do well; he liked the Vietnamese, but preferred to work with Americans. The forty-two men under his command were a rugged and motley lot, bringing to mind one of those posses assembled from the worst saloons on Main Street in the Grade B horse operas. Unshaven, dirty, unlettered, mean, nervous; one was in flight from his third wife, another (so the story went) from the police, a third was in Vietnam because he liked to kill Charlie Cong. Some of the others had the spirit of buccaneers, fugitives from a safe society. They liked the adventure, and the weapons. One of them regularly sent the ears of dead Viet Cong to his wife, through the army postal system. Half the platoon was Negro. One of these, informed that a journalist would be along on the patrol, became helpless with laughter. He doubled up, face shaking with mirth at the madness of it all. "Sheet," he said. "Shee-it."

While the men got their gear together, checked weapons and gathered up food and ammunition, I prowled around the edges of the artillery base. There were dark streaks of blood where men had been carried off the night before. Part of a torso lay just beyond the security perimeter. On the top of a small rise I looked north, and saw high hills without signs of life. There were no villages in this part of Kontum. There were some Montagnard tribesmen, but nothing else. In the old days of the French occupation, the hills were often used for tiger hunts. We loaded into helicopters and were off.

The land north of Dak To was rugged and uneven, high hills and thick jungle laced with trails. It was cool as we were dropped at four o'clock in the afternoon in a high stand of elephant grass. The trees had two growths of branches, one about six feet up the trunk and the other about twelve feet. They blotted out the sun. The light appeared to come through a great green-glass bottle without rays or beams. Higinbotham and I moved beneath one of the trees, and waited until the rest of the forty-two were accounted for. There was another captain there, and Higinbotham intro- duced him as Chris Verlumis, a 27-year-old career man from Oakland, California. Verlumis was the commander of head- quarters company, to which the Tiger Force was technically attached. It was Verlumis's first week in Vietnam, and his first patrol. Higinbotham was not happy about the arrangement, because Verlumis technically outranked him—or was, in any case, in command of a larger unit. If there was trouble, and there was bound to be trouble, Higinbotham did not want to have to worry about another captain. And he didn't want to be second-guessed. Higinbotham had told all this to Hackworth. But Verlumis wanted to come, and so Verlumis came.

We moved out along a trail north and west roughly in the direction of the Laos border. Right away we fell upon a two-man position carved into a bush. It was deserted. The trail was well-traveled, and almost immediately there was another small hut ("hootch," to American soldiers in Vietnam) and then a third. Then, as we wound up the trail, there was a small base camp, perhaps large enough to accommodate a squad of a dozen men. In Vietnam action usually comes without warning. All of these installations on the trail were signs, warning signals that enemy troops were there. Higinbotham knew it and the men knew it. I knew it.

We were moving quickly, winding up the trail as the light faded and noting all the signs of enemy occupation. Then there was a burst of machine-gun fire, a shout, and all of the men flopped, and scurried off the trail into the shelter of the trees and bushes. The firing had come from the rear of the column, three fast bursts and now it was silent. Higinbotham urgently radioed his rear squad. One enemy soldier was dead, but one of our own men was hurt.

Private First Class Richard Garcia was lying off the trail, blood leaking from a wound in his chest. Three men stood over him, while the medic punctured his arm with a morphine needle. The men moved their feet and talked quietly to Garcia, although he was nearly unconscious. He had been hit by one of our own bullets; it is difficult to see in the jungle. No one knows where the enemy is, and the frightened man sprays with his weapon. He fires it in bursts, and none too accurately. One of these had caught Garcia in the lung. The medic was working frantically, muttering and cursing under his breath. Suddenly Garcia sat up, and looked straight at the medic: "I can't breathe. I am going home. I am going to be OK." Then he was dead.

Fifty yards away, the men of the rear squad were looking after the dead Vietnamese. He had been shot in the chest, but that was only the most recent wound. His head had been bandaged, and so had his leg. Higinbotham, looking at the body, decided he had been on his way back to the base camp for medical attention. He was probably one of those wounded in the attack on the artillery fire base the night before. Next to the body lay a battered, damaged AK–47 submachine gun. That was the standard weapon of the North Vietnamese Army, Soviet-designed and manufactured in China.

Higinbotham reported both deaths to battalion headquarters. "We've got a KIA, one of theirs and one of ours," Higinbotham said. The G–2 (intelligence officer) on the other end of the line warned him to be on the watch for more enemy. "Maybe a battalion more," the G–2 said.

The light was going, almost visibly as lights dim in a theater, and Higinbotham decided to stay where he was for the night. Garcia's body was taken down to the trail and three men prepared it for transport on a litter. His arms were folded on his chest, and his blouse pulled up tight over his face and head. Then the body, compact in the camouflaged uniform, hatless, was tied to the litter, and the pack was tied to the body; lying there that night Garcia looked comfortable. Higinbotham said it was possible he was killed by rifle fire from the Vietnamese, but most likely not; most likely he was killed from our own lines. It was a matter of fire discipline, Higinbotham said; there was never enough of it, and too many people were killed needlessly. But you couldn't prevent all of it. With all the lead flying around, people got hurt; it was not a factor you could control.

The men arranged themselves in a star-shaped defense, three to a group. One man in each group stayed awake at all times. There would be no talking or smoking and the radio would be off. The jungle in Kontum goes dark before seven. The wetness comes as it grows black, and except for the chattering of the small birds and animals it is silent; after a while the bird and animal sounds become part of the silence. Because of the rot which turns the plants to phosphorus, the jungle floor is brilliant with light, enough light to see your fingernail or read the dials on a wristwatch. I had a small flask of whiskey, which I passed to Higinbotham and Verlumis and the radio operator, Terry Grey. We talked quietly of one thing and another, colleges, life on the West Coast, and then tried to sleep. I recalled a line from A. J. Liebling that when he was in an uncomfortable or dangerous spot during World War II, and he was trying to sleep, he thought about women. It seemed a sensible and distracting idea, so from nine that night until seven the next morning I thought about women.

We awoke slowly and crawled quietly from beneath the bushes to stretch as daylight came. With it came the second omen. There was a shout, a rattle of gunfire, and we were all on our bellies in that awful initial confusion. Suddenly a sheepish private stood before Higinbotham. There were three armed Vietnamese, uniformed and not alert, the private said. They stumbled into camp, saw the Americans, and fled. The GI's, equally startled, had time for only a half-dozen rounds. The three enemy soldiers scampered across a small stream and disappeared into the bush. Higinbotham shook his head, and smiled. "Oh hell, they probably spent the night with us," he said. "They probably thought we were the 226th North Vietnamese Regiment, for crissakes." Higinbotham reported the incident to G–2, which received the information without comment.

A long-range reconnaissance patrol cannot operate once its presence is known to the enemy. Twice the Tigers had been forced to fire. Now three Vietnamese had seen them, and had escaped, and were certainly bound for their headquarters. None of this could have been foreseen, and there was nothing to be done about it. But it was terrible luck. Security, to the extent that there was any in the middle of a jungle in the middle of enemy territory, was compromised. It had to be considered compromised, although the mission itself was not in doubt. The mission went on. There was no place to go but forward, deeper and higher into the hills, discovering enemy base camps and rounding up stragglers. The patrol was still well within the range of the brigade's artillery, and the operations officer was keeping careful check on our precise location. Word has been fed back that the enemy was known to be operating in the area; but Higinbotham knew that.

The objective now was to find a landing zone for a helicopter to come in and "extract" Garcia. Garcia was a burden and there was no room now for burdens. "I don't like any part of it," Higinbotham said.

Kontum that day was marvelously cool, and we crossed half a dozen small streams on our way up the hill. There was no movement except for an occasional exquisitely colored butterfly. The men moved very quietly and carefully. A clearing was found, and Garcia lifted out; the helicopter crew left a dozen cases of C rations behind. The men dug into the cases labeled, in the weird army phraseology, MEAL, COMBAT, INDIVIDUAL—like that, with commas. They were looking for cigarette packages and fruit. Each meal carton contained a little package of condiments: salt, pepper, sugar, powdered cream, coffee, gum, toilet paper, matches, and a package of five cigarettes; the brands were Camels, Chesterfields, Salems, Newports, Winstons, or Pall Malls. At least two of the large cases were untouched, so a hole was dug and they were buried. We moved out again.

The trail meandered into deeper jungle, with base camp following base camp. Higinbotham decided by one in the afternoon that his band had uncovered a staging area capable of accommodating a regiment of 1,000 men. The knowledge was not comforting. The men, in soft hats, their faces smeared with mud, carefully cradling weapons, kept silently climbing, turning their eyes off the trail and into the bush.

In two years in the Delta, Higinbotham had acquired a passable knowledge of Vietnamese. When his lead squad found a small arrow-shaped sign with the words *Anh Ban Di Trang*, he knew we were on the right trail, the pigeons among the cats. The words translated, "friends go straight"; it was obviously an enemy message. And with the Vietnamese talent for confusion, at the point of the sign the trail forked, with no clear indication which trail was meant. One branch led upward, along the small stream. The other moved left, down the hill. At the fork there were two huts where the command group waited: Higinbotham sent patrols down each trail. The first, led by Sergeant Pellum Bryant, almost immediately saw three enemy soldiers in the khaki uniforms of the North Vietnamese Army. Bryant opened fire with his M–16, and began heaving grenades. Everyone in the command post was flat on his stomach, waiting. The firing went on for five minutes, then ceased and Bryant returned to Higinbotham. He had got one, but the others had fled. Now from the other trail the radio crackled that there was resistance, that one Tiger was seriously wounded and the others pinned down.

Strung out in a long, thin line, the men moved down the trail and up to the ridge line. The patrol that had been hit was on the other side of the hill, which was not sharp but rolling, covered by deep jungle and ending in a steep ravine. At the top of the hill the men shed their packs, and a six-man patrol headed downslope to learn the American casualties and assess the strength of the enemy. It was impossible to judge distances because of the thickness of the cover.

The patrol reported back that the enemy had moved out; there was no more firing. Higinbotham nodded and, leaving six men behind to guard the rear, began to move down the trail to the ravine. It was a two-foot-wide trail that wound down and into a tiny cleft between the two hills. It then curled up the next hill. Edgy, edgy enough that a man snarled if you stumbled and stepped on his heel, the platoon moved down. There was a wounded GI in the crotch of the hills. He had been shot through the neck beside a cache of enemy rockets and grenades. The grenades were in a cave, carefully covered with tarpaulin. Four men went down to get the wounded man, crawling past the body of an enemy soldier whose head had been blown off in the firing ten minutes before. The wounded man was hurting, and scared. The hill was very steep, and the four found it difficult to slide down.

"You don't feel no pain, baby," the medic said, putting a needle into the man's arm. "You gonna be all right, baby. You gonna see that girl." The talk was all nonsense, meant to distract. The medic was wrapping a bandage around his comrade's neck. Another medic put a plasma needle into his right arm. The man's shirt was soaked with blood from the wound.

"I knew it," the wounded man said. "I knew that my chip was cashed in."

"We gonna get the MedEvac," the medic said.

"Well, that pilot better be there when I get there." Then, "You think I got a Stateside wound?"

The medic was worrying about the stretcher.

"Litter?"

"Litter!"

"Bring the litter, goddamnit."

"I wonder why my stomach hurts so much."

"Don't worry. This happens to everybody."

The wounded man, Private First Class Frank Wills, was at the base of a 45-degree incline. But the litter was there now, and the four men struggled and worried him up to the trail which led down from the ridge line.

It was very quiet, and no movement from anything. There were no birds or animals or butterflies, and the men were still and silent. Wills had become half-delirious from pain and fear. He asked again why his stomach hurt so much. Then he told the medic he had one hundred dollars in his pocket. "Take it and hold it for me," he said. Wills was thinking about going back home to Miami.

But the medic wasn't listening. No one was. Higinbotham was worried about Wills and whether a landing zone could be carved out of the hillside. It couldn't, and Higinbotham knew that. He also knew that his patrol was deep inside enemy lines with no way to get out, except to walk out. The patrol had found what it had come to find; the problem was what to do with it now. Enemy troops were obviously all around, and they knew that the Americans were there. Higinbotham squatted on the trail and wondered what to do.

The trail wound down from the ridge line perhaps one hundred yards. There were foxholes and bunkers all along it. Six men were at the top, guarding the packs, six more at the base. Higinbotham, Verlumis, Wills, the radio operator, Terry Grey; and twenty-five regulars were strung out along about fifty yards of the trail. There were plenty of grenades and plenty of ammunition. But Higinbotham thought about the deployment, and shuddered. They were not enough, not nearly enough if the enemy attacked from the ridge line; and the assumption had to be that that was what they would do.

"Hey, Mr. Reporter!" It was the trooper who found my presence so mirth-provoking. He began to laugh again, and so did I. It was an absurd predicament.

"You picked a great patrol," Higinbotham said.

"Mr. Reporter, how much you get paid for this?" the trooper asked.

"Not enough," I said.

"Damn," Higinbotham said, looking again at his maps.

Higinbotham's worries were not mine. Since the death of Garcia the night before, I had tried to concentrate on journalism. I had worked at taking careful notes and photographs, and now reflected on the similarity of the soldier and the war correspondent, the basic text for which comes from Joseph Heller's novel, *Catch-22*. On the one hand, no one wants to get ambushed or to be where bullets are fired in anger. On the other, if nothing happens there is no story. If the patrol does not meet the enemy, there is nothing to write about. It becomes a pointless exercise, a long walk under a hot sun. If the patrol does meet the enemy you are likely to be killed or wounded, or at the very least scared to death. *Catch-23*.

It was a bad catch. I worked at disbelief. You switch off, and pull all the plugs, severing connections. Your movements become slow and deliberate, and your consciousness seems to move back in time. The point is to maintain control. With forty-one men in the middle of a clearing in the middle of Kontum in the middle of a war, you are standing—nowhere. For distraction, think about women or squat down and pick blades of grass, chew them and put a film in the camera. Focus the lens. Make pictures of the American infantry. Transcribe dialogue:

"Sheet, I wrote her back she do anything she want."

"Well, we over here and they're there."

"Fuck that noise."

"Yeah."

"You hear Tomkins get killed?"

"Yeah?"

"Sheet, a mine blew him up and there was nuthin' left but nuthin'."

"Sheet."

"I tell you, Man, this is some kind of war."

"Sumthin' else!"

"Crise, I was in a platoon and there's nuthin' left of that platoon now. I'm the only one left."

"Gimme some fruit."

"Trayja fruit for some butts."

"Fuck you."

"Three butts."

"Whyn't you pick up the butts back there when we got 'em?"

" 'Cause I was on point savin' your ass in case old Charlie come along."

"Gimme the fuckin' fruit."

"Three butts."

"Sheet, man, I ain't got but half a pack."

"Goddamn I got to get this weapon *fixed*."

"Hey, Mr. Reporter. What the fuck you doing here?"

At two-thirty in the afternoon the first grenade crashed down the ridge line. It went wide with a *thump*. Then *thump! Thumpthump!* Again, closer.

In the first fifteen minutes, three died and six fell wounded. The firing came from three sides, hitting the Americans at all points on the trail. The men guarding the packs at the top of the trail scattered under a hail of machine-gun fire. Only a few actually saw the enemy, who were maneuvering and firing as they maneuvered. Higinbotham at his command post half-way down the line knew the danger of the situation better than anybody else. He collected the first reports from his sergeants. The reports were only that there were a lot of enemy, and it was impossible to tell how many. Higinbotham called Hackworth at battalion headquarters and requested artillery fire and air support. It would come in the next four hours, 1,100 rounds of 105 and 90 rounds of 155 artillery. There would be air strikes, and the noise would be as if the world were coming apart.

No one knew then and no one knows now how many North Vietnamese there were. They did not have mortars, so the unit was probably company-sized or smaller. But they had grenades and small arms and automatic weapons, and good cover to shoot from. They fought from concealed positions and they had the element of surprise and knowledge of the terrain. It was, after all, their base camp.

American artillery shells fell in a wide semicircle just beyond the American positions. They were hitting at the ridge line and beyond, but the Vietnamese fire did not lessen. The planes attacked with a roar and without warning; because of the heavy cover they could not be seen. One fist-sized piece of shrapnel landed two feet from Higinbotham, but he did not cease talking into the field phone, precisely locating the positions of heaviest enemy fire. While the shells were landing, Americans were dying; a half dozen in the first half hour, another six in the five succeeding hours of combat.

In the command post, enemy rifle fire was hitting five feet high. We were all down, scanning the jungle and watching that part of the trail we could see. Behind us, down the line, men were maneuvering and shouting at each other. Higinbotham was superbly cool, talking quietly and easily into the field telephone which was the only link with safety. As long as the artillery held out the Vietnamese could not advance; that was our theory, desperately clung to. Meanwhile the rifle fire got heavier and closer. The bullets were sounding: *Pop!*

Verlumis had left the command post to crawl up the trail toward the heaviest fighting. Pellum Bryant, the senior non-commissioned officer, was below rallying the dozen or so who had fallen under his command. One of the other sergeants was dead. Bryant was the only unwounded man in his eight-man squad. Pinned down by an enfilade of fire, he had huddled in an enemy foxhole. When the fire slackened, he poked up his head and fired bursts. It was Bryant alone who was protecting the rear flank.

By four-thirty in the afternoon, after two hours of fire, the situation was almost lost. The fight had been following a rhythm, with heavy bursts of fire and then silence except for an occasional rattle of a machine gun. The Americans had been pushed back into a tiny area about the size of a basketball court, with Higinbotham and the radio as its nucleus. Bryant was now fighting just a dozen yards to the rear. Hackworth, speaking with Higinbotham, said there was a full company of infantry a mile away. He was ordering them to reinforce.

"You've got to try it," Higinbotham said over the radio. For the first time, his voice cracked and became unsure. There was a 26-year-old advertising account executive or civil servant or department store clerk, or a good old boy at the night baseball game, but not a captain of infantry in the U.S. Army. "If you don't get up here soon, we're all gonna die. If you don't get up here soon, I'm gonna melt."

There was another crackling over the telephone; Hackworth

had gone off. Then, barely audibly, but precisely, as if he were reading from a piece of paper, Higinbotham said: "Dear God, please help me save these men's lives."

It got worse after that, and for Higinbotham it was the worst time of all. It was his first patrol with the Tigers. He didn't know the men, either their names or where they came from or how long they had been in Vietnam. Now he had gotten them into this. Higinbotham sat with the radio, his back against a tree, and prayed that it wouldn't be as bad as he thought it was.

The sniper fire came closer, nipping the tops of the branches of the bushes. The artillery seemed to be hitting indiscriminately, as Higinbotham called it closer to the American lines. But there were no lines any more. There was only a group of men huddled silently on a trail that led nowhere down from a ridge line that did not even show on the map. Bryant was on his own, and so was Verlumis. Higinbotham was worried about the artillery, and the tactics were taking care of themselves.

A wounded infantryman, his voice loud as a bullhorn, was calling from the left flank. "You've got to get me out of here!" He was repeating it. The voice was strong and deep, but it cracked with agony and pain. He repeated it again and again. As he screamed and moaned I moved forward. I went forward about five feet and then stopped, still safe. The wounded man was probably twenty yards away, although the jungle was so thick it was impossible to tell. I had the idea that I might save his life.

I looked around at the others and then the wounded man screamed, and was silent. I waited for a minute and then crawled back the five feet. I had spent twenty minutes deciding whether to get the wounded, who had been screaming and pleading for help. Now I didn't have to think about it. He was dead. Verlumis had given me a .45 pistol and now I took it out of its holster for the first time. I was lying on my stomach handling the .45, having dismissed the wounded man from mind. It was easier holding a .45 pistol.

Fifteen yards in front of the command post there was a dip that plunged almost straight down into the ravine. From that direction a voice came: "Airborne!" No one answered. Higinbotham and the radio operator and I looked at the spot where the voice came from. The radioman unhitched a grenade from his ammunition belt, and cradled it like an apple. The voice could belong to anyone, but the odds were better than even that it belonged to a North Vietnamese. I thought of identifying questions to ask. The only two that came to mind was the name of the manager of the New York Yankees, and whether or not Marilyn Monroe was dead or alive. My mind wouldn't work. I thought of asking who wrote the Declaration of Independence, but then figured that a trooper probably wouldn't know the answer. Then I remembered that I didn't know the name of the Yankee manager. Stengel was dead. Or not dead, retired someplace. These thoughts were moving so slowly I could almost see them in my mind's eye. I was closest to the dip and now aimed the pistol straight at it, or just above it. The radioman had not thrown the grenade and all of us were in a state of suspended animation. But then a voice said, "Christ, don't shoot," and a sweat-drenched head appeared over the lip of the ravine. The head belonged to an American.

There were now seven in the command post, and a 360-degree defense. We had been joined by a young rifleman. Still inexplicably careful about journalism, I asked his name; it was Private First Class Sam Washburn, of Indianapolis. Washburn had dived over a bush and told Higinbotham: "I got two Charlies and the captain got one. The captain's dead. We were lying on the trail firing at the Charlies and I looked over and asked him how his ammo was and he was dead." Higinbotham said nothing, did not comment on Verlumis, and continued to talk the artillery in. "I don't think there's anybody else back there," Washburn said. "I mean, any Americans."

That meant that the command post, and the seven of us, *were* the front. There was no protection up the trail. The cries of the wounded were getting louder as the men pulled back into a tighter circle. The command post was filling up with wounded, those who could crawl back or who were carried back by the medics. I would hear only secondhand the horrors endured by the men up the trail; they had been under heavy bombardment for more than three hours. There was no firing from the command post because the enemy could not be seen.

But then came the grenades. They were coming closer, just off the mark. That was when the awful fear set in. It was the fear of sudden realization that the North Vietnamese were lobbing grenades and there was no way to stop them.

The faces were all drawn up tight, and there was no talking. A company of reinforcements was on its way, but had got lost. No one knew whether it would arrive in time. Hollow-eyed and distracted, the men moved slowly as in a dream; or perhaps it was me, clammed up and lying flat in that taut circle. In Vietnam if you are thirty years old you feel an old man among youngsters. I was thinking about being thirty, and holding an automatic pistol I didn't know how to fire, when Washburn leaned over and very quietly, very precisely, whispered "grenade." He probably yelled it, but I was switched off, half-deaf from the pounding of the artillery and the 500-pound bombs and it seemed to me that the warning came in a whisper. Then he gave me a push. There was a flash and a furious burst of fire; the grenade had landed a yard away.

I couldn't get my feet down. I was lying on my back, almost standing on my head, and my feet wouldn't come down. Through the numbness and the red haze, I could see Washburn firing, although his hand was blown to pieces, and the radioman using his grenade launcher. Higinbotham was firing, too; but my legs wouldn't come down. Then they were down and I yelled for a medic. "I'm hit!"

"You're OK," Higinbotham said.

"The hell I am," I said. "I'm hit."

"I mean it," he said.

"Christ almighty there's blood everywhere," I said.

"You're all right."

"Goddamnit I'm not."

There was very little pain, just shock and a terrible feeling of relief. I was out of it. The terror was in the knowledge that you might lose control. You had to keep control, and you could feel it slipping away. You were half-crazy looking at the firing. The medic had scrambled up and I called for morphine. My arms and legs were shaking uncontrollably. The medic tackled me and punched the needle into my arm and began to bandage my head and back. The morphine restored the control. My hands and legs were still shaking but I was all right. Higinbotham was grinning. The medic said to take it easy. When the shaking stopped fatigue came.

"You're all right," Higinbotham said.

"I'm not all right, goddamnit," I said.

But we were both laughing, me from shock and Higinbotham from the fact that the attack had been thrown back. The grenades fired by Terry Grey, the radioman, had done it.

"Where are the VC?" I asked.

"We stopped the bastards," Higinbotham said.

I thought that line was in the best MGM tradition, and told Higinbotham so. None of it seemed real, lying in a godforsaken jungle in the middle of a godforsaken war. There were five dead North Vietnamese on the trail a dozen yards away. That was the point of farthest enemy advance. Higinbotham told me of this, and then the firing began once more. He ducked down to work the field telephone and I crawled off beneath a tree as the rat-a-tat-tat of explosions started again. I had lost the pistol and my pack, but I had the camera and my notebook. I thought it would be all right, and anyway I was out of it. There were nineteen wounded men and a dozen dead, and I was one of the wounded. The next two hours were very slow hours. Then the company of reinforcements arrived, crashing through the jungle with banshee whoops and rifle fire.

And that black humorist.

"Where's that newspaper fella?" he asked Higinbotham.

"He got hurt," Higinbotham said.

"Hurt? Sonovabitch."

I thought it would be all right until I saw the helicopters which would take the wounded out; some, like Wills, had lain on the jungle floor for five hours. There was no landing zone, so the helicopters hovered at 100 feet and lowered a T–bar. Strobe lights illuminated the jungle as arc lights illuminate a stadium. The first helicopter took three wounded. A man was strapped onto the T–bar and slowly lifted 100 feet. You ascended alone into the eye of the light, and heard the crack and thwup of bullets, and realized that the enemy, still entrenched on the ridge line, were shooting. They were shooting at the wounded men being pulled into the helicopter. You heard the bullets as you were rising and your body went stiff and you pulled out all the plugs. You gripped the T–bar and made a number of very difficult promises if God got you safely into the helicopter. But when you got there, you said instinctively, I made it. And over and over again, Jesus Christ.

There is no real epilogue to the reconnaissance patrol of the Tiger Force. Its activities that day went unnoticed in the American press because that same afternoon, on a hill only two miles away, Captain William S. Carpenter called napalm on his position after his company had been overrun. Operation Hawthorne, which lasted the better part of a month, was said to be a success. The Americans claimed 1,200 enemy dead, to 250 of their own. In the succeeding twelve months infiltration would continue. Almost eleven months to the day after the opening round of Hawthorne, a battalion of the 173rd Airborne Brigade would get ambushed and badly mauled by a force of North Vietnamese infantry. Lew Higinbotham, who by then had been transferred from the 101st to the 173rd Airborne, was operations officer that day. "How is it?" Higinbotham asked the platoon leader. "Good clean fun," the lieutenant replied. That was at 10 A.M. At ten-twenty the radio went dead; every man in the platoon was killed, or badly wounded. The wire services said the engagement took place a few miles north of Dak To, the Special Forces camp in Kontum province.

from *To What End: Report from Vietnam*, 1968

Not a Dove,
But No Longer a Hawk

by Neil Sheehan

AMERICANS, because they are Americans, arrive in Vietnam full of enthusiasm and with the best of intentions. After a prolonged period of residence, they leave with their enthusiasm a victim of the cynicism that pervades Vietnamese life and with their good intentions lost somewhere in a paddy field. I am no exception. When I first walked across the tarmac of Saigon's Tansonnhut Airport on a warm evening in April, 1962, nervous that the customs officers might not accept the journalist's visa I had hurriedly obtained from the South Vietnamese consulate in Hong Kong, I believed in what my country was doing in Vietnam. With military and economic aid and a few thousand pilots and Army advisers, the United States was attempting to help the non-Communist Vietnamese build a viable and independent nation-state and defeat a Communist guerrilla insurgency that would subject them to a dour tyranny. This seemed to me a worthy cause and something that needed to be done if other Southeast Asian peoples were to be allowed some freedom of choice in determining their course in history. Although I often disagreed with the implementation of American policy during my first two years in Vietnam, I was in accord with its basic aims.

I remember distinctly the thrill of climbing aboard a U.S. Army helicopter in the cool of the morning and taking off across the rice fields with a South Vietnamese battalion for a day's jousting with the Vietcong guerrillas. There was hope then that the non-Communist Vietnamese might win their war. I was proud of the young American pilots sitting at the controls in the cockpit and I was grateful for the opportunity to witness this adventure and to report it. We are fighting now, I used to think, and some day we will triumph and this will be a better country.

There were many disappointments those first two years, but when I left Vietnam in 1964, I was still, to use the current parlance, a hawk. I returned to Saigon in 1965 for another year. Now I have left again, and much has changed. There were 17,000 American servicemen in Vietnam at the time of my first departure and there are now 317,000 and I, while not a dove, am no longer a hawk.

If I had been wiser and could have foreseen the present consequences of that earlier and relatively small-scale American intervention in the affairs of this country, I doubt that I would have been enthusiastic during those first two years. I realize now, perhaps because this past year has impressed upon me more forcefully the realities of the war and of Vietnamese society, that I was naive in believing the non-Communist Vietnamese could defeat the Communist insurgency and build a decent and progressive social structure.

At a farewell dinner before my second departure from Saigon, the conversation drifted to the endlessly discussed but never resolved problem of gaining the sympathy of the peasantry. My host was a Vietnamese general, involuntarily retired through the vagaries of Saigon politics. To amuse us, he recounted an episode that had occurred in mid-1953 while he was commander of Franco-Vietnamese troops in the province of Buichu in what is now Communist North Vietnam.

That year, the Vietminh guerrillas, as the Vietcong were formerly called, accelerated their land-reform program. Communist cadres began confiscating the rice fields of landlords and dividing them up among the peasantry. To compete with the Vietminh and to arouse some popular support for the cause of his feeble Government and for France, the pro-French Emperor, Bao Dai, issued a decree reducing land rents from the traditional 40 to 50 per cent of the rice crop to 15 per cent.

Buichu was a predominantly Roman Catholic province. The two principal landlords there were the Catholic Bishop and the father of the Interior Minister in Bao Dai's Government.

My host knew he would have to gain the Bishop's cooperation if he was successfully to enforce the decree.

"Impossible," said the Bishop. "How can I feed 3,000 priests, nuns, seminarians and coolies on 15 per cent of the crop?"

"I agree, Your Excellency," said my host, "it will be difficult. But perhaps it is better to make sacrifices now while there is still time. If we don't do something to win the sympathy of the population, you may lose more than your rice. You may lose your Bishopric, your land and perhaps even your head."

"Impossible," said the Bishop. "I will write to the Interior Minister."

Three months later, for attempting to implement the decree despite the Bishop's opposition, my friend was removed on the initiative of the Interior Minister. By the following summer, the Vietminh were so strong in Buichu that the French decided to evacuate the province. The Bishop, his priests, nuns and seminarians fled to Hanoi and thence to South Vietnam when the Geneva accords shortly thereafter sealed France's defeat at Dienbienphu and divided Vietnam at the 17th Parallel.

Over the 13 years since 1953, the United States has supplanted France in Vietnam. Yet among the Vietnamese themselves, the two opposing sides have changed little.

Precolonial Vietnam was administered by mandarins drawn from the merchant and land-owning families. When France colonized the country in the 19th century, much of this native aristocracy became, in effect, colonial civil servants, intermediaries between their own people and the foreigner. During the First Indochina War these Vietnamese, with a stake in the traditional society which a French presence would preserve, cooperated with France. Now the same Vietnamese, for identical reasons, cooperate with the United States.

Air Vice Marshal Nguyen Cao Ky, the current Premier of South Vietnam, was a French pilot. On occasional visits to the countryside he appears before the peasants in a trim black flight suit with a lavender scarf around his neck and a pearl-handled pistol at his waist—a kind of Asian Captain Marvel.

The Deputy Premier, Lieut. Gen. Nguyen Huu Co, and

other generals in the Saigon military junta, were officers or sergeants in the French colonial forces. Their fondness for French cuisine, snappy uniforms and cocktail parties and receptions creates a pale but faithful reflection of the social round of colonial days. They are the Vietnamese who have inherited the worst of two cultures—the pretentiousness of the native mandarins and the rigidity of the French colonial officers and administrators. Premier Ky and the earlier successors of Bao Dai have also promulgated rent-reduction and land-reform laws at the urging of American advisers eager for social progress. All of these measures have been sabotaged because the regimes were and are composed of men who are members of, or who are allied with, mandarin families that held title to properties they have no intention of renouncing. While there are some patriotic and decent individuals among them, most of the men who rule Saigon have, like the Bourbons, learned nothing and forgotten nothing. They seek to retain what privileges they have and to regain those they have lost.

In Vietnam, only the Communists represent revolution and social change, for better or worse according to a man's politics. The Communist party is the one truly national organization that permeates both North and South Vietnam. The men who lead the party today, Ho Chi Minh and the other members of the Politburo in Hanoi, directed the struggle for independence from France and in the process captured much of the deeply felt nationalism of the Vietnamese people. Perhaps because of this, the Communists, despite their brutality and deceit, remain the only Vietnamese capable of rallying millions of their countrymen to sacrifice and hardship in the name of the nation and the only group not dependent on foreign bayonets for survival.

It is the tragedy of Vietnam that what began as a war of independence from France developed, as a result of its Communist leadership, into a civil conflict. Attempts to describe the current war as a geographically based struggle between North and South Vietnam breaks down almost immediately when it is recalled that Premier Ky and several other important members of his Government are North Vietnamese by birth, who fled south after the French defeat, while Pham Van

Dong, the Premier of North Vietnam, was born in the South. The war is, rather, a struggle between differing elements of the Vietnamese people as a whole.

The division of the country into two separate states at the 17th Parallel in 1954 was a provisional arrangement ending one scene in the drama. Vietnam's larger political realities extended then and still extend now in both directions across the demarcation line. North Vietnam controls and supports with men and matériel the Vietcong guerrillas in the South because the Vietcong leaders, although native Southerners, are members of the Vietnamese Communist party and obey orders from the Politburo in Hanoi.

In 1958 the late President Ngo Dinh Diem organized a Committee for the Liberation of North Vietnam, and since 1960 the Saigon Government, with American connivance and aid, has been smuggling saboteurs and commando teams into the North in a so-far vain effort to instigate a guerrilla movement among the Northern Catholics and mountain tribesmen. The opposing sides, in short, have never recognized the 17th Parallel as a permanent boundary and have violated the frontier whenever it suited them.

Communist leadership of the anti-colonial movement led to the involvement of Vietnam in the larger context of the cold war and brought the intervention of the United States, first to aid the French, and then to develop and support a non-Communist administration and army in the South. For its own strategic and political ends, the United States is thus protecting a non-Communist Vietnamese social structure that cannot defend itself and that perhaps does not deserve to be defended. Our responsibility for prolonging what is essentially a civil conflict may be one of the major reasons for the considerable amount of confusion, guilt and soul-searching among Americans over the Vietnam war.

I know this is true in my own case and in the case of many Americans of my acquaintance who have lived for long periods in Vietnam. We are continually chagrined to discover that idealism and dedication are largely the prerogative of the enemy. The American soldier makes the lack of aggressiveness of the Government forces the butt of unending gibes. He grows to hate "Charlie," the G.I. slang name for the Vietcong guerrilla and the North Vietnamese regular, because "Charlie" kills his friends, but he soon learns to respect Communist bravery and cunning.

An American general recently paid a strange tribute to a Vietcong guerrilla who held up an entire U.S. Army infantry company for an hour in the jungle north of Saigon. The guerrilla was the lone survivor of several Communists defending a bunker. He fired off all his own ammunition and that of his dead comrades, and hurled back at the Americans the grenades they tossed into the bunker. He was finally killed while throwing rocks in a last gesture of defiance. "If one of our men had fought like that," the general said, "he would have been awarded the Medal of Honor."

Since the beginning of last year, Hanoi has increased the size of its regular army contingent in the South to a total of about 47,000 men. In the face of sustained bombing of the road and rail system in the North and the Ho Chi Minh Trail through Laos, the Communists continue to infiltrate men at an estimated rate of 4,500 to 5,000 a month. Many of these young men are conscripts who march south because of pressure on themselves and their families. Yet, once in the South, they fight well, and desertions are few despite the hardships and the severe losses through disease and battle. The Vietcong guerrillas have also managed steadily to expand their forces through recruitment and conscription.

The Saigon regime, on the other hand, has experienced great difficulty in increasing the strength of its armed forces because of a very high desertion rate. Desertions are greatest among conscripts, an indication that the average South Vietnamese feels little or no commitment to defend his own society. About 85 per cent of Saigon's armed forces are, consequently, volunteers who take up arms for pay. This gives the Government forces a distinctly mercenary cast that affects both their attitude toward the population and, except for a few élite units, their performance in combat.

From the contrast in behavior of the two sides, I can only conclude that Vietnamese will die more willingly for a regime which, though Communist, is at least genuinely Vietnamese and offers them some hope of improving their lives, than for one which is committed to the galling status quo and is the creation of Washington. The official assertion that the Communist soldier endures the appalling conditions of his daily life and behaves so commendably in combat out of terror of his superiors becomes patently ridiculous to anyone who has witnessed a battle. Terror may drive a man to march toward the enemy's guns, but it will not make him fight valiantly. The course of the conflict has made apparent that the Communists are able to arouse and to exploit the native Vietnamese qualities of hardihood and resilience and to convince large numbers of their people that the cause of *their* Government is just.

Most non-Communist Vietnamese are incapable, because of the values of the society in which they live, of looking beyond individual and family interests. Their overwhelming concern with "me and my relatives" deprives the society of a social consciousness Americans take for granted in their own culture and fosters the corruption and nepotism that exist throughout the administration. The disease of corruption appears to be worsening in direct proportion to the burgeoning amounts of American aid flowing into the country. Stories of embezzlement are legion and repeatedly embitter Americans.

Province and district chiefs' positions are frequently sold to the highest bidders by those responsible for making the appointments. The incumbent is then expected both to recoup the cost of his job from corruption and to make payoffs to the higher officials who sold it to him. Some American officials with long experience in Vietnam estimate that about 20 per cent of United States aid supplied for counter-insurgency projects in the countryside finds its way to the Vietcong and that another 30 to 40 per cent is diverted by Government officials. Cement, roofing, steel bars and other building materials destined for schools and refugee housing mysteriously end up on the open market or in private villas and apartment buildings. "What gets down to the poor son of a bitch in the paddy field," one official said, "is a trickle." A U.S. Army Special Forces captain once told me how he had arranged for rice to be flown in American planes to a camp of several thousand refugees in a remote area who were suffering from malnutrition. The local district chief confiscated the rice and sold it to the refugees at exorbitant prices.

While Americans worry about winning the war and creating an effective Vietnamese Government that can gain the support of its people, the mandarin families that run the regime have a different set of priorities. In one important province on the central coast this spring a rare honest and effective Vietnamese official, who was a favorite of the Americans, was fired because he began to talk about corruption by the two senior military commanders in the region. He was replaced by a cousin of one of the generals.

Numerous complaints from the American Embassy led Premier Ky to warn his fellow generals at one meeting of the junta that they were embezzling too much and should exercise some restraint. Their reply was that they had to think of their families. Vows by the Premier that corrupt officials will be shot have brought periodic headlines in the Saigon newspapers and the execution of one Chinese businessman and a half-dozen common hoodlums. Ordinary Vietnamese assume that Premier Ky has found it imprudent to arrange firing squads for some of his colleagues on the junta. One general's wife is sometimes referred to as "Queen of the Payoff."

Promises of land reform are solemnly reported in the American press and are apparently taken with some seriousness in official circles in Washington. I have often wondered why, since the promises are never carried out and the speeches made today are practically identical in content and phrasing to those made four years ago by some other Government leader. To gain their own ends, Asians frequently tell Americans what they think Americans want to hear. The Vietnamese, possibly because of their greater experience with Americans, seem to have developed a particular talent for this. Last April, during one of his more candid moments, Premier Ky told a group of correspondents: "Never believe what any Vietnamese tells you, including me."

In February, amid the hoopla following the Honolulu conference that was to lead to an intensive program of social, political and economic reform, the junta organized a "Social Revolution Day" in Saigon. Two thousand civil servants, soldiers, students and religious leaders were assembled on the lawn of the former presidential palace in the center of the city. The social reformers arrived in their Mercedes-Benz sedans and, dressed in well-tailored suits or bemedaled uniforms, began to read the usual speeches. The scene had a disturbing atmosphere of *déjà vu*. Within 10 minutes, a segment of the crowd, less polite than the rest, began walking out in boredom. The police, having apparently anticipated what would happen, had locked the gates of the palace grounds. No one was allowed to leave until the speeches had ended, despite a good deal of shouting and arguing back and forth through the steel bars.

The current social system discriminates against the poor and prevents social mobility. The mandarin families resist all efforts to change it, since it works in their favor. Although the United States has spent millions of dollars building primary schools in Vietnam, for example, it has been unable to bring about any fundamental reform of the Vietnamese educational structure, which makes certain that the sons of the prosperous, and almost no one else, will achieve the secondary education necessary to social advancement—whether in the army, the civil service or the professions.

Sending a peasant boy to primary school and then making it virtually impossible for him to achieve a decent secondary-school education fosters discontent, rather than lessening it. There is considerable evidence that many young Vietnamese of peasant origin join the Vietcong because the Communists, who have been forced by the nature of their revolution to develop leadership from the countryside, offer them their best hope of avoiding a life on the rung of the ladder where they began—at the bottom.

A friend of mine once visited a hamlet with a South Vietnamese Army major who is one of the few field grade officers to defeat the system by rising from a humble beginning. The major spoke to the farmers in peasant dialect instead of in the sophisticated urban Vietnamese most Government officials use.

"You're not a major," said one farmer in astonishment.

"Yes, I am," said the major.

"No, you're not," said the farmer. "You talk like a peasant and no peasant could become a major."

A drive through Saigon demonstrates another fashion in which the social system works. Virtually all the new construction consists of luxury apartments, hotels and office buildings financed by Chinese businessmen or affluent Vietnamese with relatives or connections within the regime. The buildings are destined to be rented to Americans. Saigon's workers live, as they always have, in fetid slums on the city's outskirts.

Since 1954, the United States has poured more than $3.2-billion of economic aid into South Vietnam, but no Saigon regime has ever undertaken a low-cost housing project of any size. The Singapore Government, in contrast, is erecting thousands of low-cost housing units for its people.

While Vietnamese with influence prosper in the cities and towns, the war has created a different world in the countryside. It is a world in which the masses of the peasantry no longer live—they endure.

Each afternoon, in the air-conditioned press-briefing room in Saigon, the United States Military Command releases a communiqué reporting that 300 or more "enemy structures" have been destroyed by American fighter-bombers or by the guns of Seventh Fleet warships that day. The statistics imply sound military progress until a visit to the countryside reveals that what is meant by an "enemy structure" is usually a peasant hut in a hamlet the Communists control, or which the American and South Vietnamese authorities suspect the Communists control.

No comprehensive statistics on civilian casualties are available. The nature of the war would make the assembling of such statistics very difficult, but the military authorities have also never seriously attempted to gather them.

An indication of what civilian casualties may be, however, is given by the fact that American and other foreign medical teams working in three-quarters of the country's 43 provinces treat 2,000 civilian war-wounded each month. If one accepts the normal military ratio of one dead for two wounded, the monthly figure is 1,000 civilian dead.

The number of wounded handled by the medical teams, I

believe from my own observation, is merely a fraction of the total. The medical teams treat only those wounded who reach the hospitals in provincial capitals. There are undoubtedly many more who never get that far. These victims are helped at Government district headquarters or militia outposts, or by Vietcong field hospitals and dispensaries—or they simply survive, or die, without treatment. Most of the wounds I have seen in the provincial hospitals are the type a victim could survive for two or three days without medical attention. Wounds that require rapid treatment are not usually in evidence, presumably because the victims die before they can obtain hospitalization.

Although civilians are being killed and wounded by both sides, my own investigations have indicated that the majority of civilian casualties result from American and South Vietnamese airstrikes and artillery and naval gunfire. Last November, I found one fishing village in Quangngai province, on the central coast north of Saigon, in which at least 180 persons—and possibly 600—had been killed during the previous two months by aircraft and Seventh Fleet destroyers. The five hamlets that composed the village, once a prosperous community of 15,000 people, had been reduced to rubble.

The gun and the knife of the Vietcong assassin are, in contrast, far more selective than cannon and fragmentation bombs; the victims are usually limited to Government officials and sympathizers. It has been estimated that, over the past decade, about 20,000 persons have been assassinated by Communist terrorists. This is a gruesome total, but the annual average is a great deal lower than the probable yearly number of ordinary civilian victims of the war.

Lack of sufficient American troops to occupy and hold ground when it has been wrested from the Communists is one of the major reasons for the extent of damage to civilian life and property. Once a battle has ended, the American and South Vietnamese troops withdraw. The theoretical follow-up by South Vietnamese territorial forces, police and administrators to pacify the region does not materialize except in a very limited number of instances, and the Vietcong guerrillas and their North Vietnamese allies move in again. The Americans eventually return and the same region is thus fought over repeatedly.

It would be easy to blame the American military authorities for the destruction, but this would not be fair. The Vietcong and the North Vietnamese regulars habitually fortify hamlets with elaborate trenchwork and bunker systems. Infantry attacking in classic style across open paddy fields would suffer prohibitive casualties. Under these circumstances, military commanders can only be expected to use whatever force is at their disposal.

Gen. William C. Westmoreland, the United States military commander in Vietnam, has ordered that all possible care be taken to avoid killing and wounding the innocent and that, whenever feasible, civilians be warned to leave their hamlets prior to airstrikes and artillery bombardments. Unfortunately, General Westmoreland's order has sometimes been ignored by subordinate commanders.

Hamlets are also habitually bombed and shelled at the request of a South Vietnamese province or district chief who has been told by some paid informer that Communist troops are present there. Information from informers is notoriously unreliable, the peasants are often not responsible for the presence of the Communists and, since ground units do not exploit the bombings and shellings, these attacks seem to have negligible military value. American officials excuse the practice by claiming that the Vietnamese, as the legal authorities, have the right to destroy their own hamlets, even if Americans perform the destructive acts—a fine bit of legalism that ignores the basic moral issue. I have occasionally thought that the practice results largely from the cynicism of South Vietnamese officialdom and a superfluity of aircraft and artillery.

The extraordinary firepower of American weaponry, whose ferocity must be witnessed to be comprehended, is another contributing factor to widespread civilian suffering. On an average day, U.S. warplanes alone loose 175 to 200 tons of explosives on the South Vietnamese countryside. Then there are the thousands of artillery and naval shells and the hundreds of thousands of rounds of mortar and small-arms ammunition. The cratered landscape seen from an airplane window is an

excellent advertisement for the ingenuity of American munitions makers.

The flow of refugees from the countryside is the most eloquent evidence available of the gradual destruction of rural
society under the impact of the war. The number of refugees
has now passed the million mark. It takes a great deal to make
a Vietnamese peasant forsake his land and the graves of his
ancestors.

Most refugees I have questioned told me that the Vietcong
taxed them and made them work harder than usual, but that
they could live with the Communists. They left their homes,
they said, because they could no longer bear American and
South Vietnamese bombs and shells.

If resettled properly, the refugees could conceivably develop
into an asset for the Saigon Government. Yet, true to its usual
behavior, the regime neglects them and the majority are left
to shift for themselves. Refugee slums have risen in the cities
almost as fast as G.I. bars.

Deserted hamlets and barren rice fields, now a common
sight, are other evidence of what the war is doing to rural
South Vietnam. In several provinces on the northern central
coast as much as one-third of the rice land has been forsaken.
The American policy of killing crops in Communist-held areas
by spraying them with chemical defoliants from aircraft is has-
tening this process. During the first six months of this year
59,000 acres were destroyed.

The corrosive effect on the country of the American presence is not confined to military operations. Economically and
culturally, the advent of the Americans has introduced mala-
dies only time can cure. One is inflation. The primitive economy, already seriously disrupted by the war, has now been
swamped by the purchasing power of tens of millions of dollars being dispensed for the construction of bases, airfields and
port facilities and by the free spending of the individual American soldier.

This year the United States will pump a minimum of
$140-million into the Vietnamese economy to cover the

locally generated costs of the construction of new bases and the maintenance of existing ones. This sum constitutes about one-seventh of the country's entire money supply. American troops are themselves currently spending another $7-million a month.

The moral degeneration caused by the G.I. culture that has mushroomed in the cities and towns is another malady. Bars and bordellos, thousands of young Vietnamese women degrading themselves as bar girls and prostitutes, gangs of hoodlums and beggars and children selling their older sisters and picking pockets have become ubiquitous features of urban life. I have sometimes thought, when a street urchin with sores covering his legs, stopped me and begged for a few cents' worth of Vietnamese piastres, that he might be better off growing up as a political commissar. He would then, at least, have some self-respect.

Rarely in any war has the name of the people been evoked more by both sides than in the Vietnam conflict. Yet the Vietnamese peasantry, who serve as cannon fodder for Communists and non-Communists, remain curiously mute—a hushed Greek chorus to their own tragedy.

The conditions of life in Vietnam will probably always make an accurate assessment of the peasants' attitudes toward the war impossible to obtain. I have received the impression, however, on visits to accessible hamlets, that many of the peasants are so weary of the fighting they would accept any settlement that brought them peace.

Last March, I spent two days in one hamlet south of the port of Danang on the central coast. A company of U.S. Marines had seized the hamlet from the Vietcong six months previously, and a Government pacification team, protected by the Marines, was working there. In three years, the hamlet had changed hands three times. There were almost no young men in the community. Roughly half of the families had sons, brothers or husbands in the Communist ranks. The remaining families were about equally divided between those with neutral attitudes and those who were Government sympathizers.

The morning after I arrived, the peasants, under the supervision of the Government pacification workers, began constructing a fence around the hamlet perimeter to keep out Vietcong infiltrators. Through an interpreter, I asked two farmers among a group of old men, women and children digging postholes if they thought the fence would be of any use.

"Maybe it will," one said, "but I don't think so. A fence won't keep out the Vietcong."

"What did the Vietcong make you do when they controlled the hamlet?" I asked.

"They made us pull down the fence we had put up before, and dig trenches and lay booby traps," the second farmer said.

"Well, if you don't think the fence will do any good," I asked, "why are you putting it up?"

"We are just plain farmers," the first peasant said, glancing apprehensively at a policeman a few feet away with a carbine slung across his arm. "We have to obey any Government here."

As he spoke, a Vietcong sniper, hidden in a patch of sugar cane beyond the paddy fields, fired two shots. The old men, women and children scurried for cover, their fear and lack of enthusiasm for fence-building evident on their faces.

During a tour of South Vietnam in 1963, Gen. Earle G. Wheeler, chairman of the Joint Chiefs of Staff, referred to the conflict as a "dirty little war." While the Vietnam conflict may be even dirtier now than it was in 1963, it can no longer be termed little.

Reliable statistics are very elusive in Vietnam, but I would estimate that at least 250,000 persons have been killed since the war began in 1957. Last year, according to official figures, 34,585 Communists were killed and the Saigon Government forces suffered 11,200 deaths. Through mid-September of this year, again according to official statistics, 37,299 Vietcong and North Vietnamese regulars have died in battle and 7,017 Government troops have been killed.

American losses remained at a relatively low level until 1965, when the Johnson Administration committed ground combat units and began to create an expeditionary corps. That year, 1,369 American servicemen died in North and South Vietnam and neighboring Laos, and 6,114 were wounded. This year, as American offensive operations have picked up stride with the strengthening of the logistical apparatus, casualties have soared to 3,524 killed and 21,107 wounded, through mid-September. American dead are now averaging nearly a hundred a week and can be expected to increase as the expeditionary corps grows and more Americans are exposed to hostile fire.

The attitudes of the leadership in Hanoi and Washington indicate that the contest is far from being resolved. The rate at which North Vietnam is infiltrating its regular troops into the South and the willingness of the United States to engage its own ground forces and to escalate the air war against the North portend several more years of serious bloodshed. The world may hope for peace, but neither side has yet hurt the other sufficiently to prevent it from continuing. Both sides are trapped in a dilemma created by their history and political and strategic considerations. Washington cannot withdraw its troops from South Vietnam, as Hanoi demands, without making certain an eventual Communist seizure of power there and negating all the efforts of the last decade to maintain a friendly Government in Saigon.

Hanoi's best chance of winning now lies in prolonging the bloodletting to the point where the American public will tire of a war for a small land whose name most Americans cannot even pronounce correctly (they tend to say "Veetnam"). If the North de-escalates the fighting it will remove the principal source of political pressure on the Johnson Administration— the number of coffins being flown home from Saigon. Without the killing, the United States might be able to occupy South Vietnam indefinitely. The fact that 60,000 U.S. troops are stationed in South Korea brings no demonstrators into the streets and arouses no anxiety among American mothers, because the shooting in Korea has stopped.

A year ago, I worried that the patience of the American people would run out, that Ho Chi Minh would have his way and that the United States would lose the Vietnam war. This fear no longer troubles me nearly as much. I have the feeling that somehow we can muddle through this grim business. We may not win in Vietnam as we won in World War II, yet we may well prevail. Given our overwhelming military superiority, it is entirely possible that Washington, over a period of years, may be able to destroy the Vietcong and North Vietnamese main-force units in the South, and to transform what is currently a militarily sound but politically weak position into one of some, if doubtful, political strength.

Rather, my quiet worry concerns what we are doing to ourselves in the course of prosecuting and possibly some day winning this war. In World War II and in Korea the aggression of one state against another was an established fact. The United States acted with clear moral justification and Americans fought as they always like to think they fight—for human freedom and dignity. In Vietnam this moral superiority has given way to the amorality of great power politics, specifically, to the problem of maintaining the United States as the paramount power in Southeast Asia. The Vietnamese people have become mere pawns in the struggle. Whatever desires they might possess have become incidental. The United States can no longer make any pretense of fighting to safeguard South Vietnam's independence. The presence of 317,000 American troops in the country has made a mockery of its sovereignty and the military junta in Saigon would not last a week without American bayonets to protect it.

Precisely because the Saigon Government represents nothing beyond its administration and army, the United States has had to fall back on its own military force to maintain its position and to win the war. Washington can dispense the latest in weaponry, but the First Air Cavalry Division and the Third Marine Amphibious Force cannot inspire the loyalty of the Vietnamese peasantry, and General Motors cannot manufacture decent non-Communist Vietnamese leadership, effective government and dedication. Only Vietnamese can supply these and the non-Communist Vietnamese have proven themselves incapable of providing them.

Thus, in the final analysis, American strategy in Vietnam consists of creating a killing machine in the form of a highly equipped expeditionary corps and then turning this machine on the enemy in the hope that over the years enough killing will be done to force the enemy's collapse through exhaustion and despair. This strategy, although possibly the only feasible alternative open to a modern industrial power in such a situation, is of necessity brutal and heedless of many of its victims.

Despite these misgivings, I do not see how we can do anything but continue to prosecute the war. We can and should limit the violence and the suffering being inflicted on the civilians as much as possible, but for whatever reasons, successive Administrations in Washington have carried the commitment in Vietnam to the point where it would be very difficult to prevent any precipitate retreat from degenerating into a rout. If the United States were to disengage from Vietnam under adverse conditions, I believe that the resulting political and psychological shockwaves might undermine our entire position in Southeast Asia. We shall, I am afraid, have to put up with our Vietnamese mandarin allies. We shall not be able to reform them and it is unlikely that we shall be able to find any other Vietnamese willing to cooperate with us. We shall have to continue to rely mainly on our military power, accept the odium attached to its use and hope that someday this power will bring us to a favorable settlement.

But I simply cannot help worrying that, in the process of waging this war, we are corrupting ourselves. I wonder, when I look at the bombed-out peasant hamlets, the orphans begging and stealing on the streets of Saigon and the women and children with napalm burns lying on the hospital cots, whether the United States or any nation has the right to inflict this suffering and degradation on another people for its own ends. And I hope we will not, in the name of some anti-Communist crusade, do this again.

The New York Times Magazine, October 9, 1966

"Unrepentant, Unyielding"

An Interview with Viet Cong Prisoners

by Bernard B. Fall

LAI-KHÉ, SOUTH VIETNAM
TWO YEARS AGO, Lai-Khé was a tranquil place hardly an hour's ride from Saigon, and the home of the *Institut de Recherches du Caoutchouc du Vietnam,* a research institute jointly financed by the French rubber plantations in Vietnam. There was some rubber production as such, but the low, yellow-stuccoed laboratory building with its neat rows of glittering instruments and vats full of creamy latex, the clean native village of the rubber tappers, and the spacious villas for the French scientists and administrators, gave the whole place the air of a well-funded American agricultural college. The war changed all that, for Lai-Khé is at the edge of a forest complex situated between two rivers which eventually merge about 20 miles from Saigon, thus forming a triangle pointing at South Vietnam's capital. In a series of swift attacks on the Vietnamese Army posts at the edge of the forest in late 1964, the Viet Cong had completely dismantled the whole government, civilian and military apparatus in the area and taken over the town of Ben-Suc, a pleasant little place inside a meander of the Saigon River, big enough to appear on most maps of Vietnam.

Repeated attempts by the Vietnamese to retake the area failed (the stripped hulls of three American M-113 armored personnel carriers lost to accurate Viet Cong fire still lie near the road to Ben-Suc), and even a push by the US 173rd Airborne Brigade in 1965 yielded no tangible results. Progressively, the 210 square miles of forest between Ben-Suc and Ben-Cat acquired its sinister reputation as the "Iron Triangle," said to contain not only crack VC elements, but also the command structure of MR-4, the Liberation Front's 4th Military Region covering the Saigon area. It was from the Iron Triangle that the repeated successful VC penetrations of Saigon's huge Tan Son Nhut airbase had come. As long as the Iron Triangle existed, Saigon itself would be exposed to the threat of attack. The decision was therefore made late in 1966 to destroy the Iron Triangle in the largest concentrated attack by US Forces since the Vietnam war began. The operation, begun on January 8, opened with the 1st Infantry in position on the Iron Triangle's northern base, with the 25th Infantry Division 196th Light Brigade blocking all escapes on the left flank across the Saigon River, while the ARVN's 5th Division and parts of the 173rd Airborne Brigade held the right flank. Other units, including the ARVN 8th Infantry which, the year before, had broken at Ben-Suc, further reinforced the assault units. In all, 28 combat battalions—over 30,000 men with their logistical support—and 35 artillery batteries (140 field guns) had converged on the Triangle. But the key actors, on the American side, were not the men, but the unleashed machines.

For days before the actual attack, the windows of Saigon had been rattling from concentrated B-52 raids on the Triangle, at least 13 of them in eight days, unloading hundreds of tons of heavy explosives on every raid, plowing under the Viet Cong's incredibly extensive network of underground tunnels and depots. Thanks also to American technology, the Air Force cartographers are capable of providing the military with fantastically detailed photo maps *in color* within a few hours after the strikes. On these maps, the trails of the bomb carpets in the jungle look like the tracks of tiger claws on an animal's skin—claw marks that are three miles long and over 100 feet wide. Whenever the strategic bombers were not over the Triangle, artillery barrages and the hammering of the light fighter-bombers saw to it that no Viet Cong would try to break out from the hell that the Triangle had become.

But the newest weapon of them all and, in its own way, the most incredibly impressive for all its civilian normality, was an assemblage of perhaps 80 bulldozers, in many cases airlifted into the midst of the jungle by huge "Skycrane" helicopters or the somewhat smaller "Chinooks." Their job was simple:

eliminate the jungle once and for all. By the third day of the battle, huge yellow scars had begun to be clearly visible in the deep jungle green as the bulldozers began to plow down the jungle as if some insane developer were suddenly hell-bent on covering Vietnam with Levittowns or parking lots. Such Viet Cong hideouts or tunnels as there were, either were crushed or their exits bulldozed shut, for in many cases the adversary (as well as civilians) hiding in the tunnels disappeared in their deepest recesses rather than surrender. "Tunnel rats," American soldiers specially picked for their small size and equipped with gas projectors and what looked like flamethrowers, sometimes penetrated for hundreds of meters into the burrows, looking for what was said to be a veritable "subway" crossing the whole Triangle. It was never found and perhaps never existed.

Inexorably, the bulldozers bit into the countryside, cutting huge swaths of cleared land right across the Triangle. They were followed by flamethrower tanks and teams on foot, destroying the felled trees with fire. And not only the trees: every human inhabitation within the beaten zone, be it an isolated hut which may have been used by the Viet Cong, or a whole little hamlet inhabited for years by charcoal kilners—nonwhite Saigon cooks with charcoal almost exclusively—went up in flames. There was one day toward the end of the week in which the air was totally still and the sky as transparently fresh and pure as on a spring day in America. Yet as I joined a new unit within the Triangle by helicopter, the whole sky, literally in a 360° circle, was framed in by perfectly straight black columns: the earth was being scorched on the whole perimeter of the Iron Triangle. And the town of Ben-Suc was among them.

Ben-Suc had been occupied in less than two minutes by two battalions of the 28th Infantry, followed by Vietnamese troops, while overhead loudspeaker helicopters instructed the population to stay put, for "anyone seen running away will be considered a Viet Cong." The 3,500 women, children and old men (there was not one able-bodied man in the lot) stayed put as Vietnamese Navy landing craft beached in front of the village and began to take aboard the population for a 10-mile ride downstream to a temporary refugee camp at Phu-Cuong.

They went without offering resistance, believing that they would merely be taken away temporarily until the operation was over. But Operation "Cedar Falls" (the code name for the whole undertaking) was, in the words of a briefing officer, an "operation with a real difference"—there would be no coming back, because Ben-Suc would be put to the torch and then razed with bulldozers, just like the forest and part of the rubber plantation. A clamor arose as the women begged to be allowed to return long enough to dig up their meager treasures, for as in Europe during the Thirty Years War, the peasants of Vietnam have long resorted to burying their money and jewelry in earthenware jars to keep them from being pilfered by government troops or taxed away by the Viet Cong. The respite was granted and the American troops even made arrangements to evacuate the most precious movable belongings of the villagers, their buffaloes and wagons.

"Make damn sure the buffaloes stay with the refugees and don't end up in the market place," I overheard the earnest young major in charge of the evacuation say to one of his subordinates escorting the landing craft.

As the burning houses began to collapse and the bulldozers methodically bit into the remaining standing walls, a new town seemed to emerge altogether from the debris. Ben-Suc was honeycombed with tunnels, trenches and stone-lined bunkers, and every house was built atop huge rice caches carefully lined with wicker mats. There were hundreds of tons there (the total "take" in the Triangle was 3,170 tons), far in excess of what Ben-Suc could have produced, let alone saved from previous crops.

"You see," said the young major, "Ben-Suc was a major transit point of supplies both for War Zone 'C' and probably the VC's central headquarters. The stuff would come up here by motor sampan and the population then transfers it on its buffalo carts and off it goes into the deep jungle in escorted convoys."

"Look at the rice," he said, picking up a handful which he carried in the breastpocket of his combat jacket, "there are at least 20 different brands here from all over South Vietnam and probably from the US, too. I've sent a batch down to Intelligence. They'll find out where it came from."

He looked back on smoking Ben-Suc with real affection as he held its rice in his hand.

"Would you believe that we offered the women that they could take the rice with them as their own if they told us where the rice caches were? *Not one* of them spoke up. Now *that's* loyalty."

As he spoke, he opened his hand to let the golden rice grains fall on the ground, stopped in mid-gesture, and put the rice back into his pocket. I scooped up a handful from the smoldering heap to my right and put it in one of my pockets. That much of Ben-Suc would stay alive. Later, what was left of Ben-Suc would be obliterated by Air Force bombers in order to destroy whatever underground caches and depots had been missed by the bulldozers.

In the evening at the mess tent, the day's doings were toted up as officers from nearby units came in for briefing and for a hasty bite to eat. There were over 400 dead by "body count," 62 prisoners, 18 machine-guns (including three brand-new American M-60's), more than 200 individual weapons (there would be close to 400 by the end of the operation, along with 508 enemy dead and 6,000 displaced civilians), and miles and miles of destroyed tunnels.

A whole jungle hospital, with two levels below ground and one above ground, had been captured.

"You should have seen the equipment," said the G-2. "Some of the stuff was good enough to be used in our hospital. West German surgical scissors at $45 apiece by the trunkful; French antibiotics."

Now, according to an order issued by General Westmoreland, on September 20, 1966, in compliance with Article 33 of the 1949 Geneva Convention, "captured or abandoned medical supplies or facilities will not be destroyed intentionally." I was told, however, how the field hospital had been disposed of.

"Well," said an eyewitness, "we removed all the medical equipment, and then all there was left was just another empty bunker and tunnel system. So we destroyed it like everything else." The same also happened to a smaller VC aid station.

An NBC television crew with a neighboring outfit witnessed and photographed the mutilation of a dead enemy soldier, but the NBC hierarchy in New York, mindful of the uproar created more than a year ago when an enterprising CBS cameraman filmed the burning of a village with cigarette lighters, "killed" the sequence. Conversely, a reporter for a Texas newspaper was wounded that day by a VC sniper while he was flying about in a med-evac helicopter clearly marked with large red crosses. It is this kind of mutual barbarization, the needless cruelties inflicted far beyond military necessity, which will make the Vietnam war stand out in modern history.

"You should see 'em," said the burly prison camp commander. "Unrepentant, unyielding. The only thing they're sorry for is that they got taken alive."

He was referring to Professor Vinh Long and Middle-Level Teacher Tran Van Tan, captured in the Iron Triangle, and probably the highest-ranking Liberation Front cadres thus far to fall into American hands. Both were native Southerners, Vinh Long being born in Danang, and Tan in the province of the Iron Triangle. Both had gone to North Vietnam in 1954 when the country was partitioned, and both had gone on to higher studies. Long got his AB in physics and mathematics in 1963, Tan an AB in education in 1962. Both were "finds" in their own right, since they were involved in running the general education department of MR 4. [*For security reasons, we have substituted fictitious names for the real names of the prisoners interviewed by Mr. Fall.*—THE EDITORS]

The prisoner-of-war enclosure of the 1st Division was a small clearing in the rubber tree forest, surrounded by concertina barbed wire in which two squad tents had been erected. Within the enclosure was an even smaller enclosure, housing three captive women, one of them a pretty 19-year-old Eurasian girl with long red hair and freckles, but almond-shaped eyes. "She was a cook in the outfit," explained an escort.

Vietnam can be bitingly cold in January and we were shivering in our jungle combat uniforms, particularly after a night spent rolled in a poncho liner. The prisoners were lying on normal Army cots and had been issued three woolen blankets each, and each of them seemed to have his share of C-rations. Courteously sitting up on their cots as we approached, they looked, wrapped in their blankets, like green-clad desert Arabs. Intelligent, ascetic faces with deep-burning eyes, showing no fear—just curiosity as to what next. I first sat down with Vinh Long, flanked by a Vietnamese sergeant acting as an interpreter and an American captain. The captain was showing signs of a very bad cold, sneezing and fumbling through his pockets for an absent handkerchief. The Vietnamese prisoner picked up the C-ration box, searched around in it and came up with the tiny roll of toilet paper it contains, which he handed to the captain.

Long said that he spoke no French, but he spoke Russian. I explained to him in Russian that I was a college professor myself, not a soldier, and that I was not interested in military information. I also apologized for my bad Vietnamese and for the fact that I'd have to use an interpreter. That's all right he said, now clearly relaxed. Who had ordered him to return South?

"The party. But I would have gone in any case because I wanted to. I was happy. I visited Hanoi before I left."

He had left the North in December 1963 for the Duong Minh Chau area—the headquarters area of the Liberation Front. Before his departure from the North, where he has been stationed with the 338th Division at Xuan-Mai (he offered no information on units except those already known from papers captured with him), he had been briefed on the war here.

"We were given an accurate picture of what was going on in the South and told that victory would be easy. Of course, with the Americans here, it's not so easy." He picked up a cigarette in the C-ration carton, offered the others around, and then looked straight at me.

"But we'll win, anyway. Every country in the world helps us. Look at the American, Morrison, who committed suicide because he disagreed with American policies."

True, I said. But how about the other 200 million Americans who don't kill themselves?

"The Liberation Front forces will win in any case, because all the Vietnamese people help us. This war can only be settled among the Vietnamese themselves. The Americans and their allies must go."

But he had seen the Americans, now. Realistically, could they be made to go?

"Lots of American soldiers do get killed in battles, look at Chulai, Pleiku, Tayninh. We can do it."

To the Viet Cong, those battles, which we either claim as having won ourselves (Chulai), or as having suffered only minor losses (Pleiku), represent major victories. I said that I feared he was confusing the Americans with the French. The French weren't one-tenth as powerful as the Americans.

"Oh, I know the French were weaker than the US is, but we'll still win because our cause is right. Do the Americans think they can stay with this kind of war for 30, 40 years? Because that is what this is going to take."

The members of the Front are known to practice self-criticism. If he were to criticize himself for his activities over the past year, would he do something differently? There was a momentary lowering of the head, and a great deal of pride in the short answer: "I wouldn't change a thing."

And what would he do after all this was over?

"When I get out of this a free man, I will again work for the Liberation Front."

There was a poem, in wartime France, about a resistance member who had given exactly that answer to a German military court:

> Et si c'était à refaire
> Je referais ce chemin . . .

Yes, but that was 23 years ago, and the Nazis were the bad guys, and here the Free World is fighting the good fight with billions of dollars' worth of firepower against bad guys like Long and the freckle-faced cook.

"I told you," said the captain. "Unrepentant. Unyielding."

Tan was less tense than Vinh Long; perhaps because we had switched from a Vietnamese interpreter to an American GI (one of the few real side-benefits of this whole mess is that the US Armed Forces are going to have more Vietnamese linguists than all the universities of the whole world taken together; and that is *not* a figure of speech). Tan, in addition to education, had minored in anatomy and physiology and had been the inspector of the VC's educational system for the military zone. Though having fought in the Viet Minh against the French since 1950, he only joined the Communist Party here in South Vietnam in 1966, and like Vinh Long, he was sure that his side was winning.

"It's only natural that we should receive help from North Vietnam. After all, we're all Vietnamese, aren't we? Just as the Saigon government gets American help, the Front gets help from the socialist countries." There was a pause, and Tan said with great emphasis: "And it will never stop. *Never.* Even if their help does not rise above the present level, we'll win."

How did he feel he was being considered in the movement, being an intellectual, I asked. Wasn't he treated with a certain amount of suspicion?

"Oh, there is a certain amount of suspicion against intellectuals, but that is understandable. After all, being intellectuals, they are divorced from the masses and the working class, in particular.

"We Southern cadres are not discriminated against by the Northerners, although it did happen that some of the 're-groupees' [Southerners who went to the North in 1954 and then were reinfiltrated. B.F.] would desert from homesickness once they came South again. It doesn't affect our status at all."

But as a man trained in dialectical materialism, how could he dismiss American power so lightly in his estimates of the outcome of the war? That, to him, was no problem at all:

"After all, the Front is fighting a just war, as a true representative of the South Vietnamese people. This being a just war, we shall win."

But other "just wars" were lost in other places . . .

"Indonesia?" he interjected helpfully.

No, I said, but Greece, Malaya and the Philippines for example. As an intellectual, he could not dismiss these defeats lightly, unless he felt that these wars weren't "just wars."

"Not at all. They were just wars, to be sure, and the people were defeated, but only temporarily. The will to fight on remained in their hearts and they surely will rise again. But here, there won't be even such a temporary setback. The party has been active in South Vietnam for 36 years and thus defeat of its organization is impossible now.

"Here, the guerrillas will become stronger and stronger with the help of the socialist countries."

Yes, but did not the Sino-Soviet split introduce a weakening factor in this aid effort? Now he was on the defensive for the first time.

"Those struggles for greater socialist unity no more affect the socialist camp's effort in Vietnam than the French-American dispute affects power relationships in the West."

Come now, I said, if you read *Pravda* and the *Peking Review* and the incredibly severe mutual accusations between Peking and Moscow, you wouldn't describe this as a "struggle for greater unity."

"Let's not get into this. We'll win in any case."

Even if South Vietnam is totally destroyed in the process by American artillery and bombers? He had seen what happened here. It's happening all over the country. There was a hurt look in his eyes as the implication sunk in: "If South Vietnam is lost, we have got nothing left to live for. We would rather be dead than live as slaves. Have *you* ever seen anybody who wants to live as a slave?"

No, I had never seen anybody who wanted to, but I'd seen plenty of cases where people *had* to because they were given no choice. And I cited, on his side of the fence, the Budapest uprisings, and on our side, the Dominican Republic operation.

"These are small things," was his reply. And what did he think of how this whole war got started, I asked.

"Ah, the Americans are sly and clever," said Tan, whereupon the Americans present broke out in uncontrolled laughter. The interpreter explained to Tan that the Americans themselves never thought of themselves as either sly or clever. He nodded pensively, as if this were an important revelation.

"You know, they never smile," said the captain to me. I told him that considering their position and what was in store for them—transfer to the far-from-tender South Vietnamese—I wouldn't smile, either.

"The Americans," Tan went on, "took over military planning for the Saigon government. Their economic experts forced the South Vietnamese to work for them and Diem persecuted everybody. He would have killed us all, and that is why we revolted."

Tan, who had been silent for a moment, looked up and asked the interpreter if he, too, could ask me a few questions since I was a professor. Of course, he could.

"Do you know whether we will be treated as prisoners according to the Geneva Convention?"

Obviously, word must have gotten around among the Viet Cong about how badly most of the prisoners are still treated on this side, all promises of improvement notwithstanding, with the Americans reluctant to intervene once the prisoners have been transferred. All that I could say lamely was that he was being treated according to the Convention right now.

"Do American families approve of their soldiers here killing innocent people?"

Most of them weren't aware of innocent people being killed here, I said. As for the soldiers themselves, they were carrying out orders just as he was.

"Yes, but I'm here as a Vietnamese, in my own country. Why are the Americans all over the place, in Greece, in Laos?"

Well, they were helping their own allies, just as he expected the socialist camp to help him. But the socialist camp's aid was "political," he retorted. To which I answered that the Chinese weapons we had captured yesterday did not look "political" to me. A quick fleeting smile conceded the point to me.

"You may be right on that, but after all, it is the Americans who are the aggressors."

Why were the North Vietnamese so difficult about negotiations? I asked. On this, he was probably to the left (or was it right?) of official Front and North Vietnamese policy. Like Ambassador Henry Cabot Lodge here, who feels that negotiations are pointless if "victory by fade-out" can be achieved—a point which he has repeatedly made ever since September 1965—Tan felt that there was little to negotiate since his side was winning and since Vietnam was "one country."

Contrary to the Front's and Hanoi's avowed programs, he felt that reunification would come rapidly if the Americans were to leave. In fact, he did not believe that a divided Vietnam would "work." I told him that, for the sake of world peace, both Germany and Korea had accepted more or less permanent division.

"That's all right for them. But we rose up and fought for our own independence. We don't want to stay divided."

Yet, when asked what he would have done differently, Tan said that he would have negotiated last year, before the massive input of American troops, and he came through with a small truth which confirmed what intelligence specialists here had been wondering about for quite a while:

"You know, this is no longer the 'Special War' General Taylor talked about, but a new type of war [here the interpreter was faced with one of those party neologisms for which there was no acceptable single word] where outside forces became primary.

"The decision that the character of the war had changed was made late last year here in the South, either by the People's Revolutionary [i.e., South Vietnamese Communist] Party, or by the Central Committee of the Liberation Front. But when I was captured I did not yet know what this decision entailed."

As far as is known, the decision entails the maintenance of large units in reserve at more or less secure bases, while small forward units inflict heavy losses on the allied forces. How well this tactic works was shown this week, when the US suffered the highest casualties of the war (1,200 in one week)— all as a result of dozens of pinprick attacks.

But Tan knew that he was on the right path. As I was getting up to leave, he said earnestly: "We are not fighting here to have a cease-fire and prolonged division. It is the Americans who sent their troops here. They will have to make the decision to leave. Nobody can make it for them."

As I walked out, after he had ceremoniously shaken hands with the captain, the interpreter and me, Tan said something very rapidly.

"He's asking you to thank the American people and Lord Russell for what they are doing."

Back at Division, reports were still filtering in. Ben-Suc was now totally evacuated. A herd of 61 reluctant buffaloes which proved intractable to adult Americans—it seems to be true that buffaloes find the white man's smell offensive—had required the re-airlifting in of 10 Vietnamese buffalo-boys aged six to 10 who rounded up the two-ton beasts without much difficulty. The town was now bulldozed flat and awaited its final airstrike.

Standing in his map tent, the brigade commander was going through the details of the pull-out, for after all the blood and the firepower spent here, the Iron Triangle would not be held.

"We just haven't got the troops to stay here, and the Arvins [for ARVN, the South Vietnamese Army] simply won't."

"In other words," I said, "the VC will move right back in again."

"Sure," said the general. "But they'll find their dugouts smashed, huge open lanes in the forest, and at least we'll have helicopter LZ's [landing zones] all over the place. Next time's going to be easier to get back in."

As I walked out of the command post, a short, whitewashed obelisk caught my eye, standing at the entrance to Lai-Khé. It was a monument to the dead of the 2nd Moroccan Spahi Regiment, the 2nd Cambodian Mobile Battalion, the 3rd and 25th Algerian Rifle Battalions, and 3rd Battalion, 4th Tunisian Rifles; who had died for the Iron Triangle between 1946 and 1954.

The New Republic, February 4, 1967

U.S. Marines Seize 3d Hill
in Vietnam After 12-Day Push

by Jonathan Randal

HILL 881 NORTH, South Vietnam, May 5—Weary and grimy United States marines today secured this last major height commanding the isolated airstrip and valley of Khesanh. Nearly half the American combat troops here were killed or wounded in the 12-day campaign.

Gen. William C. Westmoreland, the American commander in Vietnam, echoed Marine fears when he warned during an inspection visit to Khesanh: "I don't think the battle is necessarily over. I anticipate further fighting in the general area."

The general spoke of "tremendous" casualties suffered by the 95th and 18th Regiments of North Vietnam's 325th Division. American spokesmen said they had lost 570 confirmed dead, with 598 more deaths listed as probable.

But General Westmoreland said nothing about casualties in the two marine battalions here, officially given as 160 dead and 746 wounded.

The final assault on Hill 881 North began yesterday afternoon. By nightfall, Company E of the Second Battalion, Third Marine Regiment, held part of the crest. Once heavily wooded, the hill was now a wasteland pounded by hundreds of tons of bombs and thousands of artillery shells.

At dawn, Company E pushed off to take the final bit of enemy territory. But shortly after 7 A.M. the marines ran into sporadic fire from small arms and automatic weapons.

Rather than risk the kind of infantry assault that had cost them dearly earlier in the fighting, the marines pulled back again. This time they shelled and bombed the North Vietnamese position for two and a half hours.

But when the marines advanced, again they met enemy fire from five bunkers that had somehow survived the full might of American air power and artillery over four days. In the final fighting, three North Vietnamese soldiers were killed, seven United States marines were wounded and 17 enemy weapons were captured.

"How they got through 1,000-pound bombs is what gets me," said First Lieut. Jack Adinolfi of Greenville, N.Y.

His comment reflected the thoughts of many marines who were surprised by the aggressiveness of the enemy troops since the start of fighting for the triangle of hills dominating the approaches to the Khesanh airstrip, five miles to the southeast.

The triangle is strategically important because from here, American 175-mm. guns can fire shells 20 miles, reaching almost to the Laotian border in the west and 15 miles into North Vietnam.

This makes it dangerous for the North Vietnamese to mass a large force in the area for an all-out attack on military outposts in South Vietnam. It also inhibits the enemy's movements of supplies.

The dusty red hills—861, 881 South and 881 North—take their designations from map markings showing in meters their elevation from sea level. The plateau has been struck by more than 2,000 mortar rounds and 1,200 artillery shells since the Americans dug in here two months ago.

At no point did the enemy flee the battlefield as he has often done in Vietnam, although by the time Marine riflemen reached the summits, bombs and artillery had reduced the opposition to sporadic firing.

Hill 861 was taken a week ago. Hill 881 South was occupied Tuesday.

After the marines took 881 North, General Westmoreland said the enemy had definitely come from Laos across the mountainous border that lies seven miles northwest of the hill triangle.

To strengthen Marine fire power, 4.2-inch mortars were moved to Hill 881 South and a battery of 105-mm. howitzers advanced from the airstrip farther west in the coffee-growing valley.

Marine officers said they would start extensive patrolling in the mountains surrounding the triangle.

The cost of the campaign is illustrated by the casualties suffered by Lieutenant Adinolfi's company. Since its arrival in Vietnam two weeks ago, it has lost 89 men dead or wounded out of 220.

Standing in the valley, where many North Vietnamese bodies still lay unburied, the lieutenant said, "I never cease to marvel at what marines do."

"We learned our lesson real hard and real fast," he said, "and if any of those S.O.B.'s are crazy enough to come up here tonight, they're going to get killed."

His company learned its lesson before dawn Wednesday when two North Vietnamese companies dented its perimeter along the southeastern slope of Hill 881 North. The company lost 22 dead and 69 wounded, but ultimately held its line.

The company commander and a medical corpsman were wounded and the air observer was killed by shrapnel from an armed Marine helicopter that accidentally sprayed their position.

The lieutenant assumed command. "Some of the guys had their boots off and it was raining when they hit at 4:30 A.M.," he said. "It was a real nightmare."

"I was sitting in the command bunker just praying for it to get light and for another Marine company to help re-establish the defense perimeter," he said. The enemy had pushed within 45 yards of his command post.

The marines counted 82 enemy dead including 15 snipers whose heavy bolt-action rifles were fitted with telescopic sights.

During the attack the marines were momentarily thrown off guard, the lieutenant said, by North Vietnamese dressed in American uniforms and helmets stripped from the dead.

"They were shouting out in English things like 'Corpsman! Corpsman!'" the lieutenant said. "One of our medical corpsmen fell for it, and was killed."

"There were marines out there in the trees," he added, "wounded, screaming and fighting like crazy for their lives. Our chief corpsman was in the command post. He wanted to go out and help them, but we could not spare him. He damn near cried himself to death."

By now, the lieutenant said, his company is accustomed to

everything the enemy can throw out. "Once you get mortared—and it usually happens here at dawn and dusk—you
just get used to it."

What the men of his company found harder to accept was
a message they discovered in bunkers studding the hill.

"There was one pamphlet in English," the lieutenant said,
"showing a Vietnik demonstration at home, with a woman
holding a sign saying: 'My son died in vain. Don't fight. Go
to prison.'"

On the other side were excerpts from speeches by Senators
Wayne Morse of Oregon and Ernest Gruening of Alaska and
an anti-American statement by the British philosopher
Bertrand Russell.

The New York Times, May 6, 1967

from *The Military Half:*
An Account of the Destruction in Quang Ngai and Quang Tin

by Jonathan Schell

AT THE BEGINNING of 1967, American officials in Vietnam, both military and civilian, commonly expressed the view that the "generation of refugees" was an unfortunate but unavoidable consequence of conducting effective military operations. By August, most officials were declaring that the removal of people from their original homes and villages was in itself a valuable tactic in the struggle against the National Liberation Front. Military men, in particular, were fond of quoting Mao Tse-tung's dictum that in guerrilla warfare the guerrillas are the fish and the people are the water. They argued that they could catch the fish only by drying up the water. I heard Mao Tse-tung's metaphor mentioned in this connection on at least five occasions in Quang Ngai. In an article titled "The Cause in Vietnam Is Being Won," which appeared in the issue of *The New York Times Magazine* of October 15, 1967, General Maxwell D. Taylor, former chairman of the Joint Chiefs of Staff and former United States Ambassador to South Vietnam, explains the logic of population control and, without naming the camps as such, describes the advantages to the South Vietnamese government of having from three million to four million of the country's population of roughly seventeen million in or around government-controlled camps:

As an indicator of progress in pacification, there has been an encouraging increase in Government control in rural areas in recent months. Indeed, since mid-1965, there has been an increase of some 3 million people in rural areas clearly under Government control. About 1,200,000 of this increase has occurred in the last six months.

Concurrently, the Vietcong-controlled population has decreased by more than a million since 1965, the remaining Governmental gains having come from contested areas. In that year, it was estimated that 26 per cent of the total population (including the cities) was under Vietcong domination; now it is down to 14 per cent. If one includes the cities, the total population under secure Government of Vietnam control has increased from 6.6 million in mid-1965 to 10.8 million in mid-1967. . . .

Population liberated from Vietcong control is a double asset from our point of view. Not only are these people freed from the tyranny of Vietcong domination, but they are withdrawn from among the human assets so necessary to support the guerrilla movement. The Vietcong are necessarily parasitic upon the rural population from whom they drew recruits, porters, food and other forms of help. Without this rural support, the local guerrilla movement risks atrophy and progressive attrition.

I met a young American lieutenant colonel in Binh Son District who was discouraged by the current situation in the province but thought that things would improve greatly if a sweeping plan he had in mind should be put into effect. After talking for over a year with Vietnamese whose command of English was poor, the colonel had developed a very slow, careful style of enunciation and had come to employ a minimal basic vocabulary. This way of speaking had become such a habit with him that at times he used it even with Americans, especially when he was trying to elucidate difficult points. His slowness of speech was accompanied by strong emphasis on every important word and a tense, passionate gesticulation with his fists that expressed his total dedication to his work. Sometimes he would expend so much energy explaining an idea about the future of the province that he would have to slump back in his chair with a weak smile of exhaustion when he had finished.

While I was with the colonel, I heard him tell an observer from the American headquarters for Pacification in Saigon, who had come to evaluate the "potential" of the province for Revolutionary Development, which is the South Vietnamese government's response to the Vietcong's political-indoctrination program, and is usually abbreviated as revdev, or R.D., "Look, the V.C. get their people to support them. They *or-*

ganize the people. Those people are *alive*; they are highly *mo-tivated*. But the people who are supposed to be on our side are just *blobs*." He screwed up his face in chagrin and clenched his fists in front of him. "The refugees sit around all day doing *nothing*, and *we are doing nothing about it*," he continued, coming down hard on every word. Then he outlined his plan for reconstruction. "We've got to get these people out where they can get killed," he said, then stopped himself, smiled, and added, "Don't get me wrong. I don't want them to suffer any more than they are suffering now. They've suffered too much already, but what I mean is, we've got to give them some *reason* to support the government. We have to give them some motivation to defend themselves. Now they don't have any jobs, or houses, or anything that they can get excited about, and I don't blame them for being apathetic. Look at the camps. *Anybody* would be apathetic." The first require-ment for reconstruction, as he saw it, was security, and for this he envisaged a vast, superbly conducted training program for the local young men, who would learn a new self-confidence and the will to defend their villages against the National Lib-eration Front. Next, the villages would have to be physically rebuilt—"preferably by the villagers themselves." He said, "The Vietnamese have to do it themselves. We always try to do it for them, to give it to them. I know what a tremendous temptation it is to give candy to kids. It makes you feel good inside. You're No. 1. But for every piece of candy you give a kid, you're destroying the kid's faith in his father, who can't give him any candy. I have seen so many cases of Americans who want to play Santa Claus and feel warm all over, but this kind of thing is only corrupting, and it destroys the people's pride. If only we could learn that!" The next part of the plan involved the creation of a democratic village government, chosen by the people themselves and responsive to their as-pirations. Finally, the change at the local level would be ac-companied by the total abolition of corruption at the provincial level, and the beginnings of a nationwide change-over to civilian rule. In short, the colonel wanted to see a vigorous, democratic, prosperous, happy, entirely new and changed society rise from the ashes of Quang Ngai to resist the National Liberation Front because the local villagers felt a spontaneous love for their new life and a deep enthusiasm for a wholly reformed government of South Vietnam.

I pointed out to the colonel that approximately seventy per cent of the villages in the province had already been destroyed, and asked if he saw this as a serious obstacle to the realization of his plan.

"I know it," he said. "In the fifteen-kilometre stretch of coast of our area of operation there are just *two* villages still standing, and if anyone tells you there are more they are liars. One thing is that the Vietnamese can rebuild their houses very quickly, with very little trouble at all." He then patiently described to me in detail how the thatch-roofed houses that had made up about eighty per cent of the homes in the province were constructed. "The thing is, we've got to change the population patterns," he went on. "It's these widely dispersed *population patterns* that allowed the V.C. to get going in the first place. So we won't necessarily move the people back to their original villages. If we could change the population patterns, getting people consolidated into tighter areas, we could put up defenses, and the government could control them more easily. We could check them every night for I.D. cards, and in that way keep the V.C. from infiltrating."

When the colonel had concluded his remarks, the observer from Saigon said that he would like to spend a day and a night in a village of the district with his Vietnamese interpreter, to judge for himself whether conditions were ripe for a Revolutionary Development Program, and he asked the colonel to recommend a village. Clapping a hand to his forehead, the colonel laughed in dismay, and said, "You can't sleep in a village. I couldn't let you do that. We don't have any villages an *American* could spend the *night* in."

AFTER completing Operation Malheur II in the Song Ve Valley, the 1st Brigade of the 101st Airborne Division took another hop in its drive northward and launched Operation Hood River in the Song Tra Khuc Valley. The hope was to trap a large unit of the enemy by landing on the hills above the valley and sweeping down into it from all sides, but, as in the two earlier operations, the trap closed empty. Sporadic contact with the enemy was common during these sweeps, but this time it was lighter than usual. The official figure for enemy killed during the two weeks of the operation was seventy-eight, and the figure for American casualties was three killed and thirty-eight wounded. The troops, and the artillery and aircraft that supported them, did, however, destroy most of the villages in the river valley and on the coastal plain at its mouth.

In mid-August, when I first arrived at the Chu Lai base, which is situated just north of Quang Ngai Province, in the southern part of Quang Tin Province, and which was the headquarters for Task Force Oregon at that time, I was given a briefing on the composition of the enemy in Quang Ngai Province by the head Information Officer for the task force, Major Patrick H. Dionne, who is a portly man with a round face and a smile that appears, along with an outstretched hand, as soon as someone enters his office—a greeting that seems to say, "We're going to get along fine!" (Throughout my stay in Quang Ngai, I was given perfect freedom to see whatever I wanted, and was encouraged by Major Dionne and other Information Officers to fly in FAC planes and accompany operations on the ground as often as possible.)

"We're here to sell the government of South Vietnam to the people in this province," Major Dionne said. "The trouble is, they don't *want* to have the government sold to them, so what we are really doing is cramming the government down their throats. This place has been V.C. ever since the Japanese, so they've never really had any contact with the government." Picking a pink card out of a desk file for reference, he continued, "There are from seven hundred thousand to a million people in Quang Ngai. About half of these are under G.V.N. control and a quarter are V.C. supporters. We've got quite a large number of refugees in the province. They fled the V.C. or left their area because of combat, and now the G.V.N. controls them. We've got both local V.C. and N.V.A. units in the province. The 3rd N.V.A. Division is based in Duc Pho District."

I asked if these North Vietnamese Army soldiers had infiltrated into South Vietnam recently.

"Actually, these are the ones that came down in 1954 and

stayed, and they organized the local people to support Hanoi," Major Dionne said. "You might say that the people are North Vietnamese–oriented—living on this side of the D.M.Z. The N.V.A. here are the old Vietminh who stayed on. They have their families down here and don't really have too much to go back to up North. Then, there's the V.C.—the local-force guy and the main-force guy. The local-force guy lives at home and is poorly armed—a squad might have two rifles and six hand grenades—but he's highly motivated, and does the political cadre work. As opposed to the N.V.A., the local V.C. is a loner—with a lot of other loners. They feel pretty sure that they are going to succeed. The main-force guy is organized in units and roves around. He's better armed."

When I spoke with American officers about the civilians who were sometimes killed in our bombings of villages judged to be hostile, they often brought up the fact that the Vietcong also mistreated and killed civilians in *their* operations. During my month in Quang Ngai Province, two incidents of this kind figured heavily in Army press releases, in battalion newspapers, and in Psychological Warfare posters and leaflets. On August 9th, the Vietcong had attacked a village along Route 1 that was supposed to be protected by Popular Forces stationed there. The Popular Forces had fired at the Vietcong, but without venturing outside their fortified positions, and the Vietcong had destroyed a dozen houses with satchel charges and killed and wounded several villagers; they had, however, left the medical dispensary, which was financially supported by Americans, untouched. Army photographers arrived the next morning to take photographs of civilians wounded or killed in the attack. Later, these photographs were printed on propaganda posters and were also released to the press. The other incident was the discovery of two men that the Vietcong had held prisoner for several months. The August 16th edition of the *Screaming Eagle* reported the discovery as follows:

Duc Pho—"God, they were a mess," said one paratrooper. "They looked like something out of those World War II prison camps." The 101st Airborne trooper was shocked at the physical condition of two

South Vietnamese soldiers liberated from a Viet Cong prison camp near here during Operation Malheur II. The prisoners were emaciated, haggard and beaten. Eyes and cheeks were sunk into their gaunt faces and their voices weak and inaudible due to lack of strength. Both suffered from malnutrition and exhaustion.

"They were in pretty bad shape," said Lt. Corky Boswell, Chico, Calif. "The VC had beaten them, used them for laborers, and fed them just enough to keep them alive. And that wasn't very much, as you can see. . . ." The two former prisoners, exhausted, and limited in their knowledge of enemy movements, were of little help. "We can't help you," said Xuan.

"We just dug tunnels. They watched us carefully all the time and never talked in front of us."

Major Dionne expressed deep disgust with the Vietcong for attacking the village on Route 1. "O.K., so maybe one of our artillery rounds goes astray and hits a friendly village every once in a while," he said. "But I don't know." Major Dionne's expression became disturbed. "With a hidden device—a V.C. mine . . . I mean, *I* get paid to wear the uniform, so if something happens to me it's not so bad. But these poor old buzzards don't get paid for that. I don't know . . ."

Every few weeks or so, the Vietcong overran another village along Route 1 that was supposed to be under the protection of the Popular Forces. In October, I asked U.S. AID officials in Washington how many village officials had been assassinated by the Vietcong in 1967 in Quang Ngai Province. When AID or any other government agency gives statistics on "village officials" killed, these may include officers of the Popular Forces and members of the Combat Youth—these are both lightly armed groups of villagers recruited to defend their own villages against the Vietcong—and Revolutionary Development workers, Civic Action cadres, interfamily chiefs, security agents, and a great variety of other types of individuals. For the period from January 1st to October 1st, AID listed a total of eighteen "village officials" as having been killed by the Vietcong in Quang Ngai. They consisted of three Revolutionary Development workers, three hamlet chiefs, two Youth Cadre members, one Civic Action cadre, four Popular Forces officers, one Combat Youth member, one chief of a rehabilitation center, one former village security agent, one village security agent, and one former interfamily chief. Usually, the Vietcong were careful to bomb only the houses of government employees, and several Americans expressed horror at the coldblooded premeditation of these assassinations. "We may have accidents," said one, "but we never set off a mine or shoot a bullet with some specific guy's name written on it in advance."

Major Dionne told me that Task Force Oregon's proudest nonmilitary achievement was the opening of Route 1 to traffic. When the task force arrived, it found that the Vietcong had blown up almost all the bridges on the road. Task Force Oregon engineers rebuilt the bridges and then opened the road to public traffic in a big ceremony, with several high-ranking officers of Task Force Oregon and the province chief present. Several times each week, American teams swept the road for Vietcong mines, finding an average of two a week. A light traffic of bicycles and motor scooters began to travel between certain towns, although other stretches were still unused.

Later on, Major Dionne told me, "When I get to wondering what this war is all about, I take a trip up to the base hospital. You know—a guy smilin' at you, saying that he's going to be up in a few weeks, when what he doesn't know is that he's lost the use of his legs and is crippled for life. And when I see what these boys are willing to sacrifice, that really makes me see what it's all about over here."

I also spoke briefly with an Intelligence captain assigned to the FAC control desk about the character of the enemy. "They have a parallel structure," he told me. "The orders originate in Hanoi and go to COSVN." He pronounced it "Cosvin" and explained that it meant the Central Office of South Vietnam.

I asked if he would tell me what he meant by a parallel structure.

"O.K., let's take a look at Communism—at North Vietnam, the U.S.S.R., and China," he said. "They all have a front organization that tells the people that the government has moral objectives that are sound. All these countries have that in common."

"What does the front organization consist of?" I asked.

"It's the fact that they have a President."

"How does this apply to the National Liberation Front?"

"I don't know precisely how the front and the real government are related, but the front is the organization that tries to tell them that Communism is a good deal."

"If there is a parallel structure, what is parallel to what?" I asked.

"The Front is one—the National Liberation Front—and the other . . . Oh, hell, I can't think of the other. Did you read Allen Dulles' book about intelligence?"

I said I hadn't.

"It's described in there. There's the apparatus that spreads Communism. But I forget what they call it here." (That night, the captain came in to tell me he had done some research and had found the name that had eluded him earlier—it was the People's Revolutionary Party.)

Conversations in Vietnam tend to become muddled because many meanings are attached to a few favorite terms, as in the above conversation, in which the Intelligence captain often failed to make it clear when we meant "front" in the sense of the National Liberation Front and when we meant it in the sense of a cover, or front, organization. Later, I was talking with the same captain about "the V.C. infrastructure," and I suddenly realized that this term, which he had used at the beginning of the conversation to mean the political organization of the Vietcong at the local level, had changed as we talked to mean the wood-and-packed-mud "infrastructure" of the Vietcong's tunnels and bunkers. "Parallel structure" is another of the favorite terms, and it can apply to the Vietcong governmental apparatus, which "parallels" the South Vietnamese government, or to the American advisory system, which also "parallels" the South Vietnamese government, or, as in my conversation with the captain, to the "parallel structure" of all Communist governments, including the National Liberation Front. (The word "structure" is itself a favorite in Vietnam. The military refer to all Vietnamese houses as "structures.")

AFTER completing Operation Hood River, the 1st Brigade of the 101st Airborne Division was to move north once again and launch Operation Benton, in the southern part of Quang Tin

Province. I flew over the Song Tra Khuc Valley in FAC planes—assigned by the Air Force to the 1st Brigade of the 101st Airborne Division—during the last two days of Operation Hood River. FAC pilots had two duties. The first was to fly over specified areas noting anything that seemed suspicious to them and choosing targets to recommend for air strikes. The targets were not further examined at first hand, and unless they were found to be near friendly troops or in "no-strike zones" they were bombed. Some FAC pilots flew over a certain area every day for several weeks at a time, acquainting themselves with it as thoroughly as they could from the air with the aid of maps. Other pilots would be assigned to the brigade, and would fly over the brigade in all its operations, wherever it went. The FAC pilots' second duty was to guide fighter-bombers to their targets. Air Force spokesmen were always careful to stress the point that a FAC pilot could not, on his own authority, call planes to bomb a target—that the Army had to give its clearance in every case. In practice, this meant that when a FAC pilot spotted something he wished to have bombed he would radio its position to the DASC (Direct Air Support Center) office for his military corps area and enter a request for a flight of fighter-bombers. DASC would weigh the urgency of the mission against other requests made for fighter-bombers at that particular time, and decide which of the requested targets should be bombed by the limited number of planes that were aloft or "on hot pad alert," ready for immediate takeoff. The Air Force divided all air strikes into two categories, which it termed "pre-planned strikes" and "immediate strikes." A pre-planned strike was scheduled anywhere from twenty-four hours to two weeks in advance of the time of the bombing, and an immediate strike was carried out within a few hours, at most, of a call from ground troops or from a FAC pilot who had spotted what he judged to be enemy activity. In conversation with a FAC pilot, I once said "planned strike" instead of "pre-planned strike," by mistake, and was swiftly corrected. When I asked what the difference between the terms "planned" and "pre-planned" was, the pilot answered, "*All* our strikes are *planned*. We *have* no *unplanned* strikes."

At the Danang airbase, I received a briefing from a major

on the role of FAC pilots in I Corps. When I asked what kinds of targets were usually hit by pre-planned strikes, he answered, "In the mountains, just about anything that moves is considered to be V.C. We've cleared most of the people out of there, and anything that's left has got to be V.C. No one else has got any reason to be there. We go after enemy base areas and V.C. r.-and-r. centers." The Army refers to the overnight way stations where Vietcong soldiers are believed to sleep as "r.-and-r. centers," after the Army's own practice of sending its troops for one week of "rest and relaxation" each year in a foreign capital, like Bangkok, Tokyo, or Sydney. "Most of the action is in the lowlands," the major continued. "There we hit mostly the bunkers and fortifications. The V.C. hide in there, and store their supplies in there, too. Of course, we can never hit *all* the bunkers. Also, we hit fortified villages. In some of these villages, the lines of trenches and bunkers are amazing. It looks like World War I. These fortified villages are all known to be enemy installations. I mean, they've been shooting at people and harboring the V.C. But before we hit any place we send a Psy War craft in to warn the villagers to escape. We used to drop warning leaflets, but they didn't do much good, so now we've switched over to announcing. We give the people at least a good ten or fifteen minutes to get out of there before we put in a strike. But it's the immediate strike that gives the best results. That's where you get your K.B.A.s." The initials stand for "Killed by Air." "Of course," the major added, "enemy troops in the open are the kind of target that we all like the best."

I asked him what was involved in getting clearance for an air strike.

"First, we check the area for friendly troops, and then, when the request goes in to DASC, the province chief has to give his O.K.," he said. "We *never* put in a strike without first getting permission from the province chief. He's a Vietnamese, and he knows the local conditions, so he's the man in the final analysis who knows who's friendly and who's unfriendly. And, after all, it's their country, so they ought to know what's going on." (Later, I asked Province Chief Hoang Dinh Tho, of Quang Tin Province, about the specific steps that were usually taken in securing his clearance, and learned that at the beginning of each operation in his province he designated certain regions—typically, those surrounding district capitals—as no-strike zones, and gave the ground commanders of the operation a free hand in deciding which targets to bomb in the rest of the area of operation.)

The major explained that the Vietnam Air Force (or VNAF, pronounced "Veenaf" by the Americans) had its own organization, separate from the United States Air Force but flying out of the same bases. VNAF supported ARVN with A-1 propeller-driven fighter-bombers—a type of plane that was last used by our Navy in the Korean war. "VNAF has its own FACS," the major told me. "They work just the way we do. One-half of the base is for VNAF and one-half for us."

I asked what VNAF FACS did, mostly.

"VNAF FACS usually cover convoys," the major replied. "They're pretty much tied up with that. But it's a very necessary function—to cover those convoys. VNAF uses one side of Danang. We built the facilities just the same as the American facilities, but separate. But they don't know how to take care of something nice. You go over there now, and it's a stinking mess. You know what one of the first things they did was? They unscrewed the taps and spigots in the bathrooms and took them into town and sold them."

I asked whether American FACS guided the VNAF fighter-bombers to their targets.

"Those old A-1s that VNAF uses are a lot slower than our planes, and more accurate, so they don't use any FACS for that," the major answered.

I learned that ideas for targets of the American fighter-bombers were gathered mainly from the recommendations of ground commanders, FAC pilots, and "agent reports"—the name given to most other sources of information. Occasionally, a province chief would order a town burned or bombed. All targets were described to DASC in terms of their coördinates on a military map, and DASC would relay these coördinates to the FAC pilot who was guiding the air strike. The FAC pilot would locate the target point on a similar map that he carried with him in the plane. The maps were crosshatched by a grid. The horizontal lines, spaced two centimetres apart, were numbered from 01 to 99, and the vertical lines were

similarly spaced and numbered. Each square formed by the
lines represented one square kilometre on the ground. The
coördinates were given in six figures divided into two groups
of three—691 873, for example. The first two digits of the first
group of three designated a vertical line, and the first two
digits of the second group of three designated a horizontal
line. The third digit of the first group indicated a distance, in
hundreds of metres, east of the vertical line on the map, and
the third digit of the second group indicated a distance, in
hundreds of metres, north of the horizontal line. However,
the hundred-metre intervals were not drawn on the map, so
the pilot had to estimate for himself what one hundred, or
three hundred, metres along the lines amounted to. And even
if the pilot estimated accurately, the smallest area that could
be designated by this system was a hundred metres square.
(Everything within the hundred-metre square northeast of the
coördinates 691 873 was designated by those coördinates.) On
about half the missions, DASC would give the FAC pilot a description of the type of target that was to be located in the
hundred-metre-square area designated by the coördinates.
Some of the official descriptions, such as "bunkers," "military
structures," and "enemy hamlet," referred to targets that
could sometimes be spotted from the air, but other descriptions, such as "V.C. r.-and-r. area," "suspected enemy troop
concentration," and "infiltration route" did not, and in these
cases the pilot had to rely entirely on his coördinates. Once
the pilot had found the target area on his map, he would plot
its position on the ground by using as reference points prominent topographical features that showed on his map; in the
mountains he would use the configurations of the ridgelines
as reference points, and in the flatlands he would use rivers,
roads, and villages. After finding the target on the ground, he
would relay the coördinates by radio to the fighter-bombers
when they came overhead. Just before the strike, he would
"mark" the target by hitting it with a phosphorus rocket,
which sends up a highly visible cloud of white smoke and also
splashes burning phosphorus over a twenty-yard area. Then,
using the smoke as a guide, the fighter-bombers would fly
over the target, dropping their bombs or cans of napalm, or
hitting it with rockets or strafing fire. The FAC plane mean-

while circled slowly nearby, watching the strike and telling the pilots of the fighter-bombers by radio how far from the target they were hitting. Usually, there were two or three fighter-bomber planes on a mission, and each plane flew two or three passes, depending on what armament it was carrying. When the strike was completed, the FAC pilot would fly over the area again and make a Bomb Damage Assessment Report—usually called the B.D.A. Report—to DASC and to the fighter-bomber pilots. The B.D.A. Report included the percentage of "Bombs on Target" and the percentage of "Target Destroyed." The pilot would also report any "Military Structures Destroyed." When there were friendly ground troops in the area near the target, the ground commander would radio the coördinates of their position to the FAC pilot, who would relay the information to the pilots of the fighter-bombers. The FAC pilot would make contact with the commanders of nearby artillery batteries, too, to check the trajectory of artillery shells being fired at that moment, so that he would be able to avoid them. A FAC pilot told me that one in twenty FAC pilots was killed during 1966, but he explained that he and his fellow-pilots felt less fear than many G.I.s on the ground who had a smaller chance of being hit. In the air, you didn't know when you were being shot at until a bullet came very close to the plane, or actually hit it, the pilot said, and he described a bullet passing close by as making a snapping sound, "like someone closing an ashtray in the back seat of your car." The fighter-bomber pilots made no decisions about targets themselves. A fighter-bomber pilot who was based at Danang told me, "We are going four or five hundred knots, and we can't see much ourselves. I've never seen a body or a person yet, and I've been on over a hundred missions. It's virtually impossible to see any movement on the ground. The FAC is the expert. We're only experts on delivery."

In August, there were six FAC pilots detailed to the 1st Brigade of the 101st Airborne Division. During Operations Malheur I and Malheur II, they had flown out of Duc Pho, but as the brigade moved north for Operation Hood River and Operation Benton, the FAC pilots shifted their base of operation north to Chu Lai. While the brigade was conducting an operation, the FAC pilots always kept one plane aloft over the area of operation during daylight hours. Each pilot usually flew a three-hour shift each day, though occasionally, when an emergency called for it, each would fly a six-hour shift. From August 10th to August 21st, I flew with the FAC pilots attached to the 1st of the 101st almost daily, lived with them in their quarters, and ate my meals with them on the base.

On August 10th, the next-to-last day of Operation Hood River, I flew in the early morning with a FAC pilot from Texas who had a thin face and a slight frame and was about thirty years old. I shall call him Captain Reese. The standard FAC plane was a Cessna O-1 Bird Dog. It seated two, one in front and one in back; had a single propeller; and was armed with four tubes containing phosphorus rockets, two tubes being mounted under each wing. It could fly as slowly as forty miles an hour, and could hold an extremely tight corkscrew turn when the pilot wanted to look at one small area of ground for a sustained period. Before climbing into the plane, Captain Reese picked up a flak vest, a helmet, a submachine gun, and a survival kit, the last two for use in case the plane was hit and had to make a forced landing. On the flight line, where the planes sat enclosed by steel walls to protect them from shrapnel in mortar or rocket attacks, three young mechanics lounged shirtless in the heat, waiting to refuel O-1 planes or repair their engines. Although it was against the rules, the pilots occasionally let the mechanics climb into the pilot's seat and taxi the planes across the fifty-yard stretch of asphalt between the fuel pump and the protective walls.

Just before our plane went out on the runway, one of the mechanics, who was pulling safety rods from the rocket tubes on the wings, asked Captain Reese, "You gonna get any of 'em today, Captain?"

"I dunno," answered Captain Reese.

The mechanics often asked the pilots about their missions, but they rarely got answers any more revealing than this. During most of the day, the mechanics sat on wooden boxes around a soft-drink cooler that was protected by a canvas roof, and read back issues of *Stars and Stripes*, or looked for the hundredth time through a few thumb-greased copies of *Sir!* and *Escapade* magazines. Beyond their little spot of shade stretched a landscape of hot asphalt, shimmering corrugated metal, and airplanes. Part of their job was to assemble phos-phorus rockets and load them under the wings of the FAC planes. The rockets were about a yard long and came in three pieces, which the mechanics had to screw together. I once asked a mechanic who had just dumped a case of four rockets on the asphalt whether a rocket would explode if he tossed it up in the air and let it fall onto the runway. He picked up a front section, which was marked "Warhead," and, dangling it about five feet off the ground, said, "It would go off if I dropped it from here. If it gets on you, it'll burn right through you for days and it won't go out with just water. You have to put it out with a special chemical we've got over there in the shed." The mechanics did not learn about any military op-eration that the FAC planes supported until four or five days after it had been launched, when a copy of the Task Force Oregon mimeographed *News Sheet* might reach them, and they could read, for example, "The infantry units mounted a three-pronged attack, and in the ensuing ground action tallied 44 enemy killed, bringing the body count to 65 for the action north of Duc Pho," or "Two Chinese mines were discovered by the airborne-infantrymen as they searched for the enemy in heavy jungle west of Quang Ngai City. One detainee, suf-fering a bullet wound in the back, was turned over to au-thorities. The paratroopers captured three enemy weapons and one and one-half tons of rice." Every once in a while, one of the mechanics would get a word or two out of a FAC pilot about a current operation, and he would relay the in-formation to the other mechanics with studied nonchalance, as though he always had an inside line on what was going on. But usually the mechanics just fuelled the planes, watched them disappear in the sky, read old magazines, and listened to the day-long thunder of bombs on the other side of the mountains.

When Captain Reese and I had strapped ourselves into our seats, a young mechanic waved us forward onto a siding of the runway. Captain Reese had to wait for an F-4 fighter-bomber to take off ahead of us. The F-4 was mottled with green and brown camouflage paint and had a heavy, sharklike body with stubby wings, downward-slanting tail fins, and a drooping black nose, which was just rising off the runway as the plane crossed our bow. For a few seconds, the deep roaring of its engine filled one's head completely, overpowering thought. In a quarter of a minute, the orange-tipped blue flames of its afterburners were vanishing in the distance as it rose at a steady steep angle.

Captain Reese taxied onto the runway, and our small plane lifted off the asphalt after running only a hundred yards or so down the runway, which was two miles long and stretched out of sight in front of us like a turnpike in a desert. As soon as the plane was off the ground, Captain Reese turned southwest and started a climb to fifteen hundred feet. According to regulations, the FAC pilots were not supposed to fly below that altitude, but almost all of them frequently broke this rule, and sometimes they went down as low as a hundred feet. ("As soon as I heard that rule, I knew that it was one of the rules made to break," a FAC pilot once said to me. "You can't even see people from one thousand feet. You can't see anything unless you go down there.") Captain Reese guided the O-1 over the brown, abandoned rice fields and blackened ruins of the villages in the western part of Son Tinh District. There was a heavy, high gray overcast.

Using a headset and a microphone wired for the back seat, I asked Captain Reese what types of target were most common and what the targets of the present mission were.

Speaking through a microphone the size of a lima bean that reached around on a small metal arm from the side of his helmet almost into his mouth, Captain Reese answered, "Oh, usually we get a V.C. base camp, burn off a village, or hit a supply depot. Today, we're going to hit a suspected enemy troop concentration at 324 733." (All figures given for coördinates in this account have been changed.)

I asked how it had been decided to bomb this target.

"I don't know. An agent reported it, or something, I guess," he said.

We crossed a small ridge of hills and came out over the Song Tra Khuc Valley. The cultivated fields were pale green, and the forests on the mountain slopes were a vivid deep green under a sky that was darkening before rain. Several miles to the west, where the valley vanished into the mountains, curved plumes of rain trailed down from the cloud cover, and to the east more plumes of rain descended into the sea. The air below the clouds seemed oddly clear, and tall, bluish mountains were visible far to the west, above the delicate ridges of nearer, smaller mountains. The line between the sea and the sky was lost in a uniform grayness, and a large blue island, clearly visible twenty or more kilometres offshore, seemed to be floating in the sky. The tops of four or five of the low mountains on the north and south sides of the valley were bald and blackened. Captain Reese explained that intensive bombing and machine-gun fire were usually directed at hilltops—often starting forest fires—in order to kill anyone there before our troops made a landing. In the valley, the cultivated fields were marked with craters of all sizes. Five or six thin, straight columns of smoke rose from the valley floor. "They're burning off some hootches. This is a solid V.C. area," Captain Reese told me. He circled lower, for a closer look. In that part of the valley, widely separated clusters of houses stood along a line of trees bordering a small stream. Troops were advancing across a rice field and entering a courtyard that was surrounded by three houses. A minute later, as they reappeared in a field on the other side of the yard, a spot of flame began to spread on the roof of one house, then on the roof of another, and soon all three roofs were collapsing in flames. Captain Reese brought the plane back to fifteen hundred feet and headed southwest again, toward his target area. Below us, the gray squares of freshly burned houses dotted the ground. Arriving over the target area, Captain Reese found that the hundred-metre square designated by the coördinates included a wooded ridge and a small ravine lying halfway up a mountain about three thousand feet high. The side of the ravine across from the ridge was lined with rows of crops stretching up the steep mountain slope.

"They want us to hit that ravine," Captain Reese said. "That's the target."

At eight-forty-five, the flight commander of three F-4 fighter-bombers radioed to say that they had arrived over the general area.

"Tell me what ordnance you've got, and all that jazz," the Captain said.

"We've got six napes, six seven-hundred-and-fifty-pounders,

and six two-hundred-and-fifty pounders. Can you use it?" the flight commander answered.

"We can use all that. I'll mark the target for you," the Captain replied.

Throughout most of the strike, the pilots communicated in relaxed, genial voices and with a perfectly flat intonation, which came across the headsets with a nasal, buzzing quality, perhaps because the pilots placed their lips against the tiny microphones as they talked. Captain Reese spotted the three F-4s through the clear roof of the cockpit as they cut under the clouds above us. Wheeling his plane over the target, he went into a sharp dive, and threw a switch to fire a phosphorus rocket from a tube under his wing. The rocket did not fire. "Damn. Won't fire today," he said. He banked around again, brought the plane into another dive, and threw another switch. Once more, the rocket failed to fire. On his next pass, he dropped a smoke grenade by hand out the window, and it failed to explode. He dropped three more grenades in succeeding passes, and these, too, were duds. The fifth grenade trailed a thin line of smoke from the plane down to the top of the ridge, and a large puff of white smoke soon appeared over the trees. "I want it right down in that valley. You can come in from the east and break west," Captain Reese told the flight commander, and then he began to fly in a tight circle a few hundred yards from the target. As the O-1 was closing its second full circle, he lined up the first fighter-bomber in his front windshield, and he held it in view while it went into a low dive over the cleft. The bombs travelled diagonally earthward and landed on the wooded ridge. A visible shock wave sprang outward from the point of impact, and a cloud of brown smoke shot up several hundred feet above the woods. The fighter-bomber pulled up at a sharp angle, presenting its belly, with the bombs grouped under its stubby wings, to our view. "Real fine!" exclaimed the Captain. "That's right in there! Next time, try to get it fifty metres south, down in the valley." The next plane, diving from the same angle, landed its bombs farther up the ridge. "That's real fine," said the Captain. The third plane sent two silver canisters of napalm toppling down, end over end, and they also landed on the wooded ridge. A pillar of black smoke, with a thick column of orange fire boiling briefly at its core, puffed up over the trees, and red globs of burning jelly splashed outward over the jungle. The next two loads were also napalm, and they also hit the top of the ridge. After the third napalm strike, the flight commander asked, "Do you want it down pretty much in the ravine?" and Captain Reese answered, "Yes, right down there in the ravine." The next three passes put bombs in the ravine, filling it with brown smoke. With that, the strike was over, and the Captain flew back across the target area. Large brown holes had been opened up in the woods, with blasted trees lying in pieces around the edges. Globs of napalm still burned in patches on the ground and in tree branches. At the bottom of the ravine, two bombs had landed directly on a tumbling stream. Above the trees, a flock of birds flying in tight formation wheeled swiftly in circles. One bomb had landed on the cultivated side of the ravine. "I don't see anything," the Captain observed to me, in a tired voice. Then, to the flight commander, he reported, "A hundred per cent of Bombs on Target. Fifty-per-cent Target Coverage. Thank you very much, sir. I've never marked this area before, and I don't seem to mark it very well."

"Not at all," answered the flight commander. Throughout this strike, as in most of the strikes I accompanied, the FAC pilot and the flight commander addressed each other in polite, almost humble tones.

I asked the Captain who had cultivated the fields.

"That's just Montagnard farming. You'd be amazed at the places they farm," he said.

Captain Reese headed the plane back eastward over the Song Tra Khuc Valley. The line of smoking houses along the river was now a kilometre long, and led away from the river into the fields, where two flaming houses marked the troops' advance units. Since the Captain had no further need to talk with the flight commander, he listened in on fragments of conversations on the ground. Communications between ground units crackled into our ears between bursts of static.

"We've captured one Charlie, but we haven't interrogated him yet," said a voice.

"Did he have a weapon?" asked another.

"He had on the black pajamas, short type, but he didn't

have a weapon," the first voice replied. "Most likely he hid it somewhere. We found him four hundred metres south of where we were last night."

To me, the Captain said, "Yesterday, five of them ran into a hole, and came out shooting, and got killed. All the villages around here have foxholes and bunkers under them. This place is almost entirely V.C.-controlled, or pro-V.C."

I asked whether the bunkers did not also serve as bomb shelters for the general populace.

"No," he said. "The V.C. build them—or force the people to build them—strictly for the V.C.'s own protection."

Below us, the lines of smoke from the burning houses had mingled to form a thin haze, which drifted eastward down the valley. DASC at Chu Lai radioed to say that the fighter-bombers assigned to the second target had been diverted to a more urgent mission and would not be coming.

"Well, we'll have to hit it tomorrow, or something," Captain Reese remarked to me.

I took advantage of the lull to ask him about the bombing policy—that is, the policy on the bombing of villages—that he, as a FAC pilot, helped carry out.

"We've got two kinds of strikes—pre-planned and immediate," he answered. "The pre-planned strikes are when we say, 'O.K., you people have been bad now for two or three months, and we haven't been able to talk you into being good, so we're going to wipe you out. You've got twenty-four hours to get out.' Usually, we give them twenty-four hours. That's the pre-planned. Then there's the immediate strike. Now, when there's an Army unit near the village, and they get fire from the village, they say, 'O.K., you people quit shooting or we're going to hit you now—right now.' Of course, that would be in a case where almost everyone in the village is pro-V.C. Technically, the village doesn't have to be warned of a strike when we are flying in conjunction with an operation, like we are now."

While we were talking, we had reached the entrance of the valley, where the river flowed out onto the coastal plain. Here, also, smoke was rising from a roadside, and houses were aflame. The lines of smoke were spreading westward, toward the troops of the 1st Brigade of the 101st, who were moving eastward as they burned more houses. "Those guys down there burning off those hootches are Civilian Irregular Defense Forces," Captain Reese said. "They're Montagnards trained by the Special Forces."

A single main road ran the length of the valley, following the meanderings of the river. Between the villages being burned by the Civilian Irregular Defense Forces and the villages being burned by the 1st Brigade, the road was crowded with cattle and with people carrying double loads on shoulder poles. Near the road, a Special Forces camp had been dug into the bald summit of a round hill that stood alone on the valley floor, overlooking a large village where houses were jammed together inside a small fortified square. Captain Reese said he thought that the village was probably a "new-life" hamlet and would be spared destruction.

As we turned westward again, I asked him about his aerial-reconnaissance duties, and how he distinguished houses and trails used by the enemy from those used only by civilians.

"You look for changes—something that's different," he said. "Normally, you're at fifteen hundred feet, searching for trails and tree lines, and looking for hootches. It's almost a fact that anything out in the open is friendly, so anything you see in the trees you suspect is unfriendly, because it might be V.C. We report hootches that are hidden in tree lines."

I pointed out that, except in the "new-life" hamlets, almost all the houses were built in the shade of tree lines.

"Yeah, they'll be built in the tree lines," he said. "But out in the sticks, if you spot a hootch with no fields around, it's probably V.C. Maybe a rice-storage house."

I asked who lived in the mountains.

"Just the Montagnards and a lot of Vietnamese," he said. "They've taken most of the people out of the mountains, so nobody has any business being here except the V.C. Even the Montagnards here are kind of coöperating with the V.C. We watch for trails up in the mountains, too."

I had noticed that many of the hilltops were cultivated and that most of these were laced with webs of foot trails, and I inquired about the trails.

"I'll look real close at the trails," the Captain said. "If someone walks through one, the grass gets bent."

I asked whether he could spot freshly bent grass from his airplane.

"Oh, yeah, you can tell," he said.

DASC called again, to say that a flight of two fighter-bombers had not expended all its bombs in a previous strike and had been looking for a target for the rest, so DASC had suggested Captain Reese's second target.

To get to the second target, we headed south and crossed a thousand-foot ridge into a small, high abandoned valley, where the rice fields—thickly terraced ones—had already gone wild and the house foundations were half overgrown. Four straight, mile-long avenues of craters from B-52 strikes crisscrossed the valley. The path of craters from one strike began on the ridge on the north side of the valley and marched across the fields and a stream, straight up the southern hillside, and out of sight beyond. The coördinates described a hundred-metre square in a wide stretch of woods on the southern hillside. "We're going to hit a place the troops were in a week ago," Captain Reese said. "They found some hootches and burned them off. Then, yesterday morning, a FAC pilot spotted some smoke comin' out of there. There wasn't supposed to be any smoke comin' out of there, so we're going to hit it today." Then, looking at his control panel, he exclaimed, "Hell, I forgot to pull the safety switch on the rockets! *That's* why they wouldn't fire." He went on, "You can see that they've hit this target before." He indicated scores of bomb craters and irregular splashes of brown and black from napalm strikes that scarred the woods in the target area. "It's a V.C. base area," he said. "It's got a number. All the base areas have got numbers."

The fighter-bombers for the second strike arrived over the valley and radioed that, all told, they were carrying six five-hundred-pound bombs and four tubes of rockets, with nineteen to a tube. Captain Reese brought the O-1 into a dive, and there was a sharp metallic explosion as a phosphorus rocket fired off our right wing. This was followed by the appearance of a pillar of white smoke rising from the woods. The Captain instructed the flight commander that the F-4s should land their bombs forty metres west of the smoke. Two bombs sent down in the first pass hit a hundred metres east of the smoke. The bombs sent down in the second pass landed fifty metres east, and in the third, and final, bombing pass the bombs landed within thirty metres of the white smoke. The strike continued with four volleys of rockets. Each volley spread over sixty or seventy metres of the woods, sending up puffs of brown smoke, and the rockets were all on the target or within thirty metres of it. Afterward, Captain Reese guided the O-1 into a descending tight spiral over the bomb craters to observe the damage. At the edge of one hole in the woods he saw a pile of debris that he judged to be the remains of a hut, and in his Bomb Damage Assessment Report he mentioned one "Military Structure Destroyed." At eleven o'clock, he headed our plane back to Chu Lai.

The Chu Lai base had expanded steadily since it was founded, in 1965, and by August of 1967 it was about ten miles long and five miles wide, and occupied what must be one of the world's most beautiful stretches of coastline. A wide beach of pure-white sand runs the length of the base in a gently curving crescent, and the water of the South China Sea is a bluish green, even on cloudy days. Along parts of the shore, a warm surf rolls evenly toward the beach across long sandbars; a mountain island lies off the coast. The area occupied by the base had once been heavily populated. A three-mile-long hilly promontory forming the northern tip of the base had been the site of a dense conglomeration of fishing villages. As the base expanded, leaflets were dropped on these villages announcing that they were going to be destroyed in order to make room for the base. (In the catalogue of leaflets used by the Marines and Task Force Oregon I saw several leaflets of this kind.) The people were evacuated, the villages were bulldozed away, and the Americans laid out their installations on the stretch of bare earth.

Upon landing, Captain Reese started back to headquarters in a jeep. The twenty-minute drive from the FAC flight line to the Task Force Oregon headquarters led through several miles of bulldozed fields of sand and dirt dotted with warehouses, munitions dumps, and repair sheds, and then ran along the beach for a mile or so. The sky was still overcast, and the beach was empty. Beer cans were strewn on the sand around simple canvas roofs on pole frames, which served as canopies for evening cook-outs. (When the sun was out, the waves were usually dotted with heads and with men riding the surf on air mattresses, and the beach was usually covered with sun-tanned soldiers in bright-colored boxer-style bathing trunks.) Beyond the beach, the road continued up a hill and out onto the rocky promontory at the northern tip of the base. At the top of the promontory, Captain Reese turned right and drove into the command complex of Task Force Oregon. In the center of a dirt parade ground that was surrounded by low, tin-roofed barracks, the American flag and the South Vietnamese flag (three horizontal red stripes on a yellow ground) flew at exactly the same height on two flagpoles standing side by side. Two gaily painted Buddhist shrines, each about ten feet tall and adorned with Chinese characters, also stood on the parade ground. These were the only traces of the Vietnamese villages that had once stood on the site of the base.

Captain Reese had a light lunch and then went to his quarters for a long nap. At just about any time of day after eleven in the morning, two or three of the six pilots could be found sprawled on their beds, asleep in the breeze of an electric fan. The pilots took turns standing by at a central control desk, which was in one of the barracks on the parade ground. It was in constant communication with DASC and with the FAC pilot who was aloft. Although the FAC pilots almost never flew after dark, one of their number helped supervise, from the central control desk, any bombings carried out at night, and coördinated night flights of AC-47s (this was the military version of the DC-3, and was nicknamed Spooky) that supported troops on the ground with heavy fire. On nights when the fighting on the ground was particularly intense, a pilot would have to stay up all night at the control desk and sleep the next day.

Except when the FAC pilots were flying missions, they lived entirely within the confines of their base. It would have been perfectly possible for any one of them to pass his entire one-year tour of duty in Vietnam without ever talking to a Vietnamese or setting foot inside a Vietnamese village or city other than Saigon. Except for their r.-and-r. trips to foreign cities, and occasional expeditions in the FAC planes to the Danang airbase to buy beer and soft drinks, on what they called "the soda-pop run," the pilots' daily lives revolved solely around their missions, their quarters, the central control desk, and the dining halls, bars, and movie theatres in the officers' clubs. The FAC pilots' quarters, which they called the Hootch, consisted of one of the several rows of tin-roofed barracks, which had mosquito netting serving as the upper half of the walls. The barracks was partitioned into three rooms, containing four beds each, and the beds were separated by tall metal clothes cabinets. Most of the pilots had decorated their walls with *Playboy* Playmates of the Month. On the wall next to one major's bed, Miss May of 1967, who is shown standing on a sun deck with her pink shirt open, dwarfed a dozen small snapshots of the major's wife, in one of which she was standing, arms akimbo, in a bathing suit on a beach, and of his eight-year-old son, shown standing beside a lake and holding a small fish up to the camera. On the major's desk were a can of spray insecticide, a Reader's Digest volume of condensed books (featuring President Eisenhower's book "At Ease," which is subtitled "Stories I Tell to Friends"), a can of Pepsi-Cola, a softball, a dozen loose bullets, and a life-size wooden carving of a fist with the middle finger upraised. The Vietnamese do not use the gesture of raising the middle finger, and this kind of sculpture had been developed especially for American soldiers looking for souvenirs of Vietnam. Sometimes the younger pilots played darts on a board that hung on one door, and they also occasionally played Monopoly. A refrigerator was kept stocked with beer and soft drinks. Because of the heat, most of the pilots had at least two beers or soft drinks a day. Each was on his honor to put fifteen cents in a common refreshment fund in a box in the back of the refrigerator every time he took a drink, but someone who, it seemed, had not been wholly able to put his trust in an honor system had halfheartedly attempted to revise it by taping to the front of the refrigerator door a sheet of paper with everyone's name on it, on which each person was supposed to mark down the number of drinks he had taken and the number he had paid for.

Around the central control desk, and in other places where

the pilots gathered, an atmosphere of perpetual low-keyed, comradely humor prevailed. There was a steady stream of light remarks. One man who was standing idly around said to another, with weary joviality, "It's a beautiful, beautiful war!" The second man said, "It's the only one we've got." A FAC pilot entered a room full of FAC pilots and said, "Here are our hard-working FAC pilots," in a tone that indicated neither that they were hard-working nor that they weren't. In this way, the FAC pilots rarely talked about the war directly, and yet never quite got away from the subject, either. The relaxed style of their humor was, I thought, caught quite precisely in their choice as their squadron's emblem of Charles Schulz's comic-strip dog Snoopy, who daydreams of fame as a First World War flying ace. On the outside of the door of the central-control-desk office, Snoopy was depicted, in a sketch, wearing goggles and a scarf that trailed out behind him as he went into a dive in a First World War Sopwith Camel biplane. Cartoon bombs exploded below him. (On a wall of the Duc Pho central-control-desk office, there was a large painting of Snoopy accompanied by a speech balloon that had him saying "Curse you, Charlie Cong!" The Task Force Oregon *News Sheet* reproduced one episode about Snoopy in each of its issues, and the pilots of the 20th Tactical Air Support Squadron in Danang carried calling cards that depicted Snoopy in his biplane firing a machine gun. On a wall of the squadron's office was a large color poster that bore a reproduction of a painting of an American pilot walking sadly through a prisoner-of-war camp. A vow not to give the enemy any information that was not required by international law was printed below the picture. The pilots, who flew regularly over North Vietnam, had pencilled a beard and mustache on the grave, pious, spotlighted face of the captured American.)

At the Chu Lai officers' club for Task Force Oregon, drinks were twenty cents each, and the pilots usually had three or four rounds each evening before supper. One pilot observed, "At these prices, you can't afford *not* to drink." On the evening of August 10th, the FAC pilots drove to the Marine dining hall, which was a favorite of theirs among the base's many dining halls. Ham, chops, steak, and chicken were served there. They were all prepared in the dependably appetizing

style of an excellent truckers' diner on a big American highway, and you could have as much as you could eat. Some
Korean officers sat grouped together at several tables. Most
of them were enjoying the Korean version of r. and r.—a visit
to an American base like Chu Lai, where they were allowed
to eat in the American mess halls, shop in the American PX,
and swim on the safe stretch of beach occupied by the base.
Conversation at dinner usually revolved around matters having to do with the flying life. Often, the pilots discussed the
day's events, sometimes criticizing or praising the accuracy of
certain missions of fighter-bombers. They stuck fairly closely
to day-to-day events and to the technical problems of bombing missions, such as what altitude is best to bomb from and
how to tell if a bomb is "hung" on the wing after the bomb
release has been triggered. This evening, they discussed an
incident in which a pilot had spotted a man on the ground,
had judged him to be a Vietcong soldier when he attempted
to escape observation by running into a grove of trees, and
had called in planes to bomb the trees. This incident, which
in itself was quite ordinary, had one unusual aspect: the
FAC pilot had been flying outside his assigned area, and
the bombs had only just missed some American troops
nearby.

Another pilot said that he, too, had spotted a Vietcong soldier and had later guided an air strike onto the woods the
man had disappeared into.

I asked him how he had been able to tell that the man was
a Vietcong soldier.

"Well, he walked real proud, with a kind of bounce in his
gait, like a soldier, instead of just shuffling along, like the
farmers do," the pilot answered.

During my stay with the FAC pilots, they never discussed
the progress of the war as a whole, nor did they ever express
any hatred for the enemy. They talked a lot about pensions
and salaries, they complained about the administrative slop-
piness of the promotion procedures, and they discussed the
advantages of various cities for r.-and-r. tours (Thai women
had good figures; Hong Kong had good cheap clothes, hi-fi
equipment, and cameras). The pilots laughed when they read
in the *News Sheet* that lectures on venereal diseases, and how

to tell if you had any of them, were going to be given to the men just before they went on r.-and-r. tours. The armed services displayed a completely tolerant attitude toward the soldiers' patronage of brothels in Vietnam and in the Asian cities used for r.-and-r. tours. In Hong Kong, until very recently, the Army employed a prostitute of mixed Chinese and Portuguese parentage, who spoke understandable English, to brief the soldiers on how to pick up prostitutes among the city's bar girls without getting into fights or getting fleeced. The briefing was intended to minimize the ugly incidents that occur when a soldier is overcharged or misunderstands a girl's intentions. The pilots talked a great deal about the living conditions and the food on other bases. Once, at dinner, Captain Reese got into a long discussion about food with another pilot, and as he ate a plateful of ham, he gave a detailed description of a chicken dinner he had eaten at the Duc Pho base. Then, beginning on a piece of cake, he described to me the breakfast at the Marine dining hall in which he was eating at that moment. "They have terrific breakfasts here," he said. "Every day, they have eggs, bacon, pancakes with butter and maple syrup, toast, milk, raspberry jam, grapefruit juice, coffee, and tea—the works. Real fine breakfast."

Although the pilots never spoke angrily of the Vietcong, they often spoke disparagingly of the Army, compared to the Air Force; they called Army men "grunts." Their feeling about the Army seemed very much like one ball club's or college fraternity's feeling about a rival, but occasionally they expressed a bitterness that went beyond such friendly rivalry. One pilot told me, "The Army guys sometimes don't care what you have to do, so long as they get an air strike. But I'm not going to send men on an impossible mission to get killed like that. I'm responsible to the Air Force, too, and I've got to think of Air Force safety. Sometimes it's kind of hard, because you have to look a general in the eye and say, 'No, sir, I can't do that.'" I was surprised at the intensity of the rivalry not only between the services but between units in the same service. The men of the 1st Brigade of the 101st Airborne, who were extremely proud of their paratrooper training, referred contemptuously to all infantrymen as "legs." Once, when I was driving inside the Chu Lai base on a cruelly hot afternoon with a paratrooper of the 101st, he refused to pick up a hitchhiking soldier, on the ground that the soldier was a "leg," and "no leg is worth picking up." High officers of the 101st and the 3rd of the 4th maligned each other, in my presence, by claiming that the other brigade's body count was falsified. "The 3rd of the 4th count the probables in their body count," an officer of the 101st told me. "We don't deal with probables. We only deal with confirmed kills counted by sight. That's the only way." On another occasion, an officer of the 3rd of the 4th made the same charge about the 101st, and added that the 101st's "weapons-kill ratio" was much worse than the 3rd of the 4th's, the implication being that the 101st was far less discriminating than the 3rd of the 4th when it came to deciding whom to kill. Men of both the Army and the Air Force made derogatory remarks about the Marines. One soldier of the 101st told me that the Marines were "no different from the Vietcong" in their handling of prisoners. I asked if he meant that they beat the prisoners. "Hell, *we* work 'em over before we talk to 'em," the soldier said. "The Marines are a lot worse than that. They're just like the V.C."

After dinner that evening, the pilots had a choice of two movies, one at an outdoor theatre on the beach near the Marine dining hall and the other up at the Task Force Oregon officers' club. The officers' club stood on the crest of a five-hundred-foot hill, overlooking a brushy meadow that swept down to the sea. A number of tables with chairs were arranged in a large, three-walled room under a broad, barnlike palm-leaf roof; the front was open to the ocean. In back, there was a long bar with a television set at one end, swivelling barstools, a dart board, and bartenders who wore gaudy Hawaiian shirts. Movies were shown in front. The club commanded a view of the entire twenty-kilometre crescent of beach. Even on the hottest, stillest day, a fresh breeze blew in off the water. At night, out on the ocean, the lamps that all local fishing boats were required to keep burning after dark glowed from miles away. On most evenings, the booming of artillery and bombing sounded steadily, sometimes lighting up the night sky down the coast. During some operations, flares, which are fired by artillery or dropped from planes, and descend slowly on parachutes, seemed to be hanging over the mountains throughout the night. Two hundred yards from the club, the helicopter landing pad for the base hospital sat on a high ridge, from which there was a sharp drop to the sea. Several times each day, a helicopter would fly up the coast at full speed and settle rapidly onto the asphalt, which was in full view of the front of the officers' club and looked from there like a small black stage. Two figures would run up to the helicopter and then run back to the hospital, bearing a man on a stretcher. If the cloth over the man covered him only up to his shoulders, the man was wounded, but if the cloth covered his face the man had died. Inside the club, the hospital landing pad was visible only from a few front tables, and most of the officers did not notice when a helicopter arrived, but when the officers were standing in front of the club at their weekly outdoor barbecue, tending their steaks in the charcoal pits, the arrival of a helicopter at the hospital caused a brief slackening in the din of conversation as the officers looked up from their drinks and steaks to watch the two figures bearing a wounded or dead man into the hospital.

Once every few weeks, on nights that did not precede military operations or important pre-planned strikes, some of the FAC pilots, I was told, would get together to get drunk. One evening, Captain Reese and two other pilots, whom I will call Major Nugent and Captain Leroy, returned to the FAC pilots' quarters from the officers' club talking in booming voices and laughing loudly at everything any of them said. Major Nugent had apparently half-seriously yielded to an Army officer's urging that he enter airborne training school, and Captain Reese was snickering and teasing him about it. "Why would anyone want to jump out of a perfectly good airplane? You must be out of your gourd!" he exclaimed seven or eight times, provoking a more uproarious laugh with each repetition. His idea that you should stay in an airplane until it was shot down reflected his loyalty to the Air Force and his contempt for paratroopers. About midnight, when Captain Leroy was on his way to bed, he tripped over someone's box of gear and fell on the floor. Later that night, an unidentified person threw a glass of water on another pilot as he slept.

from *The Military Half: An Account of the
Destruction in Quang Ngai and Quang Tin*, 1968

A Day in the Life

by Michael J. Arlen

SAIGON

ONE Thursday morning recently, very early—about six o'clock—but with the sun already up and the air already sticky and warm, John Laurence, who is twenty-seven years old and a correspondent with C.B.S. News, pulled himself out of bed at the slick but not notably comfortable Marine-built press center at Danang, put on his green combat fatigues, filled up his two canteens with purified water in the kitchen, and, together with his cameraman, a twenty-five-year-old named Keith Kay, and his sound man, a thirty-one-year-old Vietnamese named Pham Tan Dan, headed off in the direction of Con Thien, a Marine artillery outpost three-quarters of a mile south of the Demilitarized Zone. Con Thien isn't very far from Danang—about a hundred miles—but it is hard to get to nowadays. Laurence and his crew took one of the big C-130 transports that make regular thirty-minute flights to the Marine base at Dong Ha, then boarded a truck in a convoy that leaves Dong Ha each morning on the westerly route along what's still called Route 9, toward the village of Cam Lo. There were about twelve vehicles in the convoy, mostly trucks, and mostly carrying ammunition, food, water, mail, and some Marines who had been on leave or in hospitals and were being returned to duty at the artillery batteries. Laurence rode in an open truck with a dozen Marines, his sound man, Dan, nearby, and Kay, the cameraman, perched on the cab, half-leaning against a machine gun mounted there. The young Marines read the comics from last Sunday's paper and talked easily among themselves. One asked Laurence what he was doing there, and he said he was going out to do a show about Con Thien.

"When's it going to be on?" the Marine asked.

"With any luck, in two or three days," Laurence said.

235

A couple of them joked about that. It can take between seven and ten days for letters to go from a soldier in the field in Vietnam to the States, and one man had wanted to write his family and tell them there was going to be a TV show about his base.

"Anyhow, you can't be sure," said Laurence. "You never know what's going to get on."

Another asked him, "What kind of film are you using?"

"Sixteen-millimetre color," said Laurence.

The Marine thought for a moment. "If you're shooting color, you really ought to go down to Khe Sanh, because of the beautiful greens and browns," he said. "You know, they have six different shades of green down there."

After about a forty-minute drive, the convoy stopped at Cam Lo, which was once a village but is now just another Marine artillery battery. The road from Dong Ha to Cam Lo is reasonably safe these days (except at night), but the road from Cam Lo north to Con Thien hasn't been so successfully pacified as yet. There had been two ambushes within the last ten days—some Marines had been killed in the first one—so the convoy waited for two tanks and two ONTOS (an ONTOS is a track vehicle, a little smaller than a tank, mounting a cluster of six 106-mm. rifles, six 50-calibre spotting rifles, and one 30-calibre machine gun) to come up and join it. During the ride from Dong Ha, Laurence had noticed a seemingly introspective young Marine, sitting toward the front of the truck, who had something written on the back of his flak jacket, and while they were stopped he asked him about it. The Marine—Corporal Edward Broderick—said it was a poem he'd written a few months before. Laurence asked him if he would recite it on camera. The Corporal nodded. Kay clambered down from the cab of the truck, Dan adjusted his sound equipment, and Laurence held the mike.

"I don't know that I can remember it right off," the Corporal said, looking at Laurence's mike.

"Well, try it once on your own," said Laurence.

The Corporal took off his flak jacket, read the poem, then put the flak jacket back on again. "O.K.," he said.

Kay's camera started whirring. The Marine stared straight ahead and recited. "When youth was a soldier," he began, his voice low and flat, "and I fought across the sea,/We were young and cold hearts, of bloody savagery,/Born of indignation, children of our times,/We were orphans of creation, and dying in our prime." Everyone in the truck was very silent.

Kay was shooting back through Laurence and the Corporal to the other trucks in the convoy.

"What made you write that poem?" Laurence asked.

"Well, just the way things are," the Corporal said. He then went on to say some things about how it was better anyway to be in the front lines at Con Thien than back at some base camp like Danang.

Laurence asked him what his overriding feeling about the war was right now.

The Corporal thought for a moment. "Better to be fighting the Communists here than fighting them back in San Diego," he said.

Two tanks appeared, rumbling down the road from Cam Lo, and Laurence called to Kay that he was going to try to do an "open" (meaning an opening for the film piece) before the convoy got under way.

"We don't have much time," Kay said.

"I'll ad-lib it," Laurence said. He moved to the seat in the truck that was nearest the tailgate. Kay once again took up his station near the cab and started up his camera. Laurence, still holding the mike, stared at the floor for a moment. "The convoy for Con Thien goes once a day, and it does not stay long. It is the only source of supply for the Marine outpost on the Demilitarized Zone; it rides the only road that goes there," he began. "The convoy carries food, water, and ammunition, and returns the few men who have been lucky enough to get away for a few days. . . ."

When the convoy started up again, the Marines seemed to be in a changed mood. Some went back to reading comics, but the road was really too bumpy, and for the most part they just sat in silence and stared out at the muddy, reddish-brown dirt on either side of the road, the dry-looking scrub, the rolling, dark-green hills extending into the distance. Shortly, one by one, they started inserting ammunition clips in their M-16s and putting them on safe. Laurence nodded at Kay, and Kay's camera began whirring. Twenty minutes farther on, at a place called Charlie Two, near the entrance to a Marine battery, the convoy passed the burned hulk of a light tank, lying abandoned twenty feet off the road. One of the Marines took hold of Laurence's arm and started telling him about the ambush ten days before (he'd been one of its victims), pointing to where it had happened, describing how the tank had been hit, telling him in an intense, informative way what a serious fight it had been. The men had now stopped every other activity, and were only looking out on either side of the road with peering, impassive faces. The convoy bumped along. The sun grew hotter. For the first time, some of the men began to sweat a little.

Around noon, the trucks reached Con Thien—the end of the road. The road points directly toward the camp, then stops at the base of a slight hill. The convoy stopped, and there was a good deal of discussion among the drivers as to how far the trucks should go up toward the camp, because of the accuracy of the enemy artillery across the D.M.Z., and because of the mud, and because many of the trucks were carrying ammunition. "Hell, let's take 'em right up," the driver of Laurence's truck said, and the trucks roared up the hill.

Everybody quickly clambered out. Beyond the hill is a shallow valley, and in the valley sit the gun emplacements, just the barrels of the guns showing, the rest hidden behind sandbags, and everything in view—sandbags, terrain (there are no trees, no vegetation, just sandbags, guns, empty shell cases, and boxes of ammunition)—light brown, the color of dry dirt. Laurence and his crew walked down the hill, each man wearing a pack, and Kay and Dan carrying their equipment besides. Laurence asked someone which was the command bunker (since most of the men were either naked to the waist or wearing olive-colored T-shirts, it was hard to tell rank), and the man pointed to the largest bunker in the camp, built right into the side of the hill. The executive officer came out to greet them—a Marine major in his mid-thirties, who seemed a bit tense.

"Hi," said Laurence. "I'm Jack Laurence, of C.B.S. News.

We've come up to take pictures of you winning the war up here."

"How long are you planning to stay?" the major asked.

"Oh, just as long as we need to get some action," said Laurence. "A day, a week."

"You really want to spend the night up *here*?" the major said. "We haven't had any press around in about three weeks."

Laurence and his crew threw their packs off outside the bunker and followed the major in. Inside, it was very dark; a few men were sitting silent at tables, with candles for light. Four military-band field radios were squawking. There was a large map standing upright in the center of the bunker, about eight feet high and divided into three panels, like a screen.

"What about something to eat?" Kay whispered to Laurence. "I haven't had anything all morning."

The major walked over. "Come on," he said, "I'll give you a briefing."

Laurence and Kay and Dan stood in front of the big map, and the major pointed out the various places where the battalion's companies were now operating.

A soldier came hurrying in with a message for the major.

"Kilo Company is in contact with snipers," the major said, and showed them where Kilo Company was on the map.

The major finished the briefing at last, and Laurence, Kay, and Dan (whose Vietnamese face had been stared at suspiciously by some of the officers in the bunker) stumbled out into the sun, where the sergeant major came over and handed them each a can of C rations—in this case, something described on the label as "turkey loaf."

A man in a green T-shirt who had a bright-red mustache came over and introduced himself as Captain Jansen, and began to tell Laurence about how to take cover during an artillery barrage. "Above all, don't follow me when you see me running down the side of the hill," Jansen said. "I like to be off by myself when the shells come in. I have this feeling that the round that has your number on it shouldn't kill anyone else—and I certainly don't want to get someone else's round. Actually, the best thing for *you* to do is watch the other guys.

When they start running, hurry after them." Jansen went off to sit on the ground nearby and read *Stars & Stripes*.

Everything seemed relaxed. Laurence took out his pocket compass and fooled around with it. A soldier came up to him and said that Lieutenant Colonel Lee R. Bendel, the battery commander, was still tied up but would be available shortly. Laurence wandered off to take a look around, walking away from the command bunker up toward the top of the hill, and stepping over cast-off shell cases and the ruins of the Colonel's shower, which had been destroyed by an incoming round. At the top, he stood for a moment trying to figure out from his compass where true north was. From a bunker nearby, a voice was saying, "I swear I got the actual word. We're going in four days. Colonel's orders." Other voices chimed in from other bunkers. "Hey, we're getting out. We're getting out of here."

A corporal came up and asked Laurence to come down the hill a bit and see the new infrared radar beam—a large green machine, on the order of a searchlight, that was mounted on a jeep. The corporal explained in a proud manner how the infrared beam worked—you turn it on at night and wear infrared goggles, and then you can see the V.C. when they move across the ground in the dark. Suddenly, in midsentence, the corporal's head turned toward the north. He quickly got down on his knees and seemed to be looking at the ground. He glanced up at Laurence. "Hell, no sense staying out here," he said. "Let's get in a bunker." Laurence and the corporal started walking quickly, then ran. From somewhere, a voice yelled, "Incoming!" There was a large explosion quite far away. Laurence and the corporal tumbled into a bunker where there were about twelve other men. Everyone else seemed very casual.

"I'm Jack Laurence, from C.B.S. News," said Laurence.

"Have a beer," said one of the men.

Some of them were talking about the war, and Laurence took out a small tape recorder and turned it on. "What do you think of the enemy?" he asked.

A big Southern corporal leaned forward. "When we first came up here, we used to call the enemy Victor Charlie," he said. "But now we call him Charles. Mister Charles."

"Lord Charles," somebody else said, and laughed.

The men talked on—with Laurence recording their words —about their frustrating efforts to get at the enemy artillery. "Our shelling don't seem to have much effect, because those enemy guns keep hitting the camp every day," said one. "Often, we get about a hundred rounds a day."

"Why are you crazy enough to come up to Con Thien?" one man asked Laurence.

"You're here," said Laurence. "We might as well tell the people back home how well you're doing."

After about twenty minutes, in which there was no more shelling, the corporal in charge of the infrared radar machine told Laurence it was O.K. to leave. "I'll show you the observation post," he said. They walked toward it—the sun now very hot, everything hot and dry. A voice again yelled, "Incoming!," and Laurence and the corporal ran forward and tumbled into a small, open bunker, with a telescopelike object, a field radio, and two young soldiers all lying on the bottom. This turned out to be the observation post. There was another big explosion, also far away. The two soldiers didn't seem to be frightened, but they both had their heads flat to the ground. A voice came over the field radio. "Do you see where those rounds are coming from?" One of the soldiers raised his head sufficiently to reply to the radio. "No, sir. Don't see a thing," he said, and he grinned at Laurence. "Every time we get incoming, that lieutenant calls on the radio and asks us if we see where it's coming from, and every time we say, 'No, sir, we don't see a thing.' The fact is, those damned guns of theirs are firing from the back slopes in the D.M.Z., and they're too far away and too well camouflaged for us to do much about them."

After ten minutes or so, when the shelling again seemed to have stopped, Laurence got out of the observation post and ran back to the command bunker to look for Kay and Dan. Colonel Bendel was there. Kay was seated on the floor inside the bunker, reloading his camera, and when he had finished plugging it into the battery pack over his shoulder, Laurence and his crew went outside again, quickly following the Colonel, who had muttered something about wanting to get a "better vantage point" from which to see his two companies.

The better vantage point turned out to be on the rim of the same hill Laurence had been standing on earlier, only on the far side, in the direction of the road, away from the camp and out of sight of it. It was a lonely-seeming spot, which had obviously not been much used—at least, not by Americans. Near where they were standing, Laurence spotted five small foxholes dug into the side of the hill. The shelling now seemed to have stopped completely. The Colonel was standing on a small, jutting piece of ground, peering below him through binoculars. "You can see Kilo Company moving down there," the Colonel said. "Look—three fingers to the right of this tree." He pointed. "See them?"

Laurence, who wears glasses, peered below him and, about three-quarters of a mile away, saw a line of Marines walking in the open across a field. Just at that moment, there was a loud, sharp pop, pop, pop-pop-pop, pop, and a few seconds later a string of mortar rounds exploded in a line across the field, in the midst of the Marines. There was a moment of absolute silence.

"Are you sure those are *our* troops?" Laurence asked the Colonel incredulously. "Aren't *we* shelling *them*?"

Some of the Marines in the field could now be seen to run forward, and a few seconds later another barrage of shells exploded, this time making a much deeper sound. Laurence heard Kay's camera whirring, and turned back to him to ask, "How much of that can we get?"

"Just the smoke," Kay said. "The damned lens isn't long enough."

"Well, get a little of the smoke out there," Laurence said. "Perhaps it can be used."

"O.K.," said Kay. "But it's not going to be very clear."

Captain Jansen came up with a field radio on his back and stood beside the Colonel. The Colonel alternately listened to chatter coming out of the radio and peered down through his binoculars at the again silent field. Laurence dropped on one knee to get out of Kay's picture, and extended his mike toward the Colonel.

"Every time we move, we take heavy fire," a man's voice said over the radio.

"O.K., it looks like we've got the grid on the one that's

getting—that you're getting the incoming from," the Colonel replied. "Hold your present positions. I hope you're in holes there as best you can."

Two jets suddenly appeared above the Marines in the field—narrow, pointed F-4Cs, circling at about five thousand feet. Kay aimed his camera toward them. One of the jets went into a dive, came in very low—no more than a couple of hundred feet above the ground—passed over the field, and then climbed again.

"A dud," said Captain Jansen.

The second jet came in and made the same pass, and suddenly the far edge of the field exploded with a black-and-orange flash, and a bright sheet of fire rushed forward very fast.

"Maybe that will show up," said Kay. "But don't count on it."

The radio was now very active, with several excited voices talking back and forth. "We're in very heavy contact here," one man's voice was saying tensely.

The Colonel, speaking calmly, asked the man to tell him which way he was facing and where his platoons were.

"Tell him to make his strafing runs one hundred metres in another direction!" a second voice called.

"We're *still* in very heavy contact!" the first voice called.

The Colonel put down his binoculars and held the radio. "O.K., Bill," he said, speaking in a fatherly tone. "Just try to pull your people together and get them linked up to Mike Company. This is still your show."

There was silence for a moment. Then the voice came back: "I think we may have to have help. We might get overrun."

"All right, Bill," the Colonel said, still in a fatherly voice. "I'm going to try to bring Mike Company up to you. I'm positioning tanks to fire in your support. But I *have* to have your coördinates—your position."

Just then, somebody yelled, "Incoming!," and Laurence, who until that instant had been kneeling on the ground beside the Colonel trying to tape the dialogue, jumped into one of the foxholes, and so did Kay and Dan. Kay's camera was still whirring, although he was holding it to cover his face. A shell exploded somewhere on the other side of the hill. Laurence looked over the edge of the foxhole and saw the Colonel and his staff all flattened out on the ground, the radio chattering but none of the Marines talking—just olive-green backs on the ground.

"We've *got* to get some of this," Laurence said to Kay.

Kay raised his head from the foxhole and pointed his camera at the Colonel and his staff. At that moment, Captain Jansen turned his head and saw Kay, and then immediately the staff jumped to its feet as several shells burst with great thumping noises. The Captain organized the staff into separate foxholes. Laurence moved forward into the foxhole now occupied by the Colonel and Captain Jansen, and motioned to Kay to continue taking pictures. The artillery barrage was coming in steadily, with two or three very loud, ground-shaking explosions at a time. The staff were all crouched low in the foxholes, except for the Colonel, who was standing up, with one foot on the edge of the hole, and leaning forward. Laurence huddled low over his microphone and spoke in a soft voice: "You don't spend long in Con Thien before the action starts. Some time ago, two companies from the battalion defending this outpost ran into enemy contact, and it has become increasingly heavy. Colonel Bendel is watching the action less than a mile away and moving his troops into position."

"O.K., look," the Colonel was saying to an officer who had come up. "Do you see where that smoke is?"

"Yes, sir."

"That far, where the shells landed, is about three hundred metres," the Colonel was saying. "Right where that big tree is out there, three hundred to four hundred metres southeast."

The noise from the battlefield now became very intense as the air strikes continued: a loud roaring of jet engines, sounds of gunfire and machinegun fire, the constant explosions of the shells, and then some strange little buzzing sounds, which, Jansen explained to Laurence, were made by bullets going by very close. The Colonel, who was on the radio again, trying to get Mike Company to move around toward Kilo Company, also appeared a little mystified and irritated by the buzzing. "Don't worry about them," said Jansen. "They're almost spent."

In the middle of the shelling, a major appeared, running across the hill. "I've got to have those coördinates!" he yelled. "I can't fire if I don't have those coördinates!"

The Colonel repeated the request over the radio, and a voice came back apologetically: "I didn't have my map, but I have it now. I'm trying to figure where we are."

The major turned to go back, caught his foot on the wire running between Laurence's mike and Dan's sound box, and sent the mike spinning out of Laurence's hand and across the ground. "Goddam wire!" he said.

The Colonel turned. "Look, some of you people just move on back."

"You're all right where you are," Jansen said to Laurence.

Kay, in the meantime, had run back to the command bunker to get some more equipment, and was now crouched in his foxhole trying to change film inside his changing bag—a black cloth affair with two sleeves in which he had inserted his arms. It took about five minutes, and he finished just as a fresh barrage hit, apparently right inside the camp.

More and more bullets were now buzzing by. The Colonel continued to stand with one foot on the edge of the foxhole. Jansen was seated on the edge. Laurence got up beside Jansen, and, with Kay's camera on the three of them, again spoke softly into the mike. "That whistling sound you hear is incoming artillery fire," he said. "You may actually be able to see it landing."

Kay somehow overheard him and quickly panned his camera from right to left, and just at that point four artillery rounds burst, with great crashes, inside the camp. The Colonel looked around. "Let's make sure we spread out here," he said.

"That one landed about one hundred and fifty yards away," Laurence said into his microphone, and then glanced back and saw that Kay was furiously taking his camera case apart.

"Goddam camera won't work!" Kay yelled to Laurence. In a moment, he had it working again.

Two helicopters came into view and landed beside the camp, their engines roaring, the dust blowing up around them. Soldiers appeared from within the camp carrying men on stretchers—men who had been wounded by the artillery bombardment. Kay's camera was rolling on them; then, once again, he stopped and began to pull his camera apart. This time, it wouldn't start up again. Kay was cursing and muttering as he and Dan crouched in their foxhole, pieces of Arriflex littered around them.

"What is it?" Laurence called.

"It's the battery pack," said Dan. "It's out of power."

Kay and Dan continued to fiddle with the camera. More shells landed nearby. Captain Jansen remained seated on the edge of the foxhole. One shell landed very close by, shattering the ground, and sending off shock waves. Laurence, with nothing to do and suddenly edgy, tumbled back into the hole. "It's O.K.," Jansen said to him. "It's not close enough to hurt you, and the next shell won't be in on top."

Kay called to Laurence that the camera was really dead.

"Are you sure?" Laurence asked.

"I'm sure," said Kay.

"If you want to get out of here, you can go back with the convoy," Jansen said.

Laurence considered for a moment. "O.K.," he said. "I guess we will."

The three C.B.S. men got all their gear together, while the Colonel went on directing Mike Company up to a position on Kilo Company's flank. "Now, if you'll just get everyone linked up . . ." the Colonel was saying into the radio. Jansen formed Laurence, Kay, and Dan into a line, spaced about ten feet apart, and walked them down the side of the hill toward the road. The Colonel looked at them over his shoulder. "That's a real fine squad you got there, Jansen," he said. Jansen, seeming embarrassed, waved at him. Just as they neared the foot of the hill, another incoming round came in, and they all dived into a tiny three-foot-deep pit, sprawling on their backs on top of each other—except for Jansen, who sat on the edge, remarking, "I'll know when it's going to hit us." An incredibly loud explosion burst nearby, making the ground shake, and they all looked up, to see that a fire had started in the midst of a stack of wooden crates containing 105-mm. ammunition.

A sergeant appeared, running. It was the convoy sergeant,

who had just brought the ammunition up. "If that stuff blows, we're dead," he said.

A lieutenant also appeared on the run. "Get back! Get back!" he yelled. "It's going to blow!"

A number of men rushed out of the nearby bunkers and ran away from the fire. No one had told Laurence what to do, and he stood transfixed beside Jansen, who continued to sit still, watching. A Marine with a small hand-held fire extinguisher appeared briefly, made some dancing motions toward the fire, and then sped off.

A captain appeared a little distance away, yelled, "Everybody in the hole!," and disappeared.

The fire continued to blaze.

"For Chrisake!" the convoy sergeant said. "*Somebody's* got to put it out!"

"Incoming!" a voice yelled, and this time Laurence and Jansen both dived into the tiny hole with the others. When they stuck their heads up again, the convoy sergeant was walking back across the ground toward them holding an empty five-gallon water can. "Fire's out," he said. He dropped the can on the ground. "If you're all coming with me," he said, "let's get the hell out of here." He pointed to a jeep about fifty yards away and started to run toward it.

Laurence, Dan, and Kay chased after him, their packs bouncing on their backs. The sergeant clambered into the jeep, which was a small one, and the others began to fall in after him.

A voice in the distance yelled, "Incoming!"

"Everybody in?" the sergeant called, starting to pull away as Laurence dived into the back, his legs sticking out behind the tailgate. A couple of shells landed nearby—great crunches. The sergeant had his foot all the way down on the accelerator and was tearing across the terrain—skidding, turning, with all four wheels sometimes leaving the ground as they hit a bump—muttering incessantly, "Don't worry. We're going to make it." A huge explosion hit just behind, shaking the jeep. "Goddammit, they're trying to get us," he said, and added excitedly, "But they're gonna have to catch us!" He pushed the accelerator to the floor again and, reaching down between the legs of the man beside him—it was Kay—picked up a submachine gun and handed it back to Laurence, saying, "Hey, kid, know how to use this?"

Laurence took the gun, looked at it in bewilderment, and passed it to one of the soldiers, who put it on the floor beside him. Two more loud explosions hit, off to one side of the jeep. The sergeant was driving at top speed, the jeep screeching around the curves of the hill. In a couple of minutes, he reached the rest of the convoy—a line of trucks parked at the edge of the road, with Marines standing beside them.

"Everybody onto the trucks!" the sergeant yelled. "Let's get the hell outa here!"

Laurence, Kay, and Dan climbed onto a truck with six or seven Marines, and in a second all the trucks were moving, with Marines hanging on to the backs and sides and being hauled inside by friends. The convoy hurtled south along the road to Cam Lo.

About halfway to Cam Lo, gunfire started from the right side of the road, its source invisible—sharp cracks and pings, a few at first, and then more and more. The Marines fired back as they sped by. One truck was hit and caught on fire. The rest of the convoy reached Cam Lo in forty minutes, and stopped. The sergeant came around the truck to see Laurence. His eyes were very bright, and his right hand was bleeding. "I've had enough today," he said. "I'm not going any farther." He glanced abstractedly at his hand. "Come on and stay with us tonight," he said. "I'll buy you boys a beer." It was about six o'clock.

Laurence went into one of the tents, took off his pack, sat down on a bed, and started to write in a small notebook. The sergeant brought him a can of beer, which Laurence placed on the floor beside him, and when he had finished writing he called to Dan, who was just outside the tent setting up his sound equipment, that he was now ready to do the "voice-over," meaning a tape of his voice to be used with various filmed sequences of action. Laurence thereupon took a pillow from one of the beds, put it in the center of the bed, put his microphone on the pillow, and sat down on the edge of the bed.

"Level," called Dan from outside the tent. .

"The enemy is one hazard, nature another. . . ." Laurence said.

"O.K.," said Dan.

Laurence took a breath. "Convoy to Con Thien," he said into the microphone. "Narration. Cameraman, Kay. Sound man, Dan." He paused. "The enemy is one hazard, nature another," he began, glancing at the notebook, which was on the bed beside him. "Two days of rain have nearly washed out the soft dirt road. It will be impassable within a month, with the coming of the fall monsoon. The convoy arrives safely, unloads quickly, and turns around, because the camp is continually under artillery attack." He paused again for a moment. "Every few minutes, and sometimes every few seconds, the guns go off, their guns and our guns, whistling and pounding with the incessant, methodical efficiency of a carpenter hammering nails. In the battle outside the camp, at least twenty men are killed on both sides, perhaps a hundred wounded, as each recovers its casualties quickly and prepares for the night of shelling, and the following day of fighting."

The convoy spent Thursday night in Cam Lo, and the next day it went back to Dong Ha, running into a company of Marines along the way—in a field a few hundred feet off to the side of the road—who were being shelled by rockets. Kay's camera was working again (he had had it recharged with a generator in Cam Lo), and, crouching with Laurence and Dan in a hole by the side of the road, he photographed some of the action—tanks racing out of range, soldiers running—for the few minutes that the shelling lasted. The convoy reached Danang an hour or so later.

Laurence called Edward Fouhy, the C.B.S. bureau chief in Saigon, who asked him to ship the film down to him right away, in the hope of getting it home in time for the Saturday-evening news. Then Laurence ran back inside the C.B.S. hut in the Danang press center and quickly scribbled out a "voice-over close," and, with his mike on the bed, as at Cam Lo, and Dan outside the door with his equipment, recited it in a measured voice: "The next day, on the road to Con Thien, another American company is shelled in an open field a hundred yards ahead, again with amazing accuracy, this time with rockets.

One tank is hit, a tread knocked apart, and the rest of the tanks, vulnerable to rockets, pull back out of range. They carry away some of the casualties from the rocket attack—some of the young men the Corporal wrote his poem about." He paused, then added, "John Laurence, C.B.S. News, on the road to Con Thien."

After that, Laurence packed the cans of film and tape in a big yellow net bag and took them to the Danang airbase, where he put them aboard an Air Force flight to Saigon. A C.B.S. man in Saigon rushed them onto the Pan American flight to San Francisco, where they were put aboard a United Airlines flight to New York. The film didn't arrive in time for the Saturday news, so it was shown on Monday night, when it ran for four minutes and prompted a congratulatory telegram to Laurence, Kay, and Dan from Walter Cronkite.

The New Yorker, September 30, 1967

from *The Armies of the Night*

by Norman Mailer

5: *The Witches and the Fugs*

SINCE the parking lot was huge as five football fields, and just about empty, for they were the first arrivals, the terminus of the March was without drama. Nor was the Pentagon even altogether visible from the parking lot. Perhaps for that reason, a recollection returned to Mailer of that instant (alive as an open nerve) when they had seen it first, walking through the field, just after the March had left the road on the Virginia side of the Potomac; there, topping a rise, it appeared, huge in the near distance, not attractive. Somehow, Mailer had been anticipating it would look more impressive than its pictures, he was always expecting corporation land to surprise him with a bit of wit, an unexpected turn of architectual grace—it never did. The Pentagon rose like an anomaly of the sea from the soft Virginia fields (they were crossing a park), its pale yellow walls reminiscent of some plastic plug coming out of the hole made in flesh by an unmentionable operation. There, it sat, geometrical aura complete, isolated from anything in nature surrounding it. Eras ago had corporation land begun by putting billboards on the old post roads?—now they worked to clean them up—just as the populace had finally succeeded in depositing comfortable amounts of libido on highway signs, gasoline exhaust, and oil-stained Jersey macadam—now corporation land, here named Government, took over state preserves, straightened crooked narrow roads, put up government buildings, removed unwelcome signs till the young Pop eye of Art wept for unwelcome signs—where are our old friends?—and corporation land would succeed, if it hadn't yet, in making nature look like an outdoor hospital, and the streets of U.S. cities, grace of Urban Renewal, would be difficult to distinguish when drunk from pyramids of packaged foods in the aisles of a supermarket.

For years he had been writing about the nature of totalitarianism, its need to render populations apathetic, its instrument—the destruction of mood. Mood was forever being sliced, cut, stamped, ground, excised, or obliterated; mood was a scent which rose from the acts and calms of nature, and totalitarianism was a deodorant to nature. Yes, and by the logic of this metaphor, the Pentagon looked like the five-sided tip on the spout of a spray can to be used under the arm, yes, the Pentagon was spraying the deodorant of its presence all over the fields of Virginia.

The North Parking Lot was physically separated from the Pentagon by a wide four-lane highway. Corporate wisdom had been at work—they might have been rattling about in the vast and empty parking lot of a modern stadium when no game is being played. Being among the first hundred to arrive, they found themselves in a state of confusion. No enemy was visible, nor much organization. In the reaches of the parking lot where they had entered was some sort of crane, with what appeared to be a speaker's platform on the end of its arm, and that was apparently being gotten ready for more speeches. Lowell, Macdonald, and Mailer discussed whether to remain there. They were hardly in the mood for further addresses, but on the other hand, combat was getting nearer—one could tell by the slow contractions of the gut. It was not that they would lose their courage, so much as that it would begin to seep away; so the idea of listening to speeches was not intolerable. There would be at least company.

But a pleasant young woman accompanied by her child had come up to greet Lowell, and she now mentioned that the hippies were going to have a play at the other end of the parking lot and music seemed by far the better preparation for all battle, and music was indeed coming from that direction. So they set out, a modest group in the paved empty desert of the North Parking Area, and strolled toward the sounds of the band which were somehow medieval in sound, leaving behind the panorama of marchers slowly flowing in. On the way, they agreed again that they would be arrested early. That seemed the best way to satisfy present demands and still get back to New York in time for their dinners, parties, weekend parts. The desire to get back early is not dishonorable in Lowell and Macdonald; they had stayed on today, and indeed probably had come this far because Mailer had helped to urge them, but Mailer! with his apocalyptic visions at Lincoln Memorial and again on the March, his readiness to throw himself, breast against breast, in any charge on the foe, why now in such a rush? Did he not respect his visions?

Well the party that night looked to be the best coming up in some time; he simply hated to miss it. Besides, he had no position here; it was not his March on the Pentagon in conception or execution; he was hardly required to remain for days or even hours on the scene. His function was to be arrested—his name was expendable for the cause. He did not like the idea of milling about for hours while the fine line of earlier perception (and Vision!) got mucked in the general confusion. Besides, he was a novelist, and there is no procurer, gambler, adventurer or romantic lover more greedy for experience in great gouts—a part of the novelist wished to take the cumulative rising memories of the last three days and bring them whole, intact, in sum, as they stood now, to cast, nay—shades of Henry James—to *fling* on the gaming tables of life resumed in New York, and there amass a doubling and tripling again. He was in fact afraid that within the yawning mute concrete of the parking lot this day which had begun with such exultation would dissipate into leaderless armies wandering about, acting like clowns and fools before the face of the authority; or worse, raw massacres, something more than bones broken: actual disasters—that was also in the air. He did not know if he was secretly afraid too much would happen or too little, but one thing he knew he hated—that would be to wait, and wait again, and nerve up to the point of being arrested, and get diverted and wait again while the light of the vision went out of the day and out of his head until hungry and cold they would all shamble off shamefacedly to New York on a late plane, too late for everything all around. One could not do that to this day. Great days demanded as much respect as great nights—Victorian, no Edwardian, were Mailer's more courtly sentiments.

And in his defense, one decent motive. He had the conviction that his early arrest might excite others to further effort:

the early battles of a war wheel on the hinge of their first legends—perhaps his imagination, in lockstep to many a montage in many an old movie, saw the word going out from mouth to ear to mouth to ear, linking the troops—in fact cold assessment would say that was not an inaccurate expectation. Details later.

Yes, Mailer had an egotism of curious disproportions. With the possible exception of John F. Kennedy, there had not been a President of the United States nor even a candidate since the Second World War whom Mailer secretly considered more suitable than himself, and yet on the first day of a war which he thought might go on for twenty years, his real desire was to be back in New York for a party. Such men are either monumental fools or excruciatingly practical since it may be wise to go to every party you can if the war is to continue for two decades. Of course, the likelihood is that the government— old corporation land—knew very well how wise it was to forge an agreement in negotiation to stage (dump) the marchers on arrival in the North Area's parking—coming off the March and into the face of a line of troops at the Pentagon, Mailer along with a good many others would not have been diverted with thoughts of New York whereas the parking area was so large and so empty that any army would have felt small in its expanse.

Well, let us move on to hear the music. It was being played by the Fugs, or rather—to be scrupulously phenomenological—Mailer heard the music first, then noticed the musicians and their costumes, then recognized two of them as Ed Sanders and Tuli Kupferberg and knew it was the Fugs. Great joy! They were much better than the last time he had heard them in a grind-it-out theater on Macdougal Street. Now they were dressed in orange and yellow and rose colored capes and looked at once like Hindu gurus, French musketeers, and Southern cavalry captains, and the girls watching them, indeed sharing the platform with them were wearing love beads and leather bells—sandals, blossoms, and little steel-rimmed spectacles abounded, and the music, no rather the play, had begun, almost Shakespearean in its sinister anouncement of great pleasures to come. Now the Participant recognized that this was the beginning of the exorcism of the Pentagon, yes the papers had made much of the permit requested by a hippie leader named Abbie Hoffman to encircle the Pentagon with twelve hundred men in order to form a ring of exorcism sufficiently powerful to raise the Pentagon three hundred feet. In the air the Pentagon would then, went the presumption, turn orange and vibrate until all evil emissions had fled this levitation. At that point the war in Vietnam would end.

The General Services Administrator who ruled on the permit consented to let an attempt be made to raise the building ten feet, but he could not go so far as to allow the encirclement. Of course, exorcism without encirclement was like culinary art without a fire—no one could properly expect a meal. Nonetheless the exorcism would proceed, and the Fugs were to serve as a theatrical medium and would play their music on the rear bed of the truck they had driven in here at the end of the parking lot nearest to the Pentagon some hundreds of yards from the speaker's stand where the rally was to take place.

Now, while an Indian triangle was repeatedly struck, and a cymbal was clanged, a mimeographed paper was passed around to the Marchers watching. It had a legend which went something like this:

October 21, 1967, Washington, D.C., U.S.A., Planet Earth

We Freemen, of all colors of the spectrum, in the name of God, Ra, Jehovah, Anubis, Osiris, Tlaloc, Quetzalcoatl, Thoth, Ptah, Allah, Krishna, Chango, Chimeke, Chukwu, Olisa-Bulu-Uwa, Imales, Orisasu, Odudua, Kali, Shiva-Shakra, Great Spirit, Dionysus, Yahweh, Thor, Bacchus, Isis, Jesus Christ, Maitreya, Buddha, Rama do exorcise and cast out the EVIL which has walled and captured the pentacle of power and perverted its use to the need of the total machine and its child the hydrogen bomb and has suffered the people of the planet earth, the American people and creatures of the mountains, woods, streams, and oceans grievous mental and physical torture and the constant torment of the imminent threat of utter destruction.

We are demanding that the pentacle of power once again be used to serve the interests of GOD manifest in the world as man. We are embarking on a motion which is millennial in scope. Let this day, October 21, 1967, mark the beginning of suprapolitics.

By the act of reading this paper you are engaged in the Holy Ritual of Exorcism. To further participate focus your thought on the casting out of evil through the grace of GOD which is all (ours). A billion stars in a billion galaxies of space and time is the form of your power, and limitless is your name.

Now while the Indian triangle and the cymbal sounded, while a trumpet offered a mournful subterranean wail, full of sobs, and mahogany shadows of sorrow, and all sour groans from hell's dungeon, while finger bells tinkled and drums beat, so did a solemn voice speak something approximate to this: "In the name of the amulets of touching, seeing, groping, hearing and loving, we call upon the powers of the cosmos to protect our ceremonies in the name of Zeus, in the name of Anubis, god of the dead, in the name of all those killed because they do not comprehend, in the name of the lives of the soldiers in Vietnam who were killed because of a bad karma, in the name of sea-born Aphrodite, in the name of Magna Mater, in the name of Dionysus, Zagreus, Jesus, Yahweh, the unnamable, the quintessent finality of the Zoroastrian fire, in the name of Hermes, in the name of the Beak of Sok, in the name of scarab, in the name, in the name, in the name of the Tyrone Power Pound Cake Society in the Sky, in the name of Rah, Osiris, Horus, Nepta, Isis, in the name of the flowing living universe, in the name of the mouth of the river, we call upon the spirit . . . to raise the Pentagon from its destiny and preserve it."

Now spoke another voice. "In the name, and all the names, it is you."

Now the voice intoned a new chant, leaving the echo of the harsh invocation of all giants and thunders in the beat of cymbals, triangles, drums, leather bells, the sour anguish of a trumpet reaching for evil scurried through the tents of a medieval carnival.

Then all the musicians suddenly cried out: "Out, demons, out—back to darkness, ye servants of Satan—out, demons, out! Out, demons, out!"

Voices from the back cried: "Out! . . . Out! . . . Out! . . . Out!" mournful as the wind of a cave. Now the music went up louder and louder, and voices chanting, "Out, demons, out! Out, demons, out! Out, demons, out!"

He detested community sing—an old violation of his childhood had been the bouncing ball on the movie screen; he had
wanted to watch a movie, not sing—but the invocation delivered some message to his throat. "Out, demons, out," he
whispered, "out, demons, out." And his foot—simple American foot—was, of course, tapping. "Out, demons, out." Were
any of the experts in the Pentagon now shuddering, or glory
of partial unringed exorcism—even vibrating? Vibrating experts? "Out, demons, out! Out, demons, out!" He could hear
Ed Sanders' voice, Ed of the red-gold head and red-gold
beard, editor and publisher of a poetry magazine called *Fuck
You*, renaissance conductor, composer, instrumentalist and
vocalist of the Fugs, old protégé of Allen Ginsberg, what
mighty protégés was Allen amassing. Sanders spoke: "For the
first time in the history of the Pentagon there will be a grope-
in within a hundred feet of this place, within two hundred
feet. Seminal culmination in the spirit of peace and brotherhood, a real grope for peace. All of you who want to protect
this rite of love may form a circle of protection around the
lovers."

"Circle of protection," intoned another voice.

"These are the magic eyes of victory," Sanders went on.
"Victory, victory for peace. Money made the Pentagon—melt
it. Money made the Pentagon, melt it for love."

Now came other voices, "Burn the money, burn the money,
burn it, burn it."

Sanders: "In the name of the generative power of Priapus,
in the name of the totality, we call upon the demons of the
Pentagon to rid themselves of the cancerous tumors of the
war generals, all the secretaries and soldiers who don't know
what they're doing, all the intrigue bureaucracy and hatred,
all the spewing, coupled with prostate cancer in the deathbed.
Every Pentagon general lying alone at night with a tortured
psyche and an image of death in his brain, every general, every
general lying alone, every general lying alone."

Wild cries followed, chants: "Out, demons, out! Out, demons, out! Out! out! out! Out, demons, out."

Sanders: "In the name of the most sacred of sacred names
Xabrax Phresxner."

He was accompanied now by chants of, "hari, hari, hari,

hari, rama, rama, rama, rama, Krishna, hari Krishna, hari, hari, rama, Krishna."

"Out, demons, out."

They all chanted: "End the fire and war, and war, end the plague of death. End the fire and war, and war, end the plague of death." In the background was the sound of a long sustained Ommmm.

On which acidic journeys had the hippies met the witches and the devils and the cutting edge of all primitive awe, the savage's sense of explosion—the fuse of blasphemy, the cap of taboo now struck, the answering roar of the Gods—for what was explosion but connections made at the rate of 10 to the 10th exponent of the average rate of a dialogue and its habitual answer—had all the TNT and nuclear transcendencies of TNT exploded some devil's cauldron from the past?—was the past being consumed by the present? by nuclear blasts, and blasts into the collective living brain by way of all exploding acids, opiums, whiskies, speeds, and dopes?—the past was palpable to him, a tissue living in the tangible mansions of death, and death was disappearing, death was wasting of some incurable ill. When death disappeared, there would be no life.

Morbid thoughts for the edge of battle, thoughts out alone without wings of whiskey to bring them back, but Mailer had made his lonely odyssey into the land of the witches, it had taken him through three divorces and four wives to decide that some female phenomena could be explained by no hypothesis less thoroughgoing than the absolute existence of witches. A lonely journey, taken without help from his old drugs, no, rather a distillate of his most difficult experience, and he had arrived at it in great secrecy, for quondam Marxist, nonactive editor of a Socialist magazine, where and how could he explain or justify a striking force of witches—difficult enough to force a Socialist eye to focus on what was existential. Now, here, after several years of the blandest reports from the religious explorers of LSD, vague Tibetan lama goody-goodness auras of religiosity being the only publicly announced or even rumored fruit from all trips back from the buried Atlantis of LSD, now suddenly an entire generation of acid-heads seemed to have said goodbye to easy visions of heaven, no, now the witches were here, and rites of exorcism, and black terrors of the night—hippies being murdered. Yes, the hippies had gone from Tibet to Christ to the Middle Ages, now they were Revolutionary Alchemists. Well, thought Mailer, that was all right, he was a Left Conservative himself. "Out, demons, out! Out, demons, out!"

"You know I like this," he said to Lowell.

Lowell shook his head. He looked not untroubled. "It was all right for a while," he said, "but it's so damn repetitious."

And Macdonald had a harsh glee in his pale eye as if he were half furious but half diverted by the meaninglessness of the repetitions. Macdonald hated meaninglessness even more than the war in Vietnam; on the other hand, he lived for a new critical stimulation: here it might be.

But to Lowell it was probably not meaningless. No, probably Lowell reacted against everything which was hypnotic in that music. Even if much of his poetry could be seen as formal incantations, halfway houses on the road to hypnosis and the oceans of contemplation beyond,

> O to break loose, like the chinook
> salmon jumping and falling back,
> nosing up the impossible
> stone and bone-crushing waterfall—

yes, even if Lowell's remarkable sense of rhythm drew one deep into the poems, nonetheless hypnotic they resolutely were not, for the language was particular, with a wicked sense of names, details, and places.

> . . . Remember playing
> Marian Anderson, Mozart's *Shepherd King,*
> *il re pastore?* Hammerheaded shark,
> the rainbow salmon of the world—your hand
> a rose . . . And at the Mittersill, you topped
> the ski-run . . .

Lowell's poetry gave one the sense of living in a well, the echoes were deep, and sound was finally lost in moss on stone; down there the light had the light of velvet, and the ripples were imperceptible. But one lay on one's back in this well, looking up at the sky, and stars were determinedly there at night, fixed points of reference; nothing in the poems ever permitted you to turn on your face and try to look down into the depths of the well, it was enough you were in the well—now, look up! The world dazzled with its detail.

Lowell, drawn to hypnosis, would resist it, resist particularly these abstract clackety sounds like wooden gears in a noise-maker, "Hari, hari, hari, hari, rama, rama, Krishna, hari, rama, Krishna," and the whoop of wild Indians in "out, demons, out!" Nothing was more dangerous to the poet than hyp-nosis, for the *style* of one's entrance to that plain of sleep where all ideas coalesced into one, was critical—enter by any indiscriminate route, "Om, Om, Om," and who knows what finely articulated bones of future prosody might be melted in those undifferentiated pots—no, Lowell's good poetry was a reconnaissance into the deep, and for that, pirate's patrols were the best—one went down with the idea one would come back with more, but one did not immerse oneself with open guru Ginsberg arms crying, "Baa, baa, slay this sheep or en-rich it, Great Deep," no, one tiptoed in and made a raid and ideally got out good. Besides, the Fugs and Hindu bells and exorcisms via LSD were all indeed Allen Ginsberg's patch; poets respected each others' squatter's rights like Grenadiers before the unrolled carpet of the King.

But of course Lowell's final distaste was for the attraction itself of these sounds (which were incidentally lifting Mailer into the happiest sense of comradeship). Without a drink in him, he was nonetheless cheering up again at the thought of combat, and deciding it would be delightful to whack a bar-ricade in the company of Ed Sanders with the red-gold beard who had brought grope-freak talk to the Village and always seemed to Mailer a little over-liberated, but now suitable, yes, the Novelist was working up all steam in the "Out, demons, out."

But now these meanderings were interrupted by a sight to the rear of them and a battle cry, except there was not really a cry at all, just the unheard sense of a cry in the silent rush, the intent silence of a group of near a few hundred men, some wearing motorcycle helmets or fencing jackets or football shoulder pads, who were walking very rapidly, in fact almost at an odd run, in a long wedge perhaps two hundred feet long, forty or fifty wide at the base, and at the front, at the point, in the vanguard two or three carried standards, two or three blue and gold flags of the N.L.F., yes the American branch of the Vietcong was rushing across the parking lot for a first assault on the unseen Pentagon at a point not fifty yards from where the Fugs were playing.

On came the rush, the men carrying the standard running at an odd angle, as if the weight of the flag and pole brought their bodies and arms out too far ahead of their legs, so that they gave the impression, like Groucho Marx, of having torsos too large and too humped over for their limbs, (or perhaps this image came from the protection and stuffing they wore) and behind them were men carrying other standards and posters, a sea of slogans, (which could later be used for weapons—sticks and shards of broken masonite) nearly all the men at that odd incline forward from the vertical as if keening at the wind, and Mailer knew where he had seen this before, this posture of men running in a charge, yes it had been in the photographs by Mathew Brady of Union soldiers on the attack across a field, and on they came now, rolled up in some collective wave of purpose, their individual bodies seeming so much larger than their limbs, because their bodies were part of a mass, and one became aware of their feet as something more fragile and separated from them. The attack came on, The Wedge ran forward, this was a bona fide attack, a prepared attack, yes, and it jammed forward into some narrow exit out of the parking lot, some neck of road and fence and embankment and small pines and the body of troops in this attack, flags in the lead, charged by, went out of sight, and the rear of The Wedge galloping behind, rushed into a jam of bodies on the embankment, heaved to, pushed them forward, heaved, succeeded, pushed again, and ground finally to a straining equilibrium, then a halt.

For a few minutes, nothing happened. It was impossible to see what was going on at the head of the column, and the Fugs continued to play, "Out, demons, out!" From all over the parking lot, people were now streaming toward them to see what the attack had developed, many more people had arrived while they were listening to the music, and a man who knew Lowell or Macdonald came up to Mailer and said with a smile, "They're looking for you to speak at the other end."

But the other end was hundreds of yards away, far away from this unresolved action at their elbow. "Yes," said the man with a grin, "they said, 'will the real Norman Mailer stand up?' " It was a reference to two photographs he had used on the jacket of *Why Are We In Vietnam?*

"I'll get over in a while," said Mailer. It was mildly fatiguing to one specialized portion of the brain to keep preparing these variations on an extempore speech he still had not made. In fact, he had about decided he really did not wish to speak. It seemed a suggestion absurd in the face of the action now building, exactly the sort of thing to expect of a literary man. But his vanity was tempted. In a day of so many speeches, they ought to hear one piece of unorthodoxy.

Still, he did not want to leave. That sense of thin air and exaltation burning in the lungs, that intimation of living at high altitude had come back. "Let's try to see what's going on with that attack," he suggested.

They now left the Fugs and walked to the rear of the column jammed at that unseen exit. The men above were obviously packed too tightly for any late arrival to work himself up high enough to comprehend what was happening. It seemed foolish somehow to stand at the rear and ask questions, and they walked a few feet away and debated whether to go to the far end of the parking lot and hear speeches. The day was hovering again on anticlimax.

Abruptly—no warning—the men at the base of the stairs, the very troops who had carried the N.L.F. flags, were running toward the rear in a panic. Mailer had then that superimposition of vision which makes descriptions of combat so contradictory when one compares eyewitness reports—he did not literally see any uniformed soldiers or marshals chasing this civilian army down the embankment, there was nothing but demonstrators flying down toward them now, panic on their faces, but Mailer's imagination so clearly conceived MPs chasing them with bayonets that for an instant he did literally see fixed bayonets and knew in some other part of himself he didn't, like two transparent images almost superimposed. Then he saw nothing but the look of terror on the faces coming toward him and he turned to run in order not to be run down by them, conceiving for one instant MPs squirting Mace in everybody's eyes. Then panic was on him too. He didn't want Mace. He sprinted a few steps, looked over his shoulder, stepped in a drainage trough where the parking lot concrete was hollowed, almost fell with a nasty wrench of his back and abruptly stopped running, sheepishly, recognizing that some large fund of fear he had not even felt for a minute these three days had nonetheless lived in him like an abscess quick to burst now at the first mean threat. He was furious, furious at himself for fleeing and this shame was not balmed by the quick sight he had over one shoulder of Dwight Macdonald standing calm and still, while tens of people scrambled around him in panic. Macdonald had the quiet look on his face of a man who had lived his life, and had learned what he learned, and was not going to run from anyone.

They reassembled. It was confusing. Nobody knew why the men on the stairs had suddenly begun to flee. An attack had been mounted, had been stopped, and a retreat had gone off in their faces, partly swept them up in the terror and now had dissipated itself. His worst perspectives were being fulfilled. The one sequence he did not wish to follow on this late afternoon was in full prospect now—they would wander unattached to any troop or effort, always on the fringe, always ignorant of the next move, always confused. Then it would be dark. He had a picture again of three notables, silly to themselves, walking about with a candle, looking to be copped.

"Listen," Mailer said, "let's get arrested now." Stating the desire created it, and put a ligature across the rent in his nerve.

"Look, Norman," said Lowell, "if we're going to, shall we get away from here? I don't see any good that's accomplished if we're all picked up right next to a Vietcong flag."

This was not to be contested. Mailer had never understood how demonstrating with an N.L.F. flag was going to spark a mass movement to end the war. He could not argue with Lowell. The remark was sensible, and yet he felt uneasy, as if one should never be too sensible in war. Still—it was difficult enough for people to take him seriously without standing next to *that* flag!

So they moved on, looking for a line to cross, or a border, or a fence at the extremity of the parking lot, and came upon one in no time at all. To their left, perhaps fifty yards from where the attack had jammed, was a grassy field with United States MPs stationed in it. To their front was a low rope, not a foot off the ground. Protestors from the parking lot were standing behind this rope, two or three deep. Lowell, Mailer, and Macdonald worked into position until they had nothing in front of them but the rope, and the MPs.

6: A Confrontation by the River

It was not much of a situation to study. The MPs stood in two widely spaced ranks. The first rank was ten yards behind the rope, and each MP in that row was close to twenty feet from the next man. The second rank, similarly spaced, was ten yards behind the first rank and perhaps thirty yards behind them a cluster appeared, every fifty yards or so, of two or three U.S. Marshals in white helmets and dark blue suits. They were out there waiting. Two moods confronted one another, two separate senses of a private silence.

It was not unlike being a boy about to jump from one garage roof to an adjoining garage roof. The one thing not to do was wait. Mailer looked at Macdonald and Lowell. "Let's go," he said. Not looking again at them, not pausing to gather or dissipate resolve, he made a point of stepping neatly and decisively over the low rope. Then he headed across the grass to the nearest MP he saw.

It was as if the air had changed, or light had altered; he felt immediately much more alive—yes, bathed in air—and yet disembodied from himself, as if indeed he were watching himself in a film where this action was taking place. He could feel the eyes of the people behind the rope watching him, could feel the intensity of their existence as spectators. And as he walked forward, he and the MP looked at one another with the naked stricken lucidity which comes when absolute strangers are for the moment absolutely locked together.

The MP lifted his club to his chest as if to bar all passage. To Mailer's great surprise—he had secretly expected the enemy to be calm and strong, why should they not? they had every power, all the guns—to his great surprise, the MP was trembling. He was a young Negro, part white, who looked to have come from some small town where perhaps there were not many other Negroes; he had at any rate no Harlem smoke, no devil swish, no black, no black power for him, just a simple boy in an Army suit with a look of horror in his eye, "Why, why did it have to happen to me?" was the message of the petrified marbles in his face.

"Go back," he said hoarsely to Mailer.

"If you don't arrest me, I'm going to the Pentagon."

"No. Go back."

The thought of a return—"since they won't arrest me, what can I do?"—over these same ten yards was not at all suitable.

As the MP spoke, the raised club quivered. He did not know if it quivered from the desire of the MP to strike him, or secret military wonder was he now possessed of a moral force which implanted terror in the arms of young soldiers? Some unfamiliar current, now gyroscopic, now a sluggish whirlpool, was evolving from that quiver of the club, and the MP seemed to turn slowly away from his position confronting the rope, and the novelist turned with him, each still facing the other until the axis of their shoulders was now perpendicular to the rope, and still they kept turning in this psychic field, not touching, the club quivering, and then Mailer was behind the MP, he was free of him, and he wheeled around and kept going in a half run to the next line of MPs and then on the push of a sudden instinct, sprinted suddenly around the nearest MP in the second line, much as if he were a back cutting around the nearest man in the secondary to break free—that was actually his precise thought—and had a passing perception of how simple it was to get past these MPs. They looked petrified. Stricken faces as he went by. They did not know what to do. It was his dark pinstripe suit, his vest, the maroon and blue regimental tie, the part in his hair, the barrel chest, the early paunch—he must have looked like a banker himself, a banker gone ape! And then he saw the Pentagon to his right across the field, not a hundred yards away, and a little to his left, the marshals, and he ran on a jog toward them, and came up, and they glared at him and shouted, "Go back."

He had a quick impression of hard-faced men with gray eyes burning some transparent fuel for flame, and said, "I won't go back. If you don't arrest me, I'm going on to the Pentagon," and knew he meant it, some absolute certainty had come to him, and then two of them leaped on him at once in the cold clammy murderous fury of all cops at the existential moment of making their bust—all cops who secretly expect to be struck at that instant for their sins—and a surprising force came to his voice, and he roared, to his own distant pleasure in new achievement and new authority—"Take your hands off me, can't you see? I'm not resisting arrest," and one then let go of him, and the other stopped trying to pry his arm into a lock, and contented himself with a hard hand under his armpit, and they set off walking across the field at a rabid intent quick rate, walking parallel to the wall of the Pentagon, fully visible on his right at last, and he was arrested, he had succeeded in that, and without a club on his head, the mountain air in his lungs as thin and fierce as smoke, yes, the livid air of tension on this livid side promised a few events of more interest than the routine wait to be free, yes he was more than a visitor, he was in the land of the enemy now, he would get to see their face.

from *The Armies of the Night*, 1968

Hill 875

by Peter Arnett

HILL 875, Vietnam AP—Hour after hour of battle gave the living and the dead the same gray pallor on Hill 875. At times the only way to tell them apart was to watch when the enemy mortars crashed in on the exhausted American paratroopers.

The living rushed unashamedly to the tiny bunkers dug into the red clay.

The wounded squirmed toward the shelter of trees blasted to the ground.

The dead—propped up in bunkers or face down in the dust—didn't move.

Since Sunday the most brutal fighting of the Vietnam war has ebbed and flowed across this remote hill in the western sector of the Dak To battleground. The 2nd Battalion of the 173rd Airborne Brigade went up 875 first. It nearly died.

Of the 16 officers who led the men across the ridgeline Sunday, eight were killed and the other eight wounded. Eleven of the 13 medics died.

The battalion took its first casualties at midday Sunday as it crested Hill 875, one of the hundreds of knolls that dot the ridges in the Dak To fighting region near the Cambodian-Laotian border.

All weekend as the paratroopers moved along the jungle hills enemy base camps were uncovered. The biggest was on 875 and D Company lost several men in the first encounter with the bunkers.

A Company moved back down the hill to cut a landing zone and was chopped to pieces by a North Vietnamese flanking attack.

The remnants fled back to the crest of the hill while a paratrooper propped his gun on the trail and kept firing at the advancing enemy, ignoring orders to retreat with the others.

"You can keep gunning them down, but sooner or later

when there is enough of them they'll get to you," said Pfc. James Kelly of Fort Myers, Fla., who saw the machine gunner go down after killing about 17 North Vietnamese.

D Company, hearing the roar of battle below it, returned to the crest of the hill and established a 50-yard perimeter "because we figure we were surrounded by a regiment," one officer said.

As the battalion was regrouping late in the afternoon for another crack at the bunker system, one of the American planes striking at the nearby enemy dropped a 500-pound bomb too soon. About 30 of the paratroopers were killed.

"A foul play of war," said one survivor bitterly.

From then until a reinforcing battalion arrived the following night, the paratroopers on the hill dug in desperately. Only one medic was able to work on the many wounded, and the enemy kept driving off the rescue helicopters.

The relief battalion made it into the tiny perimeter on 875 Monday night. In the moonlight bodies of the dead lay spread-eagled across the ground. The wounded wimpered.

The survivors, hungry and thirsty, rushed up eagerly to get food and water, only to learn that the relief battalion had brought enough supplies for one day only and had already consumed them.

Monday night was sleepless but uneventful. On Tuesday the North Vietnamese struck with renewed fury.

From positions just 100 yards away, they pounded the American perimeter with 82mm mortars. The first rounds slapped in at daybreak, killing three paratroopers in a foxhole and wounding 17 others on the line.

For the rest of the day, the Communists methodically worked over the hill, pumping rounds in five or six at a time, giving new wounds to those who lay bleeding in the open and tearing through bunkers. The plop of the rounds as they left the enemy tubes gave the paratroopers a second or two to dash for cover.

The foxholes got deeper as the day wore on. Foxhole after foxhole took hits. A dog handler and his German shepherd died together. Men joking with you and offering cigarettes writhed on the ground wounded and pleading for water minutes later. There was no water for anyone.

Crouched in one bunker, Pfc. Angel Flores, 20, of New York City said: "If we were dead like those out there we wouldn't have to worry about this stuff coming in."

He fingered a plastic rosary around his neck and kissed it reverently as the rounds blasted on the ground outside.

"Does that do you any good?" a buddy asked him.

"Well, I'm still alive," Flores replied.

"Don't you know that the chaplain who gave you that was killed on Sunday?" said his buddy.

The day's pounding steadily reduced the platoon commanded by 1st Lt. Bryan Macdonough, 25, of Fort Lee, Va. He had started out Sunday with 27 men. He had nine left by noon Tuesday.

"If the Viets keep this up, there'll be none left by evening," he said.

The enemy positions seemed impervious to constant American air strikes. Napalm fireballs exploded on the bunkers 30 yards away. The earth shook with heavy bombs.

"We've tried 750 pounders, napalm and everything else, but air can't do it. It's going to take manpower to get those positions," Macdonough said.

By late afternoon a new landing zone was cut below the hill. The enemy mortars searched for it but the helicopters came in anyway. A line of wounded trudged down the hill and by evening 140 of them had been evacuated.

The arrival of the helicopters with food, water and ammunition seemed to put new life into the paratroopers. They talked eagerly of a final assault on the enemy bunkers.

As darkness fell flame throwers were brought up. The first stubborn bunker yielded, and the paratroopers were at last started on their way to gain the ridgeline which they had set out to take three days earlier.

AP wire copy, November 22, 1967

The Truest Sport:
Jousting with Sam and Charlie

by Tom Wolfe

DOWN a perfectly green tunnel, as cool and quiet as you can possibly imagine—no, it's not a tunnel, it's more like a hall of mirrors—but they're not mirrors, those aren't reflections, they're openings, one after another, on and on—just a minute! it's very familiar!—out of this cool green memory comes a steward, a tiny man, in uniform, a white jacket, perfectly starched and folded and creased like an envelope over his crisp little bones. Who doesn't know him! Here comes Bye Borty-bibe—

"Bye borty-bibe!"

He's saying it!

Dowd wakes up and it's 5:45 on the button, as always, and he looks across the stateroom at the steward. The steward is a little Filipino in a white jacket who hesitates, so as to make sure Dowd actually wakes up at bye borty-bibe, as he always pronounces it, and then he disappears down the passageway.

There is something eccentric in the way the day begins. It's terribly genteel!—having a little servant in a white jacket come by and respectfully summon you into consciousness so you can go hang your hide out for human skeet and sweat horribly. More servants will come in after Dowd leaves and make up his bed and clean up the stateroom and dust off the TV and the safe and clean off the desk and take out the laundry. *Only your laundryman knows for sure!* That was the usual joke, but there were some men who came aboard for the first time, and after a couple of hops north they would actually wonder whether it could get so bad—whether a man could get so frightened that he would literally lose control—*only your laundryman knows for sure!*—and whether later, in the bowels of

270

the ship, in the laundry room, there might actually be some little laundry humper, some sweatback, some bye-bye steward of the soul, who would, in fact, *know*.

In the first moments, when you wake up, it's as if you're furiously scanning, painting all the stray trash on the screen, although usually that begins to fade as soon as you're on your feet. In a moment Dowd would be out in the good green passageway. The passageway is a very cool and immaculate green, not luxurious, you understand—in fact, every twenty feet there is a hatchway with a knee-knocker you have to step over, and as you look on and on through these hatchways, one after the other, it's like a hall of mirrors—but it is green and generally pleasing to the nervous system. Actually . . . that is not all there is to it. It is also good because, if the truth be known, being on this good green passageway means that you are traveling first-class, sleeping in a stateroom, with only one roommate, and you have the aforesaid servants standing by. It is not even a subject that one thinks about in so many words. And yet the ship is constructed in such an obvious fashion, in layers, that one can't help but know that down below . . . they are living in quite another way, in compartments, with thirty to forty souls to a compartment, and they wake up to a loudspeaker and make up their own bunks and run along to a loudspeaker through gray-and-beige tunnels and eat in a gray-and-beige galley off trays with scullion gullies stamped into them, instead of in a wardroom.

A wardroom!—also genteel in its way. Like the rest of them, Dowd is usually doing well if he gets up in time to make it to breakfast with his guy-in-back, Garth Flint, in the smaller wardroom, where they eat cafeteria-style. More than once he hasn't even managed that and has departed with nothing in his gullet but a couple of cups of coffee, notwithstanding all the lectures about the evil consequences this has for your blood-sugar level. But when they come back, Dowd and Flint and the others can enjoy the offerings of a proper wardroom, the formal one. They can take off the reeking zoom-bags, get dressed, sit down at a table with a white tablecloth on it, write out their orders on club slips, after the fashion of a men's club in New York or London, and more little Filipino stewards in white jackets will pick up the orders and serve dinner on china plates. The china has a certain dignity: it's white with a band of blue about the rim and a blue crest in the center. The silverware—now, that's rather nice! It's ornamental and heavy, it has curlicues and a noble gravity, the sort of silverware one used to see in the dining room of the good hotel near the railroad station. So they have dinner on a field of white and silver, while little stewards in white jackets move about the edges. The bulkheads (as the walls are known here) are paneled with walnut rectangles framed with more walnut; not actual wood, which is forbidden because it is inflammable, but similar enough to fool the eye. Off to the side are clusters of lounge chairs upholstered in leather and some acey-deucey tables. Silver and heavy glass wink out of a manly backdrop, rich as burled wood and Manila cigars; for here in the wardrooms of the *Coral Sea* the Navy has done everything that interior decoration and white mess jackets can do to live up to the idea of Officers & Gentlemen, within the natural limits of going to war on the high seas.

The notion often crosses Dowd's mind: *It's like jousting.*

Every day they touch the napkins to their mouths, depart this gently stewarded place, and go forth, observing a checklist of written and unwritten rules of good form, to test their mettle, to go forth to battle, to hang their hides out over the skeet shooters of Hanoi-Haiphong . . . thence to return, after no more than two hours . . . to this linenfold club and its crisp starched white servitors.

One thing it is not good to think about is the fact that it would be even thus on the day when, finally, as has already happened to 799 other American aviators, radar-intercept officers, and helicopter crewmen, your hide is blown out of the sky. That day, too, would begin within this same gentlemanly envelope.

Fliers with premonitions are not healthy people. They are known as accidents waiting to happen. Now, John Dowd and Garth Flint are not given to premonitions, which is fortunate and a good sign; except that it won't make a great deal of difference today, because this is that day.

To get up on the flight deck of the *Coral Sea*, Dowd and Flint usually went out through a hatch onto a catwalk. The catwalk hung out over the side of the ship just below the level of the deck. At about midships they climbed a few feet up a ladder and they would be on the deck itself. A simple, if slightly old-fashioned, procedure, and by now second nature—

—but what a marvelous low-volt amusement was available if you were on the *Coral Sea* and you saw another mortal, some visitor, some summer reservist, whoever, make his first excursion out onto that deck. He takes a step out onto the catwalk, and right away the burglar alarm sounds in his central nervous system. Listen, Skipper!—the integrity of the circuit has been violated somewhere! He looks out over the railing of the catwalk, and it might as well be the railing of the god-damned Golden Gate Bridge. It's a sixty-foot drop to the sea below, which is water—but what conceivable difference does that make? From this height the water looks like steel where it picks up reflections of the hull of the carrier, except that it ripples and breaks up into queasy facets—and in fact the horizon itself is pitching up and down . . . The whole freaking Golden Gate Bridge is pitching up and down . . . the big wallowing monster can't hold still . . . Christ, let's get up on the deck, away from the edge—but it's only when he reaches the deck itself and stands with both feet planted flat that the full red alert takes over.

This flight deck—in the movie or the training film the flight deck is a grand piece of gray geometry, perilous, to be sure, but an amazing abstract shape dominating the middle of the ocean as we look down upon it on the screen—and yet, once the newcomer's two feet are on it—ge*ome*try—my God, man, this is a . . . skillet! It *heaves*, it moves up and down underneath his feet, it pitches up, it pitches down, as the ship moves into the wind and, therefore, into the waves, and the wind keeps sweeping across, sixty feet up in the air out in the open sea, and there are no railings whatsoever—and no way whatsoever to cry out to another living soul for a helping hand, because on top of everything else the newcomer realizes that his sense of hearing has been *amputated entirely* and his voice is useless. This is a *skillet!*—a frying pan!—a short-order grill!—not gray but black, smeared with skid marks from one end to the other and glistening with pools of hydraulic fluid and the occasional jet-fuel slick, all of it still hot, sticky, greasy, runny, virulent from God knows what traumas—still ablaze!—consumed in detonations, explosions, flames, combustion, roars, shrieks, whines, blasts, cyclones, dust storms, horrible shudders, fracturing impacts, all of it taking place out on the very edge of control, if in fact it can be contained at all, which seems extremely doubtful, because the whole scorched skillet is still *heaving* up and down the horizon and little men in screaming red and yellow and purple and green shirts with black Mickey Mouse helmets over their ears are skittering about on the surface as if for their very lives (you've said it now!), clustering about twin-engine F-4 fighter planes like little bees about the queen, rolling them up a stripe toward the catapult slot, which runs through the deck like the slot in the back of a piggy bank, hooking their bellies on to the shuttle that comes up through the slot and then running for cover as the two jet engines go into their shriek and a huge deflection plate rises up behind the plane because it is about to go into its explosion and quite enough gets blown—quite enough!—quite enough gets blown off this heaving grill as it is, and then they explode—both engines explode into full afterburn, 37,000 pounds of force, and a very storm of flame, heat, crazed winds, and a billion blown steely particles—a very storm engulfs the deck, followed by an unbelievable shudder—*kaboom!*—that pounds through the skillet and destroys whatever may be left of the neophyte's vestibular system, and the howling monster is flung up the deck like something out of a red-mad slingshot, and the F-4 is launched, dropping off the lip of the deck tail down with black smoke pouring out of both engines in its furious struggle to gain altitude—and already *another* plane is ready on the *second* catapult and the screams and explosions have started again and the little screaming-yellow men with their Mouseketeer ears are running once more—

—and yet this flaming bazooka assembly line will, in the newcomer's memory, seem orderly, sublimely well controlled, compared to the procedure he will witness as the F-4's, F-8's, A-4's, A-6's return to the ship for what in the engineering stoicisms of the military is known as recovery and arrest. To say that an F-4 is coming back onto this heaving barbecue

from out of the sky at a speed of 135 knots . . . that may be
the truth on paper, but it doesn't begin to get across the idea
of what a man sees from the deck itself, because it perhaps
creates the notion that the plane is *gliding* in. On the deck
one knows different! As the aircraft comes closer and the carrier heaves on into the waves and the plane's speed does *not*
diminish—one experiences a neural alarm he has never in his
wildest fears imagined before: This is not an *air*plane coming
toward me, it's a brick, and it is not *gliding*, it's *falling*, a
fifty-thousand-pound brick, headed not for a stripe on the
deck, but for *me*—and with a horrible *smash!* it hits the skillet,
and with a blur of momentum as big as a freight train's it
hurtles toward the far end of the deck—another blinding
storm!—another roar as the pilot pushes the throttle up to
full military power and another smear of rubber screams out
over the skillet—and this is normal!—quite okay!—a wire
stretched across the deck has grabbed the hook on the end of
the plane as it hit the deck tail down, and the smash was the
rest of the twenty-five-ton brute slamming onto the deck, as
if tripped up, so that it is now straining against the wire at
full throttle, in case it hadn't held and the plane had "bolt-
ered" off the end of the deck and had to struggle up into the
air again. And already the Mickey Mouse helmets are running
toward their fiery monster . . .

The obvious dangers of the flight deck were the setting, the
backdrop, the mental decor, the emotional scenery against
which all that happened on the carrier was played out, and
the aviator was he who lived in the very eye of the firestorm.
This grill was *his* scenery. Its terrors rose out of his great moments: the launch and recovery. For that reason some crewmen liked to check out the demeanor of the aviators during
these events, just as they might have in the heyday of the
chivalric code.

When John Dowd and Garth Flint came out on deck
in their green flight suits, carrying their helmets and their
knee-boards, they were an unmistakable pair. Dowd was the
tallest pilot on the ship, almost six feet five. Six years ago he
was captain of the Yale basketball team. He was so tall, he had
to slump his way through the physicals in order to get into
flight training, where six four was the upper limit. He looked

like a basketball player. His face, his Adam's apple, his shoulders, his elbows—he was a tower of sharp angles. Flint was Dowd's radar-intercept officer. He was five eight and rather solidly built. He was not small, but next to Dowd he looked like a little jockey.

Today they were to go out on a two-ship formation, with Dowd's roommate, Dick Brent, flying a second F-4B. Dowd's would be the lead ship; Brent's the wing. The usual monsoon overcast was down within about five hundred feet of the deck. It was another day inside the gray pearl: the ship, a tight circle of the waters of the Gulf of Tonkin around it, a dome of clouds, fog, mist, which was God's great gift to the North Vietnamese.

They climb aboard and Dowd eases the power on to taxi the ship toward the catapult, while the aircraft directors nurse it onto the slot. The catapult officer is out there on the deck with his Mousketeer ear baffles on and his yellow jersey flapping in the wind. Assuming the preliminary stages have been completed correctly, the catapult officer is supposed to hold up five fingers to show the pilot that all looks good for launch. If the gauges look okay, the pilot then shows that he is ready for his little slide-for-life . . . by saluting. At this point three things are supposed to happen in a very rapid sequence: the catapult officer drops to one knee (to avoid having his head removed by the wing) and throws his hand forward like a cheerleader doing the "locomotive"; the pilot cuts on full afterburn; and a seaman on a catwalk across the deck presses a black rubber button and throws both hands up in the air. This somewhat hopeless-looking gesture says: "It's done! We've fired the catapult! You're on your way! There's no stopping it!"

To Dowd this is another eccentric note. This man who fires the slingshot—or who seems to—actually he's signaling the steam-catapult crew below deck—this man, who appears to flick you into the sky or the sea with his finger, according to how things work out, is some little swabbo making seventy-eight dollars a month or whatever it is. Somehow this fact puts just that much more edge on the demeanor of the pilot's salute, because what that salute says is: "I hereby commit my hide to your miserable care, sir, to you and your sailor with

the button and your motherless catapult. I'm a human can-
nonball, and it's your cannon."

So it is that today, just before he cuts on full afterburn and
sets off the full 37,000-pound explosion and consumes the
skillet in the firestorm and braces the stick so he won't lose
control in the bad lurch of the slingshot, just before the big
ride, in the key moment of knightly correctness, Dowd rolls
his salute off his helmet with a languid swivel of his wrist, like
Adolphe Menjou doffing his hat . . . a raffish gesture, you
might say, with a roll to it that borders on irony . . . but a
friendly note all the same . . . For this is a good day! They
are flying again! There is no bomb load—therefore less
weight, therefore an easy launch! . . . a good day—otherwise
he might have, or would have been entitled to, according to
the unwritten and unspoken rules (especially since he has
more than one hundred missions behind him)—he might have
ended that cool rolling salute by leaving his middle finger
sticking up in the air, in an accepted fashion that tells one and
all: "You're only giving me the grand goose. Why should I
salute? (Here's one for you.)"

But this is a good day!—and Dowd surrenders to the catapult without even an ironic protest, and he feels a tremendous compression, so great that the surface of his eyeballs
flattens and his vision blurs, and the F-4B shrieks, and he and
Flint hurtle down the stripe and off the bow of the ship, half
blind and riding a shrieking beast, into the gray pearl. It
couldn't have been a smoother launch; it was absolutely
nominal.

Dowd heads on through the pearl, through the overcast,
with Brent's plane about five hundred yards back. The ride to
the coast of North Vietnam will take them about twenty
minutes. Just how high the cloud cover will be up around
Haiphong is impossible to say, which means that the game of
high-low may be a trifle too interesting. The weather has been
so bad, nobody has been up there. Well . . . now somebody's
going up there. Already, without any doubt, the Russian
trawlers in the gulf have painted the two aircraft on their radar
screens. *Painted!* Such a nice word for it! The phosphorescent
images come sliding onto the screen, as if a brush were doing

it. And with those two delicate little strokes on a Russian radar screen somewhere out there in the muck, the game is on again.

American pilots in Vietnam often ran through their side of the action ahead of time as if it were a movie in the mind . . . trying to picture every landmark on the way to the Red River delta, every razorback green ridge, all that tropical hardscrabble down below, every jut in the coast, every wretched misty snake bend in the Red River, every bridge around Haiphong harbor, every change of course, the angle of every bomb run from the assigned altitude . . . But just try to imagine the enemy's side of it. Try to imagine your own aircraft (encasing your own hide) sliding onto their screens like a ghost stroke (observed by what Russian?) and the trawler signaling the coast and the cannon crews and SAM battalions cranking up in the delta and devising (saying what exactly?) their black trash for the day, which could be inexplicably varied.

One day flying over Haiphong would be "a walk in Haiphong Park," as Dowd would put it. The next day the place would erupt with the wildest storms of ground fire since the bombing of Berlin, Merseburg, and Magdeburg in the Second World War, absolute sheets of 37-millimeter, 57-millimeter, and 85-millimeter cannon fire, plus the SAM's. The antiaircraft cannons now had sights that computed the leads instantly and automatically, and they were more accurate than anything ever dreamed of in the Second World War or the Korean war. But it was the SAM's that were the great equalizer. It was SAM's that made aerial combat in Vietnam something different from what the aces of wars gone by—admirable innocent fellows! —had ever known.

Dowd used to say to himself: "The SAM's come up, and the boys go down." One way or the other! The SAM's, the Russian surface-to-air missiles, were aimed and guided by radar. They climbed at about Mach 3, which was likely to be at least three times as fast as your own ship was going when you heard the warning over your radio ("I have a valid launch!"). The SAM's were not fired at random—each had a radar lock on your aircraft or somebody else's. The only way to evade a SAM was to dive for the deck, i.e., the ground. The SAM's own G-forces were so great they couldn't make the loop and come back down. "The SAM's come up, and the boys go down." And the merriment has just begun. The dive brings you down so low, you are now down into the skeet range of that insidiously well-aimed flak! This, as they say, put you between a rock and a hard place. Sometimes the North Vietnamese also sent up the Mig-21's. But they were canny about it. The Migs went up mainly to harass the bombers, the F-105's, A-4's, and A-6's, to force them to jettison their bomb loads (in order to gain speed to evade the Migs) before they reached the target. But occasionally the F-4's got a chance to tangle with them. What a luxury! How sporting! How nice to have a mere Mig to deal with instead of the accursed SAM's! Of course, you just might have both to contend with at the same time. The North Vietnamese were so SAM-crazy, once in a while they'd fire them up in the middle of a hassle and hit their own planes.

Dowd saw his first SAM last year when he was on a flak-suppression run. Other aviators had always told him they looked like "flying telephone poles," but the only thing he saw at first was a shower of sparks, like the sparks from a Roman candle. That was the rocket tail. And then he could make out the shaft—all of this happening in an instant—and it was, in fact, like a pale-gray telephone pole, moving sideways through the sky as if skidding on its tail, which meant the ship it was after had already dived for the deck and the SAM was trying to overcome its own momentum and make the loop. You were always reassured with the statement, "If you can see it"—meaning a SAM—"you can evade it"—but there were some pilots who were so egotistical they believed that the one they saw was the one that had their name on it. A fatal delusion in many cases!—for the SAM's came up in fans of six or eight, fired from different sites and different angles. "The SAM's come up, and the boys go down"—and Dowd and his whole formation hit the deck and got out of there. Not long after that, Dowd and Flint were hit by ground fire for the first time—it was to happen four more times—in the same sort of situation. They had just come down out of the dive when they took hits in the port ramp and intake duct. Fortunately it was 14.5-millimeter fire, instead of one of the big cannons, and they made it on back to the ship.

High-low! In what?—ten minutes?—Dowd will have to start playing the same game again this morning. Soon he will have to decide whether to go above the overcast or right on the deck. Above the overcast they will be safe from the gunners, who need visual sightings in order to use their automatic lead mechanisms. But right above the overcast is where SAM rules like a snake. More aviators have been wiped out by SAM's popping out of the clouds they're sitting on than any other way. Rather than contend with that automated blind beast, some pilots prefer to come in low over the terrain in the eternal attempt to get in "under the radar." But what is it really, a strategic defense or a psychological defense?

Such was the nature of the game that Dowd and every other pilot here had to play. Many of the pilots who flew over Vietnam had been trained by instructors who had flown in the Korean war. What tigers those old Korea jocks were! What glorious memories they had! What visions those aces could fill your skull with! What a tangy taste they gave to the idea of aerial combat over Southeast Asia! The Korean war brought on the first air-to-air combat between jet fighters, but it turned out to be dogfighting of the conventional sort nonetheless, American F-86's versus Soviet-built Mig-15's mainly —and it was a picnic . . . a field day . . . a duck shoot . . . American pilots, flying F-86's in all but a few dozen cases, shot down 839 Korean and Chinese Mig-15's. Only fifty-six F-86's were lost. Quite a carnival it was. Morale among American ground troops in Korea slid like the mud, but the pilots were in Fighter Jock Heaven. The Air Force was producing aces—fighter pilots who had shot down five planes or more—as fast as the Communists could get the Migs up in the air. By the time the war stopped, there were thirty-eight Air Force aces, and between them they had accounted for a total of 299.5 kills. High spirits these lads had. They chronicled their adventures with a good creamy romanticism such as nobody in flying had dared treat himself to since the days of Lufbery, Frank Luke, and Von Richthofen in the First World War. Why hold back! Jousting is jousting, and a knight's a knight. Colonel Harrison R. Thyng, who shot down five Migs in Korea (and eight German and Japanese planes in the Second World War), glowed like Excalibur when he described his Fourth Fighter-Interceptor Wing: "Like olden knights the F-86 pilots ride up over North Korea to the Yalu River, the sun glinting off silver aircraft, contrails streaming behind, as they challenge the numerically superior enemy to come on up and fight." Lances and plumes! Come on up and fight! Now there was a man having a wonderful time!

In Vietnam, however, the jousting was of a kind the good colonel and his knights never dreamed of. The fighter plane that the Air Force and the Navy were now using instead of the F-86—namely, the F-4—was competing with the new generation of Migs and was winning by a ratio of two to one, according to the air-to-air combat scoreboards, regular league standings, that were kept in various military publications. That was nothing like the fifteen-to-one ratio in Korea, of course—but more than that, it was not even the main event any longer. Not even the heroic word "ace" carried the old wallop. The studs-of-all-the-studs in Vietnam were not the pilots in air-to-air combat but the men who operated in that evil space between the rock and the hard place, between the SAM's and the automatic cannon fire.

In the past three years—1965, 1966, and the year just ending for John Dowd, 1967—the losses had been more brutal than the Air Force or the Navy had ever admitted. Jack Broughton, an Air Force colonel and commander of a wing of F-105's flying over Hanoi-Haiphong from out of Thailand, described the losses as "astronomical and unacceptable," and they were increasing sharply each year. What made the North Vietnamese game of high-low—SAM's and ground fire—so effective was a set of restrictions such as no combat pilots had ever had to contend with before.

Flying out over Hanoi and Haiphong was like playing on some small and sharply defined court. These two cities were by far the major targets in North Vietnam, and so there was very little element of surprise along the lines of switching targets. They could only be approached down a ridge of mountains ("Thud Ridge") from the west, out of Thailand, which would be the Air Force attacking with F-105 fighter-bombers, or across a wide-open delta (perfect for radar defenses) from the east, which would be the Navy attacking from carriers in the gulf. The North Vietnamese and the Russians packed so much artillery in around these two cities that pilots would come back saying, "It was like trying to fly through a rainstorm without hitting a drop."

God knows how many planes and pilots were lost just trying to knock out the North Vietnamese ground fire. The Air Force had Wild Weasel or Iron Hand units made up of pilots in F-105's who offered themselves as living SAM bait. They would deliberately try to provoke launches by the SAM battalions so that other ships could get a radar lock on the SAM sites and hit them with cluster-bomb strikes. This became the ultimate game of radar chess. If the SAM battalions beamed up at the Wild Weasels and committed too early, they stood to get obliterated, which would also allow the main strike force to get through to its target. On the other hand, if they refused to go for the bait, recognizing it for what it was, and shut down their beams—that might give the strike force just enough time to slip through unchallenged. So they'd keep shutting on and off, as in some lethal game of "one finger, two fingers." Their risk was nothing, however, compared to that of the Wild Weasel pilots, who were the first in and the last out, who hung around in the evil space far too long and stood to get snuffed any way the game went.

Navy pilots, Dowd among them, were sent out day after day for "flak suppression." The North Vietnamese could move their flak sites around overnight, so that the only way to find them was by leading with your head, as it were, flying over the target area until you saw them fire the cannons. This you could detect by the rather pretty peach-pink sparkles, which were the muzzle explosions. The cannons made no sound at all (way up here) and seemed tiny and merely decorative . . . with their little delicate peach-pink sparkles amid the bitter green of the scrabble. Dowd and his comrades could not unload on these flak sites just anywhere they found them, however. As if to make the game a little more hazardous, the Pentagon had declared certain areas bomb-free zones. A pilot could hit only "military targets," which meant he couldn't hit villages, hospitals, churches, or Haiphong harbor if there was a "third-party" ship there. So, naturally, being no fools, the North Vietnamese loaded the villages up with flak sites,

loaded the churches up with munitions, put SAM sites behind
the hospitals, and "welded a third-party ship to the dock" in
Haiphong harbor, as Garth Flint put it. There always seemed
to be some neutral flag in port there, with one of North Vietnam's best customers being our friends the British. One day
one of Dowd's *Coral Sea* comrades came in for a run on a
railroad freight depot, pickled his bombs too soon, went long,
and hit a church—whereupon the bitter-green landscape
rocked with secondary and tertiary explosions and a succession of fireballs. The place had gone up like an arsenal, which
of course it was. Every now and then Dowd would be involved in a strike aimed at "cutting off" Haiphong harbor.
This was not to be done, however, by mining the harbor or
blowing the docking facilities out of the water or in any other
obvious and easy manner. No, this had to be accomplished by
surgically severing the bridges that connected the port with
the mainland. This required bomb runs through the eye of a
needle, and even if the bridges were knocked out, the North
Vietnamese simply moved everything across by barge until the
bridges were back.

If you were a pilot being flung out every day between the
rock and the hard place, these complicated proscriptions took
on an eerie diffidence, finally. They were like an unaccountable
display of delicate manners. In fact, it was the Johnson Administration's attempt to fight a "humane" war and look
good in the eyes of the world. There was something out-to-
lunch about it, however. The eyes of the world did not flutter
for a second. Stories of American atrocities were believed by
whoever wanted to believe them, no matter what actually occurred, and the lacy patterns that American bombing missions
had to follow across Hanoi-Haiphong never impressed a soul,
except for the pilots and radar-intercept officers who knew
what a difficult and dangerous game it was.

If the United States was seriously trying to win the battle
of world opinion—well, then, here you had a real bush-league
operation. The North Vietnamese were the uncontested aces,
once you got into this arena. One of the most galling things
a pilot had to endure in Vietnam was seeing the North Vietnamese pull propaganda coup after propaganda coup, often
with the help, unwitting or otherwise, of Americans. There

was not merely a sense of humiliation about it. The North Vietnamese talent in this direction often had direct strategic results.

For example, the missions over N—— D——. Now, here was one time, in Dowd's estimation, when they had gotten the go-ahead to do the job right. N—— D—— was an important transportation center in the Iron Triangle area. For two days they softened the place up, working on the flak sites and SAM sites in the most methodical way. On the third day they massed the bomb strike itself. They tore the place apart. They ripped open its gullet. They put it out of the transport business. It had been a model operation. But the North Vietnamese now are blessed with a weapon that no military device known to America could ever get a lock on. As if by magic . . . in Hanoi . . . appears . . . Harrison Salisbury! Harrison Salisbury—writing in *The New York Times* about the atrocious American bombing of the hardscrabble folk of North Vietnam in the Iron Triangle! If you had real sporting blood in you, you had to hand it to the North Vietnamese. They were champions at this sort of thing. It was beautiful to watch. To Americans who knew the air war in the north firsthand, it seemed as if the North Vietnamese were playing Mr. Harrison Salisbury of *The New York Times* like an ocarina, as if they were blowing smoke up his pipe and the finger work was just right and the song was coming forth better than they could have played it themselves.

Before you knew it, massive operations like the one at N—— D—— were no longer being carried out. It was back to threading needles. And yet it couldn't simply be blamed on Salisbury. No series of articles by anyone, no matter what the publication, could have had such an immediate strategic effect if there weren't some sort of strange collapse of will power taking place back in the States. One night, after a couple of hops, Dowd sank back into an easy chair in the wardroom of the *Coral Sea* and picked up a copy of some newspaper that was lying around. There on the first page was William Sloane Coffin, the Yale University chaplain, leading a student antiwar protest. Not only that, there was Kingman Brewster, the president of Yale, standing by, offering tacit support . . . or at least not demurring in any way. It gave Dowd a very strange feeling. Out in the Gulf of Tonkin, on a carrier, one was not engulfed in news from stateside. A report like this came like a remote slice of something—but a slice of something how big? Coffin, who had been at Yale when Dowd was there—Coffin was one thing. But the president of Yale? There was Kingman Brewster with his square-cut face—but looked at another way, it was a strong face gone flaccid, plump as a piece of chicken Kiev. Six years before, when Dowd was a senior at Yale and had his picture taken on the Yale Fence as captain of the basketball team . . . any such Yale scene as was now in this newspaper would have been impossible to contemplate.

The collapse of morale, or weakening of resolve, or whatever it should be called—this was all taking place in the States at the very moment when the losses were beginning to mount in both the Navy and the Air Force. Aviators were getting shot down by the hundreds. Sometimes, at night, after dinner, after the little stewards in white had cleared away the last of the silver from off the white line, after playing a few rounds of acey-deucey in the lounge or just sinking into the leather billows of the easy chairs, after a movie in the wardroom, after a couple of unauthorized but unofficially tolerated whiskeys in somebody's stateroom—after the usual, in short, when he was back in his own quarters, Dowd would take out his mimeographed flight schedule for the day just completed and turn it over to the blank side and use it to keep a journal. In 1966 and 1967 more and more of these entries would make terse note of the toll of friends: "We lost Paul Schultz & Sully— presumably captured immediately on landing in parachute. Direct hit from SAM coming out of clouds—site near Kien An." Or: "Bill C. got it over Ha Tinh today—body seen bloody on ground."

Or they were about how John Dowd hadn't gotten his: "The Lord giveth and the Lord taketh away. I think today was a *give* day. 8 SAM's or so fired from multiple sites and it looked like a few had my no. on them. However they missed their mark & so this entry is made . . . Doc H. presented those who participated in the 'A' strike with a little vial of J. W. Dant cough medicine."

*

In light of all that, it may be of interest to note one fact concerning the mission to Haiphong and points north that Dowd has just headed off on: he did not merely volunteer for it—he thought it up!

For four days, which is to say, ever since Christmas Day, the coastal ports of Haiphong, Cam Pha, and Hon Gay have been socked in with bad weather. Dowd suggested and volunteered for a weather-reconnaissance hop to find out how bad it actually was, to see if the soup was moving at all, to see if the harbors were by any chance clear of third-party ships and therefore eligible for bombing, and so on. If anyone had asked, Dowd would have merely said that anything was better than sitting around the ship for days on end, doing make-work.

But *any*thing—even playing high-low with SAM over the North?

The answer to that question perhaps leads to the answer to a broader one: How was it that despite their own fearsome losses in 1965, 1966 and 1967, despite hobbling restrictions and dubious strategies set by the Pentagon, despite the spectacle of the antiwar movement building back home—how was it that, in the face of all this, American fliers in Vietnam persisted in virtuoso performances and amazing displays of *esprit* throughout the war? Somehow it got down to something that is encoded in the phrase "a great hop."

The last time Dowd and Garth Flint were out was four days ago, Christmas Day, during the American Christmas cease-fire; and what a little tourist excursion that was. They flew a photo run over Route 1A in North Vietnam, came in under the cloud cover, right down on top of the "Drive-In," as it was called, fifty feet from the ground, with Garth taking pictures, and the Charlies were down there using Christmas Day and the cease-fire for all it was worth. The traffic jam at the Phun Cat ferry, going south to the Ho Chi Minh Trail, was so enormous that they couldn't have budged even if they thought Dowd was going to open up on them. They craned their heads back and stared up at him. He was down so low, it was as if he could have chucked them under their chins. Several old geezers, in the inevitable pantaloons, looked up without even taking their hands off the drafts of the wagons they were pulling. It was as if they were harnessed to them. The wagons were so full of artillery shells, it was hard to see how one man, particularly so spindly a creature, could possibly pull one, but there they were in the middle of the general jam-up, in with the trucks, bicycles, motorcycles, old cars, rigs of every sort, anything that would roll.

Now, that was a good hop—and Dowd so recorded it in his journal—an interesting hop, a nice slice of the war, something to talk about, but merely a photo hop . . . and not *a great hop*. There was such a thing as a great hop, and it was quite something else.

Sometimes, at night, when Dowd would write on the back of his flight schedule, he'd make such entries as:

"Great hop! Went to Nam Dinh and hosed down the flak sites around that city. Migs joined in the caper, but no one got a tally. Think I lucked out in a last-minute bomb run & racked up a flak site pretty well."

The atmosphere of the great hop had something about it that was *warlike* only in the sense that it was, literally, a part of combat. A word that comes closer is *sporting*. Throughout his tour of duty on the *Coral Sea*, no matter how bearish the missions became, Dowd seemed to maintain an almost athletic regard for form. Even on days he spent diving from SAM's and running the flak gauntlets, even on days when he was hit by flak, he would wind up his journal entries with a note about how well (or how poorly) he drove his F-4 back down onto the carrier, and often with a playful tone: "2nd pass was a beauty but only received an OK—which was an unfortunate misjudgment on the part of the LSO [landing signal officer]." Or: "Went to Haiphong Barracks. 3 SAM's launched—one appeared to be directed at yours truly—however with skill & cunning we managed to avoid it, although it cost us our first bombing run, which was in question due to lack of a target—no flak to suppress. After whifferdilling around we rolled in on a preplanned secondary target. What deleterious havoc this bombing caused the enemy is questionable. However the overall mission was quite successful . . . RTB good approach except for last ¼ mile. Received *cut*-1 for my efforts."

A great hop! *With skill & cunning we managed to avoid*

. . . death, to call it by its right name. But pilots never mentioned death in the abstract. In fact, the word itself was taboo in conversation. So were the words "bravery" and "fear" and their synonyms. Which is to say, pilots never mentioned the three questions that were uppermost in the minds of all of them: Will I live or die? Will I be brave, whatever happens? Will I show my fear? By now, 1967, with more than a hundred combat missions behind him, Dowd existed in a mental atmosphere that was very nearly mystical. Pilots who had survived that many games of high-low over North Vietnam were like the preacher in *Moby Dick* who ascends to the pulpit on a rope ladder and then pulls the ladder up behind him.

Friends, near ones and dear ones, the loved ones back home, often wondered just what was on the minds of the fliers as the casualties began to increase at a fearsome rate in 1966 and 1967. Does a flier lie on his back in bed at night with his eyes wide open, staring holes through the ceiling and the flight deck and into outer space, thinking of the little ones, Jeffrey and Jennifer, or of his wife, Sandy, and of the soft lost look she has when she first wakes in the morning or of Mom and Dad and Christmas and of little things like how he used to click the toggles on his rubber boots into place before he went out into the snow when he was eight? No, my dear ones back home—I'm afraid not! The lads did not lie in their staterooms on the *Coral Sea* thinking of these things—not even on Christmas Eve, a few days ago!

Well . . . what was on their minds?

(Hmmmm . . . How to put it into words . . . Should it be called the "inner room"?)

Dowd, for one, had entered the Navy in 1961 without the slightest thought of flying or of going to war. The Navy had no such designs for him, either. Quite the contrary. All they asked was that he keep playing basketball! At Yale, Dowd had been an aggressive player, the sort who was matched up against other college stars, such as Dave De Busschere of the University of Detroit (later of the New York Knicks). At the end of his last season, 1961, Dowd was drafted by the Cleveland entry in the new American Basketball Association. He had his naval R.O.T.C. obligation to serve out, however, and the Navy sent him to Hawaii to play ball for the fleet. This he did; his team won the All-Navy championship in 1962. There was nothing to stop him from playing basketball for the rest of his service stint . . . just putting the ball in the hoop for Uncle Sam in heavy-lidded Hawaii.

Now that he was in the military, however, Dowd, like many service athletes, began to get a funny feeling. It had to do with the intangible thing that made sports so alluring when you were in school or college, the intangible summed up in the phrase "where the action is." At Yale, as at other colleges, playing sports was *where the action was*—or where the applause, the stardom, and the honor were, to be more exact. But now that he was in the Navy, something about sports, something he had never thought about, became obvious. Namely, all team sports were play-acting versions of military combat.

It is no mere coincidence that the college sport where there is the greatest risk of injury—football—is also the most prestigious. But the very risk of injury in football is itself but a mild play-acting version of the real thing: the risk of death in military action. So a service athlete was like a dilettante. He was play-acting inside the arena of the real thing. The real thing was always available, any time one had the stomach for it, even in peacetime. There were plenty of ways to hang your side out over the edge in the service, even without going to war. Quite unconsciously, the service athlete always felt mocked by that unspoken challenge. And in the Navy there was no question but that *the* action-of-all-actions was flying fighter planes off carriers.

In his last year at Yale, Dowd had married a girl named Wendy Harter from his home town, Rockville Centre, Long Island. About a year and a half later they had a son, John Jr. And then, out in Hawaii, on those hot liquid evenings when the boy couldn't go to sleep, they would drive him out to Hickam Field to watch the airplanes. Both commercial liners and military fighters came into Hickam. By and by Dowd was taking his wife and his son out there even when the boy was practically asleep in his tracks. One night they were out at Hickam, and Wendy surprised Dowd by reading his mind out loud for him.

"If you like them so much," she said, "why don't you fly them?"

So he started training . . . with a vague feeling of *pour le sport*. This was 1963, when the possibility of an American war in Vietnam was not even talked about.

A man may go into military flight training believing that he is entering some sort of technical school where he is simply going to acquire a certain set of skills. Instead, he finds himself enclosed in the walls of a fraternity. That was the first big surprise for every student. Flying was not a craft but a fraternity. Not only that, the activities of this particular brotherhood began to consume all of a man's waking hours.

But why? And why was it so obsessive? Ahhhhh—*we don't talk about that!* Nevertheless, the explanation was: flying required not merely talent but one of the grandest gambles of manhood. Flying, particularly in the military, involved an abnormal risk of death at every stage. Being a military flight instructor was a more hazardous occupation than deep-sea diving. For that matter, simply taking off in a single-engine jet fighter, such as an F-102, or any other of the military's marvelous bricks with fins on them, presented a man, on a perfectly sunny day, with more ways to get himself killed than his wife and children could possibly imagine. Within the fraternity of men who did this sort of thing day in and day out—within the flying fraternity, that is—mankind appeared to be sheerly divided into those who have it and those who don't—although just what *it* was . . . was never explained. Moreover, the very subject was taboo. *It* somehow seemed to be the transcendent solution to the binary problem of Death/ Glory, but since not even the *terminology* could be uttered, speculating on the answer became doubly taboo.

For Dowd, like every other military pilot, the flying fraternity turned out to be the sort that had outer and inner chambers. No sooner did the novitiate demonstrate his capabilities in the outermost chamber and gain entrance to the next . . . than he discovered that he was once again a novitiate insofar as entry through the *next* door was concerned . . . and on and on the series goes. Moreover, in carrier training the tests confronted the candidate, the eternal novitiate, in more rapid succession than in any other form of flying.

He first had to learn to fly a propeller-driven airplane. Perhaps a quarter of an entering class might be eliminated, washed out, at this stage. Then came jet training and formation flight. As many as 50 percent of those left might wash out at these stages. But in naval flying, on top of everything else, there was the inevitable matter of . . . the heaving greasy skillet. That slab of metal was always waiting out in the middle of the ocean. The trainees first practiced touching down on the shape of a flight deck painted on an airfield. They'd touch down and then gun right off. This was safe enough—the shape didn't move, at least—but it could do terrible things to, let us say, the gyroscope of the soul. *That shape—it's so damned small!* And more novitiates washed out. Then came the day, without warning, when they were sent out over the ocean for the first of many days of reckoning with the skillet. The first day was always a clear day with little wind and a calm sea. The carrier was so steady it seemed to be resting on pilings—but what a bear that day was!

When Dowd was in training, aviators learned to land on the flight deck with the aid of a device that bore the horrible, appropriate name of the "meatball." This was a big mirror set up on the deck with a searchlight shining into it at a 3-degree angle—the angle of the flight deck—so that it reflected at the same angle. The aviator was to guide himself onto the deck by keeping the great burst of light, the meatball, visible in the center of the mirror. And many, many good souls washed out as they dropped like a brick toward the deck and tried to deal with that blazing meatball. Those who survived that test perhaps thought for a brief moment that at last they were regulars in Gideon's Army. But then came night landings. The sky was black, and the sea was black, and now that hellish meatball bobbed like a single sagging star in outer space. Many good men "bingoed" and washed out at this juncture. The novitiate was given three chances to land on the deck. If he didn't come in on his first or second approach and flew by instead, then he had to make it on his third, or the word "bingo!" would sound over his earphones—and over the entire flight deck, as he well knew—meaning that he would have to fly back to shore and land on a nice, safe immovable airfield . . . where everyone likewise knew he was a poor sad Bingo coming in from the carrier. It didn't take many bingos to add up to a washout.

One night, when Dowd had just started night training, the sea and the wind seemed to be higher, the clouds seemed lower, the night blacker than he thought possible. From up in the air the meatball seemed to bob and dart around in a crazy fashion, like a BB under glass in one of those roll-'em-in-the-hole games you hold in the palm of your hand. He made two passes and leveled off a good two hundred feet above the ship each time. On the third time around . . . it suddenly seemed of supreme, decisive, eternal importance that the word "bingo" not sound over *his* earphones. He fought the meatball all the way down in a succession of jerks, shudders, lurches, and whifferdills, then drove his plane onto the deck through sheer will, practically like a nail. The fourth and last deck wire caught him, and he kept the throttle pushed forward into the "full military power" position, figuring he was on the verge of boltering off the end and would have to regain altitude instantaneously. He had his head down and his hand thrust forward, with his engine roaring—for how long?—God knows—before it dawned on him that he was actually down safe and could get out. The whole flight deck was waiting for him to shut off his damned engine. As he climbed down from the aircraft, he heard the skipper's voice boom out over the speaker system:

"How do you like flying now, Lieutenant?"

He noted with some satisfaction, however, that they then closed down the deck because of the weather. And was he *now* in the fraternity at last? . . . Hardly. He was just *beginning*. Everything he had learned to do so far became merely the routine. He was now expected to perform such incredible stunts day in and day out, under conditions of fleet operations and combat.

Being a carrier pilot was like being a paratrooper in that it took a while to learn how many different ways you could be killed in the course of an ordinary operation. A fellow F-4 jock, a friend, an experienced aviator, comes in one night low on fuel, not sure he has enough for a second pass, touches down long, bolters, tries to regain altitude, can't, careens off the far end of the deck, fifty thousand pounds of metal and tubes, and sinks without a trace. It all happens in a matter of seconds, *just like that*. Another friend, with even more experience, a combat veteran, *gets his* without moving a muscle. He's in his F-4, in the flight line, waiting for his turn on the catapult, when the ship up ahead somehow turns at the wrong angle, throttles up without a deflection shield behind it, and the whole fifteen tons of thrust hits his F-4, and the man and his guy-in-back and the ship are blown off the deck like a candy wrapper and are gone forever—in an instant, a snap of the fingers, *just like that*.

Yet once an aviator was in combat, all that, too, became simply the given, the hazards of everyday life on the job, a mere backdrop. From now on one found new doors, new tests, coming up with a mad rapidity. Your first day in combat . . . your first bombing run . . . first strafing run . . . the first time you're shot at . . . the first time you see a SAM . . . which also means the first time you dive for the deck straight into the maw of the flak cannons . . . the first time your ship gets dinged by flak . . . and the first time you *see someone else* in your own formation blown out of the sky over the North—and in many ways what an aviator saw with his own eyes was more terrible than the sudden unseen things happening to himself.

For Dowd and Garth Flint this came one day during a bombing run near the Iron Triangle. They were closing in on the target, barreling through the eternal cloud cover, unable to see even the ships in their own wing, when all at once a great livid ghost came drifting straight across their path, from left to right. It was an F-4. It had taken a direct hit, and smoke was pouring out of the cockpit. The smoke enveloped the fuselage in the most ghostly fashion. The pilot had cobbed it to starboard in a furious effort to reach the water, the gulf, to try to bail out where Navy rescue planes could reach them. In the blink of an eye the ghastly cartridge disappeared, swallowed up by the clouds. They would never make it. Dowd and Flint plowed on to the target, following their wing command, even though the gunners below obviously had dead range on the formation. To have done anything else would have been unthinkable.

Unthinkable, to be sure. By late 1967 thinkable/unthinkable played on a very narrow band. The options had been cut back sharply. Both Navy and Air Force fliers were *getting theirs* at a rate that was "astronomical and unacceptable," by ordinary logic, as Jack Broughton had said. But fliers with a hundred missions over the North were people who by now had pulled the rope ladder up into the pulpit. Somehow they had removed their ties with the ordinary earth. They no longer lived on it. Home and hearth, loved ones and dear ones—it wasn't that they had consciously lost their love or dear regard for such folks and such things . . . it was just that the dear folks back home were . . . so far away, back there through such an incalculable number of chambers and doors. The fliers over the North now lived in, or near, the fraternity's innermost room. Or, at the very least, they now knew *who it was*, finally, who had access to that room. It was not merely he who could be called "brave." No, it was he who was able to put his hide on the line in combat and then had the moxie, the reflexes, the experience, the coolness to pull it back in the last yawning moment—and then was able to go out again *the next day*, and the next day, and every next day, and do it all over again, even if the series proved infinite. It was the *daily routine* of risking one's hide while operating a hurtling piece of machinery that separated military flying from all other forms of soldiering and sailoring known to history.

Even *without going into combat* career Navy fighter pilots stood one chance in four of dying in an accident before their twenty years were up, and one chance in two of having to punch out, eject by parachute, at some point. In combat, especially in Vietnam, God knew what the figures were. The Pentagon was not saying. No, the Pentagon itself seemed bent on raising the ante to ridiculous heights, imposing restrictions that every aviator knew to be absurd. And "the nation"? "our country"? "the folks back home"? They seemed to have lost heart for the battle. But even that realization seemed . . . so far away, back through so many doors. Finally, there was only the business of the fraternity and the inner room.

All of the foregoing was out-of-bounds in conversation. Nevertheless, there it was. The closest aviators came to talking about it was when they used the term "professionalism." Many extraordinary things were done in the name of profes-

sionalism. And when everything else went wrong, this professionalism existed like an envelope, in the sense that each
airplane was said to have a certain "performance envelope."
Inside, inside that space, the aviators remained one another's
relentless judges right up to the end, when not a hell of a lot
of people outside seemed to care any longer. They were like
casebook proof of something an English doctor, Lord Moran,
had written forty years before. Moran had been a doctor treating soldiers in the trenches during the First World War, and
he wrote one of the few analytical studies ever addressed specifically to the subject of bravery: *The Anatomy of Courage*.
In the wars of the future, he said, aerial combat, not soldiering, would have "first call on adventurous youth." But the
bravery of these adventurers, he said, would have a curiously
detached quality. For the pilot, "love of the sport—success at
the game—rather than sense of duty makes him go on."

The unspoken things! *Bye borty-bibe* . . . every morning
when he woke up and rolled out of bed in his stateroom, the
components of the game of high-low lit up in every aviator's
brain, and he would all too literally calculate the state of his
soul that morning by the composition of his bowel movement, with diarrhea being the worst sign of all. Well, not quite
the worst; for occasionally one would hear some poor soul in
another cubicle of the head . . . vomiting. One would be
curious . . . but in another way one would just as soon not
know who it was. (After all, he might be in my wing.) Since
none of this could be spoken, demeanor was everything. (*Only
your laundryman knows for sure!*) It *was* like jousting! One
did return to the carrier like a knight! . . . or as near to
knightly status as was likely to be possible in an age of mimeographed flight assignments and mandatory debriefings.

The most beautiful possible moments came when you
brought your aircraft back to the deck from battle half shot
up. Just a few weeks ago Dowd and Garth Flint came back
with an 85-millimeter shell hole shot clear through a rear stabilizer wing. It looked as if you could put your arm through
it, and it was no more than a yard from the fuselage. Dowd
and Flint had scarcely opened the cockpit before the Mouse-
keteers, the deckhands, were gaping at the damage. Dowd
climbed down to the deck, took off his helmet, and started

walking away. Then, as if he'd just remembered something, he turned about and said to the onlookers: "Check that stabilizer, will you? Think maybe we caught a little flak."

How gloriously bored! The unspoken, unspeakable things! All the gagged taboos!

No doubt that was what made American airmen, while on leave, the most notorious bar patrons in the Philippines, Japan, and Thailand during the Vietnam years. In keeping with a tradition as old as the First World War, drink and drunkenness gave pilots their only license to *let it out*. Not to talk about the unspoken things—not to break the taboo—but to set free all the strangled roars, screams, bawls, sighs, and raving yahoos. Emotion displayed while drunk didn't count. Everybody knew that. One night Dowd was drinking at a bar at Cubi Point with an A-4 pilot named Starbird. It was getting to that hour of the night when you're so drunk you can't hear any more. Your skull itself is roaring and your screams and songs get beaten back by the gale. The bartender announces that the bar is now closed. He slides a brass pole under the handles on the tops of the big beer coolers behind the bar and locks them shut. Starbird reaches across the bar and grabs the brass pole and emits a roar of sheer gorilla fury and pulls it up out of its mooring, until it's looped in the middle like a piece of spaghetti, and announces: "The bar just reopened."

After a long season of such affronts by many roaring souls, Navy bars and officers' clubs in Subic Bay began ruling themselves off limits to pilots returning from tours in the North (Yankee Station). Then came a gesture from on high that Dowd would never forget. Admiral Red Hyland himself sent out a directive to all clubs and pubs within the purview of the Fleet, saying: It has come to my attention that the cocktail lounge conduct of aviators returning from Yankee Station has occasioned some negative responses. This is to inform all hands that the combat conduct of these men has been exemplary, despite the most trying conditions, and now hear this: THEY WILL BE ACCORDED THE FULL PRIVILEGES OF OFFICERS AND GENTLEMEN! (For you I bend the brass! The bars just reopened!)

At last!—someone had come close to saying it! to putting

it into words! to giving a tiny corner of the world some actual inkling that they just might have . . . the ineffable . . . *it!*

That memo, like all memos, soon vanished down the memory hole. Yet it meant more to Dowd than any medal he ever got.

High or low? The weather doesn't get any better as they pull closer to Haiphong, and Dowd decides to play it low. It looks like the kind of overcast the SAM's like best, high and solid. Dowd, with Brent off his wing, comes into Haiphong at about two hundred feet at close to Mach 1. Suddenly they break out of the mist and they're over the harbor. They bank for one turn around it, which immediately cuts their speed down to about 450 knots. It's peaceful, just another inexplicable stroll in Haiphong Park. The overcast is down to four hundred feet, meaning it's hopeless so far as a bombing strike is concerned. Besides, the inevitable third-party ships are welded in . . .

The weather is so bad, it's as if the enemy has decided to take a holiday from the war, knowing no bombers will be coming in. There's no sense loitering, however, and Dowd heads out for a look at Cam Pha and Hon Gay, two ports north of Haiphong. High or low . . . Dowd stays down low. There's nothing below but a smattering of islands.

All at once Dowd sees a streak of orange shoot up over the nose on the port side. Garth Flint, in the back seat, sees another streak come up under the nose on the starboard . . . They both know at once: tracer bullets . . . *They go to school with the tracer bullets* . . . The tracers show the gunners whether or not they're near the mark . . . and without any doubt they're near the mark. Then they hear a sound like *twack* . . . It sounds like nothing more than a good-size rock hitting an automobile . . . the shot hit the bottom of the nose section . . . Dowd immediately cobs it, gives it full power in a furious bid to get up into the cloud cover and out over the gulf. Every warning light on the panel is lit up red, but he still has control of the plane. Smoke starts pouring into the cockpit. The heat is so intense he can barely touch sections of the panel. It's so hot he can hardly hold the controls. The fire seems to be in the hydraulics system of the wheel well. He tries to vent the cockpit, but the vent doesn't work. Then he blows the canopy off to try to clear the smoke, but the smoke pours out so heavily he still can't see. Everything metal is becoming fiercely hot. He wonders if the ejection mechanism will still work. He can hardly hold the stick.

For Garth Flint, in back, with the canopy gone, it's as if a hurricane has hit, a hurricane plus smoke. Maps are blowing all over the place, and smoke is pouring back. It's chaos. They're going about 350 knots, and the rush of air is so furious Flint can no longer hear anything on the radio, not even from Dowd. He wonders: Can we possibly get back onto the carrier if the smoke is this bad and Dowd can't hear radio communications? Oddly, all his worries center on this one problem. An explosion right in front of him! In the roiling smoke, where Dowd used to be, there's a metal pole sticking up in the air. It's made of sections, like a telescope. It's something Flint's never seen before . . . the fully sprung underpinning of an F-4 ejection system, sticking up in the air as they hurtle over the Gulf of Tonkin. This spastic pole sticking up in the front seat is now his only companion in this stricken ship going 350 knots. Dowd has punched out!

Flint stares at the pole for perhaps two or three seconds, then pulls the ring under his seat. He's blasted out of the ship, with such force that he can't see.

Meanwhile, Dowd's furious ride is jerked to a halt by his parachute opening. He assumes Garth is floating down ahead of him. In fact, Dowd had yelled over the radio for Garth to eject and assumed he was on his way, not knowing Garth couldn't hear a word he said. Considering the way he had cobbed the engine and turned the plane to starboard and out over the gulf, Dowd expects to see water as he comes down through the clouds. Instead, little islands—and the live possibility of capture—are rising up toward him.

Reprieve! The wind carries him about a quarter mile from shore. Just the way the survival training told you, he prepares to shuck his parachute before he hits the water, at the same time keeping his life raft uninflated so the people onshore can't spot him so easily. He hits the water . . . it's surprisingly cold . . . he inflates the flotation device he's wearing—but feels himself being dragged under. The water, which looked

so calm from above, is running five- to seven-foot swells. It
pitches up and down in front of him and beneath him, and
he's being dragged under. He can't comprehend it—the parachute, which he thought he had so skillfully abandoned at
the textbook-proper second, has somehow wrapped around
his right leg in the slosh of the swells and he's going under.
He pulls out the knife that they're issued for just such a situation. But the nylon cords are wet and the damned knife
won't cut them. He's going under. For the first time since
the flak hit, the jaws of the Halusian Gulp have opened. *I'm
going to die.* At first it's an incredible notion. Then it's in-
furiating. To die by drowning out in this squalid pond after a
ten-cent shoot-down on a weather-recce mission—it's humiliating! Another fly-boy disappears into the Cosmic Yawn! He's
swept by a wave of the purest self-pity. It's actually about to
happen—*his death*—the erasure of John Dowd from human
existence—in a few seconds—*just like that!* The ineffable talent, the mystical power—*it!*—that let him hang his hide out
over the Jaws and always pull it back—he *doesn't* have it, after
all!—he is no more special than the hundreds of other pilots
who have already been swallowed up over the North! It's pathetic. It's a miserable and colossal affront. His whole life does
not roll before his eyes—only the miserable pity of the here
and now. He does not think of home and hearth. He does
not think of Mom at the shuttling sewing machine late at
night or the poignancy of seeing one's own child daydream-
ing. No, there is only the here and now and the sum total of
this total affront to all that comprises John Dowd—being
dragged down in a fish pond by a parachute, holding in his
hand a knife that the Navy issued for a task that it won't
perform—it's utterly piteous and pathetic! . . . *Jesus! How I
pity myself now!* . . . And that makes him furious. He gives
the parachute a ferocious yank. Whuh?—in that very explosion
of the final anger he discovers something: the damned thing
is caught—not around his leg but on his knee-board! . . .
The board is attached to his flight suit so he can jot down
figures, keep charts handy, whatever . . . one last breath! Now
he's completely underwater . . . He can't see . . . He grabs
the knee-board and rips it off his flight suit . . . a miracle!
. . . he's free! . . . The parachute is gone . . . the death

anchor . . . He bobs back to the surface . . . Christ! . . . the hell with the colossal affront of fate . . . There's only *now!* . . . Never mind! . . . He inflates the raft, as it says in the manual . . . He's on the side of manual now! . . . Oh yes! . . . Navy-issue! . . . Why not! . . . He climbs on the raft . . . He's not drowning any more, he's on his belly on a raft swooping up and down with the swells of the gulf . . . Never mind the past! . . . He scans the water and the nearby island . . . Not miserable Fate, but islanders with guns . . . That's what he's looking for . . . Is that one of them? . . . But on the water . . . there's Garth! . . . Flint is on a raft about two hundred yards away, bobbing in and out of Dowd's line of vision . . . It's all shaping up . . . Never mind Fate! The hell with colossal affronts! He's pulled it back after all—out of the Jaws . . .

Meanwhile, Dick Brent, in the other F-4B, has seen Dowd and Flint eject. After about fifteen minutes of diving and fishing down through the clouds, Brent spots them on the water below and radios the position. Brent sees a few people on the shore of an island, looking out toward the two men, but the islanders don't seem to be making any attempt to go out by boat to retrieve Garth and Dowd, which also means capture them. (In fact, the islanders had long since learned to leave well enough alone. American pilots in the water were often followed by screaming rescue aircraft that blew every boat out of the tub.)

After about another thirty minutes Spads are coming in low over the water. To Garth Flint it appears as if the Spad pilots don't see him, only Dowd. Over his emergency radio Flint says: "If you see two pilots, rock your wings." One of the Spads rocks its wings. The Spads call in a helicopter known as a Big Mother. The helicopter, too, heads straight for Dowd. A morose thought crosses Flint's mind: "He's a lieutenant, I'm only a lieutenant (j.g.)—so they're picking him up first."

Then it dawns on him that they're going after Dowd because he's in closer to shore and therefore more vulnerable to gunfire or capture. Hell, it's going to be okay.

Back on the *Coral Sea* Dowd and Flint were debriefed in the ready room. They drank coffee and tried to warm up. The china had a certain dignity. It was white with bands of blue about the rims and blue crests here and there. The silverware—now, that was rather nice. It was ornamental and heavy. The questions came, one after the other, and they went through everything that happened. Yet during this debriefing the two men were waiting for *something else*. Surely, they would mention *something else*. But they didn't. It was a debriefing much like *every* debriefing. Just the facts! No quarter given! No slack in the line! Then the commander of their squadron said, with a note of accusation: "Why were you flying so low?"

Now, that was really too much! Why . . . you *bastard*! But they said nothing except the usual. What they wanted to say . . . well, how could they have put it into words? How, within the inner room, does one say: "My God, man, we've just been into the Jaws!—about as far into the goddamned Jaws as you can go and still come back again!—and you want to know why we flew so low! We've just been *there*! at the lost end of the equation! where it drops off the end of the known world! Ask us about . . . *the last things*, you bastard, and we will enlighten you!" There were no words in the chivalric code for such thoughts, however.

But all at once the skipper of the *Coral Sea*, the maximum leader, a former combat pilot himself, appeared—and he smiled! And that smile was like an emission of radio waves.

"We're glad to have you back, men."

That was all he said. But he smiled again! Such ethereal waves! Invisible but comprehensible, they said, "I know. I've been there myself." Just that!—not a sound!—and yet a doxology for all the unspoken things. How full my heart, O Lord!

Flint took one day off before going out on his next mission, on New Year's Eve. Dowd had suffered a back injury in the ejection from the F-4B, and so it was another two days before he climbed back into the metal slingshot, got slung off the skillet, and went flying over North Vietnam again.

from *Mauve Gloves & Madmen,*
Clutter & Vine, 1976

from *Tet!*

by Don Oberdorfer

The Plan

IN SEPTEMBER of 1967 an important meeting was held in a pagoda at Tay Ho hamlet, four miles east of the city. The man in charge was Hoang Van Vien, known as "Ba," secretary of the Hue City Committee of the Communist Party. Ba explained to his coworkers that the revolution against the Americans and their Saigon puppets was developing very fast, that conditions were ripe for the General Offensive and General Uprising and that preparations must be undertaken immediately to prepare for the liberation of Hue.

Comrade Son Lam, thirty-five years old and a native of the Hue area, was assigned the task of organizing the uprising for the Right Bank, the section of the city south of the Perfume River. He had joined the anti-French Resistance while attending high school in Hue in 1948, became a member of a Viet Minh secret intelligence cell in 1950, was ejected from the intelligence service in 1952 when his well-to-do parents were denounced as "oppressors of the people," regrouped to North Vietnam after the country was divided in 1954 and infiltrated south in 1962 as the head of a nine-man group of Hue-area natives working for the Party. Despite the fact that his older sister was married to a government policeman, Lam lived safely in his native hamlet just east of the city.

After receiving his instructions, Lam selected as aides the men who could work best within the city and sent them to prepare the way. One night in mid-October, he walked to Hue accompanied by a squad of bodyguards and took up residence in a rented house at the edge of town. He was an ideal organizer: he knew the city and the people, he understood them and they understood him. He began making the rounds of old friends and acquaintances and, with the aid of letters of introduction, called on Hue citizens whose relatives were working for the Party.

Within a week or two he had organized five cells of residents in the Right Bank district—two cells of small-business men and three cells of youths, including the framework of a "Young People's Democratic Group" to be unveiled at the proper moment. He went back to the countryside, where his recruits joined him in small groups for a week's instruction on the aims and organizing principles of the Party. Lam did not tell them when the General Uprising would erupt; he himself had been led to believe that N day would be sometime in March.

On January 26 the leadership committee of the Party completed an eight-page plan for the offensive and uprising in the Right Bank district, specifying general missions as well as targets, the jobs of particular leaders, headquarters locations and policy guidelines. The plan suggests that the leadership did not expect to be able to hold Hue for very long, for it emphasized destruction of "the enemy" over establishment and consolidation of the new order. As set forth in the Party plan, the general missions were:

1. Destroy and disorganize the enemy's restrictive administrative machinery from the province and district levels to city wards, streets and wharves. To pursue until the end spies, reactionaries, and reactionaries who exploit Catholics in and outside the country. To prevent them from escaping and to punish scoundrels, hoodlums, and robbers who kill the people and disturb peace and honor.

2. Motivate the people to take up arms, to pursue the enemy and to seize power and establish a revolutionary government.

3. Make every effort to establish strength in the military, political and economic fields in order to conserve the government. Our immediate mission is to pay particular attention to armed and security forces.

4. Make positive efforts to develop [our forces] in the city wards, streets and wharves in order to expand the guerrilla war.

5. Encircle the reactionaries who exploit Catholics and isolate them. Pay special attention to the Phu Cam area, Thien Huu and Binh Linh schools and at the same time try to gain the support of the Buddhist sects of Tu Dam and Bao Quoc pagodas.

6. Promptly motivate the people to participate in combat, transportation and supply activities and to serve the wounded soldiers, etc.

7. Maintain order and security in the city and stabilize the people's living conditions.

The plan divided the Right Bank into four tactical areas, each with its own priority targets and special missions, its own organization and assigned leaders. The forces were given an activity schedule for their first three days of occupation and specific instructions for handling prisoners in different categories. Important prisoners of war were to be closely guarded and evacuated from the city at the first opportunity; they were to be killed on the spot only if evacuation were impossible. "Cruel tyrants and reactionary elements" were to be imprisoned separately and moved outside the city for "punishment," a euphemism for execution. As for foreign civilians such as teachers, newsmen and artists, the attack force was instructed to "gain the sympathy" of the French residents but to arrest Americans, Germans and Filipinos.

Viet Cong agents had prepared a profusion of reports on the defenses and defenders of the city, the deployment and habits of military and police patrols at night, the identity and activities of political opponents, government officials and foreigners and even the schedule of doctors on duty at the Central Hospital. Working from this mass of information, Viet Cong intelligence prepared two documents for security forces moving into the city. One was a target list for each area of the city of United States and "puppet" civil and military installations. The other list, more detailed and important, included 196 targets in the city to be given priority attention, arranged by street location. For example, these were the items for Duy Tan Street on the Right Bank:

> The Garrison Town Office is located on Duy Tan Street at the corner and adjacent to Truong Dinh Street.
> U.S. personnel live at No. 4 Duy Tan Street.
> Thua Thien [Province] Sector Headquarters is located at Phan Sao Nam Camp, No. 3 Duy Tan Street.
> Pham Tra Dang, native of Quang Nam, teacher at the high school, long-standing Vietnamese Nationalist Party member, an extremely anti-revolutionary element, lives at No. 34 Duy Tan Street.
> U.S. personnel live at Thuan Hoa Hotel, No. 5 Duy Tan Street.
> A house used by U.S. personnel is at No. 21 Duy Tan Street.
> No. 52 Duy Tan Street is the house of the concubine of Captain

Pham Lien, Phu Thu District Chief. He was formerly Duc Hoa District Chief and was active against us. He usually sleeps at his concubine's house at night.

No. 71 Duy Tan Street is the home of Nguyen Giang, father of Nguyen Vi Hoc. Hoc is chief of the Psywar office of the Province Rural Development Group. Hoc is also a member of the Dai Viet Party. He usually comes and stays at his father's house.

No. 59 Duy Tan Street is the home of Nam, a member of the National Police Service, Nam Hoa District.

Comrade Son Lam, who moved back to the city from the countryside in early January, was awakened by a messenger in the night at 2 A.M. on January 30, the first day of Tet. His presence was required immediately outside of town. At a meeting in a family chapel north of the city he was informed for the first time that the General Offensive and General Uprising would coincide with the Lunar New Year. The troops were moving, the hour of attack was close at hand. In order to maintain security, no one was permitted to leave the meeting.

The main force units began arriving shortly after dark. Lam was assigned as liaison officer between the troop units which would occupy the Right Bank and the political organization he had built. The provisional battalion, composed half of North Vietnamese regulars and half of South Vietnamese Liberation Army forces, began its march a little after 10 P.M., crossing rice fields, highways and streams and arriving at the jumping-off point after midnight. There in darkness and in silence the soldiers waited at the edge of a rice paddy only a few blocks from the headquarters of the American advisers. Son Lam was excited and anxious, but he was not fearful. He had waited twenty years for this day. His ears were eager for the "signal from above," the mortar and rocket barrage which was to be the call to battle.

United States and South Vietnamese government intelligence, charged with keeping up with threats to the city, was confused, uncoordinated and ineffective. The government police, headed by a former sports announcer who kept a bottle of Johnnie Walker Black Label on his desk, did not customarily exchange intelligence—if indeed it had any—with the 1st

South Vietnamese Division. The small CIA station in the city, which advised the police, rarely exchanged information with the U.S. military advisory team which worked with the provincial troops. The forces within the city rarely received any intelligence of value from the U.S. air, logistical and ground installation at Phu Bai, just eight miles southeast of the city along Route 1.

On January 22 the U.S. Command in Saigon informed the Pentagon in Washington of good evidence in hand that the enemy would attempt a multibattalion attack on Hue. Whatever the good evidence was, it did not reach the people most immediately endangered. Both United States and Vietnamese government forces in Hue were unprepared for a major attack.

About January 28 a U.S. military adviser in Huong Thuy district just east of the city reported signs that three North Vietnamese/Viet Cong battalions had recently left their mountain base camp and were now located in his lowland district. The officer was known at U.S. advisory headquarters in Hue as a habitual worrier and, in the absence of corroborating information, his report was discounted. The following night many of the American and Vietnamese military intelligence officials celebrated New Year's Eve at a party in the back room of the best Chinese restaurant in the city. There was plenty of food and drink, and not a whisper of impending disaster.

On January 30, New Year's morning, Brigadier General Ngo Quang Truong, commander of the 1st South Vietnamese Division, attended the flag-raising ceremony near the Emperor's Gate of the Citadel to mark the coming Year of the Monkey. Shortly after the ceremony he received reports of the attacks on Da Nang, Nha Trang and other cities during the night just past. Many of Truong's men were on Tet holiday, but he placed his remaining forces on alert and called his division staff officers to their posts at division headquarters for the night. This precautionary action preserved the command structure of the division and saved the lives of many staff officers whose residences were in unprotected areas of the city.

At this point, strong evidence of Communist troop movements converging on Hue was in U.S. hands at nearby Phu Bai, but neither Truong nor the U.S. advisory team in Hue was aware of it. The evidence consisted of telltale signals from radio transmissions, picked up by the U.S. radio intercept field station at Phu Bai on January 30. Under Army procedures of the time, this information was not forwarded directly to Hue but was sent back to Da Nang regional headquarters for posting and analysis before being relayed from there to Hue via teletype. The usual bureaucratic delays at headquarters were compounded by the attack on Da Nang itself. By the time the radio intercept reports arrived in Hue, the "signal from above" had already been fired, the Communist units had attacked from all sides and nearly the entire city had been taken over.

Marked Men

The first travail was of those who had been named as targets on the Viet Cong intelligence lists: Vietnamese officials, military officers, political figures and functionaries and Americans and foreigners other than the French. Most of them tried to hide and some of them managed to flee, but many were caught in their homes. They were marched down the nearly empty streets, their arms bound behind their backs, to prisoner collection points in the city.

Lieutenant Colonel Pham Van Khoa, the province chief, fled from his house and made his way in the darkness to Central Hospital six blocks away. There he hid for a week in an attic while a Viet Cong unit conducted the business of a command post on the floor below. Khoa, who had risen to high authority from a lowly position as a personal retainer of the Diem family, was badly shaken by the experience. He was relieved of his post a few weeks later and ultimately assigned to a less important military job in Da Nang.

The senior American adviser in Hue, Philip W. Manhard, radioed the U.S. Command in Saigon on the first morning that his house was surrounded and that he and two assistants were going into a hiding place within the residence. Manhard, a veteran Foreign Service officer, was captured and taken away. As this is written, he has not been heard from since.

Stephen H. Miller, a twenty-eight-year-old Foreign Service officer assigned to Hue as a United States Information Agency representative, had dinner the night before with James R.

Bullington, a Foreign Service classmate who had previously served in Hue and was engaged to marry a Hue girl. The girl's uncle, the son of an old mandarin, had heard rumors that the night would be very dangerous, but the two young Americans had heard such talk before and they were unconcerned. They stayed up late drinking and singing college songs before Miller went home to his house on Phan Dinh Phung Street.

All hell broke loose during the night and in the morning a neighbor boy reported to Miller that many, many Viet Cong were about, including more than thirty at the very next corner. Miller was invited by Vietnamese friends to flee with them to the big Catholic cathedral nearby, but he decided to remain in his house. When his friends returned, the house was occupied by a platoon of Viet Cong who said they had discovered the Foreign Service officer and another American hiding in a closet. Miller's body was found a few days later in a field behind a Catholic seminary which had been used as a prisoner collection point. His arms had been tied and he had been shot to death.

Bullington was luckier. Since he was not regularly assigned to Hue at the time, he was staying in the guesthouse of a friend, who hid him, in turn, with Vietnamese neighbors who had no connection with the government or the Americans. For eight days he watched North Vietnamese troops in khaki patrol the neighborhood and once saw men in black pajamas rumbling down the street in a captured American tank. On the ninth day the North Vietnamese fled and U.S. Marines liberated the house where he was hidden.

Courtney Niles, an NBC International official serving under contract as a radio-television technical adviser, was staying with a U.S. Army communications crew in a house in the Right Bank area. For two days nothing happened. On the third day a Viet Cong team marched up to the house and pounded on the front door. One of the Americans opened fire, a Viet Cong soldier fell dead and the rest of the team withdrew. The Americans gathered their weapons and steeled themselves for a last stand—but again, nothing happened. The invaders were all over the area, walking back and forth through the streets with leafy camouflage hanging from their shoulder packs, carrying mortar tubes and projectiles, machine guns and other weapons, but they simply ignored the Americans in the marked house.

Two or three nights later the attack on the house came, beginning with dynamite charges which blew out a wall without warning. Niles and several others fled. The NBC official was hit in the legs but made it nearly to the church where he had decided to seek refuge. A friend saw him fall in the street. His body was found after the area was cleared. Some of the other Americans in the house surrendered; they were bound and marched off to the Ashau Valley and have never been heard from since.

Father Elizalde, a Spanish Jesuit who lived two blocks from the U.S. advisory compound, was awakened by the barrage in the night and then by a message from the invading troops—delivered by his cook—to open all the doors or suffer the consequences. The troops swarmed in, setting up machine gun posts and mortar pits. The Spaniard and his superior, a Belgian, retreated to the little villa behind their garden while the war erupted around them.

During a pause in the fighting on the third day, a Viet Cong patrol shot off the lock on their door and a political officer summoned them, in broken English, to come outside with their hands in the air. The leader wore khaki shorts and shirt with a green and red arm band and a Ho Chi Minh medal, and he carried a clipboard full of papers describing inhabitants of the area. Copies of identity card pictures were pasted on many of the sheets. He handed the Jesuits a pamphlet printed in English containing the Communist version of American activities all over the world and of the cries of people that "Americans go home."

The priests protested that they were not Americans and that the school had nothing to do with politics or the war, but their arms were bound and they were marched across a field and through a nearby seminary, crowded with North Vietnamese soldiers, to the residence of the senior American adviser. Manhard was nowhere to be seen but five other Americans were crowded into temporary confinement in the shower stall, their arms bound behind them. The priests were searched and then interrogated. The Spaniard said he was from "south of France" and the Belgian from "north of France" and both repeated the humanitarian and non-political nature of their mission. They were vouched for by Vietnamese university students of their acquaintance who seemed to be working with the invading troops. After a while the senior Viet Cong commander on the scene wrote out a safe-conduct pass and let them go. The Americans were later marched away, except for one badly wounded civilian who was left behind.

Dr. Horst Gunther Krainick, a German pediatrician and professor of internal medicine, had come from the University of Freiburg in December of 1960 to help establish a medical school at Hue University. With the assistance of the German and Vietnamese governments, teams of German doctors—mostly from Freiburg—had labored under increasing difficulties to bring first-class medical education to a region and nation woefully short of physicians. Dr. Krainick and his wife, Elisabeth, were torn between their love of Hue and the memories of the happy early years and the growing hostility and bureaucratic difficulties at the university. They were planning to return to Germany as soon as the school year ended and the small class of senior medical students had graduated.

During the Buddhist uprising of 1966, the Germans had been left alone and as non-combatants and medical workers they felt certain they would be left alone at Tet. They placed their German identification on their door in the university faculty apartments and watched the Viet Cong from the windows. They had no way to know that the Viet Cong order was to pick up Germans and that they were listed—though not by name—in Item 65 of the Right Bank target list.

On Sunday morning, the fifth day of the occupation, a well-armed squad wearing red arm bands, neat uniforms and boots arrived in a jeep and a cream-colored Volkswagen bus and began searching the building. The Krainicks stayed put and the Viet Cong went away. Three hours later they returned and entered the Krainicks' apartment. Elisabeth Krainick screamed and when she and her husband were led away she was heard to shout in English, "Keep your hands off my husband." The couple and the two other German doctors in residence, Dr. Raimund Discher and Dr. Alois Altekoester, were taken away in the Volkswagen bus. The four bodies were found later in a shallow grave in a potato field a half mile away, all victims of executioner's bullets. Vietnamese nuns who knew them gently washed the bodies and wrapped them in black cloth and then white cloth in traditional fashion for the long trip home to Germany.

Father Urbain and Father Guy, two French Benedictine priests at the Thien An Mission in the tall pines on a bluff south of the city, had been able to coexist with the local Viet Cong who dominated the area. When the fighting began, several thousand local peasants flocked to the monastery seeking refuge, and they were followed by Communist troops. Father Urbain's body was found in a common grave with ten other victims near the monumental tomb of the Emperor Dong Khanh (1883–89), who was installed on the throne by the French and whose reign was marked by a bloody Vietnamese attack on the French at Hue. Father Urbain had been bound hand and foot and buried alive. Father Guy's body was found nearby. His cassock had been removed and he had been allowed to kneel before being shot in the back of the head.

Three fourths of Hue's Roman Catholics lived in the Phu Cam area of the Right Bank, and the Right Bank plan contained special instructions to "destroy the power and influence of reactionary ring leaders" there. On the fifth day troops came in force to Phu Cam Cathedral and ordered out about four hundred men and boys, some by name and others apparently because they were of military age or prosperous appearance. When the group was assembled, the Viet Cong leader told everyone not to fear, they were merely being taken a half mile away to Tu Dam Pagoda, headquarters of their Buddhist adversaries, for political reorientation. They marched away to Tu Dam and two days later troops returned to the cathedral to ask the women to prepare packages of food and clothing for their loved ones. After this was done, the group disappeared, marching south, and was not heard of for a long time.

Nineteen months later three Viet Cong defectors led the U.S. 101st Airborne Brigade through the royal tombs area, across a river and through some of the most rugged country of central Vietnam to a creek bed deep in double-canopy jungle ten miles from Hue. There spread out for nearly a hundred

yards in the ravine were the skulls, skeletons and shards of
bone of the men of Phu Cam, washed clean and white by the
running brook. The skulls showed they had been shot or
brained with blunt instruments. Hue authorities later released
a list of 428 victims. About 100 were South Vietnamese servicemen, including two officers; about 100 were students; the
rest were civil servants, village and hamlet officials, government workers and ordinary citizens.

Of all instances of Catholic leaders singled out for slaughter,
none was more poignant than that of Father Buu Dong, the
radiant and popular parish priest of a village east of the city.
The area was inhabited by many Viet Cong, and Father Dong
worked hard to stay on good terms with both sides in the war.
In 1967 he invited Viet Cong and government soldiers to sit
down together for Christmas dinner and, according to local
legend, he carried it off. He kept a picture of Ho Chi Minh
in his room and told his parishioners that he prayed for Ho
because "he is our friend too." At the same time, he accepted
sewing machines for the people from the American AID
program.

On the first day Viet Cong troops led Father Dong to a
nearby pagoda for questioning but released him after a passionate appeal by the elders of the parish. Five days later the
troops returned. They searched the rectory, seized his binoculars, camera, typewriter and his picture of Ho Chi Minh and
led Father Dong and two seminarians away.

The remains of his body were found twenty-two months
later in a shallow grave in the coastal sand flats along with the
remnants of three hundred other victims. In the priest's eye-
glass case were three letters. One was to his aged parents,
another to his brothers, sisters and cousins. The third, to his
parishioners, said:

My dearly beloved children,
This is my last chance to write to you my children and remind you
of the lesson of St. Peter on the boat in the storm (three illegible
words) the faith.
My words of greeting at this beginning of Spring are a hope that
my works in the faith among you will make you remember (two
illegible words) as my life is about to end by the will of God.
Love one another and forgive my wrongs, thanking God with me.

Ask God to forgive all my sins and remember to love and pray for me that I will live in belief and patience during difficulties to bring about the peace of Christ and serve the spirit of God and the interests of everyone in Mother Mary.

Please pray that I will be serene and clear-headed and brave in every adversity of the spirit and of the body and will send my life to God through the hands of the Blessed Mother.

With a promise to meet again in Heaven,

I hope for grace for all of you, my children.

From the position of his body and the lack of visible wounds, it is believed that Buu Dong was buried alive and left to die.

from *Tet!*, 1971

from *Dispatches*

by Michael Herr

Hell Sucks

DURING the first weeks of the Tet Offensive the curfew began early in the afternoon and was strictly enforced. By 2:30 each day Saigon looked like the final reel of *On the Beach*, a desolate city whose long avenues held nothing but refuse, windblown papers, small distinct piles of human excrement and the dead flowers and spent firecracker casings of the Lunar New Year. Alive, Saigon had been depressing enough, but during the Offensive it became so stark that, in an odd way, it was invigorating. The trees along the main streets looked like they'd been struck by lightning, and it became unusually, uncomfortably cold, one more piece of freak luck in a place where nothing was in its season. With so much filth growing in so many streets and alleys, an epidemic of plague was feared, and if there was ever a place that suggested plague, demanded it, it was Saigon in the Emergency. American civilians, engineers and construction workers who were making it here like they'd never made it at home began forming into large armed bands, carrying .45's and grease guns and Swedish K's, and no mob of hysterical vigilantes ever promised more bad news. You'd see them at ten in the morning on the terrace of the Continental waiting for the bar to open, barely able to light their own cigarettes until it did. The crowds on Tu Do Street looked like Ensor processioners, and there was a corruption in the air that had nothing to do with government workers on the take. After seven in the evening, when the curfew included Americans and became total, nothing but White Mice patrols and MP jeeps moved in the streets, except for a few young children who raced up and down over the rubbish, running newspaper kites up into the chilling wind.

*

We took a huge collective nervous breakdown, it was the compression and heat of heavy contact generated out until every
American in Vietnam got a taste. Vietnam was a dark room
full of deadly objects, the VC were everywhere all at once like
spider cancer, and instead of losing the war in little pieces over
years we lost it fast in under a week. After that, we were like
the character in pop grunt mythology, dead but too dumb to
lie down. Our worst dread of yellow peril became realized; we
saw them now dying by the thousands all over the country,
yet they didn't seem depleted, let alone exhausted, as the Mission was claiming by the fourth day. We took space back
quickly, expensively, with total panic and close to maximum
brutality. Our machine was devastating. And versatile. It could
do everything but stop. As one American major said, in a
successful attempt at attaining history, "We had to destroy
Ben Tre in order to save it." That's how most of the country
came back under what we called control, and how it remained
essentially occupied by the Viet Cong and the North until the
day years later when there were none of us left there.

The Mission Council joined hands and passed together
through the Looking Glass. Our general's chariot was on fire,
he was taking on smoke and telling us such incredible stories
of triumph and victory that a few high-level Americans had to
ask him to just cool it and let them do the talking. A British
correspondent compared the Mission posture to the captain
of the *Titanic* announcing, "There's no cause for alarm, we're
only stopping briefly to take on a little ice."

By the time I got back to Saigon on the fourth day a lot
of information from around the country had settled, and it
was bad, even after you picked out the threads of rumor: like
the one about the "Caucasians," obviously Americans, fighting for the VC, or the one about thousands of NVA executions in Hue and the "shallow graves" in the flats outside the
city, both of which proved true. Almost as much as the grunts
and the Vietnamese, Tet was pushing correspondents closer
to the wall than they'd ever wanted to go. I realized later that,
however childish I might remain, actual youth had been
pressed out of me in just the three days that it took me to
cross the sixty miles between Can Tho and Saigon. In Saigon,
I saw friends flipping out almost completely; a few left, some

took to their beds for days with the exhaustion of deep depression. I went the other way, hyper and agitated, until I was
only doing three hours of sleep a night. A friend on the *Times*
said he didn't mind his nightmares so much as the waking
impulse to file on them. An old-timer who'd covered war since
the Thirties heard us pissing and moaning about how *terrible*
it was and he snorted, "Ha, I love you guys. You guys are
beautiful. What the fuck did you think it was?" We thought
it was already past the cut-off point where every war is just
like every other war; if we knew how rough it was going to
get, we might have felt better. After a few days the air routes
opened again, and we went up to Hue.

Going in, there were sixty of us packed into a deuce-and-a-
half, one of eight trucks moving in convoy from Phu Bai,
bringing in over 300 replacements for the casualties taken in
the earliest fighting south of the Perfume River. There had
been a harsh, dark storm going on for days, and it turned the
convoy route into a mudbed. It was terribly cold in the trucks,
and the road was covered with leaves that had either been
blown off the trees by the storm or torn away by our artillery,
which had been heavy all along the road. Many of the houses
had been completely collapsed, and not one had been left
without pitting from shell fragments. Hundreds of refugees
held to the side of the road as we passed, many of them
wounded. The kids would laugh and shout, the old would
look on with that silent tolerance for misery that made so
many Americans uneasy, which was usually misread as indifference. But the younger men and women would often look
at us with unmistakable contempt, pulling their cheering children back from the trucks.

We sat there trying to keep it up for each other, grinning
at the bad weather and the discomfort, sharing the first fear,
glad that we weren't riding point or closing the rear. They
had been hitting our trucks regularly, and a lot of the convoys
had been turned back. The houses that we passed so slowly
made good cover for snipers, and one B-40 rocket could have
made casualties out of a whole truckload of us. All the grunts
were whistling, and no two were whistling the same tune, it
sounded like a locker room before a game that nobody wanted

to play. Or almost nobody. There was a black Marine called Philly Dog who'd been a gang lord in Philadelphia and who was looking forward to some street fighting after six months in the jungle, he could show the kickers what he could do with some city ground. (In Hue he turned out to be incredibly valuable. I saw him pouring out about a hundred rounds of .30-caliber fire into a breach in the wall, laughing, "You got to bring some to get some"; he seemed to be about the only man in Delta Company who hadn't been hurt yet.) And there was a Marine correspondent, Sergeant Dale Dye, who sat with a tall yellow flower sticking out of his helmet cover, a really outstanding target. He was rolling his eyes around and saying, "Oh yes, oh yes, Charlie's got his shit together here, this will be *bad*," and smiling happily. It was the same smile I saw a week later when a sniper's bullet tore up a wall two inches above his head, odd cause for amusement in anyone but a grunt.

Everyone else in the truck had that wild haunted going-West look that said it was perfectly correct to be here where the fighting would be the worst, where you wouldn't have half of what you needed, where it was colder than Nam ever got. On their helmets and flak jackets they'd written the names of old operations, of girlfriends, their war names (FAR FROM FEARLESS, MICKEY'S MONKEY, AVENGER V, SHORT TIME SAFETY MOE), their fantasies (BORN TO LOSE, BORN TO RAISE HELL, BORN TO KILL, BORN TO DIE), their ongoing information (HELL SUCKS, TIME IS ON MY SIDE, JUST YOU AND ME GOD—RIGHT?). One kid called to me, "Hey man! You want a story, man? Here man, write this: I'm up there on 881, this was May, I'm just up there walkin' the ridgeline like a movie star and this Zip jumps up smack into me, lays his AK-47 fucking right *into* me, only he's so *amazed* at my *cool* I got my whole clip off 'fore he knew how to thank me for it. Grease one." After twenty kilometers of this, in spite of the black roiling sky ahead, we could see smoke coming up from the far side of the river, from the Citadel of Hue.

The bridge was down that spanned the canal dividing the village of An Cuu and the southern sector of Hue, blown the night before by the Viet Cong, and the forward area beyond the far bank wasn't thought to be secure, so we bivouacked in the village for the night. It had been completely deserted, and we set ourselves up in empty hootches, laying our poncho liners out over broken glass and shattered brick. At dusk, while we all stretched out along the canal bank eating dinner, two Marine gunships came down on us and began strafing us, sending burning tracers up along the canal, and we ran for cover, more surprised than scared. "Way to go, motherfucker, way to pinpoint the fuckin' enemy," one of the grunts said, and he set up his M-60 machine gun in case they came back. "I don't guess we got to take *that* shit," he said. Patrols were sent out, guards posted, and we went into the hootches to sleep. For some reason, we weren't even mortared that night.

In the morning we crossed the canal on a two-by-four and started walking in until we came across the first of the hundreds of civilian dead that we were to see in the next weeks: an old man arched over his straw hat and a little girl who'd been hit while riding her bicycle, lying there with her arm up like a reproach. They'd been lying out like that for a week, for the first time we were grateful for the cold.

Along the Perfume River's south bank there is a long, graceful park that separates Hue's most pleasant avenue, Le Loi, from the riverfront. People will talk about how they'd sit out there in the sun and watch the sampans moving down the river, or watch the girls bicycling up Le Loi, past the villas of officials and the French-architected University buildings. Many of those villas had been destroyed and much of the University permanently damaged. In the middle of the street a couple of ambulances from the German Mission had been blown up, and the Cercle Sportif was covered with bullet holes and shrapnel. The rain had brought up the green, it stretched out cased in thick white fog. In the park itself, four fat green dead lay sprawled around a tall, ornate cage, inside of which sat a small, shivering monkey. One of the correspondents along stepped over the corpses to feed it some fruit. (Days later, I came back to the spot. The corpses were gone, but so was the monkey. There had been so many refugees and so little food then, and someone must have eaten him.) The Marines of 2/5 had secured almost all of the central south bank and were now fanning out to the west, fighting and clearing one of the major canals. We were waiting for some decision on whether or not U.S. Marines would be going into the Citadel itself, but no one had any doubts about what that decision would be. We sat there taking in the dread by watching the columns of smoke across the river, receiving occasional sniper rounds, infrequent bursts of .50-caliber, watching the Navy LCU's on the river getting shelled from the wall. One Marine next to me was saying that it was just a damned shame, all them poor people, all them nice-looking houses, they even had a Shell station there. He was looking at the black napalm blasts and the wreckage along the wall. "Looks like the Imperial City's had the schnitz," he said.

The courtyard of the American compound in Hue was filled with puddles from the rain, and the canvas tops of the jeeps and trucks sagged with the weight of the water. It was the fifth day of the fighting, and everyone was still amazed that the NVA or the Cong had not hit the compound on the first night. An enormous white goose had come into the compound that night, and now his wings were heavy with the oil that had formed on the surface of the puddles. Every time a vehicle entered the yard he would beat his wings in a fury and scream, but he never left the compound and, as far as I knew, no one ever ate him.

Nearly 200 of us were sleeping in the two small rooms that had been the compound's dining quarters. The Army was not happy about having to billet so many of the Marines that were coming through, and they were absolutely furious about all the correspondents who were hanging around now, waiting until the fighting moved north across the river, into the Citadel. You were lucky to find space enough on the floor to lie down on, luckier if you found an empty stretcher to sleep on, and luckiest of all if the stretcher was new. All night long the few unbroken windows would rattle from the airstrikes across the river, and a mortar pit just outside fired incessantly. At two or three in the morning, Marines would come in from their patrols. They'd cross the room, not much caring whether they stepped on anyone or not. They'd turn their radios on and shout across the room to one another. "Really, can't you

fellows show a bit more consideration?" a British correspondent said, and their laughter woke anyone who was not already up.

One morning there was a fire in the prison camp across the
road from the compound. We saw the black smoke rising over
the barbed wire that topped the camp wall and heard automatic weapons' fire. The prison was full of captured NVA and
Viet Cong or Viet Cong suspects, the guards said that they'd
started the fire to cover an escape. The ARVN and a few
Americans were shooting blindly into the flames, and the bodies were burning where they fell. Civilian dead lay out on the
sidewalks only a block from the compound, and the park by
the river was littered with dead. It was cold and the sun never
came out once, but the rain did things to the corpses that
were worse in their way than anything the sun could have
done. It was on one of those days that I realized that the only
corpse I couldn't bear to look at would be the one I would
never have to see.

It stayed cold and dark like that for the next ten days, and
that damp gloom was the background for all the footage that
we took out of the Citadel. What little sunlight there was
caught the heavy motes of dust that blew up from the wreckage of the east wall, held it until everything you saw was filtered through it. And you saw things from unaccustomed
angles, quick looks from a running crouch, or up from flat
out, hearing the hard dry rattle of shrapnel scudding against
the debris around you. With all of that dust blowing around,
the acrid smell of cordite would hang in the air for a long
time after firefights, and there was the CS gas that we'd fired
at the NVA blowing back in over our positions. It was impossible to get a clean breath with all of that happening, and
there was that other smell too that came up from the shattered
heaps of stone wherever an airstrike had come in. It held to
the lining of your nostrils and worked itself into the weave of
your fatigues, and weeks later, miles away, you'd wake up at
night and it would be in the room with you. The NVA had
dug themselves so deeply into the wall that airstrikes had to
open it meter by meter, dropping napalm as close as a hundred meters from our positions. Up on the highest point of

the wall, on what had once been a tower, I looked across the Citadel's moat and saw the NVA moving quickly across the rubble of the opposing wall. We were close enough to be able to see their faces. A rifle went off a few feet to my right, and one of the running figures jerked back and dropped. A Marine sniper leaned out from his cover and grinned at me.

Between the smoke and the mist and the flying dust inside the Citadel, it was hard to call that hour between light and darkness a true dusk, but it was the time when most of us would open our C rations. We were only meters away from the worst of the fighting, not more than a Vietnamese city block in distance, and yet civilians kept appearing, smiling, shrugging, trying to get back to their homes. The Marines would try to menace them away at rifle point, shouting, "Di, di, *di*, you sorry-ass motherfuckers, go on, get the hell away from here!" and the refugees would smile, half bowing, and flit up one of the shattered streets. A little boy of about ten came up to a bunch of Marines from Charlie Company. He was laughing and moving his head from side to side in a funny way. The fierceness in his eyes should have told everyone what it was, but it had never occurred to most of the grunts that a Vietnamese child could be driven mad too, and by the time they understood it the boy had begun to go for their eyes and tear at their fatigues, spooking everyone, putting everyone really uptight, until a black grunt grabbed him from behind and held his arm. "C'mon, poor li'l baby, 'fore one a these grunt mothers shoots you," he said, and carried the boy to where the corpsmen were.

On the worst days, no one expected to get through it alive. A despair set in among members of the battalion that the older ones, the veterans of two other wars, had never seen before. Once or twice, when the men from Graves Registration took the personal effects from the packs and pockets of dead Marines, they found letters from home that had been delivered days before and were still unopened.

We were running some wounded onto the back of a half-ton truck, and one of the young Marines kept crying from his stretcher. His sergeant held both of his hands, and the Marine kept saying, "Shit, Sarge, I ain' gone make it. Oh damn, I'm gone die, ain't I?" "No you ain't gonna die, for Christ's

sake," the sergeant said. "Oh yeah, Sarge, yeah, I am."
"Crowley," the sergeant said, "you ain't hurt that bad. I want
you to just shut the fuck up. You ain't done a thing except
bitch ever since we got to this fucking Hue City." But the
sergeant didn't really know. The kid had been hit in the
throat, and you couldn't tell about those. Throat wounds
were bad. Everyone was afraid of throat wounds.

We lucked out on our connections. At the battalion aid
station we got a chopper that carried us and a dozen dead
Marines to the base at Phu Bai, and three minutes after we
landed there we caught a C-130 to Danang. Hitching in from
the airfield, we found a Psyops officer who felt sorry for us
and drove us all the way to the press center. As we came in the
gate we could see that the net was up and the daily volleyball
game between the Marines assigned to the press center was on.

"Where the hell have *you* guys been?" one of them asked.
We looked pretty fucked up.

The inside of the dining room was freezing with air-
conditioning. I sat at a table and ordered a hamburger and a
brandy from one of the peasant girls who waited tables. I sat
there for a couple of hours and ordered four more hamburgers
and at least a dozen brandies. It wasn't possible, just not possible, to have been where we'd been before and to be where
we were now, all in the same afternoon. One of the correspondents who had come back with me sat at another table,
also by himself, and we looked at each other, shook our heads
and laughed. I went to my room and took my boots and
fatigues off and got into the shower. The water was incredibly
hot, for a moment I thought I'd gone insane from it, and I
sat down on the concrete floor for a long time, shaving there,
soaping myself over and over. I dressed and went back to the
dining room. The net was down now, one of the Marines said
hello and asked me if I knew what the movie was going to be
that night. I ordered a steak and another long string of brandies. When I left the correspondent was still sitting alone. I
got into bed and smoked a joint. I was going back in the
morning, it was understood, but why was it understood? All
of my stuff was in order, ready for the five-o'clock wake-up.
I finished the joint and shuddered off into sleep.

*

By the end of the week the wall had cost the Marines roughly one casualty for every meter taken, a quarter of them KIA. 1/5, which came to be known as the Citadel Battalion, had been through every tough battle the Marines had had in the past six months, they'd even fought the same NVA units a few weeks before between Hai Vanh Pass and Phu Loc, and now three of its companies were below platoon strength. They all knew how bad it was, the novelty of fighting in a city had become a nasty joke, everyone wanted to get wounded.

At night in the CP, the major who commanded the battalion would sit reading his maps, staring vacantly at the trapezoid of the Citadel. It could have been a scene in a Norman farmhouse twenty-five years ago, with candles burning on the tables, bottles of red wine arranged along damaged shelves, the chill in the room, the high ceilings, the heavy ornate cross on the wall. The major had not slept for five nights, and for the fifth night in a row he assured us that tomorrow would get it for sure, the final stretch of wall would be taken and he had all the Marines he needed to do it. And one of his aides, a tough mustang first lieutenant, would pitch a hard, ironic smile above the major's stare, a smile that rejected good news, it was like hearing him say, "The major here is full of shit, and we both know it."

Sometimes a company would find itself completely cut off, and it would take hours for the Marines to get their wounded out. I remember one Marine with a headwound who finally made it to the Battalion CP when the jeep he was in stalled. He finally jumped out and started to push, knowing it was the only way out of there. Most of the tanks and trucks that carried casualties had to move up a long straight road without cover, and they began calling it Rocket Alley. Every tank the Marines had there had been hit at least once. An epiphany of Hue appeared in John Olson's great photograph for *Life*, the wounded from Delta Company hurriedly piled on a tank. Sometimes, on the way to the aid station the more seriously wounded would take on that bad color, the gray-blue fishbelly promise of death that would spread upward from the chest and cover the face. There was one Marine who had been shot through the neck, and all the way out the corpsmen massaged his chest. By the time they reached the station, though, he was so bad that the doctor triaged him, passed him over to treat the ones that he knew could still be saved, and when they put him into the green rubber body bag there was some chance that he was clinically alive. The doctor had never had to make choices like that before, and he wasn't getting used to it. During the lulls he'd step outside for some air, but it was no better out there. The bodies were stacked together and there was always a crowd of ARVN standing around staring, death-enthralled like all Vietnamese. Since they didn't know what else to do, and not knowing what it would look like to the Marines, they would smile at the bodies there, and a couple of ugly incidents occurred. The Marines who worked the body detail were overloaded and rushed and became snappish, ripping packs off of corpses angrily, cutting gear away with bayonets, heaving bodies into the green bags. One of the dead Marines had gone stiff and they had trouble getting him to fit. "*Damn*," one of them said, "this fucker had big feet. Didn't this fucker have big feet," as he finally forced the legs inside. In the station there was the youngest-looking Marine I'd ever seen. He'd been caught in the knee by a large piece of shrapnel, and he had no idea of what they'd do with him now that he was wounded. He lay out on the stretcher while the doctor explained how he would be choppered back to Phu Bai hospital and then put on a plane for Danang and then flown back to the States for what would certainly be the rest of his tour. At first the boy was sure that the doctor was kidding him, then he started to believe it, and then he knew it was true, he was actually getting out, he couldn't stop smiling, and enormous tears ran down into his ears.

It was at this point that I began to recognize almost every casualty, remember conversations we'd had days or even hours earlier, and that's when I left, riding a medevac with a lieutenant who was covered with blood-soaked bandages. He'd been hit in both legs, both arms, the chest and head, his ears and eyes were full of caked blood, and he asked a photographer in the chopper to get a picture of him like this to send to his wife.

But by then the battle for Hue was almost over. The Cav was working the northwest corner of the Citadel, and elements of the 101st had come in through what had formerly been an NVA re-supply route. (In five days these outfits lost

as many men as the Marines had in three weeks.) Vietnamese
Marines and some of the 1st ARVN Division had been moving
the remaining NVA down toward the wall. The NVA flag that
had flown for so long over the south wall had been cut down,
and in its place an American flag had been put up. Two days
later the Hoc Bao, Vietnamese Rangers, stormed through the
walls of the Imperial Palace, but there were no NVA left inside. Except for a few bodies in the moat, most of their dead
had been buried. When they'd first come into Hue the NVA
had sat at banquets given for them by the people. Before they
left, they'd skimmed all the edible vegetation from the surface
of the moat. Seventy percent of Vietnam's one lovely city was
destroyed, and if the landscape seemed desolate, imagine how
the figures in that landscape looked.

There were two official ceremonies marking the expulsion
of the NVA, both flag-raisings. On the south bank of the
Perfume River, 200 refugees from one of the camps were
recruited to stand, sullen and silent in the rain, and watch
the GVN flag being run up. But the rope snapped, and the
crowd, thinking the VC had shot it down, broke up in panic.
(There was no rain in the stories that the Saigon papers ran,
no trouble with the rope, and the cheering crowd numbered
thousands.) As for the other ceremony, the Citadel was
thought by most people to be insecure, and when the flag
finally went up there was no one to watch it except for a
handful of Vietnamese troops.

Major Trong bounced around in the seat of his jeep as it drove
us over the debris scattered across the streets of Hue. His face
seemed completely expressionless as we passed the crowds of
Vietnamese stumbling over the fallen beams and powdered
brick of their homes, but his eyes were covered by dark glasses
and it was impossible to know what he was feeling. He didn't
look like a victor, he was so small and limp in his seat I was
afraid he was going to fly out of the jeep. His driver was a
sergeant named Dang, one of the biggest Vietnamese I'd ever
seen, and his English was better than the major's. The jeep
would stall on rubble heaps from time to time, and Dang
would turn to us and smile an apology. We were on our way
to the Imperial Palace.

A month earlier the Palace grounds had been covered with dozens of dead NVA and the burned-over leavings of three weeks' siege and defense. There had been some reluctance about bombing the Palace, but a lot of the bombing nearby had done heavy damage, and there had been some shelling, too. The large bronze urns were dented beyond restoring, and the rain poured through a hole in the roof of the throne room, soaking the two small thrones where the old Annamese royalty had sat. In the great hall (great once you'd scaled it to the Vietnamese) the red lacquer work on the upper walls was badly chipped, and a heavy dust covered everything. The crown of the main gate had collapsed, and in the garden the broken branches of the old cay-dai trees lay like the forms of giant insects seared in a fire, wispy, delicate, dead. It was rumored during those days that the Palace was being held by a unit of student volunteers who had taken the invasion of Hue as a sign and had rushed to join the North Vietnamese. (Another rumor of those days, the one about some 5,000 "shallow graves" outside the city, containing the bodies from NVA executions, had just now been shown to be true.)

But once the walls had been taken and the grounds entered, there was no one left inside except for the dead. They bobbed in the moat and littered all the approaches. The Marines moved in then, and empty ration cans and muddied sheets from the *Stars and Stripes* were added to the litter. A fat Marine had been photographed pissing into the locked-open mouth of a decomposing North Vietnamese soldier.

"No good," Major Trong said. "No good. Fight here very hard, very bad."

I'd been talking to Sergeant Dang about the Palace and about the line of emperors. When we stalled one last time at the foot of a moat bridge, I'd been asking him the name of the last emperor to occupy the throne. He smiled and shrugged, not so much as if he didn't know, more like it didn't matter.

"Major Trong is emperor now," he said, and gunned the jeep into the Palace grounds.

from *Dispatches*, 1977

Life in the V Ring

by John T. Wheeler

KHE SANH, Vietnam (AP)—The first shell burst caught the Marines outside the bunkers filling sandbags. More exploding rockets sent showers of hot fragments zinging. The Americans dove for cover.

"Corpsman! Corpsman!"

The shout came from off to the right.

"We've got wounded here!"

"Corpsman! Corpsman!" The shouts now came from the distance. You could see the men dragging a bleeding buddy toward cover.

Inside the bunkers the Marines hugged their legs and bowed their heads, unconsciously trying to make themselves as small as possible. The tempo of the shelling increased and the small opening to the bunker seemed in their minds to grow to the size of a barn door. The 5,000 sandbags around and over the bunker seemed wafer thin.

Although it could increase their chances of survival only minutely, men shifted their positions to get closer to the ground.

Some measured the angle to the doorway and tried to wiggle a bit more behind those next to them.

There were no prayers uttered aloud. Two men growled a stream of profanity at the North Vietnamese gunners who might snuff out their lives at any moment.

Near misses rocked the bunker and sent dirt cascading down everyone's neck.

Outside the random explosions sent thousands of pounds of shrapnel tearing into sandbags and battering already damaged messhalls and tent areas long ago destroyed and abandoned for a life of fear and filth underground.

This is the life in the V Ring, a sharpshooter's term for the inner part of the bull's eye. At Khe Sanh the V Ring for the

327

North Vietnamese gunners neatly covers the bunkers of Bravo
Company, 3rd Reconnaissance Battalion. In three weeks, more
than half the company had been killed or wounded. It was
recon's bad luck to live in an area bordered by an ammunition
dump, a flightline loading area, and the 26th Marine Regiment's command post.

Shrapnel and shell holes cover the area. The incoming
rounds could hardly be noticed once the barrage stopped,
such is the desolation.

And then the shells did stop. Silent men turned their faces
from one to the other. Several men scrambled out of the
bunker to see if more dead or wounded men from their unit
were outside. Medics scurried through the area, crouching
low.

Inside one bunker a Marine returned to his paperback
book, a tale of Wild West adventure. Another man whose
hand had stopped in the midst of strumming a guitar resumed
playing. Two men in a card game began flipping the soggy
pasteboards again.

The shelling wasn't worth discussing. It was too commonplace and none from Bravo Company had been hit this time.
Like jungle rot, snipers and rats, artillery fire was something
to be hated and accepted at the same time.

But the shellfire had taken its toll. Minutes before the barrage opened, Army Spec. 4 William Hankinson had drifted off
from the other members of his communications team assigned
to this Marine base.

When the first shell hit, he dived into a Marine bunker.
After the explosions stopped, he talked with the Marines
awhile before starting back to his bunker.

A white-faced Leatherneck joined the group.

"You look kind of sick," a Marine buddy said. "What
happened?"

"The whole Army bunker got wiped out," he replied.
"Jesus, what a mess."

Hankinson started to run toward the smashed bunker
where his friends' shattered bodies lay. Marines caught and
blocked him. Then with a tenderness not at all out of place
for hardened fighting men, they began to console the Army
specialist, a man most had never spoken to before that day.

One dud mortar round was half-buried in the runway of the airstrip. Planes carrying priority supplies had to be waved off until the round could be removed.

Two demolition experts raced from shelter with fire axes and chopped it out of the aluminum sheet runway. Neither would give his name. Both had told their families they were safely out of the war zone.

"An awful lot of Marines are big liars on that point," one said.

The men of No. 2 gun, Charlie Battery, didn't think of cover when the shelling began. After what they had been through when the main ammunition dump 200 yards away exploded during an earlier barrage, "This is coasting," one gunner said.

And alone of the Marines at Khe Sanh, the artillery could fire back at the enemy. No 2 gun, commanded by Cpl. Anthony Albo, kept pouring out 105mm rounds even though a shell splinter had started a fire in the gun's ready ammo bunker.

At Charlie Med, the main casualty clearing station, wounded were coming in. Some were on stretchers, some hobbled by themselves, some were hauled in across the shoulder of a comrade.

One prayed, a few cried, some were unconscious. Many showed shock on their faces.

In between shellings, Lance Cpl. Richard Noyes, 19, of Cincinnati, Ohio, roughhoused on the dirt floor of his bunker with a friend. Noyes lives with five buddies in the center of the V Ring. The war was pushed far into the background for a moment as ripples of laughter broke from the tangled, wrestling forms.

Then the first shell of a new barrage hit.

Both men recoiled as if a scorpion had been dropped between them. Even though they were underground in a bunker, everyone put on helmets. Across the front of his "brain pot," Noyes long ago had written in ink, "God walks with me."

A blank stare in the eyes of some is not uncommon at Khe Sanh where the Communists have fired up to 1,500 rounds of rockets, artillery and mortar shells in a single day.

It is called the 1,000-yard stare. It can be the sign of the beginning of combat fatigue.

For Noyes and thousands of others at this surrounded combat base, the anguish is bottled up within tolerable limits.

Noyes had had luck, lots of it. A rocket once drove through the bunker's sandbags and exploded, killing 4 and wounding 14 of the 20 men inside. Noyes was slightly wounded.

It was Noyes' second Purple Heart. One more and he automatically would be sent out of Vietnam under Marine regulations. Noyes doesn't want the third medal.

Despite heavy casualties, the survivors of the recon company are frightened but uncowed. When the call for stretcher bearers comes, the young Marines unhesitatingly begin wriggling through the opening in their bunker to help.

At night the men in Noyes' bunker sit and talk, sing, play cards, almost anything to keep from being alone with their thoughts. During a night when more than 1,000 rounds hit Khe Sanh, Noyes turned to a buddy and said:

"Man, it'll be really decent to go home and never hear words like incoming shells, mortars, rifles, and all that stuff. And the first guy who asks me how it feels to kill, I'll . . ." A pause. Then: "You know, my brother wants me to go duck hunting when I get home. Man, I don't want to even see a slingshot when I get out of here."

Lt. C. J. Slack of Carlsbad, Calif., said: "When I get back to California, I'm going to open a bar especially for the survivors of Khe Sanh. And any time it gets two deep at that bar, I'll know someone is lying."

Noyes smokes heavily and his hands never seem to be entirely still. Looking at the side of a cigarette pack, Noyes said with a wry smile, "Caution, Khe Sanh may be hazardous to your health. Oh, man, yeah."

Still later, he called out, "Okay, we're going to sing now. Anyone who can't sing has to hum. Because I said so. Okay, let's hear it."

Lance Cpl. Richard Morris, 24, of North Hollywood, Calif., began playing a guitar. Two favorites that night were "Five Hundred Miles" and "Where Have All the Flowers Gone?"

A hard emphasis accompanied the verse that went: "Where

have all the soldiers gone? To the graveyard every one. When will they ever learn? When will they ever learn?"

Finally the two small naked light bulbs were turned out and the Marines struggled toward sleep.

AP wire copy, February 12, 1968

Hanoi—March 1968

by Mary McCarthy

"Attachez vos ceintures, s'il vous plaît." "Fasten your seat belts." The hostess, plump, blonde, French, brown-eyed, in a light-blue smock, passed through, checking. It was funny to find a hostess on a military plane. Like the plane itself, loaded with mail, canned goods, cases of beer, she was a sort of last beep from the "other" world behind the mountains in Vientiane. Born in Hanoi, she had been making the run from Saigon with the I.C.C.—Poles, Indians, Canadians, of the inspection team—six times a month, weather permitting, for thirteen years, practically since the Geneva Accords.

As the I.C.C. plane, an obsolete non-pressurized Convair, circled in the dark above Hanoi, waiting to get the OK to land, out the window, by stretching against our seat belts, we could see tiny headlights of cars moving on the highways below and then the city all lit up like a big glowworm. In Phnom Penh, at the North Vietnamese Delegation, where they issued our visas, they had prepared us for this surprise, but it remained a surprise nonetheless. I thought of the Atlantic coast during World War II and the blackout curtains we had had to buy on the Cape—a Coast Guard order designed to foil enemy submarines. When the Convair taxied to a stop, it instantly doused its lights, though, and the hostess held a flashlight for the boarding officials to examine our papers. But then the airport, brilliant white and blazing with electricity. "You really don't have a blackout!" I exclaimed to the delegation from the Vietnamese Peace Committee who had come to meet us, with bouquets of snapdragons, pink sweet peas, pale-pink roses, larkspur, and little African daisies. A Japanese author and a journalist from a Tokyo paper were receiving bouquets, too. The Vietnamese did not know the word "blackout," and I tried *couvre-feu.* They dismissed the term "curfew" with laughter. "Passive defense!" In fact, there was no curfew of any sort in Hanoi—except the bell that rang at eleven o'clock nightly, closing the hotel bar—though there was one in Saigon. It was only when the sirens blew that the lights of the city went out and the cars and trucks halted and waited for the All Clear.

On the way from Gia Lam Airport into the city, we had our first alert—a pre-alert, really, given by loud-speakers; the pre-alert usually means the planes are sixty kilometers away; it is not till they are within thirty kilometers of the center that the sirens scream. Suddenly, still deep in the countryside, the driver braked the car; he had heard the pre-alert on his radio. He turned off the engine. I sat in the back seat, holding my bouquet in my lap and feeling quite apprehensive. On March 17, two days before, the much-feared swing-wing F-111A's had appeared in Thailand; there had been pictures of them in the Bangkok papers. The driver got out of the car. "He is looking for the shelter," one of my companions explained. "He has found the shelter," they announced a few minutes later, and we all climbed out of the car. In the moonlight, we could see the remains of a brick house, with its roof torn off; up the lane, there had been a hamlet, but now there were only indistinct masses of debris and, somewhere in the dark, the shelter, which I never actually saw. It was enough to know that it was there.

Outside Hanoi, the driver's first job, I discovered, was to look for a shelter for the passengers whenever the alert or the pre-alert sounded. Every hamlet, sometimes every house, is equipped with a loud-speaker, and the alarm is rung out by the hamlet bell—the same bell that calls the peasants to work in the fields. When there is no hamlet nearby, a band of young soldiers, tramping along with a transistor radio, may warn you that the planes are coming. Once, in Hoa Binh Province, out in the west, I sat huddled in the car with the thin, large-eyed young woman interpreter while the driver conducted the search; he came back, and there was a quick conference in Vietnamese. "Here there is no shelter," she whispered, gravely touching my arm, as we listened to the bombs, fortunately some miles off. Though the shelter may be only a hole in the ground, the assurance that there is such

a burrow handy gives a sort of animal comfort—possibly not
unlike the ostrich's. Or maybe it is a grateful sense that somebody, an unknown friend, has thought about your safety; even
if the uncovered earth shelter cannot protect you from a direct
hit, the thought, as they say of small presents, is what counts.

In the city, there are individual cement cylinders, resem-
bling manholes, every few feet, with round fitted covers of
cement or of plaited reeds—good against fragmentation
bombs. In a pinch, they will accommodate two small Vietnamese. But what happened, I wondered, if there were more
people on a given street when the alarm sounded than there
were shelters to hold them? As in a game of going to Jerusalem or musical chairs, who would be left outside? It is a
schoolmen's problem, that of the outsider, which is posed in
the scramble of extreme situations, and I was curious—anxious, even—about the socialist solution. But I never was able
to observe for myself what did in fact occur: in my two and
a half weeks in North Vietnam, it chanced that only once was
I in the city streets during an alert and then only long enough
to see the people scattering as our driver raced toward the
hotel and its communal shelter. And I felt that it would be
somehow impolite to express my curiosity in the form of a
point-blank question; there are many questions one does not
want to ask in Hanoi.

In any case, the target of the Hanoi government is one
shelter per person within the city limits—I am not sure
whether this ratio takes into account the communal shelters
attached to institutions. During my stay, hundreds of brand-
new cylinders were lying along the sidewalks, waiting for the
pavement to be dug up and holes sunk to contain them, and
every day trucks kept dumping more. Production and delivery
were ahead of the picks and shovels. "Manufacturing shelters
is one of our principal industries now," people remark, rather
ruefully, watching the gray cylinders being put into place.
What can be done with these grim manholes, war memorials,
when and if peace comes? The only answer I could think of
was to plant flowers in them.

Johnson's speech of March 31—and the subsequent eerie
absence of alerts—did not cause even a momentary flagging
in the shelter program. Yet, so far as I could tell, the shelters

were more a symbol of determination than places to scuttle
to when the planes approached. The city population had a
certain disdain for using them. "There are toads in them," a
pretty girl said, making a face. Like the white-gowned surgeon
I met, a Hero of Labor, who had calculated the statistical
probabilities of being killed by a bomb in the night and decided that he preferred to stay in bed, to be fresh for operating
the next morning, many people in Hanoi decline to leave their
beds or their offices when the peremptory siren shrills; it is a
matter of individual decision. Only foreign visitors are hustled
to safety by their guides and interpreters and told to put on
their steel helmets or their pellet-absorbent hats of woven
reeds or straw. A pellet in the brain is the thing most dreaded
by the Vietnamese—a dread that as a brain-worker I more
than shared; unfortunately the hat they gave me was too small
for my large Western head, and I had to trust to my helmet,
hurriedly strapping it on as I trotted down the hotel stairs to
the communal shelter and glad of the excuse of social duty to
do what private fear was urging.

Your guides are held responsible by the authorities if anything happens to you while you are in their care. This applies
particularly to guests invited by North Vietnamese organizations (which we were); accredited journalists are allowed more
rein. I was asked not to go out into the street alone, even for
a short walk, though the rule was relaxed when the bombing
of Hanoi stopped on April 1—Hanoi time. This of course
limited one's bodily freedom, but I accepted it, being a law-
abiding person. Our hosts of the Peace Committee told us
that they had been severely reprimanded because some frisky
young South Americans had eluded their control last summer
and roved unsupervised about the country; one got a pellet
in the brain and had to be sent by plane to Moscow to be
operated on; he lived. Whenever we traveled, one of the comrades of the Peace Committee made sure I had my helmet by
personally carrying it for me. I was never alone, except in bed
or writing in my room. In the provinces, when we stayed at
a guest house or came to inspect a village, each time I went
to the outlying toilet, the young woman interpreter went with
me as far as the door, bearing my helmet, some sheets of tan
toilet paper she had brought from Hanoi, and, at night, the

trusty flashlight. She waited outside till I was through and then softly led me back.

That first night, driving in from the airport, everything was novel. The driver had left the radio turned on in the car when he switched off the lights. We could hear it talking, as if to itself, as we paced up and down, and I had the foolish notion that the planes, wherever they were, might hear it, too. Other shadowy sedans and passengers were grouped by the roadside; there had been a great influx at the airport that night because for over three weeks, four times running, the I.C.C. flight had not been able to make it down the narrow air corridor from Vientiane to Hanoi. On the road we had passed several cars with diplomatic license plates, one, surely, containing the Indonesian ambassador, who had boarded the plane with his golf clubs; he used them to exercise on his lawn. Now abruptly all the headlights went on again; motors started. "They are going away. They are going away," the radio voice had said in Vietnamese; the pre-alert was over.

Activity resumed. A chattering stream of people, mostly young, was flowing along the highway from the city, walking or riding bicycles and motor bikes: boys in work clothes or uniforms, with camouflage leaves in their helmets, girls and women, some riding pillion, carrying baskets of salad greens and other provisions; now and then a wrinkled old peasant, in black, with balance-pole on shoulder or pushing a cart. A cow raised its head from a field. All that nocturnal movement and chatter gave an impression of revelry, as if a night ball game or a theater had just let out; probably a work shift had ended in the factories. Along the road's edge cases of supplies were stashed, covered with jute or tarpaulin. Jeeps and military trucks, some heavily camouflaged, were moving steadily in the opposite direction.

We were passing pretty rows of small, compact trees—perhaps pruned fruit trees; it was too dark to tell—a pre-alert to the fact that Hanoi is a shady, leafy city, like Minneapolis or Warsaw; like Minneapolis, too, it has lakes, treated as a municipal feature, with parks and promenades. The people are proud of the trees, particularly of the giant camphor, wreathed in a strange parasite with dangling coinlike leaves. Near the bombed brick house where we waited during the alert, there was a big bare blasted trunk, maybe an oak, which was putting out a few new leaves; my companions eagerly pointed them out, making sure I did not miss the symbol of resistance and rebirth. To the North Vietnamese, I soon became aware, everything is now a symbol, an ideogram, expressing the national resolve to overcome. All of Nature is with them, not just the "brother socialist countries." Nodding their heads in time with a vast patriotic orchestra, they are hearing tongues in trees, terrible sermons in stones and the twisted metal of downed aircraft. In Hung Yen Province, you eat a fresh-caught carp under a red-and-white-nylon canopy, like a billowing circus tent enclosing the whole room; it is the giant parachute of the pilotless reconnaissance plane they have shot down. Near Hanoi, in a village co-operative, raising model pigs and making handicrafts, they show you a small mute cluster bomb, olive drab, and, beside it, the mute rusty primitive soil-scratching implement the young peasant was using in the co-operative fields when pellets from the cluster bomb killed him. Visual education, they feel, for the people, and they are not afraid of hammering the lesson in. But it is Johnson, finally, they wish to give food for thought.

Growth statistics, offered everywhere, on bicycle ownership, irrigation, rice harvests, maternity clinics, literacy are the answer to "the war of destruction," which began February 7, 1965; a bombed oak putting out new leaves is a "reply" to the air pirates of the Air Force and the Seventh Fleet. All Communist countries are bent on furnishing growth statistics (it is their form of advertising), but with Hanoi this is something special, carrying a secondary meaning—defiance. On a big billboard in the city center, the number of U.S. planes shot down is revised forward almost daily in red paint—2,818, they claimed when I left, and the number keeps growing. In villages, the score is kept on a blackboard. Everything they build is dated, down to the family wells in a hamlet—a means of visibly recording progress, like penciling the heights of children, with the dates opposite, on a door. And each date has a clear significance in the story of resistance: 1965 or 1966, stamped on a well, proclaims that it was built *in spite of* the air pirates.

Hanoi, it is whispered, is going underground, digging shelters, factories, offices, operating theaters, preparing for "the worst," *i.e.*, for saturation bombing by the B-52's or even—draw a deep breath—for atom bombs, although if you mention those to one of the leaders, he tersely answers that Johnson is not crazy. This feverish digging, while dictated no doubt by a very practical mistrust of the Pentagon, seems to have a secondary meaning, too—mythic, as though the city were an allegorical character. Hanoi appears to be telling its people that it is ready to go underground, harrow hell, to rise again like the rice plants from the buried seed. To a Westerner, this sounds fantastic, so much so that I hesitate to bring it up; after all, you can tell me, Hanoi's leaders are Marxists, and Marxists do not believe in resurrection stories.

Yet the Vietnamese folk beliefs are highly animistic; they venerate (or did) the souls of their ancestors, resting in the rice fields, and the souls of rocks and trees. Their classic relief sculpture surprises you with delicate, naturalistic representations of plants, birds, animals, and flowers—much more typical of Vietnamese art than grotesque images of gods and the Buddha. The love of Nature is strong in their literature, too, and is found even in the "captured enemy documents" the U.S. is fond of distributing for publication. This helps explain their root-attachment to the fatherland, as every observer has noticed, going deeper than politics, into some sphere of immanence the foreigner is almost embarrassed to name—"spiritual," "religious"? Much is made in the North of the fatherland's sacred, indivisible unity, and, despite or because of a history of partitions like Poland's, the sentiment of being one country seems to be authentic and shared, incidentally, by the South Vietnamese firebrands who would like to "march on Hanoi." As a symbol of that unity, the North has planted the coconut palm; the visitor may be slow to grasp the significance of this. "Coconut trees." "Yes, I see them." "Before, here in the North, we did not have the coconut tree. It is a native of Saigon."

In Hanoi you find cabbages and tomato plants growing in the ornamental garden of a museum, in parks, around an anti-aircraft unit; the anti-aircraft battery has planted a large flower garden as well and it has chickens running around the gun-emplacements. Today the abundant use of camouflage—exuberant sprigs of plants, fronds, branches, leaves of coconut and banana on helmets, anti-aircraft, military vehicles, even tied to the backs of school children—cannot be meant entirely to fool the enemy overhead. For one thing, the foliage on the anti-aircraft artillery does not begin to conceal the guns' muzzles. This camouflage, snatched from Nature, must be partly a ritual decoration, a "palm" or "laurel" of prowess and connected with ancient notions of metamorphosis—pursued by a powerful enemy, you could "survive" in the verdant form of a tree. In Hanoi, the innocent protective mimicry of coconut leaves "disguising" military hardware always made me think of Palm Sunday in a Catholic country and the devout coming out of church with palm leaves or olive branches—a pre-Easter mood. In the country, a column of army trucks and half-tracks proceeding under its thatch of greenery made me feel that Birnam Wood was rolling on to Dunsinane: "Your leavy screens throw down,/And show like those you are."

The determination of Hanoi appears at first incredible—legendary and bizarre; also disturbing. We came eventually to the pontoon bridge, floating on bamboo, the replacement, for automobiles, of the Paul Doumer Bridge that still hangs, half bombed, like a groping tentacle, over the Red River. On the bridge, the traffic goes single file, and you wait for the oncoming cars to finish their turn before a policeman gives you the signal to advance. This waiting in line by the river's edge is scary—there has been a lot of bombing in the area, as you can see by looking around—and it is even scarier when you start across the frail, wavy bridge; traffic moves very slowly, with many halts, and if the bombers should come while you are there, suspended over the water, there would be no escape; useless to look for shelters on the insubstantial bridge, obviously, and you could not jump into the dark, quite swift river. You just have to put your mind on something else, make conversation; I always dreaded this crossing, the sense of being imprisoned in a metal box, a helpless, all-but-motionless target, and I had the impression that the Vietnamese did not care for it either; each time, there was a general easing of tension when the bridge was finally negotiated.

In the hotel, to my stupefaction, there was hot water, plenty of it. During nearly a month spent in South Vietnam the year before, I had had *one* hot bath—on the U.S.S. *Enterprise*. In my room at the Continental in Saigon, there was only cold water, and when I was once offered a bath in the room of a New York *Times* correspondent, the water ran dark red, too rusty to get into. In theory, they had hot water in the Marine Press Base at Da Nang, but in practice they didn't. Other luxuries I found at the Thong Nhat Hotel were sheets of toilet paper laid out on a box in a fan pattern (keys at the desk were laid out in a fan pattern, too), a thermos of hot water for making tea, a package of tea, a teapot, cups and saucers, candies, cigarettes, and a mosquito net draped over the bed and tucked in; in Saigon, I had been tortured by mosquitoes.

It was obvious that the foreigners at the Thong Nhat lived better than the general population, but this could be said, too, of the foreigners at the Continental, who moreover had to pay for what they got, whereas in Hanoi a guest of a Vietnamese organization was not allowed to pay for anything—I never had to change so much as a dollar bill into dongs. The knowledge of living much better than others (the meals were very good) and at the expense of an impecunious government whose food-production areas were being pounded every day by my government produced a certain amount of uneasiness, which, however, wore off. There was nothing to be done about it anyway, and I soon was able to verify that outside no families were sleeping in the streets, as they had been in Saigon, nobody was begging or in rags, and the people appeared healthy, though tired in some cases, particularly those who were old and had doubtless been hungry a good part of their lives.

On opening the window, I found that there was an extraordinary amount of traffic, extremely noisy traffic, though nobody in Hanoi owns a private car—only bicycles and motor bikes. The honking of horns and screeching of brakes went on all night. To someone who lives in a European city where it is against the law to honk your horn, the constant deafening noise seems very old-fashioned. My ears had forgotten those sounds, as they had forgotten the clanging of streetcars and the crowing of cocks at 4:00 A.M. Hanoi still has both cocks and streetcars, and you can hear the whistle of trains, as well as the more up-to-date noise of MIGs overhead and the

almost continuous voice of the loud-speakers, invariably fem-
inine and soothing, sugared, in tone. Unless you know Vietnamese, you cannot guess whether they are announcing an air
raid or telling you the planes have left or simply giving a news
broadcast or a political diatribe.

There is a good deal in North Vietnam that unexpectedly
recalls the past. Waiting to cross the Red River recalled my
first trip to Italy, just after World War II, when most of the
bridges were down ("Bombed by the Liberators," in Italian,
was scrawled all over the devastated cities and towns) and our
bus crossed the Po or the Adda on a tremulous pontoon
bridge; the loud-speaker outside the hotel window ("Attention, citizens, attention") recalled the loud-speakers in
Florence during a spring election campaign (*"Attenzione, cit-
tadini, attenzione"*). Jouncing along a highway deeply pitted
by pellets from cluster bombs made me think of my childhood: bumpy trips in northern Minnesota; Grandma in a mo-
toring hat and duster; and how each time we struck a pothole
her immense white head, preceded by the hat, would bounce
up and hit the car's canvas top. North Vietnam is still pioneer
country, where streams have to be forded; the ethnic minor-
ities, Meos, Muongs, and Thais, in the mountains of the wild
west, though they do not wear feathers, recall American Indians. The old-fashioned school desks and the geometry lesson on the blackboard in an evacuated school, the kerosene
lamps in the villages, the basins of water filled from a well to
use to wash up before meals on an open porch, the one- or
two-seater toilets with a cow ruminating outside brought back
buried fragments of my personal history. I was aware of a
psychic upheaval, a sort of identity crisis, as when a bomb lays
bare the medieval foundations of a house thought to be
modern.

The daytime alerts in the hotel reminded me very much of
fire drill in school. During my stay there was no bombing near
the hotel, though the siren sometimes sent us to the shelter
as often as six times in twenty-four hours. After a while you
estimate the distance of the explosions you hear—six kilometers, ten, fifteen—and you think you can tell the dull, re-
sounding noise a bomb makes from the crackle of ack-ack. In
the hotel, I began to have a feeling of security, like the veteran

correspondents who usually did not bother to get up during night raids or who, if they were up already, wandered out into the street to watch the anti-aircraft activity. In the daytime, it became a slightly tiresome routine to walk, not run, to the shelter, where a delegation of Chinese in gray uniforms—who never spoke to anyone—were always the first arrivals, and wait for the All Clear. And as in the case of fire drill, I began to half wish for some *real* excitement, for the bombs to come a bit nearer and make a louder bang. It got to be a disappointment if the alert was a false alarm, *i.e.*, when you simply sat in the shelter and heard no action at all. The other foreigners must have felt the same way, for when the explosions were noisy and the guns replied, the conversation in the shelter became much livelier, and there were giggles.

An alert was also a social event; you saw new faces and welcomed back old friends—that is, people you had known a few days—reappearing from a trip to Haiphong or Nam Dinh. One day in the shelter I met the Danish ambassador to Peking, and another time a whole diplomatic dinner party, men in dark suits, large, freshly waved ladies from the bloc countries in low-cut silks and satins, an Indian lady in a truly beautiful blue sari, joined us drab "regulars" on the underground benches, having left their double rows of wine glasses and their napkins on the table of the hotel's private dining room, reserved for parties—this eruption, as of a flight of butterflies, was a momentary wonder in our somewhat mothy, closet-like existence.

The late-night alerts were different. Though I had concluded that there was no real danger of bombing in the immediate neighborhood of the hotel—unless Johnson escalated again, with B-52's or "nukes," in which case my personal survival was not of any interest; I would not care to survive—at night, when the shrilling of the siren waked me, I forgot and would jerk up from the pillow with my heart pounding, grope my way out of the mosquito netting, find the flashlight in the dark, slippers, dressing gown, et cetera, and stumble, still unnerved, down the stairs and out through the hotel garden, pointing my flashlight down, searching for the entrance to the shelter. Those late-March night raids made everybody angry. According to the Vietnamese, who were experts on such matters, they consisted of one or two planes only, whereas before they had come in large purposeful waves; their object now must be psychological—without any military pretext—to harass the population at random, deprive it of sleep, while at the same time lessening the risk to themselves of being shot down, for it is harder to hit a single plane in the sky than to pick off one or two out of a serried dozen or twenty.

No planes, so far as I know, were shot down over Hanoi during my stay, though one, they said, an Intruder, had been shot down the day of our arrival. The foreign correspondents agreed that the bombing was slowing down, at least in the region of Hanoi, and they wondered whether the Americans could be short of planes, on account of the number destroyed or damaged in the late-January Têt offensive. The date of manufacture stamped on a shot-down plane was always of great interest; if a plane manufactured in July was shot down in August, this suggested that stocks were low.

In fact, though we did not know this in Hanoi, the "return" of the bombing, in dollars terms, had been added up early in the year by the accountants in Washington. The April number of *Foreign Affairs* was revealing that it had cost the U.S. six billion dollars to destroy an estimated 340 million dollars' worth of facilities: clearly a low-yield investment. The cost in lives of U.S. pilots in comparison with estimated North Vietnamese losses seems not to have been computed—where, on the balance sheet, would the lone target, working in a rice field, of an anti-personnel bomb figure? Left out of the calculations also—surely an oversight?—was the cost to the North Vietnamese government of the shelter program, not to mention the cost of the loud-speakers and the personnel to man them.

Only once in the city while I was there did a bomber "sneak through" the warning system. It happened once in the country, but there it was less spectacular to hear the thud of bombs before, so to speak, listening to the overture of the sirens; in the country, as I said, there are no sirens anyway and surprises were to be expected. In Hanoi, it happened one evening at the Museum of War Crimes, when we were sitting down to little cups of tea at a long table following a tour of the exhibits. Suddenly, there was a long-drawn-out, shrill, banshee-like, shrieking noise, succeeded by a shattering explosion. At the same time, out the window, we could see a plane streak across the sky. The museum director, an officer in uniform, rushed us out into the garden; guiding me by the arm, he was propelling me toward the shelter. Big red stars looking like skyrockets were bursting in the dark overhead. Then the siren must have blown, though I have no memory of hearing it. In the museum's shelter, we heard more bombs exploding. "The museum is near the bridge," the interpreter murmured, as if to excuse the fact that a raid had come so close. When the All Clear sounded, we went in and found the tea cold in our cups. Back at the hotel, during the next alert, one of the guests told us that there had been three bombs and a Shrike.

To return from a shelter to a disarrayed table where the tea has grown cold in the cups and resume a conversation at the precise point it had left off ("You were saying . . . ?") is a daily, sometimes an hourly, occurrence in the North—inevitably so, since tea is served visitors on every ceremonious occasion, and all occasions, however sickening or painful, are ceremonious. Hospitality requires that tea should be served at the beginning and end of any visit: tea, cigarettes, candies, and long slender little cakes that taste of bananas. The exceptions were the Journalists' Union and the War Crimes Commission, both of which served beer, and the prison where the captured pilots were held, which offered a choice of beer or a soft drink, plus bananas. I could never make out the reason behind these slight variations of an otherwise inflexible precept. It was easy to guess why beer was served to journalists (newsmen drink), while the Writers' and Artists' Union served tea, but why beer at the War Crimes *Commission* and tea at the War Crimes *Museum*? Maybe beer is more expensive, and Mr. Luu Quy Ky of the Journalists' Union and Colonel Ha Van Lau of the War Crimes Commission had bigger budgets than the others. In some instances, tea was followed by coffee.

Perhaps I should have asked, but the Vietnamese are sensitive, and to wonder aloud why beer was served instead of the customary tea might have been taken, I thought, as a criticism of the hospitality: "Why did they *not* serve tea?" In the same way, I was reluctant to ask why in some co-operatives, factories, and associations there were portraits of Marx, Engels, Lenin, Stalin, and Ho, while in others there was only Ho. Was it a matter of personal preference on the part of the administrator? That did not appear likely. Once, in a village co-operative I thought I saw Marx, Engels, Lenin, and Ho, and no Stalin—which made a joyful impression on me—but when I got up from my chair, I found that Stalin had been behind me all along, chuckling. The explanation may be that if the center you are visiting is a branch headquarters of the Lao Dong (Workers') Party, you get the whole pantheon; otherwise, only Ho. The absence of portraits of Mao and of the current Soviet leaders seemed self-explanatory ("Vietnam asserts its independence"), but it could not be remarked on, any more than you can remark to a host on the absence of certain persons who you might have thought would be invited to a party.

In the War Crimes Museum, that evening, among the exhibits they had showed us a Shrike, so that the sudden advent of the live missile had the air, to us, of a coincidence ("Speak of the devil . . ."), but of course, to the North Vietnamese, nearly all the exhibits in the museum "matched" what was befalling them regularly. The museum, unlike that at Auschwitz, is strictly contemporary. There were cluster bombs—guavas and pineapples—some of the delayed-action type, regarded as the most fiendish, ordinary placid TNT bombs of varying weights, ranging from babies of 200 to big daddies of 3,000 pounds, rockets, an assortment of missiles, crop-spraying powders (with the results in a bottle), tear gases, front and rear views of patients hit by a spray of pellets from the "mother" bomb, X rays of pellets in human skulls, photos of napalm and phosphorus victims (napalm has not been used in the vicinity of Hanoi and Haiphong, or, as the Vietnamese say, "not yet"), quite a collection of exhibits. And shuffling about among the displays was a small middle-aged Vietnamese woman in a bunched sweater, wide trousers, and sandals, who was staring, as if drawn by some morbid, fascinated curiosity, at the weapons and devices in the glass cases, at the big bombs arranged, like modern metal sculptures, on the floor; she bent to read the labels, sometimes furtively touched. They told us, lowering their voices, that she had been haunting the museum ever since she had lost her twenty-year-old son early in the year.

An American apologist might claim that she was an exhibit, too, a "plant" to invoke the sympathy of soft-headed pacifists and other bleeding hearts, but in fact the museum personnel seemed somewhat put out by her presence and by the occasional snuffling, sobbing noises she made, interrupting the scholarly presentation of the material. In short, they reacted like museum officials anywhere who were not lacking in heart but had their professional duties, which included discouraging nuts and people with "troubles" from intruding on official visits. It was true, she *was* causing our attention to stray. Then, as if guiltily conscious of being a disturbance, she would hastily quiet down and regain her composure, peering into the glass cases with an air of timid wonder, like a peasant viewing the tools of modern civilization and wondering what they were for. She seemed to be trying to put her lost son and these efficient implements together in some satisfactory manner, as though to make a connection and localize the source of her pain. Sometimes, appearing to find it for a moment, she actually smiled and nodded to herself.

She had gone, I guess, when the Shrike came. Perhaps one of the museum employees had persuaded her to go home finally or given her some tea in the kitchen. To tell the truth, when the Shrike came I forgot about her; I had got used to the fact that during an alert the ordinary Vietnamese—chambermaids, cooks, waiters, desk clerks, tea servers—vanished from sight, only to reappear when the alert was over. Either they proceeded to their own shelters, separate from those for foreign guests, or, like the chambermaids in the hotel who doubled as militia, they shouldered guns and went up to the roof, or they continued quietly with their jobs, like the cook I once glimpsed in the hotel sitting in his white apron and hat at the kitchen table when the All Clear blew. The siren was a Last Trump separating the sheep—us—from the nimble goats. At the National Liberation Front Delegation, the distinction was marked by a heavy dark-brown curtain dividing the communal shelter between personnel, on one side, and, on the other, the Chief of Mission, his immediate staff, and his guests. To an American, such a frank distinction appears *ipso facto* undemocratic.

At the museum, in a parting ceremony, they presented us with rings made from downed U.S. aircraft. Like a wedding ring, mine is engraved August 1, 1966—the day the plane was shot down—and has the initials H. Y., which must stand for Hung Yen Province. They also gave me a woman's comb of the same material. Such souvenirs seem to be popular in Hanoi, but though, as they watched, I murmured *"Merci beaucoup"* and hurriedly, like one rapidly swallowing medicine, tried the blunt ring on my finger, I instantly slid it off and dropped it into my handbag; luckily, I had the excuse that it was a man's ring: too big. Back in the hotel, I shut it up in a drawer out of sight, but it kept troubling my mind, making me toss at night, like an unsettled score. For some reason, the comb, scalloped in the Vietnamese style, did not bother me.

Perhaps, if I had had the courage, I might have declined to take the ring, handed it back to the Vietnamese as soon as I realized what it was. As my grandmother tried to teach me, one need never be afraid to say no. But from their point of view, it was a symbol of friendship, a medal pinned on my chest. They were proud to bestow it. What was it that, deeper than politeness, which was urging me to do so, made it impossible for me to keep it on my finger, even for a few minutes—just not to give offense? Maybe the premonition that if I once put it on, I could never take it off; I could not sport it for the rest of my stay and then get rid of it as soon as I left the country—that would be base. Yet equally repugnant to my nature, to my identity, whatever that is, to the souls of my ancestors, would be to be wedded for life or at least for the duration of this detestable war to a piece of aluminum wreckage from a shot-down U.S. war plane. Or was it just the fact that it did not "go" with my other jewelry?

Nor could I drop it in the wastebasket of my hotel room. The chambermaids would find it and return it to me: *"Votre bague, madame."* Or, worse, they would feel that, to me, their friendship band was rubbish. But if respect for the feelings of others forbade my junking it in a wastebasket of the Thong Nhat Hotel, then there was no sea anywhere deep enough for me to drop it into. I had to keep it. The comb, presenting no problem, a simple keepsake and rather pretty, remained openly on my bureau in the Thong Nhat with my other toilet articles. Yet I now slowly realize that I never passed it through my hair. Mysterious. I cannot explain the physical aversion, evidently subliminal, to being touched by this metal. Quite a few of the questions one does not, as an American liberal, want to put in Hanoi are addressed to oneself.

from *Hanoi*, 1968

The U.S. Negro in Vietnam

by Thomas A. Johnson

SAIGON, South Vietnam—The Army sergeant with the coal-black face muttered: "What in the hell am I doing here? Tell me that—what in the hell am I doing here?"

But there was a smile on his face.

At the moment, he and the men of his under-strength platoon—about half of them Negroes—were crouching on a jungle trail as artillery shells pounded the brush 100 yards away.

At the same time, some 50,000 other Negroes in Vietnam were unloading ships and commanding battalions, walking mountain ranges and flying warplanes, cowering in bunkers and relaxing in Saigon villas.

They were planning battles, moving supplies, baking bread, advising the South Vietnamese Army, practicing international law, patrolling Mekong Delta canals, repairing jets on carriers in the Tonkin Gulf, guarding the United States Embassy, drinking in sleazy bars and dining in the best French restaurants in Saigon, running press centers, digging latrines, driving trucks and serving on the staff of Gen. William C. Westmoreland, the American commander.

They were doing everything and they were everywhere. In this highly controversial and exhaustively documented war, the Negro, and particularly the Negro fighting man, has attained a sudden visibility—a visibility his forefathers never realized while fighting in past American wars.

Fourteen weeks of interviews with black and white Americans serving here reveal that Vietnam is like a speeded-up film of recent racial progress at home. But Vietnam also demonstrates that the United States has not yet come close to solving its volatile racial problem.

Why was the sergeant—a 34-year-old career soldier—in Vietnam?

349

He talked with good humor of the "good Regular Army" to a Negro correspondent, he shuddered with anger recalling that his home-town paper in the Deep South called his parents "Mr. and Mrs." only when referring to their hero son, and he pointed out that he had stayed in the Army because his home town offered only "colored" jobs in a clothing factory where whites did the same work for higher pay.

Most often, Negro and white civilians and career soldiers see Vietnam as a boon to their careers and as a source of greater income than at home. It was not unusual to hear civilians and career soldiers—Negro and white—express such views as, "Hell, Vietnam's the only war we've got."

For the Negro there is the additional inducement that Southeast Asia offers an environment almost free of discrimination.

One civilian remarked, "Bread and freedom, man, bread and freedom."

To the ordinary Negro fighting man, Vietnam means not only integration but also an integral role in American life—or at least this aspect of American life.

" 'The man' can't overlook talent when he wants the job done," said S. Sgt. James Frost, a 29-year-old Negro from Youngstown, Ohio.

In the job of battle, fighting prowess and dependability quickly erase color barriers. Staying alive becomes more important than keeping stateside racial patterns.

During the battle for Hue in February, a knot of white and Negro marines stood knee deep in the mean red mud beside their tank. They were grimy-faced, beard-stubbled and grease-spattered.

They peered across the Huong (Perfume) River, where, more than 300 yards away, unseen North Vietnamese gunners had just given up a mortar and artillery duel.

"They're through for now," said Sgt. Eddie Dailey, a Negro from York, Pa.

"It looks like it," said a white marine with field glasses.

It was 9 A.M., but from somewhere a bottle of liberated Black and White scotch was produced and passed around. "Integration whisky," someone commented.

"And that's just what's winning this Goddamn battle," the Negro sergeant said.

A white lance corporal agreed. "You're damn straight, bro," he said. The Negro shorthand for "soul brother" seemed to slip out naturally.

As the corporal, John Tice of Savannah, Ga., passed the bottle, a tattoo could be seen on his bare right arm. It showed a Confederate flag and the words "Johnny Rebel."

"That's just what's gonna win this Goddamn war," Sergeant Dailey spat. "Integration, Goddamn it."

With the integration of the armed forces in the late nineteen-forties and early fifties, the military quickly outdistanced civilian efforts at breaking down color barriers. This has continued to a point where young Negro men flock to military service for the status, careers and security that many cannot find in civilian life.

A junior infantry officer, who is white, commented:

"It's an awful indictment of America that many young Negroes must go into the military for fulfillment, for status—and that they prefer service overseas to their homeland."

The war in Vietnam is filled with ironies, and one of the biggest is that the ordinary Negro fighting man—and especially the teen-age front-line soldier—is not aware of the Negro's participation in previous American wars.

An 18-year-old Marine private at Dongha said proudly: "The brother is here, and he's raising hell. We're proving ourselves."

Officers in Saigon at the headquarters of the Military Assistance Command, Vietnam, say the heavily Negro 173d Airborne Brigade is the best performing unit in Vietnam.

This correspondent went in with the second helicopter wave when the Fourth Battalion of the 173d struck a Vietcong supply base in a thickly forested area of Phuyen Province.

Taking cover in tall grass, he found himself with a young Negro paratrooper, a private first class whose face had not yet sprouted a serious growth of beard.

"What you doin' here, bro?" the paratrooper asked. "You gonna do a story on the Fourth Battalion?"

Without waiting for an answer he kept talking.

"You tell them that the 173d is the best Goddamn outfit on this rock. We were the first brigade-size combat unit in Vietnam."

His squad was ordered forward, but he kept talking:

"Tell them we made the first combat jump in Vietnam on Operation Junction City, and that the Fourth Battalion is the best in the 173d. You tell them that—tell them we took Hill 875 at Dakto and that we are steadily kicking Charlie's rear."

Only then did the paratrooper stand up, and as he ran with his squad he called back:

"You tell them, you hear?"

Capt. Robert Fitzgerald, a Harlem-born intelligence officer on General Westmoreland's staff, commented:

"They feel they're the first Negroes to fight because their history books told only of white soldiers, and their movies showed that John Wayne and Errol Flynn won all American wars."

The 31-year-old officer went on: "The only uniform they've seen on Sidney Poitier was a chain-gang suit, and—oh, yes—that of an Army truckdriver once."

Talk of race often leaves white servicemen bored, embarrassed or annoyed. Many say the problem is overly stressed, and many Negro servicemen, especially the teen-aged, first-hitch foot soldiers, say the same thing.

But a Negro sailor stationed in Saigon noted:

"The question of race is always there for the Negro. He would either be blind or insane if it were not. But Vietnam is a buffer or isolation ward to the whole question of race as we know it."

If Vietnam is an isolation ward, then combat is a private room off the ward where the ordinary G.I. can bring to bear the special skill for which he has been trained—killing. And white or black, the G.I.—usually referred to here as a "grunt" or a "crunch"—is adept at his specialty. The élite units—the airborne, Marines, air cavalry and Special Forces—to which Negro youths flock are among the best of these specialists.

A paratroop officer commented:

"The crunch wants to fight, pure and simple. He's one hell of a fighter, and we couldn't win any war without him because he lives, eats and sleeps to fight. You don't fight wars

with gentlemen—that is, you don't win wars with gentlemen."

The grunt is no gentleman.

His average age is 19, and he left high school without fin-
ishing. His skills are with the M-16 rifle, the M-60 machine
gun, the M-79 grenade launcher, hand grenades and bayonets.

He brags and swears and swaggers, and he runs to a fight.
He runs into battle when the first shot is fired, screaming or
cursing, as if he does not believe he can be killed.

He can be, however, and he is.

He is killed and wrapped in a green paper blanket and put
off to one side until a truck or a helicopter can take him to
the rear.

Then he is remembered during quiet times by other young
soldiers and marines who still rush into battle, screaming and
cursing as if they cannot be killed.

And during those quiet times other things come out.

Like that night in a pitch-black front-line bunker, when it
was comforting to hear one another's voices, and the correspondent learned how it was after the Fourth Battalion of the
173d took Hill 875 from a determined enemy force, a force
that "had chewed up the Second Battalion."

"We hugged and kissed one another like Girl Scouts, and
we cried," said a voice in the darkness.

An Army chaplain comments: "Their anxiousness to prove
themselves as men makes them quickly absorb the lesson the
military is anxious to teach."

That lesson, an infantry platoon sergeant said, "is to make
every man feel that he's in the best army, the best division,
the best brigade, the best battalion, the best company, the best
platoon, the best squad—and that he's the best Goddamn
man in that squad."

And the Negro youngster—from the high-school basketball
team, the sharecropper's farm or the riot-ready slums—has
consistently volunteered for the élite of the military fighting
forces.

"You take a good look at an airborne rifle company and
it'll look like there ain't no foreign [white] troops there," one
Negro commented.

Dr. Kenneth B. Clark, the Negro psychologist, has noted

that a "status not readily available in civilian life" causes Negroes to join the military service at a rate two to three times greater than that for whites, and then to volunteer for élite units.

"There is no chance of asserting his manhood and demonstrating his sense of worth in civilian life," said Dr. Clark, who heads the Metropolitan Applied Research Center in New York.

Dr. Clark said the ferocity demonstrated by young frontline soldiers could be related to their youth and their eagerness to prove themselves. He noted that after the 1943 riots in Harlem he interviewed a youth who "got a terrific boost out of the destruction."

Dr. Clark added: "A few months later he was a soldier, in uniform and with a riding crop, and getting an even bigger kick out of potential destruction he could legally cause."

The Negro makes up 9.8 per cent of the military forces in Vietnam, but close to 20 per cent of the combat troops and more than 25 per cent of such élite Army units as the paratroops. Estimates of Negro participation in some airborne units have been as high as 45 per cent, and up to 60 per cent of some airborne rifle platoons.

A Negro private first class in the Fourth Battalion of the 173d Airborne Brigade said that when he joined the unit in the summer of 1967 "there were 20 brothers and 8 foreign troops" in his platoon.

About one in every four of the Army's front-line supervisors in the grades of sergeant first class and master sergeant is a Negro, a fact attesting to the higher Negro re-enlistment rate in the armed forces in general and the Army in particular.

The re-enlistment rate for first-term Army men in 1965 was 49.3 per cent for Negroes and 13.7 per cent for whites; in 1966 the figures were 66.5 and 20.0. Re-enlistment figures for 1967 have not been completed, a Pentagon spokesman said. Generally, the rate in the Army runs at least three times as high as for whites, and in the other services two times as high.

The present Negro death rate in Vietnam is 14.1 per cent of total American fatalities; for 1961 to 1967 it was 12.7 per cent. Late in 1965 and early in 1966 the Negro death rate soared to about 25 per cent, and the Pentagon ordered a cut-back in front-line participation by Negroes.

It is in the front lines that commonly shared adversity has always sprouted quickly into group loyalty and brotherhood. And whether between white and white, Negro and Negro, or Negro and white, Vietnam is no exception to the tradition of battlefield brotherhood.

"The stereotypes they had believed just sort of melt away," said Capt. Richard Traegerman, a 25-year-old West Pointer from Philadelphia. "Whites see Negroes are as intelligent and brave as anyone else, and Negroes see whites are just guys with the same strengths and weaknesses as anyone else."

A Negro soldier said he felt that the Negro underwent more of a change than the white.

"The Negro sees the white boy—really sees him—for the first time," he said. "He's just another dude without all those things to back him up and make him bigger than he is—things like a police department, big job or salary."

And a long-time front-line observer said:

"It's the most natural thing in the world to come out closer than brothers after a few days on the line. Up here it's a real pleasure to just be warm and dry or to feel a cool breeze; to have fresh water, a heat cube for C rations; to wash or take off your shoes or to be alive when others are dying. This will make any two people brothers."

For the most part, Negroes in Vietnam say that the closest thing to real integration that America has produced exists here.

"It's the kind of integration that could kill you, though," a Negro sailor remarked.

There are reports of racial discrimination, racial fights and instances of self-segregation, but most Negroes interviewed said these instances were greatly outweighed by racial coop-eration.

In effect, while participating in a war that pits yellow people against yellow people, America is demonstrating that its black and white people can get along.

So pervasive is this demonstration that some Negroes, in discussing the prejudice of lowland Vietnamese toward the

mountain-dwelling and usually primitive montagnard tribesmen, convey the idea that discrimination against Negroes has
ended at home as well as in Vietnam.

Oscar Roberts, an Army captain stationed at Pleiku as an
adviser to the South Vietnamese Army, pointed up this attitude when he remarked: "The montagnards are treated the
way we used to be treated back home."

But then he smiled and added: "The way we used to be
and still are treated some places back home."

Other Negroes did not remember, or smile, or correct
themselves.

Race is quite often a laughing matter among servicemen in
Vietnam.

Sgt. Charles C. Hardy, a 21-year-old marine from Chicago,
was on duty one night in Danang and gave his bed to a visiting white friend, but not without some specific admonitions.

"That sack has lots of soul," he said. "It's a soul-recharging
station, so you'd better be careful. I don't want to see you
wake up tomorrow morning thinking you can talk trash and
trying to dance the boogaloo and the philly dog, you hear
me?"

Some of the "brothers" in an airborne unit held a "soul
session" to "cuss Chuck," the white man. When a late-arriv-
ing brother inquired what a "couple of Chucks" were doing
attending a soul session, it was explained that they were "hon-
orary souls," and the Chuck-cussing continued.

And after watching a plea for brotherhood on a television
set in a bunker in the Central Highlands, a youth of Mexican
origin spoke up.

"All right," he said. "Which one of my Goddamn brothers
is going to buy me a beer?"

He got the beer, but not before the whites and Negroes
unleashed a barrage of anti-Mexican remarks that included:
"Give me, give me, give me! A Goddamn spec 4 in the Regular Army and he still thinks he's on relief! Give me, give me,
give me!"

Even the highly potent taboo on interracial sex is much less
a taboo in Vietnam than it was in the military in past years.

A white officer from North Carolina visited the luxurious
Saigon apartment of a Negro officer from Illinois, carrying a

dozen red roses for the Vietnamese Lunar New Year, Tet. Their friendship dated from the time they both commanded segregated airborne companies at Fort Bragg, N.C., in the late forties.

While discussing a double date with Vietnamese girls that the Negro was arranging, they reminisced about the "German broads" and Japanese women they had known.

Walls and lockers, from neat hotels in Saigon to red-earth bunkers in Khesanh, have both white and Negro pinups, regardless of the race of the serviceman.

Some bars tend to be predominantly white or predominantly Negro. This is especially true in the rear areas where the permanently assigned and normally noncombatant troops gather every day. In Saigon, for example, it is mostly whites who frequent the bars along Tu Do Street, while Negroes predominate in the Khanh Hoi area across the Saigon River along Trinh Minh The Street.

It is not uncommon, though, to find both races in both locations, and to see integrated teams making "skivvy runs"—forays in search of bar girls. And white and Negro servicemen talk to the same bar girls.

Still, there is much off-duty separation of the races, and most of it is voluntary separation by Negroes. There are several reasons, not the least of which was expressed by a high Negro civilian official:

"Wherever you have a lot of American whites with a lot of time for relaxing," he said, "then you can figure that the brother is in for a little difficulty."

A German in Vietnam asked a Negro civilian if he was aware of how some American whites talked about Negroes when they were alone. The Negro said he was.

"Do you know that they call you animals," the German said, "that they say you have tails and that they seem especially anxious that foreigners—myself and the Vietnamese—hear this?"

"I know," the Negro said.

"What's wrong with them?" the German asked.

"They're white Americans," he was told, "a strange breed of people."

A Negro field-grade officer said he relaxed only around

Negroes and put up an "aloof" and "even unfriendly" front around whites.

"You don't want to overextend yourself because you never know when whites are for real," he explained. He went on to suggest that the Negro officer must often be a "super Negro."

"I see white officers bringing Vietnamese girls into our quarters and getting away with it," he said, "and I wouldn't think of joining them. Whites prove every day how vulnerable the 'successful' Negro is in our society. If they can go to such great length and bend the rules to kick Adam Powell out of Congress and take Cassius Clay's title, they can certainly get to me. I don't intend to give them the chance."

Still, separation and aloofness are not rigid situations and attitudes.

A Negro specialist 4 in an infantry outfit said:

"I got some white friends who are 'for real' studs, and, hell, they could call me anything and do anything they want, because I know they are for real. I know some other Chucks who I'd most likely punch in the mouth if they said good morning to me, because I know they are some wrong studs."

A rear-echelon Negro private first class, sitting in a bar in Saigon's Khanh Hoi with a white friend with a Deep South accent, started to discuss why Negroes segregate themselves.

"White people are dull," he said. "They have no style and they don't know how to relax."

"What do you mean?" the white youth interrupted.

"Shut up," the Negro said. "I'm not talking about you, nigger. I'm talking about white people."

Another Negro, explaining why he frequented the Negro-owned "soul food" places in Saigon—such as the L & M and the C.M.G. Guest House, both of which have white and Negro clientele—said:

"Look, you've proven your point when you go out and work and soldier with Chuck all day. It's like you went to the Crusades and now you're back relaxing around the Round Table—ain't no need bringing the dragon home with you."

The term "soul session" is often used here to describe Negro efforts to "get away from 'the man,'" to luxuriate in blackness or to "get the black view." These sessions occur in front-line bunkers and in Saigon villas, and quite often they include some "for real" whites.

Negro V.I.P.'s who come to Vietnam find that despite full schedules a "brother" will get to them with a dinner invitation so the visitors can get "down to the nitty-gritty."

Senator Edward W. Brooke of Massachusetts, Whitney M. Young Jr. of the Urban League and the Rev. Ralph D. Abernathy of the Southern Christian Leadership Conference are among those who have got the benefit of the black view.

"Sometimes it doesn't do too much good, from what some of the black V.I.P.'s have said when they got back home," one soul-session advocate said later.

Self-segregation does not attract all Negroes, and there are some who shun any appearance of Negroes' getting together, no matter what the purpose.

There are Negro officers and civilians in Saigon hotels who prominently display record albums by Mantovani and Lawrence Welk and hide albums by such soul-sound purveyors as James Brown and Aretha Franklin.

"A lot of the brothers feel they can't be themselves and integrated," said Lieut. Col. Felix L. Goodwin, a Negro veteran of 27 years of Army service.

"This dates back to the time the Army was first integrated and we all felt we had to show whites we were not prejudiced," the colonel added. "Most of us feel comfortable enough now to be both black and integrated, and we think this is healthy."

While integration is fairly recent in the military, Negro participation in American wars is as old as the country's history.

Negroes were with Columbus, the Conquistadors and Henry Hudson. They fought the Indians in Nieuw Amsterdam and the English in the Revolutionary War. Three thousand fought in the War of 1812, and Commodore Oliver H. Perry described them as "insensible to danger."

In the Civil War, more than 200,000 black men wore Union uniforms, and the Confederacy began organizing Negro units toward the end of the war.

Negroes were at Little Big Horn with Custer. They helped to chase the Sioux into Canada, they captured Geronimo and they pursued Billy the Kid across the Southwest. Some runaway black slaves and their descendants fought on the side of the Indians.

Ten thousand Negroes fought in the Spanish-American War, and a group of Negro cavalrymen rescued Theodore Roosevelt's Rough Riders in the battle of El Caney.

A controversy over the fighting qualities of the Negro combat soldier began in World War I. The all-Negro 369th Infantry Regiment stayed under fire for 191 days without relief—longer than any other American unit—and was the first to fight its way to the Rhine.

But the 368th, also all Negro, was sent to the rear as a result of confusion and disorder after five days at the front in the Oise-Aisne offensive.

The controversy was renewed in World War II as a result of reports that the all-Negro 92d Infantry Division in Italy "melted" when it met German troops. After an investigation a Negro aide to the Secretary of War reported that some units—not all—had made "panicky and disorderly" retreats and had shown "a lack of will to fight."

But the report also pointed out that many of the men did not know how to use their weapons, and the Army learned during World War II that the efficiency of any unit fell off sharply when more than 10 per cent of its men had scored in the lowest grade of the general classification test. The 92d went into battle with 50 per cent of its men in the lowest grade and 90 per cent in the two lowest.

The controversy subsided during the Korean war as a growing number of units were integrated racially.

The Negro's ability and willingness have not been questioned in the war in Vietnam, and have in fact been consistently praised.

In a speech to fellow South Carolinians last year, General Westmoreland said: "The performance of the Negro serviceman has been particularly inspirational to me. They have served with distinction. He has been courageous on the battlefield, proficient, and a possessor of technical skills."

Courage—and often bravado—is the young combat soldier's long suit.

"When America invented the grunt, she legalized thuggery," one front-line observer said. "When I'm out with grunts and the Vietcong fires on us, I'm damn glad she invented them."

A young Negro marine in war-ravaged Hue typified the grunt's bravado, his eagerness to fight, his disbelief that he can be hurt or killed.

The marine sat on a naval landing craft on the Huong River, bound for the Citadel, once the seat of the Vietnamese imperial government and now, during the Tet fighting, South Vietnam's major killing ground.

"Put me in your paper," the marine told a correspondent.

"What can I say about you?" the newsman asked.

"You can say Lance Cpl. Raymond Howard, 18, better known as 'Trouble,' from Bay Manette, Ala., squad leader, Second Platoon, Delta Company, First Battalion, Fifth Marine Regiment, is going 'cross the river to kick him a few behinds."

The New York Times, April 29, 1968

A Small Contribution

by Kevin Buckley

EARLY in the morning, while the mist still clung to their base camp at Loc Ninh, about 180 men of Alpha and Delta companies, First Battalion of the 28th Infantry, First Infantry Division, set off on what seemed likely to be nothing more than a grueling trudge in the mud. Their mission was to reconnoiter the scene of an earlier battle in the vast rubber forest west of the camp and to make sure that all North Vietnamese troops had left the area.

For the first few hours, the going was easy. The sun was not yet overhead, and the earth, dark in the shade of the rubber trees, was cool and soft. In the distance, we heard the rattle of gunfire, and soon the radio crackled with the news that another unit, patrolling south of Loc Ninh, had run into an ambush. But for us, the only disconcerting experience came when Delta Company, which was in the lead, spotted what appeared to be a partially concealed land mine and sent a man up to detonate it. The "mine" turned out to be an overturned rubber dish, a soup-bowl-shaped container that workers hang from the trees to collect the sticky, white latex.

By late morning we had reached the scene of the earlier fighting. There were big gouges in the rubber trees, and caved-in enemy bunkers were everywhere. But there seemed to be no sign of life and Delta Company passed through the battleground without incident. Then, as Alpha Company came up, the whole area erupted. North Vietnamese automatic-weapon fire came pouring out of the jungle and we all scrambled for cover. Curiously, one of the first things that caught my eye were tracer bullets—ricochets from enemy sniper fire—floating up into the trees like strange, glowing embers.

As the men of Alpha Company began to return the fire, Lt.

362

Edward J. Knoll, 21, the company commander, strode out into the open and started to pump round after round into the underbrush. Then, suddenly seized by doubt, he stopped. "Cease fire, cease fire," he shouted. "That might be Delta in there . . . Cease fire, damn you!"

There was a moment of stillness and then a fresh burst of enemy fire came blasting out of the jungle, trimming the leaves over our heads. "Screw it! Fire! They're gooks all right," yelled Knoll. "Gimme a blooper [grenade launcher] quick. We're gonna get some gooks."

The din resumed, louder and more intense than before. Up ahead, Delta Company was exploding smoke grenades to mark the edges of its position so that Alpha would not fire in that direction. With enemy fire chipping the bark off the trees around him, Sp/4 Washington Norfleet, a Negro from Baltimore, raced up to Knoll and handed him a blooper. "Move down! Cut them off!" screamed Knoll. Then he and Norfleet—who had taken over the lieutenant's sawed-off M-16—moved out ahead, pumping bullets and grenades into the jungle.

After a while, Knoll called a halt to the firing and shouted for a South Vietnamese interpreter who was along with us. Knoll wanted the interpreter to call on the enemy to *chieu hoi*—give themselves up. But the Vietnamese, who had "Make Love, Not War!" written on his helmet, was flat behind a tree, his head wrapped in his arms, and he refused to budge. "No chieu hoi. Just kill them," he called out. Then he raised himself slightly, spoke the words "chieu hoi" and flopped down again. At this point, possibly out of disgust, Knoll indulged in pure bravado by relieving himself against a tree in what seemed to me to be full view of the enemy troops.

Strangely enough, the Communists seemed to hold their fire until Knoll was through. Then they opened up again. "I don't think they want to chieu hoi," said Knoll reflectively—at which point someone shouted, "There they go." A handful of enemy soldiers were trying to make a run for it from the brush jungle to bunkers and interconnecting spider holes, and Alpha, moving after them, opened up with everything it had. "Good work, good work," I heard Knoll say over and over.

"I saw one little bastard," he said to one man. "He peeked out from behind that tree and started going and I got him with my blooper right in the head."

Finally, the shooting stopped again. What was left of the enemy unit had fled, and now, at Knoll's order, we moved forward to investigate. There were four enemy dead—all disfigured with gaping wounds. "OK, you mother, you tried to kill my buddies, didn't you," said one GI as he hefted the corpse of the first dead North Vietnamese we came to. "Look at that. He's got a hat made out of one of our poncho liners. The rotten little bastard. I'm gonna wear that hat now, blood and all."

Quickly, the men of Alpha Company stripped the dead enemy soldiers of their gear—star-buckled belts, knives and AK-47 assault rifles. Then they placed "Big Red One" shoulder patches on each dead face before leaving the battlefield for the trip back to camp. "We let those people know who's been through the area," Norfleet said as we moved out.

Newsweek, October 14, 1968

"We Lived for a Time Like Dogs"

by Zalin Grant

Frank Anton: Willie Watkins slowly took over as camp leader. He was the strongest. When there was work to be done he did it. From there it grew to his having the crucial say about what and when to cook. He then began to make other decisions too. It was never outward that he ran the place. He didn't say, "I'm the chief." But he was. I guess you would call Watkins a good-looking Negro. He was a little over six feet tall, lanky, with very dark skin and penetrating eyes. He kept his hair short and himself neat. He was wiry and hard as a rock, could carry two sixty-pound baskets of manioc easier than I could walk. And he seemed never to get sick.

At the beginning Kushner, Williams, and myself got together and discussed what we should do. The person who led the camp had to be physically strong. None of us was. We decided to try to use our influence as a group. We made no attempt to create a military organization. The VC warned us individually several times that if we did we would be punished. Moreover, we weren't sure of our legal rights in the matter. Kushner was a captain but a doctor and therefore a noncombatant. I was a warrant officer, a pilot with no command responsibility. Williams was a first sergeant but wounded.

Eventually Watkins let us know that since we couldn't work our decisions would be limited. Some of the others followed him, saying, "That's right. Anybody who tells me what to do has to work at least as hard as I do." Willie had the Negroes organized on some questions. He got them off to the side and spoke to them about what they should do. I don't know what they talked about, but it was bad for our morale. At times they took care of each other. At other times they were split.

No racial comments were made in camp, although a couple

of guys didn't like Negroes. Joe Zawtocki, for example, didn't talk about Willie being a Negro but being Watkins. "I hate that black sonofabitch," he would say. Strictland got along with the blacks okay because he could work. Harker did too but he didn't like Willie. Actually it came down to who could work and who couldn't.

The Vietnamese went to Willie when they wanted to know something about the camp or to organize an activity. Watkins got the information from them and told us. In this respect he had pushed out Russ Grissett, who served at first as our communications link with the VC because he'd been there longest and spoke a little Vietnamese. But the VC hated Russ and they liked Willie. They liked him mainly because he worked hard and never talked back. Willie, unlike most of us, always called Garwood Mr. Dao, as the VC ordered us to do. He hated Garwood, that was obvious, but he kept it to himself. He was very secretive.

Daly. Russ Grissett told us when we first got to camp, "In the jungle the lion is king. To survive you must live like an animal." Kushner and I tried to argue that it didn't have to be that way. But eventually it was exactly as Grissett said. We fought and carried on. We lived for a time like dogs. I even took part in it myself, yes.

Anton. Watkins could have whipped anybody in camp—that was the point. Everyone thought so. Davis, who was several inches shorter and also very strong, had a certain influence over Watkins. Frequently Davis disagreed with him but they never fought. Willie liked Davis. He would bargain and barter with him before it came to blows. Several people tried to fight Willie. Lewis was one. Watkins took care of him with a single lick.

Daly. That's true. Everybody was afraid of getting beat. Watkins once pounded the stew out of Joe Zawtocki. Kushner and Anton swore they would make Watkins pay for it if they ever got back to the States. They didn't say this in front of Watkins, though. I thought since we were a military group the leadership responsibility should have been Captain Kushner's. He always said the obligation was not his because he was a noncombatant. He said the one who should be in charge was Sergeant Williams. But Williams was wounded. Many people felt Kushner was using this as an excuse to avoid responsibility.

We all admired Captain Kushner. He helped us with his medical advice. But the man was lazy. The first time we argued was when I told him it was his turn to sweep the hootch floor. He refused. He said he hadn't gone to college for so many years to sweep floors. I said, "Wait a damn minute. I didn't go to school for twelve years to sweep either. But everyone has to take his turn." He also said that before he would carry manioc he wouldn't eat them. You couldn't believe he was so lazy. But he did change. Anton never did.

Harker. Dr. Kushner was an intellectual caught in a situation where physical strength was the chief virtue. He was, as his wife Valerie said in *Life* magazine, the type of guy who would tell her to mow the lawn because he didn't want to mess up his hands. I was famous for jumping on his back. I guess I was letting off steam. Davis was the serious type. He believed, like Watkins and Strictland, in working or else. He would get into hassles with Kushner but Kushner would sweet talk him out of it. It was true that Kushner and Anton were sick. But we were all sick. And sometimes you simply had to push yourself beyond your limitations.

Watkins. Kushner was a nice guy, easy to get along with, but he was soft, and I was especially suspicious of him. I felt he was strong enough to pick manioc. All of us felt that way. We thought it was mainly laziness. He said he couldn't go. We said, "If you don't bring back more than two or three that will be helping." He said walking was bad for his feet, that he could hardly make it. We said we felt the same way. Still, if we didn't pick them we would probably starve. Finally we told him, okay, no work, no eat.

Anton. I didn't like Watkins but I had respect for him. What he did was wrong. Yet he didn't do it with malice. He did it because he was strong and lacked judgment. He took over without really trying. He did a lot for people who were sick, so much that I would have to overlook the bad part. He helped people when they were down and did not say anything about it whether he thought they were faking or not. Willie hated Williams. Why we could never figure out. Yet he helped Williams. He carried him to the latrine when he was down. He was that type of guy; he could hate but still help you.

Everybody at first tried to work. That's my opinion. Right away people got sick. I myself was sicker than the others because I didn't eat rice in the beginning. Kushner and I went down fast. We remained weak after that. At first we went for firewood. We had to get it every day because we could never get enough, and there were no complaints. Then my load got smaller and smaller. If I carried a piece the other prisoners wanted to know why I couldn't carry ten pieces. If ten pieces, why not twenty? When I carried none I heard the snide comments, "Last time you carried some, why can't you do it now?" I didn't mind it so much when it was said to my face. But I knew they were talking behind my back. I couldn't pick manioc at all.

Kushner didn't think that being a doctor excused him from working. He was sicker than everybody realized. All they understood was that "I'm doing all the work and he's eating half the food." That's the way it was. Kushner confided to me he felt terrible about not being able to help more. He would get depressed and go off by himself. The VC jumped on him more than anybody else. Some of this, of course, was his own fault. He would argue with anybody about anything.

The Vietnamese saw what was happening to us. I don't know whether they planned it. But there were signs they encouraged our antagonisms. I remember Mr. Ho said that so and so doesn't work yet he eats as much as the others. He told Watkins and Davis they should have more because they did half the work.

Yet it was not the VC but a skin disease that pushed us into our darkest period and caused a near-fatal split between us. Daly came down with it first, which was unusual since the blacks were less susceptible than we were to disease. But he was lighter-skinned than the other four, a coffee-and-cream color, and though big, perhaps more fragile. It quickly spread, some catching it worse than others.

Harker. The disease was probably caused by a lack of vitamins and oil. It was unlike anything ever seen by Dr. Kushner. The epidermis cracked open with water-blister-type sores that first ran clear serum and then pus. Scratching was almost sexual in its relief but only made the disease worse. The pus dried, gluing our pajamas to our backsides. The pain was horrible. Eighteen of us were jammed together on the bed. It was excruciatingly hot. But we had to sleep under our blankets to ward off hordes of mosquitoes. Men cried out at night, "Kill me! I want to die!" Guys began to schiz out in the daytime by pulling blankets over their heads to shut out the world. The disease was combined with our growing dysentery and malaria. The hootch smelled like a septic tank. It was best not to get up at night unless absolutely necessary. Probably you would step in excrement while walking down the aisleway.

The skin disease broke out before Mr. Ho arrived. It jumped from man to man. Ho saw the condition we were in. It was he who ordered the VC to build us another hootch. The VC had divided us several months earlier into two nine-man squads. At the time it meant nothing. The squad leaders were mostly responsible for giving the VC a head count in the mornings and evenings. Now Watkins' squad was moved to the new hootch. Our squad, headed by Strictland, who replaced Grissett, stayed in the old hootch.

Ho possibly had ideas about Strictland, and maybe that was why he was made a squad leader. All of us thought constantly about being freed. But even though you wanted to go along with the VC for this reason things sometimes got so ridiculous that you questioned them before you could catch yourself. "You don't understand," the VC would say. "You imperialists have aggressed us."

"Oh, yeah, how could I ever forget?"

Strictland made few mistakes of this sort. He was quiet and went along without arguing. He was rather short, boyish-looking, with cool blue eyes and light freckles. He was strong as a bull and a hard worker. He had been brought up on a tobacco farm in North Carolina and was drafted after high school. That's what the VC liked about him. Their idea of a "progressive" was someone who killed himself working.

Strictland. I did anything they said. Other guys argued with them. Some they'd have to hit in the head to make them get out of bed. The VC might come to the hootch and say, "We need five guys to carry grass to build us a house."

I'd say, "I'll go." Watkins and this guy Davis, we'd go do it. I didn't mind. I felt like I was just getting by. Surviving.

Anton. The VC separated the two nine-man squads into two hootches and it just so happened that most of the strong and healthy men were concentrated in one squad. Watkins, Davis, Denny, Joe Zawtocki. In fact myself and Long, who was captured when a special forces camp was overrun, were about the only ones in our squad who couldn't work. But almost everyone in the other squad was sick with the skin disease or other ailments. Harker and Strictland were the stronger members of the second squad. Harker had a terrible case of the skin disease. Strictland had serious kidney trouble, he was pissing blood.

Separating us into two hootches turned out to be like putting us into two different countries. We became enemies. At first there was a compromise about work. Watkins told the other hootch, "You send two guys on a manioc run and we'll send three or four." Then it got to the point where we'd send three and they'd send just one. Resentments built up. I irritated the other squad because I wasn't working, yet my squad was complaining about them. No one said much about Long because he was ill from the moment he arrived in camp.

The VC killed a pig on September 2 to celebrate North Viet Nam's Independence Day. Before going to eat with the Vietnamese, Grissett said, "Let's show them today how Americans act. No reaching and grabbing. Two people serve and no one eats till everyone has his food." Everyone agreed. The food was placed on the table. Grissett and someone else began politely serving the others.

Suddenly Grissett said, "Fuck this," and dumped half a plate of meat into his bowl, squatted on his haunches, and began to shovel it in. The meal deteriorated into the usual reach and grab.

That's where we were at this point. Our mental condition had begun to match our physical condition. We had no shoes, toothpaste, soap, or mosquito nets. All of us had bed sores from the hard bamboo. Rats ran rampant through the hootch at night. They were unbelievably brave. Sometimes they crawled up and sat on our arms. I guess they sensed we were one of them.

Davis. The split began one day in my hootch. Watkins, Denny, and Joe Zawtocki were talking about the guys in the other hootch being lazy. Everybody had the skin disease. We returned from manioc runs with our hands swollen and bleeding. Petty irritations became hard resentments and then anger. Some of my squad thought some of the other squad were goofing off. Some thought Dr. Kushner had too much education to work. Everybody was sick and feeling sorry for themselves, that's what it was. So we said why don't we split up and let each hootch worry about itself.

Harker. We hadn't had to work while Ho was there. The Vietnamese had done everything for us so we could attend class. The quality and quantity of our food was a little better during this time. The vacation ended and we had to face the reality of scrambling for ourselves again. The skin disease and the separation into two hootches opened the way for the breach.

The split started the day after the September 2 celebration. The other hootch said they had taken a vote at the end of August and had decided that my squad must henceforth gather its own firewood and manioc and do its own cooking.

We said, "You're crazy. Somebody will die."

They said, "This is the way it's going to be."

I was mad at Watkins. I later found that Denny had a big say in the matter too. It was like a slap in the face. I thought Watkins didn't understand the situation. A lot of men in my squad were deathly sick.

The decision to split apart was theirs. But we played the game like them. All of us played. Things became competitive and petty. Some of my squad were in the Vietnamese kitchen after the September 2 celebration and saw a pot of leftover pig fat. We brought it back to our hootch. Instead of going eighteen ways, it went nine.

Anton. We had one kitchen, a small shed with a mud-packed stove and an underground chimney to disperse the smoke. During the split we took turns using it. The other squad took an extra long time when they cooked. Whether on purpose or not I don't know. In retaliation the people cooking for us also took an extra long time. We ended up eating only two meals a day instead of three. And for about a week each group had only one meal; one group in the morning, the other in the afternoon, because they couldn't get into the kitchen till then.

Harker and Strictland did most of the work for the other squad. Harker had lost a lot of weight and like myself was very thin. He was of medium height, with a shock of brown wavy hair, a full mouth, and teeth that could have used braces when he was a kid. He was basically a loner. He and I simply ignored each other at first and seldom spoke. He was a hard worker, though, and good with his hands. Everybody respected him for this.

Davis. There was animosity. Some guys from one squad didn't talk to the other squad while the split was on; but I did.

McMillan. My foot hadn't completely healed. A lot of people said I was shamming. They thought I should have gotten up quicker. But I couldn't walk well, it was impossible to hump up and down the rocks. Kushner would go on a manioc run and couldn't bring back but two or three. He wasn't built for it, he just couldn't do it. Daly couldn't carry a heavy load either, would stumble and fall and tear up two manioc baskets before he got off one run. Fred could do nothing; he was swollen with edema. Even Grissett had fallen very sick.

Watkins did a lot of things to piss people off. It wasn't that he was sympathizing with the VC. But, goddamn, he was trying to cover his ass in the long run. He didn't do that much to be progressive. Kushner did everything to be done because he was an officer and the VC were always on his back—they forced him to do it. Watkins didn't do any more than Kushner. But the fact was Watkins was truthful about the things he did. He was honest. That was one reason why the Vietnamese liked him.

But he didn't understand our situation. Even before the split Watkins told Kushner, Daly, and myself that either we worked or he would cut off our chow. In fact he did cut us for one day. It surprised me as a black man that he would do that to another black man. I said, "This dude must be crazy." Any man in his right mind could have seen we weren't able to work. If he had a little sympathy he would have known.

Will didn't look at things that way. He was hard. One day

I walked into the kitchen to get some water when he was cooking. He told me to wait a few minutes till chow was ready. I tried to get the water anyway. He said, "If you get it I'm gonna knock your teeth down your throat."

Damn, man, I'm looking up at a big dude, almost twice as big as I am. Plus that he had once boxed in the Golden Gloves. I said, "Okay, man, if that's the way you want it."

Davis was in that squad with Watkins and Denny. Davis wanted to get along with everybody and he did; everybody liked him. But as I said to Kushner, "If a man tells Davis to jump off a mountain, he'll jump." I told Davis this to his face. I said, "If I'm in a situation where a man told me not to cook your rice and said he would beat me if I did, I wouldn't cook for you. But I would at least take some of my rice to you."

During the split, don't get me wrong, some guys were talking to each other. But I wasn't speaking to no damn body.

Davis. I didn't want any part of the camp leadership. I didn't want to be always hassling others about what they should do. We were all men. I was about as strong as Watkins. If it had come down to a fight it would have been a pretty good one. He never gave me any static. Maybe because we were both black and there was a mutual respect.

Harker. I got up before dawn early in September and went to take a leak. When I returned I saw Cannon lying on the floor near the firepit. He often sat up at night and slept in the daytime. He was in terrible pain and there was so little room on the bed that his movements disturbed the others. He was making a strange noise. I went to investigate. He said, "I'm trying to get back on the bed." But he wasn't moving. I realized he was in a sad state. He went into a coma later that day, and passed away after a few hours.

The VC made a bamboo coffin. We dug his grave. They came to the hootch and said, "Here are some white clothes to bury him in."

We said, "Take your clothing back. We don't want anything. You didn't give him anything when he was alive." They were insulted, and left.

They must have realized that we felt very strongly about it for us to talk back to them. Later they called us to a meeting.

The camp commander said, "Why do you think Cannon died?"

We said, "Because he did not have proper medical care or adequate food."

The VC said, "No, he died because of his wounds and because he didn't clean himself."

We argued with them. They became irritated. We backed off.

Anton. Williams had grown weaker after the political course. He had a bad case of edema. The fluid had swollen his testicles to three times their normal size, they were unreal, watery looking; his legs and stomach were swollen and the fluid had begun to press toward his heart. If Kushner had had the simple diuretics available in any pharmacy, he could have saved his life. It was especially hard on him watching men die whom he knew he could save if medicines were available. But nothing was available, or if it was the VC waited as usual until it was too late.

Williams lay fatally ill some days. Watkins carried him to the latrine, others washed him. The VC gave him a can of condensed milk. Kushner warned him not to drink it without diluting it because it was too sweet in concentrated form and would complicate his dysentery. By this time, however, Williams was practically incoherent. He drank it straight. One morning several weeks after Cannon died we awoke to hear Williams breathing strangely. In a couple of hours he was dead.

A few weeks after Williams it was Sherman's turn. He had never recovered from the time spent in stocks after the escape attempt. He had hung on the following months like a walking zombie, sitting outside when the sun was out, inside on the bed when it wasn't. We reminded him of his Marine Corps stories, trying to make him talk and take an interest in living. He couldn't remember them. Sometimes he laughed and smiled. But he wasn't there. And finally he died.

McMillan. Usually the two squads didn't talk to each other but that night in November we did. Joe Zawtocki was up by the kitchen when he called me. Me and Joe got along pretty good because Joe blew pot. All the guys who blew got along,

I associated with them. Anyway, Joe says to me, "Hey, Ike, want some pussy?"

I said, "Yeah, man."

He said, "You're gonna have to eat it."

I went to see what he wanted. He had the camp cat with him. Grissett, Harker, and Strictland had planned to kill the cat and eat him. Trouble was, nobody could catch him. I returned and told everyone we had the cat.

Somebody asked, "Who's gonna kill him?"

I said, "I'm not gonna kill him. I've done had enough of bad luck with cats."

They said, "What do you mean?"

I remember when I was small I used to aggravate cats—set them on fire, shoot them with my BB gun. I'd do this for devilment. My grandfather used to beat me. Ohhh, did he beat me! One time I caught this cat and poured kerosene on his back and lit him up. He looked like a shooting star. That night when I was asleep, that same cat jumped on my bed. I grabbed a window stick and started beating him. He didn't move. I got a Coke bottle and threw it at him. He still didn't move. I screamed for my grandmother. When she came the cat disappeared. I knew I had seen the cat, but now he was gone.

You can ask my wife. If a cat crosses me I'll turn around and go the other way. Any cat. That's me today. I respect cats. And it went through my head that I shouldn't bother this VC cat. But I said, "Hell, I can't have no worse luck than I'm having right now."

Davis. I didn't want them to kill it actually. I liked the cat and thought it was bad luck to kill one. I also knew the camp authorities would miss it. I told them to let me hold the cat. They said, "No, you'll turn him loose." And I would have too.

The cat was miaowing loudly. He knew something was up, all the guys were gathered round petting him. They tried first to drown him in a pot a boiling water. But he jumped out scratching and spitting and almost got away. Then Grissett said, "I'll kill him."

McMillan. Russ took the cat outside. Two or three minutes later we heard this *ka-loomph!* He returned. The cat's head was bashed in. Someone got a rusty razor blade and began to skin it. Kushner was detailed to hide the fur and entrails in the latrine. Strictland watched for the guards.

Some guys from Watkins' hootch were there and we said, "Hey, there are too many of us here. Somebody should go." They left.

We started jiving around, wondering how it would taste because it was all lovely pink meat.

"Jeez, look at those thighs!"

Strictland whistled a warning. We stashed the cat. A guard arrived. He asked us what we were doing.

"Boiling water," we said. "We're thirsty." It looked strange because we weren't supposed to have a fire at night. He told us to go to bed. Then he left.

We resumed our work. Ten minutes later a guard we called College Joe slipped in without Strictland seeing him. He walked up behind us, scaring us half to death. He saw the cat but didn't recognize it. He said, *"Tot lam,"* and laughed. He thought we had killed some sort of wild animal.

Then Qua the montagnard guard came in and began poking around.

He spotted the paws, which we hadn't been able to skin, and shouted, *"Meo! Meo!"* All of us ran from the kitchen and left the cat laying there. Went to our hootch and jumped on the bed.

The VC and Garwood arrived with lamps. They ordered us outside. Fred was the only one from our hootch who hadn't been in the kitchen, he was too sick. Before we left the hootch we agreed that no matter what happened we wouldn't admit anything. Outside, they called me and Harker to the front.

"Who killed the cat?" Mr. Hom asked.

"I don't know, Mr. Hom," I said.

He asked Harker.

Harker said, "I don't know, Mr. Hom."

He went down the line asking each person. Everybody stood firm.

Anton. We watched from our hootch. It was an eerie scene. The lamp light distorted the Viet Cong's features and made them appear even more sinister.

They said, "You have killed the camp's cat. The camp com-

mander loves his cat. All the guards love the cat." It was ridiculous. They had loved the camp dog too. Yet one day
several months earlier when meat was in short supply they had
beaten their lovable dog to death with sticks and eaten him.
They had had a pet parakeet they were going to teach to talk.
It too had disappeared into their pot. "The baby loved the
cat." The younger cook, Hannah, had a two-year-old boy
who ran around the camp bare-assed. "You must tell us who
killed the cat."

McMillan. We stood firm for half an hour. Then Russ said,
"I killed the cat. I heard a noise by the john and I threw a
rock and accidentally killed him." That wouldn't wash. The
VC jerked him out of line. They kicked and beat him. He fell
to the ground. They pounded him terribly.

Harker. Garwood came down the line and punched me in
the ribs. He said, "Somebody's gonna pay for letting Russ
take all the blame." The blow stunned me. Not because it was
thrown hard but because I was weak. I stumbled backward.
A guard removed Kushner's glasses and slapped him brutally.

McMillan. The VC tied us up. Daly and I were fastened to
a pole so tightly as to cut off our circulation. I started vomiting. The medic girl ran to see what was happening. The VC
untied me. Several hours later they untied everyone but Grissett. Several guys were made to bury the cat. Next morning
the supply director worked Grissett over with a cane. It was
his cat, brought to camp to keep the rats out of the rice supply. As the guards passed by they kicked Grissett and pinched
his ears. Around noon they untied him. The camp commander
called us to a meeting. He asked for our opinions about what
had happened the night before.

Kushner told him the guards were cruel savages. The camp
commander had this slinky look on his face. That's why we
called him Slime. He giggled like the Vietnamese do when
they're nervous and asked the others what they thought.
Everyone said the same thing. Then Slime apologized for the
beatings we'd received. He said if he had been there it
wouldn't have happened. It was true—he wasn't there. Ol'
Ratface, the North Vietnamese, was in charge. He didn't care
what happened. Slime was like that. When someone died he
came around and apologized. The ARVN POWs told us he

was dangerous, that he would execute you, and we believed he would. But at least Slime seemed to show a little sympathy. The rest didn't.

Anton. We could not understand why Grissett confessed to killing the cat. It wasn't necessary. He never recovered from the incident. Perhaps he'd been hurt more deeply than we realized when he lost his influence over us as Watkins assumed the role of camp commander. I know his failure to be released after Ho's indoctrination course hurt him. And then taking that terrible beating must have made him give up all hopes of being freed. He became quiet and meek. He quit talking about going home, stopped eating, and began to regress. He lay on his bed all day long in the fetal position with a blanket pulled over his head, sucking his thumb and whimpering like a baby.

Strictland. After we learned the camp routine we didn't want Grissett to tell us what to do. Someone like him needed to have authority. A lot of guys said that was what caused him to go downhill.

If Grissett decided not to work, he wouldn't even though he might be in better shape than others. Some mornings he said, "I'm sick." He'd tell so and so he could have his rice. If someone offered you rice, you grabbed for it. You always gave your rice to someone in your squad. You looked after them first; that was natural. Anyway, after the other guys went to work Grissett would get up and say, "Where's my rice?"

We said, "We thought you were sick and gave yours to someone."

He said, "I'm better now." He had a morning sickness called work disease. He was the type of guy to take his rice back.

Grissett would get hungry and say he was going on the next manioc run.

"Okay, I'm going too," I'd tell him. Manioc might not have done me any good but I was sure going to carry them so I could eat them.

Russ would get a basket of manioc. When he returned he wouldn't let anybody touch them. He would eat them himself. And when he finished he wanted somebody else's.

Then we said, "You didn't let us eat any of yours. Now you can't have any of ours."

At the last Grissett squatted in a corner of the bed with a blanket pulled over his head. The medic girl had four or five dull needles. She bulled them but it didn't do any good. When she gave a shot, half of it wouldn't go in. She gave me one and my shoulder got infected. I still have a hole in it. The VC brought doctors in when people started dying. Kushner told them what the prisoner needed to survive and after the guy was about dead they brought the medicine. When Grissett was unconscious they let Kushner give him I don't know how many shots. But it was too late.

Davis. Everybody pitched in when someone was really down. Personal differences were forgotten. Russ had dysentery very badly. We washed his clothes and brought food to his bed. He developed a case of bronchial pneumonia. We thought he was gone. Suddenly he popped out of it. One morning he awoke and began to move around, did some exercises and looked like his old self. He said he was going to be all right. Then several days later he sank back into it. We tried to make him eat, make him get up and move about. We were fighting against impossible odds. At a certain point in starvation a lack of vitamins brings a loss of appetite. A man will ultimately lie down and die staring at food piled in front of him.

Harker. Russ went harder than anyone. Kushner and I stayed up all night with him. He fought it so. He knew he was dying. He asked us to tell his sister that he loved her. He passed away about 3:30 in the morning the day before Thanksgiving. The medic girl came to the hootch. At first when we got to camp she had been cool toward us. But as people fell ill, as she saw she could do nothing to help because of her lack of knowledge and equipment, she became sympathetic; and we began to consider her our friend. We could see she was truly sad that Russ had died.

Several days after Thanksgiving it was Bill Port. You could tell by his bone structure that Port had once been a very big guy. He was from the First Cav. He was taking a squad from LZ Baldy to reinforce a unit getting hit. Just as they jumped from the choppers mortars started coming in. And then a ground attack. There was mass confusion. Port remembered seeing Viet Cong darting around the landing zone. He was hit by a mortar round. One of his ears was half blown off, his toes were completely ripped away, and his left arm had a deep wound that drained continually. He had powder burns on his face and severely limited vision in his left eye. At dusk he would be almost blind and someone had to lead him to the latrine. After he was first captured the VC took him to a field hospital. There they treated his wounds and fed him eggs and monkey meat regularly. He improved a little. But not enough to justify their transferring him to our camp. Why they did that we never knew. Through it all Port kept a good sense of humor. He was taken in his sleep.

McMillan. The split between the two squads lasted till people started dying like hell. Nobody brought it up to anyone's face. But the people in the other squad who wanted the split saw what was happening. They started thinking. They could see others were run-down and might die too. It didn't end all of a sudden. We gradually got back together in early December. The Vietnamese had something to do with ending it. They moved us five blacks into another hootch, making it three squads instead of two. They also told us we had to have two permanent cooks. After the split was over and we were back together I didn't say anything about it. But I was still mad. I intended to get even with some of those guys.

Harker. The VC half-stopped it in a way, and we did too. The split was so absurd and should never have happened; and didn't. No one spoke about it.

Daly. The Vietnamese separated us into three groups because they could see we weren't getting along. From the very first moment they reorganized us, people got together and things began to change. The VC tried to make us black fellows think they did this because we were sort of special. Mr. Ho had given us this idea one night in July when he called us to his hootch. He didn't say so directly. But he asked had we heard of the Black Panthers and when we said no, he told us all about them. That's all Ho talked about, black this and black that, how the Front sympathized with the blacks. He said, "You should be in the States to tell of your experiences. What would you do if we released you?"

We said, "Oh, good night! We would tell about the war and what's happening over here and everything!" We thought when they moved the blacks together in a third hootch that maybe they were preparing to release us.

During the split everything was filthy. It wasn't so much the fault of the Vietnamese as our own dirty sanitation. One group would cook and wouldn't wash the pans. The other squad would do the same thing. Overnight rats and bugs ate what was left in the pans and we got up and cooked out of them again. Nobody wanted to wash the rice before cooking it. If you didn't wash it sometimes almost half the ration was rat feces. Still, people cooked without washing it. The Vietnamese claimed that was why people were getting sick. So they said they wanted us to have only two cooks. And mama-san was assigned to teach us how to cook properly.

The POWs voted for whom they wanted as cooks. Harker and I were elected. Since I had prior cooking experience I became head cook. The assistant cook was responsible for preparing the fire and making sure enough wood was on hand. Harker didn't mind the work but he hated to get up at 3:00 A.M. After several weeks he quit. Lewis came on. He lasted till he had an argument with mama-san. Lewis didn't eat manioc. Sometimes when mama-san cooked she mixed them with the rice. She was doing this one day and Lewis said, "No, no, we no eat this way." She continued what she was doing. Lewis pulled off the pot top. Mama-san went hollering to the VC area. Mr. Hom came down and chewed Lewis out. The VC removed him as assistant cook. McMillan took over.

We had three large pots. One was for boiling water, another for cooking rice, and the third for manioc. First thing each morning we made drinking water. We had washed the rice and cut the manioc and covered it up the night before, so everything was prepared. The rice took about ten minutes to cook. Some guys wanted manioc and rice together, others wanted them separately. Some wanted a few, others forced themselves to eat a lot just to be full. Occasionally if we had extra cooking oil I cooked manioc patties or manioc soup. We ate with chop sticks we carved ourselves. Later we received American-made spoons.

Every day, three hundred sixty-five days a year, someone came to me and said, "What're we having for lunch?"

I started cussing. "What do you think we're having? Manioc and rice!"

There were times we cooked three times a day, times we cooked twice or once, and times we didn't cook at all. It was sort of an unwritten rule when it came your time to cook under the old rotation system that you screwed everybody else. But the truth is, when I became permanent cook I never took any extra. Guys kidded me about tasting the manioc soup too much. I guess everybody thought I looked surprisingly healthy. I never lost much weight like everybody else. I was five foot eleven and most of the time weighed about a hundred seventy. But that was the story of my life, it has always been like that.

Anton. I practically went into a state of shock when people started dying. Most of those who died had beriberi to some extent, and I had it too. Beriberi is primarily caused by a severe deficiency of vitamin B_1. The disease is inevitable when you have a steady diet of polished rice. It killed many American POWs in Asian camps during World War II and Korea. You get dysentery at the outset, then a swelling called edema, which is caused by a retention of body fluids. My legs ballooned up. My testicles looked like baseballs. I moved in slow motion. The edema retarded respiration. The VC gave me B_1 and iron shots. I received a hundred shots in two months. None I thought did any good.

McMillan. Anton was lazy long before he got to Viet Nam. He said after he graduated from warrant officer's school his father, an air force colonel, told him that was the first successful thing he had ever done. Anton was tall and so skinny that we called him Bones. He weighed about a hundred ten pounds. He had a thin mouth and bushy black eyebrows that moved up and down like dark thunderclouds when he grumbled, and he talked in a nasal tone. He thought we were down on him because we tried to make him get up and do. He lay under his blanket all day long. If we hadn't pushed him and made him get up, he would have died. All of us knew that.

Harker. We had a small celebration Christmas Eve. The VC gave us a banner with a star on it. We hung it behind the bed in Joe Zawtocki's hootch and found a little tree and decorated it with bits of paper. We listened to Radio Hanoi that afternoon. Several pilots held in Hanoi read beautiful warm messages about how they missed home and the children who were growing up without them. We allowed ourselves to linger over thoughts of our families. The VC returned to Watkins his New Testament, and he read the Christmas Scriptures. We said the Lord's Prayer and sang a few carols. Bob Garwood was there, he was a friend of Joe's, and he sang with us.

The camp commander made a brief speech. "You are allowed to enjoy Christmas because of the Front's lenient and humane policy. We are sorry you are not with your family. But Johnson prolongs the war. Maybe next year you will be back home." He didn't promise but he sounded almost certain that Nixon, who had been elected the month before, would end the war. We clutched at his optimism. Our spirits rose.

Anton. The Vietnamese gave us some candy. We divided it into equal shares. Garwood saw we had split it up. He reported us to the Vietnamese. The camp commander told us collect the candy, said we had to eat it community style.

"Put it in the middle of the bed and you can have it at midnight."

We said, "Midnight?"

They wanted us to stay up because captured U.S. pilots were to sing Christmas carols over Radio Hanoi at 12:00.

The pilots already had read messages saying they had ham, turkey, and cranberry sauce. We said, "If we could have but one bite of it!"

We tried to be happy but couldn't. People were showing tears. Anyway, when the camp commander said we couldn't split the candy we said, "It's our Christmas. If we can't divide it the way we want, you keep it. Or give it to Garwood."

Finally he gave in.

Harker. We received an extra can of rice for our Christmas meal and two chickens. On New Year's we had another celebration, with extra rice and several cans of U.S. Army B-ration ham. But if our spirits were rising, they suddenly fell the next day.

Anton. Fred was captured on his first mission. He had been in Viet Nam six days. He was on the tail end of the patrol and fell asleep from exhaustion during a ten-minute break. The others were gone when he awoke. He seemed to think they had left him on purpose because they didn't like him. He didn't smoke, didn't drink, didn't swear. He wasn't an average marine. He had been an excellent student and had won a scholarship to Notre Dame. He was having problems at home. He considered his father weak. His mother wore the pants in the family. Instead of going to Notre Dame, he joined the Marine Corps to prove he was a man.

Harker. You watch the changes in him. His legs swell with edema. You see his hair becoming frizzy, it stands up on his head. His eyes begin to bulge. Before he was a nice-looking guy. Now he looks foreign, strange. Kushner punched me one night. Five of us were in the hootch, McMillan had built a fire, and we had let Fred come over to sit by it. For being a good boy that day. It gets down to the ridiculous but you try to develop some sort of incentive for making them want to live. "Fred you can have your blanket if you wash yourself." Or "Fred you can sit by the fire if you don't crap in your pants today." He had that faraway look in his eyes. When he saw us watching he smiled gently. I wanted to cry.

Anton. He began to make a lot of noise at night, crying over and over, "Mama, oh, Mama . . . I want my Mama."

Once in the middle of the night someone, I don't remember who, yelled, "Die, motherfucker, die!"

No one was shocked. Several people laughed. It was that kind of situation, so pathetic, but the realism of the moment because nobody could get any sleep. Later people talked about it and said what a rotten thing to do.

Harker. You could confront him with it. "You're dying, Fred. You've got to try. You've got to get back. Your mom wants to see you, your dad does too. You mean so much to them."

He'd reply, "Yes, I want to. But I can't. I just can't."

"Why? You can. All you have to do is eat."

"Doesn't taste good."

"The food doesn't taste good to any of us. But you've got to eat to live. You ate it before."

"All I want is to be warm. Please let me sit by the fire."

Prison didn't change him as it did others, didn't make him harsh and nasty, foulmouthed like many of us became. He kept his manners through the hardest of times, always said thank you for the smallest gestures, and remained a devout Catholic when others had their faith shaken. When he died the day after New Year's all of us realized that some part of ourselves had died with him. He was nineteen.

from *Survivors*, 1975

A SMALL TOWN MOURNS ITS DEAD:
SPRING 1969

Our Town: The War Comes Home
to Beallsville, Ohio

by Jeffrey Blankfort

WASHINGTON (AP) *The Pentagon has rejected a plea to withdraw from Viet-Nam combat the servicemen from a little Ohio town that had five native sons killed in action. . . .*

[Congressman Clarence] Miller made the request in letters to Laird and President Nixon after residents of the town of 450 expressed fear their younger generation was being decimated.

I WENT to Beallsville a little more than a month after the town had buried its fifth son, Naval Corpsman Robert Lucas, in a plot of ground overlooking the high school where he and the four other boys had been schoolmates. Three of them now lie with him in the same graveyard and another is buried a few miles away.

Beallsville, on the fringes of Appalachia, is a sleepy southeastern Ohio town, made up of a general store, churches, a post office, farms, frame houses and a cemetery. Intersected by three state highways, it is located 12 miles up a winding road from the Ohio River. The road is State Highway 556, but in Beallsville it is known as Rural Route 3.

Viet-Nam has taken a toll from Beallsville that is 75 times the national average. ("They won't be getting many more of our boys," said Mayor Gramlich. "They drafted the last one of draft age this month.") The war has come home to Beallsville with unique severity, and America's confusions and contradictions about it are sharpened there: the acute consciousness of the waste, against the ingrained heartland patriotism; deep resentment over the lost sons, against the need to be proud of their sacrifice.

I talked to the parents about their sons and the war.

The Pittmans live in a two-story, many-gabled frame house on a farm six miles up the road from the Beallsville Corporation limits. With no one but themselves now, they use only the first floor. Mr. Pittman works at the Ormet Aluminum plant in Hannibal. In the fall they can peaches from their orchard.

Mrs. Maegene Pittman—whose son Jack was drafted at nineteen, was sent to the infantry and became the town's first casualty—expressed it this way: "They just took him and that was it. We never knew there was a Viet-Nam or anything until he had to go. And to think in eight months we had him back and buried."

Hurt and bitter at the loss of their only child, Mrs. Pittman and her husband, Earl, refused a military funeral. "Jack would have wanted it that way," she said. "He didn't understand the Viet-Nam thing any more than we do. We were bitter. We didn't want no part of a military funeral. I just think we have no business over there. If they were attacking our country, that's different."

Her husband saw things differently: "They're fighting over there with their hands tied behind them is the way I look at it. I always thought they ought to declare war and do it right if they're going to be over there."

"Why do you think we are there?" I asked.

He smiled. "Politics."

And you, Mrs. Pittman?

She looked over at her husband and then back at me. "It's a political war."

As I talked with the Pittmans, I sat beneath a case containing a photograph of their son and the trophies he had won at Beallsville High where he had been captain of the football and basketball teams. Before he was drafted, his mother said, he had taken "a little team of eighth graders under his wing to teach them basketball. He was a good Christian boy.

"Being our only son, we just gave everything we had to our country. We've got each other," said Mrs. Pittman, exchanging glances with her husband. "But when you get our age you look for your grandchildren, your family to multiply.

Now both of us is left with, we might as well say, no future. When you lose your only child, you don't have any future."

II

On the same road, back toward town, Kenneth and Betty Rucker live in a blue frame house on the edge of a small farm. Their son Richard was killed on Memorial Day last year. Also drafted at nineteen, he had served eight months in combat with the infantry.

Mr. Rucker works, when work is available, as an electrical lineman. A veteran of World War II, he was eager to talk about his son:

"He was very clean-cut. All his hobbies were clean. He didn't smoke, he didn't chew, he didn't drink, and he didn't specially want to go to the service much. But he was a boy that wouldn't object. Whatever he had to do, he did it and did it willingly."

What do you think about the war, Mr. Rucker? What would you do?

"There is not much you can do," he replied. "I do what they tell me, but I see this thing is out of hand and we shouldn't have been involved—which he didn't want to be. But he was that kind of boy. He wouldn't shirk no part of his American body for communism."

Betty Rucker, Richard's stepmother who raised him from the first grade, broke down in tears when she started to talk about him.

"There's just no sense to it. Just a slaughter. A lot of young kids going over there to get killed for no reason at all. We have no business over there.

"They hadn't even started their lives yet. They give them a few weeks training and they say, 'Well, you're ready, boy, go ahead.' What can you do? They don't know anything. Only kill or be killed. That's all Rich thought about, kill or be killed.

"They tell us we're over there to fight communism," she said. "If the South Vietnamese want to fight, let them fight their own battles."

Richard, in his last month of combat, had been showing signs of mental fatigue. "They checked him and said he was just a little nervous," said his father, "and then in three days he was killed."

Two days before he died, Richard wrote home:

"Well, we got into the shit again here. This is near suicide. Every day I say, you are going to make it Rich, you are going to make it."

"I gave my boy a full military funeral," said Kenneth Rucker, "but it was rough."

III

Duane Greenlee joined the Marines in January, 1966, at the age of eighteen. He was sent to Viet-Nam that July and served 44 days before he was killed.

Shortly after Duane's death, his parents separated. His father, Duane Sr., moved to Bellaire, Ohio, a few miles from Wheeling, while his mother, three brothers and four sisters relocated in Clarington, 12 miles from Beallsville.

I talked with Mrs. Greenlee over her morning cup of coffee.

"It don't seem like Duane's gone yet. It's really hard. It hits me at times and it's pretty hard to take. I know what all the other mothers feel like. I wanted to go to each one of their funerals but I just couldn't. I just stayed away and thought about it as though they were my own boys. It's hard to talk about it.

"I knew all the boys but Jack. The others had all been to my house with Duane at different times.

"I'm certainly proud of my boy. All his life he wanted to be a Marine. When he was home on furlough before he went over, we asked him if he was scared. He said he wasn't scared but he'd rather go there and fight for mom and dad and his brothers and sisters than have them come over here and fight.

"I have a son thirteen coming up and he can't wait to get in the Marines. He's going to. They're all real proud of their brother."

Do you know, or did Duane know, why he was over there?

"Duane really wanted to go and help out but he said he didn't know what he was going over there for. He wrote home in letters he didn't know what he was fighting for. He didn't see any sense in it and I don't see where we've gained anything at all by any of them being over there. I just wish it was all over.

"I believe if I had been President," she said, and dropped her voice, "I would have done like Hiroshima."

IV

"Our kid, he done most of the farming," Mr. Ernest Schnegg recalled. "I was doing construction work down at the Norton mine. Charles worked three days a week at Timken Roller Bearings in Cincinnati and when he was off he came home and took care of things."

Ernest and Esther Schnegg now live and work in Barnesville, 19 miles north of Beallsville. Their farm in Beallsville, on which they raised eight children, can no longer support them. Mr. Schnegg works seven days a week at a greenhouse and Mrs. Schnegg is a nurse's aide at Barnesville Hospital.

Charles, their oldest son, was drafted on December 5, 1966, and one day short of a year later was killed, serving with the infantry in Viet-Nam.

Their oldest daughter, Shirley, seventeen, and Roger, now their oldest son at sixteen, live on the farm and attend Beallsville High School.

Mr. Schnegg was tired. He had been working hard all day and his pants were rolled up and his feet were bare.

"I was counting on Charles to work on the farm. He was a farmer. Charles was all I had. The government took him and didn't give anything in return."

V

On March 7 of this year, the day before his son died in Viet-Nam, Robert Lucas Sr., age thirty-eight, had a heart attack. As a result he could not attend the funeral. Lucas lives with his wife and his remaining three sons and three daughters in a gaunt, gray two-story farmhouse eight miles outside of Beallsville.

Mr. Lucas came out to the back porch as I drove up, wearing the green work uniform that is a familiar sight in the area. I asked him how he felt. As far as the heart, all right, he

guessed. He told me that his wife didn't want to talk to reporters so we sat down on the edge of the porch while his
two dogs studied me curiously and we talked for a few
minutes about his son and the war.

"Well, I hope to think he died for a purpose."

Do you have any feelings about what the purpose was?

"No."

You have a thirteen-year-old boy. Will he have to go, too?

"Well, I hope not, but if there ever comes a time when he
has to defend his country, why I'm sure he'll do it."

Do you think the other boys from Beallsville should be
moved from the combat zone?

"Well, the Defense Department, whatever you call it, can't
do anything like that, can't favor one boy and put another in,
they just can't do it. It's a business same as anything else."

What do you think we should do in Viet-Nam?

"Well, I know what I would do."

What?

"If I had my way, in a week's time it would be over. I'd
draw the boys out of there and there wouldn't be no Viet-
Nam to it."

YOU'VE HEARD OF APPALACHIA?

After the death of young Lucas, Keith Harper, the Beallsville undertaker, called Monroe County Treasurer Ray Starkey,
and said, "Ray, you've got to do something." Starkey, a 50-
year resident of the Beallsville area, called their congressman,
Clarence Miller. Miller said he would "see if he could 'get the
boys moved around a little bit so this won't happen again
right away,'" recalls Starkey, "or maybe I said that to him.
Doesn't make any difference who said what, that's what he
undertook to do."

Congressman Miller contacted the Department of Defense
and was turned down.

I asked Starkey about the standard of living in Beallsville.

"It's certainly not plush. You can see that. This is Appalachia. You've heard that term? That's exactly what it is.

"The economic level isn't good here at all. 'Course now

the mine has helped the area a bit in the past couple of years. Prior to that, no. Now the aluminum plant complex we've had since '56 has been a big help. If it hadn't been for that I couldn't envision, in the name of peace, what this place would be like. I heard one guy say we'd be making change in possum skins, if it weren't for the plant."

Starkey was referring to the Olin Mathieson Chemical plant in Hannibal, Ohio, 16 miles southeast along the Ohio River, and its adjacent subsidiary, Ormet, owned jointly with Revere Copper and Brass. Ormet has 2500 employees, approximately 90 from the Beallsville area. Olin Mathieson has about 50 employees from Beallsville.

The chemical plant fabricates aluminum sheeting, plating and coil and Ormet turns it into everything from Revere pots and pans to shells for Viet-Nam. The wage scale at both plants runs from $2.84 to $4.60 an hour.

The only other large-scale employment for the area comes from its coal mines operated by North American Coal Company and Ogilby-Norton.

Due to the presence of the mines and aluminum plants, Monroe County workers earn the highest weekly wage of any county in Ohio, an average of $127 a week—for those who get work. But there is also widespread unemployment and, according to Ralph Yoss, county welfare director, 40 per cent of the 4500 families in Monroe County have annual incomes below the official poverty level of $3000.

In the Beallsville area, which is defined by the limits of the Beallsville School District and includes approximately 1000 people, 87 families are receiving some form of federal or local assistance. Besides Beallsville, the school district includes the towns of Malaga, Jerusalem, Aladonia, Switzer, Ozark and Armstrong Mills, crossing over a short way into Belmont County. It is from this general area with its larger population that the five boys originate.

There are at least six more boys from Beallsville stationed in Viet-Nam and several more apparently on their way.

In the first group is Randy Gramlich, son of Beallsville Mayor Ben Gramlich. "I'm not a dove," the mayor told me. "I never said I was a hawk, either. Still, this war, I can't see where it's any different than the rest. It's just to preserve freedom in the world."

Mr. Gramlich owns one of the town's two cafes, Jacqueline's Place, which is run by his wife. In the back he maintains the "J.F.K. Recreation Center," a free pool hall for Beallsville teenagers. Since the restaurant cannot bring in enough business to support the family, the mayor works the night shift at Olin Mathieson.

A short distance down the street I heard a sharp note of dissent from Ferrell McClelland. Tall and lean, in his late fifties or early sixties, he has spent 30 years in the coal mines. His youngest son, Roger, enlisted in the Army and has been in Viet-Nam since December.

"We ain't got no damn business over there to start with," he snapped. "I can't see what good they're gonna do over there. The one tape we got from him [Roger] said 'we don't know what we're over here for'; said 'it wouldn't be so bad if we knew what we were fighting for.' "

Beallsville Postmaster Vern Jeffers is a World War I veteran and an active member of his American Legion post. He delivered mail in Beallsville for 40 years and has been postmaster for the past eight. He is gray and bespectacled, with the voice and manner of an old family doctor.

"I enlisted in World War I. I was the youngest enlistee from Monroe County. We had as a slogan then, 'the war to end all wars.' We attended the American Legion 50th anniversary banquet recently and one of the boys said to me, 'Well, you were an enlistee, would you do it again?' Yes, I told him, under the same circumstances I would, because I really thought it was going to end all war, but we see—we have seen all these years since—that the slogan was meaningless.

"So, under the present circumstances I don't think I would enlist. If I were drafted, I certainly would go without hesitation. I wouldn't enlist because I don't feel, and I think I represent practically everybody in the community, I don't think this is a war to defend America or to make America a better place to live in. I just don't see it that way.

"I don't think it justifies the lives of these boys, over and above the expense of the war. Doesn't justify it at all. There was not a boy that really wanted to go over there that was killed. I know. I've known every one personally, all these years, since they were born. Most of the boys were from small farms and they didn't want to go over there and fight.

"And when we have been told we are working with one of the most corrupt governments in the whole world, it makes it still harder for us to believe we should sacrifice the lives of our boys for that cause."

Referring to his fellow legionnaires, Jeffers told me, "Almost, not unanimously, but by far the greater majority of them, do not think there is any justification for the war.

"I don't mean we should draw them out now," he added. "Anyone knows that would be the wrong thing. But I do think they should take definite and positive steps to bring it to a close. What we need is diplomacy.

"Diplomats," he said almost confidentially, "we're short of."

Mrs. Jean Nelson, the first woman to serve on the Beallsville Council, is serving as secretary on a committee for building a flagpole monument and memorial park in honor of the five boys who have been killed. "I feel so bitter about the war in Viet-Nam," she told me, "because it seems such a useless war, that my feeling is, any guy who can get out of it for whatever reason, more power to him.

"I don't think, however, that there has been a single solitary person in this community that has ever thought of protesting. What should we hope to accomplish? It's not going to bring our boys back.

"So many street marches! This is the type of person I would like to see shipped to Viet-Nam. Then he could be doing some good for his country!"

This strong reaction to public protest seemed to be universal in Beallsville, and there is little likelihood of a draft resistance movement forming there at the present time.

The principal of Beallsville High School, Timothy Haught, described to me what happened when a reporter from the Wheeling News-Register interviewed the senior boys after the last two deaths.

"Some expressed the fact that the war seemed at a considerable distance. Some expressed the fact that they were not entirely aware of all the implications of the war. But generally speaking, in both classes, the boys reflected the view that if called upon, they would serve."

There are 24 boys in the current Beallsville senior class.

Ramparts, July 1969

Black Power in Viet Nam

by Wallace Terry

BEFORE the war went stale and before black aspirations soared at home, the black soldier was satisfied to fight on an equal basis with his white comrade-in-arms in Viet Nam as in no other war in American history. But now there is another war being fought in Viet Nam—between black and white Americans. "The immediate cause for racial problems here," explains Navy Lieut. Owen Heggs, the only black attorney in I Corps, "is black people themselves. White people haven't changed. What has changed is the black population."

When an American force stormed ashore south of Danang this summer, young blacks wore amulets around their necks symbolizing black pride, culture and self-defense. They raised their fists to their brothers as they moved side by side with white Marines against their common Communist enemy. "Ju Ju" and "Mau Mau" groups have organized to protect themselves against white prejudice and intimidation. In remote fire-support bases near the Cambodian border, blacks register their complaints as a group. Tanks fly black flags. At Danang, Black Power Leader Ron Karenga's followers have designed a flag: red for the blood shed by Negroes in Viet Nam and at home, black for the face of black culture, and green for youth and new ideas. Crossed spears and a shield at the center signify "violence if necessary," and a surrounding wreath "peace if possible" between blacks and whites.

White pinups have been replaced by black ones. One all-black hootch in Danang sports more than 500 such photographs. "I don't want any stringy-haired beast* broad on my wall. Black is beauty." In a Saigon "soul kitchen," blacks greet

---

*"Beast," a term that originated with the Black Panthers, is rapidly replacing "Chuck" as the black soldier's standard epithet for the white man.

each other over spareribs and chittlins with 57 varieties of Black Power handshakes that may end with giving the receiver "knowledge" by tapping him on the head or vowing to die for him by crossing the chest, Roman legion style.

Many of today's young black soldiers are yesterday's rioters, expecting increased racial conflict in Viet Nam and at home when they return. Elaborate training in guerrilla warfare has not been lost upon them, and many officers, black and white, believe that Viet Nam may prove a training ground for the black urban commando of the future. As in America, the pantheon of black heroes has changed. The N.A.A.C.P.'s Roy Wilkins is a "uniform tango"—military phonetics for U.T., or Uncle Tom—and Massachusetts Senator Edward Brooke is an "Oreo" cookie—black on the outside, white on the inside. "The N.A.A.C.P., Urban League and Martin Luther King were good for their time and context," says Marine Corporal Joseph Harris of Los Angeles, "but this is a new time." King and Robert Kennedy, once among the young black soldier's idols, have died violently. Says Wardell Sellers, a rifleman from New York: "They were trying to help the brothers—you can see what that got them." Now many blacks see the case of Edward Kennedy as a plot to remove one more hope. "Just like King and Bobby Kennedy," says Pfc. Carl Horsley, 19. "They gon' try to hang Teddy 'cause he was on the side of the brothers." To most black soldiers, Nixon doesn't even bear discussion. "If he were a brother," says Ronald Washington, a black sailor from Los Angeles, "he'd be the number one Uncle Tom."

In the jungle lies death for a cause that many black soldiers don't understand or dismiss as white man's folly. "Why should I come over here when some of the South Vietnamese live better than my people in 'the world'?" asks a black Marine. "We have enough problems fighting white people back home."

Black racism is strong, but so are provocations by white soldiers. Soon after Martin Luther King was killed, crosses were burned at Danang and Cam Ranh Bay. Confederate flags still fly from barracks and trucks, and are even worn as shoulder patches on the uniforms of helicopter pilots stationed at

Phu Loi. Black soldiers at Con Thien grimace when whites call a Negro sergeant "brown boy" and a mongrel puppy "soul man." Base club operators who accept country and western but not soul music from their entertainers have paid a toll. Clubs were wrecked in Chu Lai, Qui Nhon and a dozen other places in the past twelve months. Two white sailors were recently tried for inciting a riot at the Tun My Club.

Violence has reached such a peak in the Danang area that lights have been installed on the streets of Cap Tien Sha to curb roving bands of white and black sailors who were attacking each other at night. At Dong Tam in the Delta and Dien Hoa north of Saigon, bands of black soldiers still waylay whites. A white officer in Danang was critically injured when a black Marine rolled a grenade under his headquarters. At the officer's side was a black sergeant with a reputation for not tolerating Afro haircuts and Black Power salutes.

Unrest among the blacks often turns on real discrimination or the failure of the military to accept the trappings of black soldiers bent on "doing their thing." Promotions, awards and coveted rear-area assignments are too often slow in coming the black soldiers' way, however well they fight or however high their proportion of casualties. Some 13% of battle deaths are black, while Negroes make up 11.1% of the American population and 9.2% of the military.

For all that, the black soldier in the bush still helps his white comrade and wants his help as well. At Phuoc Vinh, a black 1st Cavalry trooper recently dragged a wounded white from a rocketed hootch when no other black or white dared to venture in. A black Navy medic who had been in Viet Nam only two weeks fell on a grenade near Danang to save a white Marine and lost his own life. When black Lieut. Archie Bigger was three times wounded capturing enemy artillery pieces, eleven whites held him aloft above the suffocating napalm smoke until a rescue chopper arrived. On Hamburger Hill, a white paratrooper tried vainly to breathe life into a fallen black medic.

Yet the violence at home and in "the Nam" leaves the black man with radically divided loyalties. Thus, says Lieut. Colonel Frank Peterson, the senior black officer in the Marine Corps, "the average black who has been here and goes back to the

States is bordering somewhere on the psychotic as a result of having grown up a black man in America—having been given this black pride and then going back to find that nothing has changed."

Personal interviews conducted with 400 black enlisted men from Con Thien to the Delta provide a measure, though by no means a scientific sample, of the attitudes of black men in Viet Nam.

▶ 45% said they would use arms to gain their rights when they return to "the world." A few boasted that they are smuggling automatic weapons back to the States.

▶ 60% agreed that black people should not fight in Viet Nam because they have problems back home. Only 23% replied that blacks should fight in Viet Nam the same as whites.

▶ 64% believed that racial troubles in Viet Nam are getting worse. Only 6% thought that racial relations were improving. "Just like civilian life," one black Marine said, "the white doesn't want to see the black get ahead."

▶ 56% said that they use the Black Power salute. Only 1% condemned its use.

▶ 60% said they wear their hair Afro style. 17% wanted to, but said their commanders refused to let them. One Marine reported that he had been reduced in rank for refusing to get his hair cut closer.

▶ 55% preferred to eat their meals with blacks, 52% preferred to live in all-black barracks.

▶ 41% said they would join a riot when they returned to the U.S. However, a nearly equal number, 40%, said they would not.

▶ 28% said they believed that weapons would help the black cause back home, while 35% thought that they would be harmful to it. "What the beast has done for me which is going to screw him," said a black Marine, "is teach me how to use a weapon. The Marines taught me how to improve."

Combat inevitably sharpens both emotions and rhetoric. It is an incendiary combination to be young, black, armed, 10,000 miles from home and in persistent danger of death in "a white man's war." When the men return to "the world," their perspective may shift, and doubtless many black soldiers will become so busy with their own affairs that their militance will fade somewhat. Even in Viet Nam, 53% of the black men interviewed said that they would not join a militant group such as the Black Panthers when they return to the U.S. Says Major Wardell Smith: "A lot of what they say they will do, they just won't. They won't be so closely knit, and they will have girls, wives, families and jobs to worry over." Nevertheless, a significant number seems likely to continue to believe that the U.S. owes the black soldier a debt both for his service in Viet Nam and his suffering at home. These men are a new generation of black soldiers. Unlike the veterans of a year or two ago, they are immersed in black awareness and racial pride. It is only this fall and winter that they will be returning to civilian life in the cities. If they find that nothing has changed there, then they could constitute a formidable force in the streets of America, schooled and tempered in all the violent arts as no generation of blacks has ever been.

Time, September 19, 1969

A Long, Leisurely Drive Through
Mekong Delta Tells Much of the War

by Peter R. Kann

SAIGON—The war drags on. President Nixon has ruled out
any quick withdrawal, and enemy attacks seem to be increasing once again. No progress is reported in Paris. But if there
is no progress at the peace table, is there at least progress on
the battlefield?

There isn't a clear answer. "Progress" is measured here in
many ways. The Air Force computes the tonnage of bomb-
loads dropped. The Army tots up enemy bodies. Pacification
planners neatly categorize hamlets on computerized evaluation charts. Psychological warriors conduct mini-Gallup Polls
among taxi drivers. Economists plot curves on the shipments
of rice. Embassy officers sip tea with Saigon legislators and
seek to divine their Delphic utterances.

And still, Vietnam seems to defy analysis. The Vietnam war
remains a kaleidoscopic conflict over a splintered society in a
fragmented nation, and the bits of Vietnam that one man sees
probably are no more typical—and no less valid—than the
fragments perceived by another.

With such thoughts in mind, three Americans recently set
out in a 1954 Volkswagen on a week-long drive through the
Mekong Delta, that densely populated rice bowl of Vietnam
where, it has often been said, the war ultimately will be won
or lost. The trip covered some 400 miles by road, with side
trips on motor launches, sampans and helicopters. The route
ran from Saigon southwest to Can Tho, the administrative
hub of the Delta; then westward through the tranquil province of An Giang and on to Chau Doc province along the
Cambodian frontier; then back through one-time Vietcong
base areas of Sandec province and finally northeast back to
Saigon.

The trip offers some glimpses of recent progress and of perennial problems, of new threats like North Vietnamese battalions and of more esoteric dangers like a nine-nostriled water monster allegedly loose in the Mekong River. The trip provides no grand conclusions, only the observation that three unarmed Americans were able to spend a week driving through rural Vietnam without being shot at. That, perhaps, is progress.

Scenically, the Delta is both beautiful and boring, a lush green blanket of marshy rice paddies stretching to the horizon. The flat monotony sporadically is broken by small mounds of earth encasing tombs, by narrow belts of palm trees and by the small clusters of thatch houses that constitute Vietnamese hamlets. Less frequently, one passes larger villages, usually with an aluminum-roofed schoolhouse (courtesy of U.S. aid), a pastel pagoda and a bustling marketplace crammed with delicacies like river eel and skinned paddy rat. Crisscrossing this landscape at intervals of every few miles are the French-built canals, which, far more than the potholed roads, serve as the Delta's economic lifelines.

Despite the war, there is an overwhelming sense of peacefulness and prosperity about the Delta. The Delta has a way of enveloping, almost swallowing up, the war. Conflict seems to encroach upon the peaceful Delta setting only as isolated incidents—here a Vietcong raid on a mud-walled militia outpost, there a string of U.S. helicopters swooping down to strafe a tree line. Unlike the dusty plateaus and jagged hills of the northern areas, the placid green Delta seems unsuited to a war.

The Delta traditionally has been an area of "low profile" U.S. involvement, with Americans serving only to advise and support Vietnamese troops in a slow-paced struggle against locally recruited Vietcong. In mid-1968, this pattern was jarred when the U.S. Ninth Division moved into the upper Delta, chalking up staggering (some skeptics say unbelievable) Vietcong body counts. Then, this past summer, the Ninth was shipped home as the first instalment on President Nixon's troop-withdrawal promise.

Wherever two or more American officials gather together these days the talk is of "Vietnamization," the turning over of a greater share of the war burden to the Vietnamese. So it goes in Can Tho, the Delta administrative center, where visitors can be briefed on everything from Vietnamese adaptation to the M-16 automatic rifle to Vietnamese receptivity to participatory democracy. The prevailing new theme is sounded by Maj. Gen. Roderick Wetherill, ranking American in the Delta, who says: "The Vietnamese have just about everything we can give them. Now it's up to them, and we're confident they can hack it."

But if the talk of Can Tho is Vietnamization, the visible evidence still bespeaks Americanization. The massive USO building near the center of town has just unveiled a new barbecue pit, dedicated with military honors. Down the street is the even busier Hollywood Bar where GIs can buy "Saigon tea" from miniskirted, de-Vietnamized girls. Nearby is Palm Springs, a Hawaiian-style enclave for U.S. civilian advisers on everything from hog raising to intelligence gathering. Like the American military compound across town, Palm Springs boasts a well-chlorinated swimming pool.

Driving west out of Can Tho you pass several miles of impressive testament to American logistical capabilities: An airbase, warehouses, storage depots, helicopter fleets, truck yards, a naval support base, office buildings for civilian contractors. Scores of American trucks and jeeps clog the narrow road. A giant American road grader rumbles along, its treads cracking the pavement of this road even as it heads off to build a new road somewhere else. For perhaps five miles the Vietnamese are visibly represented only by a few militiamen rooting through the American tin cans on a roadside garbage heap.

A few miles farther on, the rural Delta re-emerges, and the view once again is of small boys draped over the backs of water buffalo, which are wallowing in the wet green paddies. A two-hour drive over relatively smooth road (potholes no deeper than six inches) brings you into An Giang province, heartland of the Hoa Hao religious sect. This sect's militant anti-Communism (the result of the sect's founding father's having been decapitated by the Vietminh) makes An Giang the most pacified province in Vietnam.

Indeed, the senior American adviser in An Giang, an

Agency for International Development official named Bill
Small, sleeps alone in an unguarded house on the outskirts of
the province capital. (He's considerably more confident than
several dozen U.S. military advisers working under him; they
live in a well-armed, walled compound defended by a platoon
of Vietnamese militiamen, a minor incongruity in light of the
American priority program to get Vietnamese troops off static
defense.)

Mr. Small has been seeking to reduce the U.S. advisory
presence in An Giang, but with limited success. One problem:
The An Giang advisory team is required to file 144 separate
reports to Can Tho and Saigon every month, and many Americans are needed here just to fight this paper war. Another
problem is the "adviser cult" that has developed among Government of Vietnam (GVN) officials. "To rate a U.S adviser
means status to a Vietnamese. To be Vietnamized out of your
adviser is to lose much face," explains a young American.

With Mr. Small, the American visitors board an outboard
motor launch for a spin through An Giang's inland waterways.
There's a stop in a Cho Moi district capital where Lt. Col.
Nguyen Quang Hanh, the urbane district chief who holds a
French passport and has a son studying in Paris, welcomes
visitors to his office, its walls gaily decorated with red, yellow
and green paper flowers of the sort associated with the Eugene
McCarthy campaign.

Breaking out a sealed bottle of Chivas Regal shortly before
10 a.m., Lt. Col. Hanh volunteers the view that because of
the death of Ho Chi Minh, the war will be over by the end
of this year. "There will be a couple of months of power struggle in Hanoi and then the war will end, militarily and politically, end completely," he says with absolute assurance.

Cho Moi district has been peaceful recently—except for the
appearance several months ago of the nine-nostriled water
snake. The snake is said to have been raised by a Cho Moi
necromancer who let it loose in the Tien Giang River. The
snake rapidly grew to a length of 15 feet, and it is rumored
recently to have gobbled up an old fisherwoman. Reports on
the river monster have circulated as far as Saigon. To many
Vietnamese, magic and monsters remain far more interesting
subjects than politics and war.

Taking a shortcut down a network of narrow canals, the motorboat runs afoul of some floating weeds and the engine jams in reverse. Luckily there's a Vietnamese Popular Force (PF) militia outpost nearby, and the boat backs over for assistance.

It's a fairly typical PF outpost, thick mud walls built around a tin-roofed shack in which the 12 PF soldiers and their families all live together. Startled by this surprise mid-afternoon visit, the PF scurry off to locate their new M-16s, to strap on ammunition belts and to don their steel helmets (most of which had been put to use collecting rainwater).

The PF return and try to look vigilant. One is asked if the outpost has had any contact with the Vietcong. "Oh, yes." When was the most recent contact? "The VC fired a mortar at us two years ago." (To be a PF in An Giang province is to be a lucky PF. In less secure provinces, the PF take heavier casualties than any other allied unit.)

The outpost is hardly equipped to handle motor repairs, and so, to the delight of laughing PF lining the mud walls, the Americans begin backing their way home. Pride is forgotten soon enough, and the costly American speedboat is strapped to the side of a Vietnamese sampan with a tiny put-put engine and is towed on home.

The next morning's drive brings the Americans into Chau Doc province, which has a common border of nearly 50 miles with Cambodia. Chau Doc is often called Vietnam's "Wild West" because it was one of the last Vietnamese frontier areas to be settled and because it has a tradition of professional banditry, smuggling and general lawlessness that predated the present war and no doubt will continue long after it is over.

Cambodia and South Vietnam have no diplomatic or legalized trade relations, but there is a considerable cross-border commerce greased by bribes to Vietnamese, Cambodian and Vietcong officials. At the small village of Nui Sam, some 500 beef cattle are milling and mooing as local merchants negotiate sales with Saigon buyers. The cows have recently been smuggled into Chau Doc from Cambodia through a complex procedure involving cross-border communication by coded message and Indian-style smoke signals.

At Nui Sam's only soup kitchen–coffee house, one can

watch the last coats of grease being applied to the cattle smuggling operation. The Cambodians and Vietcong already have been paid off. The GVN district chief at the crossing point has pocketed 200 piasters ($1.60) per head (enough money so that after three months in his lucrative job he is said to have built new homes in Chau Doc, Saigon and the seaside resort of Vung Tau).

In the soup kitchen, official papers are now being drawn up for the approval of the local GVN police chief, tax agent, economic service chief, animal husbandry representative and village chief—all of whom are accustomed to a small gratuity for their services. The room is crowded with old women clutching sheafs of paper, young clerks with stamps and chops, buyers and sellers exchanging wads of cash. Vietnamese soldiers meander among the tables cadging cigarets. Under the table, dogs, chickens and pigs poke around on the earthen floor looking for scraps of food. Perhaps $150,000 of business will be transacted here today. And as a result Americans and wealthy Vietnamese will continue to be able to buy beefsteak in Saigon restaurants at $10 a plate.

But cattle and other commercial commodities being smuggled across the border are of little concern to U.S. officials. "Hell, it's just honest smuggling," says a military officer in Chau Doc. American concern is focused on the infiltration of enemy troops and supplies across the border, and this sort of smuggling is on the rise.

In recent months, nearly two North Vietnamese regiments—up to 3,000 men—have crossed into Chau Doc from their Cambodian sanctuary. This represents the first appearance of regular North Vietnamese Army (NVA) units in the Mekong Delta and is doubly significant, and doubly dangerous, since it has occurred hard on the heels of the withdrawal of the U.S. Ninth Division. Some of the NVA troops are ensconced in cave and tunnel complexes on several of the heavily forested "Seven Sister" mountains, which dot the otherwise flat riceland of Chau Doc; others have moved south of Chau Doc into the swamp areas of the lower Delta.

There are conflicting interpretations on practically everything in Vietnam, and the NVA influx is no exception. In Saigon, some American military officers believe the Delta Vietcong have been so badly battered in the past year or so that the NVA have been called in as a "desperation move." Some U.S. diplomats think the NVA are moving in to solidify enemy control of long-time base areas in anticipation of a future cease-fire and territorial settlement. In Can Tho, senior U.S. officers suggest the NVA may move up into the eastern Delta and attempt to overrun several district capitals—a sort of "mini-Tet" campaign—and thereby score a propaganda coup.

In Chau Doc, some officials believe the NVA may break down into small units and spread across the Delta, combining with local VC forces to attack targets far more diverse and widespread than a few district capitals. "We better get over this Tet-mini-Tet psychology because I think Charlie has," says one Chau Doc officer.

In any case, whichever tack the NVA take, it likely would serve the political and psychological purpose of demonstrating South Vietnamese military vulnerability at a time of perhaps too much, too optimistic talk about Vietnamization. It could also serve to warn President Nixon that Hanoi isn't about to make American withdrawal pains any easier.

How the NVA are infiltrating the Delta is seen next day at a small village near the border. It's 9 a.m., and a military operation is in progress. Vietnamese Regional Force (RF) troops in helmets and flak jackets are cautiously moving up a hillside just off the road. They're searching for the remnants of a Vietcong unit that in the early morning hours overran a PF outpost on the hilltop, killing four PF along with a PF wife and four children. The PF had deployed no troops to set up night ambushes outside their outpost, a move that might have intercepted the enemy attack.

Lying at the edge of the road, caked in dust and crusted blood, are a wounded PF and a little girl, her face split open by a grenade fragment. Three-wheeled Lambretta buses, packed with passengers and sacks of brown sugar smuggled from Cambodia, rattle down the road. The war-hardened passengers barely bother to glance at the wounded or at the RF troops moving up the hillside 20 yards away.

The significant thing about this Vietcong attack isn't the body count. The VC attack was merely one of a dozen encounters around Chau Doc province the previous night with the aim of diverting allied forces—and particularly helicopter gunships—from border surveillance to defensive support. The local VC were attracting allied attention so the NVA regulars could slip smoothly across the border. The plan succeeded: An NVA battalion crossed from Cambodia during the night, it was later learned.

American military men have long been frustrated by the sanctuary that enemy troops have in Cambodia. A helicopter flight along the Vinh Te canal, which separates Chau Doc from Cambodia, illustrates the point. A mile or two inside Cambodia are several clusters of buildings considerably larger than thatched peasant huts. "That over there is an NVA supply depot. And that one there is a VC training center," says a young American major, casual as a tourist guide.

Allied military forces, of course, aren't permitted to attack enemy troops or facilities in Cambodia. This is partly to avoid angering Cambodia and forcing it actively into the war on the side of the Communists. And, while allied strikes might yield instant tactical dividends, the longer range result likely would be to widen the scope of the war and necessitate still more U.S. troops.

The chopper swings away from the border and lands at Tre Ton, one of five district capitals of Chau Doc province. A district is the smallest military-administrative division of Vietnam, and it is the American advisory team at this level (generally four to eight men) that has the worm's eye view of how the war is going. The senior U.S. district adviser in Tre Ton is Maj. William R. Fields, an exceptionally able two-year veteran of Vietnam.

The town of Tre Ton lies in the shadow of Nui Co To, one of the dark, forbidding Seven Sister mountains. Nui Co To is both Tre Ton's most dramatic success story and one of its most persistent problems. For nearly two decades, the Vietcong dominated the mountain. Last year the allies mounted a major campaign for Nui Co To and by April of this year succeeded in capturing the enemy's vast cave and tunnel complexes. Some 250 allied troops, many of them Cambodian mercenaries working for the U.S. Special Forces, died in the campaign.

Next, the allies tried to render the caves and tunnels uninhabitable, by pounding them with B52 air strikes, by exploding tons of TNT, by trying to fill the holes with motor oil and even snakes. The rock vaults proved indestructible. Consequently, to keep the 100 or so VC who still roam the mountainsides from moving back into their former refuges, Vietnamese troops are occupied in static defense positions in the caves, a waste of much-needed mobile manpower.

An intense pacification program in hamlets at the base of Nui Co To has made modest gains. Most of these hamlets were solidly controlled by the Vietcong seven months ago but now have at least a daytime GVN presence. Driving through these hamlets one is met by sullen stares. "These people don't know yet if the GVN is here to stay or if the VC are coming back. They haven't decided which way to lean yet, but at least they're debating it for the first time," says Maj. Fields.

It's dusk, and along the road a thin line of peasants, many leading cows or water buffalo, is moving away from the mountainbase hamlets and toward the town of Tre Ton. These people feel reasonably secure farming their fields by day but dare not sleep in their home hamlets for fear of VC reprisals or allied artillery fire. It's a chancy business being a Vietnamese civilian in a "contested" area. This same morning, for example, two civilians had been killed by an American helicopter as they ran across a rice paddy to try and retrieve a parachute that had been used to drop a flare the night before.

Throughout the district, the most significant progress, says Maj. Fields, has been in providing village and hamlet security through the Popular Self Defense Force (PSDF) program. Begun last year, this program provides minimal training and hand-me-down weapons to the residents of villages and hamlets and thus, for the first time since the war began, permits them to defend their homes and families.

"PSDF is the single best investment ever made in this country. Most people here wouldn't support the VC if they had a reasonable choice. PSDF gives them that choice. It lets them make and defend that choice," the major says. He recounts the case of a VC tax collector who sauntered into a long-compliant village one recent night to pick up monthly tax revenues. He was nabbed by the newly formed PSDF unit and hacked to death on the spot.

While the PSDF gets rave reviews from Americans here, Vietnamese army units seem more of a mixed bag. Regular army troops (ARVN), who operate only sporadically in the district, haven't been noticeably aggressive in seeking out enemy forces on the mountains. The district's Vietnamese Regional Force companies generally operate only by day and return to static defense positions at night.

And in the critical struggle to root out the Vietcong infrastructure, it's the U.S.-controlled Provincial Reconnaissance Units (PRU) that have proved highly effective at unorthodox night strikes, while the GVN-controlled National Police Field Force operates only in the late afternoon between the end of siesta and dinnertime.

Thus, here in Tre Ton, as elsewhere, the truth about the Vietnamese armed forces lies somewhere between the view of a Can Tho colonel who calls them "a bunch of little tigers" and the opinion of a Chau Doc sergeant who says "the only way to get them to move is to stick a bayonet up their rear ends."

The small U.S. advisory team in Tre Ton has one domestic problem all its own. As told by Sgt. James Smith: "We had the mother of all rats living in our outhouse. That damned rat must have measured three feet long, weighed maybe 40 pounds. It flipped our big, old tabby cat half way 'cross the compound. Haven't seen that cat since. Dogs were scared to go near that mother rat. We had this master sergeant visiting one time, and he went out to the outhouse at night, and next thing we hear is pots flying and water splashing and old sarge comes screamin' out of that outhouse. From then on that mother rat owned that outhouse after dark. Man, that rat used to eat poison like it was bread. We finally got the mother, but it took enough poison to kill a couple of cows."

If U.S advisers at the district level get thoroughly involved in both the mundane and arcane aspects of Vietnamese life, there are other American units that could profit by a bit more contact with the Vietnamese.

For example, back in Chau Phu, capital of Chau Doc province, the U.S. Navy, which helps patrol the Delta's rivers and canals, has arranged a demonstration of military gadgetry to impress the Vietnamese province chief. The gadget is an MSD (mine sweeper drone), an unmanned, remote-controlled, armor-plated boat about 15 feet long. Directed by radio waves from a black control box, the MSD can drag a chain across waterways to cut enemy mines. ("We could also use it to ram and explode enemy sampans, but that would get pretty expensive," says a Navy officer. An MSD costs about $45,000, he adds.)

The province chief and entourage are welcomed aboard a U.S. Navy patrol boat by a natty USN lieutenant commander and his well-starched staff. The black control box is unveiled and the MSD is made to loop, circle, turn right-angle corners and zig-zag back and forth across the river. The province chief, a worldly colonel who has spent the better part of three years studying in the U.S., including a term at the National War College, and who consequently speaks fluent English, is in excellent humor. At least he is until the lieutenant commander calls on a young U.S. seaman to explain the MSD controls.

"You see boat. Hard work boat. Boat go far away. No good. Boat go quick quick. Good. Stop boat push button. Box make stop go. Make boat go. Quick quick. Same same other boat no men . . ." rattles off the proud young seaman in flawless pidgin English of the sort that snows Vietnamese bargirls but not Vietnamese colonels. The innocent U.S. Navy officers smile on happily. The province chief manages a forced smile. And so ends the U.S. Navy's public relations program for this particular day.

The return trip to Saigon is remarkably uneventful, interesting only in that the road through Sandec province is now considered reasonably safe whereas 10 months ago it assuredly was not. At mid-afternoon, nearing Saigon, the Americans drive past three companies of regular ARVN soldiers, accompanied by armored personnel carriers, marching down the middle of the road—hardly the place to locate and engage enemy forces. "Maybe it's a parade," murmurs an optimist.

It's nightfall, and the dusty Volkswagen rolls into downtown Saigon. At the city's busiest intersection, directly in front of the colonnaded National Assembly Building, a beefy American construction worker in a gray Chevrolet collides with two Vietnamese soldiers on a Honda who are trying to run a red light.

The American rolls up his windows and accelerates, dragging along the battered Honda that has hooked on the Chevy bumper. The two Vietnamese soldiers give chase. They run alongside the moving car, pounding on the windshield and screaming "dirty American bastard! stinking American son of a bitch!"

Downtown Saigon's normal assemblage of dirty picture peddlers, sidewalk money changers, barhopping GIs, prostitutes, pickpockets and beggars go on blissfully about their business. Home again.

The Wall Street Journal, November 10, 1969

The My Lai Massacre

by Seymour M. Hersh

Lieutenant Accused of Murdering 109 Civilians

FORT BENNING, Ga., Nov. 13—Lt. William L. Calley Jr., 26 years old, is a mild-mannered, boyish-looking Vietnam combat veteran with the nickname "Rusty." The Army is completing an investigation of charges that he deliberately murdered at least 109 Vietnamese civilians in a search-and-destroy mission in March 1968 in a Viet Cong stronghold known as "Pinkville."

Calley has formally been charged with six specifications of mass murder. Each specification cites a number of dead, adding up to the 109 total, and charges that Calley did "with premeditation murder . . . Oriental human beings, whose names and sex are unknown, by shooting them with a rifle."

The Army calls it murder; Calley, his counsel and others associated with the incident describe it as a case of carrying out orders.

"Pinkville" has become a widely known code word among the military in a case that many officers and some Congressmen believe will become far more controversial than the recent murder charges against eight Green Berets.

Army investigation teams spent nearly one year studying the incident before filing charges against Calley, a platoon leader of the Eleventh Brigade of the Americal Division at the time of the killings.

Calley was formally charged on or about Sept. 6, 1969, in the multiple deaths, just a few days before he was due to be released from active service.

Calley has since hired a prominent civilian attorney, former Judge George W. Latimer of the U.S. Court of Military Appeals, and is now awaiting a military determination of whether the evidence justifies a general court-martial. Pentagon officials describe the present stage of the case as the equivalent of a civilian grand jury proceeding.

Calley, meanwhile, is being detained at Fort Benning, where his movements are sharply restricted. Even his exact location on the base is a secret; neither the provost marshal, nor the Army's Criminal Investigation Division knows where he is being held.

The Army has refused to comment on the case, "in order not to prejudice the continuing investigation and rights of the accused." Similarly, Calley—although agreeing to an interview—refused to discuss in detail what happened on March 16, 1968.

However, many other officers and civilian officials, some angered by Calley's action and others angry that charges of murder were filed in the case, talked freely in interviews at Fort Benning and Washington.

These factors are not in dispute:

The Pinkville area, about six miles northeast of Quang Ngai, had been a Viet Cong fortress since the Vietnam war began. In early February 1968, a company of the Eleventh Brigade, as part of Task Force Barker, pushed through the area and was severely shot up.

Calley's platoon suffered casualties. After the Communist Tet offensive in February 1968, a larger assault was mounted, again with high casualties and little success. A third attack was quickly mounted and it was successful.

The Army claimed 128 Viet Cong were killed. Many civilians also were killed in the operation. The area was a free fire zone from which all non-Viet Cong residents had been urged, by leaflet, to flee. Such zones are common throughout Vietnam.

One man who took part in the mission with Calley said that in the earlier two attacks "we were really shot up."

"Every time we got hit it was from the rear," he said. "So the third time in there the order came down to go in and make sure no one was behind.

"We were told to just clear the area. It was a typical combat assault formation. We came in hot, with a cover of artillery in front of us, came down the line and destroyed the village.

"There are always some civilian casualties in a combat operation. He isn't guilty of murder."

The order to clear the area was relayed from the battalion commander to the company commander to Calley, the source said.

Calley's attorney said in an interview: "This is one case that should never have been brought. Whatever killing there was was in a firefight in connection with the operation."

"You can't afford to guess whether a civilian is a Viet Cong or not. Either they shoot you or you shoot them.

"This case is going to be important—to what standard do you hold a combat officer in carrying out a mission?

"There are two instances where murder is acceptable to anybody: where it is excusable and where it is justified. If Calley did shoot anybody because of the tactical situation or while in a firefight, it was either excusable or justifiable."

Adding to the complexity of the case is the fact that investigators from the Army inspector general's office, which conducted the bulk of the investigation, considered filing charges against at least six other men involved in the action March 16.

A Fort Benning infantry officer has found that the facts of the case justify Calley's trial by general court-martial on charges of premeditated murder.

Pentagon officials said that the next steps are for the case to go to Calley's brigade commander and finally to the Fort Benning post commander for findings on whether there should be a court-martial. If they so hold, final charges and specifications will be drawn up and made public at that time, the officials said.

Calley's friends in the officer corps at Fort Benning, many of them West Point graduates, are indignant. However, knowing the high stakes of the case, they express their outrage in private.

"They're using this as a Goddamned example," one officer complained. "He's a good soldier. He followed orders.

"There weren't any friendlies in the village. The orders were to shoot anything that moved."

Another officer said "It could happen to any of us. He has killed and has seen a lot of killing . . . Killing becomes nothing in Vietnam. He knew that there were civilians there, but he also knew that there were VC among them."

A third officer, also familiar with the case, said: "There's this question—I think anyone who goes to (Viet) Nam asks it. What's a civilian? Someone who works for us at day and puts on Viet Cong pajamas at night?"

There is another side of the Calley case—one that the Army cannot yet disclose. Interviews have brought out the fact that the investigation into the Pinkville affair was initiated six months after the incident, only after some of the men who served under Calley complained.

The Army has photographs purported to be of the incident, although these have not been introduced as evidence in the case, and may not be.

"They simply shot up this village and (Calley) was the leader of it," said one Washington source. "When one guy refused to do it, Calley took the rifle away and did the shooting himself."

Asked about this, Calley refused to comment.

One Pentagon officer discussing the case tapped his knee with his hand and remarked, "Some of those kids he shot were this high. I don't think they were Viet Cong. Do you?"

None of the men interviewed about the incident denied that women and children were shot.

A source of amazement among all those interviewed was that the story had yet to reach the press.

"Pinkville has been a word among GIs for a year," one official said. "I'll never cease to be amazed that it hasn't been written about before."

A high-ranking officer commented that he first heard talk of the Pinkville incident soon after it happened; the officer was on duty in Saigon at the time.

Why did the Army choose to prosecute this case? On what is it basing the charge that Calley acted with premeditation before killing? The court-martial should supply the answers to these questions, but some of the men already have their opinions.

"The Army knew it was going to get clobbered on this at some point," one military source commented. "If they don't prosecute somebody, if this stuff comes out without the Army taking some action, it could be even worse."

Another view that many held was that the top level of the military was concerned about possible war crime tribunals after the Vietnam war.

As for Calley—he is smoking four packs of cigarettes daily and getting out of shape. He is 5-foot-3, slender, with expressionless gray eyes and thinning brown hair. He seems slightly bewildered and hurt by the charges against him. He says he wants nothing more than to be cleared and return to the Army.

"I know this sounds funny," he said in an interview, "but I like the Army . . . and I don't want to do anything to hurt it."

Friends described Calley as a "gung-ho Army man . . . Army all the way." Ironically, even his stanchest supporters admit, his enthusiasm may be somewhat to blame.

"Maybe he did take some order to clear out the village a little bit too literally," one friend said, "but he's a fine boy."

Calley had been shipped home early from Vietnam, after the Army refused his request to extend his tour of duty. Until the incident at Pinkville, he had received nothing but high ratings from his superior officers. He was scheduled to be awarded the Bronze and Silver Stars for his combat efforts, he said. He has heard nothing about the medals since arriving at Fort Benning.

Calley was born in Miami, Fla., and flunked out of the Palm Beach Junior College before enlisting in the Army. He became a second lieutenant in September 1967, shortly after going to Vietnam. The Army lists his home of record as Waynesville, N.C.

An information sheet put out by the public affairs officer of the Americal Division the day after the March 16 engagement contained this terse mention of the incident: "The swiftness with which the units moved into the area surprised the enemy. After the battle the Eleventh Brigade moved into the village searching each hut and tunnel."

St. Louis Post-Dispatch, November 13, 1969

Hamlet Attack Called "Point-Blank Murder"

WASHINGTON, Nov. 20—Three American soldiers who participated in the March 1968 attack on a Vietnam village called Pinkville said in interviews made public today that their Army combat unit perpetrated, in the words of one, "pointblank murder" on the residents.

"The whole thing was so deliberate. It was point-blank murder and I was standing there watching it," said Sgt. Michael Bernhardt, Franklin Square, N.Y., now completing his Army tour at Fort Dix, N.J.

Bernhardt was a member of one of three platoons of an Eleventh Infantry Brigade company under the command of Capt. Ernest Medina. The company entered the Viet Cong–dominated area on March 16, 1968, when on a search-and-destroy mission. Pinkville, known to Vietnamese as Song My village, is about six miles northeast of Quang Ngai.

The Army has charged Lt. William L. Calley Jr., Miami, one of Medina's platoon leaders, with the murder of 109 South Vietnamese civilians in the attack. A squad leader in Calley's platoon, Sgt. David Mitchell, St. Francisville, La., is under investigation for assault with intent to murder.

At least four other men, including Medina, are under investigation in connection with the incident. Calley and his attorney, George W. Latimer, Salt Lake City, have said that the unit was under orders to clear the area.

Bernhardt, interviewed at Fort Dix, said he had been delayed on the operation and fell slightly behind the company, then led by Calley's platoon, as it entered the village. This is his version of what took place:

"They (Calley's men) were doing a whole lot of shooting up there, but none of it was incoming—I'd been around enough to tell that. I figured they were advancing on the village with fire power.

"I walked up and saw these guys doing strange things. They were doing it three ways. One: They were setting fire to the hootches and huts and waiting for people to come out and then shooting them up. Two: They were going into the hootches and shooting them up. Three: They were gathering people in groups and shooting them.

"As I walked in, you could see piles of people all through the village . . . all over. They were gathered up into large groups.

"I saw them shoot an M-79 (grenade launcher) into a group of people who were still alive. But it (the shooting) was mostly done with a machine gun. They were shooting women and children just like anybody else.

"We met no resistance and I only saw three captured weapons. We had no casualties. It was just like any other Vietnamese village—old Papa-san, women and kids. As a matter of fact, I don't remember seeing one military-age male in the entire place, dead or alive. The only prisoner I saw was about 50."

An Army communique reporting on the operation said that Medina's company recovered two M-1 rifles, a carbine, a short-wave radio and enemy documents in the assault. The Viet Cong body count was listed as 128 and there was no mention of civilian casualties.

Bernhardt, short and intense, told his story in staccato fashion, with an obvious sense of relief at finally talking about it. At one point he said to his interviewer: "You're surprised? I wouldn't be surprised at anything these dudes (the men who did the shooting) did."

Bernhardt said he had no idea precisely how many villagers were shot. He said that he had heard death counts ranging from 170 to more than 700.

Bernhardt also said he had no idea whether Calley personally shot 109 civilians, as the Army has charged. However, he said, "I know myself that he killed a whole lot of people." Residents of the Pinkville areas have told newspapermen that 567 villagers were killed in the operation.

Why did the men run amuck?

"It's my belief," the sergeant said, "that the company was conditioned to do this. The treatment was lousy . . . We were always out in the bushes. I think they were expecting us to run into resistance at Pinkville and also expecting them (the Viet Cong) to use the people as hostages."

A few days before the mission, he said, the men's general contempt for Vietnamese civilians intensified when some GIs walked into a landmine, injuring nearly 20 and killing at least one member of the company.

Why didn't he report the incident at the time?

"After it was all over, some colonel came down to the fire-base where we were stationed and asked about it, but we heard no further. Later they (Medina and some other officers) called me over to the command post and asked me not to write my Congressman."

(The Army subsequently substantiated Bernhardt's accusation. In a private letter dated Aug. 6, 1969, Col. John G. Hill Jr., a deputy for staff action control in the office of Army Chief of Staff William C. Westmoreland, wrote that Medina acknowledged that he had requested Bernhardt to wait until a brigade investigation of the incident was completed. Nothing came of the investigation.)

Bernhardt said that about 90 per cent of the 60 to 70 men in the short-handed company were involved in the shootings. He took no part, he said. "I only shoot at people who shoot at me," was his explanation.

"The Army ordered me not to talk," Bernhardt told the interviewer. "But there are some orders that I have to personally decide whether to obey; I have my own conscience to consider.

"The whole thing has kind of made me wonder if I could trust people any more."

His opinion, he said, is that a higher ranking officer must have ordered the destruction of Pinkville. "Calley's just a small fry," he said.

Bernhardt said the Army must have known at high levels just what did happen at Pinkville.

"They've got pictures. Some dude went along on the mission and shot pictures," he said.

Bernhardt said the photographs were shown to him in the Article 32 proceeding, which concluded that the charges against Calley were justified.

"They showed a mass of people . . . this pile-up of people. I don't see how anybody could say it was artillery or crossfire that killed those people," he said.

(The Cleveland Plain Dealer printed today photographs showing South Vietnamese civilians allegedly killed in the incident. It said the photographs came from a former Army combat photographer, Ronald L. Haeberle, Cleveland.

(Haeberle said in a copyright story that he joined the company just before it entered the village and heard from the men that the villagers were suspected of being Viet Cong sympathizers. He said he saw men, women and children killed.)

Another witness to the shootings was Michael Terry, Orem, Utah, then a member of the C Platoon of Medina's company and now a sophomore at nearby Brigham Young University. Interviewed at his home, Terry said he, too, came on the scene moments after the killings began.

"They just marched through shooting everybody," he said. "Seems like no one said anything . . . They just started pulling people out and shooting them."

At one point, he said, more than 20 villagers were lined up in front of a ditch and shot.

"They had them in a group standing over a ditch—just like a Nazi-type thing . . . One officer ordered a kid to machine-gun everybody down, but the kid just couldn't do it. He threw the machine gun down and the officer picked it up . . ." Terry said.

"I don't remember seeing any men in the ditch. Mostly women and kids."

Later, he and the platoon team he headed were taking a lunch break near the ditch when, Terry said, he noticed "some of them were still breathing . . . They were pretty badly shot up. They weren't going to get any medical help, and so we shot them. Shot maybe five of them . . ."

Why did it happen?

"I think that probably the officers didn't really know if they were ordered to kill the villagers or not . . . A lot of guys feel that they (the South Vietnamese civilians) aren't human beings; we just treated them like animals."

Apparently one officer, who was not from Medina's company, attempted to halt the shootings. Terry and Bernhardt both reported that a helicopter pilot from an aviation support unit landed in the midst of the incident and attempted to quell it.

The officer warned that he would report the shootings. On the next day, the pilot was killed in action and the subsequent investigation started by officials of the Eleventh Brigade was dropped after one and a half days because of insufficient evidence.

Terry said he first learned of the present investigation when he was interviewed last spring by a colonel from the Army Inspector General's office. Bernhardt was not questioned until

a team from the Army's Criminal Investigation Division visited him two months ago.

The third witness to the Pinkville shootings cannot be identified. He is still on active duty with the Army on the West
Coast. But he corroborated in detail the Bernhardt and Terry
descriptions of that day in March 1968.

"I was shooting pigs and a chicken while the others were
shooting people," he said. "It isn't just a nightmare; I'm completely aware of how real this was.

"It's something I don't think a person would understand—the reality of it just didn't hit me until recently, when
I read about it again in the newspapers."

All three GIs were read key excerpts from a three-page letter
sent in March by a former GI, Ronald Ridenhour, to the Army
and 30 other officials, including some Senators. The letter outlined the Pinkville incident as he understood it. It was Ridenhour's persistence that prompted the Army to begin its
high-level investigation in April.

Ridenhour, now a student at Claremont (Calif.) Men's College, was not in Medina's company and did not participate in
the shootings. He relied on information from Terry and Bernhardt, among many others, to draft his letter.

Calley's attorney refused to comment on the new charges
brought out in the interviews. But another source, discussing
Calley's position, said, "Nobody's put the finger yet on the
man who started it."

The source said also that he understood that Calley and
other officers in the company initially resisted the orders but
eventually did their job. Calley's platoon led the attack on the
village, with the other units forming a horseshoe-shaped cordon around the area, to prevent enemy troops from fleeing.

"I don't care whether Calley used the best judgment or
not—he was faced with a tough decision," the source said.

St. Louis Post-Dispatch, November 20, 1969

Ex-GI Tells of Killing Civilians at Pinkville

TERRE HAUTE, Ind., Nov. 25—A former GI told in interviews
yesterday how he executed, under orders, dozens of South

Vietnamese civilians during the United States Army attack on the village of Song My in March 1968. He estimated that he and his fellow soldiers shot 370 villagers during the operation in what has become known as Pinkville.

Paul Meadlo, 22 years old, West Terre Haute, Ind., a farm community near the Illinois border, gave an eyewitness account—the first made available thus far—of what happened when a platoon led by Lt. William L. Calley Jr. entered Pinkville on a search-and-destroy mission. The Army has acknowledged that at least 100 civilians were killed by the men; Vietnamese survivors had told reporters that the death total was 567.

Meadlo, who was wounded in a mine accident the day after Pinkville, disclosed that the company captain, Ernest Medina, was in the area at the time of the shootings and made no attempt to stop them.

Calley, 26, Waynesville, N.C., has been accused of the premeditated murder of 109 civilians in the incident. Medina, as commander of the Eleventh Infantry Brigade unit, is under investigation for his role in the shootings. Last week the Army said that at least 24 other men were under investigation, including Calley's chief noncommissioned officer, Sgt. David Mitchell, 29, St. Francisville, La., who is being investigated for assault with intent to commit murder. Calley was ordered yesterday to stand general court-martial.

Here is Meadlo's story as given in interviews at his mother's home near Terre Haute:

"There was supposed to have been some Viet Cong in Pinkville and we began to make a sweep through it. Once we got there we began gathering up the people . . . started putting them in big mobs. There must have been about 40 or 45 civilians standing in one big circle in the middle of the village . . . Calley told me and a couple of other guys to watch them.

" 'You know what I want you to do with them' he said," Meadlo related. He and the others continued to guard the group. "About 10 minutes later Calley came back. 'Get with it,' he said. 'I want them dead.'

"So we stood about 10 or 15 feet away from them, then he (Calley) started shooting them. Then he told me to start shooting them. . . . I started to shoot them, but the other guys (who had been assigned to guard the civilians) wouldn't do it.

"So we (Meadlo and Calley) went ahead and killed them. I used more than a whole clip—actually I used four or five clips," Meadlo said. (There are 17 M-16 shells in a clip.) He estimated that he killed at least 15 civilians—or nearly half of those in the circle.

Asked what he thought at the time, Meadlo said, "I just thought we were supposed to do it." Later, he said that the shooting "did take a load off my conscience for the buddies we'd lost. It was just revenge, that's all it was."

The company had been in the field for 40 days without relief before the Pinkville incident on March 16, and had lost a number of men in mine accidents. Hostility to the Vietnamese was high in the company, Meadlo said.

The killings continued.

"We had about seven or eight civilians gathered in a hootch, and I was going to throw a hand grenade in. But someone told us to take them to the ditch (a drainage ditch in the village into which many civilians were herded—and shot).

"Calley was there and said to me, 'Meadlo, we've got another job to do.' So we pushed our seven to eight people in with the big bunch of them. And so I began shooting them all. So did Mitchell, Calley . . . (At this point Meadlo could not remember any more men involved). I guess I shot maybe 25 or 20 people in the ditch."

His role in the killings had not yet ended.

"After the ditch, there were just some people in hootches. I knew there were some people down in one hootch, maybe two or three, so I just threw a hand grenade in."

Meadlo is a tall, clean-cut son of an Indiana coal mine worker. He married his high-school sweetheart in suburban Terre Haute, began rearing a family (he has two children) and was drafted. He had been in Vietnam four months at the time of Pinkville. On the next day, March 17, his foot was blown off, when, while following Calley on an operation, a land mine was set off.

As Meadlo was waiting to be evacuated, other men in the

company had reported that he told Calley that "this was his (Meadlo's) punishment for what he had done the day before." He warned, according to onlookers, that Calley would have his day of judgment too. Asked about this, Meadlo said he could not remember.

Meadlo is back at a factory job now in Terre Haute, fighting to keep a full disability payment from the Veterans' Administration. The loss of his right foot seems to bother him less than the loss of his self-respect.

Like other members of his company, he had been called just days before the interview by an officer at Fort Benning, Ga., where Calley is being held, and advised that he should not discuss the case with reporters. But, like other members of his company, he seemed eager to talk.

"This has made him awful nervous," explained his mother, Mrs. Myrtle Meadlo, 57, New Goshen, Ind. "He seems like he just can't get over it.

"I sent them a good boy and they made him a murderer."

Why did he do it?

"We all were under orders," Meadlo said. "We all thought we were doing the right thing. . . . At the time it didn't bother me."

He began having serious doubts that night about what he had done at Pinkville. He says he still has them.

"The kids and the women—they didn't have any right to die.

"In the beginning," Meadlo said, "I just thought we were going to be murdering the Viet Cong." He, like other members of his company, had attended a squad meeting the night before, at which time Company Commander Medina promised the boys a good firefight.

Calley and his platoon were assigned the key role of entering the Pinkville area first.

"When we came in we thought we were getting fired on," Meadlo said, although the company suffered no casualties, apparently because the Viet Cong had fled from the area during the night.

"We came in from this open field, and somebody spotted this one gook out there. He was down in a shelter, scared and huddling. . . . Someone said, 'There's a gook over here,' and

asked what to do with him. Mitchell said, 'Shoot him,' and
he did. The gook was standing up and shaking and waving
his arms when he got it.

"Then we came onto this hootch, and one door was hard
to open."

Meadlo said he crashed through the door and "found an
old man in there shaking.

"I told them, 'I got one,' and it was Mitchell who told me
to shoot him. That was the first man I shot. He was hiding
in a dugout, shaking his head and waving his arms, trying to
tell me not to shoot him."

After the carnage, Meadlo said, "I heard that all we were
supposed to do was kill the VC. Mitchell said we were just
supposed to shoot the men."

Women and children also were shot. Meadlo estimated that
at least 310 persons were shot to death by the Americans that
day.

"I know it was far more than 100 as the U.S. Army now
says. I'm absolutely sure of that. There were bodies all
around."

He has some haunting memories, he says. "They didn't put
up a fight or anything. The women huddled against their children and took it. They brought their kids real close to their
stomachs and hugged them, and put their bodies over them
trying to save them. It didn't do much good," Meadlo said.

Two things puzzled him. He vigorously disputes the repeated reports of an artillery barrage before the village was
approached.

"There wasn't any artillery barrage whatsoever in the village. Only some gunships firing from above," he said.

The South Vietnamese government said Saturday that 20
civilians were killed in the Pinkville attack, most of them victims of tactical air strikes or an artillery barrage laid down
before the U.S. troops moved in. The government denied
reports of a massacre.

Meadlo is curious also about the role of Capt. Medina in
the incident.

"I don't know if the C.O. (Company Commander) gave
the order to kill or not, but he was right there when it happened. Why didn't he stop it? He and Calley passed each other

quite a few times that morning, but didn't say anything. Medina just kept marching around. He could've put a stop to it anytime he wanted."

The whole operation took about 30 minutes, Meadlo said.

As for Calley, Meadlo told of an incident a few weeks before Pinkville.

"We saw this woman walking across this rice paddy and Calley said, 'Shoot her,' so we did. When we got there the girl was alive, had this hole in her side. Calley tried to get someone to shoot her again; I don't know if he did."

In addition, Calley and Medina had told the men before Pinkville, Meadlo said, "that if we ever shoot any civilians, we should go ahead and plant a hand grenade on them."

Meadlo is not sure, but he thinks the feel of death came quickly to the company once it got to Vietnam.

"We were cautious at first, but as soon as the first man was killed, a new feeling came through the company . . . almost as if we all knew there was going to be a lot more killing."

St. Louis Post-Dispatch, November 25, 1969

Massacre at Takeo

by T. D. Allman

Yesterday's Prisoners Lie Dead in
Bloody Cambodian Schoolyard

TAKEO, Cambodia, April 17—Before, there had been about 200 Vietnamese men and boys crowded into the enclosure. Now there were less than 50.

Bodies lay to one side.

"They killed them last night at 7:30," a Vietnamese man told us.

We had driven our small car into the school compound. From a distance of 40 feet, we could see the blood-stained walls.

We jumped out of our car and ran, nearly slipping in the blood, into the enclosure.

"Where are the others?" I asked an old Vietnamese man with a wispy Ho Chi Minh beard.

"They killed them all last night. They will kill us all tonight. They say we are Vietcong. But we are just shopkeepers," the man said.

It was the third mass killing of ethnic Vietnamese discovered in Cambodia in recent days.

I and another reporter found it today after we had recalled seeing 200 Vietnamese men and boys crowded into an open-walled building yesterday and decided, "Let's go see those Vietnamese to see if they're all right."

The hour's drive from Phnom Penh to Takeo passes through tranquil countryside, with jitney busses competing with cows and bullock carts for a place on the road.

Except for a convoy of ammunition trucks near Phnom Penh, we saw nothing to remind us that Cambodia is at war.

Even in Takeo, there was the typical air of peace that characterizes the tranquility of a lazy afternoon in a Cambodian market town.

And then we found the scene at the school.

"They took the bodies away at 2 in the morning. Two truckloads of the dead and badly wounded—150 in all," a Vietnamese said.

"Can you save my brother?" he pleaded. A man about 30 with at least five bullet wounds in him lay on the concrete floor, the straw mat upon which he lay soaked with blood. He and the others had received no medical attention although Takeo has a hospital.

Near him lay a boy, about 10 years old, with two bullet wounds in his mangled leg.

Cambodian soldiers came up and motioned us away. They seemed tired and scared.

"Are you Vietcong?" I asked the Vietnamese.

"We have lived here all our lives. We are not Vietcong," said the old man. "Stay with us, or they will kill us too."

The old man and his friends spoke calmly and with no emotion in their voices.

My companion, Time correspondent Robert Anson, talked to the guard while I planned.

"Can we take the child?" I asked.

Answered another man, "Take all the wounded, or they will die."

We took the child and lay him on the back seat of the car.

"We'll be back in two hours," we said. "Before dark."

"If you don't," the old man answered, "you will find us dead."

We roared back to Phnom Penh, not stopping at any of the checkpoints. The Vietnamese boy held my hand tightly. Anson kept asking, "He's not dead is he?"

We stopped at the first Catholic church we found in Phnom Penh. The French priest led us to a French hospital near the Hotel Le Royale.

After fretting about who would pay the bills for the boy, the nurses finally let him in.

Then a French doctor came.

"Who are you?" he asked. "Who are his parents? He has a gun wound."

"You know," he said as he gave the child oxygen, "you must not think it is only the Cambodians who do this. I was down in Takeo last week and I patched up 15 Cambodians wounded by a Vietcong grenade."

I ran out to get back in the car to reach Takeo by dark. Already the journalists had heard Anson, and were rushing to their cars.

At Takeo, I asked one of the soldiers, "Was there an attack here? Is that why you killed them?"

He seemed ashamed, but said: "No, we were ordered. The Vietcong are our enemies and all Vietnamese are Vietcong. They were ready to help the Vietcong if they came."

The madness of the catastrophe that has overtaken Cambodia since March 18, in a way, is summed up in the tall, unshaven and totally placid exterior of a Cambodian paratroop captain who so far has refused to give his name to the press.

The man stands more than six feet tall, rare for a Cambodian, and he describes military events tersely and unemotionally, like a professional.

But in less than one month, he has ordered the deaths of about 40 Vietnamese civilians—men, women and children. Journalists interviewed him following the Prasaut massacre in Svay Rieng province nearly two weeks ago.

At that time, he admitted ordering the mass slayings there "because they were Vietcong."

The officer was transferred to the until now placid little provincial capital of Takeo, 50 miles south of Phnom Penh and about the same distance from the South Vietnamese border.

It is the major town in the province, which has an estimated 10,000 North Vietnamese and Vietcong troops dug into sanctuaries along the border.

Takeo was also the scene of major pro-Sihanouk demonstrations in the days immediately after the March 18 coup. Officials estimated that there were almost 4,000 pro-Sihanouk demonstrators at one time or another.

One of the first acts by the tall Cambodian captain after his transfer to Takeo was to order the 200 Vietnamese men and boys rounded up and held in detention.

It was after a sumptuous French lunch, topped off with a

chocolate souffle, by the palm-fringed swimming pool at the venerable Hotel le Royale that we had decided today to drive out to visit the Vietnamese prisoners and the paratroop captain whom we had jokingly called "Killer."

The paratroop captain was nowhere in sight during our brief, rushed visit to Takeo, but Cambodian soldiers lounged around eating bananas just 50 yards from where the bodies lay.

I must stop writing now, fill my car with gas and get back to Takeo before dark.

"We will take all the wounded you can bring us," said the French doctor. If we are lucky tonight, we shall have more wounded for him to stitch up. If we are not, all we will have are dead Vietnamese shopkeepers and small farmers, all born and raised in Cambodia, for the photographers to take pictures of.

The Washington Post, April 18, 1970

The Aftermath of a Massacre: Newsmen Rescue 7

TAKEO, Cambodia—"Please rent a truck in Phnom Penh to take us away," the old Vietnamese pleaded.

He was one of the 50 survivors of the Thursday night massacre of 140 Vietnamese in a walled schoolyard here.

It was now after dark Friday, and the old man was watching me and my colleague, Robert Anson of Time Magazine, prepare to head back to Phnom Penh with seven other survivors, four little boys and three wounded men.

I asked a Cambodian if he would rent us a truck, but he wanted 12,000 riels (over $200) and we didn't have enough.

"Get out of here before the police stop you," other Western newsmen who were staying behind told us.

We started off in our car with the seven survivors. It was the second such trip of the day. Earlier, after coming upon the bloody massacre site almost by accident, Anson and I had rushed back to the capital with a wounded 8-year-old boy.

We had also rallied several of our colleagues from the Royale Hotel to get them to go to Takeo in hopes their presence might be protection for the remaining Vietnamese.

Over the past several days, several Cambodians had told me that they considered all Vietnamese to be Vietcong, the hated invaders of the country.

During the 50-mile ride to Phnom Penh on the second trip, the Vietnamese showed no emotion at all. The least wounded of the men told me his life story:

"I was born in Takeo 42 years ago. I am not a Vietcong. None of us are. I passed the eighth grade and I have the certificate. In 1942, I worked for the French officers in Takeo. That is why I can speak to you now.

"I had a small shop.

"They came and took all the men and boys—from six up to the old grandfathers. Then they shot us. My sons are dead. This is my brother on the seat. Are they killing Vietnamese in Phnom Penh too?"

We passed a convoy of Cambodian recruits, singing and shouting on buses in the darkness, as we headed north to the city.

On the outskirts of town, the car engine failed, then started, then failed and started again. It was the spark plugs. We inched along a little further and then police surrounded us.

"These are Vietnamese," said one policeman. "I want to see their identity cards."

"They are all wounded, let me pass," I said. The other journalists had stopped too, and while they distracted the police I drove off, but the car would not go faster than 25 miles an hour.

A police motorcycle overtook us, and as we passed by the airport, one of the policemen was waving an automatic pistol.

"Don't you know we have orders to shoot?" he asked. "You all could have been shot dead."

The police captain arrived. "These people were badly hurt in an accident," I shouted. "If you do not let us pass, I will tell your superiors and they will punish you."

"What kind of an accident?" the police chief wanted to know.

He finally agreed to let us proceed, on the condition that we went to the commissariat of police in town. I agreed, but had no intention of going anywhere but to the hospital.

At the main intersection in Phnom Penh I turned left, toward the hospital, rather than going straight on to the police station.

The police blew their horns and pulled out their guns. I slammed on the brakes and ran over to the police chief's jeep.

"Go ahead, shoot me," I shouted in French. "Right here in the heart. But I am going to the hospital."

It was an utterly calculated move, which I had been planning for about ten minutes—and utterly devoid of risk. The Cambodian police would never have shot a white man down on the main boulevard of Phnom Penh. They followed us to the hospital.

At the hospital, the Vietnamese were all taken, where they joined the other little boy I had brought up earlier. Two hours later, they were still operating on the most seriously wounded man. The others seemed in good shape.

After a drink, about 20 of us went to the sumptuous suburban villas of the minister of information, Trinh Hoanh, and of the deputy prime minister, Prince Sisowath Sirik Matak.

At both places, the leaders refused to see us, though at the deputy prime minister's house, I was allowed to talk to the head bodyguard, a young Cambodian army officer, fluent in French, who wore his revolver in a holster belt around his waist, like an American cowboy.

"The deputy prime minister will give a press conference on April 20," he said. "You can see him then."

He added, "All the time the press harps on the fact that we massacre Vietnamese. You never report that the Vietnamese are attacking us, that they kill us."

"The men in Takeo killed no one," I said. "This will hurt you in America now that you want arms," I said.

He answered: "They are all Vietnamese. The Germans bombed London, didn't they?"

"But there was no fighting at Takeo," I said. A simple telephone call to Takeo could save those still living.

He replied: "It is all the same." As for telephone calls, the days of one-man rule are over in Cambodia. The provincial authorities are in charge.

It was, of course, those same provincial authorities who had ordered the massacre. The local commander, who refused to give his name, had claimed the victims were killed in a crossfire during a Vietcong attack, but even his own soldiers denied this. "There was no attack," one sergeant told me. "We just shot them."

We walked back to my car. "I can only tell you this will hurt you in world public opinion and in the United States," I said.

"We still find out who our friends are," the captain said. "Prince Sirik Matak talked for an hour yesterday with your charge d'affaires, Monsieur Rives. He was very sympathetic."

Indeed, many diplomats in Phnom Penh have attempted to make allowances for or otherwise explain the killings.

"These things happen," one Western ambassador told me. "War is new to Cambodia. There's bound to be some initial fumbling."

On the morning before we discovered the Takeo massacre, an American official told me, "All this can be exaggerated. I have the feeling these incidents are going to die down."

Indeed, Western officials, in their enthusiasm for the new anti-Communist government here, seem unwilling or unable to accept the fact that slaughters of innocent civilians are taking place, seemingly with government encouragement.

"Did you really see all these alleged killings?" a Western diplomat demanded of me irritably today. "Some of you people will do anything for a story."

At the gate, the Cambodian bodyguard of the deputy prime minister said, "We want the journalists to see everything. We have nothing to hide. Come to the press conference on the 20th. You can ask any question you want."

The Washington Post, April 20, 1970

from
Kent State: What Happened and Why

by James A. Michener

What happened on Monday

THE CRUCIAL EVENT at Kent State was, of course, the action of the National Guard on Monday, May 4. Here is what happened.

At 11:00 in the morning of a bright, sunny day, students began collecting on the commons as their 9:55–10:45 classes ended. They came casually at first, then in larger numbers when some of their 11:00–11:50 classes dismissed early because the confusion on campus made it too difficult to teach. Many students wandered by, as they always did, to check on what might be happening. Another set of classes, 12:05–12:55, would soon convene, and it was traditional for students who were involved either in leaving one class or heading for another to use the commons as their walkway. Without question, they had a right to be on the commons. But were they entitled to be there this day? A state of emergency had been declared by Satrom, presumably outlawing any unusual gatherings. Classes would meet, and that was about all. Yet testimony from students is overwhelming that they believed their campus to be operating as usual. On Friday a rally had been openly announced for Monday noon, and invitations to attend it had been circulated on succeeding days; in fact, announcements for this rally had been scrawled on certain blackboards and were seen by students when they reported for classes on Monday. Furthermore, those students and faculty who had left the campus Friday afternoon could not have listened to local radio stations and would have had no personal knowledge of what the situation was. Later we shall watch several professors, absent over the weekend, as they specifically instruct their students, with the most laudable intentions, to leave class and observe the campus rally. The rally may have been forbidden, but there were too many who either were not aware of this fact or did not believe it.

At 11:15 leaders of the National Guard, in discussion with school officials, became aware of this confusion and asked that the university radio station WKSU and the school intercom announce: 'All outdoor demonstrations and gatherings are banned by order of the governor. The National Guard has the power of arrest.' This was repeated several times but reached only a small proportion of the students, because the intercom system operated in only certain classrooms and none of the dormitories. But the rally had been forbidden; everyone knew it except the students.

At 11:30 General Canterbury, fresh from the inconclusive and even contradictory meeting with university and town officials, arrived at the burned-out ROTC building, surveyed the commons which lay before him, and concluded that the crowd was orderly and did not constitute any kind of significant threat. He could not at that moment have known that the impending dismissal of the 11:00–11:50 class would promptly crowd the commons.

At 11:45 General Canterbury, unaware that the radio broadcast canceling the rally had been heard by so few people, and not knowing about the normal movements of students going from class to class, was astonished to see so many students proceeding as if the rally were still authorized. The crowd was growing larger every minute. He saw about 600 students massing not far from his troops and became justifiably concerned. Giving a clear order, he commanded that the students be dispersed. This order was given before any rocks had been thrown.

At 11:48 someone began ringing the Victory Bell. Two students climbed onto its brick housing to issue frenzied calls to action. The bell continued clanging intermittently during the next fifteen minutes, and this coincided with the end of another class period, so that a constant press of new arrivals kept pouring onto the commons, while a much larger group watched from various walkways, driveways and porches of classroom buildings.

At 11:49 Officer Harold E. Rice, of the campus police, stood by the ruins of the ROTC building and read the riot act over a bullhorn: 'Attention! This is an order. Disperse immediately. This is an order. Leave this area immediately. This is an order. Disperse.' Unfortunately, he was so far away from the students that they could not hear him, and his words had no effect.

At 11:50 a National Guard jeep was driven up, with a driver at the wheel and two armed Guardsmen perched high atop the rear seat. Officer Rice climbed into the right front seat and with his bullhorn proceeded to read the riot act repeatedly as the jeep moved slowly along the edges of the crowd: 'This assembly is unlawful. This crowd must disperse immediately. This is an order.' (Later, certain students would claim that Rice *asked* them to break up the crowd but did not *order* them to do so, and it is possible that in one or another of the repetitions he may have used those words, but the evidence is overwhelming that he recited the version, as given, at least eight times.) The jeep was greeted with catcalls, boos, cursing and a shower of rocks; few of the latter reached the jeep and none appear to have struck any of the four passengers.

At 11:52, as the jeep made its slow progress, with Rice still shouting over the bullhorn, he spotted in the crowd someone he recognized as a leader of riots on the two preceding nights, and he wanted to arrest him. So the driver edged the jeep right into the edge of the crowd, but the young radical saw what Rice was up to and slipped away. So that all students might be properly warned, the jeep made three complete circuits.

At 11:55 the order was passed to the Guardsmen: 'If you have not already done so, load and lock. Prepare for gas attack. Prepare to move out.'

At 11:58 it was obvious that Rice in the jeep was accomplishing nothing, so Major Harry Jones ran out, banged on the jeep with his baton, and ordered it to return to the ROTC building.

At 11:59 General Canterbury gave the order: 'Prepare to move out and disperse this mob.' There is considerable variance in published reports as to the number of troops he had at his disposal. Inaccessibility of accurate records makes any estimate arbitrary; some seem much too low. It would appear that the total contingent contained 113 Guardsmen, disposed as follows: three senior officers, Brigadier General Robert H. Canterbury, Lieutenant Colonel Charles Fassinger, Major Harry D. Jones in command of three units of troops arranged in this order. On the left flank, nearest to the tennis courts, Charlie Company, First Battalion, 145th Infantry, consisting of two officers (Captain Ron Snyder, Lieutenant Herthneck) and 34 enlisted men; in the center, headed for Taylor Hall, G Troop, Second Squadron, 107th Armored Cavalry Regiment, consisting of two officers (Captain Raymond J. Srp, Lieutenant Stevenson) and 16 enlisted men; on the right flank, headed toward Johnson Hall, Alpha Company of the 145th, consisting of three officers (Captain John E. Martin, Lieutenant Klein, Lieutenant Fallon) and 51 enlisted men, but to Alpha Company, two members of Charlie Company (Richard Love and Richard Lutey) had attached themselves because their own unit had moved out before they could catch up with it. The contingent therefore included 10 officers and 103 enlisted men.

According to the plan that General Canterbury had worked out with his commanders, the Guardsmen were to sweep the commons toward the southeast, driving all demonstrators across the crest of Blanket Hill, keeping Taylor Hall on their left, the pagoda on the right. The troops would then push the students down the far slope of the hill toward the practice football field, and the operation would be completed. Captain Snyder had suggested an additional detail: his left-flank Charlie Company would sweep left of Taylor Hall and take a holding position between it and Prentice while the center and right flank completed the main sweep on the other side of Taylor. To this General Canterbury assented, adding, 'Before you step off, fire a barrage of tear gas.'

It is important to visualize the number of students confronting the Guard. At 11:45 Colonel Fassinger had estimated the number of students on the commons—that is, in position to constitute a threat of some kind to the Guard—as 'more than 500.' In the interval this number had grown to 600 and then to something over 800. Now it might number as high as 1,100; for students were piling in from all directions as their classes ended. But a much larger crowd had assembled on the terraces of halls like Johnson and Stopher to the west, Prentice and Engleman to the east. And the largest group of all filled the open spaces directly in back of ROTC toward Administration. All of these must be considered as spectators only, and they could have numbered as many as 2,500. Included among them were townspeople, high-school children, professors and, of course, university students. As they were situated that morning they formed a gigantic amphitheater focusing upon a small stage of green.*

At 12:00 sharp, before the order to march could be given, an unidentified spokesman for the students, perhaps a faculty member, ran up to Canterbury and said, 'General, you must not march against the students,' to which the general replied that the students congregated illegally. 'These students,' he told the intercessor, 'are going to have to find out what law and order is all about.' Then he nodded to his commanders; the first slim gray tear-gas canisters popped out in their long parabolas toward the demonstrators, and 103 Guardsmen plus 10 officers stepped off into the history of contemporary America. The three senior officers, apparently by accident, distributed themselves among the units: Major Jones stayed with Charlie Company on the left flank; Colonel Fassinger marched with G Troop in the center; General Canterbury went with Alpha Company on the right flank.

At 12:01 Captain Snyder positioned himself on the extreme right of his men, so that when the gas stopped and his troop broke off from the other units for the drive to the east end of Taylor Hall, he would be anchor man on the right flank. Following his custom, he kept up a barrage of tear gas. A tear-gas canister launched by an M-79 is a most effective crowd-control device; if fired on a level trajectory (none were), it has sufficient velocity to kill a man at twenty-five yards. A sudden cross wind blew up to spread it across the field and up the Taylor Hall slope—before long the smoke would be inhaled

*Eszterhas and Roberts believe the crowd to have been much larger: 'By a few minutes before noon nearly fifteen hundred students had gathered around the bell. Another two thousand to three thousand students were assembled on the opposite side of the commons behind the National Guard lines. Another two thousand were on the northern edge of the commons near the tennis courts.' One member of the research team, working independently, came up with almost these same estimates, but other members, reviewing each available photograph, convinced him that his figures were too high.

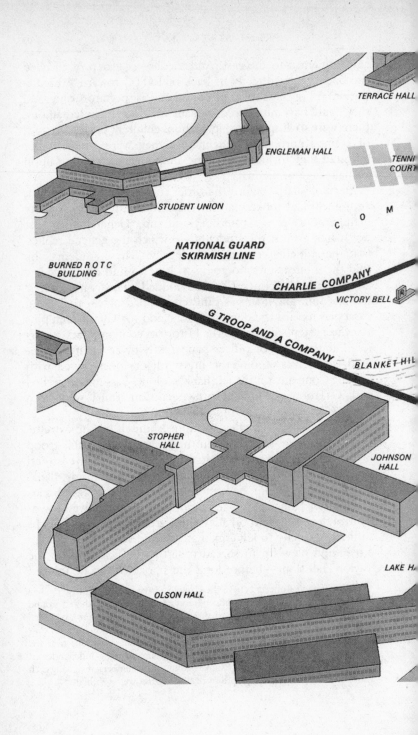

TERRACE HALL

ENGLEMAN HALL

TENNI
COURT

STUDENT UNION

C O M

NATIONAL GUARD
SKIRMISH LINE

BURNED R O T C
BUILDING

CHARLIE COMPANY

VICTORY BELL

G TROOP AND A COMPANY

BLANKET HIL

STOPHER
HALL

JOHNSON
HALL

LAKE H

OLSON HALL

VERDER HALL

N S

PRENTICE HALL

MIDWAY DRIVE

TAYLOR HALL

PARKING LOT

1. 2. 5
4
3

STATUE

FENCE

TROOPS FIRE

PAGODA

KNEELING POSITION

PRACTICE FIELD

MONDAY, MAY 4, 1970

THE FIVE STUDENTS: 1. Jeff Miller
2. Doug Wrentmore 3. Allison Krause
4. Bill Schroeder 5. Sandy Scheuer

GYMNASIUM

into the Taylor Hall air-conditioning system, filling that building and affecting all those inside. Now, as Snyder's men moved ever closer to the crowd, those among the more daring demonstrators came darting forward, seizing the hot canisters and flinging them back. Most of these fell short of the approaching Guardsmen. One says *most* because certain unusually aggressive—or brave, if you prefer—young men not only grabbed the canisters but also ran good distances with them back toward the troops, throwing them from such short range that canisters sometimes landed in the ranks.

At 12:02 Snyder's men reached the point at which they would detach themselves from the center unit for the swing left. As they reached the Victory Bell a 'bushy-haired young man' (Snyder's description) came darting down out of the trees on the slope and gave the bell a final swing. Then he wound up and hurled a fistful of small stones. Ron Snyder turned his back on the stones, spun around and brought his baton down across the boy's shoulders with such force as to snap off the tip of the baton. The young man then reached in his pocket and brought forth a piece of metal with four finger holes—a brass knuckle. Snyder hit him again. He dropped the piece of metal and dashed back up the hill.

At 12:03, as Charlie Company began to climb up through the trees, they could see a number of demonstrators along the brow of the hill. They fired more tear gas in that direction and kept climbing. At the top they beheld an even greater number of students gathered below them in the Prentice Hall parking lot, and here Snyder decided to form his line. He placed his men in a single row from the northeast corner of Taylor toward the nearest corner of Prentice, leaving twenty yards open at the Prentice Hall end as an escape route.

At 12:04 they were in the position they would hold for the next twenty minutes, and we shall leave them there as we follow the center unit, but before we do so, one incident should be noted. Clustered in front of Snyder's formation were a number of frantic coeds, and he began calling to them through the voice emitter in his M-17-type gas mask (all officers and non-coms were equipped with these special masks, through which voice instructions could be issued). He shouted to them, 'Come on, come on! It's safe.' Like a herd of frightened deer, the girls suddenly made their decision and bolted through the opening and around the side of the building. In the next few minutes Snyder estimates that he let upward of 100 students pass, all trying to escape the agony of drifting tear gas.

At 12:04, as Captain Snyder's troops were reaching their final position at the east end of Taylor, Captain Srp's center unit of eighteen soldiers was approaching the pagoda, undergoing as they marched a heavy barrage of curses and their own tear-gas canisters thrown back at them by determined students. The canisters were of little consequence to the Guardsmen, who, having anticipated this maneuver, were wearing gas masks, but this in itself posed a problem. As one Guardsman says, 'It was a hot day, and this was the hottest part of the day. The gas masks were heavy, and as soon as you put yours on, you were hemmed in and sweating. Your vision was restricted to a narrow field and sometimes you couldn't even see the man next to you. It was like being tucked away in a corner . . . sweating.' To the outsider, seeing a Guardsman in mask evoked a sense of the unreal, the mechanical, the monster from outer space, and this was an advantage, for it frightened the observer; but to the man inside the mask, there was a sense of remoteness, of detachment, of being alone in a crowd, and that was a disadvantage, for it cut a soldier off from his fellows and from reality.

At 12:05 the unit reached the pagoda, where it was met by a good deal more than returning gas canisters. Students began throwing rocks at them, and chunks of wood studded with nails, and jagged hunks of concrete. Where did they get such missiles? At least two witnesses swear they saw girls carrying heavy handbags from which they distributed rocks to men students, and some photographs would seem to substantiate this charge. At a nearby construction site some students had picked up fragments of concrete block. And some of the students had armed themselves with bricks. In addition, there were a few—not many—small stones and pebbles available on the campus itself, but these were inconsequential; on a normal day one could have searched this commons fairly carefully, without finding a rock large enough to throw at anyone.

Did any of the missiles hit the troops? Not many. The dis-

tances between the mass of the students and the Guards were
later stepped off by expert judges, who concluded that students would have required good right arms like Mickey Man-
tle's to have reached the Guardsmen with even small stones.
But as with the canisters, some students were bold enough to
run back down the hill and throw from close range, and their
stones did hit.

Worse, in a way, than the missiles were the epithets, especially when launched by coeds. A steady barrage of curses,
obscenities and fatal challenges came down upon the Guard,
whose gas masks did not prevent their hearing what they were
being called. Girls were particularly abusive, using the foulest
language and taunting the Guardsmen with being 'shit-heels,
motherfuckers and half-ass pigs.' Others called them less explosive but equally hurtful names: 'toy soldiers, murderers,
weekend warriors, fascists.' During the half hour that the
Guardsmen were in action, this rain of abuse never let up.

In addition, a special few among the students—perhaps a
dozen men and four girls—kept running at the Guardsmen,
daring them to retaliate. One young man, with extremely long
hair held in place by a beaded band, displayed a large black
flag at the end of a pole, and with extreme bravado waved it
at critical moments at the troops, almost in their faces, retreating to eight or ten yards at other times. Guardsmen behind their masks were unsure whether it was a Vietcong flag
or not. Certainly it was not any with which they were familiar.

As this central detachment reached the top of Blanket Hill,
they found that the mass of students had melted away before
them. Never were the students very close, except for the daring ones, and people who have studied the facts and the photographs become irritated when someone asks, 'Why didn't
the Guard surround the students and arrest them?' The
Guards were never within a hundred yards of being able to
surround this ebbing and flowing mass of people, and besides,
there were not nearly enough men to have done so had they
desired. It was like asking a group of six people why they
didn't surround a flock of pigeons who kept flying in all directions.

At 12:06, with the central unit perched atop the hill, the
officers faced an awkward decision. They now stood between

Taylor Hall on their left and the cement pagoda on their right, with almost the whole body of students, who a few minutes ago had been on the commons, facing them in the various open spaces that lay ahead. Also, many hundreds of additional students who could have known nothing of the preceding sweep, now arrived from their 11:00–11:50 classes, which had been held in buildings at distant parts of the campus, or were on their way to 12:05–12:55 classes in buildings nearby. For any-one to say of these students 'They had no right to be on the campus' is to misunderstand the nature of a university; they had every right to be precisely where they were, but they did add to the visual confusion. If at this crucial moment the Guard had returned to their ROTC station, they would have had an absolutely clear escape route, but in all likelihood the radical students would have followed behind them, so that the situation would have wound up exactly as it started, with the Guard at ROTC and the students occupying Blanket Hill.

So an understandable decision was reached that the Guard would push on and try to clear the large area that lay ahead, an open field used for practice football, with a soccer goal at the south end and a baseball diamond at the north. What none of the Guardsmen apparently realized was that along the eastern side of this field, ran a sturdy six-foot-high chain-link fence, topped by three strands of heavy barbed wire. What was worse, at the baseball end this fence took a right-angle turn to the west to form a catcher's backstop; it would be difficult to find on the campus a more perfect cul-de-sac. It was inconceivable that soldiers would march with their eyes open into such a trap, where they would be subjected to hostile students who would have large numbers of rocks at their disposal. But this is what happened.

At 12:07 the center unit, led by Colonel Fassinger and re-inforced by large numbers from Captain Martin's Alpha Company on the right flank, marched down from the pagoda and smack against the steel chain-link fence. They had placed themselves in a position from which they could escape only by retreating, which, when it happened, would have to be interpreted by the watching students as a defeat for the Guard. How large was this combined unit? Photographs show at least 69 Guards against the fence, but one meticulous investigation augments that number. There were 75 Guards present, comprised as follows: two senior officers (Canterbury, Fassinger) with 53 men from Alpha Company, including three officers, plus the two casuals from Charlie Company, to which were added 18 men from G Troop, including two officers. However, Major Jones now ran across the grass to join the group. We have seen that he started with Charlie Company, which halted at the far end of Taylor Hall, so that during the first few minutes when the Guard stood penned against the fence, he had been with Captain Snyder. But quickly he discerned what was developing; elbowing his way through the crowd of students, he joined the larger contingent at the fence, where he would play a conspicuous role in what was to follow. The unit therefore consisted of 68 enlisted men led by 8 officers.

As soon as the students saw that the Guard was pinned against the fence, they began to close in from the parking lot to the north, cursing, throwing rocks, waving flags and tossing back gas canisters. The word *surrounded* has often been used to describe the Guard's condition at this moment. Nothing could be more inappropriate. To the east, across the fence, there was no one but Mike Alewitz, the socialist leader whose presence there will be explained later. To the south—that is, behind the Guardsmen on the practice field—there was no one for more than a hundred yards, as numerous photographs attest. And to the west, over the path to the pagoda which the Guard had just traversed, students had not yet re-formed. Far from being surrounded, the Guard had empty space on all sides.

At 12:10 the Guard underwent a heavy assault from the north, where students had grown bolder and were dashing in close to unload. What happened next remains obscure, but the sixteen enlisted men of G Troop, plus one other, believing their supply of tear gas to have been exhausted, knelt on one knee and assumed a firing position, aiming their rifles directly at the gadfly students who were pestering them. It appears that they must have been ordered by some officer to assume this frightening and provocative position, and if a further command had been given at this moment, students on the parking lot would have been mowed down, but no such command was uttered. (Actually, the beleaguered troops had more gas. Specialist Russell Repp of A Company still carried eight canisters, a fact known by his immediate superiors, Srp and Stevenson, but not by those in command.)

The brazen young man with the black flag ran close and waved it before the silent rifles, daring the Guardsmen to fire. When they refrained, he and others were convinced that they would never shoot, that even if they did, the bullets were blanks. That much of the situation is ascertainable; what is still unknown is what took place at the core of the unit, where General Canterbury discussed this dangerous and ridiculous situation with his officers.

At 12:18 Colonel Fassinger issued the order: 'Regroup back at ROTC.' And the contingent began to form up for retreat, assuming the pattern of a flying wedge, point foremost and flanks trailing, with officers inside the V. (It may seem strange that a colonel should have been issuing orders to the troops when a general was present, but this was not unusual. In the navy, for example, it is customary for a five-star admiral attended by three- and two-star admirals to choose some warship as headquarters afloat; when they do so, they are technically under the command of whatever captain is in charge of the ship they occupy, and all personnel attached to that ship take their orders from the captain and not from the admirals.)

At 12:19 Fassinger radioed: 'For the third time I am asking for more tear gas.'

At 12:22 Fassinger gave the order to march, and his unit left the fence, where they had suffered much humiliation, some of it at their own hands, crossed the service road, and at an increasing speed, hurried back up to the pagoda. They were hot, and angry, and disgusted at having been pinned down against the fence, infuriated by the students who had challenged them, and bitterly resentful of the girls who even now trailed them up the hill, cursing and reviling them. Their gas masks prevented them from seeing just what was happening, and they were only vaguely aware of students still massed on their right flank. They had a long hot hill to climb and they were sweating. Were they in danger? On their left flank there was nobody except a few Guardsmen stationed at Johnson

Hall. In the rear there was a handful of gadflies, mostly girls, who posed no threat at all. Straight ahead the commons was almost empty. At Taylor Hall the porches were crowded with students, at least half of them girls, and some teachers who were observing the scene. On the right flank, however, at a distance of seventy yards, there was a large mass of students, including many of those who had been pestering the Guard at the practice field but also many who were merely passing by between classes. The closest student seems to have been at least twenty yards away; the bulk were more than a hundred yards distant. But there was movement, and in the confusion of the march, it could be interpreted as hostile.

At 12:24, with the escape route back to ROTC completely unimpeded and with alternate ones available either to the left flank or to the rear, some Guardsmen on the trailing right flank suddenly stopped, wheeled 135 degrees to the right— that is, they turned almost completely around—faced the students who had collected on the south side of Taylor Hall, and dropped their rifles to a ready position. It so happens that three tape recorders, operated by would-be reporters from the School of Journalism, were running at this moment, and their testimony as to what happened next is incontrovertible.

There was a single shot—some people heard it as two almost simultaneous shots—then a period of silence lasting about two seconds, then a prolonged but thin fusillade, not a single angry burst, lasting about eight seconds, then another silence, and two final shots. The shooting had covered thirteen seconds, which is a very long time under such circumstances, and fifty-five M-1 bullets seem to have been discharged, plus five pistol shots and the single blast from a shotgun. Twenty-eight different Guardsmen did the firing, but this fact should be remembered: If each of the men had fired his weapon directly at the massed students, the killing would have been terrible, for a steel-jacketed M-1 bullet can carry two miles and penetrate two or four or six bodies in doing so. Fortunately, many of the men found it impossible to fire into a crowd and pointed their rifles upward—avoiding what could have been a general slaughter.

But some Guardsmen, fed up with the riotous behavior of the students and in fear of their lives, did fire directly into the crowd, and when the volley ended, thirteen bodies were scattered over the grass and the distant parking area. Four were dead, and nine were wounded more or less severely.

On the afternoon of the shooting, a governmental agency took careful measurements (which have not previously been released); here are the dry statistics. Thirteen young people shot: eleven men, two girls. All were registered at the university and all were attending classes formally. If the wounded were arranged in order of their nearness to the Guard, the closest young man was 71 feet away from the rifles, the farthest 745 feet away, or nearly two and a half football fields. The seventh body—that is, the median one—happened to be Doug Wrentmore, who was 329 feet away. The distances of the four dead at the time they were hit are as follows:

Jeffrey Glenn Miller, fifth closest	265 feet
Allison B. Krause, eighth closest	343 feet
William K. Schroeder, tenth closest	382 feet
Sandra Lee Scheuer, eleventh closest	390 feet

Of the thirteen who were struck by bullets, two were shot in the front, seven from the side, and four from the rear. Ten of the wounded were struck directly, three by ricochets. We came upon fairly strong evidence that a fourteenth student was hit in the left arm, but not seriously; he fled the area with his wound concealed, apprehensive lest he become involved with police or FBI investigations. He was more than 600 feet away when hit, and obviously not involved in the immediate action, though what he might have been doing earlier, we have no way of knowing.

Ascertaining the correct time of the firing is difficult, for whereas most of the other events can be confirmed with minute accuracy, often by three or four people, it is impossible to state precisely when the shooting occurred, even though hundreds of eyewitnesses observed it. The time indicated here is by no means a consensus, but it does represent the best-educated guess. Estimates vary from 12:12, which hardly gives the Guard time to cover the distances involved, let alone take action at any of the resting points, to 12:45, which is the solid report of one of the most careful investigating committees but which seems ridiculously late to those who participated. A highly placed Guard officer who was in position to know what was happening, who looked at his wristwatch at the moment of firing, and who was responsible for calling the information in to the command post, affirms, 'The shooting took place at exactly 12:20, for I checked it as it occurred.' But the official log of the action recording his report times it at 12:26. The apparent impossibility of determining a precise time is not critical; if an early time is used, it means only that the Guardsmen had conducted all their operations on the practice field in less than three minutes, which seems impossible; if a late time is used it means that they dallied there for more than half an hour, which seems contrary to evidence and common sense. The time given here was noted by a journalism student at Taylor Hall, who made no great claim for its accuracy, but it does conform to the judgment of many.

At 12:25 (or 12:46, if the extreme time is accepted) the firing ceased, thanks to the energetic efforts of Major Jones, who can be seen in photographs beating his troops over their helmets with his swagger stick, pleading with them to stop. General Canterbury can also be seen, turning in surprise from the direction in which he had been heading—down the hill to safety—which lends credence to the theory that if an order of some kind had been given to fire, he at least had not been informed of it.

At 12:29, after a lapse of at least four minutes, during which frantic officers did their best to restore order, the unit re-formed, retreated in orderly fashion to their staging area at ROTC, and surrendered their guns for registry and inspection. Jack Deegan, a Marine Corps reservist majoring in history, who had followed the unit at extremely close range all the way from the link fence, reports, 'I saw one young Guard lying on the ground, tossing himself back and forth in hysteria and moaning something I couldn't hear.' He may have been William Herschler, whom the FBI reported as having cried, 'I just shot two teenagers.' At this point a veil of silence descended over the Guard.

Letters to the editor

WHEN Harold Walker left the field of the dead, he suspected that on his many rolls of film he might have captured some compelling shots, but like John Filo, he could not be sure until he saw them developed. So he did what he had been taught in journalism: 'If you think you have a scoop, get in touch with the newspaper you know best.' In his case it was *The Gazette and Daily*, of York, Pennsylvania, one of America's real odd-ball journals. Operating in the heart of the conservative Pennsylvania–German country and surrounded by people who vote Republican, it is liberal and outspoken. It is also interesting in that it is edited on a devil-may-care basis, with the editor saying pretty much what he likes. Among the American newspapers from cities its size, it has no peer. That many of its subscribers consider it communistic is a cross it has to bear.

Its reaction to the Walker photographs was typical. Calling Walker on the phone as he worked at Kent State, the editor said excitedly, 'These photos are too good to waste on a small-town paper like this. I've alerted the *Washington Post* and they want you to fly to their offices immediately.'

With some excitement young Walker caught a plane at Akron, and entered the *Post* editorial offices to find the entire staff gazing in bewilderment at the shots which he himself had not yet seen. 'How did you get such photos?' some of the older men asked in admiration, but before Walker could explain, one of the senior editors delivered the crushing decision: 'We're not going to use any of them.'

'Why not?' several assistants asked.

'Because we think they may have been faked.'

'What do you mean?' Walker cried.

'I mean these. The ones showing the National Guard marching up the hill away from the football field.'

'What's wrong with them? I couldn't have got any closer.'

'Yes, but these photos don't show any students following the Guardsmen, and we know from all the news stories that there were students there.'

'Look at the negatives,' Walker pleaded, 'they're in sequence.'

'Yes, but we think you may have spliced in a series of shots taken on Sunday afternoon. There ought to be students visible.'

Walker, exhausted from tension and lack of sleep, looked at his amazing shots of what had happened. Of all the photographs taken that day, they best illustrated the needlessness of the tragedy. Then he looked at the disbelieving experts from the great newspaper. Then he packed up his pictures and went back to York, where they appeared in the *York Gazette and Daily*. It scooped the world.

The York editor came up with the logical idea of having Walker accompany his photographs with a verbal account of what had happened, and the young newsman ended his essay in the way most sensitive men his age would have done: 'I think that when people look at the situation—students shot without warning; the dead and the wounded—there will be sympathy across the nation, no matter what the political beliefs. As for the city of Kent, the whole town seems to be in sympathy with the students.' He concluded: 'I believe the incident may bring the student and the adult communities together. It may bring about mutual understanding.'

Never in his future career as newspaperman will Harold C. Walker, Kent State 1970, be more completely wrong, for even as the paper in York was printing these hopeful and constructive words, the newspaper in Kent was being forced to find space for what will be remembered as one of the most virulent outpourings of community hatred in recent decades. It seemed as if everybody in the Kent area suddenly wanted to unburden himself of resentments against young people, colleges and education which had been festering for years. The paper had to reserve a full page, day after day for several weeks, for this violent outburst, and anyone who wishes to explore the Kent phenomenon more deeply than this book allows, is directed to those terrifying broadsides, printed solid in compact type. They give a portrait of Middle America at the beginning of the 1970's that is frightening. The first group requires no comment.

Authority, law and order are the backbone of our society, for its protection. Would you want authorities to stand by if your home were threatened? Well, Kent State is my home by virtue of taxes spent funding it. What's more, it's their home by virtue of tuition paid. Playful children destroying a disenchanting toy.

How dare they! I stand behind the action of the National Guard! I want my property defended. And if dissenters refuse to obey the final warning before the punishment, hurling taunts, rocks (stones, they say), sticks, brandishing clubs with razor blades imbedded, then the first slap is a mighty sting.

Live ammunition! Well, really, what did they expect, spitballs? How much warning is needed indeed.

Hooray! I shout for God and Country, recourse to justice under law, fifes, drums, martial music, parades, ice cream cones—America, support it or leave it.

Ravenna housewife

When radical students are allowed to go through a town smashing windows, terrifying the citizens, and are allowed to burn buildings belonging to the taxpayers to the ground, I think it is high time that the Guard be brought in to stop them—and stop them in any way they can.

The sooner the students of this country learn that they are not running this country, that they are going to college to learn, *not teach*, the better.

If those students don't like this country or our colleges, why don't they go to the country from which they are being indoctrinated?

Concerned citizen

A surprising number of the writers referred to property rights and taxes. If there had been any doubt as to what values many citizens in this part of Ohio placed in paramount position, these letters settled that question.

We are paying a large percentage of our hard-earned money to support and educate these young people. For what? To let them burn and destroy property that more of our tax money has paid for? Who paid for the hose that was cut while our firemen were trying to stop a fire, set deliberately, all the while being pelted with rocks. Some innocent person's home could very well have burned while our firemen were busy fighting a fire on campus.

Concerned resident

I, and thousands of other old-timers, have been paying taxes for many years—even before some of the present troublemakers were born. These taxes were used, and are being used, to erect and equip modern campus buildings and to pay the salaries of professors (even those who support and condone the actions of the troublemakers) who have such a vital role in the educational process. How many buildings were erected and equipped from taxes paid by campus vandals? How many professors and other university personnel received salaries from taxes paid by campus vandals? This property does not belong to them. It belongs to me and thousands like me who have paid taxes for twenty, thirty and even forty years to provide the money for these facilities. We are lending them OUR facilities and we expect them to take care of OUR property. We do not expect these temporary occupants to burn, damage or destroy that which they have borrowed. We will gladly pay for these buildings, but we see red when OUR property has to be repaired or replaced because of the actions of a few irresponsible misfits who only want to damage or destroy.

A concerned old-timer

Only a small percentage of the letters printed in that period can be reproduced here, but each one chosen represents a score or more. On no subject was the comment more unanimous than on the right of the National Guard to do whatever was required to enforce discipline.

Some have questioned the need of the National Guard on campus and throughout our city. However, I shudder to think of the condition of our city today had they had not been present to protect and preserve what so many have labored endlessly to build.

Kent citizen

Are we the citizens of this fine town going to sit back and allow certain officials to persecute the National Guard for doing their duty? Are we going to accept the theory that these ones involved in this rioting and burning were JUST children?

Since when is rioting, looting, burning, assaulting a town called academic freedom? Is it freedom of expression? Why do they allow these so-called educated punks, who apparently know only how to spell four-lettered words, to run loose on our campuses tearing down and destroying that which good men spent years building up?

I plead with the citizens of Kent to take a stand, don't allow these tragic deaths to go for naught. Make your voice heard. Do not let the National Guard be blamed for something they did not create.

> Signed by one who was taught that 'to educate a man in mind and not in morals is to educate a menace to society'

Congratulations to the Guardsmen for their performance of duty on the Kent University Campus. I hope their actions serve as an example for the entire nation. The governors of our states cannot waste the taxpayers' money playing games. These men were alerted as a last resort to control mob action.

I extend appreciation and whole-hearted support of the Guard of every state for their fine efforts in protecting citizens like me and our property.

> Mother of Guardsman

Not included in this sampling are the numerous letters, submitted by committees, with hundreds and even thousands of names, approving the behavior of the Guard. One of the most interesting themes was the recrudescence of an idea that had been born many years ago and which had enjoyed frequent revival through the decades. In April, 1933, at the depth of the depression, Representative William R. Foss, of the Ohio legislature, proposed that in view of the current oversupply of teachers, more than four thousand of whom were unable to obtain work, it would be a good idea to convert one of the four large colleges—Ohio State University was excluded—into a mental asylum. 'We intend to investigate this proposition thoroughly,' Foss warned, 'and to determine which college can most readily be converted. We're not bluffing.'

After a visit to Kent on May 4 of that year, Foss reported: 'Kent State has the finest, most modern buildings and, therefore, is most adaptable to welfare work. There would be no fire hazard in connection with the structures, and this is an important feature.' Later, referring obliquely to Kent, he said that 'one of the institutions visited was so adapted to welfare needs that it would be difficult to distinguish it from those built for that specific purpose.' The proposal came to naught and Kent State was spared.

However, two years later the idea of converting the college into an asylum surfaced again, and once more, serious consideration was given to closing down the college, but an improvement in the economy saved it. Now, after the riots of 1970, the project was reopened.

I have one possible solution to the problem. Build a fence completely around KSU, put President White and his 550 faculty members inside along with all the agitators that they understand so well and let them do their thing. We could also change the name from KSU to 'Idiot Hill.' Then Dr. White and his faculty and students could assemble and throw rocks at each other and play with matches and burn things down, because they understand each other's reasoning and don't want to be bothered. So be it! I have more ideas, but what's the use. In fact, who needs KSU? Not me.

Kent taxpayer

Letters abusing student behavior were numerous. Their endless and bitter barrage startled the students and saddened the professors, who felt that a whole society was turning against the youth who would soon be constituting that society. One of the reasonable complaints against students follows:

Last night on TV were several shots of protesting students and a leader of these talked for some time about continuing the protest into the summer. The TV program showed pictures and named the student leader.

This student leader was not a student during 1968 and to October, 1969. Girls, wild parties, filthy living conditions and failure to pay bills featured this man; an acme of unreliability. Another man, said to be a leader of Kent SDS, lived with him for a time. His fine parents came to pay the bills he owed us when he disappeared. Word is that other creditors in the area were not so fortunate. Yet, this man is shown as depicting an important trend in our times.

Ravenna citizen

A surprising number of the letter-writers, and among them the most vehement, referred to themselves as members of the silent majority. Two examples follow:

When is the long-silent, long-suffering majority going to rise up in force to show the militant minority on the KSU campus exactly how they feel about them? It's hard to believe that the surly, foul-mouthed, know-nothing punks that have raised so much hell in this town the past few days are speaking for all of us, or half of us, or even one tenth of us. Yet, like any mob, they've got you outnumbered, and any sort of ideology is completely lost in the sadistic pleasure of sheer destruction. In other words, the would-be heroes are behaving exactly like the criminals they are.

As a person young enough to be more a member of their generation than that of their parents, I reject these creeps.

Anti-violent

Kent has tolerated these so-called misunderstood students long enough. The city of Kent should be off-limits to students. Keep them on the university grounds, and when they have completely destroyed it, they can go home and we will be rid of them.

If the National Guard is forced to face these situations without loaded guns, the silent majority has lost everything. The National Guard made only one mistake—they should have fired sooner and longer.

As for the parents of the dead students, I can appreciate their suffering, they probably don't know the truth. A dissident certainly isn't going to write home about his demonstration activities. Parents are learning the hard way and others should take heed. The high school photos that appeared in the paper were all very nice, but how do you explain the mother who refused to identify her own son at the hospital because of his appearance. This same boy had refused to go home on holidays.

I only hope the National Guard will be here the next time we need them. I am fully prepared to protect what is mine—property, home and life—at any cost against these mobs of dissidents in the event our law enforcement is prohibited to do what is necessary.

Ravenna citizen

Numerous letters spoke of the need for instituting some kind of vigilante movement to combat the students. Sometimes this was intimated; often it was spelled out.

There has been no other issue in recent years that has raised my wrath as much as student demonstration, including SDS leadership, against the Vietnam war and against anything else that occurs to the demonstrators.

So, it was refreshing to see a group of hard-hatted construction workers in lower New York do something about it. They went through those demonstrators like Sherman went through Atlanta, leaving sixty or seventy injured. That's exactly what we need . . . a harder line with demonstrators, not the easy, 'pat on the wrist' punishment for their crime.

I'm for raising a counterforce to neutralize the efforts of sometimes silly, and sometimes dangerous, and always unthinking students who want to go to a school without abiding by its rules.

Aurora citizen

My first reaction, and again I have been thinking of this for some time, was to arm both my home and my office. But during moments of more rational thought, I realize that probably all I would accomplish is to shoot myself in the foot. I abhor violence and I have no desire to traipse all over the country protecting other people's property. However, I feel an immediate and compelling responsibility to protect my own locality. I am thinking in the direction of a kind of citizens committee, under appropriate professional direction, who would bear arms against these people to protect our families and property. Further, I will support taxation to raise the funds to provide a capable effective force to deal with this problem.

Kent citizen

Many persons in the Kent area felt that students who dressed oddly or who wore their hair long ought to be disciplined. In fact, the bitterness which such appearance created was one of the recurrent themes in discussing the shooting. Several intimated that the penalty for non-conformity should be death.

It is too bad that a small minority of students feel that these damnable demonstrations must take place. If the slouchily dressed female students and the freakishly dressed, long-haired male students would properly dress and otherwise properly demean themselves as not to make show-offs of themselves, such trouble could be and would be avoided. It is difficult to understand why female students must get out and make such fools of themselves as they do, but it is understandable that male students do so largely to get their screwball mugs on television and in the press.

If the troublemaking students have no better sense than to conduct themselves as they do on our university and college campuses, such as throwing missiles, bottles and bullets at legally constituted police authority and the National Guard, they justly deserve the consequences that they bring upon themselves, even if this does unfortunately result in death.

Attorney-at-law

There were, of course, several letters which challenged the headlong rush to law and order. These writers endeavored to explain that the phrase required careful definition.

Where are the voices of 'law and order' when construction workers in New York City attack a peaceful, non-violent demonstration of anti-war protesters? I would suspect that the lawless action of the construction workers is condoned by the 'silent majority' because they aren't members of the 'effete corps of impudent snobs,' or they aren't 'bums.'

You see, the voices of the silent majority chose to remain silent on those issues. It would appear to me, then, that a double standard exists when people call for law and order—it's a good phrase when applied to young, long-haired dissidents and radicals, but it's a meaningless phrase when applied to the silent majority. I would submit that just as students are not above the law, neither are members of the 'silent majority.'

Ravenna citizen

And from time to time isolated writers would remind the public that four young people were dead, that something had gone fearfully wrong. They sounded like lost voices, except for the eloquence they sometimes introduced into their letters.

I am a KSU student. I am not a radical, but to quote Albert Camus, 'I should like to be able to love my country and to love justice, also.'

The letters I've been reading about the Kent deaths, and the people I've heard saying that the demonstrators deserved to be shot, frighten me. Many justify the slayings because of the property damage that had been done. But the crowd Monday was attacking no buildings. Did they shoot to avenge the burning of the ROTC building?

Revolutionaries and SDSers don't frighten me, nor do squads of police or National Guards. I am afraid of the people who say 'kill the demonstrators, because they destroyed our property.' I am afraid of these people who value property over human life. I am not afraid for my life, but for my soul, and for the sensitivity and humanity that is slowly being erased from our society.

Jesus said that no one can truly love God if he cannot love his fellow man. You people with the 'mow 'em down' philosophy, can you love God without loving Jeffrey, Bill, Sandy and Allison?

Ravenna student

On Monday, May 4, I witnessed the KSU killings. As horrible and frightening as the memories of those experiences are, they are not nearly so terrifying as the hostility that has been revealed in their aftermath. I am not a radical. I do not believe that arson and violence should go unpunished, but I know of no state in which arson carries a death sentence, and there are certainly none in which 'illegal' assembly is punishable by execution.

I have recently heard a multitude of comments such as, 'They should have mowed them all down' or 'I'll bet they think twice next time' or 'They got what they deserved.' It is in the people who make these statements that the real violence is to be found. They seem to be permeated with an intense desire to see destroyed or shackled anything they do not understand or anyone who does not concisely conform to their glorious social ideals about what is 'American.'

They are to be feared far more than are the campus dissidents, for they would destroy something far more precious than property, or even life—they would destroy freedom! And is not freedom supposed to be what America is all about?

Kent State student

It would be fruitless to reproduce all the savage attacks that were visited upon the faculty. The unfortunate resolution adopted in the Akron Church on Tuesday afternoon was referred to in a score of letters, with citizens rebuking them in harsh terms for their one-sided interpretation of what had happened on the campus. Only three letters need be cited here, a typical one of rebuke, and two reflections by university members on the tragedy that had overtaken a notable institution. They represent the kind of reevaluation that was being undertaken across the nation.

I do not understand why the teacher who was convicted of first-degree riot is permitted to teach at the university during the week and serve her time on weekends. She shouldn't even be allowed on the campus, much less be permitted to teach.

Ravenna resident

The meeting of the faculty of Kent State University held on Tuesday [in the Akron church] was deeply disturbing to me. The tone of the meeting seemed to me emotional and rhetorical—in short a mob. And I am sick of emotionalism, mobs and violence.

What is truly academic must be personal and humble. As I recall hearing it read, one of the items in the resolution stated that we will not teach under military coercion. Similarly, I don't see how we can teach under the social pressure of our own desire to reach unanimous decisions.

I want my students back, but I do not want to unite them behind any social issue or against any issue, such as the war in Indochina, even though I abhor that war. I want my students to wander a free campus, and I only want those who are 'academically inclined' to contemplate with humility and with intricacy. I am frightened of the mob—the mob in me.

Kent professor of English

The statement issued [by the faculty] from an Akron church Tuesday correctly expresses the angry mood of the majority of the faculty, but it is not enough. If academic democracy is to work, it must be self-enforcing. We must demonstrate clearly that we understand and are able to assume the responsibility for conduct of our university.

It is imperative that we defend academic freedom, which includes the right to dissent, as we have undertaken to do, but we must insure that the freedom we defend is clearly differentiated from license to destroy by violence. Our campus must remain open to those who would express unpopular ideas, but it must not be a sanctuary for those who commit felonious acts, no matter what purpose they avow.

I am not making just another appeal to 'law and order.' My position is that unless we insist upon the maintenance of orderly processes, the tragic circumstances of last Monday are the eventual and inevitable result.

All who have contributed to the blurring of the connection between the rights and responsibilities of free people must share in the guilt for the deaths of our students: those who have engaged in civil disobedience and have refused to accept the consequences, those who have cried for amnesty for those who have criminally violated the rights of others in pursuit of a worthy cause, those who have failed to understand that destroying a building is not a legitimate exercise of freedom of expression, and those who have stood silently by while this tide of passion has engulfed us in its tragic whorl.

Kent professor of journalism

The most deplorable aspect of these letters was not the explosive outpouring of hatred (which could be forgiven as an autonomic response to phenomena not understood) nor the obvious obsession with property values as opposed to human life (which is often observed in American life) but rather the willingness to condemn all students, perceiving them as a mass to be castigated. Nothing can excuse this error. We must constantly remember that only a small percentage of the Kent student body was involved. The following table has been revised continuously from the day this study started; it was refined whenever new police reports were made available or new photographs came to light. As it now stands, it incorporates the best guesses of many experts but reflects the personal conclusions of none. It is a composite.

Percentage of Student Body of 21,186 Participating in Disturbances

Incident	Total Persons Involved	Non-university Persons	University Persons	%age of Total Student Body Participating
Friday night downtown	1,000	600	400	01.9
Saturday night ROTC fire				
Passive spectators	1,500	250	1,250	05.9
Active participants	500	250	250	01.2
Sunday night sitdown	700	150	550	02.6
Monday noon rally				
Distant spectators	2,500	400	2,100	09.9
Passive on Blanket Hill	650	150	500	02.3
Active on Blanket Hill	450	50	400	01.9

from Kent State: What Happened and Why, 1971

FAIRNESS AND THE DRAFT: 1970

The American Class System

by Stewart Alsop

WASHINGTON—Last week's Supreme Court ruling on draft exemptions for conscientious objectors will make this country's system of military recruitment even more discriminatory than before. And even before the decision, the system was one of blatant class discrimination. This fact probably has at least as much to do with the radicalization of the campuses as the Vietnam war itself.

The Court upheld the appeal of a California intellectual who claimed status as a conscientious objector, not on the accepted basis of "religious training and belief"—he had crossed out that phrase on his application—but as a result of "reading in the fields of history and sociology."

As Selective Service Director Curtis Tarr has pointed out, the ruling will be of no use to the uneducated—it will be useful only to a would-be conscientious objector who has "sharpened his intellect in the matter of religion and philosophy." Selective Service anticipates a flood of CO applications from college graduates who have been busy sharpening their intellects.

Even before the decision, a college man had a far better chance of avoiding the draft, one way or another, than the poor clod who only finished high school. Last year, for example, out of 283,000 men drafted only 28,500 were college men—just over 10 per cent. Well over 40 per cent of the college-age young now go to college. The figures speak for themselves—if you can manage to go to college, your chances of not being drafted are quadrupled.

A system which produces this result is quite clearly based on class discrimination. But the story does not really end there. The radical young, especially in the prestigious Eastern Ivy League colleges, talk as though they were a lost generation, condemned by the system to be hauled away to Vietnam, and killed or wounded—this has been the theme of many a youthful valedictorian. But it is nonsense.

Yale, Harvard and Princeton, to cite three obvious examples, together have graduated precisely two—repeat, two—young men, in the whole course of the war, who were drafted and killed in action in Vietnam. The kind of men who volunteer for dangerous jobs—the Walter Mittys, if you will—still fortunately exist. Yale has had 34 such volunteering types killed in Vietnam, Harvard thirteen, and Princeton thirteen, including civilians. But the only draftees were one Army corporal (Yale) and one private first class (Harvard).

Unless they are Walter Mittys, the small minority of college men who do end up in uniform rarely see any fighting. The Army has adopted a more or less explicit policy of encouraging well-qualified and intelligent young men to "volunteer" for noncombat supply and administrative jobs, to avoid being drafted into the infantry. This system explains why the Army is so reluctant to respond to the urgings of the President and Secretary Laird to set a date after which no draftees will be sent to Vietnam. Without the threat of drafting men into the infantry, the Army fears that its whole system of attracting volunteers by promising them noncombat jobs will break down.

It is a bit strange, surely, when an army recruiting system is squarely based on promising recruits they won't have to hear a bullet fired in anger. In fact, the American Government's message to young men is something like this: "If you are smart, and go to college, you will have a good chance to avoid the draft entirely. If not, you can at least avoid getting shot at by opting for a noncombat job. Leave the fighting to the peasants and the Walter Mittys."

This is not a very inspiring message for the idealistic young. Yet the message is heeded, for entirely understandable reasons. After all, what sensible young man wants to spend two years of his life being shouted at or shot at? The young men who do end up getting shouted at or shot at are of a very different sort from the college radicals.

Their faces appeared in eleven heartrending pages of pictures in Life magazine last year. The pictures, with names and hometowns, were of 242 men who had been killed in Vietnam in one week. It was only necessary to look at those young men, peering innocently out from beyond the grave, to know what kind of young men they were.

They were not the kind of young men to whom it would have occurred to get a teaching job or to go to divinity school in order to avoid the draft, or to get a logistical or noncombat intelligence job to avoid combat. The great majority of them were obviously fresh out of high school, or off the farm or the production line. Most of them came from small towns—Poquonock, Conn., or La Farge, Wis., or Nickerson, Neb., or Morganton, N.C., or the like.

There were a scattering of marines, and three Navy men, probably volunteers for the Navy's dangerous Vietnam river patrols. The rest had been drafted and assigned to the Army specialty known as Eleven Bravo. Eleven Bravo is the infantry. Hardly anyone volunteers for Eleven Bravo, for that is where people get killed.

The United States, according to the radical young, operates under a corrupt system. They are entirely correct. The system is indeed corrupt, in two absolutely fundamental ways.

There are two things the American Government can take away from the American citizen. It can take his money, in taxes. And it can take his body, for services in the armed forces—which can mean taking his life. The taxing power is exercised in such a way that a rich man who uses money to make money, can avoid paying anything like his fair share of taxes. To cite a single example, at current rates on tax-free bonds, a rich man can enjoy an income of $18,000 on $300,000 of capital, without paying a cent of income tax, or even filing a return. A man, with a wife and two children to support, who earned that much with his brains or his muscles, would have to pay the government $3,200, if he did not want to go to jail.

There are many other ways, of course, for a rich man to avoid paying taxes a wage earner has to pay. This blatant class discrimination corrupts the democratic process. The democratic process is even more fatally corrupted when the government's power of military recruitment is also based on class discrimination.

This second corruption of power has unquestionably con-

STEWART ALSOP

tributed to the radicalization of the universities. A young man who exploits the system to duck the draft or avoid combat is only being sensible. But he can never quite shake off the knowledge that others are being shouted at or shot at in his place. In such circumstances, it is not really hard to see why many young men feel a psychic need to believe that America's role in Vietnam is wholly "obscene," and to believe also that the whole American system is rotten and corrupt. And in at least two ways, it is.

Newsweek, June 29, 1970

AN ARMY OF RELUCTANT DRAFTEES:
OCTOBER 1970

You Can't Just Hand Out Orders

by John Saar

FOR 17 DAYS at a time through monsoon rains and tropical heat, the men of Alpha Company, First Battalion, 8th Cavalry, 1st Air Cavalry Airmobile hunt NVA soldiers and supply caches close to the Cambodian border. Stealthing through the bamboo-thicketed hills, they have the same air of acquired professionalism as drafted GIs of past wars. They look the same, even smell the same: a drab green centipede of men in soiled fatigues with the same boy-man faces under the bobbing steel helmet brims.

In reality, the 118 men of Alpha are quite different. They are a microcosm of an Army in evolution, an Army trying to adjust to the winding-down war in Vietnam. Old ideas of dress, behavior, discipline and rank no longer apply. Virtually no draftee wants to be fighting in Vietnam anyway, and in return for his reluctant participation he demands, and gets, personal freedoms that would have driven a MacArthur or a Patton apoplectic. It is an Army in which all questions— including "Why?"—are permissible. Alpha Company seethes with problems, but it has not fallen into chaos. Much of the reason is that a special kind of relationship, new in the Army, exists between the "grunts"—liberated, educated, aware young draftees—and their youthful commander, Captain Brian Utermahlen, West Point class of 1968.

Captain Utermahlen lets it be known in Alpha that he came close to quitting West Point eight separate times. He still rings the bells to which youth responds: honesty, independence, resistance to authority. These are shared attitudes which give him an instinctive rapport with his men, despite his Germanic name, bearing, blond good looks and his obvious devotion to the Army.

Utermahlen's continuing problem is to find an effective

467

compromise between his own professional dedication and his draftees' frank disinterest in anything that might cost an American life. Nothing could suit them better than President Nixon's recent proposal for a cease-fire in place, for Alpha Company has no desire to go on fighting. Grunt logic argues that since the U.S. has decided not to go out and win the war, there's no sense in being the last one to die. Followed to its conclusion and multiplied by every infantry company in Vietnam, this sort of logic—and the new permissiveness—has unquestionably affected the whole Army's combat efficiency. It is no longer the pliant and instantly responsive instrument of the past. Many officers frankly doubt that they could get their men to fight another costly battle such as the 1969 assault on Hamburger Hill that took 84 lives.

"The colonel wants to make contact with the enemy and so do I," says Utermahlen, "but the men flat don't. It's frustrating, but I understand how they feel." Including himself, there are only five career soldiers in the company—"lifers," the draftees call them.

Joe Curry, aged 25, is not one of them. He wears beads and a peace medallion and is one of Utermahlen's platoon sergeants. He was drafted out of an executive job and a prosperous home in Greenwich, Conn. "The object," Curry says, "is to spend your year without getting shot at, or if you do, to get the fewest people hurt. We don't try to frustrate the captain's attempts to kill gooks, but we don't put our hearts in it. If we did we could kill a lot more. Supposedly the mission comes first. I put the welfare of the men first." Pfc. Steve Wright says succinctly: "Two of them want to kill gooks, and the rest of us never want to see any again."

Curry's view finds a partial echo up the line. "We could kill a lot more enemy than we do," says Lt. Colonel Jack Galvin, CO of the battalion of which Alpha is a part, "but we'd have to pay for it, and I won't sacrifice anybody. I won't allow my companies to charge into a bunker area. I'd rather take some criticism." Utermahlen, for the most part, sees eye to eye with the colonel. "Charging up hills," he says happily, "has gone right out of fashion."

When Alpha takes to the jungle on its 17-day missions,

Utermahlen is scarcely recognizable as a traditional Army officer. He runs his company with a "hands-off" technique that develops a subtle community self-discipline. "That way I don't have to be too much of a bad guy," he says. "They police one another." The two black bars on his lapels are superfluous. If the job went up for vote, he would be elected—probably unanimously. "These guys are no longer blindly following puppets," he says. "They're thinkers and they want intelligent leadership. It's not a democracy, but they want to have a say. If I ran this company like an old-time tyrant, I'd have a bunch of rebels. There are people in the company with more experience than I have, and if they think I'm doing something grossly wrong, I'm ready to listen."

Utermahlen has not always had Alpha's support. He relieved a very popular commanding officer. When he took over, he was half prepared for a vengeance grenade attack from his own men—a "fragging." "They told me horror stories about how bad the company was," Utermahlen remembers, "and there were signs around saying the colonel wasn't welcome. I thought, my God, I'm going to be fragged."

He gingerly settled in, but found his position threatened from above by the colonel (Galvin's predecessor) and from below by the grunts. "The colonel told me every time we had contact, we would report at least two confirmed kills. I said, 'I can't do that, sir.' It went against everything I believed in. Only a change of command saved me."

The death of three of his men when they blundered into an ambush that had been set by other GIs was a crushing blow to Utermahlen, and it almost led to a no-confidence strike by the grunts. "I still think of it as my fault," he says, "and I fully expected to be relieved."

A member of the company remembers, "Everybody I knew was pretty sore at him. The platoon the guys were from discussed not going back to the field." Utermahlen survived the immediate crisis. Gradual vindication turned to acceptance and admiration when Utermahlen outfoxed an NVA mortar crew that Alpha was chasing. When night fell, the Communists were still up ahead somewhere, and Utermahlen guessed that they might have his position pinpointed. He ordered his angry company to mount up in the darkness and crabbed them off to a flank. The NVA shells screeched into the vacated spot and exploded harmlessly.

Since the death of a favorite radio operator, Utermahlen has often voiced his hate for the NVA. "Dammit," he will say, pounding his knee, "it's nice to kill gooks." Few if any of his draftee soldiers can work up such a depth of feeling. Says Platoon Sergeant Curry, "I don't understand what makes him dislike gooks so bad he wants to kill them. He once said he had a desire to strangle a gook, and that sickened me."

Pfc. Wayne Johnson, aged 21, from Kissimmee, Fla., has asked for a transfer out of infantry: "I don't like to kill. I hate the thing they believe in, but not the people themselves. Our business is killing, but my heart's not in it."

Perhaps half of Alpha's 21 blacks agree with the alienated view of Pfc. John Munn, a tall, somber soul brother. "I have my life to preserve," says Munn, "but I have nothing against that little man out there. They're fighting for what they believe in, and you can't knock that. I lie on my air mattress at night and I say what am I doing here? I can imagine a war back in the world that I'd fight and wouldn't mind dying in—to keep your people free." Utermahlen quashed a court-martial charge against Munn after witnessing his bravery under fire. He agrees that blacks generally do not get their share of promotions.

During a meal break two grunts were calmly discussing the theory and practice of fragging NCOs:

"If you keep hassling people, tension builds and it has to bring a release."

"A can of tear gas is like a first warning . . ."

Midway through a mission the spindle-legged figure of Pfc. Duane Sedler approaches Utermahlen. Sedler has already won a Bronze Star, but now he politely announces he must refuse an order to go on night ambush. Without rancor Utermahlen tells him he will probably be court-martialed. Sedler, a California college dropout with gentle deep-set eyes and sucked-in cheeks, is obviously distressed: "Those small ambushes with people who don't know what they're doing are dangerous. It's my life and I'd like to try to keep it."

Sedler's friends are sympathetic. "Nobody owns anyone around here," says Pfc. Eugene Dillon. "If he doesn't want to go, it's up to him." Sedler stays with the company, is eventually said to have "shaped up," and the court-martial is quietly forgotten. Disciplinary action in the field is disastrous for morale—and ineffective besides. Military justice has no answer to the grunt's ironic question: "What can they do to me: send me to Vietnam?"

One episode that got under Utermahlen's skin was an odd disagreement with Pfc. Bill Johnson, who twice turned down the Bronze Star. "He's obviously sincere about not wanting any of the Army's medals, and the more I think about it, I may be the one that's screwed up. I told him, 'Don't expect any favors.' Johnson kept his cool and said, 'That's fine with me.' He made me feel," says Utermahlen, his finger and thumb an inch apart, "about that big."

One of Alpha's veteran second-tour soldiers is Sgt. Chris Manis, owner of a tigerish smile, and a special favorite of Utermahlen for his skill and aggression. Manis saw heavy fighting in 1967–68: "We make a lot less contact now, and guys are a lot more afraid. I don't know why." For a time Manis led an elite recon squad popularly known as the "Crazy Eight," until draftee members balked at the discomfort and danger. The unit dissolved.

Marty Hyland is another man who has earned a special relationship with Utermahlen. Hyland is a draftee, a high school graduate, a wearer of beads, peace symbols and generally unbarbered hair. He is also quick, intelligent, quite irreverent and cool enough to pick up, in the field, the skills of an artillery spotter. "He's come through all the problems smelling like a rose," says Utermahlen. The forward observer job is generally held by a lieutenant. Hyland is still a Pfc. The two meet easily, as equals. Utermahlen pretends not to hear when Hyland talks wistfully of civilian days: "Man, did you ever get to hear Janis Joplin at the Fillmore? Outasight. Those were the days of wine and weed."

After 17 days in the bush the company waits to be taken out. The achievements are not very exciting: hospitalization of a Vietnamese couple who surrendered to get medicine for their child; capture of an ancient NVA helmet; claim of two enemy dead, which Utermahlen himself doubts. Success depends on the conscientious execution of patrols; many of the patrols are squad-size, and all nine of the squad leaders are draftees. Sgt. Jim Sgambati is a Silver Star holder: "They screw up the old man. They go out on a patrol and avoid the enemy." And yet compared with other units in Vietnam, Alpha is an exceptionally good company.

As the fleet of Hueys dragonflies in to take them back to Firebase Betty, various men evaluate their recent mission. SP4 Dave Clark, radio operator: "It was all right. Main thing was we got through without getting anyone hurt. We didn't get anything done, but I don't care." SP4 Earl Rucker, medic: "I'm real pleased. No contact and no one got hurt." Captain Brian Utermahlen, company commander: "I'm not pleased. It's fine that we didn't get anybody hurt, but we didn't accomplish anything. Professionally I'm still hungry."

After the jungle, firebase defense is like garrison duty, and the men relish it. Alpha splits into two roughly equal groups for the evening parties: the "juicers" lay in supplies of cold beer, while the "smokers" roll their joints and pack their pipe bowls with strong Vietnamese marijuana. Estimates on marijuana users within Alpha vary from Utermahlen's low of 7% up to the senior pothead in the company's enthusiastic 85%. "We pass the pipe around," says a squad leader, "and we ask what the hell are we doing here?"

Among the grunts there is a general taboo against smoking grass in the field, although some do: "We had one guy who was on grass all the time, and he won the Silver Star. He had it down to an exact science. He'd feel the breeze blowing away from the lifers, and he'd say, 'Hey, the wind's right. Let's get nice.'"

Utermahlen is resolutely opposed to marijuana. "It has no place in the field where you rely on quick thought and reflexes. I know the people who smoke it, but I can never catch them." Marijuana smoking is so extensive that anything more than token enforcement would antagonize a dangerously high percentage of the company. No commander as perceptive as Utermahlen cares to risk confrontations of that nature in Vietnam just now. So downwind from Firebase Betty at night, it sometimes smells as though a large haystack were burning.

Utermahlen's views on military appearance are also relaxed. "What they wear or look like out in the field is very low on my list of priorities. It's one of the compromises I make. As long as a man does his job, I don't care if he wears peace beads or symbols or if he shaves."

The sudden appearance of Neanderthal man would hardly have caused a greater stir than the arrival, in the middle of the mission, of the company's new first sergeant—a 44-year-old, six-foot-two, big bellied, 257-pound giant with a bikinied girl tattooed over 12 inches of forearm. The draftees instantly read about his 25 years of Army service in his seamed face, and they avoided him like an alien being. Captain Utermahlen was uneasy, unwelcoming. It was a sad and unequal contest from the start: a high school dropout asked to administer and discipline a young company where 50% of the GIs have college time.

The first sergeant had served with the same battalion in 1965–66, until he was wounded, but the Army since then had altered beyond his comprehension. "Things have changed. Before, everyone was gung ho and wanted to mix it with Charlie. Now it seems everyone's trying to avoid him." He paused to mop the sweat from his brow with the tattooed girl. "I'm still out to kill gooks; that is what I get paid for. The only thing you can do is force men into contact, but with their attitude now, I don't think we can go on like this for long." Back at the firebase, he announced his dislike of the casual way soldiers responded to some of Utermahlen's less urgent orders. The litter of abandoned ammunition at the firebase also annoyed him. Loose talk about fragging incensed him. He finally reached an insupportable level of frustration. Twice when his patience gave out he drew and leveled his pistol to enforce orders. The second time, the young soldier he had been arguing with about garbage called his bluff and ran off to get his M16 rifle. As the two readied for an incredible high-noon showdown in the middle of the firebase, other soldiers intervened. There was no shooting but, at Captain Utermahlen's request, the first sergeant was reassigned to the States.

On occasion Utermahlen has declined to comply with Colonel Galvin's suggestions. Once, when requested to leave an ambush patrol in his rear, Utermahlen said his men were not well enough trained. The request was pressed, and Utermahlen's jaw dropped into a mulish set as he once again refused. It is this sort of blunt frankness that prompts the grunts to award Utermahlen the supreme accolade of being "a good dude."

In contrast to his men, Captain Utermahlen will probably never be happier or more fulfilled in the service of the United States Army than he is as Alpha's commander. Against the personal exultation of doing the job for which he has been educated, trained and equipped, other factors are relatively insignificant. In the jungle, where his resources, instincts and intelligence are tested to the utmost, he feels no crisis of conscience about the morality of the war. Yet Utermahlen is incapable of divorcing himself from his generation, and ahead lies the certainty of strained relations with the Army. Removed from the simplicity of the jungle, his thoughts move in new directions: "Is there such a thing as a moral war? I don't know. I think about it, and the doubt has been raised in my mind by the protest in the U.S.

"I believe 100% in the U.S. Army," he says, "but I'm not ready to compromise my principles: being honest with people and doing the best job possible for people under and over me. If that hurts my career, then it's just part of the ball game. The job I have comes before any moral judgment on the war, but if I thought it was wrong I definitely would not be fighting here. If I were given an unlawful order, I wouldn't be able to do it. I'd rather suffer the consequences. I've told my wife not to be surprised if I have to leave the Army."

Utermahlen and other officers of his caliber have the flexibility to accommodate the changing generation of soldiers. The question is whether the tradition-steeped hierarchy can in turn meet the demands that officers like Utermahlen are sure to have.

from
Who Was *Lyndon Baines Johnson?*

by Doris Kearns

Guns, butter, and prophecy

LBJ was great in domestic affairs, elder statesman Averell Harriman once observed. "Harry Truman had programs but none got through. Kennedy had no technique. FDR talked simply during the crisis but didn't act enough later. Johnson went back past the New Frontier all the way to the New Deal. He loved FDR and it was fantastic what he did. If it hadn't been for . . . Vietnam he'd have been the greatest President ever. Even so he'll still be remembered as great."

If it hadn't been for Vietnam . . . How many times this phrase has been spoken in conversations assessing Johnson's place in history. For it is impossible to disconnect Johnson from that war, and undeniable that the fighting abroad halted progress toward the Great Society. Indeed, Johnson claimed he himself foresaw and weighed the devastating consequences of war on domestic reform, but felt he had no choice but to escalate the war.

"I knew from the start," Johnson told me in 1970, describing the early weeks of 1965, "that I was bound to be crucified either way I moved. If I left the woman I really loved—the Great Society—in order to get involved with that bitch of a war on the other side of the world, then I would lose everything at home. All my programs. All my hopes to feed the hungry and shelter the homeless. All my dreams to provide education and medical care to the browns and the blacks and the lame and the poor. But if I left that war and let the Communists take over South Vietnam, then I would be seen as a coward and my nation would be seen as an appeaser and we would both find it impossible to accomplish anything for anybody anywhere on the entire globe.

"Oh, I could see it coming all right; history provided too

475

many cases where the sound of the bugle put an immediate
end to the hopes and dreams of the best reformers: the Spanish American War drowned the populist spirit, World War I
ended Woodrow Wilson's New Freedom, World War II
brought the New Deal to a close. Once the war began, then
all those conservatives in the Congress would use it as a
weapon against the Great Society. You see, they'd never
wanted to help the poor or the Negroes in the first place. But
they were having a hard time figuring out how to make their
opposition sound noble in a time of great prosperity. But the
war. Oh, they'd use it to say they were against my programs,
not because they were against the poor—why they were as
generous and as charitable as the best of Americans—but because the war had to come first. First we had to beat those
godless Communists, and then we could worry about the
homeless Americans. And the generals. Oh, they'd love the
war too. It's hard to be a military hero without a war. Heroes
need battles and bombs and bullets in order to be heroic.
That's why I am suspicious of the military. They're always so
narrow in their appraisal of everything. They see everything
in military terms. Oh, I could see it coming. And I didn't like
the smell of it. I didn't like anything about it, but I think the
situation in South Vietnam bothered me most. They never
seemed able to get themselves together down there. Always
fighting with one another. Bad. Bad.

"Yet everything I knew about history told me that if I got
out of Vietnam and let Ho Chi Minh run through the streets
of Saigon, then I'd be doing exactly what Chamberlain did in
World War II. I'd be giving a big fat reward to aggression.
And I knew that if we let Communist aggression succeed in
taking over South Vietnam, there would follow in this country
an endless national debate—a mean and destructive debate
—that would shatter my presidency, kill my Administration,
and damage our democracy. I knew that Harry Truman and
Dean Acheson had lost their effectiveness from the day that
the Communists took over in China. I believed that the loss
of China had played a large role in the rise of Joe McCarthy.
And I knew that all these problems, taken together, were
chickenshit compared with what might happen if we lost
Vietnam.

"For this time there would be Robert Kennedy out in front leading the fight against me, telling everyone that I had betrayed John Kennedy's commitment to South Vietnam. That I had let a democracy fall into the hands of the Communists. That I was a coward. An unmanly man. A man without a spine. Oh, I could see it coming all right. Every night when I fell asleep I would see myself tied to the ground in the middle of a long, open space. In the distance, I could hear the voices of thousands of people. They were all shouting at me and running toward me: Coward! Traitor! Weakling! They kept coming closer. They began throwing stones. At exactly that moment I would generally wake up . . . terribly shaken. But there was more. You see, I was as sure as any man could be that once we showed how weak we were, Moscow and Peking would move in a flash to exploit our weakness. They might move independently or they might move together. But move they would—whether through nuclear blackmail, through subversion, with regular armed forces, or in some other manner. As nearly as anyone can be certain of anything, I knew they couldn't resist the opportunity to expand their control over the vacuum of power we would leave behind us. And so would begin World War III. So you see, I was bound to be crucified either way I moved."

Did Lyndon Johnson believe all this? Yes . . . some of the time. Was it true? Some of it; and the rest was not simply pure illusion. For even Johnson's most grotesque exaggerations were always constructed on some fragment of reality, so that they could never be totally disproven by factual evidence or unanswerable logic alone, only by rejecting his judgment for one more reasonable, more consonant with the known facts.

Johnson's description of the nature of the challenge in Vietnam was, of course, a product of his unique personal qualities. But it is important to remember that many others shared this view, although they would not have expressed it with such color or hyperbole. And they, like Johnson, derived their convictions from historical experience.

Johnson's most trusted advisers on Vietnam, Robert McNamara and McGeorge Bundy, contended that step-by-step escalation would allow continuous monitoring of the reactions of China and Russia; it would emphasize America's limited objective; it might press Hanoi to negotiate in order to prevent the terrible damage which large-scale bombing would inflict. Johnson chose gradual escalation. It was a predictable choice, based, as it was, on the type of approach he found most congenial: limited bombing represented the moderate path between the competing extremes of widespread destruction and total withdrawal. Of course sometimes, as every automobile driver knows, the middle of the road is the most dangerous place to be.

In Johnson's view, limited bombing was "seduction," not "rape," and seduction was controllable, even reversible. "I saw our bombs as my political resources for negotiating a peace. On the one hand, our planes and our bombs could be used as carrots for the South, strengthening the morale of the South Vietnamese and pushing them to clean up their corrupt house by demonstrating the depth of our commitment to the war. On the other hand, our bombs could be used as sticks against the North, pressuring North Vietnam to stop its aggression against the South. By keeping a lid on all the designated targets, I knew I could keep the control of the war in my own hands. If China reacted to our slow escalation by threatening to retaliate, we'd have plenty of time to ease off the bombing. But this control—so essential for preventing World War III—would be lost the moment we unleashed a total assault on the North, for that would be rape rather than seduction, and then there would be no turning back. The Chinese reaction would be instant and total."

Johnson's metaphor suggests an effort to force the contest in Vietnam into a pattern drawn from the politics he knew so well. As long as he could use force as a means of bargaining, he could moderate his anxiety about the difficulties and unknowable dangers of this strange war in an unfamiliar land.

In the White House Situation Room—the illusion of control

JOHNSON needed to believe that the Vietnamese experience could be assimilated into his own framework; he needed to interpret everything on his own terms. This master practitioner of bargaining and negotiation was also a man who perceived the fragility of that process. He preached rationality and compromise, but continually feared and imagined the emergence of unreasoning passions and unyielding ideologies. His conduct and words expressed a will to believe, a fear of his own doubts. Johnson was always afraid that he himself might give way to irrational emotions; control came to appear a requirement of survival of the self. By treating the struggle in Vietnam as an exercise in bargaining, he sought to deny that it might exist somewhere beyond the healthy bounds of reasonable negotiations. Thus, the purpose of the bombs was not to hurt or destroy; that was a by-product. They were all means of bargaining without words. Since Johnson, if not an expert on warfare, was a master bargainer, he would retain final control over when and where to bomb so that his knowledge of detail could be both used and increased. The same attention to the minutiae of power that had characterized his relations with the Congress would now characterize his conduct of the war.

Long hours of discussion preceded the choice of each bombing target. Tracing his fingers across the map of Vietnam, the President would point to various potential targets —railroad bridges, army barracks, oil storage depots, airfields, armored truck convoys, factories—demanding to know the costs and benefits of attacking each one. "How many tons of bombs will it take to destroy this?" he would ask, while waving a photograph of a railroad bridge twenty miles from Da Nang. "How important is that [a petroleum storage depot] to the North Vietnamese? If we choose these army barracks fifteen miles from Haiphong, how can we be certain of the accuracy of our aim?" So it went: one by one. In developing his list of permissible targets, Johnson operated on the fundamental premise that he could only bomb up to a certain point. To move beyond that point—for example, to mine Haiphong Harbor or bomb the Red River dikes—might risk war with Russia or China. Suspicious that the North Vietnamese had entered into secret treaties with the Communist superpowers, Johnson lived in constant fear of triggering some imaginary provision of some imaginary treaty.

This belief was linked to, became part of, his continued magnification of the stakes. Vietnam was no longer just a "test case for wars of national liberation," a "lesson for aggressors," a necessity to "prevent the fall of Southeast Asia," or part of the "containment of China." America fought in Vietnam to prevent the otherwise inevitable onset of World War III. It was an aspect of Johnson's own dimension, the size of his personal needs and his huge ambitions to satisfy the needs of all others, that only the largest cause of all—to forestall world-wide destruction—could justify actions which were now so threatening to the public's admiration, his life as a public man, and his capacity to lead others, in their own interest, to accept his grandly benevolent intention.

"I never knew," Johnson later said, "as I sat there in the afternoon, approving targets one, two, and three, whether one of those three might just be the one to set off the provisions of those secret treaties. In the dark at night, I would lie awake picturing my boys flying around North Vietnam, asking myself an endless series of questions. What if one of those targets you picked today triggers off Russia or China? What happens then? Or suppose one of my boys misses his mark when he's flying around Haiphong? Suppose one of his bombs falls on one of those Russian ships in the harbor? What happens then? Or suppose the fog is too thick or the clouds are too high or the target too small and the bomb drops by mistake within the thirty-mile radius of Hanoi?" The more questions he asked, the more agitated he became. "I would then begin to picture myself lying on the battlefield in Da Nang. I could see an American plane circling above me in the sky. I felt safe. Then I heard a long, loud shot. The plane began to fall faster, faster, faster. I saw it hit the ground, and as soon as it burst into flames, I couldn't stand it anymore. I knew that one of my boys must have been killed that night. I jumped out of bed, put on my robe, took my flashlight, and went into the Situation Room."

After hours of being alone, he felt so weary that he sought the world of action. At 3 A.M. the Situation Room was the perfect escape. There, at any time of day or night, he could find what he needed: people, light, and talk. Around the table in the middle of the room sat five or six men on loan from the Pentagon and the CIA, responsible for receiving messages from Saigon and Da Nang. As the pilots completed their bombing missions, they would report the results over their radios to American headquarters at Saigon: mission accomplished, bridge destroyed. The message would then be transmitted to the White House in the form of a summary telegram. With these Telex reports before them, the Situation Room staff would make the appropriate markings on a giant map, indicating which strikes had destroyed what targets.

As it turned out, the classified wires and reports were endowing illusion with the appearance of precision. Johnson had reason to worry about whether the bombs were actually hitting their targets, but it was not the reason he thought. The real concern was not that a mistaken strike might provoke China or Russia, but that the bombers, flying over hundreds of hamlets and hillocks and villages, could not even begin to separate enemies and innocents, soldiers and civilians.

As the military increased its involvement and responsibility, errors in reporting became standard operating procedure. Exaggerated descriptions of American success were matched by diluted reports of North Vietnam's strength. The estimates of progress improved with each step of the journey from Army headquarters in Vietnam to the Situation Room in the White House. Soon it became almost impossible for anyone in Washington to know what was really going on in Vietnam. But Lyndon Johnson was not about to question a process of reporting that provided him with what he wanted to hear. If the enemy body count seemed inordinately high, that was to be expected when poorly trained men without photo equipment or spotting devices were engaged in battle with the most technologically accomplished civilization in the history of the world. How could America possibly fail to force the North Vietnamese into bargaining? Lyndon Johnson wanted one thing from his nightly visit—the feeling that he was still in control—and that was the only thing that the maps and the men and the messages were able to provide.

A full-scale public commitment to Vietnam would have required Johnson to accept the fact that he could not secure all of the goals he desired. It would have required him to admit that even this leader must make choices and accept limits. It would have meant defining priorities and settling the conflicts

among them. But here, as always, Johnson attempted to compromise conflict instead of choosing sides, manipulating and
orchestrating the political process in order to shape a formula
that would satisfy every competing claim.

How could Johnson have imagined that he could conduct
a major war in virtual secrecy while simultaneously summon-
ing the American people toward a Great Society? In early positions of leadership Johnson found that he could move in
contradictory directions, so long as he compartmentalized his
leadership, and kept his dealings with one group a secret from
the next. Even in the search for votes, the process of cam-
paigning permits, indeed requires, stressing some facts and
minimizing others. The politician's talent, as Johnson interpreted it, was the ability to embrace and enter into the habits
and ways of life of many different men. This required control
over information. Johnson could not allow his immediate
audience access to contradictory information about the particular "self" he was playing to them, permit a person who
had seen him in the "right" role happen upon him in the
"wrong" role. And when his leadership proved effective,
Johnson had been praised by the very Senate on which he had
practiced his deceptions. The country, then, would also reward the President for "pulling off," as he described it, "both
the war in Vietnam and the Great Society at home," even if
he hadn't told them everything at the time.

The public, Johnson reasoned, would only hurt itself by
knowing too much. Democracy demanded good results for
the people, not big debates. But the most important thing
about a democratic regime is what questions it refers to the
public for decision or guidance, how it refers them to the
public, how the alternatives are defined, and how it respects
the limitations of the public. Above all, the people are powerless if the political enterprise is able to take them to war
without their consent. The business of war involves the se-
verest sacrifices falling on the ordinary men and women in the
country. Here more than anywhere else, the people must have
an opportunity to make a choice. For in the end, no statesman
can pursue a policy of war unless he knows for what goals,
and for how long, his people are prepared to fight.

Lyndon Johnson had wanted to surpass Franklin Roosevelt;

and Roosevelt, after all, had not only won the reforms Johnson envied, he had waged a war. But there was a critical
difference: Roosevelt did not attempt the New Deal and
World War II at the same time. Only Johnson among the
Presidents sought to be simultaneously first in peace and first
in war; and even Johnson was bound to fail.

"I figured when my legislative program passed the Congress," Johnson said in 1971, "that the Great Society had a
real chance to grow into a beautiful woman. And I figured
her growth and development would be as natural and inevitable as any small child's. In the first year, as we got the laws
on the books, she'd begin to crawl. Then in the second year,
as we got more laws on the books, she'd begin to walk, and
the year after that, she'd be off and running, all the time
growing bigger and healthier and fatter. And when she grew
up, I figured she'd be so big and beautiful that the American
people couldn't help but fall in love with her, and once they
did, they'd want to keep her around forever, making her a
permanent part of American life, more permanent even than
the New Deal.

"But now Nixon has come along and everything I've
worked for is ruined. There's a story in the paper every day
about him slashing another one of my Great Society programs. I can just see him waking up in the morning, making
that victory sign of his and deciding which program to kill.
It's a terrible thing for me to sit by and watch someone else
starve my Great Society to death. She's getting thinner and
thinner and uglier and uglier all the time; now her bones are
beginning to stick out and her wrinkles are beginning to show.
Soon she'll be so ugly that the American people will refuse to
look at her; they'll stick her in a closet to hide her away and
there she'll die. And when she dies, I too will die."

The professors and the protesters

IN THE BEGINNING, Johnson had feared his country would
become obsessed with failure if Vietnam were lost. As the war
went on, the obsession he feared for his country became his
own. Indeed, as the Great Society disintegrated, the lower the
President's popularity fell, the more Johnson *had* to see his

decision to escalate as the only decision he could have made. He had committed everything he had to Vietnam. Regardless of all evidence, he simply had to be right. To think otherwise, to entertain even the slightest doubt, was to open himself to the pain of reliving old decisions, options, and possibilities long since discarded. "No, no, no," Johnson shouted at me one afternoon, as I tried to discuss earlier opportunities for peace. "I will *not* let you take me backwards in time on Vietnam. Fifty thousand American boys are dead. Nothing we say can change that fact. Your idea that I could have chosen otherwise rests upon complete ignorance. For if I had chosen otherwise, I would have been responsible for starting World War III."

In the heady days of the Great Society and at the start of the escalation, Johnson was confident that he could deal rationally and successfully with the small, scattered strands of criticism on the war. At that time, he was able to maintain a bantering, almost friendly tone—so long as those critics remained few in number and confined their critiques to private conversations.

"Well, Bill [Fulbright]," one conversation began in 1965, "what have you been doing today to damage the Republic? You say you've got a bad stomach. Well, that's because you've been so anti-Johnson lately. I told you that it's bad for you to take after me. Now you tell your wife I love her and I am sorry you're so damned cranky and grouchy all the time." But as the opposition proliferated and surfaced in the public forums, and as support for the Administration's policies plummeted in the polls, Johnson no longer debated or discussed the substance of the critics' charges. Increasingly, he endeavored to dismiss the content by discrediting the source.

Strangely, however, he was probably least harsh toward the protesting young, although he heard each taunt and chant, and they wounded him deeply. But they were not, he believed, motivated by self-interest or personal animosity; their dissent sprang from the ignorance of their youth. "Why should I listen to all those student peaceniks marching up and down the streets? They were barely in their cradles in the dark days of World War II; they never experienced the ravages of Adolf Hitler; they were only in nursery school during the fall of

China; they were sitting in grammar school during the Korean War; they wouldn't know a Communist if they tripped over one. They simply don't understand the world the way I do." And how else could he deal with the young? Certainly not as enemies. They were, after all, the future for which he had hoped to build, and for which, he believed, he was now fighting. If they marched against him because of what they did not know, then there was a chance that someday they would understand.

But Johnson could be unsparing of the professors who had failed to guide their students. All his life he had maintained a distinction between the doers and the thinkers, as if membership in one category walled off the other. Now, his mounting stress served to reinforce that wall. The thinkers were the critics, a negative chorus jealously intent upon the destruction of all he had built. "The professors believe you can get peace by being soft and acting nice. But everything I know about history proves this absolutely wrong. It was our lack of strength and failure to show stamina, our hesitancy, vacillation, and love of peace being paraded so much, that caused all our problems before World War I, World War II, and Korea. And now we're really up for grabs. We're the richest nation in the world. And the minute we look soft, the would-be aggressors will go wild. We'll lose all of Asia and then Europe, and we'll be an island all by ourselves. And when all that comes to pass I'd sure hate to have to depend on the Galbraiths and that Harvard crowd to protect my property or lead me to the Burnet Cave."

Suspicion of motive became his chief instrument in discrediting critics on the Hill. "Fulbright's problem," Johnson told himself, "is that he's never found any President who would appoint him secretary of state. He is frustrated up there on the Hill. And he takes out his frustration by making all those noises about Vietnam. He wants the nation to stand up and take notice of Bill Fulbright, and he knows the best way to get that attention is to put himself in the role of critic. He would have taken that role whichever way I moved on Vietnam. And then beside Fulbright there were all those liberals on the Hill squawking at me about Vietnam. Why? Because I never went to Harvard. That's why. Because I wasn't John F.

Kennedy. Because I wasn't friends with all their friends. Because I was keeping the throne from Bobby Kennedy. Because the Great Society was accomplishing more than the New Frontier. You see they had to find some issue on which to turn against me, and they found it in Vietnam. Even though they were the very people who developed the concept of limited war in the first place.

"And then," Johnson continued, "there were the columnists. They turned against me on Vietnam because it was in their self-interest to do so, because they knew that no one receives a Pulitzer Prize these days by simply supporting the President and the Administration. You win by digging up contrary information, by making a big splash. Truth no longer counts so long as a big sensation can be produced. Every story is always slanted to win the favor of someone who sits higher up. The Washington press are like a wolf pack when it comes to attacking public officials, but they're like a bunch of sheep in their own profession, and they will always follow the bellwether sheep, the leaders of their profession, Lippman and Reston. As long as those two stayed with me, I was okay. But once they left me in pursuit of their fancy prizes, everyone else left me as well. But the more they screamed and squawked, the more determined I was to stick it out."

Conspiracy theorist

As UNPLEASANT as it was for him to feel "done in" by his opponents, he was not accepting blame. Indeed, his ensuing feeling of martyrdom brought a temporary rise in self-esteem. That his polls were down meant only that the conspirators had been successful in creating a false image. It was one thing to look for unworthy motives, however unfairly or inaccurately described. But to believe oneself the target of a giant conspiracy was such a leap into unreason that it could only mean some disintegration of Johnson's thought, that the barriers separating reason from irrational thought and delusion were crumbling.

"No matter what anyone said," Johnson once argued, "I knew that the people out there loved me a great deal. All that talk about my lack of charisma was a lot of crap. There is no such thing as charisma. It's just the creation of the press and the pollsters. Deep down I knew—I simply knew—that the American people loved me. After all that I'd done for them and given to them, how could they help but love me? And I knew that it was only a very small percentage that had given up, who had lost faith. We had more than three million young people serving in uniform. I heard from 100 of them every day. They didn't get the attention the TV people gave the exhibitionists. They didn't have anyone to make signs for them and parade around for them. They were just there, from daylight to dark, fighting for freedom and willing to die for it.

"The problem is that I was sabotaged. Look what happened whenever I went to make a speech about the war. The week before my speech, the St. Louis *Post-Dispatch* or the Boston *Globe* or CBS News would get on me over and over, talking about what a terrible speaker I was and about how awful the bombing was, and pretty soon the people began to wonder, they began to think that I really must be uninspiring if the papers and the TV said so. They began to think that I might be wrong about the war. And gradually they stopped coming to my speeches. And then the press gleefully reported a small crowd and an uninspiring speech. Why it's just as if you were making a tour of the nation and I was an advance man going into every town ahead of you, telling people you were a prostitute, a mean woman, out to cheat them of their hard-earned money. Well, at first the people might still come to see you, dismissing all that talk as nasty rumors. But after a while, some of it would have to sink in. And then more and more. And then there would be absolutely nothing you could do to stop the tide."

Johnson's critics did in fact have a reinforcing effect upon each other. The eastern media did exaggerate the sentiments of the people. There were those in the Kennedy crowd out to get Johnson. But in the past Johnson had displayed a fine sense of discrimination about his political opponents, recognizing that his enemies today might be his allies tomorrow. Now he became unrestrained and reckless, creating a fantasy world of heroes and villains. Members of the White House staff who had listened to the President's violent name-calling were frightened by what seemed to them signs of paranoia. Suddenly, in the middle of a conversation, the President's voice would become intense and low-keyed. He would laugh inappropriately and his thoughts would assume a random, almost incoherent quality as he began to spin a vast web of accusations.

"Two or three intellectuals started it all, you know. They produced all the doubt, they and the columnists in the Washington *Post*, the New York *Times*, *Newsweek*, and *Life*. And it spread and it spread until it appeared as if the people were against the war. Then Bobby began taking it up as his cause, and with Martin Luther King on his payroll he went around stirring up the Negroes and telling them that if they came out into the streets they'd get more. Then the Communists stepped in. They control the three networks, you know, and the forty major outlets of communication. It's all in the FBI reports. They prove everything. Not just about the reporters but about the professors too.

"The Communists' desire to dominate the world is just like the lawyer's desire to be the ultimate judge on the Supreme Court or the politician's desire to be President. You see the Communists want to rule the world, and if we don't stand up to them, they will do it. And we'll be slaves. Now I'm not one of those folks seeing Communists under every bed. But I do know about the principles of power, and when one side is weak, the other steps in. And that's just what the Communists did when they realized the soft spots in the American liberal community.

"You see, the way it worked, the opponents of the war went on jags which pretty much originated in the Communist world and eventually found their way to the American critics. One jag was that we were killing civilians. The next was that we needed a bombing pause. The first bombing pause came after a Communist diplomat talked to some influential Americans. Bobby Kennedy sat with me and told me that he knew that if we ordered a pause something would happen. So I ordered a pause. We delivered a letter to North Vietnam and they threw it back the next day. Later, Senator Morse came in and told me the Soviet ambassador said that such and such would happen if we stopped the bombing. They were telling the same thing to Fulbright, Clark, Mansfield, Church, and others. Then McGeorge Bundy had lunch with Dobrynin, and suddenly he became an ardent advocate for peace. Fortas was against the pause. So was Rusk, and Clifford. I also thought it was wrong, that it would make us look like a weak sister. But I hated to see history record that I stood in the way of peace. So again I ordered a pause and again nothing happened. Isn't it funny that I always received a piece of advice from my top advisers right after each of them had been in contact with someone in the Communist world? And isn't it funny that you could always find Dobrynin's car in front of Reston's house the night before Reston delivered a blast on Vietnam?"

Sometimes it seemed as if Johnson himself did not believe what he was saying, as if all the surmises were a bizarre recreation, a way to relax. But at other times, his voice carried so much conviction that his words produced an almost hypnotic effect. Conversations with Cabinet members would begin with the question, Why aren't you out there fighting against my enemies? Don't you realize that if they destroy me, they'll destroy you as well? Discussions on legislation would be interrupted by diatribes against "the critics." Private luncheons and dinners would be dominated by complaints about "the traitors."

In 1967, Secretary of Defense Robert McNamara began to move away from the President's policy of escalation. As McNamara now saw the situation in Vietnam, the war was going badly and should be capped. But as McNamara's pessimism grew, his access to the President diminished. Johnson did not want to hear other people's doubts. He needed loyalty and support. So, in November 1967, the President suddenly announced that McNamara was leaving the DOD to accept the directorship of the World Bank. Here again Johnson conjured an explanation which precluded the necessity for dealing directly with the content of McNamara's doubts.

"McNamara's problem," Johnson later said, "was that he began to feel a division in his loyalties. He had always loved and admired the Kennedys; he was more their cup of tea, but he also admired and respected the presidency. Then, when he came to work for me, I believe he developed a deep affection for me as well, not so deep as the one he held for the Kennedys, but deep enough, combined with his feelings about the office itself, to keep him completely loyal for three long years. Then he got surrounded by [Assistant and Deputy Assistant Secretaries of Defense] Paul Warnke, Adam Yarmolinsky, and Alain Enthoven; they excited him with their brilliance, all the same cup of tea, all came to the same conclusion after old man Galbraith. Then the Kennedys began pushing him harder and harder. Every day Bobby would call up McNamara, telling him that the war was terrible and immoral and that he had to leave. Two months before he left he felt he was a murderer, and didn't know how to extricate himself. I never felt like a murderer; that's the difference. Someone had to call Hitler and someone had to call Ho. We can't let the Kennedys be peacemakers and us warmakers simply because they came from the Charles River.

"After a while, the pressure got so great that Bob couldn't sleep at night. I was afraid he might have a nervous breakdown. I loved him and I didn't want to let him go, but he was just short of cracking and I felt it'd be a damn unfair thing to force him to stay. When he told me in November that the only job he really wanted then was the World Bank, I told him any job he wanted in the Administration he could have. Now the man who deserved that bank job all along was Henry Fowler; he'd been waiting for it all the way through. When I told him McNamara was going to get it, tears came to his eyes. But at that point, I had no choice."

LBJ's reasons why

THE DEPTH of Johnson's feelings about Vietnam, and the distance between his view and that of those who opposed the war, were brought home to me in a long conversation with him during the summer of 1970. In the course of the conversation, I expressed a feeling that, too often, the debate about Vietnam was confined to tactical questions, focusing on the means of war—the effectiveness of bombing, the viability of strategic enclaves, the success or failure of pacification—at the expense of understanding the rightness or wrongness of the ends. After I finished, Johnson talked uninterruptedly for nearly three hours.

"How in the world can you and your friends say that South Vietnam is not a separate country with a traditionally recognized boundary? That boundary was created and internationally recognized by the Geneva Accords. Fifty nations recognized it; the Communist states recognized Hanoi's regime as a sovereign entity. The final decision specified two zones. That's that. Oh, sure, there were some Koreans in both North and South Korea who believed their country was one country; yet was there any doubt that North Korean aggression took place? And does the belief of some within a country determine the legality of the boundaries? . . . It's just perverted history to claim that it's civil war, just pure bad history manufactured by the Harvards and the Galbraiths. No understanding of the thirty years before. There was no insurrection before the Communists decided to take part. Ho was a Communist all his adult life. He was trained in Moscow Communist headquarters. He was the founding father of the Communist party in Indochina. After the Geneva Accords thousands of guerrillas moved from North to South, waiting word from Ho. All under Communist discipline, directly under Ho's command. The myth these professors have that it's a nice family fight, papa and mamma and children, is pure crap. Why, the decision to renew the fight was made in Hanoi in 1959. The NLF was organized by the central committee of the Communist party in Hanoi, and announced from Hanoi. Sure, there's some free movement, but look at who controls it, who determines its direction. It is Hanoi, loud and clear.

"As for the argument that it was our aggression, not the North's aggression, against the people's will, well, that's just nonsense and naïveté. What better proof do you want of 'the people's' will than the elections in September, 1967? What better proof of the existence of a large fraction of dedicated anti-Communists in the South than their struggle in this war? And when you and your friends speak of the peasants physically suffering at the hands of the South Vietnamese government, just compare that with the suffering at the hands of the Vietcong—where every village chief, teacher, and doctor is killed to destroy the infrastructure.

"And when you all speak of a consensus among well-informed writers that the pro-Vietcong element is larger, just recognize the stake that Lacouture, a Frenchman, has in seeing it that way, and the academics and journalists make money and sell papers not by agreeing with government policy but by disagreeing with it. And you people read their history. While we read the security and intelligence reports of the CIA, the State Department, the DOD—men whose interest it is to find out what's really happening over there. You see, we just read different histories, that's all.

"You see, I deeply believe we *are* quarantining aggressors over there, just like the smallpox. Just like FDR and Hitler, just like Wilson and the Kaiser. You've simply got to see this thing in historical perspective. What I learned as a boy in my teens and in college about World War I was that it was our lack of strength and failure to show stamina that got us into that war. I was taught that the Kaiser never would have made his moves if he hadn't been able to count Uncle Sam out because he believed we'd never come in. Then I was taught in Congress and in committees on defense preparedness and by FDR that we in Congress were constantly telegraphing the wrong messages to Hitler and the Japanese—that the Wheelers, the Lindberghs, the LaFollettes, and the America Firsters were letting Hitler know he could move without worrying about Uncle Sam.

"So I knew that if the aggression succeeded in South Vietnam, then the aggressors would simply keep on going until all of Southeast Asia fell into their hands, slowly or quickly, but inevitably at least down to Singapore, and almost certainly to Djakarta.

"Oh, sure, I recognize your argument about the diversity of communism and your claim that nationalism is strong as well as communism, but the question is, which is stronger? And I believe that the Communists—in terms of resources, skill, leadership, and training—have the upper hand in every battle against nationalist uprisings. I wish it were otherwise. It would certainly make the world a safer place. But look at Czechoslovakia. Now there you had a deep and strong, solid nationalist faith, but in the crunch of Soviet tanks how did that faith hold up? 'Spirit' cannot stand up to superior force. You've got to understand the facts of power.

"And then you all speak of a united Vietnam as the best bulwark against Communist aggression, and you talk approvingly of social revolution as a base for popular government. Well, you tell me when was the last major social revolution that came out successfully while a country was carved up in a war? Well, that's something for your sociologists. And don't give me the Bolshevik Revolution, that's a lot different. And to talk about Vietnam as a bulwark against Communist China—that's sheer Fulbright nonsense. Only slightly less nonsense than Dulles' claim that Laos was a bulwark of democracy. Vietnam ain't a bulwark of anything right now. It's in the midst of a struggle against communism. And if you think it is, it's just because you don't understand the country. You don't understand the way in which the Communists control the resources over there. You simply see a different country than I do. First, we've got to get the Communists out, and *then* begin the process of building South Vietnam as a stronghold.

"But the most unfair part of all is your constant screeching about the bombing, like I wanted to bomb civilians. There is nothing I wanted less, which is why I made sure that I had more control over the generals than any other civilian President in history. I insisted on that. I knew what the generals wanted. To saturate the whole area. To bomb the hell out of the North. Look at what's happening under Nixon. He's already dropped more bombs than I did in all my years. I spent ten hours a day worrying about all this, picking the targets one by one, making sure we didn't go over the limits.

"As for your criticism of our pacification, you are right that war is devastating. But we were doing everything we could to limit that. We rebuilt as we went along. That was our Mekong River Delta project. Hospitals, schools, technology. We wanted to modernize Vietnam society. You talk of land enclosure as a good thing. Well, I see it as an enclosure of spirit and mind. The promise of America has always been freedom from narrow boundaries. The frontier. The future. And technology is essential for that freedom and that future. Sure, the

Vietnamese will never be the same again, but they've had a whole world opened to them. More choices. Freedom from superstition. The freedom of alternative lives. You can't talk about the quality of life until food and basic minimums are provided. We *will* get those things there. As soon as this conflict is peaceably settled. America will do it. You'll see. We've got in our history a tradition of benevolence. It will show up here too. I am as certain of that as I am of anything in my life."

The Meo of Laos

by John E. Woodruff

CIA Alliance Brings Ruin to Proud Race

BAN SON, Laos—A decade of feeding men into the only aggressive pro-government army in Laos has made totally dependent refugees of the hundreds of thousands of once fiercely independent hill tribesmen now gathered about this malaria-infested valley.

"I don't know why we carry on with these people," an Air America pilot shouted over the whine of his helicopter high above a cloud bank somewhere over northern Laos. "They won't fight any more, but we just go on dropping rice and medicine to them, just like in the old days."

In Vientiane, a top American official discusses the relationship with the Meo and other hillmen who make up the Central Intelligence Agency's clandestine army:

"Look, they came to us for help [in 1960] and we have given them plenty of help."

He then hastens to assure his questioner that the United States can accept it philosophically if rank-and-file Meo finally make the uncomfortable accommodation with the North Vietnamese that he feels sure must inevitably come some day.

The accommodation is one that some Americans insist the tribesmen would have made several years and tens of thousands of lives ago had the Americans not armed them and exhorted them to keep fighting.

Until 1960, the Meo of Laos lived much as their grandfathers did—in primitive freedom and disease, on hilltops seldom lower than 3,500 feet, in villages of no more than 20 or 30 thatch houses.

Since the mid-1800's, when they came from Yunnan province of China, where most Meo still live, they had often carried their flintlocks and crossbows down to the valleys to

defend their independence against their Lao and other neighbors. The fights earned them a reputation as aggressive, cruel
attackers.

The alliance with the Americans radically changed their way
of fighting—and their way of living.

It turned the Meo into a far more modern and potent army
than they could have imagined in 1945—long before the
Americans came—when they added a few European rifles left
over from World War II to their own primitive arsenal and
won their first fight with the North Vietnamese.

For the Americans, it also provided the badly needed military punch that officials readily acknowledge was the main
strength of all United States policy in Laos for the last 10
years.

But to many who have long watched the war in Laos, the
new strength provided by the Americans seems, in ironic ret-
rospect, to have been the tribesmen's downfall: it made them,
these observers say, a force the North Vietnamese had to crush
in order to maintain the Laotian Communist control of the
"liberated zones" of the country.

Today, a fourth of the Meo, maybe more, are dead—
thousands of soldiers from combat and tens of thousands of
civilians from exhaustion or illness as they walked for weeks
on end to escape the enemy they have fought for 10 years as
allies of the United States.

More than half the Meo mountain tribesmen of Laos are
gathered here now, and it is virtually impossible to find anyone
here who has not lost at least one close relative to the long
war.

Semi-official estimates—based on recorded death benefit
payments—list 10,000 Meo, Lao Thung, Yao and Thai Dam
tribesmen killed in combat, from an army that has probably
never numbered more than 15,000 men at any one time.

But by far the greater death toll has been exacted by long
walks forced upon entire villages in recent years since the Lao
Peoples' Revolutionary Army and North Vietnamese troops
began systematically removing both the CIA army and the
Meo population from traditional Communist territory.

Some villages have walked for as long as three weeks with
little rest and scant food to escape enemy pressure. Some have

had to move as many as six times in a single year as one outpost after another fell to the Communists.

A few village leaders tell gory tales of reprisal massacres in which, they say, North Vietnamese soldiers methodically slaughtered the women, children and old men who make up most of the refugees.

But these incidents seem to have been the exception. The most efficient killer has been the sheer torture of the long marches.

Weakened by exposure to hot sun or monsoon rains, exhausted by days or weeks of walking with only nominal rest stops, sometimes hungry for days on end until pilots with the United States Agency for International Development can find their trail and drop rice to them, the refugees soon fall victim to the chronic malaria which their bodies have learned to resist under normal conditions.

The very young and the very old tend to die on the trail. So do mothers weakened by pregnancy or recent childbirth—and their number is far larger than in the West, for many Meo women bear children almost annually.

Many of those who survive the walk soon fall victim to the new strains of malaria or dysentery in their new home—or to the tuberculosis, pneumonia and dozens of other diseases to which the malaria and dysentery leave them susceptible. American refugee workers say that whenever they take a census at the end of a major move, between 10 and 15 per cent of the population is dead a year later.

Edgar L. Buell, a retired Indiana farmer who has worked with the Meo hill people since 1960, believes that the Meo and other hill tribes have lost a fourth of their population in refugee moves and combat.

A combination of his estimate with the aid agency's figures showing about 200,000 tribal refugees now under American care suggests that more than 65,000 tribesmen have died— the vast majority of them Meo civilians forced to leave their villages. A few officials give lower estimates; most run far higher.

The Meo of Southeast Asia—there there may be as many as 4 million of them altogether, scattered in tiny hilltop villages across northern Thailand, Burma's Shan plateau, northern Indochina and eastern Yunnan and western Kwei-chow provinces in China—are traditionally among the richest of the many hill tribes that complicate the region's teeming ethnic divisions and subdivisions.

In Laos, their most famous source of wealth was the poppy, from which they took the opium sap by processes their ancestors brought from China when they came to Laos just over 100 years ago.

The opium of Sam Neua province, now the Communist "capital" of Laos, is known to all the world's smuggling rings as some of the best there is.

The $100 or so a Meo farmer was able to get for his annual crop enabled some men eventually to adorn their wives with as many as five or six of the heavy, ornate silver necklaces Meo women use to dress up their traditional black shirts and long pants. Even infant daughters—and sometimes sons—commonly wore two or three lighter necklaces, and sometimes a bracelet.

By primitive tribal standards, the Meo also were skilled at raising livestock and fruits, and their herbs and orchards were measures of prestige as well as wealth.

All of that is lost now to the Meo of the CIA army.

The poppy fields and the orchards, if they are still being farmed, are well inside the Lao Communists' territory. The livestock gradually has been left behind in the chaotic mass escapes of the last three years.

Even most of the silver jewelry has been sold off for money. All that is left is American aid.

American officials in Vientiane are quick to point out the spectacular Western-style efforts that the Agency for International Development has made to help the Meo.

Heroic pilots of Air America and Continental Air Services, they point out, have braved tiny mountain passes, incredible weather problems and Communist gunfire to drop rice and medicines to hilltop villages.

Men like Mr. Buell—whom the Meo call Tan Pop, which translates roughly as Mr. Sent-From-Above—have risked all manner of hardship and disease to live in Meo villages and bring them schools, train village medics and improve their farm tools, the Americans say.

Days in Meo refugee villages and interviews with Meo and American refugee officials fill in the details of some of these claims.

The rice distribution program to Meo villages is years old now, but refugee officials in Vientiane acknowledge that it was only under intense pressure from doctors working with the tribesmen that the Agency for International Development finally started last spring a $1 million-a-year program of distributing meats and other protein supplements.

That program, they say, is calculated to provide for about one refugee in every five now under the agency's care. It goes to tribesmen chosen by doctors according to their illnesses or their degree of malnutrition.

Some officials who work with the program acknowledge that the food the aid agency provides is calculated to fend off starvation but not to replace even the simple diet the Meo had before their constant moves cost them their livestock and farms. Every medical worker interviewed said that malnutrition is now extremely widespread among the Meo, even by primitive tribal standards.

The American-sponsored village health program has brought small, thatched-roof dispensaries and trained medics to most Meo communities.

But the refugee subcommittee of the Senate Judiciary Committee, headed by Senator Edward M. Kennedy (D., Mass.), has documented the need to which this program was the American response: It was undertaken when it became clear that the CIA army's wounded were getting virtually no care except that of the traditional Meo witch doctors, whose ancient ritual of shrieks, gongs, charms and dances quickly proved unequal to the effects of modern grenades and automatic rifles.

Pop Buell estimates that 100 of the medics trained for this ostensibly civilian public-health program have died on the battlefield. That, he says, is about one in every five.

Even the small, thatched schoolrooms Pop Buell encouraged the Meo to build have sometimes been turned to benefit the CIA-sponsored war effort, according to some U.S. aid workers.

"I was in a village one day when the neighboring village

was attacked," one aid worker says. "A naikong (village leader) came to the classroom and rounded up all the boys over 10 years old, handed them guns and flintlocks and started giving them instructions just outside the school—it was an instant recruiting pool."

But the schools also have brought the Meo arithmetic, reading, writing, which no government ever tried to give them before, and has taught them the language of the lowland Lao, the language of government in Laos. In so doing, the schools have greatly strengthened their ability to deal with the Lao, Chinese, Indian and Vietnamese merchants who have traditionally exploited their simplicity.

Baltimore Sun, February 21, 1971

U.S. Finances Victor-to-Refugee Transit

VIENTIANE, Laos—On September 25, 1945, Toubhy Lyfong received a letter from Gen. Le Thiep Hong, then Viet Minh commander of the Vinh region of North Vietnam.

It is from this letter that Mr. Lyfong, who soon afterward would be dubbed "King of the Meo" by French journalists, dates the chain of events that eventually brought his people to their current state of total dependence on United States aid.

Mr. Lyfong says the letter notified him that Viet Minh troops planned to cross into Laos through Xieng Khouang province, where he was the French-appointed chief of Meo hill tribesmen. It asked him to let them pass so they could start organizing resistance to the expected return of the French after World War II.

He refused—largely, he says, out of loyalty to the French, who had given him eight years of schooling, the most ever permitted a Meo. Two weeks later, Viet Minh troops and a few of their Lao allies fought Mr. Lyfong's Meo mountain tribesmen at an outpost near Nong Het, just inside Laos.

The fight was a chaos of aged French and British colonial weapons, Meo crossbows and flintlocks and a few Japanese and American rifles scrounged during World War II; history seems to have overlooked it, although it may well have been the seminal battle of the tragi-comic struggle that still sputters backward and forward across Laos today.

That day, according to Toubhy Lyfong's memory, the Meo were the winners.

Mr. Lyfong organized loosely run Meo guerrilla forces for the French from then until 1954, when the Viet Minh scored their spectacular victory at Dienbienphu and drove the French from Indochina.

When Mr. Lyfong went to France to retire after the war, though, his loyalty was scarcely rewarded; refused permission to transfer his $250,000 fortune to Paris from the colonial bank, he relates, he had to return to Indochina after only two weeks.

By 1960, his continued presence in Laos was to prove helpful to new foreigners: the Americans, who were starting to organize an army of hill tribesmen to supplement the pathetically ineffective Royal Lao Army they tried to build for the Vientiane government in the late 1950's.

It was in that year that Toubhy Lyfong says he cemented an alliance with the right-wing Gen. Phoumi Nosavan and Prince Boun Oum—and thus with the United States Army and Central Intelligence Agency, which then were financing and supplying the Phoumist army in southern Laos.

Throughout 1960, Mr. Lyfong lent his prestige—as well as the many local officials he had appointed while province chief and his remaining friendships from the days as a guerrilla organizer—to a little-known army major named Vang Pao.

Maj. Vang Pao, the highest-ranking Meo in the Lao Army, twice had been refused an overdue promotion to lieutenant colonel by Lao officers who could not accept the idea of a hill tribesman as their equal, according to Mr. Lyfong.

Promised better treatment by General Phoumi and Prince Boun Oum—and promised money and arms by the Americans—Vang Pao set out to build a hill-tribe army. For General Phoumi and Boun Oum, the alliance offered at last the prospect of a friendly force in parts of northern Laos that long had been largely the preserve of neutralist and pro-Communist forces with whom they frequently had quarreled.

By early 1961, as minister of social welfare under a short-lived government headed by Prince Boun Oum, Mr. Lyfong was able to give Vang Pao's infant army more tangible help. He diverted Lao and American refugee goods to the Meo of the Plain of Jars region, whom Vang Pao had regrouped according to a prearranged plan when neutralist troops took over the plain as they retreated before a drive on Vientiane by General Phoumi's men.

Soon afterward, Vang Pao became commander of Military Region II, Xieng Khouang and Sam Neua provinces, the toughest Communist-held territory in northern Laos.

Vang Pao's regroupment of the Meo onto seven strategically located hilltops surrounding the plain radically altered the course of the war in northern Laos, for it welded a large group of rugged Meo mountaineers into the beginnings of what gradually became the Vientiane government's most effective single fighting force.

It also radically altered the lives of the Meo by separating them from their tiny hilltop villages of no more than 20 or 30 houses each.

Now Vang Pao's Meo followers were gathered into settlements that soon proved too crowded for their way of farming, which consists of cutting and burning trees and brush from the sunny side of a mountain, planting rice and corn for two or three years until the soil is depleted and then starting over again on a different hillside.

The refugee supplies sent from Vientiane by Mr. Lyfong —largely rice bought in Thailand with American money—thus became the first step in the Meo's decade-long walk to total dependence on United States aid.

It is fashionable among high American officials in Vientiane today to point out that the Meo already had had some fights with the Communists before the Americans organized them and to insist that the Meo "came to us."

"Look, these people came to us for help, and we have given them plenty of help," one top-level diplomat says.

An anonymous memorandum of the Vientiane office of the agency that preceded the United States Agency for International Development presents a more complex picture.

Arguing in favor of giving the Meo help that was soon to

be justified publicly as humanitarian refugee aid, the 1960 memorandum said, in part:

"Toughened by their hard work in the high mountains, accustomed from childhood to firearms and to hunting in groups, used to traveling long distances on foot from one village to another, they become excellent fighters with a minimum of training.

"For many months now, ever since the Communists seized control of the Plain of Jars, the Meo, working together with officers and soldiers from the Lao armed forces, have been formed into regular [Laotian Army] military units. They have defended their homes and given great assistance to their brothers in arms elsewhere in Laos by harassing the enemy's convoys and military columns."

Some lower-level Americans who work with the Meo argue that the relationship established in 1960 was by nature unequal, even if it had been a simple case of responding to a Meo request for aid.

One says: "It's no help to your case if you tell the judge the 12-year-old girl invited you into her bedroom.

"The Meo were primitive people who thought for a long time that we were generously helping them defend their little hilltops and thatched huts. They know now that they are being used in something bigger, of course, but now it's too late.

"We saw the thing in terms of geopolitics—or the struggle against communism, or whatever you want to call it—from the beginning, and we were only too relieved to find some effective warriors in Laos who were willing to take on an enemy much bigger than they could ever have understood."

Whatever the precise relationship was at first, the uses to which the Meo army soon was put give little support to the "they-came-to-us" view.

By 1962, Meo units were stiffened by the presence of "white star" teams of the Green Berets and had spread the American-paid army deep into Sam Neua province, the regroupment area granted to the pro-Communists Pathet Lao by the 1954 Geneva agreements.

Edgar L. Buell, now head of the United States AID program for hill-tribe refugees, talks of this achievement by his beloved Meo with considerable pride: "When I came here in

[1960, as a $65-a-month International Voluntary Service worker], we couldn't set foot inside Sam Neua province. Within a couple of years, we were able to work the whole province."

Then the 1962 Geneva conference on Laos called for an end to the confused fighting and prohibited foreign troops on Lao soil.

But its chief effect on the American-backed Meo army was to shift it from Green Beret to CIA sponsorship.

By this time, Vang Pao's army had become a force the Communists would not ignore, and soon after the cease-fire Pathet Lao and North Vietnamese forces attacked Meo positions near the Plain of Jars, arguing that the Meo and their American advisers had been parachuted into the mountains after the cease-fire.

Baltimore Sun, February 22, 1971

A War-Exhausted People Seek a Way Out

VIENTIANE, Laos—Edgar L. (Pop) Buell believes that many Meo hill tribesmen are starting—gradually and in small groups—to make a painful peace with the Lao and Vietnamese Communists they have fought on and off for 25 years.

"I've lost about 75,000 people, Meo and others, in the last 18 months," says Mr. Buell, a retired Indiana farmer who has worked with the Meo as a civilian adviser since 1960. "Of course, some of them are dead from the war and the long walks. But most of them, I'm convinced, are Meo, and a few from other tribes, who have finally either found their way back into their old places in Communist areas or else decided the last time the Communists came that they just were not going to run any more."

Many Americans here believe that Pop Buell's figures are extravagant, but few question his sense for the trend of Meo affairs. One top military official says, "The Meo are terrifically worn down as fighters.

"Their morale is shot, and they are slow to engage in battle. If you are going to have a guerrilla Army, you have to make your move fast and clear out fast. That is what the Meo used to do best; now they just don't do it."

Another top-level official says, "If the fight goes on, and the North Vietnamese really decide to turn on the pressure, the Meo will be crushed.

"What else can they do? They are going to have to find some way to get out of the way of the battle sooner or later, and if the worst comes, many of the leaders like Vang Pao [leader of the Meo Clandestine Army] will have to come here to Vientiane or maybe even leave the country."

No one is proclaiming it as a policy, but this tacit assumption that most Meo eventually will end their decade of fighting and running under U.S. sponsorship by finding a way to co-exist with their old enemies is the stated expectation even at the very top of the U.S. mission here.

Mr. Buell is convinced that such an accommodation is possible, although it will by no means be pleasant.

"The Communists know their limits with the Meo—they know they can tax them so far, and they can get so much forced labor, and they can go just so far with the political ideas, and then they stop.

"And this isn't going to be any overnight thing—it's going to go on like it is now, a few hundred or a few thousand here and there.

"And I don't hardly expect the Meo are going to fight for the other side after all, for the Communists. It would be a big thing to just get the Meo the hell out of the war."

Many critics of American policy insist that the kind of accommodation Mr. Buell describes is what the Meo would have had to do 10 years ago—before losing their health, their wealth and much of their population—had the United States not provided the massive backing that enabled them to become a fighting force too important for the Communists to shrug off.

That argument was outlined at length last May 7 by Ronald J. Rickenbach, who served for several years as a U.S. Agency for International Development Worker at Sam Thong.

In testimony before the refugee subcommittee of the Senate Judiciary Committee, headed by Senator Edward M. Kennedy (D., Mass.), Mr. Rickenbach argued that when the North Vietnamese moved into Laos, the choices open to the Meo were to "accommodate themselves, fight or flee."

"They could not very well fight without arms and assistance; they could flee, but to nowhere as suitable to their way of life than where they already were, or they could accommodate themselves in some peaceful, subservient way to the Vietnamese presence, and thereby allow something of a local political balance to be effected in cognizance with the realities of the time."

When the Americans came on the scene with unlimited arms and extensive food supplies, he said, the Meo yielded to the temptation to fight. A primitive tribe thus "became unwitting pawns of the United States."

American officials in Vientiane generally reject this argument.

Even the Americans who now readily accept the probability that the Meo one day will have to make their peace with the Communists insist that could not have happened in 1960, pointing out that the Meo were already fighting the Communists under the French before 1954.

More recently, an intensive American effort has often been needed to keep the Meo in the fight, and that effort is invariably made, even by Americans who personally feel strongly that the Meo are a depleted and exhausted people and that their Army has a severe case of combat fatigue.

Americans at several levels are known to have visited Gen. Vang Pao many times to dissuade him from a plan he often mentions to move the Meo en masse into Sayaboury province of western Laos, where there has been little fighting. Ambassador G. McMurtrie Godley, himself is known to have made more than one such visit to General Vang Pao since becoming ambassador a year and a half ago.

One key U.S. official says: "Hell, what else could the old man have done—it's still true that without the Meo, there would just be no such thing as American policy in Laos; we just wouldn't have any force to back it up with."

The ambassador is known not to take the Sayaboury idea seriously and to regard his visits with the general as efforts to bolster the morale of a highly mercurial man who is temporarily "down in the dumps."

Americans who work with Vang Pao say that the Sayaboury move is only one of a collection of half-formulated ideas he often mentions as means of retiring the Meo from the war.

But the inability of a man who grew up a primitive tribesman to formulate a plan fully does not, they insist, mean that he does not take the problem seriously.

"It's a deep and constant preoccupation," one American says.

"Sometimes, it's as if he were the only Meo leader with the foresight to understand how important it is to their people."

Some time ago, they had an annual "meeting at Long Cheng. He spent half the day with the civilian politicians—we call them the Meo Mafia—and the other half with the top Army officers. He told them the time had come to get out, and that place was where they would go, and they should start getting ready.

"When he finished, they just sat there—both the morning group and the afternoon group—just silence, no questions, no interest, no response.

"That's how it's been a lot of times—no action until the fighting actually starts. The Meo are just that way."

Others confirm the story but insist that the Meo are not "just that way."

"They've moved so damn many times, and every time it was just this once more," one says. "How can we expect them to move again when there isn't really even a plan to follow?"

The absence of plans—or the profusion of half-coherent and conflicting plans—is as striking among the Americans as it is among the Meo.

Various responsible Americans mention at least five different parts of Laos, including Sayaboury province, as places where they expect the main body of Meo to go to escape the war.

How the Meo will get there, where they will get food and supplies to tide them over the year it will take to harvest their first crops, what will become of their weapons—all of these and other equally fundamental questions go unanswered.

The absence of planning has provoked bitterness among a few Americans who care deeply about the Meo.

"We always had plenty of plans for how they should defend our gear at Phou Pha Thi, and for scouting missions, and for how they could disrupt the North Vietnamese for us," one says. "It's only now that we seem to be running out of plans."

This bitterness is not shared by most Americans, however. Most argue that if what the Meo must do is make peace with the Communists, then too much American intervention can only poison prospects that are already bleak from a decade of bitter warfare.

Meanwhile, even the location of the Meo refugee camps is becoming controversial among the Americans, some of whom contend that the long, oval-shaped gathering of camps east of Ban Son was planned deliberately to keep the Meo in the line of Communist advance toward Vientiane.

"I don't buy that idea," one experienced American says. "If the Communists want to take Vientiane, they can skirt the Meo and come right up the Mekong."

Talks with Americans who work with the refugees suggest that most of the hill-tribe villages east of Ban Son got there mainly because the people there came from eastern Laos and simply stopped walking when they got to relatively secure territory.

However the refugees got where they are, the Communist pattern of recent years has not suggested that any direct attack on Vientiane is in their plans.

Instead, they have sought to move the battlefield from place to place north of Vientiane—and the royal capital of Luang Prabang—in a manner that creates an impression of growing pressure on the two capitals.

The areas where this tactic can be most effective are approximately the ones where the Meo are concentrated, and the increasing presence of North Vietnamese troops around Long Cheng and Sam Thong suggest that the Meo are not yet out of the way.

"I'm not going to say they're through yet," Pop Buell says. "God knows nobody thought they could make it this long—it was always just hold out for six more months, and then six more and six more."

Baltimore Sun, February 23, 1971

Copters Return from Laos with the Dead

by Gloria Emerson

KHESANH, South Vietnam, Feb. 27—The dead began to come into the emergency field hospital here today after 1 P.M.

The first South Vietnamese soldier, killed yesterday in Laos, was wrapped tightly in an American Army poncho held by bandage strips used as string. All that could be seen were his small, bare feet—dark with dust—hanging over the stretcher's edge.

He lay on the reddish earth while a Vietnamese officer of the hospital at the airborne division's forward command post looked at a large tag and wrote down one more name and unit.

Fifteen minutes later—raising a furious blizzard of dust that stings the eyes and whips the face—another United States medical evacuation helicopter landed. Two more dead, then 10 more dead.

By 3 P.M. there were 30 dead and over 200 wounded.

A small despairing scene, it is being repeated every day in the face of mounting Communist resistance to the South Vietnamese drive into Laos. This week the South Vietnamese command reported a total of 320 dead, 1,000 wounded and 99 missing in action since the operation began on Feb. 8. It is suspected that the figures are unrealistically small.

At this hospital, an emergency station with a few tents and an underground surgical bunker with only stretchers for the critically wounded, the Vietnamese orderlies stand in groups near a small helicopter pad.

They seemed uncertain of how to remove the dead and the wounded most quickly from the choppers, which are flown by American crews.

One young orderly kept rushing toward the craft holding a stretcher in front of him as a shield against the dirt, but then he dropped it as he came closer and did not seem to know what to do next.

Other orderlies did not bother with the stretchers. Some carried the wounded in a stumbling file of piggyback rides. Those Vietnamese who were wounded but could somehow walk made the few hundred yards by themselves, weaving a little in the scorching sun.

In one tent, where the day's wounded lie on American cots waiting for Vietnamese medics or Dr. Tran Qui Tram, who is 21 years old, to help them, there were more than a dozen men in the stifling heat. Some closed their eyes and were silent but others would not restrain their groans.

The most seriously wounded man, a North Vietnamese, Third Lieut. Mac Thang Nong, a member of the 35th North Vietnamese Commando Battalion, a demolition outfit, was on a wooden table as the medics dressed his wounds. They did not give him an anesthetic—no one had that.

"I was on a reconnaissance mission with three others," he said, whispering slowly in Vietnamese. "We were near Hill 30 when I was hit by fire from the hilltop. I considered myself as already dead. From now on I do not worry about anything."

He was captured by the South Vietnamese on the hill, where heavy fighting has been going on this week.

Lieutenant Nong, who said he left North Vietnam only a month ago, declined to talk about his family and closed his eyes.

The South Vietnamese wounded paid no attention to the enemy officer. They were too busy with their own thoughts and their own pain.

Pvt. Nguyen Huu Thanh, a combat engineer supporting South Vietnamese airborne troops in Laos, does not know the name of the place where he was hit by rocket fragments. The tears rolled down his face as he muttered in Vietnamese.

"Do you know whether they will amputate my arm?" he pleaded. "I am afraid they will cut off my arm here."

But he could not bring himself to put the question to the medics. When they bent his arm in a splint—no one knew whether it was fractured or only full of steel splinters—he cried out. There was no one to soothe him and no one to give him water.

Pvt. Tran Van Gu, a Ranger with the 21st Battalion, which fought on Hill 30, was wounded by North Vietnamese recoilless-rifle fire. "The North Vietnamese are frightening," he said. It was hard to hear him because of the bandage around his face.

"The North Vietnamese were hit by three waves of B-52 bombers last night, but still they survived and they shelled us early this morning," he related.

"Many of the Rangers wish that they would be ordered to withdraw," he continued, "because all of us are surrounded and cannot figure out a way to fight back against the North Vietnamese. They don't fear air strikes or artillery. I am convinced that we cannot fight them in Laos."

An infantryman with the First Division fighting at Hotel 2, where the North Vietnamese have attacked ground forces 18 miles southwest of Laobao, told of the assault.

"They fired on us day and night with rockets, mortars and recoilless rifles," Pvt. Tran Van Ngo said, sighing. "At 4 P.M. yesterday I was wounded. So were seven others. The choppers couldn't land all day to get us out because of the enemy fire."

The soldier said he was 49 years old though his papers say he is 40. "A long long time ago my father changed the age on my papers from 28 to 19 to keep me from being drafted by the French to fight the Germans," he said. "I am far too old to be in the army now as a private, with all the hardship that comes to a man. I dodged one war only to be caught finally in another."

The New York Times, March 3, 1971

Spirit of Saigon's Army Shaken in Laos

by Gloria Emerson

KHESANH, South Vietnam, March 27—The morale of many soldiers in South Vietnam's finest military units, who fought the North Vietnamese in Laos, is shattered.

Men in the crack First Infantry Division, in the marines and in the Airborne Division say that the Laos invasion was a nightmare for them and for other soldiers.

Through an interpreter they spoke of how the North Vietnamese outnumbered them and advanced in wave after wave, running over the bodies of comrades and never stopping.

In low, strained voices, the South Vietnamese spoke of what they termed the enemy's ability to survive American air strikes and B-52 bombings, which they themselves feared so much.

While these men did not say that they spoke for all the 20,000 South Vietnamese soldiers who took part in the Laos campaign, they asserted that the morale of their fellow soldiers was low. Those interviewed were in the state of dejected fatigue that is common to men coming out of a long retreat under heavy enemy fire, and perhaps their views will be less gloomy after some rest.

In Saigon, for example, a paratroop lieutenant who was wounded early in the campaign said that for the next six months his men would prefer to desert and risk jail rather than go into such a battle again, but that later, perhaps, they would be ready to face the enemy once more.

For many of the South Vietnamese soldiers, most of whom are in their twenties, the Laos campaign was their first fierce encounter with North Vietnamese ground forces; not for years has there been major fighting in South Vietnam to compare with the operation against enemy supply trails in Laos.

It was a test, and now most South Vietnamese veterans frankly admit that their forces failed. They had no chance, these men say.

Although it is not known whether the effects of the Laos operation will be permanent, some experienced South Vietnamese noncommissioned officers are wondering if their units will be able to fight well again and respect their officers.

What has dramatically demoralized many of the South Vietnamese troops is the large number of their own wounded who were left behind, begging for their friends to shoot them or to leave hand grenades so they could commit suicide before the North Vietnamese or the B-52 raids killed them.

Some soldiers who had been in the drive into Cambodia last year said they had never dreamed that the Laos operation would not be as simple. Since there was no significant fighting in Cambodia, these South Vietnamese felt that the enemy was no longer a threat. They learned differently in Laos and they will not soon forget it.

"The best units were sent in and the best units got the worst beating in combat," Sgt. Nguyen Van Lac said. "Now you see the North Vietnamese chasing us out. We lost 59 artillery pieces—105-mm. and 155-mm. howitzers—or the equivalent of three artillery battalions."

The sergeant is an artillery liaison man at the forward command post here of an American unit, the First Brigade of the Fifth Infantry Division (Mechanized).

More chilling accounts of the Laos fighting came from the men who lived through it, the tired and shaken men who said they were not prepared for what had happened.

In American helicopters they came out of Laos this week without their combat packs, their rations or their steel helmets—and sometimes without their weapons. Nothing mattered, they said, except getting out.

One of them was a 22-year-old marine who came back to South Vietnam on Wednesday after walking through the jungle for two nights and a day before the airlift.

His version of the fighting near a fire base called Delta on Hill 547, about eight miles inside Laos, told how the South Vietnamese troops ran for their lives, each man struggling for himself only.

"The last attack came at about 8 P.M.," Private Moc, the marine, said in Vietnamese. "They shelled us first and then came the tanks moving up into our positions. The whole brigade ran down the hill like ants. We jumped on each other to get out of that place. No man had time to look for his commanding officer. It was quick, quick, quick or we would die. Oh, God, now I know for sure that I am really still alive."

Private Moc asked, as did other men, that his full name and unit be withheld for he was afraid that he would be punished for telling what happened to him.

"When I was far from the hill, with about 20 other marines, there was a first lieutenant with us," he continued. "We moved like ghosts, terrified of being ambushed by the North Vietnamese. We stopped many times when there was firing —not daring to breathe. How terrible those minutes were."

Private Moc came back to South Vietnam with the legs of his pants ripped off, and his thigh showing through the tatters. A small thin man, he had only his M-16 rifle left of his equipment. He continued his account of the action in Laos:

"Only last Tuesday our group bumped into a North Vietnamese unit, and we ran again like ants. And the Lieutenant, he whispered to us 'Disperse, disperse, don't stick together or we will all be killed.' After each firing, there were fewer and fewer of us. Nobody cared for anybody else at all."

What made his blood run cold, Private Moc said, was how the North Vietnamese kept coming and coming, running over the bodies of their own men, and not stopping.

"They were everywhere and they were so daring," he said. "Their firepower was so enormous, and their shelling was so accurate, that what could we do except run for our lives."

Hearing the assault shout of the North Vietnamese, remembering how they screamed "Xung phong!" will long haunt one man, Sgt. Nguyen Minh. He fought with Brigade A of the Second Marine Artillery Battalion.

The entire brigade ran away, he said.

Its position in Laos was south of Route 9, the east-west axis of the drive, about seven miles inside the border. The brigade arrived there March 5 and stayed for two weeks before it retreated.

"For days," he related, "we had been made desperate by their constant shellings and assaults, by their strange attitude of ignoring death and always moving closer and closer to us.

Never were the marines in such trouble, and we were never so afraid.

"They knew everything about us. They shouted to us, 'We know that you are Company One of Battalion Two. Surrender, brothers. We have hot meals and hot tea for you out here!'

"And, then, hearing them shout for assault, knowing they were all around us, our fear was so great."

An infantry platoon leader who has been in the army for 18 years also discussed the terror he felt in Laos.

Sergeant Co, 38, is now AWOL. He does not care.

"All that counts is surviving the Laos operation," he said. "Being absent for a few days, getting some punishment, that is nothing to me."

There was no room on the American helicopters that came to pick up his battalion in Laos on March 6, so Sergeant Co clung to the skids of one craft.

"Each helicopter could have been the last one, so what choice was there for me?" he asked. "Only the madmen would stay and politely wait for the next helicopter."

During the last three days his battalion was in Laos, he said, 30 of the men were killed and 20 wounded. "Only about 100 men were still okay at the end out of 400," Sergeant Co said. "The North Vietnamese could have killed us all if they had wanted to do it."

A corporal in the marines who fought on Hill 547 in Laos on the night of March 22 said that many of his friends had killed themselves because they were wounded. No American helicopters could extract them because of heavy antiaircraft fire.

"The papers and the radio in Saigon kept on saying there was a Laos victory, I have learned now, but what a joke," Corporal Ti said. "We ran out like wounded dogs."

"The most heartbreaking thing," he continued, "was that we left behind our wounded friends. They lay there, crying, knowing the B-52 bombs would fall on them. They asked buddies to shoot them but none of us could bring himself to do that. So the wounded cried out for grenades, first one man, then another, then more."

"I could not bear it," he said. "We ran out at 8 P.M. and

about midnight we heard the bombs explode behind us. No more bodies! They all became dust. Some men who were wounded in the legs or arms tried to run out with us, but they could not make it."

As for the effect these experiences will have on the soldiers, a 38-year-old sergeant major who has seen combat with the infantry many times in the last 11 years is worried.

"I am afraid that we will have a lot of deserters," said the sergeant, who did not want to give his name. "When many of the men get back to the rear, and think back on what they have been through, and hear the other soldiers talk, then their fear will get worse.

"It can happen. I know this kind of thing all too well."

The New York Times, March 28, 1971

The Homecoming of Chris Mead

by Karl Fleming

CHRIS MEAD sat halfway back in the bus, staring vacantly out the mud-streaked window at the wintry Michigan countryside. The trees were black and bare. A patchy snow covered the ground. The only sounds were the whack-whack of the windshield wipers and the drowsy whine of the tires on wet pavement. Mead was wearing a brand-new Army uniform, with Sp/4 insignia on the sleeves. But the war was over for him now, and he was going home.

Mead is one of the more than 2 million U.S. military men who have served in Vietnam and returned, and, like many of them, he came back discouraged by what he had seen of war and uncertain of what he will make of peace. He had been discharged only the day before at Oakland, Calif. It took all day before he got to the last steel cage and drew $524 in discharge pay. "Is that it? Am I out now?" he asked. "That's it," the paymaster said. Mead started out, past a huge wall painting of Uncle Sam in tears. I'LL MISS YOU, it said. Mead gave the poster the finger.

That was his farewell. He had joined the Army with six classmates from Ovid-Elsie Consolidated High School near Owosso, Mich.; three are still in, two got medical discharges, one was killed in action. Mead himself took a lot of gunfire—"I was dead for sure a couple of times." He saw trucks blown up, kids maimed, women killed, buddies bleeding and dying. Once he saw a Viet Cong running away on the stumps of his shot-away legs. And now he was out, and no one said good-by or good luck. There was just the "Certificate of Appreciation" with President Nixon's facsimile signature. "I extend to you my personal thanks and the sincere appreciation of a grateful nation," it said. "You have helped maintain the security of the nation during a critical time in its history."

Only coming home, you'd never know it. Elsie, Mich., is

just the sort of Middle American town that used to welcome its boys noisily home from the wars. But when Mead's bus pulled into the dingy Indian Trails Bus Depot in nearby Owosso in a light snow, the only one there to meet him was his kid brother Greg, 19. They bear-hugged. "You've gotten so big, man," Chris said. "You're bigger than I am."

They got into the family car, a green 1967 Chrysler. Mead drove, out of town and across the tracks and past big red barns and herds of Holsteins and crossroads stores with Smith-Douglass Fertilizer signs. They didn't talk about the war at all. "Check it out: I'm 21 now," Mead said; he had turned 21 three days before his discharge. He asked about his bedroom, his record collection, his clothes. And girls. "I've got to scope me out a really neat chick. One I can rap with, not one who just wants to have babies. How's the girl situation?" Greg grinned and said, "They're still around."

And then they were home. A sign on the side of the barn said Orlo Mead & Sons, and an electric Christmas star glowed on top. "Mom turned on the light to let the neighbors know you're home," Greg said.

Mead pulled into the icy driveway. The whole family tumbled out the side door to greet him: his parents and Vicki, 14, Neil, 11, and Brad, 7. Mrs. Mead was having a new $300 linoleum-tile floor put down in the kitchen and was apologetic about the homecoming dinner. She had managed pork chops and gravy, mashed potatoes, green peas and pumpkin pie and a store-bought birthday cake. But Mead's ulcer was bothering him. "Wow, I wish I could eat," he said. "I'm not even interested in food any more."

They sat around the table and exchanged news, and finally they had to talk about the war. It came up because Mrs. Mead was worried about what Greg should do when he has to go into the service. "Join the Navy," Mead said flatly. "If you go to 'Nam you'll be a grunt for sure. If you can get out of it, don't go. You don't want to go over there and get yourself blown away. All of it is bad and scary. One minute you're talking to a buddy and the next you're out policing him up."

"We could have cleaned up this mess a long time ago," his dad said, "if we would go all-out. I don't understand fighting and not going all-out to win. It's nothing but a big political war."

"It's not worth anybody getting killed for," said Mead. "It's for nothing. The people over there don't care. They're ingrates to the max. The Arvins on the Red Ball Highway sit on their asses on the bridges and the GI's have to go in and get theirs blown away," Mead said. "All the people are interested in is money. Little kids were selling us our own soda pop for 90 cents a bottle. I know what I was fighting for: nothing."

They talked some more, the children gawking saucer-eyed at Mead, till finally he blinked and exclaimed: "Goddam! I can hardly believe it. I'm really home. It seems like it was a long, bad dream." The kids drifted upstairs to bed, and Mead got out his suitcase. His combat boots were tied to the handle. He opened the bag and started taking out his souvenirs.

One was a water pipe, ornately carved in brass and wood. His father and mother looked at each other.

"Is that for smoking marijuana?" Mrs. Mead asked.

There was a long pause. Then Mead said, "Yeah."

"I don't believe in that," his dad said.

Mead took the suitcase upstairs. There was a homemade "Welcome Home, Chris" sign with a peace symbol on his door. Stuck on the bedroom walls were old Steppenwolf and Beatles album covers and a flower he'd drawn as a child. His longbow was standing in the corner beside the ancient TV set.

Kid stuff. Mead had gone away a boy and come back a man, and now he had to start thinking about work in an economy grown suddenly inhospitable to its homecoming young. The Meads have 160 acres and used to be dairy farmers. But the profit went out of it, so they sold the cows, and now Mead's father commutes 40 miles to Flint every day to work as an electrician. Mead thought of working there too, and when he came back downstairs he asked about the chances of getting a job. But his father shook his head. "It doesn't look good at all."

Mead didn't want to worry about it—not right away. He asked for the car.

"Sure," his father grinned. "Where you going? Terrorizing?"

"A lot of girls have been asking about you," his mother
said.

He and Greg drove to the outskirts of Owosso, had a couple of coffees at the Tri-Ami Bowl, then moved on and parked
at the Elias Big Boy coffeeshop. Local kids kept circling the
block in cars. "Hey, what's happening?" they yelled at each
other. Nothing was happening, and the Meads went home to
bed.

He slept late next morning, then headed back into Owosso
to buy some clothes. He handled the car easily—he drove a
water truck and sometimes an amphibious "duck" in Vietnam—and on the way he said, "Man, I can't wait to get some
wheels. Everybody's born with something they can do well. I
like to drive." But his $524 coming-out pay wasn't enough.
He spent $84 of it on clothes at the Yankee Giant Plaza
and $291 on a Panasonic eight-track stereo-radio and a dozen
cartridges—the Grand Funk Railroad, Jethro Tull, Paul
McCartney, The Who, The Moody Blues. "Goddam," he
said. "Now I'll have to go to work right away to get some
wheels. But I have to have music to get my head back where
it was. I want some peace of mind. No hassles, no responsibilities. I'm tired of thinking about 'Nam."

That afternoon, Mead drove back to Elsie (population:
1,045). Main Street was dead, and he didn't know whether he
could settle in again. "I hate to put it this way," he said, "but
I want to be some place where there's a chance I might get
into trouble—know what I mean?" There isn't much trouble
to get into in Elsie. He bought a bottle of Cold Duck wine
for $3.11; then he bumped into a couple of old school pals
and they talked awhile. One of them, Phillip Saxton, had a
job at Vaughn Seed Co. Mead asked about work there. Saxton
didn't think they were hiring. So Mead said maybe he would
try applying at the Elsie Door and Specialty. And do something about the war. "*Something's* got to be done, man. You
just can't sit around with all this stuff going on."

Next day—the third day back—he just hung around home.
His mother, at his request, hadn't told anybody except family
that he was back. "I don't want nobody making a big deal

out of it," he said. "The people who would notice me are the ones I don't want to have anything to do with—the gung-ho types who're for the war. Anyway, I'm not proud of what I did over there. I'm sorry. I don't even want anybody to know I was there. It's lousy and there's no sense in it. I wish I hadn't even gone. Maybe I should have gone to Canada or broke a leg or something."

Newsweek, March 29, 1971

Who Wants To Be the Last American Killed in Vietnam?

by Donald Kirk

MILITARY REGION ONE.
South Vietnam.

IF THERE is any war, that is, an American war, involving American troops and costing American lives, it is mainly here in Military Region One, once known as "I Corps," whose mountains and rice fields have absorbed more American blood in the past six years than South Vietnam's other three regions combined.

"We lost 18 men in our company last month to booby traps," says a platoon sergeant encamped on one of the outcroppings of Charlie Ridge, a forbidding dark rise on the skyline some 10 miles west of here. "All we get out of it was killing two dinks in an ambush." Just two nights before I spoke with the sergeant, down the same ridge, he and his men heard the whine of Soviet-made 122-millimeter rockets whistling overhead—aimed not at them but at a South Vietnamese firebase in the lowlands. "They was shootin' from the rocket belt behind us," says one of the G.I.'s, pulling out his canteen during a break on a patrol through thick underbrush toward a small stream hidden at the base of the slope. "There was nothin' we could do but call in artillery. That was some hilarious fight, listening to them rounds goin' back and forth above us."

The morning after the rocket attack half a dozen of the G.I.'s were sitting around an old shellhole eating C-rations when one of them tripped a hidden wire, setting off a booby trap concealed in the hole. Three men were wounded—two of them partially blinded, one with possible brain damage. "There all night and nothing happens," says a rifleman, recounting the incident as we pause by the stream. "Sit here and watch a buddy get blown away. The whole thing's point-less. We'll never win."

It is, in reality, a desultory kind of struggle, punctuated by occasional explosions and tragedy, for the last Americans in combat in Vietnam. It is a limbo between victory and defeat, a period of lull before the North Vietnamese again seriously challenge allied control over the coastal plain, as they did for the last time in the Tet, May and September offensives of 1968. For the average "grunt," or infantryman, the war is not so much a test of strength under pressure, as it often was a few years ago, as a daily hassle to avoid patrols, avoid the enemy, avoid contact—keep out of trouble and not be "the last Amer-ican killed in Vietnam."

"I mean, what does it accomplish—what does it gain," asks our forward observer, a captain who attended Officer Can-didates' School after having graduated from the University of Southern California in Los Angeles. "Even if we kill 500 dinks, to me it's not worth it." The F.O. calls in artillery strikes on suspected targets in the nearby hills, but he does so with no-table lack of relish. "I just saw three dinks down in that rice field," he says. "One of them was carrying a shiny tube. They were probably V.C., but maybe they were civilians with an old shell. I don't think it's right to look for some excuse for shoot-ing at them." Although the F.O. is a captain, he articulates the views of the G.I.'s with whom I go on patrol down the ridge.

"The dinks are just playin' with us, waitin' for us to go home, then they'll beat the —— out of the ARVN [Army of the Republic of Vietnam]," says the rifleman in front of me, reiterating a view held by many of his superiors. "It's a lifer's playground, a chance for the generals to test their strategies," the G.I. enlarges, in thick Georgian tones, as we scramble up from the stream bed—only to stop again a minute later so our "pigman" can test-fire his machine-gun. "Git them cows down there," another G.I. yells, grinning while the M-60 spews a torrent of bullets into the bushes in front of us. The cows, grazing on a rise half a mile away, amble off at the urging of a boy who hears the shots. A couple of the grunts idly curse all the "lifers"—the C.O., the N.C.O.'s, anyone vaguely responsible for issuing them orders and threats. "If the lifers don't get you," says one, explaining why we don't radio a false location and rest instead of walk, "then the V.C. will."

Their chatter is hardly unique. In a month visiting units in the field and rear areas around Military Region One, I found literally no young G.I.'s in favor of the war, none who didn't think we should "get out," few who didn't hate the "lifers" almost as much as the "dinks"—a term sometimes used to describe ARVN as well as enemy forces. For all the complaints, though, cases of refusal to fight or go to the field are quite rare—perhaps an average of two or three per battalion per month. Virtually every G.I. in the bush theoretically yearns for a softer job somewhere else, but almost all of them admit that time slips by faster here, that "lifers don't hassle you so much" over petty matters of haircut and dress, that drugs are less available and duty not so dull as in the rear.

Nor are there more than slim odds these days that a combat G.I. will die despite the danger of mines set and re-set daily by V.C. sympathizers—often farmers or small boys selling PX cokes by the road at 50 cents a can. Casualty figures in July receded to the lowest ebb in six years, 11 killed one week, 29 another, about 70 for the month—the first since 1965 in which the number of American "K.I.A.'s" (killed in action) was below 100. (The U.S. command now emphasizes low American casualties with the same enthusiasm that it once accorded such statistics as enemy "body counts." At a briefing in the middle of August, for instance, a military spokesman proudly disclosed a weekly average of 19 American K.I.A.'s for the previous two and a half months, "exactly half the average of 38 K.I.A.'s for the year to date." These figures, he noted happily, compared with an average of 81 killed each week of last year.) Specifically ordered to hold down casualties, commanders rarely invade traditional enemy base areas among shadowy crags and valleys to the west—and carefully disengage from battles in the lowlands if heavy losses seem inevitable or even conceivable.

Only occasional incidents or intelligence reports still remind G.I.'s—and commanders—that "a war's going on here, y'know." On the "Arizona Territory," a shell-pocked stretch of abandoned rice fields southwest of Danang, Vietcong guerrillas intermittently fire on armored personnel carriers and tanks rumbling through land that Marines failed to secure in six years before the last of them pulled out of here several months ago. One night at the end of August, for instance, the V.C. killed five and wounded seven G.I.'s sitting behind their vehicles in a circular night defensive position. Commanders put all 70,000 U.S. troops remaining in Military Region One on special alert in anticipation of small-scale attacks by North Vietnamese regulars and local terrorists bent on exploiting Vietnam's unending political problems.

But the American military posture remains basically defensive and low-keyed. No more than 8,000 U.S. troops are "beating the bush" in Military Region One these days—and they rarely pursue the enemy beyond the first few ridgelines.

"There's no longer that intense aggressiveness," laments Lieut. Col. Lee Roberts, who enlisted in 1948 at the age of 19, attended O.C.S. after having been turned down for West Point—and now commands a battalion from a mountain firebase 20 miles southwest of Danang. "Instead of going on lengthy sweeps, our companies set up defensive positions from which they send out patrols," he explains, sipping coffee from a paper cup in front of his sandbagged command bunker, overlooking an undulating velvet-green valley. "If they get into contact," he says, surveying his A.O.—area of operations—through baleful, slate-gray eyes, "they back off and call in air and artillery."

"What we're performing is defense-in-depth," summarizes the information officer at the headquarters of the Americal division, which totals some 20,000 troops south and west of Danang, including those patrolling Charlie Ridge and the Arizona territory. "We're interdicting enemy supply routes and infiltration of troops to the lowlands." Off-duty, in the officers' club behind the headquarters, built on rolling sand dunes at Chulai, for which marines fought bunker to bunker in 1965, a couple of R.O.T.C. lieutenants joke about the Americal's notorious past. First there was exposure of the massacres at Mylai, a few miles to the south, followed by the case of a former brigade commander charged with mowing down civilians from his helicopter and, late last year, revelation of the use of a chemical defoliant capable of inducing cancer. Then, in June, the commanding general was relieved in the after-math of an attack on a firebase in which 33 G.I.'s were killed.

"I'm afraid to tell anyone back in the world I'm with the Americal," says one of the lieutenants, laughing sardonically. "No one has much pride in the division. That's one reason morale is so bad."

Despite the image, however, the mission of the Americal—and the attitude of its men—is no different from those of the only other full-strength U.S. division in Vietnam, the 101st Airborne, based at Camp Eagle, midway between Danang and the DMZ. Just as the Americal defends Danang and the coast to the south, so the 101st patrols the lowlands and hills beyond the one-time imperial capital of Hue, for political and cultural reasons South Vietnam's most important city after Saigon. Once regarded as the toughest of U.S. divisions, the 101st now appears as wary of combat, as reluctant to fight, as lax in discipline, as the Americal. Commanders proudly evoke its traditional nickname "Screaming Eagles," but G.I.'s these days prefer to call it, not without a certain touch of reverse pride, "the one-oh-*worst*."

"I have seen the Screaming Eagles in action—in the jungles and air and assisting the people of northern Military Region One—and can testify that the outstanding reputation enjoyed by the 101st is completely justified," brags the division commander, Maj. Gen. Thomas M. Tarpley, somewhat defensively, perhaps, in a letter on the inside front cover of the division's slick-paper color magazine, Rendezvous With Destiny. The cover itself, however, testifies to the war-weariness of the men whom Tarpley tries to praise. In a water-color sketch of de-foliated trees etched against glowering gray clouds, three G.I.'s are standing on a truck, reaching toward a crane heli-copter hovering above them. Black peace symbols adorn drab army-green cannisters containing 155-millimeter artillery shells, and the twisted limbs of three leafless trees form the initials F.T.A., —— the Army.

Already a legend around the 101st, the cover evokes the mood of the grunts whom I accompany on a couple of patrols by a stream along which the V.C. slip men and supplies into the lowlands. The platoon leader is a gung-ho career soldier, a first lieutenant out of O.C.S., airborne, ranger and jungle schools, who inwardly regrets he's arrived in Vietnam a couple of years too late for "the real war." He has been here only three weeks, and he wants to play by the rules. Maybe, if he succeeds, there's still enough time for him to get a regular—as opposed to a reserve—commission, a promotion to captain and command of a company in the field, if not exactly in full-fledged combat.

"Shoot to capture, not to kill," the lieutenant, an athletic, lifeguard type with close-cropped hair and finely chiseled features that remind me of a carving of a Roman centurion, earnestly abjures his troops, in an upstate New York twang. The men, saddled up for a RIF (reconnaissance in force) through abandoned rice fields and one-time hamlets, erased except for occasional cement foundations by air and artillery strikes, grin and snicker. "I shoot for K.I.A.'s, not P.O.W.'s," retorts Specialist 4 Robert Latchaw, a wiry Pole from South River, N.J., laughing at the lieutenant's naiveté. "Whaddya want us to do, shoot an ear off?" jibes Doc, the medic. The lieutenant, unfazed, insists he's following policy set down by "higher higher" headquarters. "We're not after body counts anymore," he says. "We'd prefer information. K.I.A.'s don't talk." With that, we sally forth through tall grass toward a stream near which our platoon sergeant, remaining behind with a squad, swears he saw "two dinks running that way."

It is clear to everyone but the lieutenant, though, that we're not seriously pursuing "the dinks," who were fleeing a fight with some South Vietnamese near the ruins of an old French fort, first booby-trapped by the V.C. and then leveled by American bombs, dropped to set off the booby traps. "Just walkin' around don't accomplish nothin'," says Latchaw, a church-going Catholic with a wife "back in the world" who sends him weekly packages of "world food," good canned stuff to supplement the boring, bland diet of C-rations. "I been here nine months, and I ain't been in no firefight yet. Most I did was spend 100 days in the mountains during the monsoon without changing my clothes once." We are, by this time, beside the stream, filling canteens, after an hour-long stroll broken by frequent halts for rest and talk. If there are any V.C. in the area, they are as eager to keep out of our way as we are to keep out of theirs.

All of us, that is, except for the lieutenant: next morning, around 10, he leads another RIF toward the stream, this time aiming for the "draw," the ravine down which the water tumbles from the last ridgeline into the lowlands. It seems like another easy walk in the sun before we begin, but our point man is still hacking away with his machete several hours later. (Murmurs from the grunts behind me: "I want to be back in Kentucky rabbit-huntin'." "When I get back to the world I don't even care if I see another forest. I'm stayin' in the city.") The lieutenant sends a couple of riflemen—a bull-necked Chicano named Quito and the Kentuckian—into the bush in hopes of finding an easier route. They return a few minutes later. "Gettin' too theek," says Quito. "Might see some dinks we don't want to see." We plunge straight ahead, find a trickle of flowing water, fill canteens, keep going another hour until we stumble on the same stream we reached, lower down, on yesterday's patrol. Some of the men flop in, lying on their backs in the fast-running water, cleansing bodies, fatigues and socks. We would be easy marks for an ambush. No one is standing guard.

Across the stream we see clear signs of V.C. movement— little footpaths leading across open clearings. For the first time we spread apart, a routine precaution. Behind us rises the slope of the ridgeline, burned off by a fire ignited by one of the Delta Tangos—"Defensive Target" artillery rounds— called in by the lieutenant a couple of nights ago. We follow the path along the stream, wade in the water for a while, then emerge about where we'd been the day before. A couple of hundred yards from the bank a neat path cuts a straight line through the bush—the kind of trail along which guerrilla soldiers could run full-speed if necessary, dropping for cover at the sound of approaching helicopters.

"We're going to work this area really well," the lieutenant advises his men, who remain sullenly silent. "We're gonna set up ambush positions in here and set out a couple of claymore mines—get them as they fall back from fighting the ARVN." As soon as we return to our original position, the lieutenant announces his plan to our platoon sergeant, a hard-talking Midwesterner who's been with the unit only a couple of days, but knows how to handle eager young officers.

The sergeant reminds the lieutenant a resupply helicopter is about to arrive, that it'll take a while sorting out the stuff, burning off the waste. He says he's found a "beautiful N.D.P."—night defensive position—"over there by the trees." The lieutenant hesitates, wavers. He senses that his men, from the new sergeant on down, are against him. "We don't have enough men for an ambush," the sergeant argues. "We get into a fight, we'll get waxed." The lieutenant finally settles for setting a single claymore on the trail this side of the stream.

That night we hear the crackle of small arms from over near the ARVN positions, a mile or so away. Helicopters circle overhead, muttering machinegun fire, and artillery and mortar rounds thud across the fields. Next morning, the lieutenant is beside himself with anger and frustration. "Should have sent out that goddam ambush," he says, not looking at the sergeant. "Could have gotten them running away. Godammit, we gotta get moving. It's late already. This happens again, I'm gettin' everyone up at 5 o'clock."

It is 10:30 before the men are ready. Then the lieutenant gets more bad news, this time over the radio. The battalion commander, on a firebase a couple of miles away, is ordering the entire company in to guard the base perimeter. "Just routine rotation." In vain the lieutenant pleads that he needs "a couple more days to work the area by the stream." His men curse him silently. "Godammit, if no one was looking, I'd frag the sonuvabitch," says one of them.

The threat of a fragging—explosion of a fragmentation or hand grenade—in this case is probably not serious. The G.I. who makes it not only walked point the morning before but willingly went on patrol again in the evening to plant the mine. An Iowa farm boy, he criticizes the war on the grounds that "we're not fightin' it like we should." Since we failed to invade North Vietnam, H-bomb Hanoi and Haiphong and declare "free fire zones" of V.C. hamlets, he says "we oughta quit wastin' time and go home." Like most of the grunts in the field, he may lack motivation but he's not really bored— an intrinsic factor in turning casual threats into deeds.

It is mainly in the rear, among the troops whom the grunts disdainfully call the REMF's for Rear Echelon Mother ——, that talk of fragging, of hard drugs, of racial conflict, seems bitter, desperate, often dangerous. At the combat base at Quangtri, the last provincial capital below the DMZ, I walk into a dimly lit single-story barracks one afternoon hoping to find perhaps a couple of G.I.'s with whom I can talk—and count 16 of them reclined in the shadows of a lounge shielded by blankets and curtains hanging from the windows. "Welcome to the head hootch," says a thin, hollow-cheeked private first class of 18 or 20, waving me to a spot on the couch after I convince him I'm a reporter, not a criminal investigator. The G.I.'s proudly explain that their hootch is a meeting place for potheads from all over the base, but I don't smell any marijuana in the air. "How many of you smoke scag [heroin]," I ask. They all raise their hands.

Who are the heads in the hootch—and why have they "graduated" from pot to heroin? They are, for the most part, white, with 10 to 12 years of education, a few with records of juvenile delinquency or petty crime in civilian life. While some might not perform well under any circumstances, all of them seem hopelessly demoralized both by the war and by their immediate surroundings. "I was supposed to be a heavy-equipment operator but all I do is pick up beer cans," says one. "They haven't got anything for us to do," says another. "They just want to keep us busy." Several are aimless drifters, too strung out for work, awaiting courts-martial or undesirable discharges, demotions and restrictions. Many, if they report for duty at all, put in only a few hours a day before finding some excuse to return to the hootch—or else they just go back with no excuse at all.

It's far from clear whether the men are more at odds with their commanders and sergeants or the war in general. "They tell you to do something, then they yell at you for doing it," says the equipment operator. "They harass you about haircuts and beards and burn you for sleeping on guard when you've been working all day." Most of the complaints are petty, often unjustified, but they also suffer from the same sense of futility, of pointlessness, that affects thousands of other G.I.'s in the midst of withdrawal of American troops. "The gooks are winning this war," says one. "The ARVN are afraid to fight. They run away. The gooks can have the place when we leave."

While we are talking one of the heads slowly stirs a plate of "hard times," all but powerless marijuana seeds and stems. "It's what I got left," he says. "It's gettin' so hard to score marijuana around here, guys have to turn to scag"—which doesn't smell, comes in much smaller quantities and is easier to hide. Another G.I. idly tells a story, verified by his friends, of ordering more than 300 vials of heroin at $2 a vial from a Vietnamese "cowboy" on a motorcycle by the gate of the base. "I gave him $200 for a hundred and robbed the rest and ran," says the G.I. "He drove away grinning, and I knew I was the one that was ripped off. It was all salt and sodium acid." The next day the G.I. armed with his M-16, bought 200 vials from a trusted pusher in a nearby village. "I sell it here for $5 a vial," says the G.I., a personable, fair-haired Midwesterner who served six months of a five-year term "back in the world" before enlisting in the Army.

That night a couple of the G.I.'s—a black and a Chicano—invite me to a pot party at a helicopter hangar on the other side of the runway. The air in the little room in the back of the hangar is heavy with the sweet smell of "dew." A helicopter pilot tells me he's been "stoned ever since getting to Vietnam"—that he performs better that way but is "scared —— of scag." Beside him is a doctor, an army captain, silently smoking pot in a corncob pipe. Some of the helicopter crewmen pass freshly rolled cigarettes around. A couple of other G.I.'s stand lookout, glancing from time to time over the walls to see if M.P.'s are coming. One of the chopper pilots argues convincingly for legalization of pot—says it's not habit-forming, is no more harmful than beer. He doesn't know it, but several of the enlisted men in the room have laced their marijuana with heroin. Some of them plan to go to "the party after the party"—an all-night get-together in one of the perimeter bunkers for speed freaks, pill-poppers who get the pills by mail from home or buy them on the local market, often at ordinary pharmacies.

It is difficult to quantify the use of drugs in the rear. It is obvious though, that a relatively high proportion of the REMF's, perhaps 20 per cent, is on the hard stuff as opposed merely to marijuana, while only a marginal few indulge in the bush. ("We see a guy using it out here, we take care of him, or the C.O. sends him back to the rear," one of the men on Charlie Ridge tells me. "Otherwise he'll be high some time when we're under attack. You can't hardly walk if you're high all the time.") The use of drugs in base camps accounts for widespread thefts—and also is a major factor in fraggings. G.I.'s on drugs will steal almost anything, ranging from stereo sets to food from the mess hall, to sell in exchange for heroin, peddled by small boys and women, cowboys on Hondas, even South Vietnamese soldiers operating near Americans.

Addicts resort to fraggings—or threats and intimidation— whenever commanders order shakedown searches, restrict them to quarters or otherwise attempt seriously to cut down the flow. At each camp I visit there are tales of incidents in which G.I.'s have blown up orderly rooms, sometimes wounding or killing the wrong man, or have merely exploded grenades outside windows for shock effect. One of the favorite techniques is to set off a tear-gas cannister—a harmless antic that creates momentary chaos and serves a warning of more violence later. At the rear headquarters of one of the battalions of the 196th Brigade, on a road leading to Freedom Hill out- side Danang, the battalion's new executive officer, in the midst of a crusade against drugs, walks into his quarters one day and finds a grenade pin on his pillow—a symbol of what may happen to him if he keeps up his campaign.

"It's like war: you take chances," says the exec, Maj. John O'Brien, a bluff, outspoken man with a strong Massachusetts edge to his voice, who served 10 years in the enlisted ranks before attending O.C.S. The major, on his second tour in Vietnam, arrived here in June totally unprepared for the new mood among G.I.'s in the rear. He found heroin vials, empty, discarded around battalion headquarters, in the latrines, under barracks. At least 20 of more than 100 men assigned to his battalion "rear" were perpetually too high and too weak to perform. At the same time, a number of others were not only opposed to the use of drugs but willing to work with him to prevent it. "We had a couple of meetings just brain- storming," says O'Brien, who, unlike many career officers, seems capable of talking with young G.I.'s on an informal basis. "We were receptive to any ideas anyone wanted to offer. The situation was so desperate, we had to be open to everything." The result was a well-balanced combination of force and propaganda.

"As of this date I'm declaring war on drug abuse in this battalion," begins the mimeographed "Open Letter to All Drug Users," posted on bulletin boards around the battalion area. "I will seek out and find every drug user and pusher" in the battalion. The letter recounts what many of the G.I.'s already know—that the major, assisted by a special "drug squad" of half a dozen men, has already confiscated more than 100 vials filled with heroin. "Things are going to get a hell of a lot tighter before the problem is satisfactorily resolved," the letter promises. "There will be more shakedowns and inspections. The flow of traffic in and out of the compound is going to be dramatically reduced. My officers and senior N.C.O.'s are now authorized to conduct unannounced search of any man on this compound." The letter invites addicts to turn themselves in voluntarily to the army's amnesty program, under which they can spend several days in a special ward getting over the immediate physical effects of the habit—or else face prosecution and court-martial.

Major O'Brien has no real illusions, however, about the long-range efficacy of his program. He thinks he's drastically reduced the use of heroin in his own compound but points out a couple of cases in which addicts went through amnesty withdrawal, only to pick up the habit again a few days later. He doesn't like to talk about the grenade pin left on his pillow—fears that publicity might encourage a fragging—but points with a grin at a copy of his "open letter," scrawled with defiant notations. "Happiness is a Vial of Smack," says one of them. "Major O'Brien is a Smack Freak," says another. "Stay A Head." Perhaps over-optimistically, the major views the comments as a good sign. "It shows they're worried," he says. "At least I'm getting a response."

Major O'Brien's program, I discover, is the exception, not the rule. By far the majority of the commanders and executive officers whom I meet are simply not aware of the scope of the problem in their own units. They tend, in many cases, to rely on the word of their N.C.O.'s—most of whom are so conservative, not to mention so hooked on alcohol, as to distort their whole attitude toward the drug problem. Another complication is that officers and N.C.O.'s also must cope with racial conflict—protests against authority by young blacks who claim the army discriminates against them. Racial tension, like drugs, is of secondary importance in the field, but it threatens to explode in base camps where blacks have time to form their own Panther or antiwar "liberation" organizations—and chafe under petty harassment by lifers who often, in fact, do reveal instinctive, subconscious, if not explicit, forms of prejudice.

The racial question is so sensitive at Camp Baxter, on a road lined with military installations and Vietnamese refugee shanties near Marble Mountain, just south of Danang, that military officers don't want me on the base. Finally the camp commander, Col. Joseph Otto Meerboth, a graying West Pointer, agrees to let me talk to G.I.'s—but asks me to "come back tomorrow" when I show up for my appointment. As I am escorted toward the gate, he orders military policemen to seal off the post to intruders and search the barracks for half a dozen blacks, whom he's convinced are plotting a major racial disturbance. The next day, Colonel Meerboth explains that the blacks transferred four days ago to another base, returned without warning to pick up their possessions—and that one of them, at least, is "extremely dangerous."

"He's organized an extralegal confederacy," says the colonel, who admits having had little experience with either drug or racial problems before his assignment to Camp Baxter last fall. "The traditional method for rendering extralegal confederacies ineffective is to dismember them. Last night I brought in three of these men one by one, talked to them and told them they had to leave. They have been escorted elsewhere." Colonel Meerboth's decision, however, has not necessarily conquered the problem, characterized by intermittent demonstrations, a couple of killings, secret meetings and threats, spread over the past 8 or 10 months. At the service club, where he reluctantly permits me to interview G.I.'s, both blacks and whites criticize the transfer of troublemakers—and claim the one singled out by the colonel as the "ringleader" was actually instrumental in keeping the blacks from staging an armed, open revolt.

"A white man just don't understand the problem," says

Sgt. Clarence Chisholm, a graduate of the Tuskegee Institute who was drafted into the Army and works as a communications specialist. "Whenever you try to explain what's happening, you're branded as a 'militant.'" Chisholm, due to rotate home from Vietnam in a couple of days, charges the white officers and N.C.O.'s with practicing *de facto* segregation by recommending transfers mainly for blacks and leaving the camp, once 20 per cent black, almost entirely white. Some of the whites whom I meet agree with Chisholm's interpretation. "Our sergeant told me it's 'open season on blacks,'" says one of them. "The thing is this Colonel Meerboth cannot control this compound," says another, shouting excitedly in the middle of a circle of white soldiers who rush to the service club to talk to me when word gets around "there's a reporter there."

The G.I.'s charge all the "undesirables"—Black Panthers, drug addicts, whatever—were transferred to three or four nearby units reputed as dumping grounds for those not wanted elsewhere. The black "ringleader," I learn, has gone to Chulai, where he's now on permanent guard duty with the 277th Supply and Service Battalion. "I'm scared to go there," says another G.I., a Chicano, who's also been transferred to the 277th but has returned to Camp Baxter to pick up his stuff—and has somehow escaped the colonel's notice. "I hear they're *all* scag freaks down there." Intrigued, I go to Chulai the next day to meet the colonel's nemesis, Specialist 4 Loyle Green Jr., a tall, polite one-time student at Malcolm X University in Chicago, who once had visions of attending O.C.S. and making a career in the Army but has since decided "to help the brothers back in the world."

"They gave us five hours to pack our bags and leave after they notified us to our transfers," says Green, whom I meet in battalion headquarters. "We started to protest, but there was nothing we could do. We were railroaded to Chulai. The majority of the transfers were from minority groups—blacks, Spanish, Indians." Green attributes his transfer to his role in leading a sit-in outside Colonel Meerboth's headquarters in protest against the pretrial confinement of a black G.I. charged with assaulting a white. "It was so tense that a lot of blacks had gotten weapons," Green recalls, "but it was going to be a peaceful protest." The blacks, he notes with pride, simply turned their backs, got up and left when Colonel Meerboth emerged to order them to disperse. "Then there was the plan to destroy the entire compound," large enough for several thousand men, says Green. "I talked to a couple of the blacks and told them there was no way. We were already infiltrated by informants. We had the weapons, grenades to do it, but we would have lost in the end."

Green, acknowledged by Colonel Meerboth as a "persuasive speaker" and a "natural leader," appears less than militant in his outlook. Rather, he displays a sensitive judgment of power realities, an understanding of the limits to which the blacks can go—and determined, passive defiance of white authority. One factor that may have cast him as a sinister figure, in Meerboth's mind, was the funeral service in March for a black killed by a white in a brawl in the middle of the camp. "The blacks didn't want the chaplain to speak," says Green. "We had 200 or 300 there. We just turned our backs to the chaplain while he kept rattling on. We chanted, 'Black Power!' and put up a liberation flag—it had a black fist in the middle with the words 'Black Unity' in black letters on top, with a red background. The colonel stood there shaking his head. I told him we didn't want any American flag there. No blacks are American. I don't consider myself an American. I consider myself a black."

Green, like many of the black G.I.'s, wears the black-power band, made of black shoelaces, around his wrist. A black-power ring, in the form of a clenched fist, gleams from the index finger of his right hand. In defiance of authority, he is growing a full-scale beard, in addition to the regulation mustache. Ironically, in view of his antiwhite, antiwar outlook, he has never been disciplined, court-martialed or reduced in rank. He does not refuse to work, as do many blacks, particularly those on drugs. "I was a clerk-typist and a driver," he says. "It was challenging at first, but there wasn't enough to do"—an explanation, combined with opposition to the war, that may account for most of the Army's problems in the rear.

Unlike Green, however, black G.I.'s whom I meet at the 277th headquarters in Chulai seem not only depressed but openly, dangerously rebellious, possibly on the verge of armed revolt. One of them, interviewed in the presence of the battalion executive officer, tells me the blacks have a "secret arms cache" and plan to start using it "if things don't let up around here." The exec, Maj. Robert De Biasio, who has been trying to work with the blacks to find the causes of their problems, listens without interrupting. Later he tells me he doesn't think the black is kidding. "We've searched those barracks time and again and found nothing much," he says. "I think they have the arms underground somewhere. The only way we could find them would be to order everyone out of the barracks early in the morning, keep them under guard and go over the whole area with a mine detector."

Major De Biasio may face a tougher problem than does Major O'Brien at Freedom Hill. At the 661st, one of four companies in his battalion, G.I.'s estimate that 20 per cent of more than 100 troops don't work at all. The company commander, a pleasant, open man with eight years' enlisted time behind him before he went to O.C.S., may be afraid to impose tight discipline. He arrived several months ago—after the fragging of the quarters of his predecessor, who escaped unharmed but severely shaken. "We have some outstanding young men here," the C.O. blandly observes, venturing that only a dozen men in the entire battalion "use drugs on a somewhat irregular basis." In view of the C.O.'s easygoing tolerance, if not essential blindness to reality, it is not surprising that many of the troops whom I meet at the 661st focus their complaints on their sergeants rather than on the officers. Ironically, the most feared of the N.C.O.'s is a black, a 33-year-old Georgian known for his skill as a boxer and judo expert and nicknamed, as a token of both respect and dislike, "Karate Joe."

Karate is sipping beer with another N.C.O., a white sergeant from Tennessee, when I see him in his hootch. He's afraid to go to the enlisted men's club—doesn't want the men thinking he's trying to harass them off-duty. He's stopped counting the times he's found grenade pins on his pillow or been threatened verbally. "It doesn't even bother me any more," he says, but it is clear he is intensely unhappy. "My first tour here, we were all together," he says. "We worked as a team. I was doing the same thing then, running the ammo

supply point, humping ammo into helicopters to take to the
field. I never had no problems with the men. This time they
don't really care no more."

Karate shouts and curses at the troops to get them to work,
but he's beginning to feel he's engaged in a lost cause. "You
discipline them so much and eventually the C.O. gets started
on getting them 212's"—discharges on grounds of unsuit-
ability or unfitness for service. "I just don't know what the
answer is," he says, clenching his beer can. "It's not the same
Army any more."

The only real answer, as far as *this* war is concerned, may
be to keep withdrawing the men on an accelerated timetable
and send only volunteers over here for the remaining advisory
and rear-area jobs. Wherever I go in the northern provinces,
whether in the field or in rear areas, I find the problem of
motivation so overwhelming as to defy rational "solutions"
and "programs" other than withdrawal. Below Charlie Ridge,
on the Arizona Territory, I talk with a young captain on his
first tour. He is a West Point graduate, in command of a troop
of armored personnel carriers—an ideal position for a career-
minded military man. He has been here only one week, but
already he is filled with doubts and questions.

"They train you, send you to schools," says the captain, as
we begin a bumpy ride through fields planted with mines and
booby traps, "but nobody's prepared to see a guy killed or
wounded. I had the most sobering experience of my life yesterday—I saw one of my men wounded with shrapnel. He's
the first guy I've ever seen wounded. Once we've decided to
get out, and then keep fighting, it seems kind of worthless.
Nobody wants to be the last guy to die in Vietnam." That
night, after the A.P.C.'s—or "tracks"—have formed a defensive circle by a small river, a lone guerrilla fires an AK-47 rifle
from a couple hundred meters in front of us, sending bright
red tracers over our position. The G.I.'s leap onto the tracks,
answering with machine guns and M-16's. Helicopter gunships arrive, spraying the bushes with bullets. It is an eerie late
show, played against the black backdrop of the sky and mountains, and it lasts for an hour.

"They got some nerve opening up against all our firepower
like that," says one of the G.I.'s as the guns fall silent and we

stretch out to sleep on cots unfolded behind our track. "Far as I'm concerned, they can have this whole country. There ain't no reason for us bein' here. We was fightin' to win, that'd be one thing, but we're just wastin' time." It is a typical G.I. commentary—one I hear countless times around Military Region One—at the butt end of a bad war.

The New York Times Magazine, September 19, 1971

A VISIT WITH GENERAL LOAN: 1971

Portrait of an Aging Despot

by Tom Buckley

"TAKE a case of beer with you," said the man who arranged the appointment. "He'll appreciate it." I thought I was being kidded, but I climbed the stairs to the third floor of the Defense Ministry with a case of Budweiser—$2.40 at the Post Exchange—on my shoulder. As I set it down in his office, Maj. Gen. Nguyen Ngoc Loan rose awkwardly on his braced leg to shake hands. He looked at me closely. At last he said, "I remember you," with a note of triumph in his voice. His eyes rolled away from me. It was only ten-thirty in the morning, but on his desk, which was clear otherwise, there was an empty bottle of Vietnamese "33" beer (so he would appreciate the Budweiser after all) and an empty glass. It was a small office at the end of a corridor, undecorated and barely furnished. Instead of a combination-lock filing cabinet for classified documents, there was a small refrigerator, in which an orderly stacked the Budweiser to chill.

Loan (say "low-ahn") had been promoted to permanent two-star rank only a few days earlier. He shrugged off my congratulations. "It is a joke," he said. "I have no troops and no duties. I am in charge of long-range planning, maybe for the next war. I ask to retire but they do not permit me to retire, so they give me two stars and a few more piasters. I can live on my salary, my wife does not complain, but I could get a good job in business. I could earn twice as much. After all, I took a management course at MIT." He pulled on his cigarette, and his laugh—almost a giggle—was broken up by a hacking cough.

It had been different the last time I had seen him, in March 1968. Loan was then the commander of the national police. From behind the walls of his headquarters compound, a sinister place that few Vietnamese approached if they could avoid it, he commanded 70,000 men—the police, the special branch, the paramilitary battalions of the Police Field Force, an army of spies and informers. His powers were those of life and death, and at his command tens of thousands of persons were imprisoned in the tiger cages of Conson Island and else-where; tortured in the dreaded provincial interrogation cen-ters; were assassinated, executed, or simply not heard from again.

But even then, two of the three events that were to lead to his fall from power had already taken place. His friend and fellow Air Force pilot, Nguyen Cao Ky, had been induced to relinquish the premiership and run for the Vice-Presidency while Gen. Nguyen Van Thieu ran for the Presidency. Then in February 1968, during the Tet fighting, Loan had the mis-fortune to be photographed shooting a bound and helpless Vietcong prisoner in the head with his revolver. Loan might conceivably have escaped the consequences of these two events, but that May, when Saigon was attacked for the second time, he became, as far as I can tell, the only South Viet-namese general to be wounded in ground combat. His right leg was shattered by machine-gun bullets as he led an attack against a guerrilla unit. Thieu took the opportunity to replace him with one of his own men.

Loan was sent to Australia for treatment, but the photo-graphs and television films of the shooting had made him no-torious. He seemed to epitomize all that was vicious and cowardly about the war in general and the South Vietnamese forces in particular, and the public outcry forced him to leave. He was taken to the Walter Reed Army Hospital in Washing-ton. The leg was saved, finally, but it was little more than a stick. Long after his recuperation, while Thieu consolidated his power, Loan and his family lived in virtual exile, in a house in Alexandria, Virginia, closely watched by the Central Intel-ligence Agency. When at last he received permission to return to Saigon, it was to a meaningless assignment and an empty office.

I first met Loan during the summer of 1967. The occasion was the graduation of a class of police recruits at Loan's head-quarters. I had been invited to attend by the senior American public-safety adviser. He was a retired captain of the New York

State Police, an amiable enough fellow, particularly in comparison with some of his subordinates, among whom were old-time members of colonial police forces in Malaya, Burma, the Dutch East Indies, and a large number of agate-eyed former Deep South sheriffs and deputies, but his talents clearly would have been better employed as a supervisor of bank guards.

Loan was seated not far from me under a canopy made from an orange-and-white cargo parachute. He was not prepossessing. His forehead sloped and so did his chin, he was losing his hair, his eyes goggled, his teeth were bad, and he was skinny and stoop-shouldered. Senior officers, both Vietnamese and American, invariably wore immaculately starched combat fatigues and mirror-polished boots, no matter how deskbound they were, and set their faces in chin-back frowns to disguise the vast echoing hollows under their caps. Loan, by contrast, wore flopping sandals and the short-sleeved white shirt and baggy gray cotton trousers of the ordinary policeman. His homely face was alive with intelligence. Throughout the long ceremony he drank cognac and soda and joked with his subordinates, laughing so hard on occasion that his feet beat a tattoo on the ground as a reflex of his spasms. It was as though Loan were commenting on something everyone knew, that Vietnamese families paid heavily to have their sons accepted as police recruits, since it was generally a much safer job than the infantry and in time the opportunities were considerable for augmenting the small salary with all sorts of graft, notably heavy bribes from draft dodgers.

When the last medal for marksmanship and interrogation technique had been distributed, a buffet was served. The American press crowded around Loan. He seemed to enjoy the verbal sparring and he spoke English well, although he slurred his words—not just because of his drinking, I think, but because he didn't relish the taste of English vowels and consonants on his tongue. For the most part he dodged the questions, but at one point he said something rather elegant, although not, as things worked out, very accurate. "As long as Ky remains in power I will remain in power," he said, "and as long as I remain in power Ky will remain in power."

Between the election and the heavy skirmishing along the

demilitarized zone it was a busy summer. I did not see Loan again until early October. The committee on elections of the National Assembly had recommended that because of widespread cheating, the victory of Thieu and Ky should be invalidated. While the full Assembly was voting on the question, Loan slouched in a chair in a box overlooking the stage of the old opera house in Saigon where the Assembly met, his cap pushed back on his head, drinking beer and absentmindedly spinning the chambers of his revolver, a snub-nosed .38-caliber Smith & Wesson "Airweight." The committee's recommendation was rejected.

After weeks of trying I was able to arrange an appointment with Loan in early December of 1967. It was a time when American optimism about the course of the war was reaching a zenith of fatuity. General Westmoreland had gone to Washington to inform Congress that the other side was no longer capable of launching major offensive operations. Army units were pursuing the guerrillas near the Cambodian border, and the Marines had just reoccupied Khesanh in force. On New Year's Eve a group of bright young attachés at the American Embassy, calling themselves collectively "the Flower People," a term that was fresh and bright then, gave a "Light at the End of the Tunnel" costume party.

With its ten-foot concrete walls, guard towers, rusting rolls of concertina barbed wire and death's-head signs warning of mines, the exterior of Loan's compound proved to be more fearsome than the inside. At least there were no gibbets, whipping posts, or freshly dug graves. His office was on the second floor of a yellow stucco house shaded by trees that probably had been the residence of the commander when it was a regimental garrison for the French cavalry. When I entered the office, through padded double doors, Loan was reading dossiers. For fifteen minutes he did not look up. When at last he signaled me to sit on the chair in front of his desk, and ordered drinks, I asked him to tell me something about his early life. He said he had been born in Hué, the old imperial capital, in 1930, one of a family of eleven children. His father, he said, had been an engineer on the highways and railroads. It occurred to me that his status was probably sub-professional, since the French seldom permitted a Vietnamese to go higher. Nevertheless, the family must have been relatively well off as part of the small middle class created by the French, but distinct from and socially inferior to the traditional mandarin and landowning classes.

In 1951, while Loan was studying pharmacy at the University of Hué, the French became belatedly convinced after five years of war that victory or even the avoidance of eventual defeat was impossible without the formation of a Vietnamese national army. Until then the French force had been dominantly composed of troops from metropolitan France, the Foreign Legion, and colonial units from North Africa and Senegal. The 70,000 Vietnamese volunteers were formed in separate battalions, officered by Frenchmen, and were assigned mainly to defensive operations, as they were to be fifteen years later by the Americans.

Conscription was introduced, and for the first time more than a token number of Vietnamese were trained as officers. It was at this point that Loan, whose sympathies were dictated by his family's status, volunteered for officer training. Others of his generation made a different decision, fleeing into the jungle to join the Vietminh. Like many other senior Vietnamese officers I have spoken to, Loan told me that he had served briefly with the guerrillas while still a schoolboy but quit when he learned that they were Communists and not just simple nationalists fighting for Vietnamese freedom. It's a story I'm dubious about.

"At that time they didn't say a word about it," Loan said. "I was a Vietminh cadre from the time I am fourteen until nineteen, but all they say is just to fight against the Japanese, the Chinese, the French imperialists."

Loan was graduated at the top of his class, which included Ky, served briefly in the Delta, and was sent to what was then French Morocco for flight training. He also studied for a while at St. Cyr, the West Point of France. By the time he returned home, in 1955, the jungle was closing in over the wreckage of Dienbienphu, the French had signed the Geneva accords, and the new rump government of South Vietnam, headed by Ngo Dinh Diem, was being established by the United States.

The national army numbered 300,000 men at the time of the French collapse, but never became an effective fighting force. In *Vietnam: A Dragon Embattled*, Joseph Buttinger states, quite accurately, "They were poorly trained and equipped, but the major deficiency then and for a long time to come was a lack of competent officers: The best elements of the Vietnamese educated middle class had no desire to serve in an army created to fight, still under French overall direction, for a regime they despised and against people who, even if led by Communists, were still known to be fighting primarily for national independence."

It was these officers who formed the nucleus of Diem's armed forces and hold all the senior positions today, and the handicaps they began with have never been overcome. They were recruited reluctantly, trained indifferently, patronized and snubbed first by the French and then by the Americans and throughout by the social and intellectual elite of their own country, who reflected the traditional view in the Orient that military men are down near the last rung on the social ladder. And in the eleven years of the second Indochina war little has happened to improve their sense of self-esteem.

The Vietnamese Air Force probably did not have so pronounced an inferiority complex as the other services, mainly because the Vietcong did not have any airplanes—nothing more, in fact, until recently, than a few machine guns to challenge the old propeller-driven Skyraiders supplied by the United States. As Loan rose slowly in rank—he was promoted to major only after the fall of Diem—he did less flying and more staff work. He was sent to the United States for further training and gradually emerged as an intelligence and security specialist.

A Vietnamese who knew Loan in those days describes a figure less flamboyant than the style set by Ky, a withdrawn, seemingly rather timid young man who drank sparingly, did not have a mistress, and whose only vice was a fondness for the poker games played in an upstairs room over Brodard's Café.

The Vietnamese Air Force had a brief moment of glory in the spring of 1965. It flew the first two bombing raids against North Vietnam. Ky, the commander of the Air Force, led the attack and Loan flew as his wingman. The raids were mainly symbolic. The Skyraiders didn't go very far north of the Benhai River; and because they were clearly no match for North Vietnamese missiles, radar-directed heavy flak guns, and MiG interceptors, they were restricted to operations in South Vietnam thereafter. It was not until 1968 that the Vietnamese Air Force received even a token number of jets, and these were not suitable for operations against the North either.

("You tied our hands," Loan said when I went back to see him. "You wanted to win the war all by yourselves." What else could he say? Moreover, it seems incontestably true that until it was too late the American command *had* decided to win the war with American troops and let the Vietnamese pick up the pieces.)

In June 1965, only a few months after the raids, Ky emerged as the leader of the military junta after two years of revolving-door governments. His elevation to power occurred just as American combat troops were beginning to arrive, and their presence provided an essentially false sense of stability. Older generals were shuffled off into exile or retirement. Loan was promoted to colonel and appointed director of military intelligence and security. A year later he was given command of the national police. He was Ky's most trusted confidant and, according to many observers, second only to him in power.

The Tet attacks began in the north and center of Vietnam early in the morning of January 30, 1968. Saigon and the Delta were hit twenty-four hours later. In the absence of Thieu, who was spending the holidays at his villa in Mytho, his wife's home city, Ky and Loan took charge of the defenses of the capital.

On the afternoon of February 1 there was a skirmish in the vicinity of the Anquang Pagoda, the headquarters of the "militant" wing of the Buddhist church, which was agitating for a negotiated peace with the Vietcong. During the course of the fighting a captive was brought to Loan, who stood with his aides perhaps a half block away. Without a word, Loan snapped away his cigarette and drew his revolver. He took a marksman's stance, his right arm extended, and, at a distance of perhaps three feet, put a single bullet into the side of the prisoner's head.

In the heat of his rage, Loan had ignored the fact that Eddie Adams, the ace photographer of the Associated Press, and an NBC camera crew were focused on him. He glared at them after the shooting and it seemed certain he would order their film seized, but, inexplicably, he did not. Within hours Adams' picture sequence was being transmitted around the world. The next night the film was shown on the Huntley-Brinkley television news.

The two minutes of air time swept by, the battle receded, but the image remains. Loan, booted, armored with a flak vest, is a symbol of implacable savagery. The prisoner, smaller, frail, helpless, his hands invisible, wired together behind his back, wears only a ragged shirt and shorts. His face is distorted, pushed to one side by the impact of the bullet in his brain, his hair stands up, his mouth opens in what might be a final cry.

That was, I think, the turning point, the moment when the American public turned against the war. The Tet offensive destroyed confidence in the judgment of the men who were directing it; the murder committed by Loan sealed its moral bankruptcy. At the same time there rose to the surface a grudging admiration for the courage of an enemy that had fought for so long without a single airplane, helicopter, tank, or artillery piece against the most powerful nation in the world and mercenaries hired from all over Asia.

There was a fine irony in all this. The prisoner was identified, accurately probably, as the commander of a Vietcong sapper unit. He was said to have had a revolver in his possession when he was captured and to have used it to kill a policeman. Unlike the main force battalions that invaded Saigon, which wore khaki uniforms, and the sappers who penetrated the United States Embassy, who wore red armbands, the prisoner had no similar identification. As a practical matter, his end was probably merciful, since he escaped the gruesome torture that would have almost certainly been a prelude to his death in captivity.

The killing that so shocked the United States had no similar impact in Vietnam. Few Vietnamese were even aware of it, and if they were, they could understand a certain appropriateness in Loan's action. The Vietcong frequently assassinated government officials, although giving these murders at least a semblance of legality by first convicting the victim of a capital crime in absentia in a revolutionary court and leaving a death warrant with the body. From time to time the Vietcong have carried out multiple murders. One I recall was inflicted on a village of Montagnards who had been working for the government. In Hué during the Tet fighting many hundreds of government officials, sympathizers, and members of their families were massacred. By and large, though, I think far more murders and atrocities were committed by the Allied side. For one thing, they had the firepower and mobility to strike at Vietcong villages. For another, they had the more pressing need for information about the enemy, which inevitably leads to torture and worse.

I next saw Loan a month or so after the killing, when I arranged to go on a night patrol of the city with him. The Vietcong offensive had receded but skirmishes still took place on the outskirts of the city. A "second wave" attack was anticipated, however, and Saigon remained under a strict curfew from 7:00 P.M. until dawn. A police jeep picked me up at my apartment building at 10:00 P.M. and took me to the compound, where he was waiting for me. I sat beside him as we rolled through the deserted, eerily quiet streets, one of a convoy of three jeeps.

He said that at least as far as he was concerned the assault on Saigon had come as no surprise. "We knew in advance they were going to attack," he said. "For three days before, I had meetings, meetings, meetings. On the night it happened Ky called me. 'How about you and your wife coming over?' he said. I said, 'No, thanks. I'm on combat alert.' But he insisted. So I went over for a few minutes. Ky looked at me. 'You carry a revolver in my house on the first day of the New Year?' he said. 'You know it's bad luck.'

"I only stayed for a few minutes," Loan said. "I stayed on the streets, riding around like we are doing now, until 2:00 A.M. I am just lying down on my cot at my headquarters when

I get the news. The VC are attacking all over. Ky calls me to say that Tansonhut is under attack. He says he is being advised to leave there. 'No,' I say, 'stay with the Air Force.' General Khanh, the Third Corps commander, calls me to tell me to take command in the city. I have very few troops. I send my last two armored companies to help Tansonhut. Then I round up a platoon of PFFs [the Police Field Force] and two armored cars, and we race to the radio station, which the Communists have overrun. We take it back and the man right next to me is shot dead and falls on top of me."

Loan took a pull on a highball that was mixed for him by his orderly. The ingredients were kept in a small portable bar in the rear of the jeep. Sensing that he was in an amiable mood, I asked him to explain why he had shot the prisoner. "I am not a politician," he replied. "I am not a chief of police. I am just a soldier. When you see a man in civilian clothes with a revolver killing your people . . . when many of your people have already been killed, then what are you supposed to do? We knew who this man was. His name was Nguyen Tan Dat, alias Han Son. He was the commander of a sapper unit. He killed a policeman. He spit in the face of the men who captured him. What do you want us to do? Put him in jail for two or three years and then let him go back to the enemy?

"People in the United States do not know the things we know here," he said. "I respect the Vietcong in uniform. They are fighting men like me. People know that when they are wounded I take care of them. I see they get to the hospital. But when they are not in uniform they are criminals and the rule of war is death."

We had rolled over the high-backed bridge into the port district. Behind the warehouses and storage yards was a warren of shacks and tiny truck-gardening plots that even in the best of times was highly insecure. We turned off the main road and rolled slowly into a rutted alley for 100 yards and stopped. Loan's driver pulled a dashboard switch, and a floodlight on the jeep illuminated the featureless dwellings on both sides of us. He flashed the light quickly twice more. Another 100 yards away another jeep flashed a signal in reply. We started forward again, turned two or three times and emerged in a small square in front of a police post.

Scores of police materialized out of the shadows. Groups of men and women were being led forward to stand before camp tables at which were seated members of the special branch, who carefully checked the identification cards that all Vietnamese above the age of sixteen must carry. Raids and roundups were being carried out all over Saigon during those weeks. Here, in the port, an area had been cordoned off, the houses searched, and the residents brought to this central point.

Off to one side, squatting in the shadows, was a closely guarded group of fifteen or twenty civilians. Loan slouched over. The police officer in charge of the roundup said something in Vietnamese and pointed to an extraordinarily handsome man—tall, clear eyes, a coppery sheen to his skin—who wore clean white pajamas. Loan gave a word of command and the man was brought before him. Loan turned the man's identification card over in his hands, not looking at it. He asked questions, gently, as though thinking of something else. The man replied in an equally calm tone of voice.

Then Loan stepped back. He reached into his trousers pocket. He held what looked like a small automatic. He pointed it at the man's head. I had a momentary sense of— what shall I say—of rushing time, of dreadful weight. The man's expression didn't change. Loan's finger tightened on the trigger. There was a spurt of flame. With his other hand Loan flipped a cigarette out of a pack, put it in his mouth, and turned the barrel of his funny cigarette lighter to its tip. He took a drag and put his head back and laughed. He coughed on the smoke and laughed again. A scratching, hawking giggle, a shriek. His aides laughed and the police laughed, and the man in the white pajamas stood there motionless and silent.

"When I was in Washington the photographer who took the picture came to see me," Loan was saying in his bare little office with the beer bottle on his desk. "He said that he was sorry that he had to take it. He say that he have given his prize money to some organization like the Red Cross. I tell him, 'I am finished now; my career is over, but that is all right.

What is past is past. To be alive or dead, to be liked or not liked, it doesn't matter. Life belongs to Buddha, to God, whatever it is that is higher than me.' "

Harper's Magazine, April 1972

We Have Always Survived

by Robert Shaplen

OUTSIDE the restaurant in Cholon, the Chinese section of Saigon, where a group of us were having dinner a couple of months ago, there was a sudden howl of sirens. After years in this city, I had become used to sirens, whose throbbing *wow-wow-wow* is heard constantly, and at first we paid no attention and went on enjoying our fried crab. Within a few minutes, however, it became apparent that some emergency vehicles had come to a stop directly in front of the restaurant. I went out, to find the block cordoned off, while American and Vietnamese military police carried out a house-to-house search in the glow of rotating red-and-white searchlights flashing from the tops of jeeps. Getting out my press credentials, I approached a young American M.P. who was waving his M-16 rifle like a fishing rod. He couldn't have been more than nineteen years old, and he looked as if he might have arrived in Vietnam the day before. When I asked him what was going on, he replied only, "Sir, you'll have to go back into that restaurant." A Vietnamese M.P.—an older man—muttered something in broken English about "students" and "more riot." The Saigon University residential compound, Minh Mang, was only a block away, and for the past week the students had been, as they often are, demonstrating—this time against some new rules designed to prevent just such activity. Pointing to the roof of one of the buildings across the street, the Vietnamese policeman said something about "terrorists." I again tried the young American, who was now ducking in and out of doorways and pointing his gun at anyone still on the street. He was so jittery that I was afraid the weapon could go off at any moment, and it was obvious that he was in no mood to listen to further questions from me. "Sir," he finally spluttered, "have you got a disaster pass?"

I had never heard of a disaster pass—nor, as I subsequently

found out, was there such a thing (the young M.P. was probably referring to a special pass entitling a small number of
officials to go anywhere at any time)—but the phrase has
stayed with me, and I have since reflected that, in a manner
of speaking, I have had a disaster pass for Saigon for a quarter
of a century. Between the date of my first arrival, in June,
1946, and the present highly uncertain time, I have seen the
city undergo myriad changes, almost all of them for the
worse—particularly over the past decade, during which I have
spent approximately half my time in Vietnam. From a 1946
estimate of four hundred thousand, not counting French colonial troops, the population has grown to almost three million, and that of what is called the Saigon metropolitan area,
embracing parts of Gia Dinh Province, which surrounds the
city, is more than four million. Official projections—including
one made by C. A. Doxiadis, the famous Greek city planner,
whose firm did a study of Saigon in 1965—range as high as
nine million two hundred thousand for the metropolitan area
by the year 2000. Once a gracious city of quiet streets lined
with tamarind and flame trees, with plentiful gardens and play
areas, Saigon has become a monstrous urban sprawl, full of
ugly, squalid slums, in which crime abounds. Most of Saigon's
decline and degradation, of course, can be blamed on the war,
and much of it has occurred since 1965, when the Americans
began arriving in strength. The first Indo-China war, between
the Vietminh and the French, from the end of 1946 until the
middle of 1954, affected Saigon, but not nearly as much, because the major impact was felt in North Vietnam and in the
northern parts of South Vietnam. Moreover, the French, having ruled Indo-China for a hundred years, blended into the
scene; they and the Vietnamese had developed their own
peculiar love-hate relationship and were used to each other.
The Americans, though, were, as in so many other parts of
the world, out of place and ill at ease in Vietnam—something
that is even more apparent today, when they are leaving.

In the time of the French war, long before the booming
blasts of rockets, mortars, and artillery were regularly heard
and orange flares filled the sky at night, Saigon was at least as
dangerous as it has been since. This was chiefly because there
was much more random terrorism. One sat in one or another

of the cafés on the main thoroughfare, the Rue Catinat (which was named after one of the first French vessels to come to the area and has now been renamed Tu Do, or Freedom Street), and several times a week, usually around eleven in the morning or five in the afternoon, young men hired by the Vietminh would hurl grenades at the cafés from bicycles. Sometimes they missed or the grenades proved to be duds, but more often than not they killed or wounded members of the motley French Army—including blacks from Africa and Foreign Legionnaires—or civilians who were foolish enough to sit outside. After a time, most of the cafés put up protective metal screens. There were, in the beginning, none of the modern *plastique* explosive devices, which can rip apart whole buildings, but over the months the grenades took their steady toll. Even so, the war never had much visible effect on the easy way of life centering around the cafés and the two main clubs, the Cercle Sportif and the Cercle Hippique. The official American representatives in those days, whose number grew from about a score when I first arrived to several hundred by the time of Dien Bien Phu and the French surrender, shared the pleasant life of Saigon, whose charm was enhanced by the lovely, lithe Vietnamese women, in their native *ao dais*—the traditional long-sleeved dresses with their long skirts slit in two panels to show wide trousers underneath—and by lovely Frenchwomen, too. There was, moreover, a constant feeling of excitement, a genuine sense of adventure. One could arrange clandestine meetings with Vietminh agents in teahouses on the outskirts of town, to which one travelled by *cyclo*—pedicab—and where one sat and sipped tea and discussed the theory and practice of revolution. In Saigon in those days, which now seem impossibly far off, there was none of the tawdriness and none of the dementia that the city reveals today.

General D. used to be one of South Vietnam's leading generals. He was in charge of IV Corps, in the Mekong Delta; he took part in several of the coups after the one that overthrew President Ngo Dinh Diem in November, 1963; and he once tried to mount one of his own, which petered out before it reached Saigon. Eventually, he lost his commission and sank into the limbo that has swallowed up so many Vietnamese leaders in recent years. Nowadays, dressed in stained trousers and a shirt, D. can regularly be seen on Tu Do, gesticulating and shouting wild imprecations. He occasionally comes onto the veranda or into the lobby of the Hôtel Continental—a rambling, high-ceilinged, musty, comfortable remnant of French colonialism, at which I have always stayed while in Saigon. Once, he went behind the room clerk's counter and started handing out room keys to everyone who walked in. The manager—a good-natured man named Philippe Franchini, who is part French and part Vietnamese, and who inherited the hotel from his French father—let him alone, and in time D. grew tired of his game and went off, still shouting. He is a victim of paresis.

There are demented people all over Saigon—most of them simply victims of war. One crazy woman who usually wanders around Tu Do wears an American Indian headdress and is always giggling. No one knows who she is, but she has become a daily feature of the landscape. There are deranged war widows who rant and rave, like General D., but they tend to be more bitter, and they deliberately squat to relieve themselves in front of hotels where Americans stay. Then there is a woman who directs a group of deaf-and-dumb prostitutes—most of them fourteen and fifteen years old, some even younger. They cluster nightly at the corner of Tù Do nearest the Continental, usually just before the curfew hour, which is 1 A.M. At this time of night, there are prostitutes—among them some whom I have watched grow old and tight-faced in the last ten years—standing at street corners all over town, hoping to be picked up by late-cruising customers. At this hour, too, pimps haul their girls around on the backs of motorcycles and offer them at bargain prices. They are scarcely bargains, though; the venereal-disease rate among prostitutes in Saigon is now estimated to be sixty-five per cent.

More tragic than the prostitutes, to my mind, are the street boys of Saigon—wild, tough youngsters, many of them as young as nine or ten, and many of them orphans who have no homes other than the doorways they sleep in at night. Some who work part time as shoeshine boys are as pestiferous as flies and, if finally given in to, curse their customers unless they get what they consider enough piastres. Some sell news-papers, peanuts, pencils, or postcards, or do any momentary job offered them. Most of the time, though, there is nothing for them to do, and increasingly often they steal—from black-market sidewalk stalls, from the open-air stores, from the pockets of careless pedestrians. They spend much of their time smoking cigarettes—marijuana if they can get it—and playing cards for money in the alleyways. Many seem beyond re-demption; some actually want to be arrested and to live in prison, even under the worst of conditions. An American friend of mine carried out an experiment last year. For several months, he had watched one particular boy, who was about nine, and whose life on the streets had not yet totally oblit-erated a look that was almost angelic. Each afternoon, the boy was to be seen around Tu Do, wearing the same tattered shirt and short pants, doing occasional begging or sometimes sell-ing newspapers. My friend took him home, gave him a bath, fed him, and dressed him in some new clothes. The boy thanked him and then asked if he might leave. An hour later, he was back at his station on Tu Do, wearing the old, dirty clothes.

Beggars are all over Saigon, and they range in age from three to three score and ten. Some are the children of refu-gees, and wander about with infant sisters or brothers strapped to their backs, and some are native Saigonese who have made a profession of begging during all the years of the war. Many of them are crippled, either born so or maimed in battle, and they sit on street corners where Americans are most likely to pass by, holding out their hats or cups, smiling and bobbing their heads. They are profuse in their thanks if someone gives them ten or twenty piastres (from three to five cents), but if they are ignored, they, like the shoeshine boys, will hurl curses—which they can be pretty sure the Americans won't understand. Saigonese beggary has become more than an ex-pression of poverty and despair. There is a special quality of self-degradation to it—of self-hatred and hatred of the foreigner who has reduced the whole society to shame and dependence. There is occasionally, of course, actual self-immolation, carried out by young Buddhist monks and nuns who burn themselves to death by soaking their robes in gasoline and then igniting them. The beggars, too, sometimes perform horribly self-destructive acts. One day, while I was walking along Tu Do with a friend, I saw a middle-aged man who had just cut his arms and legs with a knife and lay bleeding on the sidewalk, still holding out his hat. I said, "Oh, my God—only in Vietnam!" My companion, an American who has been in and out of the country for as many years as I have and is married to a Vietnamese woman, rebuked me. "Have you ever seen a big American city late at night, with all its brutality and ugliness and violence?" he asked. He paused, and then added, "It's true, though, that both we and the Vietnamese have a strong feeling of having sinned—against each other and against ourselves. Poor Vietnam is the whore, America the pimp."

Now that the Americans are withdrawing, a sense of impending change is everywhere. My Vietnamese friends—even those who have been closest to us—are bewildered and worried. Most of them have been making good money, but they have not let themselves become part of what I call the American-privileged Vietnamese class, which has grown up over the past five or six years, and which differs noticeably from the privileged Vietnamese class that the French created. My friends have not been motivated primarily by the urge for profit, as have the contractors who have built apartment houses and villas and rented them to Americans at exorbitant prices, or as have those Vietnamese who have taken jobs at high salaries with American construction companies or the American bureaucracy—to say nothing of the thousands of prostitutes, taxi-drivers, and café operators, or the countless black marketeers selling goods pilfered from the docks or stolen from the post exchanges. My friends are people who have simply made the most of the opportunity given them by the huge American presence to earn five, ten, or twenty times as much as they had ever earned before or will ever earn again. Some of those I am speaking of, many of whom are journalists, have remained ardent nationalists; some are strict neutralists; and some accept, with a sense of transcendent fate, the prospect of a Communist victory—mainly because they are so disillusioned by the ineptitude of successive local governments. Disillusion, in the case of the Thieu government, has become contempt; they consider it "Diemist" without Diem's redeeming attributes, which were, in the beginning at least, those of a true nationalist and patriot. There is today a universal distrust of the Army, which runs the country—of the corruption it promotes and countenances, and, in particular, of the money that the wives of generals and other high officers are making from such activities as the disposal of scrap bullet and bomb casings and of Army steel and cement. Such business, of course, has always existed as an adjunct to war, but there is something especially sleazy about the way it is carried on here now, and about the naïve, even bland, acceptance of it by the Americans. A conservative estimate is that fifteen thousand Americans, in uniform or out, have been involved in this process of corruption. These Americans have encouraged the black-marketing of all sorts of goods, have encouraged pilferage for payoffs, have raked in huge profits from the smuggling of drugs and other goods, from the illicit trade in dollars, from the operation of night clubs, from the importation of American call girls, and so on. The prevalence of corruption has its comic as well as its depressing aspects. A few months ago, a group of fifty angry women marched to the National Assembly building and staged a brief, shrieking demonstration to protest the demolition of their black-market street stalls by the police. The police take such action sporadically—and the stalls always reappear as soon as the police disappear. Many of the women who run the stalls are the wives of Army officers, and although they have the protection of their husbands they do not necessarily have that of the police, who obey their own instructions or their own instincts. However, the anger of the women on the march to the Assembly was directed not at the police so much as at the Americans and, indirectly, at the American post exchanges. As long as the Americans permitted various goods to be sold, or stolen—so ran the argument of the women—why blame them for selling those same goods?

The cynicism that dominates Saigon today is notably exemplified by the role that the Vietnamese and American draft-dodgers and deserters play there. Most Vietnamese Army deserters return eventually to their own units or to other units, but some flee to the cities—most often to Saigon—where they hide in the slums or, in some cases, obtain work under assumed names and at unusually low wages in Vietnamese or American companies. Occasional roundups are conducted, but since the ranks of the police are filled with men who are also seeking to avoid military service, the deserters and draft-dodgers are not too assiduously pursued. In addition to the thousands of Vietnamese deserters, there have been hundreds of American deserters in and around Saigon; now, of course, their number has dwindled. Most of the American deserters hide out in the slums, including an infamous area known as Hundred-P. Alley (the "P." stands for "piastre"), which is near Tan Son Nhut Airport and derives its name from the ease with which one may procure anything there—a girl, opium, heroin—for a relatively small fee. The American and Vietnamese police conduct sporadic raids on the place, and seize guns, dope of various kinds, forged leave passes, blank flight authorizations to leave the country, and so forth, all stolen from American bases. It is a world unto itself, one of many such enclaves that survive no matter what action the police take.

There are other spots where, in the receding tide of the American presence, total permissiveness has set in. Among them are night clubs and bars on Plantation Road, near Tan Son Nhut. Late last year, one of the underground G.I. newspapers in Vietnam, *Grunt Free Press*, printed a story about life on Plantation Road headed "Happiness Is Acid Rock." It dealt mostly with one of the more popular rock-and-roll places where young Vietnamese and Americans gather nightly, noting, "There is an empathy between them found nowhere else in Vietnam." The story continued:

The vibrations are there in the flashing lights and the cool music and the hot air and smoke and crowding. It's a warm scene, as warm as any found in Haight-Ashbury, Greenwich Village, Santa Monica, Des Moines, London, Paris, Berlin, Tokyo, and anywhere else where under-thirties groove together. . . . "You know, it's like this [one American soldier said]. Some G.I.s bitch and moan about Vietnam, but, man, it ain't so bad as all that. Gimme a place like this and it don't matter if I'm in Saigon or Sioux City. There's some good thing going for us here, man, but you got to know where it's at. . . . It's the vibrations. I dig the vibrations here. There's something mellow about these people when I come in here. And I don't get it anywhere else."

Nearby, in a restaurant on the upper floor of a run-down tenement, other G.I.s sit and smoke opium or hashish or marijuana while stereo tapes blare out the latest pop tunes. Marijuana can be bought virtually anywhere, in phony cigarette packs. A popular brand just now is Park Lane; the names tend to change as crackdowns increase. Another underground G.I. paper, *Rolling Stone* (no relation to the domestic sheet of the same name), last fall quoted a G.I. as saying, "They couldn't *pay* me to leave here before my enlistment's up. This place is a gold mine. Hell, scoring grass here is easier than buying a loaf of bread."

Advertisements like these still appear every day in the Saigon *Post* or the *Vietnam Guardian*, the two main English-language papers:

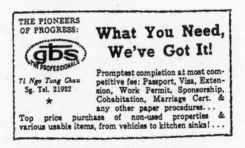

THE PIONEERS OF PROGRESS:

gbs THE PROFESSIONALS

71 *Ngo Tung Chau* Sg. Tel. 21922

★

What You Need, We've Got It!

Promptest completion at most competitive fee: Passport, Visa, Extension, Work Permit, Sponsorship, Cohabitation, Marriage Cert. & any other paper procedures. . .

Top price purchase of non-used properties & various usable items, from vehicles to kitchen sinks! . . .

(Cohabitation papers allow a Vietnamese girl to live legally with a man—usually an American—though they are unmarried.)

One of the first victims of Vietnamization may be said to be Miss Lee. Until early in 1970, the main part of her business consisted in finding suitable girl partners for American servicemen and other foreigners in town. She kept files on about fifty women, including young widows, "companions," and middle-aged women. Her advertisements promised "beautiful

ladies of charm and class, for company, conversation, or . . ."
For five hundred piastres—about two and a half dollars—a
customer had the right to look through her album of photographs. Another five hundred entitled him to meet a girl
and look her over at the office of the agency. For fifteen hundred, a date would be arranged. If a marriage ensued, Miss
Lee took a further cut of twenty-five hundred piastres. The
following advertisement shows what Miss Lee is reduced to
today in the way of offering services:

MISS LEE:
— Needs to buy AIR-
CONDITIONERS &
CARS Top prices paid.
—Has **CAR FOR RENT**
monthly,   weekly,
daily with insurance:
TOYOTA,   MAZDA,
DATSUN. VOLKSWA-
GEN, JEEP, MICROBUS
Sedan, Pick-up, mic-
robus)—GOOD CONDI-
TION,   SEASONABLE
PRICES.
—SERVANTS, COOKS.
DRIVER LICENCE
—VILLAS   APART-
MENTS, HOUSES
FOR RENT
Please Ask for:
MISS LEE
12-Bis Chi-Lang
GIA-DINH
PTT: 23.637
Daily: 08.00 2·000
including Sundays
and Holidays

Inevitably, the departure of the Americans has also meant
the closing down of many bars, hotels, night clubs, and restaurants in the main sections of Saigon that have thrived on
G.I. patronage. Some of these places, hoping to attract the
Americans' young Vietnamese hangers-on, have changed their
names from such things as Tennessee Bar, Texas, or G.I. Dolly
to Vietnamese ones—street names or the names of local movie
heroes or heroines. One straitlaced Vietnamese I know, who
regards the presence of the G.I.s as a necessary evil but the

self-degradation of his young countrymen as an unnecessary one, said of this transformation, "The rats have taken over."

Welcome To Happy Room
413—415 Phan-Thanh-Gian St.
Saigon   Tel.: 90305
Air Conditioned ★ New Decoration

TURKISH BATH: NIGHT CLUB:
★ Excellent Service   ★ State side Music
★ Pretty Girl Massager ★ Magicial & Sexy Show
★ Private Steam Tubs   ★ Experienced Band &
                         Beautiful Singer
Here reserved the foreigner only.
Open every day from 09.00 AM To 24.00 PM.

There is also literal truth in this statement. The rat population has increased tremendously in the last two years, despite improvements in the garbage-collection system. One sees rats by the hundreds, especially at night, even around the best restaurants and homes, scurrying across streets, chasing and jumping over each other. Owing to a sad lack of medical facilities—there are approximately five hundred registered M.D.s in Saigon, along with hundreds of Chinese practitioners—illnesses caused by filth and rats are a mounting problem. In 1968, the infant-mortality rate was one in twenty; today, of twenty thousand recorded deaths each month more than half are those of children under five. A large number of deaths, particularly those of infants, go unrecorded. (It recently was revealed, incidentally, that some Saigon surgeons, who had earlier been sent to the United States for training as Army doctors, were devoting much of their talent and time to cosmetic surgery on local women who wanted to look more Occidental.)

Despite all this, and beneath the unrest that one feels today in Saigon—only a fraction of which takes the form of overt demonstrations by students, veterans, and others—one senses something else: an intense determination to endure. Again and again, the Vietnamese reveal a capacity for surviving almost anything: poverty, disease, bombed-out homes, loss of members of the family. Everywhere, Americans bemoan our failures and condemn both the Vietnamese and themselves either for becoming so deeply involved in the war to begin with or for not having fought "the right kind of war." There is a constantly growing awareness among the Americans in Saigon of the policies that have led us to disaster—and the publication of the Pentagon Papers, of course, added to this. But the Vietnamese think differently; among the Vietnamese in Saigon, the Pentagon Papers scarcely caused a ripple. They tended to shrug the revelations off with typical fatalism and cynicism. Whatever they now think of us, their attitude is expressed over and over again in the words "We will survive. We have always survived."

Saigon may be the most heavily polluted city in the world, not excluding New York or Los Angeles. There are approximately a million registered vehicles in the area, and probably at least as many more come and go. In addition to private cars, small Renault taxis, and buses, there are several thousand three-wheeled motor scooters and many thousand three-wheeled *pousse-pousses*—motorized versions of pedicabs. All these smaller motor vehicles, as well as many of the larger ones, use kerosene or low-grade gasoline for fuel, so the Saigon air is constantly full of smoke and fumes, and a haze never leaves the sky. To make matters worse, there are now thousands of motorcycles, almost all Japanese-made, which swarm like locusts and make life more hazardous than ever for pedestrians. A wild Jet Set of Honda-riding youths races down Tu Do each night, or along the Bien Hoa Highway, outside town, and then the young men pile their motorcycles on the sidewalks while they go to cafés or movies. The city now has a considerable number of traffic lights, but in many places streams of vehicles still seem to come from all directions at once, and the ability to maneuver across a busy street at the height of the morning, noon, or evening rush hour is the mark of a veteran resident.

From my window at the Continental, I am mesmerized by the noise and variety of the traffic flow and pedestrian dash. Roaring convoys of American-made trucks, driven either by G.I.s or by Vietnamese, are likely to be followed by screaming police cars escorting some high government official or rushing to some new disaster. Amid all this, small blue taxis scuttle about like water bugs, and motorcycles dart in and out. Vietnamese women seem to handle motorcycles more skillfully than men—or, at least, less dangerously. They sit straight and prim in the saddle, often wearing colorful little hats, and their natural grace is even enhanced by their adept control of the sputtering machines. The motorcycles serve as family jitneys, taking children to school and parents to work. Partly owing to the kerosene fumes—and to the fact that some of the kerosene containers were once used for defoliants—Saigon has lost many of its lovely old trees; others have been cut down to widen the streets. The fumes have also affected the normal bird population. A friend of mine bounced into my room one afternoon recently, exclaiming, "Guess what! I just saw a pigeon."

In the past few years, Saigon has acquired an elaborate hippie culture and language. The hippies are categorized by age groups. A *hippie choi choi* ("*choi*" means "play") is a very young hippie, a teenybopper; a *hippie xom xom* is a twenty-year-old boy or girl; and a *hippie lau lau* is an old-time hippie, in his or her late twenties. *"Bui doi,"* which literally means "dust of life," denotes a general hippie attitude, and also is used to describe street youngsters. *"Quan voi"* means "elephant pants"—bell-bottoms. *"Trong cay si,"* literally "to plant love trees," means that one is madly in love. *"Xai tien nhieu my"* means "to spend money like the Americans," to live lavishly, and is used to describe not only the American way of life in Saigon but the American conduct of the war—the indiscriminate use of artillery and planes to achieve a non-achievable objective. *"Bay buom"* means "to fly like a butterfly," as from girl to girl. *"Cao boi,"* the most common term, is a Vietnamese phoneticism of "cowboy," meaning a young hoodlum or tough. In the past two years, *cao bois* have become increasingly numerous, wandering the streets in gangs. They have encouraged much of the increasingly overt anti-Americanism, sometimes jumping American soldiers or civilians on the street and beating them up, for no apparent reason or because they have been hired by somebody holding a grudge against the victim. They are also responsible for other growing street crime, including robberies; many are good at

deftly snatching watches off the wrists of pedestrians. Most of
the hippies, however, are harmless. They meet in cafés and sit
and talk and drink Coca-Cola or beer, complaining about the
futility of life or bragging about how they can stay in school
and out of the Army for two more years because their parents
have lied about their age. Like hippies the world over, they
favor long hair, and the boys have a special fetish—expensive
shoes. These may cost as much as fifteen dollars a pair—a very
high price in Saigon. Last fall, during an anti-crime campaign
that lasted three months, the police arrested more than two
thousand hippies, along with four hundred young men described as *cao bois* and hooligans, but the hippies—arrested
ostensibly because they refused to cut their hair—were quickly
released. During that campaign, almost a quarter of a million
people were apprehended, about half of them for alleged traffic violations. In Saigon nowadays, when one is driving a car
it is commonplace to be stopped by the police for failing to
obey some sort of traffic sign in Vietnamese. Almost always,
a five-hundred-piastre note—worth a bit more than a dollar
at the new official rate—will spare you a trip to the police
station. This, of course, is one way the vastly underpaid policemen make ends meet. In last year's crackdown, the second-
largest group of those apprehended consisted of polluters and
litterers. Then came illegal residents, "military troublemakers" (for the most part, veterans who had engaged in anti-
government demonstrations), draft-dodgers, people with false
identification papers, gamblers, and deserters. The campaign
was launched as a result of a decree, issued late in 1970, that
gave Lieutenant General Nguyen Van Minh, the head of the
Capital Military District, the right to do almost anything to
maintain order in the city, but since most of those arrested or
questioned were released, nothing much came of it all. It was
like the sporadic anti-corruption campaigns in Saigon. Every
now and then, there is a hue and cry about corruption, and
a scapegoat—a Chinese merchant, a Vietnamese found stealing at the docks, or someone caught at the airport in the act
of smuggling heroin or black-market dollars in or out of the
country—is arrested and tried. Then the hullabaloo is over,
and everything continues as before.

Whether they are hippies or not, virtually all of Saigon's

young people are deeply embittered by what the war has done to them and their country, but, except for a relatively small element of revolutionary activists, they hold their bitterness tightly to themselves. Among the activists, some have covertly established direct liaison with the Communists, and others have made indirect contacts. In the past year, the Communists have stressed the importance of trying to build up the youth movement in the city. Since there are plenty of urgent political, social, and economic issues to be concerned about, a considerable number of high-school and college students have been aroused by the activists. This has been particularly true at times when the government has moved high-handedly, as it often has, to arrest student leaders and subject them to imprisonment and torture. Largely because of their contempt for the Saigon government, a good number of young people still feel admiration for the late Ho Chi Minh, whom most of them respect as a nationalist who led the Vietnamese to victory over the French, rather than as a Communist.

Recently, I talked with a student at the Buddhist Van Hanh University who expressed such admiration. The youth, whom I will call Thanh, was a senior, studying politics. At first, he said that the only people he admired were his parents; his father was a contractor, he told me, and his mother was "in the trading business." Then he observed that the only "world personage" he admired was Ho. When asked why, he replied, "Ho Chi Minh spent his life for Vietnam. He freed Vietnam from world domination. History will judge his actions. But as a very young man, with empty hands, he went to France, worked so hard to get what he got. I admire him on this point. That is what today's youth should learn from him." Like many other young men, Thanh said he liked the Americans as a people but felt they had done his country more harm than good.

The most activist, or most curious, of the Saigon youths go out into the countryside during their summer vacations and during Tet (the New Year period) and join the Vietcong. Whether or not they become Communist operatives, their action is, as much as anything, an expression of their disgust at the degraded, profiteering way of life in Saigon—and, in many cases, at their own parents' participation in it. Similarly, some girls from good middle-class or lower-middle-class families whose incomes are inadequate because of inflation are sent to work in bars and restaurants, and they occasionally sleep with Americans they like while retaining their ties with their families and their Vietnamese boyfriends. Young men from good families, while deprecating their parents' profiteering, are glad to have those parents pay bribes to keep them out of the Army, and they make a point of adeptly juggling the amounts of time they devote to leisure and to attending overcrowded classes so they can avoid military service.

These youths are not to be confused with the rich hippies whose parents keep them out of the service through sheer pull, or with a minority of serious and deeply troubled young men who object to the war. On a number of occasions over the past two years, I have had dinner with a group of six or seven of these serious young people. All are college graduates in their late twenties, and most have done graduate work in law, engineering, education, or administration. One of them works in the Presidential Palace, for one of Thieu's aides. "I have long legs," he says, with a sad smile, implying that he is used primarily as a messenger boy. Another is a lieutenant commander in the Navy, holding down a dull desk job. None of them are doing anything like the work for which they are qualified by their education and ability, and this is part of the tragedy of Vietnam today. The bureaucracy is still French-oriented, immobilized, so although some younger people have been elected to the House of Representatives or to provincial and village councils, the appointive jobs are mostly held by older men. Thus, most of the considerable younger talent that exists is being wasted. "The generation gap is very bad," one of my young friends said. "We are the transitional ones. Those younger don't care or aren't ready for anything. Most of them feel abandoned, and that's why, though they are really disillusioned, they pretend to be full of bravado, like the hippies and *cao bois*. The older intellectuals are lying low or have given up. We have nowhere to turn except to politics, which remains corrupt. The French created their privileged Vietnamese class—the *doc phu su*, or mandarin element—but they left the peasants and the middle class untouched. And they used the civil servants they created as just that—servants. When I was

twenty-one, I had a sense of direction—of behavior and morality. Now anything goes. There is a loss of faith in Vietnamese historical traditions. We know what's wrong here, but
there's nothing we can do about it. No one lets us. At least,
the French allowed the Vietnamese culture to exist, in its own
way, but you Americans have made us a nation of operators.
We're in a void. We're empty."

I reflected afterward that although there has been plenty of
repression of political prisoners and censorship of the press in
Saigon over the past few years, there has also been a greater
degree of freedom of expression—certainly more than there
was in the days of Diem. In the early sixties before Diem's
overthrow, the sort of discussion I easily had on my own with
this group of young men was occasionally possible but had to
be arranged with the utmost care to safeguard the participants. Nowadays though newspapers are regularly banned,
they usually reappear after several days or a week, and continue their criticism of the Thieu government until they are
banned again, and the process repeats itself. It is a kind of
endless anarchy—neither freedom nor total repression. Much
of the published dissent is dissent for dissent's sake—what is
called in Saigon *nham nho*, a phrase translated for me by one
Vietnamese as "bold and brazen talk that's out of place." This
is not to say that some important issues have not been raised
in the press. Considerable attention was given two years ago
to the arrest, trial, and sentencing of the opposition deputy
Tran Ngoc Chau, for example, and to the more recent arrest
of his fellow-deputy Ngo Cong Duc. Duc is the owner of the
most popular opposition paper, *Tin Sang*, which has achieved
the distinction of having been banned most often. (Duc was
defeated for re-election in August, but he continues his broadsides against Thieu.) *"Nham nho"* is also widely used to describe the so-called new culture, which consists largely of
cheap novels and an increasing amount of pornography. This,
like everything else meretricious, is blamed on the influence
of the Americans—and with similar justification.

Lately, however, there has been an awakening of something
new, perhaps best defined as an awareness of anger. This was
apparent a few months ago in an exhibition of paintings,

drawings, poems, scrolls, and pamphlets by students at the College of Arts and Letters of Saigon University. Most of the paintings and sketches were naturally concerned with the war, and many of them had a harsh, "Guernica"-like quality. One large panel depicted Americans as eagles, hawks, and wolves devouring the countryside. There were many paintings or drawings of cemeteries and skulls, of bare bones in fields, of people on the run. One poignant painting, called "Going Back," showed a group of boys returning to an empty village in the war-ravaged wilderness. Another, which showed shackled prisoners, was entitled "Victory of the U.S. Over Prisoners of War," and a slogan in Vietnamese read "Hate calls for hate, blood for blood, skull for skull." A Vietnamese friend I went to the exhibition with remarked that it was a display of "the weapons of the weak." Without guidance, sense of direction, or much talent, the young artists and poets were venting their wrath against the Americans because, as my friend said, "they have no other way to say anything—they can't attack the government, but the government lets them attack the United States." There have been more and more anti-American cartoons in the newspapers recently. Still, it is surprising to me that the anti-American sentiment has risen so slowly. In Saigon, the slowness can be explained partly by the fact that, with rare exceptions (such as an American jeep leaving the scene of an accident, or a few G.I.s getting into fights with Vietnamese in bars), the American troops have behaved well, and that over the past two years fewer and fewer G.I.s have been allowed to come to the capital. (Several other big cities have been declared off limits entirely.) The worst instances of American brutality, epitomized by My Lai, have occurred in the countryside; the number of smaller but similar incidents will never be known but must run into the thousands. On the other hand, one must say that the average American who has served in Vietnam for a year or eighteen months, though he may have failed to understand the Vietnamese, has generally left them alone. In the earlier days of the war, some friendships were established between Americans and Vietnamese, but they were nearly always surface relationships. The Vietnamese are not easy to know, and they like to emphasize their inscrutability to the Americans, who shuttle in and out of their lives so quickly. After my twenty-five years of contact with the country, I have perhaps a score of close Vietnamese friends, all of them in Saigon.

One reason that the Vietnamese are not easy to know is that there has been a deplorable slowness in instituting systematic Vietnamese-language training for our people here. Vietnamese is extremely hard to learn, because of its many tones—some words can be pronounced five or six different ways, tonally, and have five or six altogether different meanings. Matters could have been improved quite easily, however, if we had subsidized the widespread teaching of English to the Vietnamese instead of letting them acquire it in local, often rather expensive, fly-by-night schools. For those under forty, English, rather than French, is the second language in Saigon, but it is not spoken as well as French was, and still is. Indeed, one of our greatest failures in Vietnam has been in the field of education in general. We have built schools all over the country, yet there are not enough teachers, books, or equipment. Though the Vietnamese, like the Chinese, are hungry for education, attendance in four of eleven Saigon school districts is less than fifty per cent of those eligible. This is because the city now has slightly more than a thousand classrooms in public and private elementary schools, with an enrollment of two hundred and fifty-seven thousand. A third to a half of the classroom space is operated on three shifts a day, which means that many of the children who are able to attend school at all are there for only three hours. There are twenty-five hundred teachers, or one teacher for more than a hundred pupils. Not surprisingly, then, only fifty-eight per cent of the children who enter school finish even the elementary grades.

The situation in the universities is in some ways even worse. Saigon University—one of eight universities and colleges in the country—has about thirty-five thousand students and three hundred and fifty teachers, or one teacher for about seventy-seven students. Many, if not most, of the professors and instructors devote only three hours a week to their Saigon classes, because they have to travel the length and breadth of the country to teach at other universities scattered from Hué, in the north, to Can Tho, in the south. Lectures are ordinarily handed out in mimeographed form, and there is virtually no classroom discussion. Moreover, there is so little scientific equipment that twenty-two thousand of Saigon University's thirty-five thousand students are enrolled in either its College of Arts and Letters or its law school—this in a country that, if it is to survive at all, needs many more engineers and scientifically trained graduates than lawyers or students of literature. One consequence of the university's inadequacy is that sons and daughters of the wealthy go abroad to study, and stay away. My friend Ton That Thien, who is a social historian and is the dean of Van Hanh University, a private Buddhist institution with thirty-six hundred students, sympathizes with those who can afford to go abroad, even while he bemoans the effects of their absence on Vietnam. "Who wants to come back to a huge prison and get killed?" he asks.

One of the idols of the younger generation is a slim, bespectacled young man, born in Hué, named Trinh Cong Son, who, at thirty-two, is the composer of some haunting antiwar songs, which, though banned in 1968 and 1969, are still played in a few night clubs and distributed on pirated cassettes. A twenty-three-year-old North Vietnamese refugee girl named Khanh Ly, whose deep, melodious voice is as haunting as the songs themselves, has helped make them famous. Perhaps the most famous of the songs is "The Love Song of a Madwoman," which contains the names of memorable battles in the long war:

I had a lover who died in combat at Pleime.
I had a lover from Zone D who died in combat at Dong Xoai.
I had a lover who died at Hanoi.
I had a lover who died in a hurry somewhere along the borders.
I had a lover who was killed in the battle of Chuprong.
I had a lover whose cadaver was floating down a river. . . .

Another of Son's songs is called "A Lullaby of Sounds of Cannon Fire in the Middle of the Night." The first part goes:

Every night the sounds of cannon fire reverberate through
    the city.
A city sweeper stands still in the street, a broom in his
    hands.
The sounds of cannon fire wake a mother from her sleep,
Fill the heart of a baby with poignant sadness. . . .
Shelters are being destroyed, laid in lifeless ruins,
Yellow skin, yellow flesh, what a tragedy being blown to
    pieces.

Trinh Cong Son, who sometimes sits in night clubs to hear
Khanh Ly sing his songs, has gained fame but little money
from them, for he has no control over the cassette distribution. What money he does make comes from sheet-music sales
of love ballads he has written. The government has more or
less left him alone, because of his popularity, but he has little
faith or trust in politicians and little interest in politics. A year
or so ago, some friends in the Vietnamese Air Force offered
him a safe assignment as an enlisted man, but he turned it
down. His songs are extremely popular with members of the
armed forces, who go to the club on Tu Do where Khanh Ly
sings them and sit and applaud her wildly. Sometimes, one
veteran, who has lost an arm, a leg, and an eye in battle, gets
up and sings the songs in a husky voice, with the spotlight
playing on him, creating a grotesque shadow play.

I spent an afternoon talking with Trinh Cong Son and listening to a few of his latest songs, which are somewhat in the
nostalgic vein of the revolutionary ballads of the Spanish Civil
War. Among the titles are "We Are Determined to Live," "We
Can Count Only on Ourselves," and "Vietnam, Rise Up."
Hearing them, I thought of the words of a Vietnamese Communist marching-and-indoctrination song I had recently read.
It was taken from the body of a North Vietnamese soldier,
and had none of the sadness of Trinh Cong Son's songs. In
contrast with it, even his latest ones sound anachronistic and
sentimental. Here is one verse:

To feel a resentment when our hatred boils,
Living is to endure misery and pain,
To be haughty, to subdue the enemy,
To roar when our people are suffering,

To be ashamed when we are defeated.
Living is to snarl in fury,
To feel a hatred when our people are in misery,
To keep away vile and shameless people.
To be proud is moving forward in combat.
Living is to put the enemy to death.

While Hanoi has always been a city with a strong identity, both political and intellectual, Saigon has never had such a well-defined role or character. A friend of mine says, "You hear people say, 'I'm a New Yorker,' or '*Ich bin ein Berliner,*' but you never hear anyone say, 'I am a Saigonese.' " Even the history of the city is ill-defined. There are a number of theories about its beginnings. The land on which it stands was once a watery waste of marshes and swamps, with a few clusters of trees and tall reeds among countless small streams. Tigers, leopards, monkeys, snakes, and crocodiles were the only inhabitants. The first human beings known to have lived there were called Phu Nam, which may mean "people from the swamps of the south," and their origin is obscure, but in recent decades archeologists have uncovered earthenware and jewelry that are believed to have been fashioned by Phu Nam. In the first century A.D., according to Vietnamese historians, ships sailing from Rome to China by way of India touched at South Vietnam, but whether any of the sailors ventured as far inland as Saigon is doubtful. The name Sai Gon was first heard by Europeans in 1675, as reported by both a British travel writer and a French travel writer of the period. An early account speaks of Tay Cong—"*tay*" from the Chinese word meaning "west" and "*cong*" meaning "tribute." The suggestion is that what is now Saigon was a small outpost paying tribute to various kings or warrior leaders, probably including Chinese, Vietnamese, Siamese, and Cambodians, since these peoples fought back and forth over the lower part of Indo-China until the French began to dominate the peninsula, in the nineteenth century. Whatever its history, Saigon was never considered a capital by the rival Vietnamese emperors based at Hanoi, the capital of Tonkin, and Hué, the capital of Annam, who fought each other for control of all of Vietnam between the sixteenth and nineteenth centuries. Instead,

Saigon recurrently served as a place of refuge—a temporary haven for an exiled or defeated ruler—or a place the ruling emperor could put in the charge of an underling.

It was not until the French formally took over the entire country, around 1880, that Saigon, as the principal city of what European explorers had christened, from an earlier Chinese name, Cochin China, gradually became one of two Indo-Chinese capitals, Hanoi being the other. Thereafter, the French governor-general divided his time between the two. Over the years, though, Saigon remained more of a commercial center than a capital city. It was a place where people went to make money. As Ton That Thien says, "People come to Saigon at the dictates of their heads, not their hearts, and they come to take, not to give." This was probably true of the first Yankee traders to complete transactions in the area—Salem sea captains named John Brown and John White, aboard the ships Marmion and Franklin, who in 1819, after considerable negotiation, sailed home with cargoes of sugar. (The Vietnamese name for Americans, Hoa Ky, stems from this visit, when the Stars and Stripes was interpreted by the local people as the "flower [hoa] flag [ky].") In 1823, White published a book on the voyage. In a passage that calls to mind today's Saigon, he describes the amount of bribery and finagling he and Brown had to use to get the sugar they wanted, through local officials and merchants. Conversely, he reminds us of anything but modern Saigon when he tells how zealously some of the womenfolk were guarded.

When the French took over the South—in 1862, twenty-three years before they gained control of the North with the ostensible purpose of using it as a springboard for the development of the China trade—Saigon and Cholon were just two scattered collections of small settlements built up along the mudbanks of small canals and the Saigon River. The settlements were connected by dirt roads and paths that ran along the canals. In the following decades, particularly after 1900, the French built their familiar stucco structures with red tile roofs that still dominate the city. Official buildings and private homes were all in the same style, with open verandas and large gardens, and they stood on wide boulevards and streets that the French planted with hundreds of trees. One thing to be said for the French colonialists is that they knew how to plan and create cities, and Saigon was probably their gem. As the capital of Cochin China—which was a colony, whereas Annam and Tonkin were protectorates—Saigon from the outset was primarily a commercial center.

Even before the First World War, the French met with a good deal of political resistance from Vietnamese nationalists, and crushed them ruthlessly, driving them from the cities into the countryside and then conducting campaigns in which whole villages were often wiped out for harboring a cell of resistance leaders. In furthering their economic objectives, the French dealt largely not with the Vietnamese but with the local Chinese, and Saigon was essentially a French-Chinese city rather than a Vietnamese one. The Chinese traders formed a comprador class, much like that employed by Europeans in China, and they were also used in administrative roles, subordinate to the French *fonctionnaire* class. However, the French did start a number of primary and secondary schools to train Vietnamese as interpreters and petty *fonctionnaires*. Largely because of the University of Hanoi, which was opened in 1917 as a branch of the University of Paris, Hanoi became the cultural and political center of Indo-China. (Saigon University was set up some thirty years later, as a branch of Hanoi University.) Saigon, for its part, was dominated by Chinese rice mills in Cholon and by a handful of powerful French trading and shipping companies, which had some Vietnamese employees. Most of the interpreters originally used by the French were Vietnamese students from the French Catholic schools, who also had some knowledge of the Latin alphabet and of Chinese characters. What Vietnamese intellectuals there were sought haven in the countryside among the local Vietnamese landowners, who led a precarious existence, because they hesitated to claim their ancestral holdings under French sponsorship for fear the French would one day be thrown out by the Vietnamese nationalists, whereupon a restored royal government would take reprisals against them as collaborators. A lot of land in the Delta thus being officially unclaimed, the French claimed it for themselves; some of it went to the local French-run Catholic Church. The *doc phu su* mandarin element were allowed to have some land, too.

During the twenties and thirties, Saigon grew and became more cohesive. Physically and politically, it was still quite distinct from Cholon, but streetcar lines now connected the two (they lasted until the mid-fifties, when they were replaced by bus lines). The two cities were not joined politically under a common administration until after the French departed, but there was commingling of commerce through the conduits of the French and Chinese comprador system. Also, in 1936 the French completed the Trans-Indo-China Railway, which ran between Hanoi and Saigon (the trip took forty hours, and a fourth-class ticket cost only a few dollars), and this helped promote commerce and trade throughout the country. By the late thirties, the *doc phu su* had become chiefs of districts or, in Saigon, subordinate officers in the French municipal bureaucracy. During the thirties, some sons of *doc phu su* went to France to study, as did the sons of rich peasants, and even a few sons of workers. Most of these foreign students returned to become teachers, lawyers, doctors, or pharmacists, but others became members of a burgeoning revolutionary element.

In the twenties and thirties, too, the French were building up rubber, coffee, and tea plantations in the south and central parts of the country, and many of them maintained luxurious villas both on their plantations and in Saigon. In town, a Frenchman, dressed in white shorts and shirt, would work a few hours a day and then retire to his home and, after a siesta, go to a café for an apéritif, after which it would be time for dinner and a visit to his club. And after rice-harvest time there could also be seen in Saigon some of the few wealthy Vietnamese landowners, dressed in rich silk robes, who were in town for a couple of weeks to shop for French luxuries and Chinese delicacies. There was also a new element arriving— the Corsicans. Some had come as servicemen and Legionnaires, others as employees of the police or customs services; in time, tougher, Mafia-type Corsicans, with international smuggling and racketeering connections, showed up. A number of Corsicans opened restaurants or ran them for French bosses, and these places, which, unlike the earlier French restaurants, served not only French food but Chinese, gave Saigon the reputation of combining the two best cuisines in the world. In general, life in Saigon and in all of Cochin China

was soft and easy, even for the peasants—in contrast to life in
the north, where the climate was more rigorous and the soil
less fertile. The peasant in what is now North Vietnam spent
many hours a day tilling his fields or fishing, but the south-
erner could turn his soil over in a couple of hours, throw in
his seeds, and just let the rice grow; when he went fishing in
his sampan, at dawn or at dusk, he would take along a lantern
and two pieces of wood, which, when he clapped them together, attracted fish. In half an hour, he would have all the
fish he could use, and, like his new French master, he could
go home and relax. As always, the people who worked hardest
were the Chinese. Cholon was already a close-knit society of
clans and family branches. One of the earliest heads of the
Chinese community was a rich merchant, Ong Tich, who
owned a fleet of boats that brought rice from the Delta to the
city along the rivers and canals. It was his chief assistant, Ma
Tuyen, who in 1963 hid the fugitive dictator Ngo Dinh Diem
and his brother Ngo Dinh Nhu before they were found by
Vietnamese officers and murdered.

Though the French took Vietnamese or Chinese mistresses,
there was little intermarriage. The good Vietnamese families
disapproved of such marriages, for the most part, and a girl
who became the wife of a Frenchman was looked down upon
and often ostracized from her own circle. There were more
marriages between Chinese and Vietnamese. A Chinese man
who came to Cholon from southern China to make money
frequently left a wife behind him but took a Vietnamese wife,
too, and raised a family there, perhaps returning to China after
ten or twenty years, leaving his Vietnamese wife behind. Some
of the Chinese who came remained, though they might revisit
China every few years—and, like all good overseas Chinese,
they regularly sent remittances to their families back home. A
Vietnamese song of the time indicates how the Vietnamese
felt toward the French and toward the Chinese. It tells of a
French boss who is returning to France and advises his Vietnamese *co-ba*, or mistress, to marry his Vietnamese interpreter.
The Vietnamese interpreters, however, were then regarded as
having prostituted themselves to the French and were held in
contempt. The song goes on, "They are not good for each
other, the girl and the interpreter, even if they both have tens

of hundreds of piastres." The song concludes with the words
"It is better for the girl to marry a humble Chinese who has
a pole and two baskets to feed his pigs."

Between the two world wars, the French prided themselves
on having defeated the national resistance movements in Vietnam—a pride that went before one of history's biggest falls.
During the mid-thirties, resistance cells managed to stay alive
in the South, though the jails were full of political prisoners,
and by the late thirties the revolutionaries had become openly
active again in the Saigon area. In 1940, what was known as
the Insurrection of Cochin China took place. The leading
Southern revolutionary at the time was Le Hong Phong, the
head of the Cochin China Committee of the Indo-China
Communist Party, which Ho Chi Minh had by then welded
together (although the Party had been outlawed in 1939 and
about two hundred members arrested). Just after the defeat
of France in Europe, the Insurrection was savagely suppressed,
and Phong and his wife were caught and executed. By the
time the Japanese invaded Indo-China, a short while afterward, the rebellion was over. The French, under an admiral
named Jean Decoux, were permitted by the Japanese to maintain control of the country's administrative apparatus, but the
Japanese actually took control. They kept most of the Vietnamese Communists in jail but sent a few nationalists to
Japan, as part of a long-range plan for indoctrinating local
leaders to help Japan build its "Greater East Asia Co-Pros-
perity Sphere."

Under combined Japanese and French control, Saigon became a city in a cocoon. Though the Japanese were clearly
the masters, life generally continued for a time at its easy pace.
Gradually, however, this gave way to a harsher discipline. With
their shaved heads and samurai swords and boots, the Japanese were privately mocked by the Vietnamese and French
alike—except for a small number of collaborators—but, by
and large, the Japanese were accepted with Oriental fatalism
by most Saigonese. There was no coal coming into Saigon
from the North because the Japanese were using it for war
purposes, so rice had to be burned as fuel, and by 1944 there
was an acute rice shortage all over Vietnam. More than a mil-

lion people in the North were starving. In Saigon and the rest
of the South, the Vietnamese were not as badly off, but they
suffered, too, and the suffering increased as time went on, for
the Japanese reduced the amount of rice grown, by forcing
the people in the countryside to raise pigs and hemp, which
the Japanese needed for food and fibre. The upper-class
French, though cut off from France, were able to make do,
and the Chinese, too, managed to survive fairly well, but the
Vietnamese poor suffered more and more as the war dragged
on. In Indo-China, the Japanese committed few atrocities
compared to what they were responsible for in other parts of
Southeast Asia, but as the war continued, a Vietnamese underground was formed to pass military information to the
Allies, and those of its members who were caught were
summarily executed. By 1944, the news that the Japanese were
losing the war had become pretty well known in Saigon. Vietnamese who worked for Japan's Domei News Agency and
members of the French Secret Service, including some double
agents, had spread the word. (There was also a small group
of Gaullists, and they helped.) By this time, American B-29
bombers, called "black tunas" because they came in from the
sea, had begun bombing the docks of Saigon and the railroad
station, and air-raid sirens were regularly heard in the city. The
Japanese became aware of a growing lack of coöperation
among the French and also of a growing Vietnamese resistance movement, led by Ho Chi Minh as head of the Vietminh, and Tokyo decided to take the administration out of
French hands almost entirely. This was done on March 9, 1945,
and the five months before the war ended constituted a twilight period. Five thousand French troops were interned by
the Japanese in Saigon, but a few *fonctionnaires* were allowed
to remain free to keep things running. The Vietnamese and
the Chinese mostly stayed in their homes, awaiting the war's
outcome.

Of the many changes that Saigon has undergone in the
course of its history, probably none was as great as that which
occurred in August and September of 1945. The first British
occupation troops—mostly Indians—arrived early in September, and were warmly welcomed by the Vietnamese, who,
moving swiftly, had already taken control of the city. For the

most part, the welcomers were members of the Vietminh People's Committee, directed by General Nguyen Binh. Ho Chi Minh had sent Binh south in 1945 to take over command of the underground from Tran Van Giau, who, in Ho's estimation, had failed to put up an effective resistance to the French and the Japanese. Binh had quickly set up separate and distinct zones for revolutionary operations and started a training center, and he had placed his men not only in Saigon but in many hamlets in the Delta and in the region north of Saigon. The British refused to deal with the Vietminh, even though the Vietminh offered to coöperate in disarming some seventy thousand Japanese who remained in the South. Instead, the British commander, Major General Douglas Gracey, declared martial law, armed the five thousand French soldiers who had earlier been interned, and ordered the disarmament of the Vietminh and the Vietnamese police. Some Japanese troops were even used to suppress the Vietnamese nationalist movement, and hundreds of ordinary Vietnamese citizens suspected of revolutionary activity were rounded up and imprisoned by the French. The Vietnamese retaliated by calling a general strike, which virtually crippled Saigon. Guerrilla fighting had already broken out in the suburbs and the surrounding countryside. Each night, there were assassinations, and the sky above Saigon was red with the flames of exploding ammunition or fuel dumps or of the homes of suspected collaborators. Toward the end of September, the French mounted a coup against the remaining Vietminh in the city, attacking their last sanctuaries—the Hôtel de Ville, the Post Office, and Sûreté headquarters. Scores of additional Vietnamese were seized and jailed; others fled to the countryside to hide and wait. The campaign of terror continued into 1946, as General Binh reorganized his forces, and in December, 1946, when the war against the French broke out in earnest, Binh had control of sizable parts of the Delta. Meanwhile, the terrorist attacks in Saigon increased month by month.

These attacks had become really serious by 1950, the year in which the Americans made their fateful decision to support the French economically and with large amounts of matériel—a decision based to a considerable extent on the fact that in Europe we were trying, through the Marshall Plan, to put

France back on its feet after the ravages of the Second World War. Of course, the drain on France would have been more easily alleviated if the French had granted the Vietnamese a real measure of autonomy and thus eased the colonial conflict. Their only step in this direction was to set up the Annamite Emperor Bao Dai as Chief of State. Bao Dai, whom I met several times, was far less of a playboy than he was reputed to be, but his efforts to gain real concessions from the French were frustrated, and the resistance intensified. As for the Americans, during this critical period our officials, except for a handful, thought we should stand behind the French, while gently prodding them to give the Vietnamese a few more independent functions. This was the real beginning of the tragic United States involvement.

Despite the atmosphere of tension, Saigon in the late forties and early fifties retained many aspects of a typical French provincial city. Except for the hours spent around the pool at the Cercle Sportif by day and at the restaurants, gambling parlors, and brothels at night, money-making was a pastime that absorbed everyone. Paris was the nerve center of the game, and vast fortunes were made by the French and their friends among the Vietnamese and Chinese on the basis of a totally unrealistic rate of exchange between the franc and the piastre. The trick was to wheel and deal in Saigon and then transfer your ill-gotten piastres to Paris by telegraph, but one had to have permits for the transfers, and huge bribes were paid to get them.

In 1954, the United States Legation became an Embassy, which brought in more Americans. Though they mingled with the French at the Cercle Sportif, they otherwise kept to themselves, leading the compound-ridden lives that official Americans—and many business people as well—lead abroad, going to their places of work by day and retiring at night into barbed-wire-protected apartment houses and villas. Long before the major war began, this barbed wire had become a common sight in Saigon, and I well remember the first enclosures behind which the Americans shielded themselves.

The stream of Saigonese life continued to flow along Rue Catinat. Day after day, one could see the whole swarm of colonial and Vietnamese society on the broad avenue, lined with cafés and elegant shops filled with the best French goods. Nearby, some thirty thousand French civilians—the chief money-makers—lived in sumptuous villas. Catinat was their meeting place, and the delicate social nuances of Saigon could be detected in the manner in which people greeted each other—in the nature of a handshake and in the quick flick of a smile, or the lack of one. French and Vietnamese women flowed by like shoals of multicolored tropical fish. Then, there were Algerians, Moroccans, Tunisians, and Senegalese from the French Colonial Army. And there were the Indians, who flocked to Saigon after the war and became merchants and moneylenders. Today, the Indians are the main money-changers—the black market is sometimes called the Bank of India —but a recent crackdown on illegal financial dealings and a revised exchange rate have somewhat diminished the trade in black-market dollars.

While the area around Catinat remained the social and commercial hub of Saigon, the spokes of the city's wheel, now stretching out for miles, made up the real Saigon. The city's population quadrupled between 1940 and 1950, and the ever-increasing swarm of people for the most part lived precariously, on the edge of poverty. On the fringes of the city were the shantytowns, huts made of straw and mud and pieces of tin, that were haunts of the poor and the displaced, the coolies and all those others who managed in some way to earn a few piastres a day. In the somewhat better areas, closer to the center of the city, there were whole blocks of what were called *compartiments*, which were narrow one-story, or occasionally two-story, structures of wood or tin about twenty feet deep; they usually contained a store of some sort in front and living quarters in back. This was lower-middle-class Saigon. Among these structures and behind them, in dank corners in an intricate maze of alleyways, were cubicles used for prostitution and abortion, or for smoking opium. There were holes leading from one *compartiment* and one alleyway to another, and these not only afforded escape routes for criminals but served as a spawning ground for Vietminh cells. It was here that General Binh's terrorists met to get their grenades and here that they hid after using them.

The main business of this labyrinthine part of Saigon—
including sections of Cholon—was gambling. The poor
gambled at least as much as the rich, and were victimized by
racketeers, who ran the gambling syndicates, as they ran everything else, including the brothels. The most famous of the
houses in the early fifties was the House of the Four Hundred,
which the French built and protected primarily for the use of
their own military, though Vietnamese, too, were eventually
allowed in. Customers could buy tickets and then choose any
one of approximately four hundred girls (who were medically
inspected every week). According to a friend of mine, "It was
more like a slaughterhouse than a bordello, and the noise was
enough to drive a man crazy." The plushest gambling casino
was the Grand Monde, which was situated on the border of
Saigon and Cholon. Initially, the major gambling houses were
controlled by Chinese or Macanese, but then the Binh Xuyên,
a local gangster organization run by a Vietnamese named Bay
Vien, moved in and took over almost all the casinos, including
the Grand Monde. With the approval of Bao Dai, he also won
control of the police, and in effect, with a further nod from
the French, became the "boss" of Saigon. He moved around
town with an entourage of fancily clad armed bodyguards, and
at night at the Grand Monde he dispensed purple chips worth
five thousand piastres to his friends and snubbed anyone he
didn't trust or who was of no use to him. At his headquarters,
he had a private zoo, including tigers and poisonous snakes,
and beneath it was a tunnel where he kept a large cache of
guns and opium. Bay Vien's power did not wane until after
the French defeat in 1954 and the assumption of power by
Ngo Dinh Diem, who was appointed Premier by Bao Dai.
After a number of bitter battles in the streets and in the
marshes around the city, where the Binh Xuyên had hideouts,
the organization was finally destroyed in 1955, and Bay Vien
fled to France (where Bao Dai, deposed as Emperor by Diem,
also settled in comfortable exile). I saw Bay Vien in Paris three
years ago. He was acting the role of a benign old man, but
the earlier soul of the gangster chief was still betrayed in his
sharp, flickering smile and his small, darting eyes.

After the French defeat in 1954 and Ho Chi Minh's full

takeover in North Vietnam, there was a vast exodus of nearly a million people from North to South. The influence of these Northerners, many of them Catholics, on the Saigonese and the other Southerners has been a lasting one. Initially, Diem's idea was to place the majority of the refugees in a sort of *cordon sanitaire* around Saigon, in the hope that they would serve as a protective screen against the Vietminh, but most of the newcomers wanted to be in Saigon. They had come South with very little in the way of money and possessions, so they had to scramble to make a living, and the best place to scramble was in the city. Many of them were uprooted intellectuals and professional people who felt out of place in the commercial-minded Southern city, and their sense of isolation was enhanced first by the unrest and violence during Diem's early struggle to gain control and later by the fact that Diem himself, who came from central Vietnam, tended to rely strongly on his own small group of intimates and on Southerners he felt he could trust. Also, against the background of political intrigue in the South, the Northerners seemed more rational and tough-minded, whereas the Southerners were less sure of themselves, more given to subterfuge, and less sophisticated. Ultimately, however, the two groups began to mingle, and the process, which continues, was both a subtle and a useful one. In many respects, it was the Southerners who succumbed to the influence of the Northerners, or, to put it differently, the Southern way of life was absorbed into the Northern framework. Many, if not most, of Saigon's newspapers, for example, were taken over by Northerners, who made them more politically aggressive and also more comprehensive. The Northerners, who as a rule were better educated, had an enlivening influence on writing and poetry—to which, in time, the Southerners responded both by adapting to the cultural change and by mass-producing lower-quality material. Novels of romance and adventure began running in the papers as serials and appearing in bookstores and on sidewalk stands; once again making money counted for more than the quality of what was sold.

As for business in general, with the French influence diminished (though by no means eliminated, since the French kept rubber plantations and shipping and trading interests) the Southern and Northern Vietnamese competed to take over what had been dominated by French and Chinese. Because the Northerners were better competitors, they often won out, but the competition was healthy and served to heighten the spirit and temper of the city. The Northerners also led the Southerners to adopt more elaborate dress and more careful and precise manners, adding further variety and zest to the city's life. And yet, despite the slow and useful interplay, the two cultures remained basically separate. As time went on, the Diem regime, especially as it came to be dominated by Diem's brother Ngo Dinh Nhu and Mme. Nhu, became more and more authoritarian. Life in Saigon became increasingly tense. The Southerners withdrew more into themselves, while the Northerners alerted themselves more. By the time I returned to the city early in 1962, after an absence of a number of years, the mounting resistance to the Diem regime could be felt in the atmosphere, and it was apparent that it was only a matter of time before there would be an explosion. It was not too difficult to arrange clandestine meetings with those opposed to Diem, in the back rooms of private homes or tiny restaurants. Finally, when the explosion came, in November, 1963, and Diem and Nhu were overthrown with American help, Saigon seemed to breathe one vast sigh of relief.

Saigon is now officially one of eleven autonomous cities in the country—that is, cities independent of provincial authorities—but its mayor, Do Kien Nhieu, is responsible militarily to General Nguyen Van Minh, for he is chief not only of the Capital Military District but also of the III Corps area, which surrounds Saigon and stretches away to the north, northeast, and northwest. Ultimately, though, President Nguyen Van Thieu is the man who runs Saigon, by means of a tightly organized palace entourage, which controls the security forces throughout the city and determines all policy matters, such as how much freedom of speech and assembly the Buddhists and the students may be allowed at any given time. Whenever there is a crackdown on demonstrations, or a roundup of

students or other dissident elements, or the arrest of an opposition political leader, one can be sure that the order for it
came directly from the palace.

All the complex problems and violent conflicts besetting the
city are compounded by tremendous overcrowding. By 1963,
the population of the Saigon metropolitan area had reached
two million two hundred thousand, and it has leaped upward
each year since, owing to the influx of refugees from the countryside. Since 1965, three and a half million people are estimated to have become refugees, and of these two million have
moved into the cities. The population of South Vietnam, approaching nineteen million, is now almost half urbanized,
whereas before the war it was eighty per cent rural. Estimates
are that perhaps a third of the present urban population will
move back to the countryside after the war; the rest, however
difficult life is in the city, will want to stay there, because of
job opportunities and the sheer excitement of cosmopolitan
as compared to rural life. Saigon's population density averages
about seventy-five thousand per square mile, but there are
some blocks where nearly two thousand people are crowded
into three or four acres. An American official who has acted
as an adviser to the Vietnamese on municipal problems for
several years has estimated that ten per cent of the city's population live in splendor and comfort, forty per cent live a
lower-middle-class life of survival, and fifty per cent live in
abject squalor. Compared to Calcutta and some other cities
in India, Saigon may not be so badly off, but there is no doubt
that the war has created a grave situation and that very little
is being done to correct it. On a number of occasions, I have
flown back and forth across the city in a helicopter at just
above housetop level and observed the growing patches of
slums in most of the districts. From the air, too, one can see
the pattern of destruction wrought by the war—mostly by the
1968 Tet offensive. Several thousand large re-settlement blocks
have been erected, the majority of them on the fringes of the
city, but they are not nearly enough to meet the demands for
veterans' housing, let alone low-cost housing for civil servants
and the general displaced public. As the city has expanded,
the number of districts has grown in the past twenty years
from five to sixteen, incorporating large parts of neighboring

Gia Dinh Province. Saigon, in its municipal housing program, has not yet discovered, as Singapore has, for example, the uses of high-rise housing—"high" here meaning four or five stories. There are, of course, a few Saigon hotels that rise to ten or eleven stories, and some office buildings that have as many as eight floors. But by and large the city is still flat and dotted—a mass of one- or two-story structures filling every available inch of space. Two-thirds of the population still occupy dwellings that lack the basic utilities, including water, which is drawn from neighborhood wells. Such dwellings—huts or shacks, usually made of a combination of mud, thatch, flattened-out beer cans, and American-donated sheets of tin—are classified by the government as unauthorized housing, and during the student and veteran demonstrations of the past two years some have been torn down by the police. In general, though, because there is no cohesive building program and no established procedure for assisting masses of the impoverished, the police and other officials turn their backs on the slum conditions—when they don't make money out of them through extortion. The city has a total of eleven public hospitals, with fewer than five thousand beds, and thirty-nine public dispensaries, and there were cholera epidemics in 1964 and 1966; it is thanks only to a mass inoculation program, mostly against cholera, that health conditions are not worse than they are, but both cholera and plague remain real threats. To collect eighty-five thousand tons of garbage and other refuse a month, the city has only a hundred and thirty modern trucks. While these have improved the sanitary situation, particularly in middle-class sections, it is still bad in the poorer areas, where there is no room for the vehicles to operate.

Facing the street on a typical slum block, or combination of blocks, in Saigon there are likely to be *compartiment*-type dwelling-workshops of a story or two, which look relatively clean and neat. In most of these, a narrow lane may lead from the street partway into the block, but it will soon dwindle into a series of narrower passageways—so narrow that it is difficult for even one person to walk through them. Packed tightly around these passageways are scores of ill-made huts, most often consisting of just one room, in which a whole family of six or seven—the average number—lives. Water is drawn from a community well, which may be several passageways distant from a family's hut, though sometimes rusty pipes carry water to communal faucets. Most likely, there will be no electricity at all, and cooking will be done over charcoal stoves. For toilets, there are nearby canals or a ditch in back of the huts. During the day and in the early evening, wandering salesmen, including venders of noodle soup, hot food, raw fish, and fruit, move in and out of this maze. Everything is crowded so close together that, except for a few square yards of open space here and there, no light enters from above, and the whole scene has an underground appearance. Children and grownups scurry about like moles.

A Vietnamese friend of mine, Nguyen Hung Vuong, who has been my assistant in Vietnam for the past decade, has lived during this time in a more middle-class lane complex, and he has given me some understanding of what life there is like and how it has changed. His house, a small one, faces a crowded lane about fifty yards long in the Third District, in the central part of Saigon. Vuong's immediate area is called Ban Co, which means "chessboard," after the manner in which the lanes are laid out. When Vuong first rented the house, in 1961—for a thousand piastres a month, plus a three-thousand-piastre down payment and another thousand to the person who arranged the deal—his lane was about six yards wide. It is less than half that now, because so many houses have been built there since, and because illegal extensions have been built on older ones. In contrast with the poorer sections of the city, Ban Co has electricity and running water, and some of the lanes, including Vuong's, have been covered with asphalt, so they seldom get flooded in heavy rains—something that happens routinely elsewhere—but to reach his home by car he has to weave his way in and out of an increasingly complex system of large and small lanes. The Vietnamese have a saying, *"Gan nha, xa ngo,"* which means, roughly, "My house is close to your house, but my lane is far from your lane."

All residents of Saigon except foreigners have to go through an elaborate identification procedure when they move into a new dwelling, and they are subject to constant checks and

rechecks by the police. Each family must have a census certificate, approved by the chief of the *lien gia*, or group of
families. The paper must then be certified by the head of
the *khom*—that is, a series of lanes or blocks, making up
something like a ward. Then the chief of the *phuong*, or sub-
district boss, has to give *his* approval. The *lien gia* system in
Saigon was adopted by the government in the mid-fifties.
(The Vietminh had used it before that, but its real origins date
back two thousand years to imperial China; it is said to have
been invented by a prime minister at the court of one of the
Eastern Chu emperors. When the minister fell out of favor
and tried to go into hiding, he was quickly discovered through
his own system and beheaded.) There are sixteen families in
Vuong's lane, and they make up one *lien gia*—an unusually
large one, the average being five or six families. Though the
head of a *lien gia* gets no salary, his position can make him
rich through the favors he is able to hand out. In Vuong's
area, an illiterate petty tradesman took the job a number of
years ago; bit by bit, he got rich, and moved from a house
without beds to one of the best houses in Ban Co, where he
serves fine meals and drinks. Vuong's guess is that he has been
involved, like so many other minor officials, in such activities
as smuggling, prostitution, handling stolen goods, or the lottery racket.

In the ten years that Vuong has been living in Ban Co, it
has increased in more than just population and size. There are
now several four- and five-story buildings in the area, and a
house near Vuong's that cost eighty thousand piastres in 1961
is now worth two million, while some multi-story ones are
selling for fifteen and twenty million. Pharmacies, which have
always been abundant in Saigon, are multiplying in Ban Co,
as elsewhere, at such a rate that registered pharmacists now
rent or sell the use of their degree to fake pharmacists, who
sell only packaged medicines—or, sometimes, dope. New restaurants, snack bars, and ordinary bars have proliferated, too,
despite the diminishing number of Americans. With the advent of new-style Western clothing, especially miniskirts, tai-
lors and dressmakers have been doing good business in the
lanes and streets of Ban Co. Barbershops are thriving, as always, for they are centers of rumor and gossip, and some of

them are used by the police and by gangsters for gathering or passing information, or are used as rendezvous points by the Vietcong. The barbershops also pass out newspapers; most people in Vuong's lane and others like it don't buy papers or magazines but rent them from the barbershops or from the stands for an hour or so. Vuong's lane is fortunate in having a school, a hospital, and a police station nearby—though the last is something of a mixed blessing, for police stations are prime targets of Vietcong terrorists. When Secretary of State William Rogers was here in the spring of 1969, a band of terrorists was discovered in the school building, preparing to launch some 60-mm. mortar shells on sites in downtown Saigon and then to attack the police station with grenades. The year before, during the Tet offensive, there was fighting within several hundred yards of Vuong's lane, and a number of his neighbors fled. One of the more noteworthy manifestations of Saigon life is the camaraderie that exists among the people of a lane. After a death, for instance, even neighbors who have not been particularly friendly contribute money to the bereaved family and gather to mourn and to discuss the life of the lane and of the whole city beyond, which is so much a part of their daily existence and yet is in many ways so far removed.

A middle-class lane such as Vuong's is also fortunate in that it has fewer deserters, pimps, *cao bois*, petty gangsters, and other troublemakers than the poorer lanes have. Vietnamese are cliquish and clannish by nature, and sometimes snobbish, too; snobbery is ingrained in them, and, especially in the South, it was encouraged by the French. The Vietnamese also tend to be xenophobic. For example, Vuong, a well-educated man and an intellectual, remarked to me once, "Luckily, though we are overcrowded where I live, there are almost no foreigners—I mean Americans, Koreans, Filipinos, Thais, and so on. The Chinese are all right. They have adapted themselves to the Vietnamese way of life. But for us Vietnamese the foreigners are quite a nuisance—especially the Koreans, Filipinos, and Thais, because they are concerned only with their own security and with making money. It is the Americans who are responsible for bringing them here. The African soldiers that the French brought caused us less trouble."

Despite Vuong's desire not to be bothered by foreigners, Saigon will probably never again be a city of separate national identities, as it was under the French. With the coming of the Americans, there are few areas that have not suffered in social and demographic as well as psychological ways. The effects of the many changes wrought by the war are bound to be lasting, no matter what happens politically, and even if the Communists take over. A Franco-Vietnamese professor of urban affairs at Saigon University remarked to me recently, "Inevitably, there will be a flattening out of classes, and the Occidental influence will remain. There is a new and probably lasting amalgamation of elements—an in-touchness that, for better or worse, will be permanent. It's a matter not only of foreign influences but of what has happened to the Vietnamese themselves. There has been a complete breakdown of traditional images. Civil servants now live in close proximity to *cyclo*- and taxi-drivers who make three or four times what they make. There may be no real contact between them now, but in time it will become unavoidable. A rich undertaker—undertakers have become rich during this terrible war—may build a five-story house on top of the one-story hut he once lived in. For the moment, he may not have any association with the poor people in the lane alongside him, but sooner or later he will. But the rich will still be rich, the poor poor, though they will be living side by side, and the taller houses will overshadow the huts and shacks. We don't know how many will stay rich, or what the impact will be of, for instance, the newly arriving Japanese businessmen, who, although they are Orientals themselves, in many respects lead a Western life. There may emerge a whole new middle class, or there may be no middle class—just well-off people and poor people."

These comments seem especially pertinent as applied in Gia Dinh Province, part of which already blends into Saigon. It has a population of roughly a million and a third, consisting primarily of people who have had to leave Saigon for economic or other reasons and refugees who have come in from farther out and have settled there instead of in the city proper, though they may work in Saigon. A Vietnamese friend recently told me, "The outskirts in Gia Dinh are like boils on Saigon's skin. In the parts of the province that are closest to the city, you have a whole new classless society. It includes small shopkeepers and a large floating element, among them many criminals and hoodlums. The Communists try to infiltrate these floating groups, because deserters, gamblers, and gangsters are hard for the government to control. Farther out of town, in the areas that are somewhat more secure, well-off people have built new brick houses with high surrounding walls. They hire guards or else pay protection to both the government police and the Communists. There is no census, no way of knowing who is moving where or what effect the bombing of the countryside has had on driving people to the suburbs or the cities. No such thing as social mobility, in the traditional sense, any longer obtains."

If there is another large-scale Communist attack on Saigon, like the one in 1968, it will undoubtedly have its genesis in Gia Dinh, throughout which the Communists are establishing new cells. Much of the drug traffic and a good many other illicit activities have shifted from the city to the suburbs as police pressure has increased in Saigon, and this move will help the Communists. Partly for those reasons, Saigon and national officials want to bring large chunks of Gia Dinh under the direct control of Saigon municipal authorities. If the plan is followed, it will mean that some thirty-four hundred hamlets of Gia Dinh will be given over to Saigon, while the remainder of the province will either survive separately or be incorporated into adjacent provinces.

The one part of Saigon that has retained its identity is Cholon, for not even the long, abysmal war has had much of an effect there. The community demonstrates once again the Chinese capacity for remaining Chinese no matter where and no matter who rules China, and the fact that the Chinese in Vietnam have survived all but intact under the French, under the Vietnamese, and throughout the American invasion merely emphasizes the point. In the case of the million and a quarter or more Chinese in Vietnam—the largest group of them in Cholon—this "Chineseness" is doubly significant because in the early days of the Diem regime they were forced to become Vietnamese citizens. Moreover, their young men have been drafted to fight for a cause that most of them do

not believe in, though this is not to say that they are pro-
Communist. They were further humiliated, in 1967, by a government requirement that all Chinese establishments—shops,
hotels, and so on—identify themselves with Vietnamese names
painted above their Chinese names in Chinese characters.

A walk through Cholon, whether by night or by day, is
vastly different from a walk through Vietnamese Saigon. For
one thing, one sees fewer Americans or other white-skinned
foreigners, if one sees any at all. There are fewer vestiges of
colonialism, in the form of the stucco buildings that the
French built elsewhere in the city. Instead, there are rows
upon rows of neat, spick-and-span shops, stacked high with
Chinese and Western goods, including many one can't find
anywhere in the rest of Saigon. Indoor and outdoor restaurants abound, serving an infinite and marvellous variety of
Chinese food. The predominant smell is one of soy sauce,
whereas among the outdoor food stands of Vietnamese Saigon
the usual smell is that of *nuoc mam*, a strong fermented fish
sauce that the Vietnamese like. There are many more Buddhist
temples than there are in Saigon proper, and there is a playground next to each. (In the Vietnamese city, there is scarcely
any room left for children to play.) Chinese music fills the
air—lilting, high-toned instrumental variations on a few similar themes—whereas elsewhere in Saigon nowadays one
seldom hears Vietnamese music, which is more melodic and
sentimental than its Chinese counterpart; instead, there is only
the blare of rock and roll. The one big change in Cholon over
the years has been that the younger generation has adopted
Western clothes—for girls, skirts and blouses instead of the
long gowns called *cheongsams*, and, for boys, tight trousers
and shirts. Some of the older people—the old men, especially—still wear long Chinese robes.

It is said that the Chinese control three-quarters of the
economy of Vietnamese Saigon, and it is probably true. Even
the wealthy Vietnamese are tied into the Chinese financial
community one way or another. The Chinese dominate the
rice trade, they pull the strings of the money markets, and
they set prices for basic commodities like fish, vegetables,
pork, cement, and textiles. The illicit traffic in gold and opium
is under Chinese control, though the Vietnamese take part in

it. Most of the Chinese look down on the Vietnamese, and have either opposed or contemned the whole long series of governments that has followed the regime of Diem—whom, though he cracked down on the Chinese, they respected, because his birth and education gave him mandarin credentials.

A significant aspect of life in Cholon is a generation gap that is in many cases much deeper culturally than the similar manifestation among the Vietnamese. The younger generation of Chinese, who are better educated than Vietnamese youngsters, because the Chinese schools are better run and there are more of them, fall into three basic groups: the Maoists; the fence-sitters, who are fuzzily pro-Kuomintang; and the so-called "Western-trippers," who increasingly prefer American and European movies, for instance, to Chinese ones depicting ancient swordsmen killing scores of enemies with a single stroke. The number of Maoists is small—probably no more than five thousand—but they are hard-core believers in the new China, and they have organized themselves into Red Guard units. During the Tet offensive in 1968, these groups harbored the Vietcong terrorist and sapper squads, and their members took part in street demonstrations in Cholon when, for periods of hours, and even days, the Communists controlled certain blocks of the area and hoisted the Vietcong flag.

Since the overseas Chinese are great accommodators, and since they have even less faith in the future of the present Saigon government than the Vietnamese have, it is probable that if a poll could be taken many people in Cholon would be found to favor Hanoi, chiefly because they feel that under its government contact with the homeland would be easier. This pro-Hanoi sentiment is also in part a product of what is, perhaps unfairly and inaccurately, called "Chinese chauvinism," and it may prove unrealistic, for it is highly unlikely that if Hanoi eventually establishes its own rule over Saigon the Chinese will be allowed to continue playing the economic role they have played for so many years.

As for attitudes toward China among the Vietnamese, all of them, North and South, fear the Chinese and would prefer to remain independent of them. After all, most of Vietnam was occupied by the Chinese for more than a thousand years, and its people are proud that their ancestors finally drove off the northern conquerors and established their independence. Moreover, the most recent Chinese "occupation" of Vietnam—in 1945 and 1946, when some of Chiang Kai-shek's Kuomintang troops were sent in by the British-American Southeast Asia Command to occupy the northern part of the country temporarily while the British occupied the south—has not been forgotten; the occupying troops plundered the area and made fortunes from opium and other illegal traffic. (Indeed, remnants of these troops are still engaged in such activities in the wild border areas of Laos and Burma.) Although the Chinese Communists are regarded as friends by Hanoi, there is little doubt that the North Vietnamese want to maintain their tenuous balance between Moscow and Peking, which Ho Chi Minh managed so well for so long. It is likely that the Cholon Chinese similarly hope to go on hedging their bets.

When it comes to movies, more of the young in Vietnamese Saigon have broken sharply with tradition than have done so in Cholon. Late last year, a Vietnamese film entitled "Chan Troi Tim," or "Purple Horizon," for the first time showed a Vietnamese hero and heroine kissing each other on the lips. While essentially innocuous compared to many contemporary productions from the West, the film nevertheless contained what for the Vietnamese were touches of neorealism, including a scene that displayed a bare bosom. There were also scenes of bar girls, deserters, and other by-products of the war, and scenes of napalming and bombing by Vietnamese pilots in American planes. The film received a lot of favorable comment from the younger generation but some severe criticism from older Vietnamese. It was a box-office success.

The Vietnamese have taken to television avidly; even some of the poorest families have sets. There are two channels, one run by the United States Army and the other run by the Saigon government, and the American one is by far the more popular among the Vietnamese, who, even if they don't understand the dialogue, enjoy the action of such shows as "Mission: Impossible," "Wild, Wild West," and "Batman." The favorite Vietnamese TV show, "Cai Luong," is a dramatic series told in classical opera form, though the story line is modern; one episode dealt with a young woman who was forced to leave home and go to work as a bar girl. The Americans show a considerable number of propaganda films but, on or off TV, have made scant effort to improve Saigon's cultural life. One exception was the presentation last year, with the financial backing of about half the sixty members of the American Chamber of Commerce, of the German opera "Hansel and Gretel," of all things. It cost seven thousand dollars to put on five performances, and considerable criticism was voiced in the American community about the amount of money spent on something so seemingly irrelevant when the same sum could far better have been used to help refugees or orphans.

With some exceptions, the only regular contact between Americans and Vietnamese is at the G.I. level, where the motivation is for the most part sexual, would-be sexual, or at best superficial. There have, however, been several thousand marriages between Vietnamese girls and American soldiers, despite the fact that they are difficult to arrange—having been purposely made so by both sides. Many of the marriages have broken up once the couple has gone off to America, where the girl has very often found herself the only Oriental in a small American community. Some Americans have also adopted Vietnamese war orphans, with the help of a number of private and public organizations sponsored by Americans and Europeans, but the number of adoptions is infinitesimal in relation to the thousands of orphans who either will have to be reared in government institutions or will remain homeless and destitute.

Something that has not altered through the long years of the war is the importance in Saigon of fortune-telling. Virtually all Vietnamese, no matter how well educated, are firm believers in soothsayers of one kind or another, and depend on them for guidance in all sorts of decisions. President Thieu, former Vice-President Ky, and all the other people I know in the hierarchy of power have made many decisions only after seeking the advice of a favorite seer—and this may be one reason American advice hasn't been taken as often as many

people at home think it has. Even the most Western-minded
Vietnamese, who pretend to laugh at the way some of their
friends depend on fortune-tellers, secretly go to fortune-tellers
themselves and cling to traditional beliefs, such as the significance of who enters their houses in the first moments of the
new year. I know a number of Americans who have visited
Vietnamese friends on the eve of the new year and have politely been asked to leave at the last moment of the old year,
because "a good Vietnamese friend of mine is coming in a
few moments and it would be unlucky if you were here." The
most popular forms of fortune-telling are astrology, phrenol-
ogy, palmistry, the reading of playing cards, and scrying in
crystal balls. Over the past years, in which one disastrous series
of events has followed another, the timing of coups and
attempted coups has invariably been determined by what fortune-tellers told the generals involved. My friends—journalists, businessmen and others—have regularly told me whether
their luck at a given time would be good or bad, and, oddly,
they have been right more often than not.

Numerology plays a vital part in these predictions, with emphasis on the basic numbers three and five. Three is lucky, and
five is unlucky; the fifth, the fourteenth, and the twenty-third
days of the lunar month are always considered unlucky. (In
the second and third of these dates, the digits—one and four,
two and three—add up to five, accounting for the presumed
ill omens.) Finally, and most important, there is the twelve-
year Vietnamese calendar cycle, similar to the Chinese cycle,
with each of twelve successive years identified by a spirit in
the form of an animal figure, and each of these being considered lucky or unlucky for each man in certain years. The year
1971 was the Year of the Hog, and in February, 1972, the whole
cycle began again, with the Year of the Mouse, or Rat. Each
year, at the start of Tet, the family home is brightly lighted to
welcome not only the first visitor but the new spirit. Tables
are laden with food, flowers are placed everywhere, and at
dawn the family honors its ancestors by sitting down to the
first banquet of the Tet period, which lasts between seven
and ten days. When the meal is over, each member of the
family dresses in his best clothes to greet relatives, especially
grandparents. Each child receives a small sum of money in a

traditional red envelope, and foreign as well as Vietnamese employers are expected to give the Vietnamese who work for them, and even hotel managers and hotel servants, Tet gifts—if not a month's salary, then a few hundred or a few thousand piastres, depending on the importance of the relationship.

Some years ago, an American friend of mine undertook a study of the significance of fortune-telling and other forms of soothsaying, and came up with some interesting results. The sites of all buildings, including the Presidential Palace (currently considered to be in a bad spot), are thought to be lucky or unlucky according to their access to light, water, and space. The fortunes of the American Embassy in Saigon definitely seemed to change from good to poor when it was moved from its site downtown, on Ham Nghi Boulevard, facing away from the Saigon River and Vo Di Nguy Street, to its present site, on Thong Nhut Boulevard. A prominent geomancer has pointed out that President Thieu was born in the Year of the Mouse, and this means that 1972 doesn't look good for him. No one knows how much faith the Communists in North Vietnam place in all this, but certainly those of my Saigon friends who are from the North believe in the whole system implicitly.

Despite Saigon's wartime transfigurations, the Vietnamese remain a ritualistic people, and one of their fundamental rituals remains the transmission, after careful evaluation, of rumor and gossip. Ever since 1960, when the first coup against Diem occurred, the chief rumor-and-gossip mill has been called Radio Catinat, and the old name has stuck. Around 1962, its headquarters were at a restaurant called La Pagode, toward the upper end of the Rue Catinat. After the fall of Diem, the veranda of the Hôtel Continental and, subsequently, the bar of the Caravelle Hotel were part of the network, but its true center since Diem's overthrow has been a small restaurant and pastry shop called Givral, across the street from the Continental. (La Pagode, a block away, is now frequented by "phantom troops"—officers and noncoms whose families are rich enough to keep them in Saigon.) Much of the talk one hears at Givral is of questionable value, for people who frequent the restaurant often plant information on each other for a purpose. Among the clientele are National Assemblymen (the Assembly building is only fifty yards away), public officials, secret police, journalists, and businessmen. It is not uncommon to see an opposition deputy and a secret-police agent sitting together and fencing verbally. Everyone who comes to Givral does so not only to exchange information but to play the subtle conversational games the Vietnamese play so much better than Americans can—testing each other, putting each other on, trying to humor somebody and to denigrate somebody else. Cabinet ministers drop by from time to time, as do other high civilian and military officials; President Thieu used to, when he was still an Army officer. Businessmen not only listen to journalists and others here but use the place to test their own agents, one against another, for veracity or the ability to plant false rumors. There are three daily "broadcast times" at Givral—one around ten in the morning, one in midafternoon, and one between five and seven, after the daily press briefings are held at the National Press Center, across the way. The morning period is concerned mostly with business rumors and reports, and the two afternoon sessions with political and military matters.

If Radio Catinat is the most central and most public place for the dissemination of information, true and false, there are other places, not far off, which are also important, each in its own way. For several mornings, I accompanied a friend of mine, Pham Xuan An, who is employed by an American news magazine and is probably the hardest-working and most highly respected Vietnamese journalist in town, on his rounds of these spots. An, who loves animals and birds—he has eight birds, four dogs, and one fish—took me first to the Ham Nghi animal-and-bird market, near the old American Embassy building. The market, which stretches for about half a block, sells monkeys, civets, ocelots, rabbits, guinea pigs, and all sorts of dogs, cats, fish, and birds—among the last being cuckoos from Africa, pigeons from France and Mozambique, owls, myna birds, parrots, skylarks, pheasants, and canaries. For those who favor ancient folk remedies, bats are available; a well-regarded cure for tuberculosis involves cutting the throat of a bat and drinking its blood mixed with rice wine. Adjacent to Ham Nghi is a street called Nguyen Cong Tru, where each morning at about ten o'clock Chinese businessmen or their Vietnamese agents meet in two or three cafés to determine collectively what the day's black-market piastre rate will be and also to set the prices of rice, pork, and other basic commodities. Within half an hour after their decisions are made, the word goes out to the two main commodity markets in Saigon and Cholon and to the dollar black market. This Chinese-dominated strip dates back to the days of the French, who operated out of the same places through their Chinese compradors. In the same block, and extending along part of Ham Nghi, is the center of the sidewalk black-market traffic in American goods. Here, despite occasional crackdowns by the police, one can buy anything available at the American post exchanges and a wide range of other foreign products as well, including Japanese cameras and hi-fi sets. Because police roundups have been more frequent in the past year or so, the more expensive items are no longer displayed, but they can be bought on a C.O.D. basis; that is, a Vietnamese woman running a stall will ask a customer whether he wants such-and-such a camera, and if he is interested he will give her his address and she will come around the next morning, camera in hand, and bargain. Almost all the goods are perfectly genuine—except the whiskey, which is usually diluted with rice wine. The markup on black-market goods ranges from forty to five hundred per cent, but some things remain cheaper at the black-market-dollar rate (now about four hundred and fifty piastres to the dollar) than they are at the post exchanges. It all depends on the subtle process of supply and demand, and on one's ability to bargain. Some of what is sold has been pilfered from the docks on its way to the post exchanges, and then the price is ordinarily kept low, but usually something like a case of beer, which sells for three dollars at the PX, will cost six or eight dollars on the black market. A carton of American cigarettes, which costs a dollar-seventy at the PX, will cost four dollars on the black market.

In the same vicinity are a number of restaurants, each catering to a different clientele, and to these An took me in his search for tidbits of information. The Victory, a spacious place on Ham Nghi specializing in Chinese food, has much the same atmosphere in the morning that Givral has in the afternoon, but is not so crowded. Politicians, journalists, and important businessmen exchange information there every morning over tea or Chinese soup. The nearby Do Thanh is more of a middle-class place, for officials of sub-Cabinet rank, field-grade officers, and the second-rung diplomatic set. An, being a journalist who, though he works for the Americans, is also trusted by the Vietnamese, makes a point of visiting at least five such places each morning before he heads for Givral; then, after lunch, he goes to the official American and Vietnamese briefings and back to Givral. "It takes a long time to build up your sources," he says. "You have to be frank and sincere, and you have to protect your sources. You must also do them favors—tell them things they want to know, buy them lunches and dinners, give them Tet gifts. Saigon operates in this pattern of social circles. If you're not qualified for one particular circle, you won't be accepted in its restaurant. The people there will just ignore you. Journalists—the good ones—are the most useful informants, because they are in a position to hear things from so many different sources. The whole thing is like a school. You can graduate from one circle to another, just as you would from one class to another, once you've passed your tests."

If rumors remain a large part of the daily life in Saigon, hard facts are what the police deal with. Whether or not their efforts are appreciated by the populace, the police have undoubtedly become more efficient in the past two years. This is chiefly thanks to the efforts of Trang Si Tan, who was appointed police chief in January, 1971. Tan, a former prosecutor, magistrate, and president judge of the Saigon Municipal Court, is in charge of about twenty thousand men, including the uniformed police, who handle traffic, administrative work, and other routine functions; the Maritime Police; the Field Force Police, who are engaged primarily in keeping order and quelling disturbances; and, finally, the Special Police, who are in charge of security. There is considerable rivalry and jealousy among the police, the Military Security Service, the Vietnamese Central Intelligence Organization, and Vietnamese Army Intelligence, just as there is among their American equivalents, yet Tan—who reports, through the National

Police Chief, Colonel Nguyen Khac Binh, to Prime Minister Tran Thien Khiem (who is also Minister of the Interior)—is widely respected by all his colleagues. A quiet, soft-spoken man with the mien of a judge, he is a tough administrator, and he operates his force with more discipline and order than it has had for a long time. A while ago, I took two trips around Saigon with him and watched him in action.

Tan's Special Police are in charge of what is called "population control and classification." The population is divided into four categories—A, B, C, and D—and each household is given a rating that supposedly reflects its loyalty to the government. Tan and I visited one of five police stations, for example, in District Six, which embraces part of Cholon and is considered one of the least secure districts in the city, and I discovered that the almost twenty-five thousand households in the substation area were rated as follows: 16,007 were A, or pro-government; 7,944 were B, or uncommitted; none were C, or openly anti-government but non-Communist nationalist; and 277 were D, or pro-Vietcong (or suspected of being so). A file is kept on each member of each household, and each must have an identity card. The A houses in District Six are mostly those of government civil servants, members of the armed forces, or the People's Self-Defense Forces—the locally recruited "home guards." The uncommitted households, which are the majority in many areas, are most difficult for the police to identify. These households consist of people who maintain that their sole interest is in earning a living, and that they are neither for nor against the government—simply not interested in politics. While Tan's Special Police and their penetration agents—that is, men out of uniform who have penetrated pro-Communist or suspected pro-Communist groups and neighborhoods—keep a constant check on these houses, no one can tell for certain that the Communists have not planted some of their workers among them. Another thing the police are anxious to know is whether members of these households would, if they were given the chance, vote for a neutralist or a Communist candidate in an open election contest. The reason there were no C households in the area we visited—and there are very few anywhere—is, of course, that hardly anyone wants to be identified as being against the government.

When I asked Tan whether all this didn't really amount to total police control, he replied that it was not unlike what the Communists had always done, and that since the 1968 Tet attack it had become the only way to determine what the Communists were up to. Tan and his American advisers readily admit that in the most sensitive areas—particularly in Cholon and some of the newer districts of the city—the system is far from fully effective. Even so, incidents of terrorism, sabotage, and other forms of Communist activity have diminished considerably since it was put into effect. Throughout the city in 1969, according to police statistics, there were a total of three hundred and seven incidents of all kinds—bombings, mortar barrages, killings of policemen, and so on. In 1971, the total number of incidents was only about sixty-five. Tan says he believes there are now probably between two hundred and five hundred Communist Party members in the city, and perhaps fifteen thousand active sympathizers. It is undoubtedly much harder for them to move about than it used to be; they do maintain a courier system, though, and they are believed to have five secret mobile radio stations in Saigon. As a result of a tighter system of checkpoints that Tan's men have established on the outskirts of Saigon, he says, it is also harder for the Communists to move people into the city.

We visited one of these checkpoints, where all vehicles were stopped and searched by both uniformed police and plainclothesmen. Former Vietcong members who were regarded as trusted returnees acted as spotters. At this particular checkpoint, Tan told me, twenty-five thousand people passed back and forth each day, and out of every five hundred perhaps ten were held for questioning. Though Tan said he did not believe that the Communists could conduct a large-scale assault on the city, he admitted that they could still conduct propaganda campaigns and carry on political activity almost anywhere, and that they were undergoing a thorough reorganization to improve their apparatus for another major attack. "As always, they will exploit the democratic process," Tan says, "and when that process is weakened by lack of authority, by lack of decent living standards, by lack of any useful long-range plans for making the city livable, the danger will remain, no matter how many checkpoints we set up or how much population control we maintain."

Although ten city plans have been drawn up for Saigon in the past ten years, almost nothing has been done to carry any of them out. After the Tet offensive of 1968, there was a brief period when the Americans and the Vietnamese got together on projects for repairing the worst damage—caused mostly by American planes bombing entrenched Communist attackers—but there has been little coördinated or long-range action since then to alleviate the overcrowding or to improve the dire condition of the slums, and the administrative organizations that were formed at the time have been allowed to die, mostly for lack of funds (though, according to Frank R. Pavich, who is one of a handful of American urban experts here, there are few Vietnamese with any real background in urban planning). A survey has been made of each block in Saigon to determine how the land is being used—for residential, commercial, or other purposes—but nothing has been done to identify the worst slum areas, to get fundamental economic-aid programs started, or to plan the construction of higher buildings as at least a temporary solution. What has happened is a considerable amount of indiscriminate, haphazard new building in various parts of the city, indicating, if nothing else, some degree of hope for the future of a non-Communist Saigon. However, there are few signs of any long-range outlook on the part of the central or municipal government. Pavich and others believe that the earlier plans, made by such experts as the Doxiadis group, to expand the city northward toward Bien Hoa, where the Americans have had their biggest airbase, are still valid, but that putting them into effect would require further detailed and constructive planning, and a lot more money. James P. Bogle, another American expert, who made a study of Saigon's growth problems a few years ago, concluded that, where urbanization was concerned, the government was facing problems familiar to all less developed countries, and that it was "extremely questionable" whether it would be able to cope with them. Unlike the North Vietnamese, who have continued to rebuild as the war has gone on, the South Vietnamese, except for the short period after the Tet offensive, have done very little to improve any of their cities.

Important as the rebuilding process is, social reconstruction and moral regeneration are more important. "We have fostered a whole new generation of drifters, who have lost all their Confucian values," one older Vietnamese in Saigon told me. "All they think of is dodging the draft, having fun, riding their Hondas." There is no doubt that the Americans have altered the entire fabric of Saigon life, and one feels that a new breakdown is inevitable unless something drastic is done. What we have done is to create a social spectrum with a *nouveau riche* class at one end, a new class of poor people, largely refugees, at the other, and in the middle a classless majority, who have lived off the American presence.

Another Vietnamese friend told me, "You Americans think you have given the Vietnamese a better material life, but it's not true. Most of the equipment you poured in here will end up as scrap. Perhaps the situation will have to disintegrate still further before something new can be built. The only hope is that a new younger group, with ideas of its own, will emerge, and that these young people will understand that both the old prewar society and the American superimposed one are finished. If we don't go Communist, it may take twenty years, or even longer, to bring about a new synthesis, but it will happen. First, though, we must undo the damage you have done. The Vietnamese like to raise monkeys. You have seen them in the animal market, in homes, in the parks. What you have done here in Saigon is create a monkey climate. The only Vietnamese you really know—the ones you have dealt with—are monkeys. Why don't you at least help us get rid of the monkeys before you go?"

The New Yorker, April 15, 1972

Report from the Inferno

by John Saar

THE LITTLE RADIO was hard to hear because 500 yards away the whole Laikhe ammo dump was erupting in gouts of fire and cataclysmic chain explosions. Through the shattering crumps and the shriek of errant metal came the urgent-voiced American Forces Radio newscast: giant B-52s were unloading high explosives on North Vietnam's port city of Haiphong. Awed and made puny by the monstrous destruction mushrooming in front of us, we realized it was the simultaneous facsimile of another horror scene 660 miles north. Fireballs, leaping in the sky like crimson tumors, dwarfed the darting ambulances, and the men who bravely wheeled loaded munitions trucks from the fiery base of a smoke column reaching 3,000 feet into the air were grimed, big-eyed and very frightened.

The message was impossible to deny—whether by a sapper's rocket in the South, or SAC's iron bombs in the North, Vietnam was again springing into flames. The difference this time is that the mindless brutality of this quarter-century war has acquired a savage new sophistication. In the intransigence of the North Vietnamese grinding on through the blood of their youth and the Vietnamized forces of the South brought to parity by U.S. air power, one senses something close to a perpetual war formula. The most depressing aspect of this new offensive to end all offensives is the patterned automatism of the bloodletting. The governments of North and South yoke their people to unyielding conflict, and the great power eminences are there at their shoulders to heap them with yet more efficient tools of destruction. The costs of the war for both North and South are now so grossly disproportionate to the size or importance of Vietnam that there can be none but Pyrrhic victories.

The early action was in the north and a civilian Air Vietnam flight let us out into the blazing sunlight of Hué's Phubai airfield where a group of wounded South Vietnamese marines were awaiting Medevac. Nearby, a group of home-going GIs lolled against a wall, staring through their shades and nodding absently to a Joplin tape. The music floated over the sorry group of South Vietnamese, heads and newly amputated limbs wrapped in grubby bandages: "Freedom's just another word for nothing left to lose. . . ." Vietnamization means the GIs go home but the Vietnamese stay, to fight on indefinitely.

The Ranger-trained adviser, brush-cut and aripple with repressed energy, is quick to defend the Vietnamese soldiers who abandoned 14 fire bases in the first retreat from the DMZ: "Hell, the Japs might have stayed under the kind of fire they were taking, Americans wouldn't. The way that 130-mm was coming in even the Russians would have *chieu hoied*." The logic makes perfect sense—why should the ARVN fight from fixed positions in bad terrain and under constant bombardment?

The road north to Dongha—the road, rail and river town where the North Vietnamese advance was eventually halted—is a gradual passage from a peaceful countryside of buffalo boys and rice harvest to the haunted desolation of a recent battlefield. Down the road toward us, tripping barefoot quick, quick, quick, came a straggle of refugees Indian-file— women, children, old men and a few dogs idling alongside. Faces scared and strained with effort—fugitive people not *going* anywhere, but fleeing *from*. The war is a beast that leaves a spoor of havoc—mounds of cartridge brass, motorcycles and bikes flattened as neatly as pressed flowers by passing tanks, ditches a confusion of hasty army litter, dried bloodstains in the brown dust, bloated corpses of dogs, buffalo and Communist soldiers. Dongha is dying in a carnival of destruction at the hands of the soldiers—from every quarter come shouts, laughter, random shots, the splintering of glass and the breaking of doors. In the darkness of a general store we find a Vietnamese marine swinging at cartons with a sugar-cane cutter. "VC," he says, thumbing at the wreckage. The contents of the shops and houses lie in the muddy streets like a knee-deep snowfall; the stuff and identity of people's lives is a thoroughfare for proliferating rats and flies. And eddying heavily over the town is the revolting odor of rotting flesh—a smell you recognize instantly but thankfully never quite remember afterward. Mouth trembling between anger and tears, Le Thi Tin, 45-year-old mother of 14, picks through the looted disorder of her home for pots and pans and the minimal wherewithal of survival for her new-old life as a refugee. Incoming Communist shells whistle overhead and in a surge of panic she sweeps her two sons and herself into a bunker. White-faced and pathetically fearful, she says she stayed in Dongha because she was born and raised there. Will she ever come back to her home? "If peace comes." She does not sound hopeful, says the interpreter. Requiem for Dongha—once a town of 30,000 people—shelled and rocketed by Communists, sacked by ARVN.

There is a new desperate tenacity to this NVA offensive. We are seeing more Communist bodies than ever before because conventional warfare requires them to stand and fight more often. On the outskirts of Quangtri one such squad fought and died to a man. Now they lie strewn over the edges of their foxholes like the petals of a spent bloom, heads blown open like eggshells. Every inch of the schoolhouse wall behind them is pitted with fire. They might as well have been stood up against it for all the chance they had.

In a busload of refugees is an old man from the Eden-like valley of Camlo, captured and held by the Communists. He has the wispy goatee of venerated age and his eyes are like faded stained glass. "I left my home and belongings and have just these clothes," he says. "Many people are being killed by VC rockets and by bombing. Many compatriots were suffering and starving when we left. I saw a human hand in a tree and parts of human beings blown apart." The bus leaves.

With the withdrawal of the American ground troops whose own tactics in other times were said to have accidentally taken the lives of thousands of Vietnamese civilians, there has been extra compensatory use of air power. B-52s and tac air are plainly less discriminatory weapons than the GI with a rifle. Thuyen is a short, swarthy soldier in ARVN's Third Division. His left leg is bandaged and his eyes are dazed. "The planes dropped bombs on Camlo city and killed two of my children and severely injured my wife. Two of my brothers were also killed." A doctor with the rank of captain stops the interview and ejects us from the hospital. Why? we ask. "Because the soldiers do not tell the truth. They will only give you propaganda."

The quotient of loss and suffering is so high in South Vietnam that wherever you go, whomever you talk to, you stumble from one dismal personal tragedy to another. After decades of incipient disaster, the adjustment and return to apparent normality is rapid, but scratch the patina and you find the unhealed wounds. Death is so casual and commonplace that people husband their sorrow for their families only. In the barren moorland country off national Route 1 a handful of white-clad druidic figures are holding a service. A girl red-eyed with grief and clutching an offering of bananas and water climbs into a bus with two priests and drives off. Crumpled at the roadside is the jeep in which her father and six others were killed when it ran over a mine. The Vietcong set the mine; the killing was as random as the Camlo bombs.

The mud-stained truck grinding through the streets of Hué was a dirty brown. The officer in the back who asked for directions was wearing his olive-drab mac. The yellow-and-red flag draped over the coffin in the back seemed glaringly bright. As the truck meandered slowly through the maze of back streets, onlookers, stricken and glum, stared and pointed. Lt. Le Van Hoan, a gravely good-looking armor officer, was bringing home the body of his friend Minh, killed at Kontum with three of his men when their vehicle detonated a mine. The truck halted finally outside a trim whitewashed villa and Minh's family surged out. Streaming tears, the dead boy's sister threw herself over the coffin while two of his brothers, also weeping, tried to comfort her. Lieutenant Hoan nervously sucked his cigarette and blew out the smoke without taking it down.

Minh's father, a 60-year-old public servant, says he was terribly upset over his son's death, but glad Minh died fighting for his country—"besides, there are so many families who have had their sons killed in battle." Swinging round in his chair he points, "Over here a family, over here a family. . . ."

Minh, the 21-year-old who used to write poetry and play the Vietnamese guitar, was drafted into the army when he dropped out of high school. The family will remember him with the flag he came home under and a picture on the family altar of a slightly out-of-focus Vietnamese boy wearing an outsize U.S. Army steel helmet. Two of Minh's brothers are in ARVN and Thang will go next: "I think the young men in the North are like the men in the South. They are obliged to go in the army but in their hearts they want peace. If I have to go it is my duty, but I don't think my death would help my country."

Out in the reed flats south of Hué a U.S. helicopter dances like a dragonfly just feet off the water in search of Vietcong. Periodically there is small-arms fire. An ARVN officer tells us that a militia force has killed five VC. He claims only one friendly dead but the interpreter clearly hears the figure eight given over the radio. A sampan glides into the bank and government soldiers heave two VC bodies quivering onto the ground. They wear threadbare shorts and shirts and Ho Chi Minh sandals cut from old auto tires. In their drenched equipment bags are patched ponchos, plastic explosive, vials of Romanian penicillin. Like the two men, the can in which they kept fried pork to supplement their rice was torn and riddled with M-16 fire.

Colonel Bo, who can sometimes speak English and sometimes not, is officially an ARVN information officer. But foreign journalists agree that his province is closer to psychological warfare. At his invitation, we interviewed NVA Lt. Nguyen Khac Soan, aged 29, captured after escaping and evading for eight days. The prisoner is hollow-cheeked and faint from hunger and has eventually to be carried out. The interview is generally worthless and a Vietnamese colleague says, "Colonel Bo twists all the questions and answers."

Vietnam is a totally mobilized country and at around the age of 18 a young man has to decide whether he wants to kill for the government or for the VC. For reasons we could not find out as he was marched, arms bound, along Route 1 with his B-40 rocket-launcher hung around his neck, 23-year-old Le Hong Sinh chose to join the VC in 1968. The mud and blood freshly crusted on his face did not hide a ruddy flow of health, and his legs were thick with muscle. He was frightened but not cowed. The interpreter said, "I wished him luck. He's going to need it, he'll have a very rough time." A well-informed Vietnamese source later confirmed that prisoners were sometimes tortured or killed: "It is necessary to get information quickly or to make the others talk." Do the North Vietnamese torture their prisoners? "I'm sure they do. They're human too."

In the air-conditioned calm of the senior adviser's comfortable quarters the war seems very distant. The M-16 is hung on the wall, the helmet with the eagle of the full colonel by the door. The requisite paperback library on guerrilla warfare is on the bedside table. On the door is the adviser's poem:

> Mine is not to run this train;
> The whistle I can't blow.
> Mine is not to say
> How far this train can go.
> I'm not allowed to blow off steam
> Or even ring the bell.
> But let this train run off the track
> And see who catches hell.

The colonel has no such apprehensions. In fact, he's cock-a-hoop: "They shot their wad and it didn't work out. Now, like they always do, they're stubbornly hanging on instead of pulling back to regroup and they're losing their asses every day." Already on this offensive, reporters have learned to be wary—an unprecedented amount of misinformation (optimistic, of course) is adrift. A trip to a fire base southwest of Hué puts the colonel's rose-tinted views in another perspective. On a fire base called Bastogne, a battalion of ARVN have had their guns knocked out, cannot evacuate their dead and wounded and are short food, water and ammunition.

"Excuse me, colonel, but as accredited MACV correspondents we are entitled to talk to these soldiers."

The colonel blocked the way. "Well, I'm not going to let you talk to them." He was as good as his word. The trucks carrying a company of the U.S. 196th Infantry rolled away moments later. In a conversation over a concertina-wire fence, other soldiers explained there had indeed been a misunderstanding and a temporary refusal by a company to go into the field. The soldiers are reasonable and rational, and after a two-hour appeal by their commanding officer they all agree to go. But the soldiers make it plain they feel no obligation to fight for Vietnam and will accept only such action as is necessary to protect themselves and other Americans.

A junior U.S. adviser, after a swift glance over his shoulder, gives his version of Anloc: "Things are getting worse and worse and the Vietnamese just aren't doing anything. The smell inside the town got so bad they bulldozed a mass grave for 300 dead ARVN. The NVA shelled the hospital and destroyed it with captured 155s and killed 61. Now they don't have a hospital or enough medical supplies and there are 500 to 600 ARVN wounded they can't get out."

At noon, Laikhe, headquarters for ARVN's Route 13 battle, was at a standstill for a two-hour lunch. No rushing trucks with badly needed ammo, no bustling staff officers with pressing plans—just the broiling 100° heat of the open, and the gentle swinging of hammocks in the beguiling shade of the rubber trees. Then a mortar round zonked into the road close to a chopper park. In the days of the U.S. war, crews would have materialized immediately to fly their birds from an insecure coop. Today the heat shimmers off the asphalt. No one appears and there are no more mortars—this time. You remember a Vietnamese friend saying, "At night the NVA run, they never walk, always they run. . . ."

The week's reporting ended with a ride back to Saigon in a U.S. Medevac helicopter. As we climbed away, black coils of smoke were rising from Laikhe's ammunition dump. It was, I imagined, pretty much like the scene over Haiphong's blazing harbor. For these people, peace seemed to be no closer than it was years ago when we, and the other side, first decided to help them with their war.

Life, April 28, 1972

The South Vietnamese Army

by Peter Braestrup

Quangtri: Anything But Easy

SAIGON—As border outposts and outlying towns fell in April and May to Hanoi's troops, President Thieu faced a harsh reality: Many of the generals he had rewarded for political loyalty had brought on near disaster as field commanders.

Thieu redeployed Saigon's forces with surprising boldness to meet battlefield crises—at Anloc, at Kontum, at Hue, he issued stronger mobilization decrees to provide 70,000 replacements for South Vietnamese losses. He flew to the forward command posts to talk with his senior officers and pin medals on the brave.

But essentially, Hanoi's initial successes—and the command weaknesses they laid bare—did not lead Thieu to change South Vietnam's military-political "system."

Instead, he has as usual tried to balance "political security" against military necessity as he reshuffles commanders amid public outcry.

In American official eyes, and those of Thieu's domestic critics, the offensive has left the 46-year-old ex-general no real choice: As U.S. support dwindles, the army leadership cannot survive and remain mostly "political" and part "professional."

Under the pressure of events, Thieu has fired two of the country's four regional commanders, replaced three of its 13 division commanders, reshuffled perhaps a dozen of his 44 military province chiefs.

The net result overall, in U.S. eyes, is "modest improvement."

The most striking change—and possibly the most difficult politically for Thieu—has occurred in the north, where potential military catastrophe in May threatened the former imperial capital of Hue.

Here, the perils of South Vietnam's military politics-as-usual became most obvious. The general in charge of Military Region I, which embraces the northern five provinces, was Lt. Gen. Hoang Xuan Lam, 44, an amiable, round-faced officer who favored a swagger stick and a tanker's black beret. The shock of the offensive was just too much for him, as for others.

This April, when the North Vietnamese came across the Demilitarized Zone (DMZ), Lam did not establish a tactical headquarters at Hue. Nor did he often visit forward regimental command posts. Instead, he commuted daily 60 miles to Hue from his Danang headquarters by (American-piloted) helicopter, returning in time for lunch or dinner.

"The situation is serious, but not critical," he told newsmen.

For a month, Lam left the battlefield coordination of mutually antagonistic armor, rangers, infantry and marine units to a deputy at Hue, but delegated no authority. A junior U.S. adviser at the Hue citadel dubbed Lam the "absentee warlord."

Many reasons have been advanced for the subsequent May 1 rout of Saigon's forces at Quangtri City—the inexperience of the under-strength 3d Division; the apparent breakdown of its highly regarded commander, Brig. Gen. Vu Van Giai; poor coordination and the shock of enemy artillery fire. Most authoritative sources ultimately blame Lam's failure to face reality and grab hold.

But Thieu did not shift Lam to a desk job in Saigon until after the Quangtri debacle. He was grateful to Lam for his political loyalty as shown in 1967, when the generals met to decide whether Thieu or Air Vice Marshal Nguyen Cao Ky would head the government ticket in the fall elections. Lam then supported Thieu, ripping off his general's stars and throwing them on the table and saying he would quit if Thieu got the second spot. Thieu got the nod.

Thereafter Lam, with close ties to the locally-influential Dai Viet Party, was Thieu's trusted political-military boss for the northern region. Lam did not fire able non-political officers, but he did bring in his protege, Maj. Gen. Nguyen Van Toan, as commander of the 2d Division, south of Danang.

In U.S. eyes, Toan was an able commander; he was also

known, briefly, in 1968, as the "Cinnamon King," for his alleged use of army trucks in a Quangngai cinnamon venture with Lam's wife.

Moreover, like his colleagues, Lam's tactical abilities as a corps commander were seldom put to the test. The U.S. battalions were handling the big-unit war shielding the frontiers at Khesanh, on the DMZ, in the Ashau Valley. For the most part, Lam could focus on his role as Thieu's regional administrative boss.

This in itself is no small burden, even for the most energetic commander. As in many other Third World countries, the officer corps not only runs the army, but also plays the dominant role in local administration. This spreads the talent pretty thin.

With a guerrilla threat present everywhere, the 44 province chiefs, 220 district chiefs and six big-city mayors under South Vietnam's centralized French-style system have long been military men. They have overall responsibility both for leading the militia in combat and for running the civil bureaucracy.

This has, willy-nilly, involved army colonels and majors as well as generals in politics. And especially during the lavish U.S. build-up, many found opportunities to boost low official incomes through collusion with Vietnamese contractors, diversion of U.S. aid, or "taxes" on local commerce.

Not all money-minded province chiefs have been incompetents or cowards; for example, Brig. Gen. Ly Tong Ba, now commander of the 23d Division at Kontum, coupled high living on a low salary with great bravery in leading his militia in Binhduong Province during the 1968 Tet offensive.

Not all officials had to be crooks to get by, but reformers—in Vietnam as in Chicago—arouse hostility.

In June, for example, local politicians in Binhdinh Province succeeded in getting Thieu to remove Col. Nguyen Van Chuc, who was not only brave, but an outspoken foe of local corruption.

Chuc's leadership is credited by his American advisers with saving southern Binhdinh Province from the North Vietnamese in May, after the regular South Vietnamese army 40th Regiment, led by an incompetent, lost three northern districts in April.

But Chuc rocked the boat, antagonizing regular army unit

leaders and local businessmen alike. He also irritated his new superior, Gen. Toan, the ex-Cinnamon King, whom Thieu has just named as regional commander.

Thieu does not admire boat-rockers. To stay in office, like many another Third World leader, he has had to maintain a kind of "politburo" consensus among key army leaders. Of necessity, he has also operated since 1967 a kind of military patronage system, easing out allies of possible rivals (E.G., Ky), repaying past favors, rewarding loyalty above all else.

Given South Vietnam's past history of military coups, counter-coups and factional jealousies, Thieu has presumably felt that he could take no chances.

In any event, first the U.S. "shield" and then the lack of any overriding military threat prior to March 30, 1972, allowed Thieu, in army matters, to put political security foremost. Thus, Gen. Lam stayed on, along with others less competent.

To replace his friend Lam in early May, Thieu rushed in Lt. Gen. Ngo Quang Truong, 43, a thin, small officer who was widely known as Thieu's best general, a "clean" military professional.

To Thieu's credit, Truong had also been promoted rapidly: from brigadier commanding the 1st Division at Hue in 1968 to lieutenant general commanding the 16-province Mekong Delta region in 1970.

By all accounts, Truong did not get promoted by bucking the system, but by leaving politics and business to others and winning battles, notably at Hue in 1968.

According to one South Vietnamese colonel, both Truong and the fellow paratrooper who succeeded him as 1st Division commander, Maj. Gen. Phan Van Phu, "learned the right things from the Americans."

Truong, alone of all Vietnam's draftee division commanders, insisted on periodic retraining for his battalions. He developed a good staff and good subordinate commanders, and insisted on joining U.S. troops in big-unit operations.

And, important to the palace, he avoided publicity and obeyed Thieu's orders.

Truong returned to Hue—where he set up forward headquarters—and his decisive leadership, together with Thieu's dispatch of airborne reinforcements, warded off catastrophe.

Yet, Thieu elsewhere did not discard political caution.

For example, as far back as 1968, Gen. Creighton W. Abrams repeatedly urged that the three lackluster divisions (5th, 18th and 25th) around Saigon be headed by stronger men, with more qualifications than simple loyalty.

Thieu demurred, then and later. These three units were crucial to any military coup in the capital.

Prior to March 30, he changed two of the three division commanders; both new men were loyal, able former province chiefs, not necessarily a qualification for high military command. One of them has turned out to be brave, while the other has already found running a 12,000-man division in a big war too much to handle. The three divisions remain below par.

Thieu's sensitivity to Saigon's political security remains acute. For example, in April he appointed a Navy vice-admiral, Chung Tan Cang, with no past exposure to ground combat, as commander of the Capital Military District, charged with the defense of the city and surrounding Giadinh Province.

Cang's appointment engendered little public enthusiasm, and some apprehension, but Cang was a Thieu loyalist, if only out of gratitude.

Early in 1965, Cang was sacked as head of the navy by Dr. Phan Huy Quat's short-lived government, after he allegedly profiteered off government-run coastal shipping.

Later that year, when the military took over (again), Thieu rehabilitated Cang, possibly as a gesture to Cang's navy friends. He gave Cang a political staff job. Five years later, the admiral was assigned to the office of Gen. Tran Thien Khiem, the prime minister (and minister of defense and interior), as chief of an anti-corruption drive urged by the U.S. mission.

Cang is close to Thieu, and according to U.S. advisers, extremely energetic in organizing the capital's defenses.

But during the first few weeks of his tenure South Vietnamese sources said Thieu's personal staff kept tabs on Cang's whereabouts and associations. Even now, he is frequently summoned to the presidential palace for detailed instructions. When it comes to Saigon, Thieu keeps a tight rein.

Thieu's right-hand man in all this is Lt. Gen. Dang Van Quang, presidential "assistant for military security." Some

South Vietnamese politicians regard Quang, without affection, as the most powerful man in Vietnam—a kind of
J. Edgar Hoover, Carmine De Sapio and Robert S. McNamara
combined.

A classmate of Thieu's in the 1948 class at Dalat Military
Academy, Quang seldom makes speeches; but he keeps an eye
on intelligence matters, the police, province chiefs, the non-
Communist opposition, promotions and demotions, and all
things military.

It is he who telephones the corps commanders and other
senior officers, speaking in Thieu's name, to check on compliance with Thieu's orders.

This leaves Gen. Cao Van Vien, 53, the widely respected
head of the Joint General Staff since 1966, something of a
"broker between warlords" on many issues, notably personnel. A lean former paratrooper, wounded in action, Vien is
regarded as Thieu's man for the "professional" side of the
military.

By all accounts, Vien is apolitical, obeys Thieu's orders as
best he can, deals with the American military and works within
the system.

Last winter, tired, ailing and frustrated, Vien was ready to
retire; but after some rest he returned to duty in time to organize the South Vietnamese army's troop shifts in response
to the North Vietnamese spring attacks.

Thieu's political security considerations aside, Vien's task is
not easy.

The South Vietnamese military is not a national army in the
sense that its forces are accustomed to fighting and living anywhere in the country. Only the Saigon-based airborne and
marine divisions—the strategic reserve force—do that.

The officers change, but most regular infantry divisions are
regionally based and recruited. The men of the 7th Division,
for example, have been in the Mekong Delta at Mytho, with
wives and children, for 10 years.

And until March 30, most regular South Vietnamese division commanders had little cause to stretch their military talents—after 1969, most of the North Vietnamese army moved
back to Laos and Cambodia.

The battalions sweated and bled, along with the militia, to

expand the government presence and tamp down the Viet-congs in the countryside. They largely succeeded.

But there was little strain at the sprawling division head-quarters inherited from the departing Americans, and the staffs knocked off for two-hour lunches. The idea was to avoid mistakes, risks and excessive losses. It was a long war.

"It is one thing to fly around in a chopper to see how a couple of your battalions are doing on a three-day sweep on familiar ground in Haunghia," observed an experienced U.S. Vietnam hand. "It's something else fending off a North Viet-namese division, shifting battalions, coordinating with other units, getting the choppers, the artillery, the airstrikes, with Saigon on your neck 24 hours a day."

Thus, the South Vietnamese army command structure—the highly centralized leadership and the relatively passive staffs—was ill-prepared for the ordeals of 1972. Despite their U.S. equipment and U.S.-style briefings, complete with map and pointer, the South Vietnamese military—like every army—reflected their own national culture and their own ex-perience.

Moreover, besides being a largely territorial force regionally recruited and based—the South Vietnamese armed forces are also a collection of military clans, reflecting a similar faction-alism among the middle class civilian politicians.

As one U.S. senior officer has noted, some of the inter-service rivalries in South Vietnam spring from "germs" left by U.S. Air Force, Navy, Army and Marine advisers over the years, as well as from past political feuds within South Vietnam itself.

"It's not easy to command airborne or Marines temporarily attached to your division," said a senior South Vietnamese colonel. "They feel free to ignore the orders of a regimental or division commander during an operation, especially when they don't admire him."

Indeed, during one sweep, he said, "the airborne did not turn on their radios, and we shouted for hours trying to get answers. Another time, they turned on the radios only to com-plain and criticize us."

One problem is that the commanders of the Marines, the Airborne, the Rangers and armored battalions do not depend on corps commanders for promotions, but on their own home headquarters, for example, the armor command in Saigon.

"When a complaint by infantry about a particular Ranger unit goes to the Ranger command" in Saigon, an infantry officer said, "it will be torn up." Over and over again this spring, U.S. advisers would find that to avoid friction, South Vietnamese armored and infantry units had not been placed under a single commander but instead told to "cooperate" —an invitation to disarray.

"The big question," said a U.S. adviser in Haunghia, "is always: who's in charge?"

In U.S. eyes, perhaps the most damaging schism is that between helicopter crews and the infantry. In the U.S. Army, the division commander controls his own army helicopters. But partly because the first South Vietnamese helicopter pilots were former air force fighter-bomber pilots, the South Vietnamese air force got all the helicopters. Their crews have nothing to fear from a division commander if they ignore his orders. He's Army and they're Air Force.

"Personal relations are very important," observed a South Vietnamese staff officer in Saigon. "If the relations [between a helicopter flight leader and a ground commander] are not good, difficulties come in the evacuation of wounded or in resupply. The helicopter pilots have many excuses—weather, engine trouble, fuel is low, ground fire is too heavy." At Anloc and Quangtri, South Vietnamese helicopters' performance ranged from fair to awful.

Some of these "command and control" weaknesses as well as political side effects came to light—at least inside the military—long before Hanoi launched its offensive at the end of May. There were hesitations and foulups in Cambodia in 1970–71.

The big snarl came during "Lam Son 719"—the three-month foray in early 1971 against the Ho Chi Minh Trail complex in southern Laos. It was Saigon's big-war operation: the marine division, the airborne, the 1st Division plus armor and rangers. Despite the press photographs of fleeing South Vietnamese GIs hanging on sides of U.S. helicopters, the basic trouble in Lam Son 719 was leadership and staff work, not the troops' willingness to fight.

Who was nominally in charge? Lt. Gen. Lam, the amiable regional political boss. There were personal rivalries: Lt. Gen. Le Nguyen Khang, the marine commander, refused to talk to Lam.

Lacking faith in their own air force, the South Vietnamese ground commanders relied heavily on U.S. air support and helicopters.

But in contrast to this year's big war, there were no U.S. advisers on the ground in Laos with the units, to report on the real situation, to guide the air strikes and talk to the U.S. helicopter pilots.

According to U.S. after-action reports, South Vietnamese army staffs "were reluctant to press for current information unless first requested by senior commanders . . . The information [reaching headquarters] was often inaccurate and usually incomplete . . . Coordination of artillery fires between units was 'difficult . . .' As the operation went on, 'political directives' (from Thieu) were frequent. South Vietnamese commanders became 'unable to assess the situation.' " The planned withdrawal from Laos in March and April of 1971 became, at best, a costly retreat—in places a rout.

According to unpublished official records, South Vietnam lost heavily of its best troops—1,550 killed, 5,500 wounded, 650 missing—along with a division's worth of U.S. equipment: 54 tanks, 300 vehicles and 96 artillery pieces.

In Laos, the North Vietnamese were slow to react and suffered heavy losses, but they showed that they could marshal tanks, artillery and hard-charging infantry even under heavy U.S. airstrikes.

The lessons of Lam Son 719 were apparently lost on Thieu. No reshuffle of commanders resulted.

The 1971 election season was on, according to some South Vietnamese sources, and Thieu was preoccupied with political problems (E.G., Ky, Big Minh), not the seemingly remote prospect of a major conventional military test.

The surprising aspect of the 1972 offensive, so far, is that the South Vietnamese high command—for all its chronic weaknesses—survived the initial surprise and shock.

They were saved by the resilience of the average "binh chi," (GI), the presence of enough good units and adequate leaders at Anloc and other key places, the massive weight of U.S. airpower, and Hanoi's crucial failure to exploit its initial gains.

Moreover, Thieu has kept logistics on the home front going: Vigorous roundups of draft-dodgers and new mobilization decrees have kept up the strength of Saigon's forces in numbers, if not in quality. The training camps are full, and the AWOL rate is about what it was last year—12,000 to 14,000 a month.

But Thieu and his advisers also made some key military decisions: For the first time in the war, they shifted ordinary draftee outfits from their home turf to fight elsewhere; the 21st Division and part of the 9th from the Mekong Delta to Highway 13 and Anloc, north of Saigon; part of the 2d Division from south of Danang to Hue.

Thieu eventually committed his entire elite strategic reserve of marines and airborne to Hue, the most vulnerable target, relying on militia and draftees to defend Saigon.

And after the collapse of the 22nd Division and its commander north of Kontum, Thieu took advantage of North Vietnamese foot-dragging to rush a fresh division—the 23d—into place, to meet the enemy thrusts.

Thieu and Vien boldly stripped large areas of regular troops and left them for the provincial Regional Forces and district Popular Forces to defend. In marked contrast to Tet 1968, these militia, by and large, have filled the gap, notably in pitched battles in Haunghia, Tayninh, Quangtri and southern Binhdinh provinces.

But the old weaknesses have cropped up even during Saigon forces' efforts to retake lost ground.

One airborne brigade commander north of Hue swore that he would put a paratrooper with a pistol on every tank to make sure the attached armored cavalry unit didn't run off. Similar coordination troubles and over-reliance on air strikes have plagued Saigon's two-month-old effort to open Highway 13 to encircled Anloc.

Except for Truong's forces around Hue, regular South Vietnamese regimental commanders have followed low-risk, go-slow tactics—which ironically has often led to higher casualties from enemy mortars. "There are plenty of weak regiments," said a senior U.S. official.

In short, despite a certain current euphoria among the presidential staff, Thieu has only gained a respite on the battlefield. He and his countrymen have survived one more crisis in a long series of crises—at great cost.

Thieu has problems.

Even if he wanted to, he could not suddenly discard the military-political system he has partly inherited, partly created. No other organized political structure exists—or can be rapidly created—to replace the armed Forces' hierarchy and the civil administration it controls.

Yet, by all estimates, Thieu can ill afford militarily to continue the old ways.

Hanoi has not given up. Key territory must be regained. The South Vietnamese army's slim resources in trained combat-worthy units leave little margin for incompetence, or even mediocrity, among combat leaders.

As never before, the U.S. mission is pressing Thieu to shed some of his political caution and put more fighters, like Truong and Phu, in key command jobs.

As these sources see it—but Thieu may not—there is little other choice if Saigon is to survive.

The Washington Post, July 9, 1972

Viet Soldier Serves Officer, Not Nation

SAIGON—"Maybe the war will die out in the next few months because the Communists can't keep it up," said Pvt. Nguyen Van Lon.

"Where I was, they fired a thousand rounds of mortar and artillery a day at the start. Now they only shoot a few hundred."

A skinny, 20-year-old draftee, Lon was convalescing from a chest wound suffered May 11 during the South Vietnamese forces' seemingly interminable ARVN struggle to open Highway 13 to encircled Anloc, 60 miles north of Saigon.

As U.S. field advisers like to point out, it was not American airpower alone, but the resilience of the South Vietnamese army's ordinary "grunts" like Lon which ultimately slowed Hanoi's massive March 30 offensive.

Wearing a white sports shirt, dark slacks and sandals, Lon

sat in an open-sided cafe near the army recuperation center in Saigon. He had let his fingernails grow long—a sign of elegance among Saigon youth—but his hair was cut short, army style. Puffing a Vietnamese Capstan brand cigarette, he talked about himself, his outfit and the war with a mixture of pride, resignation and hope.

"I never had a taste of the war until I was drafted," he said. "I saw planes and helicopters overhead sometimes. But no Communist troops ever came to the village, not even during the 1968 Tet offensive."

"All I knew about the Communists was that people said they were very harsh. They forced the people to pay taxes and to go to indoctrination courses."

To Lon, as to many another young rural Vietnamese, such notions as "the nation," "Communism" and "the government" were remote abstractions. Lon grew up in a hamlet in the prosperous Phukhuong district near Tayninh City, site of the "Holy See" of the Cao Dai sect, 75 miles northwest of Saigon.

A nominal Cao Dai, Lon was the son of a small shopkeeper who died when Lon was eight years old. His mother kept the family alive by selling fish and vegetables from a stall in the local market. Lon got a fourth-grade education in the village school—standard Vietnam—and then went to work, helping his mother and other relatives working in shops.

His older sister married a South Vietnamese ranger sergeant; his younger sister runs a flower stall at the airborne division base in Saigon.

Lon had a girl friend; she has moved to Nhatrang on the central coast and writes him every month. He had a lot of teen-age cronies; most of them dodged the draft until the police scooped them up.

"It was not a bad life," Lon said.

But at 18 he chose to be drafted into the regular army, rather than join the local Regional Forces or Popular Forces.

"I wanted to travel around the country and see new things," he said. "It was a mistake. I miss my family all the time."

In 1970, Lon was shipped off to the big Quangtrung Recruit Training Center (output: 30,000 men a year) where he got 10 weeks of basic training. After the easygoing life of the village, army discipline was a shock. He wound up in a 500-man battalion of the 25th Division, near Trangbang northwest of Saigon.

In 1970 and '71, it was not a rigorous war for Lon's unit: The allied invasion of the Cambodian sanctuaries had pushed most North Vietnamese regular battalions out of striking distance.

"Our battalion commander was easy on us, but not so brave," Lon recalled. "We did not do much hard fighting."

In those days, privates like Lon got four days' leave a month—and in some units, it is said, one could get one's leave extended, for a price.

Many of his comrades stayed longer. "They wanted to help their families, or just missed their families," Lon said.

When the errant trooper returned he wound up in a bamboo "Tiger cage," or (in the airborne) got a public beating or, in the worst cases, got sent to a penal battalion.

Since the March 30 offensive began, as Lon noted, desertions have continued. According to official sources, they now run at the rate of 12,000 a month—about the same level as last year—and the police have been fairly zealous about rounding them up.

Deserters in Vietnam do not normally defect to the Communists: They hide out with relatives or re-enlist in militia closer to home, or join the roving but Saigon-based elite marines or airborne.

Lon did not say whether he had ever gone AWOL, although his home village was only a 40-mile bus ride from Trangbang. "I often visited Saigon, with my friends," he said. He would spend a day's pay (70 cents) on a ticket to a Vietnamese movie, strong on passion and romance.

In any event, the army decided that Lon was needed further afield. He was transferred last December to the 21st Division's 31st Regiment, which was conducting a more arduous war in the swamps and canals of the Uminh forest in the Mekong Delta.

His new outfit was "better," Lon said. Why? The battalion commander, he allowed, was "not so easy on us. But he was brave and always with the troops."

With this remark, Lon touched on a theme common to all conversations in which South Vietnamese officers and U.S. advisers comment on the South Vietnamese army's fighting capacity: the extreme dependence of troops on personal leadership, in the absence of ideology, tradition or a coherent nationalism.

Indeed, another soldier, a Saigon-educated private from the 3rd Division, which was routed at Quangtri in May and now being rebuilt, said: "In the ARVN (South Vietnamese army), you are not serving the nation or the army. You are working for an individual. If he steals the rice, or mistreats the men, the unit is lousy. If he is good, the unit is good."

"In Vietnam," said a veteran U.S. adviser, "everybody looks up for direction, for inspiration. This culture puts a hell of a burden even on the good battalion commander. He's elder brother and big daddy to everybody. He decides everything. If he gets wounded or killed, the whole battalion of 500 men may fall apart."

This has caused Saigon's forces some grave losses during the current offensive. For example, the 20th Armor Battalion, newly equipped with 56 American M-48 tanks, reportedly fought well around Quangtri City in April until its commander was wounded. Then it fell apart. "The deputy who took over just didn't have the same charisma," said a U.S. adviser.

Lon's immediate superiors, by his account, were "brave" and "knew soldiering."

Most notably, his platoon leader was not a dandyish 19-year-old second lieutenant fresh out of Thu Duc Officer School —which until last year virtually guaranteed a commission to any middle-class youth who had passed his French-style baccalaureate (or university entrance exam). Nobody washed out of Thu Duc for lack of leadership qualities.

Lon's platoon was headed by a veteran sergeant first class, Danh Khuon. His company commander was a rarity in Saigon's forces, a first lieutenant promoted up from the enlisted ranks. He had been with the battalion for six years.

Lon himself became a squad leader, through seniority and the attrition of corporals and sergeants. He had only six men in his squad, instead of 10: two had been wounded, two others had been detailed to other jobs in the company.

"We get along well," he said. "We take turns cooking the rice (two meals a day) and getting the water." No senior officer, he said, levied a "tax" on the troops' $ -a-month ration allowance.

In April, Lon's division was shifted north from the Mekong Delta to the Highway 13 "front" north of Saigon. "At least we were out of the swamps," Lon said. "It was hot and flat, but it was dry."

At 9 A.M. on May 11, already tested by enemy fire, Lon's battalion joined yet another Saigon effort to open the road to Anloc. On that day, although Lon and his fellow troopers did not know it, the North Vietnamese army had begun a major assault on the battered town, coupled with a day-long barrage of some 6,000 rounds.

Lon's squad was, as usual, not briefed on the overall battalion plan, which was essentially a simple frontal push against North Vietnamese forces dug in on scrubby open terrain in deep bunkers.

The Saigon troops, then as later, had no heavy "direct fire" weapons of their own, such as 90 mm. recoilless rifles, to knock out the North Vietnamese bunkers. They had M-16s and grenades.

They had no special unit training in attacking fortified positions; Saigon's planners apparently hoped that air strikes and artillery shells, however imprecise, would do the job.

As the artillery burst over the treelines ahead, Lon said, Sgt. Khuon "pointed in the right direction, ordered us to advance, and everybody got up out of their foxholes and started moving ahead."

Seven crablike armored personnel carriers covered the advance, firing their .50-calibre machine guns.

Lon's company ran into a North Vietnamese listening post. "We had no foxholes to take cover in. We assaulted it from 30 meters away. We killed seven enemy and picked up four AK-47s," Lon said, with a touch of pride.

But the firefight alerted the enemy. The South Vietnamese skirmish line began to draw heavy fire from the main bunker line—which the bombs had once more failed to destroy.

Then 82 mm. mortar rounds began to explode among the exposed South Vietnamese infantrymen. The attack stalled.

The men went to ground. Their leaders felt that it was enough for one day in a long war.

"At noon, we pulled back to our old foxhole line and began digging deeper. The Communists kept shelling us with mortars. I got hit along with four others in the company," Lon said.

For lack of resources, Saigon's medical evacuation is a good deal less luxurious and speedy than the U.S. system. Lon was hastily bandaged and taken on a stretcher to the highway at Chonthanh.

A jolting truck ride to Laikhe got him to a division aid station where he got emergency treatment and a pain-killing shot of morphine. Only then was he lifted by helicopter, to Conghoa Hospital in Saigon.

"After 10 days in hospital," he said, "I felt better."

What's in prospect for Lon? "I'm hoping for a 30-day leave to go home," he said. "But they say only 15 days."

What after that?

"I'll go back to the unit. But maybe the war will end soon. I do not know."

The Washington Post, July 10, 1972

"WE HAVE BEEN FIGHTING ELEVEN CENTURIES": NORTH VIETNAM, JULY 1972

Letter from Hanoi

by Joseph Kraft

MORE than any other capital in the world, probably—and maybe in history as well—Hanoi has grown accustomed to living with war. The city takes its lumps less in the heroic style of London during the blitz than in the spirit of New York at rush hour. Life is unpleasant, and there is an evident need to subordinate self to a larger interest. Still, the misery wears a familiar aspect. It comes in short bursts, and people act in the certain conviction that the trouble will somehow be surmounted.

One reason trouble seems routine is that the American bombing is routine. Almost every day around noon, for instance, a pilotless reconnaissance plane flies in to photograph Hanoi. It moves so rapidly that there is no warning of its approach, and there is small chance for hits by either anti-aircraft guns or the surface-to-air missiles, known as SAMs, that the North Vietnamese have received from the Russians. Only the noise of the drone's breaking through the sound barrier announces its advent. It is a startling noise—like a sudden clap of thunder—but after almost four months of bombing hardly anybody in Hanoi bothers to look up. The drone is dismissed with a shrug as "the noon plane."

Even serious air raids—the raids of June 27th, July 4th, and July 22nd—have a regular pattern. Danger is first signalled by a pre-alert, broadcast through loudspeakers all over town, which announces that American planes have been sighted approaching Hanoi, usually from the southwest, at a distance of more than fifty kilometres—about thirty miles. A second pre-alert, soon afterward, announces that the planes are within the fifty-kilometre radius. Then, within a few minutes, the alert itself sounds—a long, wailing siren note that rises, dips, and then rises again. Minutes later, the planes come into sight—fighter-bombers, floating lazily and then diving on targets to drop bombs, which can be heard as they explode though not seen as they fall. As soon as the planes are visible, the racket of the anti-aircraft guns begins. Almost simultaneously, the SAMs can be seen, powered upward by rocket engines that give off a faint red glow. During the raid of July 4th, it was possible to follow the glow of a missile until a plane was struck and sent spinning to earth, trailing a cloud of black smoke. More often, the SAMs miss the planes, enter the upper atmosphere, and explode in a puff of white vapor. Then, suddenly, the planes are gone, and the siren is sounded on a steady note, signalling the all-clear. Several of the embassies here record the raids, both on film and on tape. The diplomats play the films and tapes over and over, and there has developed among them a kind of connoisseurs' taste in raids. One Canadian representative, before playing his recordings of the July 4th raid, remarked to me, "Visually, June 27th was a better raid, but sonically July 4th was superior." Listening to the recording, I had a chance to clock the raid; from first pre-alert to all-clear, it lasted twenty-seven minutes.

Short though the attacks are, they dominate life in Hanoi. A considerable part (some say forty per cent, some say twenty per cent) of the city's population has been removed to places of safety, in the mountains fifty miles northwest of Hanoi and elsewhere. Most of the government leaders seem to have left, apparently for a mountain hideout. Large numbers of young children have been evacuated, and the streets of Hanoi seem, by Asian standards, empty of boys and girls; when I went to change money recently at the state bank (a formidable pile that in French colonial days housed a main office of the Banque de l'Indochine), one of the women tellers had with her her little girl, who had come in from an evacuation camp for a couple of days.

As a further safety measure, virtually all public gatherings have been stopped. No films are being shown. The theatres are shut down, as are all museums. Boating on the Little Lake, a chief recreation spot in downtown Hanoi, has been suspended. The International Club, which has a pool where diplomats used to seek relief from the terrible hundred-degree heat of summer days, has been closed. Sunday Mass at the Cathedral is now said at four-thirty in the morning. The central markets have regulations to discourage shoppers from dawdling over their purchases, and an effort has been made to put decentralized, travelling markets in all neighborhoods.

The extent of the damage done by the bombing is hard to determine, especially for foreigners. We are restricted in our movements, and since even the driving of cars is forbidden, correspondents and diplomats must rely on government-assigned chauffeurs to get around. The general impression among Western diplomats is that, for reasons of morale, the government understates bombing losses. In trips I took outside Hanoi, I saw evidence of considerable destruction and death. The two main bridges leading east from Hanoi to the port of Haiphong have been bombed out, and the port itself is in ruins. All the major bridges on the road leading south to the Demilitarized Zone and the front lines have also been destroyed. The textile town of Nam Dinh, about forty-five miles southeast of Hanoi, has been badly battered, and presumably all towns farther south have been even more badly battered. South of Hanoi, I saw two spots where American bombs had seriously damaged the network of dikes that prevents the Red River from flooding in the rainy season (from mid-May through September): near Phu Ly, I saw a sluice gate that had been smashed; south of Nam Dinh, I saw a dike badly cracked and pitted by bomb craters. The hits were probably accidental, since both sites were close to more likely targets—roads and a railroad. But they did take place, and, in a sense—given the extent of the dikes (twenty-seven hundred miles), the number of bombing sorties daily over North Vietnam (about three hundred), and the probable error made by the pilots (quite substantial, in my judgment)—they were bound to take place. If the hitting of the dikes was not deliberate, it was surely predictable.

On the morning of July 8th, I visited a town thirty-six miles east of Hanoi—a trading center called Hung Wen, with a population of about twenty thousand—within twenty-four hours after it had been struck by American planes. The bombs had hit an area about a thousand yards long and five hundred yards wide in the middle of town. According to the local authorities, eighteen blast bombs had been dropped, along with four anti-personnel bombs; each of the latter contains 192,500 steel pellets, which are hurled through the air when the bomb explodes. Seventeen persons were killed and twenty-five wounded. Forty-three houses were destroyed, thirty-six by fire and seven by the force of concussion. One of the houses destroyed belonged to Vo Nguyen Dam. He and two of his children were killed; his wife and three other children survived. In the rubble of their home, I met one of the survivors, a married daughter. She had been burned in the attack, and was poking about in a dazed way. Bits of a body—a charred jawbone, a hank of hair, what looked like a leg—were lying around, and she was trying to assemble them. She kept muttering, "My brother and sister were innocent."

Another destroyed home belonged to Nguyen Van Lam, a seventy-two-year-old grandfather. He said that he was a Catholic and that his family had been saying prayers when the attack came. His wife, his only son, and his grandson had all been killed. He stood in the rubble, a toothless old man dressed in brownish-red pajamas, and raised his fists to the heavens. "I feel deep hatred against the Americans!" he shouted. "As long as I live, I will have hatred in my heart!"

All sixteen beds in the emergency ward of the local hospital were filled. As I entered, I saw a five-year-old boy, his body covered with burns. There was a thirteen-year-old girl whose left leg had been severed just above the knee. There were two children whose bodies were full of steel pellets from the anti-personnel bombs. The doctor who took me around said as we emerged from the ward, "You Americans say you do not mean to kill people. Why, then, do you use anti-personnel bombs?"

Some sections of Hanoi proper have been bombed. I was shown three public-housing projects, comprising about five hundred apartments, that had been destroyed in the raids of June 27th and July 4th. The authorities claim that the raid of July 22nd knocked out a water-purifying plant. I was told that hospitals and schools had been hit in raids during the spring. The industrial power plant for the city has been destroyed, and the electric current that emanates from the remaining power plant is feeble and subject to repeated failure. But otherwise Hanoi is remarkably intact. It bears the aspect of a nineteenth-century French provincial capital, very clean and rather drab, with broad, tree-lined avenues and airy public buildings of reddish or mustard-colored concrete. The working day starts around dawn, breaks at eleven for four hours, and resumes at three in the afternoon for another four hours. At the beginning and end of every break, the streets are filled with men and women going to and from offices, shops, and factories. The men wear sandals, cotton trousers, and short-sleeved sports shirts, usually white and open at the neck. The women are dressed in the traditional *ao dai*, and they all seem to have the lissome beauty made so familiar to Americans by the women of South Vietnam. Compared with Saigon, where the streets are messy with beggars, prostitutes, peddlers, and families cooking on the sidewalks, Hanoi has almost no street life. The police and the military, both highly visible in Saigon, are rarely seen in Hanoi; even their manning of checkpoints at the city gates—by soldiers in little huts, which they rarely leave—is discreet.

Most shopping is done in the early morning, and the closest thing to a crowd in Hanoi is the collection of housewives bustling about the central market just after dawn. By making huge purchases of food, both abroad and from peasants at home, and by rationing such goods as rice and cloth, the government keeps the prices of necessities within the reach of a consuming public whose earnings average ninety dong, or thirty dollars, a month. Rationed rice (under a system that allots thirty-three pounds a month to a worker, nineteen to a child, and thirty to a government minister) costs about six and a half cents a pound. When I visited the market, beef was going for about forty-five cents a pound, fresh carp for thirty-five cents a pound, fish sauce for twenty cents a pound, and fresh eggs for a dollar a dozen. Pineapples cost twenty cents apiece, tomatoes thirty-five cents a pound. Ducks were being sold, live, at thirty cents a pound.

Goods other than food are bought at government-controlled department or specialty stores. At one department store, I priced soap at twenty cents a bar for a Russian-made brand and forty cents a bar for a luxury item from East

Germany, conical hats at eighty cents apiece, plastic raincoats at a dollar apiece, and sleeping mats at forty cents. Sandals cost four dollars a pair, and shoes were on special sale, reduced from eight dollars a pair to six dollars. A short-wave radio cost three hundred and fifty dollars, a Russian-made camera five hundred dollars. Next to the department store was a tailor shop, and there I found shirts selling for three dollars and fifteen cents apiece, and trousers for four dollars and seventy-five cents a pair. Next to the tailor shop was a Western restaurant—the Restaurant of European Dishes. Its menu, which was displayed, in the Continental style, outside the entrance, included a beef dish for thirty cents, an omelette for thirty cents, and stuffed crab for sixty cents. I had some of the crab, and it was very good.

The availability of fresh seafood in a Hanoi restaurant bears on one of the never-ending American arguments about Vietnam. Despite the mining of the harbors since mid-May, and the intensive bombing of all internal transportation lines, North Vietnam is plainly not paralyzed. Large quantities of goods move at a fairly rapid clip all the time. Trucks provide the chief means of transport, and downtown Hanoi, where the bombing is relatively sporadic, has become a kind of national parking lot. The railways have been cut at all the major rivers, but at night I saw several trains being pulled by steam locomotives on the lines between bridges. One foreign ambassador told me that on a nighttime trip to Haiphong he had counted seven moving freight trains. I myself have no evidence that a way around the mining has been found, but the Swedish Embassy here recently received a consignment of tonic water sent by sea, and curtains sent by ship to the British mission arrived the other day. Rumors persist that the North Vietnamese are unloading freighter cargoes at sea onto landing craft and other shallow-draft wooden vessels, which pass over the mines without activating them.

Laborious individual effort, systematically organized and repeated over and over again, is required to keep transport moving. Pontoon bridges have been set up to replace most of the bombed-out road bridges. Traffic moves in one-way bursts of half an hour each; at fixed times sections of the pontoon bridges are removed to allow passage of river traffic. To supplement the pontoon bridges, ferries—usually barges pushed by river steamers—have been set up at most major crossings. Sections of the railways are constantly being demolished by bombing and are constantly being replaced. Pontoon bridges cannot replace the destroyed railway bridges, but the North Vietnamese move merchandise by rail between bridges, then load it on trucks for the river crossing, and then back on freight cars. The trucks come from all corners of the Communist world—Russia, China, Czechoslovakia, East Germany —and they have been painted brown, numbered, and incorporated into a national fleet. They move mainly by night, with headlights hooded. During the day, they line the streets of Hanoi, parked in the shadow of buildings or trees and often camouflaged with leafy branches.

Underlying this laborious effort is a furious concentration on the war and its object—reunification with South Vietnam. The foremost official expression of this well-nigh obsessive focus is the last will and testament of President Ho Chi Minh, written in May of 1969 and published at his death, on September 3rd of that year. "Even though our people's struggle against U.S. aggression, for national salvation, may have to go through more hardships and sacrifices, we are bound to win total victory," the testament begins. A subsequent passage asserts:

The war of resistance against U.S. aggression may drag on. Our people may have to face new sacrifices of life and property. Whatever happens, we must keep firm our resolve to fight the U.S. aggressors till total victory.

> Our mountains will always be, our rivers will always be,
>   our people will always be;
> The American invaders defeated, we will rebuild our land
>   ten times more beautiful.

No matter what difficulties and hardships lie ahead, our people are sure of total victory. The U.S. imperialists will certainly have to quit. Our fatherland will certainly be reunified. Our fellow-countrymen in the South and in the North will certainly be reunited under the same roof. We, a small nation, will have earned the signal honor of defeating, through heroic struggle, two big imperialisms—the French and the American—and of making a worthy contribution to the world national-liberation movement.

The six leading officials of North Vietnam—Le Duan, the First Secretary of the Workers', or Communist, Party; Truong Chinh, the President of the National Assembly; Vo Nguyen Giap, the Defense Minister; Pham Van Dong, the Prime Minister; Nguyen Duy Trinh, a Deputy Prime Minister and Foreign Minister; and Le Duc Tho, the Politburo member who sits on the North Vietnamese delegation to the Paris peace talks—have all sworn allegiance to Ho's testament. Parts of the testament are reprinted under pictures of Ho in markets, offices, and other public places. A placard bearing the line "No matter what difficulties and hardships lie ahead, our people are sure of total victory" is situated at a particularly lovely spot on the shore of the Little Lake in Hanoi. When I remarked to my interpreter that that seemed a queer place to put a call to arms, he replied that, on the contrary, it was entirely appropriate. The Little Lake, he told me, was also known as the Lake of the Restored Sword. In the early fifteenth century, at a time when Vietnam was being invaded by the Chinese from the north, the Emperor Le Loi was out boating, and a tortoise surfaced and gave the Emperor a sword. With that sword, the Emperor beat the Chinese. He then went back to the lake and returned the sword to the tortoise. "The lake," my interpreter said, "is the symbol of our will to be a nation."

Another sign of the intense national commitment to the struggle is the Vietnamese radio. The Voice of Vietnam, as the radio is called, is the principal national medium. Among the twenty-one million residents of North Vietnam, there are five hundred thousand private radios and six hundred thousand loudspeaker units to relay broadcasts to the villages and hamlets. "Our main subject is the fight against U.S. aggression," Tran Lam, the director of the Voice of Vietnam, told me. "Our whole program has as its central theme the strength of our people versus U.S. aggression." On one typical morning, broadcasting began at five with a fifteen-minute program for the peasants. The subject, according to Mr. Lam, was "how to achieve high yield in rice cultivation despite the bombing." At five-fifteen, there was a two-part news bulletin. The first part announced "victories achieved in the past twenty-four hours in North and South Vietnam." The second part dealt with "threats to the dikes by U.S. imperialists and the condemnation of their action by the world public." At five-thirty-five, an announcer read the day's lead editorial in *Nhan Dan*, the official newspaper of the Workers' Party; it dealt with an anti-aircraft unit and the techniques used against low-flying American planes. At five-forty-five, there was a children's program on the subject of "how young people in the country should receive city children who are being evacuated." So it went for the rest of the day. The last program, at eleven o'clock at night, was a study of "crimes committed by the U.S. and the lackey Thieu [as President Nguyen Van Thieu is always called here] in terrorizing the students of South Vietnam." The sign-off, at eleven-thirty, was an announcement of the number of American planes shot down —with a separate figure for hits on B-52s—since the war began.

This ceaseless concentration on a war waged against heavy odds has caused some Vietnamese, particularly in the leadership circles, to see themselves at the center of world history—a nation anointed to carry the torch of revolution. In a speech published on February 3rd, which is now deemed important as an expression of Hanoi's decision to launch the March 30th offensive in South Vietnam, Truong Chinh, the Assembly President, called Vietnam "the focus of the basic contradictions of human society." Nguyen Khac Vien, the French-educated editor of the scholarly publication *Vietnamese Studies*, with whom I had one of my rare unsupervised interviews, expounded on the theme without any evident self-consciousness. "Vietnam has become the focus of the three conflicts central to the present age," he said, as though he were stating a known fact apparent to the meanest intelligence. "It is the front line in the fight between colonialists and anti-colonialists. It is the front line in the fight between capitalists and Socialists. It is the front line in the international class struggle between the rich and the people."

Hong Chuong, an editor of the Communist monthly

theoretical journal *Hoc Tap*, made the same point with what seemed to me melodramatic self-importance. I met him in the *Hoc Tap* offices, which are in a pleasant tower-shaped building overlooking a pond. The reception room was decorated with cases full of historical mementoes, including a first edition of *Pravda*, some medals depicting Lenin and Ho Chi Minh, and some fragments of American bombs. The ashtrays in the reception room were made from bomb casings. I opened the conversation by asking for a few biographical details, and Mr. Chuong told me, "We don't speak about ourselves, because we consider each individual a drop of water in the ocean of the people. But I can tell you that I am a journalist about fifty years old."

I asked Mr. Chuong whether he was born in North or South Vietnam. He said, "We don't make that distinction. Our President, our Prime Minister, and the First Secretary of our Party were born in the South. Our country is one. The problem of partition is a problem that has been made by you American imperialists."

I asked him to tell me about the Vietnamese approach to Marxism and how it differs from the Russian and Chinese approaches. He said, "Our tradition is one of fighting, and we put it in the framework of Leninism. It is not enough to say that we have been fighting for thirty years. We have been fighting for much longer than that. We have made a contribution to Socialism in military thinking. Let me take as an example our national hero Tran Huong Dao. He rose up against the Mongol invasions two centuries before Columbus. These were the same Mongols who took China and India and Europe. They were defeated in Vietnam. Not once but three times we defeated them. And each time, I may say, we took prisoners and released them—fifty thousand each time. I once read an article by an American comparing Tran Huong Dao with Clausewitz. I think that underestimates Tran Huong Dao. Clausewitz existed in the eighteenth century; Tran Huong Dao was five centuries before him. Moreover, Tran Huong Dao was not only a great military writer, as was Clausewitz. He was also a great general of armies. I think Tran Huong Dao is a head taller than Clausewitz.

"But you asked about the originality of Vietnamese Socialism. Here is an example. In Russia, Lenin replaced Kerensky and the Czar. Lenin represented the proletariat, and Kerensky and the Czar represented the bourgeoisie and the nobles. But they were all Russians. In China, Mao Tse-tung replaced Chiang Kai-shek. Mao represented the peasants, and Chiang was a representative of the warlords. But they were both Chinese. In Vietnam, however, Ho Chi Minh replaced the Japanese Fascists and the French colonialists. President Ho was Vietnamese. They were foreigners. Our contribution to Marxism is not a question of doctrine. We have creative minds, and we are not stuck on any formula. One mistake that the Americans always make is to think that we will do what the Russians did or the Chinese did. In that sense, you are dogmatists. But we follow our own ways, and that is why you are being defeated. If there is a single piece of advice I would give to Kissinger, the adviser of Nixon, it would be: Abandon dogmatism. For instance, in chess you can imagine a board full of pieces where the right move will win. You can also imagine a board where most of the pieces are gone and where the right move will also win. We have used both tactics against the Americans."

I said that I was not sure I followed his argument, and he said, "A baby of two cannot understand an adult of forty, but an adult of forty can understand a baby of two. The United States will be two hundred years old in four years. Vietnam is now four thousand years old. Vietnam can understand the two-hundred-year-old United States. But the United States cannot understand the four-thousand-year-old Vietnam. Nixon said recently that the war had lasted eleven years and had been hard and long. For us, it has not been long enough. We have been fighting eleven centuries, not eleven years. We fought eighty years against the French. When we came to understand that we would have to fight against the United States, we were sure it would take longer. We thought it would take a century, and we are ready to fight for a century. But Nixon has only two cards to play now. He can destroy Hanoi. That is one. He can destroy the dikes. That is the other. But we are not afraid. Let him play them. After that, he will be defeated."

After that interview, I told Ngo Dien, the official of the

North Vietnamese Foreign Office who had finally approved my application for a visa to Hanoi, that some of his country-men seemed to me positively fanatical in their single-minded attention to Vietnam and the war. He said, "We are not fa-natics. If we were fanatics, we would lynch the pilots when they were shot down, not treat them correctly in prison camps. If we were fanatics, you would not be here." He went on to point out that immoderate boasting was one response of a small and backward country caught up in a war with a great power, and that another response was to show the spe-cial modesty personified by Ho Chi Minh. "The example of our President," he said, "has had a great impact on the Viet-namese people."

Perhaps by accident, perhaps by prearrangement, in every-thing that happened to me thereafter in Hanoi the softer side of the Vietnamese character emerged. A curious instance oc-curred at a dinner given for me by the Vietnamese press as-sociation. Among the guests was Colonel Ha Van Lau, the officer who negotiated the military cease-fire with the French back in 1954, and a former member of the North Vietnamese delegation to the Paris peace talks—a man whom I had come to know as the toughest of the tough. Colonel Lau is now in charge of the office that investigates what the North Viet-namese call American war crimes. In an earlier encounter dur-ing my visit to Hanoi, Colonel Lau had described American depredations against his country in the harshest terms. He had flung out his words contemptuously, the way a Spaniard spits. But at dinner he was another person. We talked about Presi-dent Nixon's visit to China and his trip to the Great Wall. I said that the President's comments had not been distinguished but that it was hard to know how an American President should respond to the sight of the Great Wall. Someone sug-gested that he should have written a poem. "Better a song," Colonel Lau put in. He said that songs were particularly suit-able to memorable places. He said there was one song that always reminded him of Paris. It was sung by an American, Josephine Baker. Did I know it? And suddenly the severe mil-itary man, who sometimes, in the fury of his nationalism, affected not to speak French, began to sing, in a voice that wasn't at all bad:

> *"J'ai deux amours*
> *Mon pays et Paris. . . ."*

The next day, an interview was arranged with Nguyen Dinh Thi, a writer, whose work ranges from a critique of Aristotle to a song that the national radio uses as its theme. One of his novels, "The Dike That Exploded," was a best-seller. As secretary of the Writers' Union, he has been in touch with literary figures the world over. Yevtushenko had been his guest during a visit to Vietnam. "I liked him very much," Thi said. "But he is an actor. I told him, 'You are the Don Quixote of world literature.' " Thi told me that "by tradition and wisdom and the teachings of Ho Chi Minh, the Vietnamese people have developed a spirit of bitter intransigence in a fight." He went on, "Our people are performing now as the victims of barbarism. I regret that you haven't seen another side of us. We are poor. We are used to a hard life. We have typhoons every year. We do the back-breaking work of cultivating rice. Our tradition is that everybody helps everybody else. We respect literature more than war in our country, and there has never been a military caste here, as there was in Japan. An expression we use all the time is '*Tinh thuong*,' which means a combination of pity, compassion, and love. We know that we live on the edges of the great powers. We see that we have to be prudent and modest. We have a great sense of humanity, a sense of the pity of humanity."

At a reception the day after that, I met Ton That Tung, a distinguished surgeon and a relative of the former emperor Bao Dai. Among other things, Dr. Tung has translated into French the works of To Huu, a leading contemporary poet, who works in the Secretariat of the Workers' Party. I told Dr. Tung that some of his countrymen seemed peculiarly harsh to me—as if fighting were the only way they knew of to achieve things. I asked him if there was anything that he found unique in the Vietnamese personality. He said, "You should notice that when we entertain we never lord it over people—we put them wholly at ease. And we don't have religious disputes;

except when foreigners were involved, we had toleration for all religions."

He asked me what other impressions I had of North Vietnam. I said something about the need to end the war. Feeling that to be banal, I added that the two sides seemed so far apart and that there was so little mutual trust that I was pessimistic about a settlement. Dr. Tung was not so pessimistic. He said, "I know your people are tired of the war. Do you think our people want to go on fighting forever?"

I found that leaving Hanoi was almost as hard as getting there. Only four regular planes a week come to Hanoi: two small Chinese planes with chancy connections through Nanning to Canton and Hong Kong; an Ilyushin 18, run by Aeroflot, which goes out through Laos; and a converted Second World War Stratoliner, which is run by the International Control Commission set up at the Geneva Conference of 1954, and which also goes out through Laos. Bad weather forced two cancellations, but finally I left aboard the Russian airliner. My chauffeur, my interpreter, and a woman guide from the Foreign Ministry who had supervised my entire trip all came out to the Gia Lam airport to escort me through customs and wait for the plane to take off. As we sipped beer and lemonade in the departure lounge, a good cross-section of the foreign diplomats and journalists stationed in Hanoi passed in review. They are cut off from normal Vietnamese life by the language barrier and various restrictions, including the prohibition against driving cars. Much as settlers in the West used to arrange their lives around the pony express, the foreign colony in Hanoi orders its life around the planes from the outside world. Among those I saw were an Arab diplomat, who assured me that a particularly tough statement put out the night before by the North Vietnamese Foreign Ministry was done for "domestic consumption," and an East European diplomat, who said the statement showed that revisionism was finally taking hold in Hanoi. A military attaché observed that he had recently been counting the number of anti-aircraft guns parked along the road from Hanoi to Gia Lam; it was down from ninety-six a week ago to sixty-two—a probable sign that the guns had been moved south, toward the front. A West European diplomat observed that though the Paris peace negotiations had resumed, they would probably not get anywhere, because the North Vietnamese did not feel for Nixon the kind of trust they felt for Pierre Mendès-France, who negotiated the Geneva settlement back in 1954. I also saw a Russian diplomat, with whom I shared a bomb shelter at the Foreign Ministry during an air-raid alert, and a Soviet journalist—one of two indistinguishable heavies representing *Pravda* and *Izvestia*, who were known to the speakers of English in Hanoi as Mutt and Jeff. As each of these passing acquaintances talked, my guide drew for me on a napkin the ideograms used to denote their countries. I asked her to draw the characters for America. She did, and then she said, "Literally, the characters mean 'beautiful country.' I wish you Americans would stop behaving in a way that is— I won't say it. I wish you would start behaving again in a way that is beautiful."

The New Yorker, August 12, 1972

from *Fear and Loathing on the Campaign Trail '72*

by Hunter S. Thompson

Dozen Protestors Do About-Face

Sgt. Roy Gates, an Army recruiter in Miami Beach, looked out his carpeted and paneled office at a sign in the window saying, "Non-delegates—Help Wanted."

In what must rank as one of the Army's finest recruiting efforts, Gates thought he had convinced 13 non-delegates during the conventions to enlist in the military.

Nine of the protesters, however, failed to pass the Army's intelligence tests.

"Their low education surprised me—around the eighth grade and wanting to change the world," he said. "They said they didn't want to go along with the hard core radicals. It's amazing the different types you find." —Miami *News*, Friday, August 25

On Tuesday afternoon my car disappeared. I left it on the street in front of the hotel while I went in to pick up my swimming trunks, and when I came back out, it was gone.

To hell with it, I thought, it was time to get out of Miami.

I went up to my room and thought for a while, sitting with my back to the typewriter and staring out the window at the big ocean-going yachts and luxury houseboats tied up across the street, at the piers along Indian Creek. Last week they'd been crawling with people, and cocktail parties. Every time the Fontainebleau lobby started buzzing with rumors about another crowd of demonstrators bearing down on the hotel from the direction of Flamingo Park, the boats across Collins Avenue would fill up with laughing Republican delegates wearing striped blazers and cocktail dresses. There was no better place, they said, for watching the street action. As the demonstrators approached the front entrance to the hotel, they found themselves walking a gauntlet of riot-equipped police on one side, and martini-sipping GOP delegates on the other.

One yacht—the Wild Rose, out of Houston—rumbled back and forth, just offshore, at every demonstration. From the middle of Collins Avenue, you could see the guests lounging in deck chairs, observing the action through high-powered field glasses, and reaching around from time to time to accept a fresh drink from crewmen wearing white serving jackets with gold epaulets.

The scene on the foredeck of the Wild Rose was so gross, so flagrantly decadent, that it was hard to avoid comparing it with the kind of bloodthirsty arrogance normally associated with the last days of the Roman Empire: Here was a crowd of rich Texans, floating around on a $100,000 yacht in front of a palatial Miami Beach hotel, giggling with excitement at the prospect of watching their hired gladiators brutalize a mob of howling, half-naked Christians. I half-expected them to start whooping for blood and giving the Thumbs Down signal.

Nobody who was out there on the street with the demonstrators would be naive enough to compare them to "help-less Christians." With the lone exception of the Vietnam Veterans Against the War, the demonstrators in Miami were a useless mob of ignorant, chicken-shit ego-junkies whose only accomplishment was to embarrass the whole tradition of public protest. They were hopelessly disorganized, they had no real purpose in being there, and about half of them were so wasted on grass, wine, and downers that they couldn't say for sure whether they were raising hell in Miami or San Diego.

Five weeks earlier, these same people had been sitting in the lobby of the Doral, calling George McGovern a "lying pig" and a "warmonger." Their target-hotel this time was the Fon-tainebleau, headquarters for the national press and many TV cameras. If the Rolling Stones came to Miami for a free con-cert, these assholes would build their own fence around the bandstand—just so they could have something to tear down and then "crash the gates."

The drug action in Flamingo Park, the official campground

for "non-delegates" and other would-be "protesters," was so
bottom-heavy with downers that it was known as "Quaalude
Alley."

Quaalude is a mild sleeping pill, but—consumed in large
quantities, along with wine, grass, and adrenaline—it produces the same kind of stupid, mean-drunk effect as Seconal
("Reds"). The Quaalude effect was so obvious in Flamingo
Park that the "Last Patrol" caravan of Vietnam Vets—who
came here in motorcades from all parts of the country—refused to even set up camp with the other demonstrators. They
had serious business in Miami, they explained, and the last
thing they needed was a public alliance with a mob of stoned
street crazies and screaming teenyboppers.

The Vets made their camp in a far corner of the Park, then
sealed it off with a network of perimeter guards and checkpoints that made it virtually impossible to enter that area unless you knew somebody inside. There was an ominous sense
of dignity about everything the VVAW did in Miami. They
rarely even hinted at violence, but their very presence was

MIAMI: AUGUST 1972   647

menacing—on a level that the Yippies, Zippies, and SDS street crazies never even approached, despite all their yelling and trashing.*

The most impressive single performance in Miami during the three days of the GOP convention was the VVAW march on the Fontainebleau on Tuesday afternoon. Most of the press and TV people were either down at the Convention Hall,

---

*Earlier that week, Lucian Truscott from the *Village Voice* and I tried to arrange a brief chat between John "Duke" Wayne and about two dozen Vets from the vanguard of the Last Patrol. They had just arrived in Miami and when they heard Wayne was holding an "open" press conference at Nixon headquarters in the Doral they decided to stop by and pick up on it.

But the GOP security guards wouldn't let them in—so they moved about a half block down Collins Avenue to a public parking lot on the edge of the ocean—where they were quickly surrounded, at a discreet distance, by a cordon of Florida state troopers.

"Say, man," a vet in a wheelchair called out to me after I'd used my press credentials to penetrate the cop-cordon, "Can you get that asshole Wayne out here to talk to us?"

"Why not?" I said. "He's tough as nails, they say. He'd probably *enjoy* coming out here in the sun and abusing you dope-addled communist dupes for a while."

"The Duke fears nothing," Lucian added. "We'll bring him out right after his press conference."

But John Wayne was not eager that day for a chat with the Last Patrol. "What the hell do they want to talk about?" he asked.

"Yeah, *what?*" said his drinking buddy, Glenn Ford. They were standing on the front steps of the Doral waiting for a cab.

"They just want to shoot the bull," said Lucian. "You know, maybe talk about the war . . ."

"*What* war?" Ford snapped.

"The one in Vietnam," Lucian replied. "These guys all fought over there—a lot of them are crippled."

The Duke seemed agitated; he was scanning the street for a cab. Finally, without looking at us, he said: "Naw, not today. I can't see the point in it."

"Why not?" Lucian asked. "They just want to *talk*. They're not looking for trouble. Hell, the place is crawling with cops."

Wayne hesitated, then shook his head again as he suddenly spotted a cab. "So they just want to *talk*, eh?" he said with a thin smile.

I nodded. "Why not. It won't take long."

"Bullshit," Wayne replied. "If they got somethin' to say to me, tell 'em to put it in writing."

Then he waved us away and eased off across the driveway to the waiting cab. "Playboy Plaza," he barked. "Jesus, I need a *drink*."

covering the "liberals vs. conservatives" floor-fight over rules for seating delegates in 1976—or standing around in the boiling mid-afternoon sun at Miami International Airport, waiting for Nixon to come swooping out of the sky in Air Force One.

My own plan for that afternoon was to drive far out to the end of Key Biscayne and find an empty part of the beach where I could swim by myself in the ocean, and not have to talk to anybody for a while. I didn't give a fuck about watching the rules fight, a doomed charade that the Nixon braintrust had already settled in favor of the conservatives . . . and I saw no point in going out to the airport to watch three thousand well-rehearsed "Nixon Youth" robots "welcome the President."

Given these two depressing options, I figured Tuesday was as good a day as any to get away from politics and act like a human being for a change—or better still, like an animal. Just get off by myself and drift around naked in the sea for a few hours. . . .

But as I drove toward Key Biscayne with the top down, squinting into the sun, I saw the Vets. . . . They were moving up Collins Avenue in dead silence; twelve hundred of them dressed in battle fatigues, helmets, combat boots . . . a few carried full-size plastic M-16s, many peace symbols, girlfriends walking beside vets being pushed along the street in slow-moving wheelchairs, others walking jerkily on crutches. . . . But nobody spoke; all the "stop, start," "fast, slow," "left, right" commands came from "platoon leaders" walking slightly off to the side of the main column and using hand signals.

One look at that eerie procession killed my plan to go swimming that afternoon. I left my car at a parking meter in front of the Cadillac Hotel and joined the march. . . . No, "joined" is the wrong word; that was not the kind of procession you just walked up and "joined." Not without paying some very heavy dues: an arm gone here, a leg there, paralysis, a face full of lumpy scar tissue . . . all staring straight ahead as the long silent column moved between rows of hotel porches full of tight-lipped Senior Citizens, through the heart of Miami Beach.

The silence of the march was contagious, almost threatening. There were hundreds of spectators, but nobody said a word. I walked beside the column for ten blocks, and the only sounds I remember hearing were the soft thump of boot leather on hot asphalt and the occasional rattling of an open canteen top.

The Fontainebleau was already walled off from the street by five hundred heavily armed cops when the front ranks of the Last Patrol arrived, still marching in total silence. Several hours earlier, a noisy mob of Yippie/Zippie/SDS "non-delegates" had shown up in front of the Fontainebleau and been met with jeers and curses from GOP delegates and other partisan spectators, massed behind the police lines. . . . But now there was no jeering. Even the cops seemed deflated. They watched nervously from behind their face-shields as the VVAW platoon leaders, still using hand signals, funneled the column into a tight semicircle that blocked all three north-bound lanes of Collins Avenue. During earlier demonstrations—at least six in the past three days—the police had poked people with riot sticks to make sure at least one lane of the street stayed open for local traffic, and on the one occasion when mere prodding didn't work, they had charged the demonstrators and cleared the street completely.

But not now. For the first and only time during the whole convention, the cops were clearly off balance. The Vets could have closed all six lanes of Collins Avenue if they'd wanted to, and nobody would have argued. I have been covering anti-war demonstrations with depressing regularity since the winter of 1964, in cities all over the country, and I have never seen cops so intimidated by demonstrators as they were in front of the Fontainebleau Hotel on that hot Tuesday afternoon in Miami Beach.

There was an awful tension in that silence. Not even that pack of rich sybarites out there on the foredeck of the Wild Rose of Houston could stay in their seats for this show. They were standing up at the rail, looking worried, getting very bad vibrations from whatever was happening over there in the street. Was something *wrong* with their gladiators? Were they spooked? And why was there no noise?

After five more minutes of harsh silence, one of the VVAW platoon leaders suddenly picked up a bullhorn and said: "We want to come inside."

Nobody answered, but an almost visible shudder ran through the crowd. "O my God!" a man standing next to me muttered. I felt a strange tightness coming over me, and I reacted instinctively—for the first time in a long, long while—by slipping my notebook into my belt and reaching down to take off my watch. The first thing to go in a street fight is always your watch, and once you've lost a few, you develop a certain instinct that lets you know when it's time to get the thing off your wrist and into a safe pocket.

I can't say for sure what I would have done if the Last Patrol had tried to crack the police line and seize control of the Fontainebleau—but I have a fair idea, based on instinct and rude experience, so the unexpected appearance of Congressman Pete McCloskey on that scene calmed my nerves considerably. He shoved his way through the police line and talked with a handful of the VVAW spokesmen long enough to convince them, apparently, that a frontal assault on the hotel would be suicidal.

One of the platoon leaders smiled faintly and assured McCloskey that they'd never had any intention of attacking the Fontainebleau. They didn't even *want* to go in. The only reason they asked was to see if the Republicans would turn them away in front of network TV cameras—which they did, but very few cameras were on hand that afternoon to record it. All the network floor crews were down at the Convention Hall, and the ones who would normally have been on standby alert at the Fontainebleau were out at the airport filming Nixon's arrival.

No doubt there were backup crews around somewhere—but I suspect they were up on the roof, using very long lenses; because in those first few moments when the Vets began massing in front of the police line there was no mistaking the potential for real violence . . . and it was easy enough to see, by scanning the faces behind those clear plastic riot masks, that the cream of the Florida State Highway Patrol had no appetite at all for a public crunch with twelve hundred angry Vietnam Veterans.

Whatever the outcome, it was a guaranteed nightmare situation for the police. Defeat would be bad enough, but victory would be intolerable. Every TV screen in the nation would show a small army of heavily armed Florida cops clubbing unarmed veterans—some on crutches and others in wheelchairs—whose only crime was trying to enter Republican convention headquarters in Miami Beach. How could Nixon explain a thing like that? Could he slither out from under it?

Never in hell, I thought—and all it would take to make a thing like that happen, right now, would be for one or two Vets to lose control of themselves and try to crash through the police line; just enough violence to make *one* cop use his riot stick. The rest would take care of itself.

Ah, nightmares, nightmares. . . . Not even Sammy Davis Jr. could stomach that kind of outrage. He would flee the Nixon family compound on Key Biscayne within moments after the first news bulletin, rejecting his newfound soul brother like a suckfish cutting loose from a mortally wounded shark . . . and the next day's Washington *Post* would report that Sammy Davis Jr. had spent most of the previous night trying to ooze through the keyhole of George McGovern's front door in Washington, D.C.

Right . . . but none of this happened. McCloskey's appearance seemed to soothe both the crowd and the cops. The only violent act of the afternoon occurred moments later when a foul-mouthed twenty-year-old blonde girl named Debby Marshal tried to ram her way through the crowd on a 125 Honda. "Get out of my way!" she kept shouting. "This is ridiculous! These people should go back where they belong!"

The Vets ignored her, but about halfway through the crowd she ran into a nest of press photographers, and that was as far as she went. An hour later she was still sitting there, biting her lips and whining about how "ridiculous" it all was. I was tempted to lean over and set her hair on fire with my Zippo, but by that time the confrontation had settled down to a series

of bullhorn speeches by various Vets. Not much of what was said could be heard more than fifteen feet from the bullhorn, however, because of two Army helicopters that suddenly appeared overhead and filled the whole street with their noise. The only Vet speaker who managed to make himself plainly understood above the chopper noise was an ex-Marine Sergeant from San Diego named Ron Kovic, who spoke from a wheelchair because his legs are permanently paralyzed.

I would like to have a transcript or at least a tape of what Kovic said that day, because his words lashed the crowd like a wire whip. If Kovic had been allowed to speak from the convention hall podium, in front of network TV cameras, Nixon wouldn't have had the balls to show up and accept the nomination.

No . . . I suspect that's wishful thinking. Nothing in the realm of human possibility could have prevented Richard Nixon from accepting that nomination. If God himself had showed up in Miami and denounced Nixon from the podium, hired gunsels from the Committee for the Re-Election of the President would have quickly had him arrested for disturbing the peace.

Vietnam veterans like Ron Kovic are not welcome in Nixon's White House. They tried to get in last year, but they could only get close enough to throw their war medals over the fence. That was perhaps the most eloquent anti-war statement ever made in this country, and that Silent March on the Fontainebleau on August 22 had the same ugly sting to it.

There is no anti-war or even anti-establishment group in America today with the psychic leverage of the VVAW. Not even those decadent swine on the foredeck of the Wild Rose can ignore the dues Ron Kovic and his buddies have paid. They are golems, come back to haunt us all—even Richard Nixon, who campaigned for the presidency in 1968 with a promise that he had "a secret plan" to end the war in Vietnam.

Which was true, as it turns out. The plan was to end the war just in time to get himself re-elected in 1972. Four more years.

from *Fear and Loathing on the Campaign Trail, '72*, 1973;
illustrations by Ralph Steadman

Who Was This Enemy?

by Fox Butterfield

When the war has ended and the road is open again,
the same stars will course through the heavens.
Then will I weep for the white bones heaped together in
*   desolate graves*
of those who sought military honors for their leaders.
>   —From a diary of an unknown
>   North Vietnamese soldier, 1965.

SAIGON. One afternoon many years ago when the Vietnam war was still new to Americans, an eager young U.S. Special Forces officer lay watching a branch of the Ho Chi Minh trail in the jungle of southern Laos. It was raining hard, and as he and his three companions waited uncomfortably under their camouflaged ponchos, a silent column of North Vietnamese soldiers suddenly materialized on the path in front of them.

"They were marching in perfect discipline, like nothing I'd ever seen before," the American officer recalled recently. "They didn't talk, shout or horse around, like G.I.'s or South Vietnamese troops; and they kept the proper distance between one another. For two hours they kept filing past; there must have been a couple thousand of them."

What particularly surprised the officer was that intelligence reports from prisoners and captured documents showed that the Communist troops on the trail were badly short of food, exhausted and homesick. "'How could they maintain discipline like that if they were in such bad shape,' I asked myself."

It is a mystery that has confounded a generation of C.I.A. agents, Pentagon planners and White House advisers. And it is precisely the problem that has made President Nguyen Van Thieu nervous about the peace settlement—for under the accord more than 100,000 North Vietnamese soldiers will be permitted to stay on in the South, men who were well-disciplined enough to march down the trail even while thinking that for the vast majority of them it would be a one-way street. They were men who subsisted for weeks at a time on little better than a handful of rice and some roasted salt. They were bombed by B-52's that fly so high they could neither see nor hear them until the bombs exploded. Once in the South they were not able to send or receive mail; and if they died, their families were not notified for years afterward, if ever.

Of the 700,000 to 800,000 North Vietnamese soldiers who have come down the trail since 1965—about 100,000 men a year—virtually none except for high-ranking officers ever got back to North Vietnam before 1968, American intelligence officials believe. Soldiers who had been sent south simply fought on until they were killed or were too badly wounded to continue, in which case they were taken to rest camps and hospitals nearby in Laos and Cambodia. After the Tet offensive of 1968, however, there was a gradually increasing flow of wounded and disabled troops back to North Vietnam, perhaps 200,000 in all. But there was little rotation of active units back to the North.

Fortunately, many North Vietnamese infantrymen kept a record of their experiences—diaries, poems, notebooks of comments by comrades, even some letters that they carried with them for months, unposted. At night, or during rests on the march, when their officers weren't listening, they read their diaries and poems aloud to entertain one another. Though usually laconic, and though often studded with what to us seem Communist clichés, they tell a poignant tale of ordinary men, with ordinary frailties, facing unremitting hardship. But judging by their accounts, even ordinary men can, at times, be transformed by a subtle chemistry of patriotism, skillful political control and sheer force of circumstances.

Date to remember forever—2:30 P.M., Jan. 4, received notice to report for induction into the army on Jan. 10.

Thus Bui Quang Vinh, a country boy from a village north of Hanoi, began his diary. Like many North Vietnamese, Vinh appears torn between patriotism and his foreboding of doom, for no one from his village had ever returned from the war in the South. Of all the events he goes on to record, he dwells longest on these last few days at home before departing for the army. But there is no mention of a farewell ceremony or parting words from his family; North Vietnamese prisoners have testified that parents often cannot bring themselves to speak when their sons leave.

Tomorrow, in a few days, I go. Go forever, with no return. Oh, let me go and get it over with. What is the use in looking back? I am only a plain soldier. I will have only superiors.

Now the cocks are crowing for the first time tonight. It is very late, why don't I sleep? It is because I am going away. Whatever hardships, whatever difficulties, I will never forget moments like this.

Why, for what reason, do they think that way? Why do they say, "He is going away, he is very happy"?

In one of the few references to his family he allows himself, Vinh thinks wistfully of his sister:

I have a younger sister named Thi Huong,
her hair streaming like sunrays and her eyes like a mirror.
She is 18 this year
and many a young man in the village finds himself
*   wondering.*

A friend writes in his diary to encourage him:

At noon on a cold winter day
you are leaving when I am on the way home from school.
We meet on the road
for the last time in our native place.
Getting down from my bicycle I shake your hands,
to say good-by and wish that
while I study hard at home,
you achieve many victories.

And more prosaically, another friend adds:

Answering the call of the country, Vinh, step up with no hesitation. Facing difficulty, don't be a coward. Vinh, be fully confident and optimistic. Someday the sunshine will be thousands of times more beautiful when the American pirates are submerged in the black mud.

Cheered, Vinh copies a patriotic poem:

Death
Though death is feared nobody can avoid it,
but a man's death must have its reason.
How to die without blackening your name—
to die of illness is an ordinary death
to die of old age is a natural death
to die of frustrated love is a shameful death
to die for the people on the battlefront,
oh, what a sacred and beautiful death!
Death comes in a second but your name is
*   remembered for thousands of years.*
This death makes everybody salute.

Many of the diaries of the North's troops, like Vinh's, were kept in tiny, pocket-sized, plastic-covered notebooks distributed by the soldiers' regiments. They bear the imprimatur "Gift of the Regiment," and the slogan, "Study and Practice the Will of the Great Uncle Ho." Inside the front cover, some of the diaries have brief texts of the most recent Central Committee resolutions, lists of important Vietnamese historical battles and distances of provinces from Saigon.

Last October Vinh's diary was found on his body by South Vietnamese paratroopers near the ruins of Quang Tri city. He had come south in August as a replacement for the 308th North Vietnamese Division but apparently dozens of his comrades deserted under the pressure of incessant artillery bombardment and air strikes. Torn to the end between duty and self, Vinh wrote in his last entry:

Today is Oct. 6 and we must again fight this war. We stay in the bunker all day, eat, sleep and relieve ourselves in the bunker. The enemy shelling is all around us. Only nine of us remain [probably out of his company of more than a hundred]. *The rest of them left in groups for the North. I do not know how to decide. In many ways I wanted to go back with them; but thinking of the honor of my family, my own honor, and the country, I had to stay.*

I don't know what my fate will be. Life and death are already too close to each other. The more I think, the more I miss my father, mother, family and friends. I wish one day that I could see my family again. But, that is too luxurious a wish. If I die,

I only regret that I have left my country, my northern land, and could never get back to it. Farewell, fatherland.

If anyone, any comrade, any friend happens to read this note, please have understanding for me. I have been so long in the war.

Of all the experiences recorded by North Vietnamese soldiers, invariably the most traumatic is the march south. The Ho Chi Minh Trail, or as the Vietnamese themselves call it, the Truong Son Route (after the range of mountains it crosses), has been highly developed since its primitive beginnings in the late nineteen-fifties. Now an intricate web of surprisingly well-built roads and paths, it has its own system of way stations—every four or five miles—hospitals with up to 200 beds and detention camps for deserters. But even for the few select groups who got to ride down it on trucks—high-ranking officers, medical units, army motion-picture teams—it was often fatal.

Luong Trong Tan, an ordinary infantryman in the 320th North Vietnamese Division, began his march south to Kon Tum Province in the Central Highlands on a chill, rainy day in December, 1971. He was 23 years old and had already been in the army and away from his family for nearly two years:

Dec. 6—I attended a political indoctrination session on the heroic example of a heroic unit in the morning and received military clothing in the afternoon. My request for home leave was disapproved again, and I felt very homesick when the regiment departed at 4 A.M.

Dec. 20—We arrived at Way Station 13 after dark and had to dig our own trenches. There was no water, so we had to fetch it from the stream and carry it up to the top of the mountain. I felt exhausted to the point where I thought the tiredness would even stop my breathing.

Dec. 25—We had to begin our march at 3 A.M. because we were going to cross a river [they were afraid of U.S. warplanes spotting them if they crossed in daylight]. *It was a tricky route in the darkness, and I felt unhappy. My feet already hurt from the earlier days' marching.*

Dec. 30—At 7:30 A.M. we arrived at Station 42. There I participated in constructing tunnels. I felt exhausted, but I had to accept the situation because I had no other choice.

Jan. 8—We climbed high slopes on the Truong Son range. I felt very tired because of the heavy load on my back, and because the road had been destroyed by B-52's. My life is getting more miserable. We have only rice, salt and water; for nearly one month I have not eaten any vegetables. I read my wife's old letter again. I miss her very much but I have no way to send mail to her. Please understand my situation. Tonight I trembled with malaria.

A poem recited by members of Luong Trong Tan's unit:

Who forced me to climb slopes and wade streams,
Who urged me to travel across jungles?
I have become a human wreck because of that,
And a deep sorrow I feel as I remember my native place.

Jan. 12—During the meal my platoon became sick from eating poisonous cassava.

Jan. 14—I have not taken a bath for 15 days. No water has been available.

Jan. 26—Upon arrival at Station 75, I dug trenches and then was given soup of taro leaves. How delicious it was, after so long without vegetables.

Feb. 5—We were shown a film on heroic soldiers. I enjoyed it very much, since I had not seen a movie for two months.

Feb. 7—The battalion gathered to listen to an orientation briefing by a cadre from the political staff. I felt a distaste for life. Probably everybody at home now is busy making preparations for Tet [the Vietnamese New Year and the biggest holiday of the year]. *Instead, we are getting ready for combat. Tomorrow I will offer my youth to the revolution. Tomorrow our country will be unified and I will enjoy a peaceful spring.*

Feb. 25—The early morning rain made the trenches wet. I felt very sad and an extreme hatred toward the war. All comrades were ravenous but could find nothing to eat. For a week we have had nothing but some bowls of rice gruel.

March 1—During the night enemy B-52's continuously bombed around the hill where we are camped, and I couldn't sleep all night.

March 8—At 9 A.M. my unit received the order for withdrawal and to destroy trenches before we left. Oh, what a dread-

*ful thing for me. As I was destroying trenches, a helicopter flew
in so low that I thought it was going to land on the hill. But it
circled the area twice and then flew away. As I was lying flat
on the ground, I could clearly see an American in the helicopter
looking down at the hill; how panic-stricken I was at that
moment.*

*March 10—I stayed in the trench all day. How miserable I
was; I was very hungry and did not have enough to eat. All I
could do was to lie down or sit with my head on my knees. How
pitiful it was for those whose rice was stolen. They had nothing
left to eat. That this critical shortage resulted from theft was a
surprise to me. If I had concealed food in another place it might
not have been lost. How I detest war.*

*March 18—The unit received orders to make preparations for
a major attack. I felt very worried writing down this note.*

It was his last entry.

Whatever the North Vietnamese soldiers' own troubles and
shortcomings, their Southern cousins have always held them
in awe, ascribing to the Northerners all the martial virtues
they themselves are not disposed toward: discipline, courage,
abstention from drunkenness and looting.

Awareness of the differences proved helpful to a Government officer, Col. Ton That Hung, last spring when troops
of the 320th North Vietnamese Division overran the Government base at Tan Canh. The South Vietnamese there gave
themselves little hope of escape. Colonel Hung, after hiding
for a week in a deserted mountain village, finally thought he
would be captured when he heard voices approaching early
one morning before sunrise. But suddenly Colonel Hung
jumped up from his hiding place, and though he still couldn't
make out the uniforms of the newcomers embraced them—
they were Government Rangers. He knew they were not the
enemy, Colonel Hung said later, because they were cursing
and shouting, and certainly no North Vietnamese soldiers
would do that on patrol.

Nguyen Van Nang, a former Vietcong lieutenant colonel,
now in a center for defectors in Saigon:

"The thing that makes the Communist army work is the political officer—everything depends on him. The troops may not like their political officer, they call him 'Mr. Argument,' but they respect him. And he is always there to watch them."

Pham Minh Phat, a company political officer, now in prison:

"What does the political officer do? He makes sure the soldiers get their rations, he calls meetings to indoctrinate them in the party line, he leads them in criticism sessions. In theory the military officer of a unit is its commander, but in fact the political officer of a unit is more powerful—he reports to higher echelons on the military officer."

A lean, ascetic-looking man with a high forehead, Phat spent 11 years in the army, and his narrow, darting eyes suggest someone constantly on the lookout for signs of trouble. He does not smile often. Asked if he could recall any jokes his men told about life in the army, he replied: "No, there were no jokes in my company. Everyone was satisfied, for discipline was strict and evenly applied to all ranks. So why would they make jokes?

"Political officers are carefully recruited on the basis of class background and ability," Phat explained. "They must be party members, be from worker or peasant families, and must be able to endure hardship better than anyone else in their unit. They can never display any lack of faith in the leadership of the party."

Pausing to light another of the cigarettes that he smokes down to the very tip, Phat continued: "It is simple, really. We indoctrinate the soldiers to realize they are struggling to liberate the nation and gain human rights for themselves. They are usually very young, and they are flattered to think that they are fighting for something great, something superhuman. Since soldiers may be killed at any moment and must ignore material comforts, they must have something to fight for more than their pay.

"There were other techniques that were useful too," Phat recalled, his deep, penetrating voice growing louder as he warmed to the subject. "We held competitions in the battalion, emulation campaigns, to see which company best followed the model of heroic units. And before a battle I always called the troops together, listing the crimes of the enemy unit against the people to make the men angry.

"Of course, sometimes there were problems. For example, when we went out on an operation, a comrade might get thirsty and climb a peasant's coconut tree to steal the fruit. But the other soldiers would accuse him later in a criticism session and force him to confess. A soldier with a high degree of political consciousness would confess even without being criticized."

Notes kept by a company political officer, Mai Tan Lam, of a regimental party committee meeting, Kon Tum Province, April, 1972, shortly before the spring offensive:

Comrades, we are facing a great opportunity for the party, and the people of the South are waiting for our army to liberate them. We have made much progress in preparing for the coming combat mission, but the majority of our cadre and soldiers are still new and inexperienced. Some are passive and wait to be assigned tasks. Some do not dig enough trenches and practice proper camouflage procedures; they leave their clothes to dry in open areas and fail to use care in dissipating smoke from cooking fires, so that enemy airplanes can locate our positions. A few comrades are afraid of violent combat—

Therefore, political cadre must classify soldiers into categories, progressive and backward, in order to facilitate indoctrination and control their thought. Each unit must control the thought of all soldiers and eliminate all illusions of peace, fear of sacrifice and liberalism. If indoctrination courses are frequently held, soldiers should have peaceful minds when going into battle—

Soldiers should be encouraged to emulate heroic units and to carry out the last will of Uncle Ho—

Before departing for the combat mission, do not disclose to personnel the schedule of movement, the participating units or the direction of movement.

Long live the People's Democratic Republic of Vietnam.

Since the Tet offensive of 1968, with a gradual return of as many as 200,000 wounded and disabled North Vietnamese back up the Ho Chi Minh trail to the North, veterans have become an increasing headache for Hanoi. On paper the Government has instituted a careful program of veterans' benefits: factories and cooperative farms must rehire all previous employes no matter what their injury; all veterans are entitled to complete their education at state expense; pensions for the disabled are to be strictly paid. But as the candid North Vietnamese press often admits, many men without arms and legs have had trouble finding jobs and acceptance in civilian society. In a lengthy article on the veterans' problem last year, the official party journal Hoc Tap decried the lack of public sympathy for wounded soldiers and the families of the dead. "Many party members do not properly understand the policy toward wounded combatants and the war dead," Hoc Tap said, "and this has adversely affected the feelings of the invalids, the families of the dead and the soldiers."

Unlike the American Government and military in Vietnam, with their light-at-the-end-of-the-tunnel philosophy, which insisted that every report show progress, the Vietnamese Communists tended to look for problems. Identify the trouble and then solve it, seemed to be the method in many captured Communist documents and newspaper articles. The resulting frequent admissions of food shortages, low morale and poor leadership often led hopeful American officials to conclude that the North Vietnamese were finished.

Perhaps the most common problem was the simplest one—most veterans had been away for at least two years and their families had little or no word of their fate.

A letter to the editor of Tien Phong, the Hanoi party youth newspaper, from a veteran, Duong Ngan:

Dear Comrade:

Previously my wife and I were in love and treated each other equally. Because of the anti-U.S. task I had to go far away. Recently I was able to return home and found that my wife had had a child by another man and that the child was already 4 years old. I was very hurt.

Some of the neighbors advised me to forgive her and make up, but others advised me to cut it off. I am a young party member and don't know what to do to sort things out. I hope you can give me some advice.

The published reply:

Dear Comrade Duong Ngan:

We have never before been faced with such a difficult question. We can see that the solution is not simple. Only a very deep love can help you overcome your heartache and forgive your wife.

You should listen to the voice of your own heart. If you do not love her, then everything is lost and you will not live happily together. We hope, however, that there is love in the heart of a young party member. A generous husband will triumph.

To prepare for their major 1972 spring offensive, Hanoi's leaders in 1971 drastically revised North Vietnam's draft law, expanding the age limits from 18–32 to 17–40 and abolishing exemptions for young men with critical skills, such as teachers, skilled workers and administrative cadre on farms and factories. For the first time, Catholics—whom the Government has always distrusted—and even some women were called up for front-line service. In some small villages where all eligible youths had already been drafted, 15- and 16-year-olds were inducted, and many boys were called out of school in the middle of semesters. In the rush to get as many troops as possible to the South for the series of large-scale conventional attacks, the usual rigorous nine-month training period was cut to three months.

One result of the new draft policies, as occurred in the U.S. Army after 1968, was a large influx of relatively well-educated and already well-established young men, especially teachers, who were not as unquestioning of authority as boys fresh off the farm. The Communists' usually small desertion rate is said to have been affected, and occasionally a new, more philosophical attitude is reflected in the soldiers' diaries.

Nguyen Van Minh, apparently a schoolteacher in civilian life, wrote a letter to his girl friend, Hoa, on July 10 last year. It was found, unposted, in September by South Vietnamese militia in Binh Duong Province near Saigon:

Dearest Hoa,

It is already summer at home, the sweet jasmine must be in bloom again and your younger brothers and sisters are playing in the garden, I imagine. Everything is so peaceful there—

You are finished teaching, now that summer is here, and your classes are over. I am always afraid that you are seeing Hai, the mathematics teacher—the way you used to look at him. He is so handsome, even with his arrogant manner and loud voice. Now you can wait for him every day at the gate after school. Probably your parents have already approved the match. Do you tell him you love him the way you told me, lying there under the trees by the river, do you remember, Hoa? Your long hair brushed my face, my golden summer butterfly.

Maybe you should get married. The enemy here is very barbarous and many comrades have been killed and lain down to sleep forever. Last week three members of our squad were buried by the Americans' B-52's. We did not know they were above us until the bombs burst around us; I was lucky to crawl into my bunker in time and only suffered a bloody nose from the concussion. My right ear still rings from the noise. Now I feel death very near whenever I see an airplane coming through the clouds.

This terrible war makes so many strange thoughts race through my head. I would like to jump straight up for thousands of miles to get away from here, from this killing. Before, I did not know what it was to kill a man; now that I have seen it, I don't want to do it any more.

But it is the duty of a soldier to die for his country, me for our fatherland, the enemy for his. There is no choice.

The New York Times Magazine, February 4, 1973

War Lingers in Hamlets
as Cease-Fire Hour Passes

by Arnold R. Isaacs

TUONG HOA, South Vietnam—Fleeing a war that was officially over, the villagers of Tuong Hoa began trudging away from the gunfire at 9 A.M. yesterday, when the Vietnam cease-fire was exactly one hour old.

At the head of the column, a woman jogged clumsily with a wailing child, bleeding from shrapnel wounds, clinging to her back. Behind her the rest filed by with frozen faces—"Vietnamese are used to suffering," a sergeant had remarked in the last village—except for one girl of 10 or 11, who wept hysterically. An old man trying to comfort her indicated with gestures that someone, possibly her mother, had been shot.

In the hamlet, the shells whirred in rhythmically, exploding every 10 seconds with the characteristic dull, metallic slams that sound as if they were landing in rain barrels. Close by but out of sight, rifles and machine guns sputtered among the houses.

At 9.05 A.M., an hour and five minutes after the war ended, two infantrymen carried a dead or badly wounded soldier out of the hamlet. They were followed shortly by an entire infantry company, apparently abandoning the hamlet to the Communists.

Before anyone could ask if all the South Vietnamese were pulling out, a flurry of rifle shots snapped the air overhead. It was clearly time to leave, and there was no way for any of us to report the result of the fight.

Tuong Hoa, about 22 miles north of Saigon, was one of scores of hamlets where the Communists had attacked in hope of being able to hold them when the cease-fire came.

Many of them, like Tuong Hoa, were the scene of bitter fighting hours after the 8 A.M. deadline—fighting that could have been merely the last spasms of a generation old war or the beginnings of a continued wave of violence.

Yesterday, Tuong Hoa was also the midpoint on a journey through the first hours of a "peace" that may have been hailed in the rest of the world but was greeted in Vietnam with wary uncertainty.

At 7 A.M., with an hour to go before the cease-fire was scheduled to take effect, the People's Self Defense Force patrols, South Vietnam's home guard, were returning to their homes after a night on guard.

Teen-agers and leather-faced old men, carrying antiquated arms and wearing only bits of uniforms, reflected the extent to which war has enveloped the entire South Vietnamese population.

Overhead, three luminous white contrails across the lavender dawn sky marked the soundless passage of a flight of B-52 bombers—certainly the last trip for those crews, maybe one of the last for any American airmen over Vietnam.

In the hamlet Chanh Hiep, the distant thumping of artillery seemed to come from all directions. A machine gun was firing just off the road; a soldier explained that the fighting had been going on since 3 A.M., when the Viet Cong approached the hamlet and called to government soldiers over loudspeakers, urging them to lay down their arms rather than fight in the last hours before a cease-fire.

Most of the people were standing in front of their homes, listening to the firing and glancing frequently at their watches, wondering if it really would stop on time.

At 8 A.M., the hour of the cease-fire, on the main street a group of soldiers—actually cadets from the Army Engineering School who were assigned to hamlet security for the expected heavy attacks during the last night—heard the time signal on a portable radio, and then President Nguyen Van Thieu began to speak, urging his countrymen to remain "vigilant" against possible Communist violations. The nearby automatic weapons fire and the distant artillery did not even slow down, and there was no emotion, neither elation nor surprise nor shock, on the faces of the villagers.

"The president can say anything, but this war will never end," a sergeant remarked bitterly.

Across the street, Duong Ba Trang was quivering with news of a more personal sort. He had come from Saigon for his usual Sunday visit with his 18-year-old son and arrived just at 8 A.M., only to be told his son had been captured by Viet Cong or North Vietnamese troops earlier in the week during savage fighting at the Michelin rubber plantation to the west.

"He is lost now," Mr. Trang said despairingly over the drone of President Thieu's voice from the radio. "There is one chance in a million of finding him. If the Viet Cong have him I will never see him again."

At each burst of firing, the soldiers looked at their watches, breaking into nervous chuckles as the time moved on to 8.15 A.M. By 8.30 A.M. there was still no halt to the shooting.

9.35 A.M.: The war had been over for 1 hour and 35 minutes. After Tuong Hoa we drove through Phu Cuong, the capital of Binh Duong province, to head back to Saigon, but beyond the city two armored cars stood on the road and there was more firing just ahead.

As we turned around, Huong, our interpreter, lighted a cigarette, and I expressed surprise. The bitterness in her voice was like ripping cloth: "It's not every day I celebrate a cease-fire."

The other road back to Saigon passes a military hospital, and two jeeps raced by with casualties. Artillery was still firing all around and alongside the road people from Communist occupied hamlets waited to see if government troops would move back in.

11 A.M.: The war had been over for three hours. On the portable radio the Armed Forces Vietnam network's news announcer was describing President Nixon's prayer of thanksgiving "for the end of the combat"—and on that very word, the car stopped suddenly at a road block just at the entrance to Long Thanh, east of Saigon.

A few hundred yards away smoke was rising from a fire set by a Communist mortar shell and there was heavy fighting at the other end of the town.

An old man argued desperately with the policeman, trying to get through the roadblock to find his wife, who was wounded two hours ago (when the war had only been over an hour) and taken away. There were no Communist troops around, and he thought it was a South Vietnamese shell that had hit his wife.

"I don't believe in anybody or anything anymore," he said bitterly.

4.15 P.M.: At the daily press briefing the U.S. military communique began: "All offensive military operations by U.S. forces in the Republic of Vietnam ended at 0800 today." For the Americans, it was the last daily communique and the last day of the "5 o'clock follies," the name by which the daily command briefings are still called though they have long since been starting at 4.15 P.M.

The follies ran for 8 years and 28 days—"The longest running show in town," Maj. Jere K. Forbus, the briefing officer, commented as he left his last performance.

Although one American was listed as killed yesterday—the fourth since the cease-fire was announced—and four pilots missing, the United States is on its way out of the war.

But the Vietnamese are not so sure they will not have a war to keep talking about. Lt. Col. Le Trung Hien, the Vietnamese Army spokesman, announced there were 53 Communist cease-fire violations yesterday—and he would be back at the press center tomorrow.

Baltimore Sun, January 29, 1973

How the POW's Fought Back

by John S. McCain III,
Lieut. Commander, U.S. Navy

THE DATE was Oct. 26, 1967. I was on my 23rd mission, flying right over the heart of Hanoi in a dive at about 4,500 feet, when a Russian missile the size of a telephone pole came up—the sky was full of them—and blew the right wing off my Skyhawk dive bomber. It went into an inverted, almost straight-down spin.

I pulled the ejection handle, and was knocked unconscious by the force of the ejection—the air speed was about 500 knots. I didn't realize it at the moment, but I had broken my right leg around the knee, my right arm in three places, and my left arm. I regained consciousness just before I landed by parachute in a lake right in the center of Hanoi, one they called the Western Lake. My helmet and my oxygen mask had been blown off.

I hit the water and sank to the bottom. I think the lake is about 15 feet deep, maybe 20. I kicked off the bottom. I did not feel any pain at the time, and was able to rise to the surface. I took a breath of air and started sinking again. Of course, I was wearing 50 pounds, at least, of equipment and gear. I went down and managed to kick up to the surface once more. I couldn't understand why I couldn't use my right leg or my arm. I was in a dazed condition. I went up to the top again and sank back down. This time I couldn't get back to the surface. I was wearing an inflatable life-preserver-type thing that looked like water wings. I reached down with my mouth and got the toggle between my teeth and inflated the preserver and finally floated to the top.

Some North Vietnamese swam out and pulled me to the side of the lake and immediately started stripping me, which is their standard procedure. Of course, this being in the center of town, a huge crowd of people gathered, and they were all hollering and screaming and cursing and spitting and kicking at me.

When they had most of my clothes off, I felt a twinge in my right knee. I sat up and looked at it, and my right foot was resting next to my left knee, just in a 90-degree position. I said, "My God—my leg!" That seemed to enrage them—I don't know why. One of them slammed a rifle butt down on my shoulder, and smashed it pretty badly. Another stuck a bayonet in my foot. The mob was really getting up-tight.

About this time, a guy came up and started yelling at the crowd to leave me alone. A woman came over and propped me up and held a cup of tea to my lips, and some photographers took some pictures. This quieted the crowd down quite a bit. Pretty soon, they put me on a stretcher, lifted it onto a truck, and took me to Hanoi's main prison. I was taken into a cell and put on the floor. I was still on the stretcher, dressed only in my skivvies, with a blanket over me.

For the next three or four days, I lapsed from consciousness to unconsciousness. During this time, I was taken out to interrogation—which we called a "quiz"—several times. That's when I was hit with all sorts of war-criminal charges. This started on the first day. I refused to give them anything except my name, rank, serial number and date of birth. They beat me around a little bit. I was in such bad shape that when they hit me it would knock me unconscious. They kept saying, "You will not receive any medical treatment until you talk."

I didn't believe this. I thought that if I just held out, that they'd take me to the hospital. I was fed small amounts of food by the guard and also allowed to drink some water. I was able to hold the water down, but I kept vomiting the food.

They wanted military rather than political information at this time. Every time they asked me something, I'd just give my name, rank and serial number and date of birth.

I think it was on the fourth day that two guards came in, instead of one. One of them pulled back the blanket to show the other guard my injury. I looked at my knee. It was about the size, shape and color of a football. I remembered that when I was a flying instructor a fellow had ejected from his plane and broken his thigh. He had gone into shock, the blood had pooled in his leg, and he died, which came as quite a surprise to us—a man dying of a broken leg. Then I realized that a very similar thing was happening to me.

When I saw it, I said to the guard, "O.K., get the officer." An officer came in after a few minutes. It was the man that we came to know very well as "The Bug." He was a psychotic torturer, one of the worst fiends that we had to deal with. I said, "O.K., I'll give you military information if you will take me to the hospital." He left and came back with a doctor, a guy that we called "Zorba," who was completely incompetent. He squatted down, took my pulse. He did not speak English, but shook his head and jabbered to "The Bug." I asked, "Are you going to take me to the hospital?" "The Bug" replied, "It's too late." I said, "If you take me to the hospital, I'll get well."

"Zorba" took my pulse again, and repeated, "It's too late." They got up and left, and I lapsed into unconsciousness.

Sometime later, "The Bug" came rushing into the room, shouting, "Your father is a big admiral; now we take you to the hospital."

I tell the story to make this point: There were hardly any amputees among the prisoners who came back because the North Vietnamese just would not give medical treatment to someone who was badly injured—they weren't going to waste their time. For one thing, in the transition from the kind of life we lead in America to the filth and dirt and infection, it would be very difficult for a guy to live anyway. In fact, my treatment in the hospital almost killed me.

I woke up a couple of times in the next three or four days. Plasma and blood were being put into me. I became fairly lucid. I was in a room which was not particularly small—about 15 by 15 feet—but it was filthy dirty and at a lower level, so that every time it rained, there'd be about a half inch to an inch of water on the floor. I was not washed once while I was in the hospital. I almost never saw a doctor or a nurse. Doctors came in a couple of times to look at me. They spoke French, not English.

For a guard, I was assigned a 16-year-old kid—right out of the rice fields. His favorite pastime was to sit by my bed and read a book that had a picture in it of an old man with a rifle in his hand sitting on a fuselage of an F-105 which had been shot down. He would point to himself, and slap me and hit me. He had a lot of fun that way. He fed me because both my arms were broken. He would come in with a cup that had noodles and some gristle in it, and fill a spoon and put it in my mouth. The gristle was very hard to chew. I'd get my mouth full after three or four spoonfuls, and I'd be chewing away on it. I couldn't take any more in my mouth, so he'd just eat the rest himself. I was getting about three or four spoonfuls of food twice a day. It got so that I kind of didn't give a damn—even though I tried as hard as I could to get enough to eat.

After I had been there about 10 days, a "gook"—which is what we called the North Vietnamese—came in one morning. This man spoke English very well. He asked me how I was, and said, "We have a Frenchman who is here in Hanoi visiting, and he would like to take a message back to your family." Being a little naïve at the time—you get smarter as you go along with these people—I figured this wasn't a bad deal at all, if this guy would come to see me and go back and tell my family that I was alive.

I didn't know at the time that my name had been released in a rather big propaganda splash by the North Vietnamese, and that they were very happy to have captured me. They told a number of my friends when I was captured, "We have the crown prince," which was somewhat amusing to me.

They told me that the Frenchman would visit me that evening. About noon, I was put in a rolling stretcher and taken to a treatment room where they tried to put a cast on my right arm. They had great difficulty putting the bones together, because my arm was broken in three places and there were two floating bones. I watched the guy try to manipulate it for about an hour and a half trying to get all the bones lined up. This was without benefit of Novocain. It was an extremely painful experience, and I passed out a number of times. He finally just gave up and slapped a chest cast on me. This experience was very fatiguing, and was the reason why later, when some TV film was taken, it looked to many people as if I had been drugged.

When this was over, they took me into a big room with a nice white bed. I thought, "Boy, things are really looking up." My guard said, "Now you're going to be in your new room."

About an hour later in came a guy called "The Cat." I found out later that he was the man who up until late 1969 was in charge of all the POW camps in Hanoi. He was a rather dapper sort, one of the petty intelligentsia that run North Vietnam. He was from the political bureau of the Vietnamese Workers Party.

The first thing he did was show me Col. John Flynn's identification card—now Gen. John Flynn—who was our senior officer. He was shot down the same day I was. "The Cat" said—through an interpreter, as he was not speaking English at this time—"The French television man is coming." I said, "Well, I don't think I want to be filmed," whereupon he announced, "You need two operations, and if you don't talk to him, then we will take your chest cast off and you won't get any operations." He said, "You will say that you're grateful to the Vietnamese people, and that you're sorry for your crimes." I told him I wouldn't do that.

Finally, the Frenchman came in, a man named Chalais—a Communist, as I found out later—with two photographers. He asked me about my treatment and I told him it was satisfactory. "The Cat" and "Chihuahua," another interrogator, were in the background telling me to say that I was grateful for lenient and humane treatment. I refused, and when they pressed me, Chalais said, "I think what he told me is sufficient."

Then he asked if I had a message for my family. I told him to assure my wife and others of my family that I was getting well and that I loved them. Again, in the background, "The Cat" insisted that I add something about hoping that the war would be over soon so that I could go home. Chalais shut him up very firmly by saying that he was satisfied with my answer. He helped me out of a difficult spot.

Chalais was from Paris. My wife later went to see him and he gave her a copy of the film, which was shown on CBS television in the U.S.

As soon as he left, they put me on the cart and took me back to my old dirty room.

After that, many visitors came to talk to me. Not all of it was for interrogation. Once a famous North Vietnamese writer—an old man with a Ho Chi Minh beard—came to my room, wanting to know all about Ernest Hemingway. I told him that Ernest Hemingway was violently anti-Communist. It gave him something to think about.

Others came in to find out about life in the United States. They figured because my father had such high military rank that I was of the royalty or the governing circle. They have no idea of the way our democracy functions.

One of the men who came to see me, whose picture I recognized later, was Gen. Vo Nguyen Giap, the hero of Dienbienphu. He came to see what I looked like, saying nothing. He is the Minister of Defense, and also on North Vietnam's ruling Central Committee.

After about two weeks, I was given an operation on my leg which was filmed. They never did anything for my broken left arm. It healed by itself. They said I needed two operations on my leg, but because I had a "bad attitude" they wouldn't give me another one. What kind of job they did on my leg, I do not know. Now that I'm back, an orthopedic surgeon is going to cut in and see. He has already told me that they made the incision wrong and cut all the ligaments on one side.

I was in the hospital about six weeks, then was taken to a camp in Hanoi that we called "The Plantation." This was in late December, 1967. I was put in a cell with two other men, George Day and Norris Overly, both Air Force majors. I was on a stretcher, my leg was stiff and I was still in a chest cast that I kept for about two months. I was down to about 100 pounds from my normal weight of 155.

I was told later on by Major Day that they didn't expect me to live a week. I was unable to sit up. I was sleeping about 18 hours, 20 hours a day. They had to do everything for me. They were allowed to get a bucket of water and wash me off occasionally. They fed me and took fine care of me, and I recovered very rapidly.

We moved to another room just after Christmas. In early February, 1968, Overly was taken out of our room and released, along with David Matheny and John Black. They were the first three POW's to be released by the North Vietnamese. I understand they had instructions, once home, to say nothing about treatment, so as not to jeopardize those of us still in captivity.

That left Day and me alone together. He was rather bunged up himself—a bad right arm, which he still has. He had escaped after he had been captured down South and was shot when they recaptured him. As soon as I was able to walk, which was in March of 1968, Day was moved out.

I remained in solitary confinement from that time on for more than two years. I was not allowed to see or talk to or communicate with any of my fellow prisoners. My room was fairly decent-sized—I'd say it was about 10 by 10. The door was solid. There were no windows. The only ventilation came from two small holes at the top in the ceiling, about 6 inches by 4 inches. The roof was tin and it got hot as hell in there. The room was kind of dim—night and day—but they always kept on a small light bulb, so they could observe me. I was in that place for two years.

As far as this business of solitary confinement goes—the most important thing for survival is communication with someone, even if it's only a wave or a wink, a tap on the wall, or to have a guy put his thumb up. It makes all the difference.

It's vital to keep your mind occupied, and we all worked on that. Some guys were interested in mathematics, so they worked out complex formulas in their heads—we were never allowed to have writing materials. Others would build a whole house, from basement on up. I have more of a philosophical bent. I had read a lot of history. I spent days on end going back over those history books in my mind, figuring out where this country or that country went wrong, what the U.S. should do in the area of foreign affairs. I thought a lot about the meaning of life.

It was easy to lapse into fantasies. I used to write books and plays in my mind, but I doubt that any of them would have been above the level of the cheapest dime novel.

People have asked me how we could remember detailed things like the tap code, numbers, names, all sorts of things.

The fact is, when you don't have anything else to think about, no outside distractions, it's easy. Since I've been back, it's very hard for me to remember simple things, like the name of someone I've just met.

During one period while I was in solitary, I memorized the names of all 335 of the men who were then prisoners of war in North Vietnam. I can still remember them.

One thing you have to fight is worry. It's easy to get uptight about your physical condition. One time I had a hell of a hemorrhoid and I stewed about it for about three days. Finally, I said, "Look, McCain, you've never known of a single guy who died of a hemorrhoid." So I just ignored it as best I could, and after a few months it went away.

The story of Ernie Brace illustrates how vital communication was to us. While I was in the prison we called "The Plantation" in October, 1968, there was a room behind me. I heard some noise in there so I started tapping on the wall. Our call-up sign was the old "shave and a haircut," and then the other guy would come back with the two taps, "six bits."

For two weeks I got no answer, but finally, back came the two taps. I started tapping out the alphabet—one tap for "a," two for "b," and so on. Then I said, "Put your ear to the wall." I finally got him up on the wall and by putting my cup against it, I could talk through it and make him hear me. I gave him the tap code and other information. He gave me his name—Ernie Brace. About that time, the guard came around and I told Ernie, "O.K., I'll call you tomorrow."

It took me several days to get him back up on the wall again. When I finally did, all he could say was, "I'm Ernie Brace," and then he'd start sobbing. After about two days he was able to control his emotions, and within a week this guy was tapping and communicating and dropping notes, and from then on he did a truly outstanding job.

Ernie was a civilian pilot who was shot down over Laos. He had just come from 3½ years' living in a bamboo cage in the jungle with his feet in stocks, and an iron collar around his neck with a rope tied to it. He had nearly lost use of his legs. He escaped three times, and after the third time he was buried in the ground up to his neck.

In those days—still in 1968—we were allowed to bathe

every other day, supposedly. But in this camp they had a water problem, and sometimes we'd go for two or three weeks, a month without a bath. I had a real rat for a turnkey who usually would take me out last. The bath was a sort of a stall-like affair that had a concrete tub. After everyone else had bathed, there usually was no water left. So I'd stand there for my allotted five minutes and then he'd take me back to my room.

For toilet facilities, I had a bucket with a lid that didn't fit. It was emptied daily; they'd have somebody else carry it, because I walked so badly.

From the time that Overly and Day left me—Overly left in February of 1968, Day left in March—my treatment was basically good. I would get caught communicating, talking to guys through the wall, tapping—that kind of stuff, and they'd just say, "Tsk, tsk; no, no." Really, I thought things were not too bad.

Then, about June 15, 1968, I was taken up one night to the interrogation room. "The Cat" and another man that we called "The Rabbit" were there. "The Rabbit" spoke very good English.

"The Cat" was the commander of all the camps at that time. He was making believe he didn't speak English, although it was obvious to me, after some conversation, that he did, because he was asking questions or talking before "The Rabbit" translated what I had said.

The Oriental, as you may know, likes to beat around the bush quite a bit. The first night we sat there and "The Cat" talked to me for about two hours. I didn't know what he was driving at. He told me that he had run the French POW camps in the early 1950s and that he had released a couple of guys, and that he had seen them just recently and they had thanked him for his kindness. He said that Overly had gone home "with honor."

I really didn't know what to think, because I had been having these other interrogations in which I had refused to cooperate. It was not hard because they were not torturing me at this time. They just told me I'd never go home and I was going to be tried as a war criminal. That was their constant theme for many months.

Suddenly "The Cat" said to me, "Do you want to go home?"

I was astonished, and I tell you frankly that I said that I would have to think about it. I went back to my room, and I thought about it for a long time. At this time I did not have communication with the camp senior ranking officer, so I could get no advice. I was worried whether I could stay alive or not, because I was in rather bad condition. I had been hit with a severe case of dysentery, which kept on for about a year and a half. I was losing weight again.

But I knew that the Code of Conduct says, "You will not accept parole or amnesty," and that "you will not accept special favors." For somebody to go home earlier is a special favor. There's no other way you can cut it.

I went back to him three nights later. He asked me again, "Do you want to go home?" I told him "No." He wanted to know why, and I told him the reason. I said that Alvarez [first American captured] should go first, then enlisted men and that kind of stuff.

"The Cat" told me that President Lyndon Johnson had ordered me home. He handed me a letter from my wife, in which she had said, "I wished that you had been one of those three who got to come home." Of course, she had no way to understand the ramifications of this. "The Cat" said that the doctors had told him that I could not live unless I got medical treatment in the United States.

We went through this routine and still I told him "No." Three nights later we went through it all over again. On the morning of the Fourth of July, 1968, which happened to be the same day that my father took over as commander in chief of U.S. Forces in the Pacific, I was led into another quiz room.

"The Rabbit" and "The Cat" were sitting there. I walked in and sat down, and "The Rabbit" said, "Our senior officer wants to know your final answer."

"My final answer is the same. It's 'No.'"

"That is your final answer?"

"That is my final answer."

With this "The Cat," who was sitting there with a pile of papers in front of him and a pen in his hand, broke the pen in two. Ink spurted all over. He stood up, kicked the chair over behind him, and said, "They taught you too well. They taught you too well"—in perfect English, I might add. He turned, went out and slammed the door, leaving "The Rabbit" and me sitting there. "The Rabbit" said, "Now, McCain, it will be very bad for you. Go back to your room."

What they wanted, of course, was to send me home at the same time that my father took over as commander in chief in the Pacific. This would have made them look very humane in releasing the injured son of a top U.S. officer. It would also have given them a great lever against my fellow prisoners, because the North Vietnamese were always putting this "class" business on us. They could have said to the others, "Look, you poor devils, the son of the man who is running the war has gone home and left you here. No one cares about you ordinary fellows." I was determined at all times to prevent any exploitation of my father and my family.

There was another consideration for me. Even though I was told I would not have to sign any statements or confessions before I went home, I didn't believe them. They would have got me right up to that airplane and said, "Now just sign this little statement." At that point, I doubt that I could have resisted, even though I felt very strong at the time.

But the primary thing I considered was that I had no right to go ahead of men like Alvarez, who had been there three years before I "got killed"—that's what we used to say instead of "before I got shot down," because in a way becoming a prisoner in North Vietnam was like being killed.

About a month and a half later, when the three men who were selected for release had reached America, I was set up for some very severe treatment which lasted for the next year and a half.

One night the guards came to my room and said, "The camp commander wants to see you." This man was a particularly idiotic individual. We called him "Slopehead."

One thing I should mention here: The camps were set up very similar to their Army. They had a camp commander, who was a military man, basically in charge of the maintenance of the camp, the food, etc. Then they had what they called a staff officer—actually a political officer—who was in charge of the interrogations, and provided the propaganda heard on the radio.

We also had a guy in our camp whom we named "The Soft-Soap Fairy." He was from an important family in North Vietnam. He wore a fancy uniform and was a real sharp cookie, with a dominant position in this camp. "The Soft-Soap Fairy," who was somewhat effeminate, was the nice guy, and the camp commander—"Slopehead"—was the bad guy. Old "Soft-Soap" would always come in whenever anything went wrong and say, "Oh, I didn't know they did this to you. All you had to do was co-operate and everything would have been O.K."

To get back to the story: They took me out of my room to "Slopehead," who said, "You have violated all the camp regulations. You're a black criminal. You must confess your crimes." I said that I wouldn't do that, and he asked, "Why are you so disrespectful of guards?" I answered, "Because the guards treat me like an animal."

When I said that, the guards, who were all in the room—about 10 of them—really laid into me. They bounced me from pillar to post, kicking and laughing and scratching. After a few hours of that, ropes were put on me and I sat that night bound with ropes. Then I was taken to a small room. For punishment they would almost always take you to another room where you didn't have a mosquito net or a bed or any clothes. For the next four days, I was beaten every two to three hours by different guards. My left arm was broken again and my ribs were cracked.

They wanted a statement saying that I was sorry for the crimes that I had committed against North Vietnamese people and that I was grateful for the treatment that I had received from them. This was the paradox—so many guys were so mistreated to get them to say they were grateful. But this is the Communist way.

I held out for four days. Finally, I reached the lowest point of my 5½ years in North Vietnam. I was at the point of suicide, because I saw that I was reaching the end of my rope.

I said, O.K., I'll write for them.

They took me up into one of the interrogation rooms, and for the next 12 hours we wrote and rewrote. The North Vietnamese interrogator, who was pretty stupid, wrote the final confession, and I signed it. It was in their language, and spoke about black crimes, and other generalities. It was unacceptable to them. But I felt just terrible about it. I kept saying to myself, "Oh, God, I really didn't have any choice." I had learned what we all learned over there: Every man has his breaking point. I had reached mine.

Then the "gooks" made a very serious mistake, because they let me go back and rest for a couple of weeks. They usually didn't do that with guys when they had them really busted. I think it concerned them that my arm was broken, and they had messed up my leg. I had been reduced to an animal during this period of beating and torture. My arm was so painful I couldn't get up off the floor. With the dysentery, it was a very unpleasant time.

Thank God they let me rest for a couple of weeks. Then they called me up again and wanted something else. I don't remember what it was now—it was some kind of statement. This time I was able to resist. I was able to carry on. They couldn't "bust" me again.

I was finding that prayer helped. It wasn't a question of asking for superhuman strength or for God to strike the North Vietnamese dead. It was asking for moral and physical courage, for guidance and wisdom to do the right thing. I asked for comfort when I was in pain, and sometimes I received relief. I was sustained in many times of trial.

When the pressure was on, you seemed to go one way or the other. Either it was easier for them to break you the next time, or it was harder. In other words, if you are going to make it, you get tougher as time goes by. Part of it is just a transition from our way of life to that way of life. But you get to hate them so bad that it gives you strength.

Now I don't hate them any more—not these particular guys. I hate and detest the leaders. Some guards would just come in and do their job. When they were told to beat you they would come in and do it. Some seemed to get a big bang out of it. A lot of them were homosexual, although never toward us. Some, who were pretty damned sadistic, seemed to get a big thrill out of the beatings.

From that time on it was one round of rough treatment followed by another. Sometimes I got it three or four times a week. Sometimes I'd be off the hook for a few weeks. A lot of it was my own doing, because they realized far better than we did at first the value of communicating with our fellow Americans. When they caught us communicating, they'd take severe reprisals. I was caught a lot of times. One reason was because I'm not too smart, and the other reason was because I lived alone. If you live with somebody else you have somebody helping you out, helping you survive.

But I was never going to stop. Communication with your fellow prisoners was of the utmost value—the difference between being able to resist and not being able to resist. You may get some argument from other prisoners on that. A lot depends on the individual. Some men are much more self-sufficient than others.

Communication primarily served to keep up morale. We would risk getting beat up just to tell a man that one of his friends had gotten a letter from home. But it was also valuable to establish a chain of command in our camps, so our senior officers could give us advice and guidance.

So this was a period of repeated, severe treatment. It lasted until around October of '69. They wanted me to see delegations. There were antiwar groups coming into Hanoi, a lot of foreigners—Cubans, Russians. I don't think we had too many American "peaceniks" that early, although within the next year it got much greater. I refused to see any of them. The propaganda value to them would have been too great, with my dad as commander in the Pacific.

David Dellinger came over. Tom Hayden came over. Three groups of released prisoners, in fact, were let out in custody of the "peace groups." The first ones released went home with one of the Berrigan brothers. The next peace group was a whole crew. One of them was James Johnson, one of the Fort Hood Three. The wife of the "Ramparts" magazine editor and Rennie Davis were along. Altogether, I think about eight or nine of them were in that outfit. Then a third group followed.

The North Vietnamese wanted me to meet with all of them, but I was able to avoid it. A lot of times you couldn't face them down, so you had to try to get around them. "Face" is a big thing with these people, you know, and if you could get around them so that they could save face, then it was a lot easier.

For example, they would beat the hell out of me and say I was going to see a delegation. I'd respond that, O.K., I'd see a delegation, but I would not say anything against my country and I would not say anything about my treatment, and if asked, I'd tell them the truth about the condition I was kept under. They went back and conferred on that, and then would say, "You have agreed to see a delegation, so we will take you." But they never took me, you see.

One time, they wanted me to write a message to my fellow prisoners at Christmas. I wrote down:

"To my friends in the camp who I have not been allowed to see or speak to, I hope that your families are well and happy, and I hope that you will be able to write and receive letters in accordance with the Geneva Convention of 1949 which has not been allowed to you by our captors. And may God bless you."

They took it but, of course, it was never published. In other words, sometimes it was better to write something that was laudatory to your Government or against them than say, "I won't write at all"—because a lot of times it had to go up through channels, and sometimes you could buy time this way.

At this point I want to tell you the story of Capt. Dick Stratton. He was shot down in May of 1967, when the American peace groups were claiming that the United States was bombing Hanoi. We were not at that time.

Dick was shot down well outside of Hanoi, but they wanted a confession at the time an American reporter was over there. That was in the spring and summer of '67—remember those stories that came back, very sensational stories about the American bomb damage?

"The Rabbit" and the others worked on Dick Stratton very hard. He's got huge rope scars on his arms where they were infected. They really wrung him out, because they were going to get a confession that he had bombed Hanoi—this was to be living proof. They also peeled his thumbnails back and burned him with cigarettes.

Dick reached the point where he couldn't say "No." But when they got him to the press conference, he pulled this bowing act on them—he bowed 90 degrees in this direction, he bowed 90 degrees in that direction—four quadrants. This was not too wild to the "gooks," because they're used to the bowing thing. But any American who sees a picture of another American bowing to the waist every turn for 90 degrees knows that there's something wrong with the guy, that something has happened to him. That's why Dick did what he did. After that they continued to keep pressure on him to say he wasn't tortured. They tortured him to say that he wasn't tortured. It gets to be a bad merry-go-round to be on.

Dick made some very strong statements at his press conference here in the States a few weeks ago. He said he wanted the North Vietnamese charged with war crimes. He's a fine man. He and I were at "The Plantation" together for a long time, and he did a very fine job there. He's an outstanding naval officer, a very dedicated American, and a deeply religious man.

I think a great deal of Dick Stratton. He just was very, very unfortunate in getting the worst that the "gooks" could dish out.

We had a particularly bad spring and summer in 1969 because there had been an escape at one of the other camps. Our guys carried out a well-prepared plan but were caught. They were Ed Atterberry and John Dramesi. Atterberry was beaten to death after the escape.

There's no question about it: Dramesi saw Atterberry taken into a room and heard the beating start. Atterberry never came out. Dramesi, if he wasn't such a tough cookie, would probably have been killed, too. He's probably one of the toughest guys I've ever met—from south Philly. His old man was a pro boxer, and he was a wrestler in college.

The reprisals took place all through the other camps. They started torturing us for our escape plans. The food got worse. The room inspections became very severe. You couldn't have anything in your room—nothing. For example, they used to give us, once in a while, a little vial of iodine because many of us had boils. Now they wouldn't let us have it because Dramesi and Atterberry had used iodine to darken their skin before they tried to escape, so they would look like Vietnamese.

That summer, from May to about September at our camp, twice a day for six days a week, all we had was pumpkin soup and bread. That's a pretty rough diet—first, because you get awfully damn tired of pumpkin soup, but also because it doesn't have any real nutritional value. The only thing that could keep any weight on you was the bread, which was full of lumps of soggy flour.

On Sunday we got what we called sweet bean soup. They would take some small beans and throw them in a pot with a lot of sugar and cook it up, with no meat whatsoever. A lot of us became thin and emaciated.

I had the singular misfortune to get caught communicating four times in the month of May of 1969. They had a punishment room right across the courtyard from my cell, and I ended up spending a lot of time over there.

It was also in May, 1969, that they wanted me to write—as I remember—a letter to U.S. pilots who were flying over North Vietnam asking them not to do it. I was being forced to stand up continuously—sometimes they'd make you stand up or sit on a stool for a long period of time. I'd stood up for a couple of days, with a respite only because one of the guards—the only real human being that I ever met over there—let me lie down for a couple of hours while he was on watch the middle of one night.

One of the strategies we worked out was not to let them make you break yourself. If you get tired of standing, just sit down—make them force you up. So I sat down, and this little guard who was a particularly hateful man came in and jumped up and down on my knee. After this I had to go back on a crutch for the next year and a half.

That was a long, difficult summer. Then suddenly, in October, 1969, there were drastic changes around the camp. The torture stopped. "The Soft-Soap Fairy" came to my room one day and told me that I would get a roommate. The food improved greatly and we started getting extra rations. The guards seemed almost friendly. For example, I had a turnkey who used to just bash me around for drill. The door would open—and he'd come in and start slugging me. They stopped that kind of thing. I attribute all this directly to the propaganda effort that was directed by the Administration and the people in the United States in 1969.

My younger brother, Joe, was very active in the National League of Families of American Prisoners of War and Missing in Action in Southeast Asia. That was the umbrella for all the POW family groups. So he has filled me in on why the North Vietnamese attitude toward the American prisoners changed, and given me this information:

As the bombing of the North picked up in 1965, 1966, Hanoi made its first propaganda display by parading beaten, subjugated American pilots through the streets. To their surprise, the press reaction around the world was generally negative.

Next, the North Vietnamese tried the tactic of forcing Cdr. Dick Stratton to appear and apologize for war crimes. But he had obviously been mistreated, and was doing this only under extreme duress. That backfired, too. They followed this by releasing two groups of three POW's in February and October, 1968. These men had been there less than six months and had suffered no significant weight loss and were in pretty good shape.

Until the Nixon Administration came to office in 1969, the Government back home had taken the attitude: "Don't talk about the prisoner-of-war situation lest you hurt the Americans still over there." Secretary of Defense Melvin Laird, early in 1969, went over to the peace talks with the North Vietnamese and Viet Cong in Paris. [Talks had begun under President Johnson late in 1968.] Laird took pictures of severely beaten men, such as Frishman, Stratton, Hegdahl—all of whom had suffered extreme weight loss. He got the photos through foreign news services. He told the North Vietnamese: "The Geneva Convention says that you shall release all sick and wounded prisoners. These men are sick and wounded. Why aren't they released?"

In August, 1969, Hanoi let Frishman come home. He had no elbow—just a limp rubbery arm—and he had lost 65

pounds. Hegdahl came out and had lost 75 pounds. Also released was Wes Rumbull, who was in a body cast because of
a broken back.

Frishman was allowed to hold a press conference and spilled
out the details of torture and maltreatment. Headlines appeared all over the world, and from then on, starting in the
fall of 1969, the treatment began to improve. We think this
was directly attributable to the fact that Frishman was living
proof of the mistreatment of Americans.

I'm proud of the part Joe and my wife, Carol, played here
at home. The temptation for the wives, as the years went by,
was to say, "God, I want them home under any circumstances." When Carol was pressed to take this line, her answer
was, "Just to get him home is not enough for me, and it's
not enough for John—I want him to come home standing
up."

I received very few letters from Carol. I got three in the
first four months after I was shot down. The "gooks" let me
have only one during the last four years I was there. I received
my first package in May of 1969. After that, they let me have
approximately one a year.

The reason I got so little mail was that Carol insisted on
using the channels provided by the Geneva Convention for
treatment of prisoners of war. She refused to send things
through the Committee for Liaison with Families run by the
antiwar groups.

This brings me to something that I want to discuss in more
detail:

As you may know, back in 1954, the North Vietnamese had
a big hand in toppling the French Government in Paris because the French voters had no more stomach for the Vietnam
war their Government was waging at the time. That was the
way the North Vietnamese won in 1954—they didn't win in
Vietnam.

The French agreed to pull out of Indo-China with no questions asked when they signed the agreement. As a result, they
got back just one third of their POW's.

I'm convinced that Hanoi hoped to win in our case by un-
dermining morale among the people at home in America.
They had to marshal world opinion on their side. I remember

in 1968 or '69 [North Vietnam Premier] Pham Van Dong's speech to the National Assembly, because we were blasted with these things on the loud-speakers. The title of his address was, "The Whole World Supports Us," not, "We Have Defeated the U.S. Aggressors," or anything like that.

In 1969, after the three guys who were released went back to the U.S. and told about the brutality in the POW camps, President Nixon gave the green light to publicizing this fact. It brought a drastic change in our treatment. And I thank God for it, because if it hadn't been for that a lot of us would never have returned.

Just one small example of the way things improved: Over my door were some bars, covered by a wooden board to keep me from seeing out, and to block ventilation. One night, around the end of September, 1969, "Slopehead," the camp commander himself, came around and pulled this thing off, so that I could have some ventilation. I couldn't believe it. Every night from then on they pulled that transom so I could get some ventilation. We started bathing more often. It was all very amazing.

In December of 1969 I was moved from "The Pentagon" over to "Las Vegas." "Las Vegas" was a small area of Hoala Prison which was built by the French in 1945. It was known as the "Hanoi Hilton" to Americans. "Heartbreak Hotel" is also there—that's the first place that people were usually taken for their initial interrogations and then funneled out to other camps.

This whole prison is an area of about two city blocks. At "Las Vegas," I was put in a small building of just three rooms called the "Gold Nugget." We named the buildings after the hotels in Vegas—there was the "Thunderbird," "Stardust," "Riviera," "Gold Nugget" and the "Desert Inn."

I was moved into the "Gold Nugget," and immediately I was able to establish communications with the men around the camp, because the bath area was right out my window, and I could see through cracks in the doors of the bath and we would communicate that way. I stayed in that one, in solitary confinement, until March of 1970.

There was pressure to see American antiwar delegations, which seemed to increase as the time went on. But there wasn't any torture. In January of 1970, I was taken to a quiz with "The Cat." He told me that he wanted me to see a foreign guest. I told him what I had always told him before: that I would see the visitor, but I would not say anything against my country, and if I was asked about my treatment I would tell them how harsh it was. Much to my shock and surprise he said, "Fine, you don't have to say anything." I told him I'd have to think about it. I went back to my room and I asked the senior American officer in our area what his opinion was, and he said he thought that I should go ahead.

So I went to see this visitor who said he was from Spain, but who I later heard was from Cuba. He never asked me any questions about controversial subjects or my treatment or my feelings about the war. I told him I had no remorse about what I did, and that I would do it over again if the same opportunity presented itself. That seemed to make him angry, because he was a sympathizer of the North Vietnamese.

At the time this happened, a photographer came in and took a couple of pictures. I had told "The Cat" that I didn't want any such publicity. So when I came back—the interview lasted about 15, 20 minutes—I told him I wasn't going to see another visitor because he had broken his word. Also at that time Capt. Jeremiah Denton, who was running our camp at that time, established a policy that we should not see any delegations.

In March, I got a roommate, Col. John Finley, Air Force. He and I lived together for approximately two months. A month after he moved in, "The Cat" told me I was going to see another delegation. I refused and was forced to sit on a stool in the "Heartbreak" courtyard area for three days and nights. Then I was sent back to my room.

The pressure continued on us to see antiwar delegations. By early in June I was moved away from Colonel Finley to a room that they called "Calcutta," about 50 yards away from the nearest prisoners. It was 6 feet by 2 feet with no ventilation in it, and it was very, very hot. During the summer I suffered from heat prostration a couple or three times, and dysentery. I was very ill. Washing facilities were nonexistent. My food was cut down to about half rations. Sometimes I'd go for a day or so without eating.

All during this time I was taken out to interrogation and pressured to see the antiwar people. I refused.

Finally I moved in September to another room which was back in the camp but separated from everything else. That was what we called "the Riviera." I stayed in there until December, 1970. I had good communications, because there was a door facing the outside and a kind of louvered window above it. I used to stand up on my bucket and was able to take my toothbrush and flash the code to other prisoners, and they would flash back to me.

In December I moved into "Thunderbird," one of the big buildings with about 15 rooms in it. The communication here was very good. We would tap between rooms. I learned a lot about acoustics. You can tap—if you get the right spot on the wall—and hear a guy four or five rooms away.

Late in December, 1970—about the twentieth, I guess—I was allowed to go out during the day with four other men. On Christmas night we were taken out of our room and moved into the "Camp Unity" area, which was another part of Hoala. We had a big room, where there were about 45 of us, mostly from "Vegas."

There were seven large rooms, usually with a concrete pedestal in the center, where we slept with 45 or 50 guys in each room. We had a total of 335 prisoners at that time. There were four or five guys who were not in good shape that they kept separated from us. The Colonels Flynn, Wynn, Bean and Gaddis also were kept separate. They did not move in with us at that time.

Our "den mother" was "The Bug" again, much to our displeasure. He made life very difficult for us. He wouldn't let us have meetings of more than three people at one time. They were afraid we were going to set up political indoctrination. They wouldn't let us have church service. "The Bug" would not recognize our senior officer's rank. This is one thing that they did right up until the end, till the day we left. If they had worked through our seniors, they would have gotten co-operation out of us. This was a big source of irritation all the time.

In March of 1971 the senior officers decided that we would have a showdown over church. This was an important issue for us. It also was a good one to fight them on. We went ahead and held church. The men that were conducting the service were taken out of the room immediately. We began to sing hymns in loud voices and "The Star-Spangled Banner."

The "gooks" thought it was a riot situation. They brought in the ropes and were practicing judo holds and that kind of stuff. After about a week or two they started taking the senior officers out of our room and putting them over in another building.

Later in March they came in and took three or four of us out of every one of the seven rooms until they got 36 of us out. We were put in a camp we called "Skid Row," a punishment camp. We stayed there from March until August, when we came back for about four weeks because of flooding conditions around Hanoi, and then we went back out again until November.

They didn't treat us badly there. The guards had permission to knock us around if we were unruly. However, they did not have permission to start torturing us for propaganda statements. The rooms were very small, about 6 feet by 4 feet, and we were in solitary again. The most unpleasant thing about it was thinking of all our friends living in a big room together. But compared with '69 and before, it was a piece of cake.

The great advantage to living in a big room is that way only a couple or three guys out of the group have to deal with the "gooks." When you're living by yourself, then you've got to deal with them all the time. You always have some fight with them. Maybe you're allowed 15 minutes to bathe, and the "gook" will say in five minutes you've got to go back. So you have an argument with him, and he locks you in your room so you don't get to bathe for a week. But when you're in a big room with others, you can stay out of contact with them and it's a lot more pleasant.

All through this period, the "gooks" were bombarding us with antiwar quotes from people in high places back in Washington. This was the most effective propaganda they had to use against us—speeches and statements by men who were generally respected in the United States.

They used Senator Fulbright a great deal, and Senator Brooke. Ted Kennedy was quoted again and again, as was Averell Harriman. Clark Clifford was another favorite, right after he had been Secretary of Defense under President Johnson.

When Ramsey Clark came over they thought that was a great coup for their cause.

The big furor over release of the Pentagon papers was a tremendous boost for Hanoi. It was advanced as proof of the "black imperialist schemes" that they had been talking about all those years.

In November of 1971 we came back from "Skid Row," and they put us in one of the big rooms again in the main Hoala Prison area. This was "Camp Unity." From that time on we pretty much stayed as a group with some other people who were brought in later. We ended up with about 40 men in there.

In May, 1972, when the U.S. bombing started again in earnest, they moved almost all the junior officers up to a camp near the China border, leaving the senior officers and our group behind. That was when President Nixon announced the resumption of the bombing of North Vietnam and the mining of the ports.

"Dogpatch" was the name of the camp near the border. I think they were afraid that Hanoi would be hit, and with all of us together in one camp one bomb could have wiped us out. At this time, the "gooks" got a little bit rougher. They once took a guy out of our room and beat him up very badly. This man had made a flag on the back of another man's shirt. He was a fine young man by the name of Mike Christian. They just pounded the hell out of him right outside of our room and then carried him a few feet and then pounded him again and pounded him all the way across the courtyard, busted one of his eardrums and busted his ribs. It was to be a lesson for us all.

Aside from bad situations now and then, 1971 and 1972 was a sort of coasting period. The reason why you see our men in such good condition today is that the food and everything generally improved. For example, in late '69 I was down to 105, 110 pounds, boils all over me, suffering dysentery. We started getting packages with vitamins in them—about one package a year. We were able to exercise quite a bit in our rooms and managed to get back in a lot better health.

My health has improved radically. In fact, I think I'm in better physical shape than I was when I got shot down. I can do 45 push-ups and a couple hundred sit-ups. Another beautiful thing about exercise: It makes you tired and you can sleep, and when you're asleep you're not there, you know. I used to try to exercise all the time.

Finally came the day I'll never forget—the eighteenth of December, 1972. The whole place exploded when the Christmas bombing ordered by President Nixon began. They hit Hanoi right off the bat.

It was the most spectacular show I'll ever see. By then we had large windows in our rooms. These had been covered with bamboo mats, but in October, 1972, they took them down. We had about a 120-degree view of the sky, and, of course, at night you can see all the flashes. The bombs were dropping so close that the building would shake. The SAM's [surface-to-air missiles] were flying all over and the sirens were whining—it was really a wild scene. When a B-52 would get hit—they're up at more than 30,000 feet—it would light up the whole sky. There would be a red glow that almost made it like daylight, and it would last for a long time, because they'd fall a long way.

We knew at that time that unless something very forceful was done that we were never going to get out of there. We had sat there for 3½ years with no bombing going on—November of '68 to May of '72. We were fully aware that the only way that we were ever going to get out was for our Government to turn the screws on Hanoi.

So we were very happy. We were cheering and hollering. The "gooks" didn't like that at all, but we didn't give a damn about that. It was obvious to us that negotiation was not going to settle the problem. The only reason why the North Vietnamese began negotiating in October, 1972, was because they could read the polls as well as you and I can, and they knew that Nixon was going to have an overwhelming victory in his re-election bid. So they wanted to negotiate a cease-fire before the elections.

I admire President Nixon's courage. There may be criticism of him in certain areas—Watergate, for example. But he had to take the most unpopular decisions that I could imagine—the mining, the blockade, the bombing. I know it was very, very difficult for him to do that, but that was the thing that ended the war. I think the reason he understood this is that he has a long background in dealing with these people. He knows how to use the carrot and the stick. Obviously, his trip to China and the Strategic Arms Limitation Treaty with Russia were based on the fact that we're stronger than the Communists, so they were willing to negotiate. Force is what they understand. And that's why it is difficult for me to understand now, when everybody knows that the bombing finally got a cease-fire agreement, why people are still criticizing his foreign policy—for example, the bombing in Cambodia.

Right after the Communist *Tet* offensive in 1968, the North Vietnamese were riding high. They knew President Johnson was going to stop the bombing before the 1968 elections. "The Soft-Soap Fairy" told me a month before those elections that Johnson was going to stop the bombing.

In May of 1968 I was interviewed by two North Vietnamese generals at separate times. Both of them said to me, in almost these words:

"After we liberate South Vietnam we're going to liberate Cambodia. And after Cambodia we're going to liberate Laos, and after we liberate Laos we're going to liberate Thailand. And after we liberate Thailand we're going to liberate Malaysia, and then Burma. We're going to liberate all of Southeast Asia."

They left no doubt in my mind that it was not a question of South Vietnam alone. Some people's favorite game is to refute the "domino theory," but the North Vietnamese themselves never tried to refute it. They believe it. Ho Chi Minh said many, many times, "We are proud to be in the front line of armed struggle between the socialist camp and the U.S. imperialist aggressors." Now, this doesn't mean fighting for nationalism. It doesn't mean fighting for an independent South Vietnam. It means what he said. This is what Communism is all about—armed struggle to overthrow the capitalist countries.

I read a lot of their history. They gave us propaganda books. I learned that Ho Chi Minh was a Stalinist. When Khrushchev denounced Stalin in the late 1950s, Ho Chi Minh did not go along with it. He was not a "peaceful coexistence" Communist.

At this particular juncture, after *Tet* in 1968, they thought they had the war won. They had gotten General Westmoreland [commander of U.S. forces in South Vietnam] fired. They were convinced that they had wrecked Johnson's chances for re-election. And they thought that they had the majority of the American people on their side. That's why these guys were speaking very freely as to what their ambitions were. They were speaking prematurely, because they just misjudged the caliber of President Nixon.

To go back to the December bombing: Initially, the North Vietnamese had a hell of a lot of SAM's on hand. I soon saw a lessening in the SAM activities, meaning they may have tied them up. Also, the B-52 bombings, which were mainly right around Hanoi in the first few days, spread out away from the city because, I think, they destroyed all the military targets around Hanoi.

I don't know the number of B-52 crewmen shot down then, because they only took the injured Americans to our camp. The attitude of our men was good. I talked to them the day before we moved out, preparing to go home, when they knew the agreements were going to be signed. I asked one young pilot—class of '70 at West Point—"How did your outfit feel when you were told that the B-52s were going to bomb Hanoi?" He said, "Our morale skyrocketed."

I have heard there was one B-52 pilot who refused to fly the missions during the Christmas bombing. You always run into that kind. When the going gets tough, they find out their conscience is bothering them. I want to say this to anybody in the military: If you don't know what your country is doing, find out. And if you find you don't like what your country is doing, get out before the chips are down.

Once you become a prisoner of war, then you do not have the right to dissent, because what you do will be harming your country. You are no longer speaking as an individual, you are speaking as a member of the armed forces of the United States, and you owe loyalty to the Commander in Chief, not to your own conscience. Some of my fellow prisoners sang a different tune, but they were a very small minority. I ask myself if they should be prosecuted, and I don't find that easy to answer. It might destroy the very fine image that the great majority of us have brought back from that hellhole. Remember, a handful of turncoats after the Korean War made a great majority of Americans think that most of the POW's in that conflict were traitors.

If these men are tried, it should not be because they took an antiwar stance, but because they collaborated with the Vietnamese to an extent, and that was harmful to the other American POW's. And there is this to consider: America will have other wars to fight until the Communists give up their doctrine of violent overthrow of our way of life. These men should bear some censure so that in future wars there won't be a precedent for conduct that hurts this country.

By late January of this year, we knew the end of the war was near. I was moved then to the "Plantation." We were put together in groups by the period when we were shot down. They were getting us ready to return by groups.

By the way—a very interesting thing—after I got back, Henry Kissinger told me that when he was in Hanoi to sign the final agreements, the North Vietnamese offered him one man that he could take back to Washington with him, and that was me. He, of course, refused, and I thanked him very much for that, because I did not want to go out of order. Most guys were betting that I'd be the last guy out—but you never can fathom the "gooks."

It was January 20 when we were moved to the "Plantation." From then on it was very easy—they hardly bothered us. We were allowed out all day in the courtyard. But, typical of them, we had real bad food for about two weeks before we left. Then they gave us a great big meal the night before we went home.

There was no special ceremony when we left the camp. The

International Control Commission came in and were permitted to look around the camp. There were a lot of photographers around, but nothing formal. Then we got on the buses and went to Gia Lam Airport. My old friend "The Rabbit" was there. He stood out front and said to us, "When I read your name off, you get on the plane and go home."

That was March 15. Up to that moment, I wouldn't allow myself more than a feeling of cautious hope. We had been peaked up so many times before that I had decided that I wouldn't get excited until I shook hands with an American in uniform. That happened at Gia Lam, and then I knew it was over. There is no way I can describe how I felt as I walked toward that U.S. Air Force plane.

Now that I'm back, I find a lot of hand-wringing about this country. I don't buy that. I think America today is a better country than the one I left nearly six years ago.

The North Vietnamese gave us very little except bad news about the U.S. We didn't find out about the first successful moon shot [in 1969] until it was mentioned in a speech by George McGovern saying that Nixon could put a man on the moon, but he couldn't put an end to the Vietnam war.

They bombarded us with the news of Martin Luther King's death and the riots that followed. Information like that poured continuously out of the loud-speakers.

I think America is a better country now because we have been through a sort of purging process, a re-evaluation of ourselves. Now I see more of an appreciation of our way of life. There is more patriotism. The flag is all over the place. I hear new values being stressed—the concern for environment is a case in point.

I've received scores of letters from young people, and many of them sent me POW bracelets with my name on it, which they had been wearing. Some were not too sure about the war, but they are strongly patriotic, their values are good, and I think we will find that they are going to grow up to be better Americans than many of us.

This outpouring on behalf of us who were prisoners of war is staggering, and a little embarrassing because basically we feel that we are just average American Navy, Marine and Air

Force pilots who got shot down. Anybody else in our place would have performed just as well.

My own plans for the future are to remain in the Navy, if I am able to return to flying status. That depends upon whether the corrective surgery on my arms and my leg is successful. If I have to leave the Navy, I hope to serve the Government in some capacity, preferably in Foreign Service for the State Department.

I had a lot of time to think over there, and came to the conclusion that one of the most important things in life— along with a man's family—is to make some contribution to his country.

U.S. News & World Report, May 14, 1973

Bomb Error Leaves Havoc in Neak Luong

by Sydney H. Schanberg

NEAK LUONG, Cambodia, Aug. 8—The destruction in this town from the accidental bombing on Monday is extensive.

Big chunks of the center of town have been demolished, including two-story concrete buildings reinforced with steel. Clusters of wood and thatch huts where soldiers lived with their families have been erased, so that the compounds where they once stood look like empty fields strewn with rubbish.

On Monday evening the United States Embassy described the damage as "minimal."

"I saw one stick of bombs through the town, but it was no great disaster," said Col. David H. E. Opfer, the air attaché at the embassy, who briefed the press then. "The destruction was minimal."

[A United States Embassy spokesman in Phnom Penh said Wednesday that American aircraft, in their third bombing error in three days, hit a village on the Phnom Penh–Saigon highway, Reuters reported. In Washington, the Pentagon denied the report.]

The nearly 400 casualties from Monday's bombing, which the Americans say was carried out by a lone B-52 with a 20-ton-plus load, make it the worst accidental bombing of the Indochina war. Official figures show 137 killed and 268 wounded, most of them soldiers and their families. The Americans originally put total casualties at around 150 but have since acknowledged their error.

However, the toll could be somewhat higher because the count does not include minor wounds. Moreover, some townspeople say they believe a few bodies remain in the wreckage. The smell of decaying flesh is still prevalent in parts of town.

The atmosphere in Neak Luong, on the east bank of the

Mekong River 38 miles southeast of Phnom Penh, is silent and sad—and bewildered at being bombed by an ally. Everyone has lost either relatives or friends; in some cases entire large families were wiped out.

Yesterday afternoon a soldier could be seen sobbing uncontrollably on the riverbank. "All my family is dead!" he cried, beating his hand on the wooden bench where he had collapsed. "All my family is dead! Take my picture, take my picture! Let the Americans see me!"

His name is Keo Chan and his wife and 10 of his children were killed. All he has left is the youngest—an 8-month-old son. The 48-year-old soldier escaped death because he was on sentry duty a few miles away when the bombs fell.

The bombs went right down the middle of the town from north to south as it lay sleeping shortly after 4:30 A.M. Over 30 craters can be seen on a line nearly a mile long, and people reported others in jungle areas outside the town that this correspondent could not reach.

Some witnesses said the bombs exploded above the ground, indicating that they might have been antipersonnel devices.

A large part of the market area in the center of town is smashed flat and many of the two-story concrete shops and apartment buildings on either side are shattered and uninhabitable, with walls and roofs reduced to rubble. Other buildings still usable have large holes.

A third of the hospital is demolished, with the rest badly damaged and unusable until major repairs are made. Several patients were wounded and some are believed killed. A bomb fell on the northeast corner of the hospital, blowing some walls down and scattering concrete, beds and cabinets.

At his press briefing Colonel Opfer, who visited Neak Luong within a few hours of the bombing, said that there was "a little bit of damage to the northeast corner of the hospital" and talked about some "structural cracks" in a wall.

The bombs also hit a compound for marines, which had a large field full of flimsy shacks in the back. The shacks were leveled and the main building, a two-story concrete structure, was turned into a stark shell, with only some walls left standing, and those badly cracked and tilted. The shacks, of thatch and wood and corrugated metal, where the marines lived with

their families, is a rubbish heap crisscrossed with fallen coconut trees.

Ammunition also exploded in this compound and many
people died. A woman's scalp sways on a clump of tall grass.
A bloody pillow here, a shred of a sarong caught on barbed
wire there. A large bloodstain on the brown earth. A pair of
infant's rubber sandals among some unexploded artillery
shells.

Colonel Opfer referred to the soldiers' shacks as
"hootches" suggesting that not much of value had been destroyed. The attaché said further that the bombing "took
place in what is essentially a small village." Actually, by Cambodian standards it is a big town; about 10,000 people live in
and around Neak Luong, half of them in the town proper.

Asked the reaction of the people when he walked through
Neak Luong, Colonel Opfer said, "They were sad, but they
understand that this is war and that in war these things
happen."

"I do not understand why it happened," said Chea Salan,
a 21-year-old soldier who lost relatives and army buddies. "Before, every time we saw the planes coming we were happy
because we knew the planes came to help us. Now I have lost
heart."

Another soldier asked, "Did the Government capture the
pilot yet."

"Why did this happen to us?" said Keo Sakhoun Tha, also
a soldier. "I want world opinion to judge what happened
here." He added, almost as an afterthought, "I am frightened
at night now when the planes come."

"At first, after the bombing, I thought it must be a North
Vietnamese plane," still another soldier commented. "I did
not believe it could be an American plane. Now I believe it."

Though several soldiers and residents said they were angry,
their tone carried no anger, and little anti-American reaction
was discernible. Rather the people were confused, hurt and
bewildered that such a disaster should befall them, and especially that it could be caused by an ally.

"I am simply desolated," said a naval ensign, Phiboun
Doutch, "but we must continue the struggle against the
enemy."

Local people, in their confusion over the bombing, continually stressed that there had been no enemy activity in the vicinity.

The bombs struck a fuel and ammunition dump. Trees for acres around are stripped of leaves and charred, with sheets of tin from soldiers' huts hanging from some of the high branches. A magic necklace, specially blessed by a Buddhist priest to ward off harm and misfortune, lay broken.

There is one unexploded bomb buried in the main street near the central market. The people are jittery about it. "When are you Americans going to take it away," a man called to a visitor.

The New York Times, August 9, 1973

A KHMER ROUGE EXECUTION: JULY 1974

"I watched them saw him 3 days"

by Donald Kirk

TUOL SAMPEOU, Cambodia—Twenty-five-year-old Sanguon Preap had been serving in the Khmer Rouge for only three months when he witnessed a display of ruthlessness that led him to flee to the sanctuary of this refugee village some eight miles southwest of Phnom Penh.

"I was very frightened when I saw the Khmer Rouge saw off the neck of a civilian with the sharp edge of sugar palm leaves," said Preap, standing amid a cluster of refugees beside a row of flimsy huts.

"They spent three days cutting his head off," said Preap. "They sawed a little one morning, and then in the evening, and finally the following day in the morning and then in the evening, and finally the following day in the morning and night.

"They made the victim stand up while they were cutting in front of hundreds of people living in the Khmer Rouge area. Then they held him up when he could stand no longer."

The episode was not just an isolated case but one of many I heard during visits to refugee camps. Khmer Rouge soldiers also have used the knife-like edges of sugar palm leaves to lop off the heads of Cambodian officers captured while overrunning nearby towns and military installations.

"They want the victims to suffer more and to serve as examples for people," said one informant. "They denounce them as traitors before the crowd."

"I had to join the Khmer Rouge army or they would have killed me," said Preap. "Those who refuse to serve they send to their deaths. They walk thru villages telling the people to follow them, and the people must obey."

Another refugee, who fled here with his wife and nine children from an area some 50 miles to the east, said that he had never personally witnessed any executions.

"They tied up people by putting both hands behind their backs and telling them they were sending them to the high command," said the refugee Lach Pech. "Whenever they did that, then we knew the man would be sent to his death in the forests. It was a secret why they killed people, and nobody dared ask why."

Lach Pech said that in his village Buddhist monks were forced to dig up the roots of large trees—and then throw bodies into the ground where roots had been.

"There is no real security around here," said one village leader. "There are government soldiers somewhere, but there are not enough of them. We worry the enemy will come back again, and we will be in danger. They are only a mile away."

Chicago Tribune, July 14, 1974

A Flight Into Hell

by Paul Vogle

DA NANG, March 29 (UPI)—Only the fastest, the strongest, and the meanest of a huge mob got a ride on the last plane from Da Nang Saturday.

People died trying to get aboard and others died when they fell thousands of feet into the sea because even desperation could no longer keep their fingers welded to the undercarriage.

It was a flight into hell, and only a good tough American pilot and a lot of prayers got us back to Tan Son Nhut air base alive—with the Boeing 727 flaps jammed and the wheels fully extended.

It all started simply enough. I asked World Airways Vice President, Charles Patterson, if he had anything going to Da Nang. He said, "Get on that truck and you've got yourself a ride."

It was a ride I'll never forget.

World Airways President Ed Daly was aboard. He was angry and tired. Daly said he had been up all night arguing with American and Vietnamese officials for permission to fly into besieged Da Nang to get some more refugees out.

Daly finally said to hell with paperwork, clearances, and caution, and we were on our way.

It seemed peaceful enough as we touched down at the airport 370 miles northeast of Saigon.

Over a thousand people had been waiting around a quonset hut several hundred yards away from where we touched down.

Suddenly it was a mob in motion. They roared across the tarmac on motorbikes, Jeeps, Lambretta scooters, and on legs speeded by sheer desperation and panic.

Ed Daly and I stood near the bottom of the 727's tail ramp. Daly held out his arms while I shouted in Vietnamese, "One at a time, one at a time. There's room for everybody."

706

There wasn't room for everybody and everybody knew damn well there wasn't.

Daly and I were knocked aside and backward.

If Ed Daly thought he'd get some women and children out of Da Nang, he was wrong. The plane was jammed in an instant with troops of the 1st Division's meanest unit, the Hac Bao (Black Panthers).

They literally ripped the clothes right off Daly along with some of his skin. I saw one of them kick an old woman in the face to get aboard.

In the movies somebody would have shot the bastard and helped the old lady on the plane. This was no movie. The bastard flew and the old lady was tumbling down the tarmac, her fingers clawing toward a plane that was already rolling.

A British television cameraman who flew up with us made the mistake of getting off the plane when we landed, to shoot the loading.

He could not get back aboard in the pandemonium. In the very best tradition of the business he threw his camera with its precious film into the closing door and stood there and watched the plane take off.

We heard later that an Air America helicopter picked him up and carried him to safety.

As we started rolling, insanity gripped those who had missed the last chance. Government troops opened fire on us. Somebody lobbed a hand grenade towards the wing. The explosion jammed the flaps full open and the undercarriage in full extension.

Communist rockets began exploding at a distance.

Our pilot, Ken Healy, 52, of Oakland, Calif., slammed the throttles open and lurched into the air from the taxiway. There was no way we could have survived the gunfire and got onto the main runway.

A backup 727 had flown behind us but had been ordered not to land when the panic broke out. He radioed that he could see the legs of people hanging down from the under-carriage of our plane.

UPI photographer Lien Huong, who was in the cockpit of that backup plane, saw at least one person lose his grip on life and plummet into the South China Sea below.

There were 268 or more people jammed into the cabin of the little 727 limping down the coast.

Only two women and one baby among them. The rest were soldiers, toughest of the tough, meanest of the mean. They proved it today. They were out. They said nothing. They didn't talk to each other or us. They looked at the floor.

I saw one of them had a clip of ammunition and asked him to give it to me. He handed it over. As I walked up the aisle with the clip, other soldiers started loading my arms with clips of ammunition, pistols, hand grenades. They didn't need them anymore. In the cockpit we wrapped the weapons and ammo in electrical tape.

There was no more fight left in the Black Panthers this day.

They had gone from humans to animals and now they were vegetables.

We flew down the coast, the backup plane behind us all the way. Healy circled Phan Rang air base 165 miles northeast of Saigon, hoping to put down for an emergency landing.

On the backup plane Lien Huong served as interpreter, radioing Phan Rang control tower that the Boeing had to land there in an emergency. The reply came back that there was no fire fighting equipment at Phan Rang so Healy aimed the plane for Tan Son Nhut.

I heard Healy on the radio, telling Tan Son Nhut, "I've got control problems." The backup plane was shepherding us in.

Huong, in the cockpit of the backup plane, told me later when we touched down safe the pilot and cabin crew on his plane pulled off their headphones, some of them crossed themselves, and all thanked God for a small miracle delivered this Easter weekend.

When we touched down the troops who had stormed us were offloaded and put under arrest. They deserved it.

A mangled body of one soldier, M16 rifle still strapped to his shoulder, was retrieved from the undercarriage. He got his ride to Saigon, but being dead in Saigon is just the same as being dead in Da Nang.

Over a score of others came out of the baggage compartment, cold but alive. Somebody told me that four others crawled out of the wheel wells alive. One died.

The last plane from Da Nang was one hell of a ride. For me. For Ed Daly. For Ken Healy. For the Black Panthers. And for two women and a baby.

But the face that remains is that of the old woman lying flat on the tarmac seeing hope, seeing life itself, just off the end of her fingertips and rolling the other way.

UPI dispatch, March 29, 1975

For Those Who Flee, Life Is "Hell on Earth"

by Le Kim Dinh

SAIGON, South Vietnam, April 1—Cam Ranh Bay, one of the most picturesquely beautiful places on the South China Sea, has become a hell on earth for the hundred thousand or more refugees who have arrived there from Da Nang and also from the whole central part of the country.

Today, they are scarcely safer than when they fled; they are starving and gasping from thirst.

Cam Ranh Bay, one of the best deep-water ports in Asia, was the main United States logistical base in Vietnam.

Some of the refugees had paid as much as $1,200 to get to Cam Ranh from the dying city of Da Nang.

At Cam Ranh, I found, money does not matter. Fortunes are stolen by some, and these are robbed by others. Piasters, gold, diamonds, bits of priceless family treasure—none of it means anything in comparison with the need to survive.

At Cam Ranh, the suffering of the civilians was far and away the worst, with babies dying on ships or ashore, with the body of an old man lying ignored all day at a pier. But the ragged remnants of the South Vietnamese forces there have their ordeal, too.

The general morale has not been buoyed by the fact that many senior officials of Military Region II have left Cam Ranh for Saigon.

The chaotic situation was alleviated somewhat by the arrival from Saigon of some shock troops, whose specialty is combat reconnaissance. They were sent in to protect the Vietnamese naval training center, the headquarters of Military Region II and the main airport.

But there were clashes between these troops and many marines and rangers who came here from Da Nang. Many of those men became bandits after they discarded rifles, equipment, ammunition and even their uniforms to swim out to the barges and other boats off the dying city.

For the last day or so there have been pitched battles between the shock troops and the men from Da Nang. All through the night last night shots rang out in Cam Ranh, some from the military men, some from looters shooting their way into buildings.

The marines scarcely seem to exist any longer as a military force.

The shock troops themselves have been doing some stealing. They have been seizing loot from the "renegades," as they call the men from the north, as they find it. Bags of money, radios, gold and other valuables taken from the bandits have been piled up near the gate of the naval center and some of the loot has been stolen once more—by the shock troops.

On a street near Cam Ranh Bay today a major recognized a captain and shouted, "Do you know where the colonel is?"

The captain replied, "I think I saw him on a fishing boat. Maybe he made it."

A lieutenant colonel who had commanded an armored brigade said, "I am not sure how many tanks and armored personnel carriers we lost, and I am not sure how many of my men succeeded in getting aboard.

"Let's not talk about it," he added. "I am exhausted and worried and I don't know where my wife is."

This morning there were 11 ships in Cam Ranh Bay waiting to unload their bedraggled cargoes of soldiers and civilians. They had been at sea two days or more.

Two small ships carried rich civilians who had paid one million piasters ($1,200) per person to come from Da Nang to Saigon, only to be told they would not be permitted to go beyond Cam Ranh Bay.

Most of them remained on the ships suffering terribly from hunger and thirst, rather than face the horrors on shore.

It was said that Saigon authorities were not willing to permit a flood of refugees into the capital, and had therefore ordered the navy to prevent the civilian ships from going farther. But some said it was just a question of money.

"When they are willing to pay another one million piasters per person, then those ships will set sail for Saigon," a military man said.

No one has any clear idea how many have died. Bodies eventually just disappear. One wealthy man is said to have been murdered on shipboard in front of his wife, and his body was thrown overboard. Four babies were reported trampled to death on another ship.

There are no Americans at Cam Ranh, and there is no help in the form of transport planes or helicopters.

For nearly everyone who traveled so far to get here, this appeared to be the end of the line—waiting and listening for the approaching rumble of North Vietnamese tanks.

The New York Times, April 2, 1975

The Fall of Phnom Penh

by Sydney H. Schanberg

Cambodia Reds Are Uprooting Millions as They Impose a 'Peasant Revolution'

BANGKOK, Thailand, May 8—The victorious Cambodian Communists, who marched into Phnom Penh on April 17 and ended five years of war in Cambodia, are carrying out a peasant revolution that has thrown the entire country into upheaval.

Perhaps as many as three or four million people, most of them on foot, have been forced out of the cities and sent on a mammoth and grueling exodus into areas deep in the countryside where, the Communists say, they will have to become peasants and till the soil.

No one has been excluded—even the very old, the very young, the sick and the wounded have been forced out onto the roads—and some will clearly not be strong enough to survive.

The old economy of the cities has been abandoned, and for the moment money means nothing and cannot be spent. Barter has replaced it.

All shops have either been looted by Communist soldiers for such things as watches and transistor radios, or their goods have been taken away in an organized manner to be stored as communal property.

Even the roads that radiate out of the capital and that carried the nation's commerce have been virtually abandoned, and the population living along the roads, as well as that in all cities and towns that remained under the control of the American-backed Government, has been pushed into the interior. Apparently the areas into which the evacuees are being herded are at least 65 miles from Phnom Penh.

In sum the new rulers—before their overwhelming victory

they were known as the Khmer Rouge—appear to be remaking Cambodian society in the peasant image, casting aside everything that belonged to the old system, which was generally dominated by the cities and towns and by the élite and merchants who lived there.

Foreigners and foreign aid are not wanted—at least not for now. It is even unclear how much influence the Chinese and North Vietnamese will have, despite their considerable aid to the Cambodian insurgents against the Government of Marshal Lon Nol. The new authorities seem determined to do things themselves in their own way. Despite the propaganda terminology and other trappings, such as Mao caps and Ho Chi Minh rubber-tire sandals, which remind one of Peking and Hanoi, the Communists seem fiercely independent and very Cambodian.

Judging from their present actions, it seems possible that they may largely isolate their country of perhaps seven million people from the rest of the world for a considerable time—at least until the period of upheaval is over, the agrarian revolution takes concrete shape and they are ready to show their accomplishments to foreigners.

Some of the party officials in Phnom Penh also talked about changing the capital to a more traditional and rural town like Siem Reap, in the northwest.

For those foreigners, including this correspondent, who stayed behind to observe the take-over, the events were an astonishing spectacle.

In Phnom Penh two million people suddenly moved out of the city en masse in stunned silence—walking, bicycling, pushing cars that had run out of fuel, covering the roads like a human carpet, bent under sacks of belongings hastily thrown together when the heavily armed peasant soldiers came and told them to leave immediately, everyone dispirited and frightened by the unknown that awaited them and many plainly terrified because they were soft city people and were sure the trip would kill them.

Hospitals jammed with wounded were emptied, right down to the last patient. They went—limping, crawling, on crutches, carried on relatives' backs, wheeled on their hospital beds.

The Communists have few doctors and meager medical supplies, so many of these patients had little chance of surviving. On April 17, the day this happened, Phnom Penh's biggest hospital had over 2,000 patients and there were several thousand more in other hospitals; many of the wounded were dying for lack of care.

A once-throbbing city became an echo chamber of silent streets lined with abandoned cars and gaping, empty shops. Streetlights burned eerily for a population that was no longer there.

The end of the old and the start of the new began early in the morning of the 17th. At the cable office the line went dead for mechanical reasons at 6 A.M. On the previous day, amid heavy fighting, the Communist-led forces had taken the airport a few miles west of the city, and during the night they had pressed to the capital's edges, throwing in rockets and shells at will.

Thousands of new refugees and fleeing soldiers were filling the heart of the capital, wandering aimlessly, looking for shelter, as they awaited the city's imminent collapse.

Everyone—Cambodians and foreigners alike—thought this had to be Phnom Penh's most miserable hour after long days of fear and privation as the Communist forces drew closer. They looked ahead with hopeful relief to the collapse of the city, for they felt that when the Communists came and the war finally ended, at least the suffering would largely be over. All of us were wrong.

That view of the future of Cambodia—as a possibly flexible place even under Communism, where changes would not be extreme and ordinary folk would be left alone—turned out to be a myth.

American officials had described the Communists as indecisive and often ill-coordinated, but they turned out to be firm, determined, well-trained, tough and disciplined.

The Americans had also said that the rebel army was badly riddled by casualties, forced to fill its ranks by hastily impressing young recruits from the countryside and throwing them into the front lines with only a few days' training. The thousands of troops we saw both in the countryside and in Phnom Penh, while they included women soldiers and boy militia, some of whom seemed no more than 10 years old, looked healthy, well organized, heavily armed and well trained.

Another prediction made by the Americans was that the Communists would carry out a bloodbath once they took over—massacring as many as 20,000 high officials and intellectuals. There have been unconfirmed reports of executions of senior military and civilian officials, and no one who witnessed the take-over doubts that top people of the old regime will be or have been punished and perhaps killed or that a large number of people will die of the hardships on the march into the countryside. But none of this will apparently bear any resemblance to the mass executions that had been predicted by Westerners.

[In a news conference Tuesday President Ford reiterated reports—he termed them "hard intelligence"—that 80 to 90 Cambodian officials and their wives had been executed.]

On the first day, as the sun was rising, a short swing by automobile to the northern edge of the city showed soldiers and refugees pouring in. The northern defense line had obviously collapsed.

By the time I reached the Hotel Le Phnom and climbed the two flights of stairs to my room, the retreat could be clearly seen from my window and small-arms fire could be heard in the city. At 6:30 A.M. I wrote in my notebook: "The city is falling."

Over the next couple of hours there were periodic exchanges of fire as the Communists encountered pockets of resistance. But most Government soldiers were busy preparing to surrender and welcome the Communists, as were civilians. White flags suddenly sprouted from housetops and from armored personnel carriers, which resemble tanks.

Some soldiers were taking the clips out of their rifles; others were changing into civilian clothes. Some Government office workers were hastily donning the black pajama-like clothes worn by Indochinese Communists.

Shortly before 9 A.M. the first rebel troops approached the hotel, coming from the north down Monivong Boulevard. A crowd of soldiers and civilians, including newsmen, churned forth to greet them—cheering and applauding and embracing and linking arms to form a phalanx as they came along.

The next few hours saw quite a bit of this celebrating, though shooting continued here and there, some of it only a few hundred yards from the hotel. Civilians and Buddhist monks and troops on both sides rode around town—in jeeps, atop personnel carriers and in cars—shouting happily.

Most civilians stayed nervously indoors, however, not yet sure what was going on or who was who. What was the fighting inside the city all about? they wondered; was it between diehard Government troops and the Communists or between rival Communist factions fighting over the spoils? Or was it mostly exuberance?

Some of these questions, including the nature of the factionalism, have still not been answered satisfactorily, but on that first day such mysteries quickly became academic, for within a few hours, the mood changed.

The cheerful and pleasant troops we first encountered—we came to call them the soft troops, and we learned later that they were discredited and disarmed, with their leader declared a traitor; they may not even have been authentic—were swiftly displaced by battle-hardened soldiers.

While some of these were occasionally friendly, or at least not hostile, they were also all business. Dripping with arms like overladen fruit trees—grenades, pistols, rifles, rockets— they immediately began clearing the city of civilians.

Using loudspeakers, or simply shouting and brandishing weapons, they swept through the streets, ordering people out of their houses. At first we thought the order applied only to the rich in villas, but we quickly saw that it was for everyone as the streets became clogged with a sorrowful exodus.

Cars stalled or their tires went flat, and they were abandoned. People lost their sandals in the jostling and pushing, so they lay as a reminder of the throng that had passed.

In the days to follow, during the foreign colony's confinement in the French Embassy compound, we heard reports on international news broadcasts that the Communists had evacuated the city by telling people the United States was about to bomb it. However, all the departing civilians I talked with said they had been given no reason except that the city had to be reorganized. They were told they had to go far from Phnom Penh.

In almost every situation we encountered during the more than two weeks we were under Communist control, there was a sense of split vision—whether to look at events through Western eyes or through what we thought might be Cambodian revolutionary eyes.

Was this just cold brutality, a cruel and sadistic imposition of the law of the jungle, in which only the fittest will survive? Or is it possible that, seen through the eyes of the peasant soldiers and revolutionaries, the forced evacuation of the cities is a harsh necessity? Perhaps they are convinced that there is no way to build a new society for the benefit of the ordinary man, hitherto exploited, without literally starting from the beginning; in such an unbending view people who represent the old ways and those considered weak or unfit would be expendable and would be weeded out. Or was the policy both cruel and ideological?

A foreign doctor offered this explanation for the expulsion of the sick and wounded from the hospital: "They could not cope with all the patients—they do not have the doctors—so they apparently decided to throw them all out and blame any deaths on the old regime. That way they could start from scratch medically."

Some Western observers considered that the exodus approached genocide. One of them, watching from his refuge in the French Embassy compound, said: "They are crazy! This is pure and simple genocide. They will kill more people this way than if there had been hand-to-hand fighting in the city."

Another foreign doctor, who had been forced at gunpoint to abandon a seriously wounded patient in midoperation, added in a dark voice: "They have not got a humanitarian thought in their heads!"

Whatever the Communists' purpose, the exodus did not grow heavy until dusk, and even then onlookers were slow to realize that the people were being forcibly evacuated.

For my own part, I had a problem that preoccupied me that afternoon: I, with others, was held captive and threatened with execution.

After our release, we went to the Information Ministry because we had heard about a broadcast directing high officials of the old regime to report there. When we arrived, about 50 prisoners were standing outside the building, among them Lon Non, the younger brother of President Lon Nol, who went into exile on April 1, and Brig. Gen. Chim Chhuon, who was close to the former President. Other generals and Cabinet ministers were also there—very nervous but trying to appear untroubled.

Premier Long Boret, who the day before had made an offer of surrender with certain conditions only to have it immediately rejected, arrived at the ministry an hour later. He is one of the seven "traitors" the Communists had marked for execution. The others had fled except for Lieut. Gen. Sisowath Sirik Matak, a former Premier, who some days later was removed from the French Embassy, where he had taken refuge.

Mr. Long Boret's eyes were puffy and red, almost down to slits. He had probably been up all night and perhaps he had been weeping. His wife and two children were also still in the country; later they sought refuge at the French Embassy, only to be rejected as persons who might "compromise" the rest of the refugees.

Mr. Long Boret, who had talked volubly and articulately on the telephone the night before, had difficulty speaking coherently. He could only mumble yes, no and thank you, so conversation was impossible.

There is still no hard information on what has happened to him. Most people who have talked with the Communists believe it a certainty that he will be executed, if indeed the execution has not already taken place.

One of the Communist leaders at the Information Ministry that day—probably a general, though his uniform bore no markings and he declined to give his name—talked soothingly to the 50 prisoners. He assured them that there were only seven traitors and that other officials of the old regime would be dealt with equitably. "There will be no reprisals," he said. Their strained faces suggested that they would like to believe him but did not.

As he talked, a squad crouched in combat-ready positions around him, almost as if it was guarding him against harm.

The officer, who appeared no more than age 35, agreed to chat with foreign newsmen. His tone was polite and sometimes he smiled, but everything he said suggested that we, as foreigners, meant nothing to him and that our interests were alien to his.

Asked about the fate of the 20 or so foreign journalists missing in Cambodia since the early days of the war, he said he had heard nothing. Asked if we would be permitted to file from the cable office, he smiled sympathetically and said, "We will resolve all problems in their proper order."

Clearly an educated man, he almost certainly speaks French, the language of the nation that ruled Cambodia for nearly a century until the nineteen-fifties, but he gave no hint of this colonial vestige, speaking only in Khmer through an interpreter.

In the middle of the conversation he volunteered quite unexpectedly: "We would like you to give our thanks to the American people who have helped us and supported us from the beginning, and to all people of the world who love peace and justice. Please give this message to the world."

Noting that Congress had halted aid to the Phnom Penh Government, he said, "The purpose was to stop the war," but he quickly added: "Our struggle would not have stopped even if they had given more aid."

Attempts to find out more about who he was and about political and military organization led only to imprecision. The officer said: "I represent the armed forces. There are many divisions. I am one of the many."

Asked if there were factions, he said there was only one political organization and one government. Some top political and governmental leaders are not far from the city, he added, but they let the military enter first "to organize things."

Most military units, he said, are called "rumdos," which means "liberation forces." Neither this commander nor any of the soldiers we talked with ever called themselves Communists or Khmer Rouge (Red Cambodians). They always said they were liberation troops or nationalist troops and called one another brother or the Khmer equivalent of comrade.

The nomenclature at least is confusing, for Western intelligence had described the Khmer Rumdos as a faction loyal to Prince Norodom Sihanouk that was being downgraded by Hanoi-trained Cambodians and losing power.

The Communists named the Cambodian leader, who was deposed by Marshal Lon Nol in 1970 and has been living in exile in Peking, as their figurehead chief of state, but none of the soldiers we talked with brought up his name.

One over-all impression emerged from our talk with the commander at the Information Ministry: The military will be largely in charge of the early stages of the upheaval, carrying out the evacuation, organizing the new agrarian program, searching for hidden arms and resisters, repairing damaged bridges.

The politicians—or so it seemed from all the evidence during our stay—have for the moment taken a rear seat. No significant political or administrative apparatus was yet visible; it did not seem to be a government yet, but an army.

The radio announced April 28 that a special national congress attended by over 300 delegates was held in Phnom Penh from April 25 to 27. It was said to have been chaired by the Deputy Premier and military commander, Khieu Samphan, who has emerged—at least in public announcements—as the top leader. Despite that meeting the military still seemed to be running things as we emerged from Cambodia on Saturday.

One apparent reason is that politicians and bureaucrats are not equipped to do the dirty work and arduous tasks of the early phases of reorganization. Another is that the military, as indicated in conversations with Khmer-speaking foreigners they trusted somewhat, seemed worried that politicians or soft-living outsiders in their movement might steal the victory and dilute it. There could be severe power struggles ahead.

After leaving the prisoners and the military commander at the ministry, we headed for the Hotel Le Phnom, where another surprise was waiting. The day before, the Red Cross turned the hotel into a protected international zone and draped it with huge Red Cross flags. But the Communists were not interested.

At 4:55 P.M. troops waving guns and rockets had forced their way into the grounds and ordered the hotel emptied within 30 minutes. By the time we arrived 25 minutes had elapsed. The fastest packing job in history ensued. I even had time to "liberate" a typewriter someone had abandoned since the troops had "liberated" mine earlier.

We were the last ones out, running. The Red Cross had abandoned several vehicles in the yard after removing the keys, so several of us threw our gear on the back of a Red Cross Honda pickup truck and started pushing it up the boulevard toward the French Embassy.

Several days before, word was passed to those foreigners who stayed behind when the Americans pulled out on April 12 that, as a last resort, one could take refuge at the embassy. France had recognized the new government, and it was thought that the new Cambodian leaders would respect the embassy compound as a sanctuary.

As we plodded up the road, big fires were burning on the city's outskirts, sending smoke clouds into the evening sky like a giant funeral wreath encircling the capital.

The embassy was only several hundred yards away, but what was happening on the road made it seem much farther. All around us people were fleeing, for there was no refuge for them. And coming into the city from the other direction was a fresh battalion marching in single file. They looked curiously at us; we looked nervously at them.

In the 13 days of confinement that followed, until our evacuation by military truck to the Thai border, we had only a peephole onto what was going on outside, but there were still many things that could be seen and many clues to the revolution that was going on.

We could hear shooting, sometimes nearby but mostly in other parts of the city. Often it sounded like shooting in the air, but at other times it seemed like small battles. As on the day of the city's fall we were never able to piece together a satisfactory explanation of the shooting, which died down after about a week.

We could see smoke from the huge fires from time to time, and there were reports from foreigners who trickled into the embassy that certain quarters were badly burned and that the water-purification plant was heavily damaged.

The foreigners who for various reasons came in later carried stories, some of them eyewitness accounts, of such things as civilian bodies along the roads leading out of the city—people who had apparently died of illness or exhaustion on the march. But each witness got only a glimpse, and no reliable estimate of the toll was possible.

Reports from roads to the south and southeast of Phnom Penh said the Communists were breaking up families by dividing the refugees by sex and age. Such practices were not reported from other roads on which the refugees flooded out of the capital.

Reports also told of executions, but none were eyewitness accounts. One such report said high military officers were executed at a rubber plantation a couple of miles north of the city.

In the French Embassy compound foreign doctors and relief agency officials were pessimistic about the survival chances of many of the refugees. "There's no food in the countryside at this time of year," an international official said. "What will they eat from now until the rice harvest in November?"

The new Communist officials, in conversations with United Nations and other foreign representatives during our confinement and in statements since, have rejected the idea of foreign aid, "whether it is military, political, economic, social, diplomatic, or whether it takes on a so-called humanitarian form." Some foreign observers wondered whether this included China, for they speculated that the Communists would at least need seed to plant for the next harvest.

Whether the looting we observed before we entered the French compound continued is difficult to say. In any case, it is essential to understand who the Communist soldiers are to understand the behavior of some of them in disciplinary matters, particularly looting.

They are peasant boys, pure and simple—darker skinned than their city brethren, with gold in their front teeth. To them the city is a curiosity, an oddity, a carnival, where you visit but do not live. The city means next to nothing in their scheme of things.

When they looted jewelry shops, they kept only one watch for themselves and gave the rest to their colleagues or passersby. Transistor radios, cameras and cars held the same toy-like fascination—something to play with, as children might, but not essential.

From my airline bag on the day I was seized and threatened with execution they took only some cigarettes, a pair of boxer underwear shorts and a handkerchief. They passed up a blue shirt and $9,000 in cash in a money belt.

The looting did not really contradict the Communist image of rigid discipline, for commanders apparently gave no orders against the sacking of shops, feeling, perhaps, that this was the least due their men after five years of jungle fighting.

Often they would climb into abandoned cars and find that they would not run, so they would bang on them with their rifles like frustrated children, or they would simply toot the horns for hours on end or keep turning the headlights on and off until the batteries died.

One night at the French Embassy, I chose to sleep on the grass outside; I was suddenly awakened by what sounded like a platoon trying to smash down the front gates with a battering ram that had bright lights and a loud claxon. It was only a bunch of soldiers playing with and smashing up the cars that had been left outside the gates.

Though these country soldiers broke into villas all over the city and took the curious things they wanted—one walked past the embassy beaming proudly in a crimson-colored wool overcoat that hung down to his Ho Chi Minh sandals—they never stayed in the villas. With big, soft beds empty, they slept in the courtyards or the streets.

Almost without exception foot soldiers I talked with, when asked what they wanted to do, replied that they only wanted to go home.

The New York Times, May 9, 1975

American's Brief Brush with Arrest and Death

BANGKOK, Thailand, May 8—Some of the foreigners who stayed behind after the American evacuation of Phnom Penh learned quickly and at first hand that the Communist-led forces were not the happy-go-lucky troops we had seen in the initial stage of the Communist take-over.

I had my first experience with the tough Khmer Rouge troops early in the afternoon of the first day of the take-over.

With Dith Pran, a local employe of The New York Times, Jon Swain of The Sunday Times of London, Alan Rockoff, a freelance American photographer, and our driver, Sarun, we had gone to look at conditions in the largest civilian hospital, Preah Keth Mealea. Doctors and surgeons, out of fear, had failed to come to work and the wounded were bleeding to death in the corridors.

As we emerged from the operating block at 1 P.M. and started driving toward the front gate, we were confronted by a band of heavily armed troops just then coming into the grounds. They put guns to our heads and, shouting angrily, threatened us with execution. They took everything—cameras, radio, money, typewriters, the car—and ordered us into an armored personnel carrier, slamming the hatch and rear door shut. We thought we were finished.

But Mr. Dith Pran saved our lives, first by getting into the personnel carrier with us and then by talking soothingly to our captors for two and a half hours and finally convincing them that we were not their enemy but merely foreign newsmen covering their victory.

We are still not clear why they were so angry, but we believe it might have been because they were entering the hospital at that time to remove the patients and were startled to find us, for they wanted no foreign witnesses.

At one point they asked if any of us were Americans, and we said no, speaking French all the time and letting Mr. Dith Pran translate into Khmer. But if they had looked into the bags they had confiscated, which they did not, they would have found my passport and Mr. Rockoff's.

We spent a very frightened half-hour sweating in the baking personnel carrier, during a journey on which two more prisoners were picked up—Cambodians in civilian clothes who were high military officers and who were, if that is possible, even more frightened than we.

Then followed two hours in the open under guard at the northern edge of town while Mr. Dith Pran pulled off his miracle negotiation with our captors as we watched giddy soldiers passing with truckloads of looted cloth, wine, liquor, cigarettes and soft drinks, scattering some of the booty to soldiers along the roadside.

We were finally released at 3:30 P.M., but the two Cambodian military men were held. One was praying softly.

The New York Times, May 9, 1975

Grief and Animosity in an Embassy Haven

BANGKOK, Thailand, May 8—For the 800 foreigners, including this correspondent, who spent two weeks in the French Embassy in Phnom Penh after the Communists took over, the time seemed like a chaotically compressed generation of life.

A baby was born, another died. A dozen marriages were performed—all marriages of convenience to enable Cambodians to get French passports so that they could escape the country and its peasant revolution.

There were days of deep sorrow. Cambodians without foreign papers had to go on the trek into the countryside. Friends were torn apart. Families broke up as Cambodian husbands were separated from their European wives. On those days sobbing could be heard in every corner of the compound.

And there were days when hopes rose, days when the rumors said that evacuation was imminent.

Heroes and knaves emerged—more of the latter than the former. There was no running water and food was limited, and out of this grew tensions and rivalries between groups.

Between French officials living well in the embassy and French civilians living in the driveways and gardens outside. Between the outside French and the French staff of Calmette Hospital, who were also living fairly well. And between the non-French foreigners, including the favorite targets—Americans and journalists—and everyone else.

There was more selfishness than sharing. A minor example: Put a pack of cigarettes on a table for 10 seconds and turn around, and it would be gone.

The first convoy of foreigners who had taken refuge in the embassy for 13 days, including this correspondent, arrived in Thailand Saturday after three and a half days on the road.

Hundreds of other refugees remained in the embassy even longer and arrived in Thailand today.

To describe what life was like in the compound is to describe sheer incongruity. A French doctor walked the hospital's pet sheep around the gardens. (The hospital's pet gibbon was taken by the Communists and led around the street outside in a pink dress.) Some of the Frenchmen in the compound fed their dogs better than other people were able to feed their children.

Our group of foreigners lived in the building that used to be the ambassador's residence, one of three buildings on the grounds; the others are a chancellery and a large cultural center. Eighteen of us, using sofa cushions and pillows as mattresses and linen tablecloths for blankets, slept on the floor of a large living room—surrounded by humming air-conditioners, an elegant upright piano, a crystal chandelier and some of the embassy's best silver, except for the silver teapots, which were used to boil water over wood fires outside.

For a few days it might have been fun—a curious experience to dine on when you got home. But as time wore on, nerves frayed more and more and hardly an hour went by without an argument somewhere in the compound, usually over something petty.

The water supply ended a few days after our arrival, after which we had to rely on water tapped from our air-conditioners and that delivered periodically in barrels by the new Government. There was never enough for bathing, and the odor of unwashed people was ripe.

With food limited and with no running water, sanitation deteriorated and there were scores of cases of diarrhea—the evidence of which filled every walkway and garden in the compound.

The compound was difficult at times, but never as difficult as was suggested by the radio news reports we kept listening to, which said our situation was "more and more precarious." Sometimes when we were hearing those bulletins we were swilling Scotch and smoking long cigars.

Though some people managed not to fare too badly, for most of those in the compound the situation was far more than a series of annoyances; there was nothing funny about it.

There was nothing funny for Mrs. Nha, an Air France employe who sat sobbing under a tree on the morning of April 19. Her mother and father were missing, and in two days she would be forced to take her young son and go into the countryside herself.

"I was an optimist," she said as the tears coursed down her cheeks. "Not only me. All Cambodians here thought that when the Khmer Rouge came it would be all welcomes and cheering and bravo and the war would be over and we would become normal again. Now we are stunned, stunned."

There was nothing funny for Mrs. Praet, a Belgian whose Cambodian husband was being forced to leave her and join the march. As she wept into her handkerchief he embraced her gently. "Courage, ma cherie. Courage, ma cherie," he whispered. She could not control herself and her small body shook with her weeping as their two little girls looked on uncomprehending.

Some Cambodian women, realizing that their infants could not survive the long trek, tearfully gave theirs to French families for foster care or adoption.

"My first baby, my only baby!" a mother in shock shrieked. "Save him! Save him! You can do it."

It was raining as the Cambodians left. The hospital's sheep, tethered to a truck, was bleating mournfully; no one paid any attention.

At one time, about 1,300 people were living in the attractively landscaped compound, which is 200 yards by 250 yards or so. Then the Communists ordered out all Cambodians without foreign passports or papers, which forced about 500 people to take to the road.

Family or not, we all lost someone close to us, and when the Cambodians trudged through the gate we foreigners stood in the front yard, weeping unashamedly.

The forced evacuation was part of an apparent campaign to make it clear to Jean Dyrac, the consul and senior French official at the embassy, and to everyone else in the compound that the new Government, not foreigners, was in charge—and under its own rules.

The first thing the Communists did was declare that they did not recognize the compound as an embassy, simply as a regroupment center for foreigners under their control. This shattered the possibility of asylum for high officials of the ousted regime who had sought sanctuary. On the afternoon of April 20, in a gloomy drizzle, Lieut. Gen. Sirik Matak, who was among those marked for execution, and a few other leading figures were taken away in the back of a sanitation truck.

Throughout our stay the Communists continued their campaign of proving their primacy—refusing to let a French plane land with food and medical supplies, refusing to allow us to be evacuated in comfort by air instead of by rutted road in the back of military trucks, and, finally, shutting down the embassy radio transmitter, our only contact with the outside world.

At the same time they did not physically harass or abuse us—the only time our baggage was searched was by Thai customs officials when we crossed the border—and they did eventually provide us with food and water. The food was usually live pigs, which we had to butcher.

Though the new rulers were obviously trying to inflict a certain amount of discomfort—they kept emphasizing that they had told us in radio broadcasts to get out of the city before the final assault and that by staying we had deliberately gone against their wishes—but there was another way to look at it. From their point of view we were being fed and housed much better than their foot soldiers were and should not complain.

But complain we did—about the food, about each other, about the fact that embassy officials were dining on chicken and white wine while we were eating plain rice and washing it down with heavily chlorinated water.

Among the embassy denizens, even in the midst of the tears and heartache, a search for the appearance of normality went on.

A Frenchwoman picked orange-colored blossoms from a bush and twined them in her laughing child's hair.

Gosta Streijffert, a former Swedish Army officer from a patrician family who is a Red Cross official, sat erect in a straight-backed chair he had carried outside and read a British news magazine with his monocle fixed.

At a table nearby a United Nations official and a Scottish

Red Cross medical team played bridge and drank whisky; someone carped loudly about the way his partner conducted the bidding.

In the midst of all this an American airplane mechanic who did not leave Cambodia on the day the United States Embassy staff was evacuated because he was too drunk had an epileptic seizure. The Red Cross doctors carried him on the run to the building where the hospital staff was quartered with their equipment.

The American recovered slowly. His case interrupted the staff's dinner—steak. We were envious, and they seemed embarrassed and angry when journalists made notes about their full larder.

Why was there not more sharing, more of a community spirit? What made us into such acquisitive, self-protective beings?

Why did all the Asians live outside, in the heat and rain, while many of the Caucasians, like my group, lived inside, with air-conditioning? We explained it by saying the living arrangements were up to the embassy, but this was clearly not an answer. Was our behavior and our segregation a verdict on our way of life?

Amid the generally disappointing behavior of the Westerners there were exceptions—people who rose above the squabbling and managed to hold things together.

There was François Bizot, a Frenchman who worked for many years in the countryside restoring ancient temples and ruins. He lost his Cambodian wife and mother-in-law, who were forced on the march. Yet his relationship with the Communists was strong and they trusted him, for he had met some in his work in the interior and he speaks Khmer fluently.

It was Mr. Bizot who, in the early days of our confinement, was allowed to scout for food and water. And it was he who successfully argued the cases of some Asians whose papers were not in perfect order. A number of people who were in the compound probably owe their futures to him.

There were others who performed constructive roles, among them Douglas A. Sapper 3d, an American with a Special Forces background who was involved in a private airline company.

Sapper, as everyone calls him, organized our group's kitchen and food rationing to make sure supplies would last. His ranger training—and his colorful language, none of which can be reproduced here—kept us eating regularly and kept pilferers out of the larder.

These special people notwithstanding, the general level of behavior remained disappointing throughout our stay. We held constant group meetings and made endless lists of who was supposed to perform what chores, and we were constantly going through the movements of organizing, but we never really got organized.

Lassitude and depression set in as the days dragged on. People lay dozing on their makeshift beds throughout the day, waiting only for the next feeding. One journalist slipped into a torpor in which he had energy only to lift his aerosol insecticide can and spray away flies.

Occasionally, however, there was an occurrence dramatic enough to break this morphic aura—such as the sighting of a Chinese plane on April 24 coming in for a landing at the airport, possibly carrying high Cambodian and Chinese officials from Peking.

There was also the unexpected arrival the day before of the seven Russians who had been holding out at the Soviet Embassy. They had been desperately trying to make friendly contact with the new Cambodian leaders to counterbalance Chinese influence.

But it was the Chinese and not the Russians who had been supplying the Khmer Rouge with arms. The Cambodian Communists rebuffed the Soviet overtures, fired a rocket through the second floor of their embassy, looted the building and ordered the Russians to the French compound.

This phase came to an end for us in the early hours on April 30 when—after an evening of sipping champagne "borrowed" from embassy stocks and singing determinedly hardy traveling songs such as "It's a Long Way to Tipperary," we were awakened as scheduled, after a few hours' sleep, and told to board the trucks.

As we stepped into the pleasantly cool air with our sacks and suitcases, we could see in the night sky the lights of many planes coming from the direction of South Vietnam and heading west. Saigon was falling, and South Vietnamese pilots, carrying their families and other refugees, were making their own evacuation journey to Thailand.

The New York Times, May 9, 1975

Evacuation Convoy to Thailand:
Arduous Trip Through the Secret Cambodia

BANGKOK, Thailand, May 8—The evacuation journey by truck to Thailand from Phnom Penh, where hundreds of foreigners had been confined in the French Embassy compound for nearly two weeks, gave a brief but revealing glimpse into the covert spy system and communally organized countryside of the Cambodian Communists—a glimpse that as far as is known no Westerners had ever had before.

We traveled on some of the well-defended dirt roads that had been built by hand and used as clandestine supply routes during the five years of the war that ended with the seizure of the Cambodian capital on April 17.

None of these roads show on maps of Cambodia, yet some were only half a mile or so from the main highways.

On the 250-mile trip we saw reservoirs, dikes, bridges—all built with hand tools. No machines or earth-moving equipment were visible.

We also saw boy militia units on patrol everywhere and male-female work crews repairing roads.

For those in the truck convoy the trip was arduous. It was especially difficult for the very young and the very old, and some fell ill. On our second day out, as we stopped in Kompong Chhnang for the night, a 9-month-old retarded child died in the bedlam of the governor's residence where we spent the night. French doctors who accompanied us said they knew before we started that the child could never survive such a trip. But the parents had no alternative—they could either take the child with them and pray for a miracle or leave him behind in Phnom Penh to die.

For the strong and healthy, the trip was tolerable. During rest stops we were able to forage for coconuts, mangoes and other fruit. And at every stop there were a few abandoned houses with big clay urns filled with rainwater, which we poured over our steaming heads.

The petty squabbling between various groups that often dominated our lives in the French Embassy compound followed us on the journey to the border. A group of Soviet diplomats refused to share their food with anyone. They even complained that they were not getting their proper convoy ration of rice.

At one point, in pique, the Russians threatened to expose stowaways on our truck. We in turn, advised them that if they persisted with their threats we would write a long story about their behavior, which, we suggested, would not go down very well in Moscow. They eased up a bit after that and offered us some vodka and tinned meat.

The French and the Vietnamese with French passports also continued to act like badly behaved zoo denizens, whenever the Communists brought us food.

If the Communists were looking for reasons to expel us as unfit and unsuited to live in a simple Asian society, we gave them ample demonstration on this journey.

The trip from the French Embassy began early on April 30 in virtually the same welter of chaos in which we had entered the embassy as refugees 13 days earlier.

In the darkness before dawn there was utter confusion in the embassy yard as more than 500 of us clambered into the 26 Soviet, Chinese and American-made military trucks for the journey.

There were supposed to be exactly 20 persons to each truck. But in the darkness and confusion some stowaways managed to sneak aboard. Five were on our truck—three Asian wives of Westerners whose papers were incomplete but who were fiercely determined to get out, a child of one of these women, and a German television correspondent.

The German sat upright, but the other stowaways slipped under our legs and we covered them with towels, bush hats and other oddments. Somehow, the officials who checked the convoy never noticed them.

At 6 A.M., with the sun just coming up, the convoy moved out. As it did, we saw a fresh battalion of troops marching single file into the city from the north.

Then the scenes changed and we met new images. The street lights burned, casting their artificial ray along the boulevards of a deserted city. Abandoned cars and assorted trash marked the trail of the departed population.

Every shop had been broken open and looted. Not a single civilian was visible—only the many soldiers camping in the shops and on the sidewalks.

We suddenly turned right—that is, west—down the road to the airport, and this was puzzling because we were supposed to be heading north and northwest toward Thailand.

We did not know it yet, but this was to be the detour that kept us from seeing that early stretch of Route 5 north of Phnom Penh that had been clogged with refugees forced out of Phnom Penh and may now be dotted with bodies.

Our convoy started southwest out of the capital down Route 4, then cut north along a rutted secondary road until we picked up Route 5 near Kompong Chhnang.

From there to the border, along Route 5, we encountered a wasteland of broken bridges, abandoned fields and forcibly evacuated highway towns.

The trip was a grueling one—with our trucks often lost or broken down for long hours either in the blistering sun or torrential downpours.

Some of these areas we passed through had been badly bombed by the United States Air Force in the early years of the war. Fields were gouged with bomb craters the size of swimming pools. But our American group and the other Westerners encountered almost no hostility from the local people.

While some sections we passed through were battered, others showed that they had been developed and organized over a long period of time and that they had remained untouched sanctuaries throughout the war.

The whole trip—with us jammed in the back of the bone-jarring military trucks—took more than three days. It was Saturday morning, after riding and bouncing all night, before we arrive at Poipet, the border town on the Cambodian side. Formalities took about an hour, but the Communist officials never searched our baggage or film or anything else we imagined they might be interested in.

Finally, at 11:20 A.M. I crossed over the rickety frontier bridge into Thailand. The first person to greet me was Chhay Born Lay, a Cambodian reporter for The Associated Press who left his country with his family on a press-evacuation flight.

As we walked forward to embrace each other, the back of my right hand caught on a roll of barbed wire marking the border and the scratch began to bleed. Lay instantly bent his head, grabbed the hand and began sucking the blood from the cut. I tried to pull my hand away, but he held tight.

This is what it is like to have a Cambodian friend. We both had left many Cambodian friends behind. We were both crying.

The New York Times, May 9, 1975

"Running Again—the Last Retreat"

by Philip Caputo

LONG BINH, South Viet Nam—This is a personal account of what must be one of the great tragedies of modern times.

What is happening here is an exodus of humanity of staggering magnitude, so staggering that no words of mine can capture anything but the smallest fraction of it.

I am writing this in a thatch hut on Highway 1, the long Vietnamese road which the French soldiers who fought in Indochina dubbed la rue sans joie, the street without joy.

Today, Sunday, it is living up to that name. A hundred yards away, North Vietnamese mortar shells and rockets are slamming into government positions guarding the bridge over the Dong Hai River, whose brown waters meander with mocking indifference thru green rice fields and murky swamps.

[The Associated Press reported that early Monday Communist sappers had seized a section of Highway 1, cutting the refugee flow into the capital from the east.]

I am writing under the pressure of those bursting shells.

Pouring over the river bridge is another kind of stream, a stream of flesh and blood and bone, of exhausted, frightened faces, of crushed hopes and loss. The long, relentless column reaches forward and backward as far as the eye can see, for miles and miles and in places 50 feet across.

These are thousands upon thousands of Vietnamese refugees fleeing the fighting in Trang Bom, east of here, the shellings in Long Thanh, south of here, the attacks near Bien Hoa, north of here. They are jammed on the blacktop in crowds as thick as those pouring out of a football stadium, but this crowd is at least 20 miles long.

They are running from what looks like the Communist drive on Saigon and that's where they're trying to go. Many of them are refugees two and three times over—people who ran from Xuan Loc, from Da Nang and Ham Tan and Qui Nhon.

Now they are running again, but this is their last retreat. This is the end of the road, for them, for South Viet Nam, and for a war that's gone on for over a generation.

They are filing past me on foot, their sandals scraping mournfully against the pavement, their heads hunched down against the driving monsoon rain that lashes them.

They are riding on motor scooters, in cars, in trucks, buses, oxcarts all piled up with crates and suitcases and ragged bundles of clothes. Sometimes the noise of the vehicles is deafening, but not so deafening as to drown out the wind-rushing sound of an incoming rocket that whips over their heads to burst in the paddylands beyond the river.

At other times, all you hear is that solemn, processional shuffling of sandled feet, bare feet, bloodied feet against the rainslick asphalt. You hear that and the chorusing of crying children.

A three-year-old boy, his face and hands covered with sores and insect bites, a toy-like sun helmet on his toy-like head, toddles thru the crowd, whimpering for his lost parents.

They find him finally and his whimpering stops as they prop him on their motor scooter.

Two enemy mortars have just exploded near the South Vietnamese bunkers and earthworks guarding the bridge. White and gray smoke is billowing upward, dissipating, wafting over the multitudes like some noxious cloud.

Some of the scenes here are almost Goyaesque in their horror. Vietnamese soldiers are picking thru slabs of meat which they will eat for supper. In the middle of the road a few yards away is the lower half of a man's leg swollen and rotting in the rain. The upper half is a mass of rended flesh indistinguishable from the meat the soldiers are preparing to cook.

An old woman with teeth turned blackish-red from chewing betel-nuts screams at a truck that seems to be slowing down to pick her up. She grabs her bundle of clothes, but it is almost as heavy as she is, and it breaks open, and as she tries to gather it up, the truck presses on.

A company of South Vietnamese soldiers and sailors stationed at the naval base on the river stumbles across the paddies into the village where the North Vietnamese mortars are emplaced.

They vanish into the trees. Soon shells are thudding in on top of them. Small arms fire crackles in between the punctuating thumps of the mortars. Then the soldiers come running out, fanning thru the sea of green rice like flushed rabbits.

A heavy shell whines in, explodes on the river bank with an ear-splitting crash.

"Ya, ya, eeyah," a farmer shouts at his herd of water buffalo as they plod across the bridge, fouling up the traffic even more, the great gray beasts tossing their horned heads and bellowing at the sound of man at war.

Mixed into the column are scores of retreating soldiers, some with their weapons, some without, all beaten.

The endless river of people flows on, part of it coming from further east on Highway 1, part from Highway 15 to the south, both parts meeting in a sorrowful confluence at this bridge.

A flight of South Vietnamese fighters screams overhead. Within minutes comes the hollow rumbling of bombs. A pillar of smoke, as if rising from an enormous funeral pyre, swirls into the leaden, sagging sky. The planes are strafing Communist tank columns rumbling up Route 15. They are only a few miles away.

A teen-age boy, behind the wheel of a rickety truck in which his parents and family sit amidst piles of belongings, looks at me and says:

"We come from Long Thanh. Many shells fall on us last night. Many VC [Viet Cong] in Long Thanh. Much fighting. Many die."

Meanwhile, all up and down the column, South Vietnamese soldiers are firing their rifles into the air in an attempt to stem the tide.

It is futile. The crowd seems to have a momentum all its own, and the sharp cracks of the soldiers' M-16s is not half as frightening as the Communist tanks that growl like armored monsters somewhere behind this procession.

A few have stopped to rest at the entrance to the National Military Cemetery. They flop down in the shadow of a statue of a South Vietnamese soldier.

He is sitting, his jaw slack with exhaustion, his helmet

pushed back on his head, his rifle lying across his knees. He is a symbol of the weariness and the pity of war.

At the base of the monument, mingled with refugees, a few living soldiers are sitting in almost the same position.

Like the statue, their pose seems to say that it is over. This is the end of the road, the end of a war. And the nearness of an end is all there is to mitigate the incalculable suffering of the Vietnamese who are making their last march down the street without joy.

Chicago Tribune, April 28, 1975

We Clawed for Our Lives!

by Keyes Beech

ABOARD THE USS HANCOCK—Tuesday morning I had breakfast on the ninth floor of the Caravelle Hotel in Saigon and watched a column of ugly black smoke framed by the tall, twin spires of the Catholic cathedral in Kennedy Square just up the street.

Tan Son Nhut airport was burning; the streets were bare of traffic, unnaturally but pleasantly quiet.

The waiters were nervous and the room boys said I couldn't have my laundry back until "tomorrow."

What tomorrow?

Six hours later I was fighting for my life and wishing I had never left the hotel. I nearly didn't make it out of Saigon.

My Daily News colleague, Bob Tamarkin, telephoned to say the embassy had ordered a full-scale evacuation—immediately. He said he hoped to see me later.

I joined others who were leaving and we went to a prearranged assembly point, a U.S. embassy building only a couple of blocks away.

Three buses were quickly filled with a mixed bag of correspondents and Vietnamese. Some of the more dignified among us held back rather than scramble for seats and waited for the fourth bus.

That was a mistake.

The first three buses made it inside Tan Son Nhut airbase and their passengers flew out. Ours never made it inside, and that accounts for one of the longest days of my life.

We heard the bad news over the driver's radio on the way out: "Security conditions are out of control at Tan Son Nhut. Do not go to Tan Son Nhut. Repeat, do not go to Tan Son Nhut."

We went on anyway, the sound of explosions and the rattle of automatic weapons growing louder by the second—incoming mixed with outgoing fire. South Vietnamese soldiers were firing wildly in the air for no apparent reason.

South Vietnamese sentries turned us back at the first checkpoint. For the thousandth time, I made mental note of the billboard legend that departing Americans see as they leave Saigon:

"The noble sacrifices of allied soldiers will never be forgotten."

We tried another approach to the airbase but were again waved back. No way, as the Vietnamese are fond of saying.

The evacuation had broken down.

It was 2 P.M. when we headed back to the city. Nobody on that bus will ever forget the next few hours. We cruised aimlessly about Saigon for at least three hours while our security escorts tried to figure out what to do with us.

We were a busload of fools piloted by a man who had never driven a bus and had to wire the ignition when it stalled because the Vietnamese driver had run away with the keys the night before.

"I'm doing the best I can," said Bill Austin of Miami, Okla., the man at the wheel, as we careened through narrow streets, knocking over sidewalk vendors, sideswiping passing vehicles and sending Vietnamese scattering like leaves in the wind.

When the back seat driving became too much, Austin, an auditor, stopped the bus and said: "If there is a bus driver aboard, I'll be glad to let him take the wheel."

There were no takers. By now we had been joined by two other buses and half a dozen cars packed with Vietnamese who figured that by staying with us they could get out of the country.

At every stop, Vietnamese beat on the doors and windows pleading to be let inside. We merely looked at them. We already had enough Vietnamese aboard. Every time we opened the door, we had to beat and kick them back.

For no reason, except that we were following another bus, we went to the Saigon port area, one of the toughest parts of the city, where the crowds were uglier than elsewhere. Police fired into the air to part the mob and let us through onto the dock.

I got off the bus and went over to John Moore, the embassy

security officer who was sitting in one of those sedans with the flashy blinker on top.

"Do you know why we are here and what you are going to do with us?" I asked him.

Moore shrugged helplessly. "There are ships," he said, gesturing toward sandbagged Vietnamese vessels lying alongside the dock.

I looked around at the gathering crowd. Small boys were snatching typewriters and bags of film. This, as the Chinese would say, looked like bad joss. I didn't know how or whether I was going to get out of Saigon, but I damned well knew I wasn't going to stay here.

I got back on the bus, which was both our prison and our fortress. And other correspondents including some of my closest friends—Wendell S. (Bud) Merick of U.S. News and World Report and Ed White of the AP—felt the same way. White's typewriter, his most precious possession at the moment, next to his life, was gone.

Again we had to fight off the Vietnamese. Ed Bradley of CBS, a giant of a man, was pushing, kicking, shoving, his face sad. I found myself pushing a middle-aged Vietnamese woman who had been sitting beside me on the bus and asked me to look after her because she worked for the Americans and the Viet Cong would cut her throat.

That's what they all said and maybe they are right. But she fought her way back to my side. "Why did you push me?" she asked. I had no answer.

Austin didn't know what to do with us so we drove to the American embassy. There the Vietnamese woman decided to get off.

"I have worked for the United States government for 10 years," she said, "but you do not trust me and I do not trust you. Even if we do get to Tan Son Nhut, they wouldn't let me on the plane." She was right, of course.

"I am going home and poison myself," she said. I didn't say anything because there was nothing to say.

For lack of anything better to do, Austin drove us to the embassy parking lot across the street. The embassy was besieged by the Vietnamese that we were abandoning. Every gate was closed. There was no way in.

I went to the parking lot telephone and called an embassy friend. Briefly, I stated the situation: "There are about 40 of us—Americans, British and two or three Japanese. We can't get in."

"Hold it," he said. A few minutes later, he came back on the phone with the following instructions:

"Take your people to the MacDinh Chi police station next to the embassy. They know you are coming. They will help you over the wall."

An uncertain Moses, I led my flock out of the parking lot, across the street and through the police barricades to the police station. They never heard of us. When we tried to talk to them, they told us to move on and fired into the air to make their point.

We dribbled around the corner to the rear of the embassy compound, where several hundred Vietnamese were pounding at the gate or trying to scale the wall. There was only one way inside: through the crowd and over the 10-foot wall.

Once we moved into that seething mass, we ceased to be correspondents. We were only men fighting for their lives, scratching, clawing, pushing ever closer to that wall. We were like animals.

Now, I thought, I know what it's like to be a Vietnamese. I am one of them. But if I could get over that wall I would be an American again.

My attache case accidentally struck a baby in its mother's arms and its father beat at me with his fists. I tried to apologize as he kept on beating me while his wife pleaded with me to take the baby.

Somebody grabbed my sleeve and wouldn't let go. I turned my head and looked into the face of a Vietnamese youth.

"You adopt me and take me with you and I'll help you," he screamed. "If you don't, you don't go."

I said I'd adopt him. I'd have said anything. Could this be happening to me?

Suddenly my arm was free and I edged closer to the wall. There were a pair of marines on the wall. They were trying to help us up and kick the Vietnamese down. One of them looked down at me.

"Help me," I pleaded. "Please help me."

That marine helped me. He reached down with his long, muscular arm and pulled me up as if I were a helpless child.

I lay on a tin roof gasping for breath like a landed fish, then dropped to the ground. God bless the marines. I was one myself in the last of the just wars.

One American offered me a cup of water and a doctor asked me if I wanted a tranquilizer. I accepted the water and declined the tranquilizer. "Are you sure you're all right?" the doctor said anxiously.

"Sure," I croaked. "I'm just fine. But my friends?"

I looked up and saw a yellow shirt coming over the wall. That was Bud Merick of U.S. News & World Report. Minutes later I saw the sweaty red face of big Ed White from the Associated Press come over.

I was very happy to see him. He is not only my friend. He was carrying my typewriter.

A tall, young embassy officer in a pink shirt looked at me and said, "Aren't you Keyes Beech?"

I admitted I was. His name is Brunson McKinley and I last saw him in Peking two years ago. We made our way through the crowd of Vietnamese evacuees gathered around the embassy swimming pool and through to the main embassy building and took the elevator to the sixth floor.

Our embassy friends seemed glad to see us and expressed awe that we had come over the embassy wall. I was pretty awed too, now that I think of it.

A retired American general who has been around here a long time, Charles Timmes, said he had been on the phone to "Big" Minh, the new president, urging him to ask the North Vietnamese for a cease-fire.

"He said he was trying but they wouldn't listen," Charlie said. "Anyway, they haven't shelled the embassy yet."

"That's nice of them," I said, slumping into a soft chair.

The man I really wanted to see was down on the third floor. His name is Graham Martin and he was our ambassador. In my view, he gambled with American lives, including mine, by dragging his heels on the evacuation.

A few minutes later I was on the embassy roof and inside a Marine helicopter and on my way to the carrier Hancock.

It was exactly 6:30 P.M.

My last view of Saigon was through the tail door of the helicopter. Tan Son Nhut was burning. So was Bien Hoa. Then the door closed—closed on the most humiliating chapter in American history.

I looked at the man next to me. He was a Vietnamese and I moved away from him. Forty-five minutes later we put down on the Hancock.

The salt sea air tasted good.

Chicago Daily News, May 1, 1975

Diary of S. Viet's Last Hours

by Bob Tamarkin

ABOARD THE USS OKINAWA—"They lied to us at the very end," said Capt. Stuart Herrington, the tears welling in his eyes. "They promised. They promised," he said, biting hard on his lip to hold the tears back.

Shirtless, he sat on the edge of the bunk, shaking his head. He continued:

"I have never received an order in my life to do something I was ashamed of. If I would have known how it was going to end, I would have refused the order."

He was speaking of the evacuation of the Americans and Vietnamese during the frantic day last Tuesday when the Americans pulled out of South Vietnam, leaving hundreds of Vietnamese in the embassy compound and thousands of others who had been promised evacuation working in Saigon and the rest of the country.

Lt. Col. H. G. Summers, a barrel-chested 250-pounder, sitting in the bunk next to Herrington, turned to me and said:

"I asked you to come here because you were the last newsman to see the end. Do you know what you saw? Do you really know what you saw?" he asked.

"I saw the evacuation of the U.S. Embassy—the last hours," I answered.

"No," Summers said, pausing. "You saw deceit. You saw how we let this country down to the very end."

Both men hadn't slept for more than 24 hours and both were emotionally drained.

The two had been assigned to the embassy to assist with the evacuation. For nearly 20 hours they organized groups of people, assuring them that they would be evacuated. They used Vietnamese firemen on standby to protect Americans should a helicopter accident occur.

In the end, even the firemen were left behind.

"We had arranged the people in groups of 70. We made them throw away their suitcases. They listened to us and believed us. They waited confidently in those rows, believing their friends would not let them down," Herrington said.

Until a few minutes before they themselves were flown out on the last choppers before the marines left, Herrington and Summers believed those 500 in the compound would be flown out. The two officers said they were told that Ambassador Graham Martin and his key aides would be leaving in the last helicopter, remaining until all evacuees were taken out. They left well before that.

"They didn't have the courtesy to tell us," Summers said. "We learned by accident the ambassador had left earlier. And we knew that those other people would not be going.

"They lied to us at the very end. One thing you don't do is lie to your own people."

There was no indication that the evacuation was going to stop until a security agent told them they would be taking the last chopper out, Summers said.

A total of 70,000 people were evacuated Tuesday. The operation employed 80 helicopters flying 495 sorties.

But as one senior diplomatic official put it:

"The big numbers are irrelevant. The rest of our lives we will be haunted by how we betrayed those people. It made me cry when I got here. There were lots of people who were crying when they got here."

On the second floor of a small annex building just behind the wall the marines had set up a 50-caliber machinegun ready to strafe the walls should the Vietnamese try storming it.

A three-foot space along the top of the wall, where the barbed wire had been pushed aside, was the only way into the massive embassy compound. The embassy was sealed.

I had gone to the embassy earlier in the day, at noon, about 90 minutes after the evacuation alert was sounded. I was late arriving at a pre-designated pickup point, from which I would have been taken by bus to the defense attache office at Tan Son Nhut Airport.

Four other Americans stood with me outside the gate, where only minutes before a portly man dressed in a blue suit had been allowed to enter. He was Gen. Dang Van Quang,

the national securities affairs adviser to former President
Nguyen Van Thieu.

I now stood with the other Americans, who were waving
passports as proof of their citizenship. We were refused entrance.

John Hogan, the embassy press officer, whom I knew, assured me I could get in. But he gave no instructions. As I was
walking away, he poked his finger at me from behind the gate
and said: "Don't write one word about this evacuation." I
returned to my hotel room and filed a story about the initial
evacuation alert.

By the time I had returned to the entrance at 25 Hog Thap
Tu St. I saw my 61-year-old colleague, Keyes Beech, scrambling to get through the three-foot space. As he was pulled
up by the marines, he was pulled back by the Vietnamese
clinging to him, hoping that somehow they would be pulled
up with him. The Marines had orders to grab Americans first,
then third-country nationals and then the Vietnamese.

The scene at the wall was brutal. Marines and other embassy
personnel threw Vietnamese people off the wall. One official
drew his revolver, stuck it point-blank in the face of a young
Vietnamese boy and screamed: "Get down, you bastard, or
I'll blow your head off. Get Down!"

The marines brought the butts of their rifles down on the
fingers of those trying to climb the walls. Elderly women and
children who were being pushed up by the sheer force of
bodies beneath them became enmeshed in the barbed wire,
their skin punctured with bloody wounds.

One official who had thrown a young girl from the wall
three times finally gave in. "I couldn't take it anymore. I feel
sorry for her," said Jeff Kibler, 24, an embassy accountant.

A bus pulled up to the gate jammed with people and with
scores more clinging to the top. Under the threat of being
machinegunned, the driver backed away.

One American woman, who had arrived from Honolulu on
Saturday to get a family of seven out of the country, arrived
at the gate, trailed by the family. She stopped, realizing the
futility of the situation.

"I couldn't put them through that," she said, the tears

welling in her eyes. She sent the family away and returned to go over the wall herself.

Most of those who were legitimately to be evacuated were ignored as the marines began pulling people up. In some cases, families were separated forever. They were hoisted up and over like sacks of potatoes, dumped wherever they landed. I got in that way.

As the only correspondent who stayed to cover the evacuation of the embassy through the departure of Ambassador Martin (I left 45 minutes after he had), I kept a diary of the events and people I met in those desperate hours.

Following is a chronology of America's last few hours in South Vietnam, as I witnessed them.

3 P.M.—The embassy was surrounded by Vietnamese who wanted to get out of the country. They were screaming, crying, trampling one another, and some clawed at the gates in their futile efforts to get inside the embassy compound.

5:39 P.M.—I was hauled through the gap in the barbed wire. It had taken me more than 1½ hours to inch through the bodies to the marines' grasp, just three yards away.

One marine was pulled off the fence by hands that grabbed his legs. At that point, the mood of the marines turned from bare tolerance into fitful rage. They began pushing back harder and screaming louder.

Security guards in the neighboring French embassy stood on walls of their compound casually watching the pandemonium. Many people ran up to them, waving their papers and cards. The French ignored them.

6 P.M.—The rampage started quietly, and then it snowballed.

A few youngsters wandered into an inconspicuous storeroom filled with 200 or so cases of soft drinks and grabbed a couple of bottles apiece. Within minutes hundreds were storming the storeroom carrying away several bottles at a time. Within minutes the storeroom had been cleaned out. The assault set the mood for what was to follow.

The fever spread into the embassy restaurant, where people began grabbing what they could. They devoured and drank anything they could get their hands on.

The binge spread to the food lockers, where frozen foods were kept. Slabs of ribs and frozen steaks and beef briskets were pounded with hammers and dull-edged knives to soften the meat to be cooked on the stoves and in the ovens, which were in control of the evacuees.

Then they found the store-room to the restaurant above the main embassy restaurant. Down they came. This time they carried off cases of canned goods, juices, boxes containing cartons of cigarets. Some were stopped by the marines, who began beating looters.

9:40 P.M.—A grim-faced Graham Martin, his hair perfectly combed, followed by four Marines, disappeared up a flight of stairs. He surveyed the pillage. The crowd did not recognize the ambassador. He came swiftly down the stairs minutes later, the marines still following closely. He disappeared through the gate that leads to the main embassy courtyard, where the helicopters land on the parking lot.

As the helicopters circled overhead, their red lights blinking off and on, orange flames and thick smoke poured out of the embassy's smoke stack. The remaining documents and papers, some collected since 1954, when the United States established its embassy in Saigon, were being burned in the incinerator.

10 P.M.—Only an hour earlier, a marine had threatened to blow the head off a young Vietnamese boy. He pointed his .45 automatic at the youth, forcing him to drop the carton of cigarets he had taken from the storehouse. Then the marines walked the same steps, stuffing cartons into their own knapsacks.

10:30 P.M.—A 30-year-old American woman named Marilyn (she would not give her last name) who came to Vietnam only a few days ago to be with a Vietnamese friend, decided she wanted to go back over the wall. She begged a marine guard to let her go. There were still thousands at every gate to the embassy, but they were quiet, sitting in the darkness, hoping they would be allowed in the next morning.

"In all good conscience, I can't let you go over the wall," the marine said. "You must get permission from the embassy officials in charge of the evacuation."

She was disappointed, but agreed.

The marines began rounding up the last few Americans in

the compound. It had been 12 hours since the evacuation began.

11:30 P.M.—The marines were ordered to round up the Americans and let them pass through to the landing pad door first. The Vietnamese sensed something might be wrong and began to stir. They began to advance toward the gate, but were stopped. The process of getting through the gate is slow. Fifty to 80 people at a time allowed to pass. A normal helicopter load is 50 people, but now they were jamming the copters with as many as 80 and 90. The sound of small-arms fire pierced the night along with the muffled sound of artillery.

MIDNIGHT—Some of the marines were edgy and a few turned sadistic. One stood before the hundreds of Vietnamese who stared blankly ahead, and said: "All right, now everybody sings." He began waving his hands through the air, conducting them. They didn't understand. He laughed loudly. They just stared in bewilderment, their faces blank. One young Vietnamese boy and a man tried to squeeze through the gate.

They were beaten, brutally.

The choppers began landing on the roof of the embassy and on the parking lot. The group I was with was led into the embassy to take off from the heliport.

1 A.M.—The inside of the embassy now appeared to have been ransacked. The marines and embassy security officials systematically went through every room tearing up, ripping out and destroying whatever might reveal anything to the enemy.

1:15 A.M.—Ambassador Martin was in the office of Conrad F. LaGeux, a special assistant. A senior diplomatic official, sipping a glass of champagne, was going over last-minute details with Henry Boudreau, counselor of administrative affairs. Martin, still in shirtsleeves, was calm. They were joined by Josiah W. Bennett, head of political affairs. Meanwhile, the deputy ambassador, Wolfgang J. Lemann, roamed throughout the embassy, walkie talkie in hand, monitoring the evacuation efforts.

2 A.M.—About 200 evacuees had been led to the stairwell of the top floor and were planted there to wait for another chopper to land. The door to the floor was locked. For more than two hours they waited, sealed in the well without water.

One man said that he had been at the embassy since 7 A.M. waiting to leave. An American who worked as a computer analyst heard on the radio at 8 P.M. that all the Americans had left. He was unaware of the evacuation.

At midnight a friend called to let him know the helicopters were still flying. He got to the embassy at 1 A.M. and was pulled over the fence.

3 A.M.—A security official said the evacuation was 12 hours behind schedule.

3:30 A.M.—Marines were stretched out sleeping on the floor of the embassy lobby, machineguns, M-16s, knapsacks, walkie talkies spread out everywhere. In a back room on the first floor was Major J. Keene, commander of the 140-man detail assigned to provide evacuation protection. He was grabbing a few minutes of sleep, his feet propped up on a desk. A young marine in a corridor gathered his gear, stuffing a paperback book into his knapsack. The book: "The Fall of Rome."

Amid the big plastic bags of shredded paper a flagless pole stood forlornly, and there were still plaques on the lobby wall. One plaque was in honor of four embassy personnel—an American woman and three Vietnamese—who were killed by a Viet Cong bomb while on duty at the embassy on March 30, 1965.

The other plaque read: "Embassy of the United States of America. Built in time of war. Dedicated to the cause of peace. In memory of those who have served their nation in Vietnam. Ellsworth Bunker Ambassador. September 1967."

4:15 A.M.—Ambassador Martin appeared in the lobby. He was wearing a light brown suit, and carried a small attache case and a folded clothes bag.

He first walked outside, but several minutes later he and top aides returned. Instead of leaving from the ground-level site, he was instructed to depart from the heliport atop of the embassy. He spoke to no one, but stood waiting for the elevator to the sixth floor for the last time. With him were special assistants, Thomas Polgar, LaGeux, and George Jacobson. An air of deep depression surrounded them as they walked into the elevator.

About 15 minutes later, a marine helicopter carried off the ambassador, his aides, two security guards, several personnel from the mission warden's office and a missionary couple, officially ending America's presence in South Vietnam.

They were on their way to the USS Blue Ridge, the flagship of the 7th Fleet.

As the Jolly Green Giant CH-53 lifted Martin and the others into the blackness, the lights of Saigon glimmered below and fires could be seen on the city's outskirts. They were from the fighting of the encroaching and overpowering North Vietnamese Army, tightening its grip for the kill. Lightning from monsoon rains in the distance lit up the sky periodically.

A stream of lights headed down from the direction of Bien Hoa, 15 miles north of Saigon, where the Communist tanks and troop trucks pushed toward the scared and panicked city. It was just a matter of time before 30 years of war would come to an end.

To the end, Martin maintained the somber aloofness that characterized him. Yet, he maintained a certain dignity.

5 A.M.—A sense of panic overtook even the marines. So far there was no actual fighting, just threats and shots fired into the air.

5:15 A.M.—The remaining American civilians—there were three of us—were instructed to go to the sixth floor. One civilian was the young woman who would not give her name. The other civilian was a portly man in his late 30s, who also refused to give his name or even his home in the States. He arrived in Saigon only on Monday to try to help some Vietnamese friends out. It was too late. Now he sulked, turned to an officer and said: "You know, I had ordered $100 worth of tailor-made clothing yesterday when I arrived, and I paid for it in advance." The soldier merely nodded.

The embassy security head appeared, a walkie talkie in hand. Martin Garrett turned to the group of army officers, marines and civilians and several other embassy security staff, and said:

"We just got orders from President Ford that the evacuation is to stop immediately. The pilots have been flying for 14 hours, and the President has ordered the commander of the 7th fleet to halt operations."

He carefully gave instructions to the marines to station themselves on the roof and to leave all their gear behind.

Those marines who were still on the embassy grounds were told to walk back into the embassy casually when the next chopper left, and secure the doors behind them. They, too, would be leaving from the heliport.

5:30 A.M.—The marines took their place on the roof. The helicopter landed, its massive propellers whooshing through the air, creating cyclonic winds, drowning out the sounds of the night.

My chopper lifted off, its red lights blinking, and headed toward the South China Sea. The passengers, including me, sat stoically in the dark, tired and numb. Some were dazed, finding it difficult to believe that the Americans were pulling out in this manner skulking away in the darkness.

Below in the courtyard, where the big choppers had been loading, the headlights from the cars and trucks surrounding the parking lot were still on to light the way for the choppers.

Hundreds of Vietnamese looked up, waiting for the next one.

It never came.

Chicago Daily News, May 6, 1975

Tenderness, Hatred and Grief
Mark Saigon's Last Days

by Malcolm W. Browne

ABOARD THE U.S.S. MOBILE, in the South China Sea, May 3 —Like a failed marriage, the Vietnamese-American relationship of the last generation has ended in a mixture of hatred and suspicion, coupled with a strong remnant of tenderness and compassion on both sides.

It ended with an embittered Saigon policeman pistol-whipping an American reporter and with Government troops and policemen taking potshots at American cars and buses, or sometimes just at any "big nose"—non-Asian.

The parting was often a time of anxiety and grief, however, and both American and Vietnamese faces were lined with tears.

There were the Americans—private citizens now—who lived and worked in Vietnam years ago and who came back before the end to do what they could. They went into debt to buy air tickets, arriving within a few days of the surrender, in a desperate effort to find Vietnamese friends or the relatives of their Vietnamese wives. Most of them failed, but at least in trying they avoided the extra load of guilt they would have felt at doing nothing.

"At least during those final hours at the gate outside the airport trying to get my own people in," an American said. "I maybe helped one woman. She was Vietnamese, with an American passport, but of course without a big nose no one was getting through on their own. I had to leave my own behind, but at least I got her through."

The tens of thousands aboard the huge evacuation armada sailing away from Vietnam have told endless stories of heroism, loyalty and love in the last hours.

But for millions of Vietnamese and not a few Americans the dominant memory will be sorrow and betrayal and guilt.

There was scarcely an American in the final weeks who was not forced to share personally in that intense feeling of guilt. For each of them had what Vietnamese call a big nose—the only real passport to salvation. Caucasian features could do almost anything: cash checks, cut through the maddening bureaucratic impediments that had been erected both by Saigon and Washington and, most of all, get a few Vietnamese to safety.

Nonetheless, countless Vietnamese, knowing they would remain despite all, worked for their American friends to the last.

On the other hand, many an American organization, private and official, locked its doors and left without any effort to help Vietnamese employes and associates.

Some, like Northrop, the airplane builder, offered help to Vietnamese employes but not to their families; in most cases this amounted to leaving the employes behind.

The Saigon branches of American banks closed, sent their records and American employes home and left tens of thousands of Vietnamese depositors unpaid.

Many organizations had some access to the "black lift"—a semiclandestine airlift of selected Vietnamese and their families that operated for about a week like an underground railroad before the frantic final exodus under fire.

Details of how it worked will have to remain secret for a time to protect the Vietnamese and Americans involved, but a considerable number of Vietnamese found out about it.

Any American, including newsmen, suspected of having anything to do with it became the object of an endless procession of supplicants, some pleading, some offering bribes, some asking for marriage. Only a handful of places were available, so the Americans involved dissembled, comforted and lied.

There were Vietnamese who could have gone and chose not to—thoughtful, courageous men and women who made their decisions after agonizing reflection. Among them was one of the principal reporter-photographers on the staff of The New York Times, Nguyen Ngoc Luong.

One of them explained: "In the end the color of the skin counts for more than politics. Anyone who has lived in either the United States or Vietnam knows this, and I have done both. The Vietcong, like me, are yellow."

For an overwhelming majority desperation and panic prevailed. Some who knew from the first that they could not leave, however much they wanted to, tried to send out last precious parts of themselves—photographs, the ashes of ancestors, keepsakes and children.

On the last day, as frantic people took to the streets despite the thunder of rockets and the popping of rifles, someone spread a blanket on the sidewalk next to the Continental Hotel, in the heart of the downtown foreign quarter. On the blanket lay a sleeping baby, beside it a small plastic bag containing ragged clothing and toys. Clearly the hope was that someone would carry it away to America, but by then it was too late.

There was the maid who, believing she could not go herself and having no living relatives, wanted to send her cat, all she had. Both were evacuated.

The prospect of leaving, real or imagined, often led to bitterness. There were those Vietnamese who had been promised that they would be evacuated but who gave way to morose suspicion—to the widespread Vietnamese belief, carefully nurtured by the Communists, that even those Americans considered the closest of friends could not be trusted.

In the long decades of American involvement in Vietnam there were an appreciable number of Americans who learned to understand and love the country. Unfortunately, it seemed to some of them, the more Americans who came the greater was the number who preferred to avoid any real relationship with the Vietnamese.

Increasingly the Americans walled themselves into compounds, command posts and official buildings, which they furnished with air-conditioning, supermarkets, swimming pools and clubs—everything possible to keep the Vietnamese reality from penetrating the American one. For most the outside represented the threat of death, robbery, disease and the hatred presumed to be lurking behind the mask of an Asian face.

Of course there were just enough such evidence as Vietnamese units abandoning or betraying American advisers under fire to lend substances to many Americans' attitudes. Americans were ambushed in supposedly safe places and killed; they were robbed and cheated.

On the other hand, there were countless cases in which Americans short-changed or cheated Vietnamese—sometimes because of misunderstandings arising from the language barrier—and instances of brutal and overbearing behavior. Not least was the killing and wounding of people seemingly without reason.

The Communists were provided with ample evidence to support their denunciations of "American imperialism."

Despite the recriminations tenuous contact was maintained between Americans and Communists through an indirect telephone link. On the final day this correspondent telephoned the Vietcong delegation after a particularly heavy shelling of the Saigon airport by their side to ask about their safety, among other things.

"I cannot tell you how grateful we are for asking, especially considering the circumstances," was the reply. "We hope you all get through this somehow."

A few minutes before one of the last groups of distraught Americans rushed from their ravaged offices and hotel rooms to look for a bus to the airport, a Vietnamese friend arrived to say farewell. Some of the Americans were in tears, and the Vietnamese, seeking to comfort them, patted their shoulders and said:

"You may hear after you leave that some here have died, perhaps even at their own hand. You must not spend the rest of your lives with that guilt. It is just a part of Vietnam's black fate, in which you, all of you, became ensnared for a time. Fate is changeless and guiltless."

The New York Times, May 6, 1975

MAPS

CHRONOLOGY

BIOGRAPHICAL NOTES

NOTE ON THE TEXTS

NOTES

GLOSSARY

INDEX

Quang Tri

Thua
Thien

Da Nang

MR I

Quang
Nam

Quang Tin

Quang
Ngai

Kontum

Binh
Dinh

Pleiku

MR II

Phu Bon

Phu
Yen

Dariac

Khanh
Hoa

Quang
Duc

Cam Ranh Bay

Phuoc
Long

Tuyen
Duc

MR III

Ninh
Thuan

Lam Dong

Phan Rang

Binh
Long

Tay
Ninh

Long
Khanh

Binh
Thuan

Binh
Duong

Binh Tuy

Hau
Nghia

Bien
Hoa

Gia
Dinh

Kien
Phong

Kien
Tuong

SAIGON

Long
An

Go
Cong

Phuoc
Tuy

Chau
Doc

An
Giang

Sa
Dec

Dinh
Tuong

Vinh
Long

Kien
Hoa

Phu Quoc
Island

Kien
Giang

Phong
Dinh

Vinh
Binh

Vung Tau

Chuong
Thien

Ba
Xuyen

MR IV

Bac Lieu

An
Xuyen

SOUTH VIETNAM
Provinces and Military Regions

VIETNAM

Chazaud

DEMARCATION LINE

MR 1

SOUTH VIETNAM

	International boundaries
	Provincial boundaries
	Military regions boundaries

THAILAND

LAOS

CAMBODIA

CENTRAL HIGHLANDS

Plateau du Kontum

Plateau du Darlac

Mekong

PHNOM PENH ★

MR 2

MR 3

CAPITAL SPECIAL ZONE

MR 4

Gulf of Thailand

SOUTH CHINA SEA

Vinh Linh
Cua Viet
Quang Tri
Con Thien
Dong Ha
Phong Dien
Tchepone (Xépôn)
Khe Sanh
Muang Nong
Hue
Phu Bai
Danang (Tourane)
A Shau
Hoi An
Xé Banghiang
Song Boung
Ben Giang
An Hoa
Queson
Tam Ky
Chu Lai
Khong Sédone
Ban Bac
Son My (My Lai)
Saravan
Chavane
Dak Sut
Quang Ngai
Pakse
Dak To
Kontum
Attapu
Plateau du Kontum
Pleiku
Tonle Kong
Virachei
Boung Long
Pleime
Qui Nhon
Tonle San
Ia Drang
Lomphat
Andaung Pech
Hau Bon
Stung Treng
Tonle Srepok
Va Hieo
Song Ba
Tonle Sap
Song Srepok
Ban Don
Tuy Hoa
Kratie
Senmonorom
Ban Me Thuot
Dai Lanh
Duc Lap
Khanh Duong
Kompong Cham
Mekong
Sre Khtum
Gia Nghia
Duc My
Ninh Hoa
Nha Trang
Snuol
Bo Duc
Khanh Hoa
Cam Ranh
Phum Krek
Mimot
Da Lat
An Loc
Phuoc Binh
Chon Thanh
Don Luan
Bao Loc
Phan Rang
Tay Ninh
Ben Cat
Phu Cuong
Phan Thiet
Kompong Trabek
Svay Rieng
Khiem Cuong
Bien
Xuan Loc
Moc Hoa
Gia Dinh
Cholon
SAIGON
Ham Tan
Takeo
Plain of Reeds
Ap Bac
Tan An
Phuoc Le
Long Xuyen
Cao Lanh
My Tho
Go Cong
Vung Tau
Sa Dec
Vinh Long
Truc Giang
Rac Gia
Can Tho
Vi Thanh
Phu Vinh
Khanh Hung
Quan Long
Bac Lieu
Ca Mau Peninsula
Con Son

0		50		100		150 km

0		50		100		150 miles

Chronology, 1940–1995

1940   Defeat of France by Germany, May 10–June 22, increases vulnerability of French Indochina to Japanese expansionism. (Indochinese Union, formed in 1887, consists of five states: Cambodia, a French protectorate since 1863; Cochin China, a French colony since 1867; Annam and Tonkin, French protectorates since 1883; and Laos, a French protectorate since 1893.) Japanese forces attack French posts along the Chinese border in northern Tonkin, September 22–24; fighting ends after French governor-general agrees to allow Japanese to station troops and use airfields in Tonkin.

1941   Indochinese Communist Party holds conference in northern Tonkin in May under chairmanship of Nguyen Ai Quoc ("Nguyen the Patriot"), the party's founder, and establishes the Viet Nam Doc Lap Dong Minh (Vietnam Independence League) as a united front organization opposed to French and Japanese rule. Vichy French sign agreement on July 22 giving Japanese military control of Cochin China, including air and naval bases that can be used to attack Malaya, the Dutch East Indies, and the Philippines. Japan begins war against the United States and Great Britain on December 8 (December 7 in the U.S.).

1942–43   Vo Nguyen Giap, a Communist activist since the 1930s, begins recruiting and training Viet Minh guerrilla forces in mountains along the Chinese frontier. Nguyen Ai Quoc is arrested during visit to southern China in 1942 and is imprisoned by Chinese Nationalists until 1943. After his release he adopts Ho Chi Minh ("He Who Enlightens") as new political pseudonym and works in southern China with the Vietnam Revolutionary League, an anti-Japanese front controlled by the Chinese Nationalists. Free French movement led by Charles de Gaulle declares in December 1943 that Indochina will assume a new "political status within the French community" after the defeat of Japan.

1944   Ho Chi Minh returns to Vietnam in August and begins planning for a general uprising under Viet Minh leadership following the defeat of Japan. Giap leads small Viet Minh force in successful attacks on two French outposts on December 24.

1945   Japanese demands for rice and other crops cause severe famine in northern and central Vietnam (as many as two million Vietnamese die from hunger by 1946). Japanese overthrow French administration in Indochina on March 9 and install Bao Dai, heir to dynasty that ascended to the throne in 1802, as emperor of puppet Vietnamese state with authority over Annam and Tonkin. Viet Minh form army in April with Giap as its commander, and work with the Office of Strategic Services, American special operations organization, to collect intelligence and rescue downed Allied airmen in Indochina. Allies divide Indochina at the 16th parallel into Chinese Nationalist and British occupation zones for the purpose of disarming and repatriating Japanese troops following the surrender of Japan. Emperor Hirohito announces Japanese surrender on August 15. Ho Chi Minh issues call for general uprising on August 16. Viet Minh seize power in Hanoi on August 19 and control most of Tonkin by August 22. Bao Dai abdicates on August 23 and uprising spreads to Saigon on August 25. Provisional government of the Democratic Republic of Vietnam is formed with Ho as its president. Ho declares Vietnam independent at mass rally in Hanoi on September 2. Chinese Nationalist army enters northern Vietnam in early September. British, Indian, and French troops begin landing at Saigon on September 12. French seize key buildings in Saigon on September 23; fighting spreads throughout Cochin China as French, British, Indian, and rearmed Japanese troops attempt to suppress Viet Minh resistance. Indochinese Communist Party is officially dissolved in November as Ho, seeking to conciliate Chinese Nationalists, negotiates with other Vietnamese nationalist factions to form new coalition government in Hanoi (Communist Party apparatus continues to control Viet Minh).

1946   French military command declares Cochin China pacified in early February. Agreement signed by Ho and French emissary Jean Sainteny on March 6 provides for French recognition of Democratic Republic of Vietnam as a "free State" within the French Union, allows the French to station 25,000 troops in northern Vietnam for five years, and calls for a plebiscite to determine the status of Cochin China. Nationalist Chinese troops begin withdrawing from Vietnam after signing of Sino-French agreement on March 14 (withdrawal is completed in October; last British forces leave Vietnam in April). Ho holds further talks on status of Vietnam in France, June–September, that leave major issues unresolved. Viet Minh suppress rival nationalist parties in the north. Ho returns to Vietnam on October 20. Clashes between Viet Minh and French in Haiphong lead to bombardment of the city by the French navy on November 23 in which as many as 6,000 Vietnamese civilians are killed. Viet Minh begin offensive against French in Tonkin on December 19.

1947–48   French gain control of major towns in Annam and Tonkin by spring of 1947 as main Viet Minh forces and leadership retreat into the Viet Bac, mountainous region north of Hanoi. Major French offensive in the Viet Bac using paratroops and armored columns inflicts heavy casualties but fails to destroy the Viet Minh, October–November 1947. Guerrilla warfare continues throughout Vietnam as French concentrate on holding the Red River and Mekong deltas, major rice-growing regions in Tonkin and Cochin China. Using captured French and Japanese weapons, Viet Minh build army made up of local village militia, regional guerrilla units, and main-force infantry battalions; by the end of 1948 Viet Minh regain control of the Viet Bac and establish base areas along the central coast and in remote regions of southern Vietnam.

1949   Bao Dai signs agreement with French on March 8 consolidating Cochin China, Annam, and Tonkin into the State of Vietnam, an "associated state" within the French Union; under its terms, Bao Dai will serve as chief of state, with the French retaining control of Vietnamese foreign policy, finances, and defense. Agreements making Laos and Cambodia associated states are signed in July and November. French Expeditionary Corps in Indochina now numbers 150,000, and is composed of troops from France, Algeria, Morocco, Tunisia, Senegal, units of the Foreign Legion, and Indochinese recruits (for political reasons, French government does not send conscripts to serve in Indochina). Communist Chinese troops begin arriving along northern Vietnamese border on December 15 following defeat of Nationalists in the Chinese civil war.

1950   Ho Chi Minh declares Democratic Republic of Vietnam to be the sole Vietnamese government on January 14. After China and the Soviet Union extend diplomatic recognition to the Democratic Republic of Vietnam, the United States recognizes the Associated States of Vietnam, Laos, and Cambodia on February 7. Viet Minh use bases in southern China to organize, train, and equip regular infantry divisions and receive new weapons, including machine guns, mortars, and recoilless rifles, from the Chinese. President Truman approves sending $15 million in military assistance to French forces in Indochina on March 10. Aid is rapidly increased after Korean War begins on June 25 (U.S. will send $2 billion in military aid to Indochina by 1954). Viet Minh regulars overrun French outpost at Dong Khe, September 16–18, opening major offensive along northeastern Vietnamese-Chinese border. French abandon Lang Son, October 18, and retreat from northeastern border region after losing 6,000 men killed or captured in border battles. During autumn French build line of fortifications around Red River delta as Giap plans general offensive designed to capture Hanoi. French sign agreement with Bao Dai regime on December 8 establishing Vietnamese National Army.

1951   Viet Minh lose more than 10,000 men killed in three major attacks on Red River delta, January–June, before abandoning general offensive (French inflict many casualties with air-dropped napalm during Red River battles). Vietnamese Communist Party is overtly reestablished in February as the Lao Dong (Workers') Party. French drop paratroops on Hoa Binh, 40 miles west of Hanoi, on November 14, beginning campaign intended to draw Viet Minh into open battle against superior French firepower.

1952   Both sides suffer heavy losses in fighting around Hoa Binh before French withdraw on February 24. French give Vietnamese National Army increasing role in counter-guerrilla operations in southern and central Vietnam as French Expeditionary Corps is concentrated in northern Vietnam for operations against Viet Minh regulars. Viet Minh begin successful offensive on October 11 in highlands northwest of Hanoi but fail to overrun fortified airfield at Na San, November 23–December 1. Major French incursion into the Viet Bac, October 29–December 1, fails to significantly disrupt Viet Minh logistics.

1953   Viet Minh begin receiving trucks, anti-aircraft artillery, and heavy mortars from the Soviet Union. Armistice is signed in Korean War on July 27. French command decides to reoccupy abandoned airstrip at Dien Bien Phu, village in valley near the Laotian border over 180 miles west of Hanoi, and use it as a base to block Viet Minh operations into Laos. Dien Bien Phu operation begins with successful French parachute assault on November 20. Giap orders major reinforcements to Dien Bien Phu and begins planning siege of French base. French command reinforces Dien Bien Phu in hopes of inflicting major defeat on Viet Minh.

1954   Viet Minh surround Dien Bien Phu garrison of 10,000 men with force of 40,000 regulars and achieve three-to-one superiority over French in howitzers and heavy mortars. Intense bombardment of Dien Bien Phu begins on March 13; by March 17 Viet Minh capture three of the eight strongpoints held by the French forces. Eisenhower administration considers, and then rejects, proposals for the U.S. to launch airstrikes in support of the French garrison. Viet Minh overrun Dien Bien Phu on May 7 and capture 6,500 prisoners; more than 2,000 French troops and 8,000 Viet Minh are killed during the battle.

International conference on Indochina opens in Geneva on May 8, attended by delegations from France, Great Britain, the U.S., the Soviet Union, Communist China, the Democratic Republic of Vietnam, the State of Vietnam, Laos, and Cambodia. Ngo Dinh Diem becomes premier of the State of Vietnam on July 7. Cease-fire agreement is signed in Geneva July 21 between representatives of Viet Minh army and the French Expeditionary Corps; it provides for the exchange of prisoners and the "regrouping" of the opposing armies within 300 days north and south of a "provisional military demarcation line" near the 17th parallel. Separate cease-fire agreements are signed for Laos and Cambodia that call for the withdrawal of Viet Minh forces from both countries. The "Final Declaration" of the conference, which calls for holding internationally supervised general elections throughout Vietnam in July 1956, is not signed by any of the delegations, and the U.S. and the State of Vietnam refuse to "associate" themselves with it. Cease-fire goes into effect throughout Indochina by August 11. French Expeditionary Corps loses 75,000 men killed, including 21,000 from metropolitan France, during the Indochina War, while the Viet Minh lose at least 200,000 dead.

French withdraw from Hanoi in October as Lao Dong Party takes control of North Vietnam. Over 900,000 refugees, most of them Roman Catholic, move south from North Vietnam by May 1955, and between 50,000 and 90,000 Viet Minh move north, while about 10,000 Viet Minh remain in South Vietnam with instructions to engage in "political struggle" toward reunification. Authority of Diem is challenged within South Vietnam by the Cao Dai and Hoa Hao, politically powerful religious sects, and the Binh Xuyen, criminal organization that controls much of Saigon.

1955   Troops loyal to Diem drive Binh Xuyen from Saigon in intense fighting, April 28–30, and begin successful campaign against military forces of the Cao Dai and Hoa Hao. Diem declares on July 6 that South Vietnam is not bound by the Geneva agreements to hold national elections in 1956. Land reform campaign conducted by the Lao Dong Party in North Vietnam results in widespread denunciations, arrests, and executions. Diem ousts Bao Dai as head of state and on October 26 proclaims himself the first president of the Republic of Vietnam. U.S. establishes Military Assistance and Advisory Group Vietnam on November 1 to train and equip South Vietnamese army (new group succeeds MAAG-Indochina, which was established in 1950 to convey aid to the French).

1956   Diem regime begins repressive campaign aimed at Viet Minh in South Vietnam that results in the death or imprisonment of thousands of suspected Viet Minh supporters by the end of the 1950s. Last French troops leave South Vietnam on April 28. Land reform campaign in North Vietnam ends in November after resulting in 10,000–15,000 deaths.

1957–58   Former Viet Minh in South Vietnam begin forming small armed units and assassinating government officials, sometimes working with remnants of the Binh Xuyen, Cao Dai, and Hoa Hao military forces. (Communist-led insurgents in South Vietnam will become known as Viet Cong, from Viet Nam Cong San, "Vietnamese Communists," a term applied to them by the Diem regime.)

1959   Lao Dong Party leadership decides to use "armed struggle" as well as "political struggle" to overthrow Saigon government and reunify Vietnam. In May North Vietnamese organize secret transportation group to infiltrate cadre who "regrouped" north in 1954 back into South Vietnam along the Truong Son Strategic Route ("Ho Chi Minh Trail"), a network of paths running through the mountains of southeastern Laos. North Vietnamese also organize transportation groups for infiltration of men and supplies into South Vietnam by sea, and for sending supplies to Laos after fighting breaks out in July between the Communist Pathet Lao movement and the Royal Lao army. Viet Cong assassinations and ambushes increase (Communist forces assassinate more than 30,000 people in South Vietnam between 1957 and 1972).

1960   Military coup in Laos on August 9 leads to increased outside involvement in the Laotian civil war, with the U.S. supplying and training rightist forces and the Soviet Union airlifting military equipment to the Pathet Lao and its neutralist allies. Formation of National Liberation Front, an alliance of opponents of Diem regime, is announced in Hanoi on December 20 (insurgency in South Vietnam remains under control of the Lao Dong Party). U.S. military personnel serving in South Vietnam total 900 by the end of the year.

1961   U.S. Central Intelligence Agency begins arming Hmong (Meo) tribesmen to fight Pathet Lao in Laotian mountains and sending teams of South Vietnamese into North Vietnam on sabotage missions. Cease-fire is declared in Laotian civil war on May 11 and international conference on Laos convenes in Geneva on May 16. In response to requests by Diem for more American assistance in fighting the Viet

Cong, President John F. Kennedy decides in November to increase the number of U.S. military personnel in South Vietnam and expand their role in counter-guerrilla operations. In December U.S. helicopter units begin carrying South Vietnamese troops on operations and American pilots begin flying combat missions in attack aircraft with Vietnamese aircrew onboard (flights are officially described as training missions). American military personnel in South Vietnam total 3,200 by the end of the year.

1962   General Paul D. Harkins becomes first commander of U.S. Military Assistance Command Vietnam (MACV), new headquarters established in Saigon on February 8 to control buildup of U.S. advisers and support personnel. U.S. special forces begin organizing paramilitary units among Montagnards in Central Highlands. With U.S. assistance, Diem regime launches strategic hamlet program designed to protect rural population from Viet Cong coercion. American helicopters and armored personnel carriers increase mobility of government troops in counter-guerrilla operations and allow the South Vietnamese to make offensive sweeps into Viet Cong base areas. Geneva conference on Laos ends on July 23 with signing of accords under which the U.S. and North Vietnam agree to observe the neutrality of Laos and refrain from using Laotian territory for military purposes. North Vietnam fails to withdraw its troops from Laos by October 7 deadline and continues to use Ho Chi Minh Trail to infiltrate men into the South. U.S. curtails overt military aid to Laotian government in compliance with Geneva agreement, but continues covert support of the Royal Lao army and the Hmong. Viet Cong begin forming battalion-sized main-force units in South Vietnam. American military personnel in South Vietnam total 11,300 by the end of the year.

1963   Viet Cong main-force troops repulse attack by numerically superior South Vietnamese force equipped with helicopters, armored personnel carriers, and heavy artillery at Ap Bac on January 2 before withdrawing from the battlefield; engagement is hailed as major victory by Viet Cong propagandists and increases doubts among some American advisers and journalists about fighting ability of South Vietnamese army. Organized Buddhist opposition to

Diem regime increases after South Vietnamese troops kill nine persons during Buddhist celebration in Hue on May 8. Buddhist monk commits suicide by self-immolation in Saigon on June 11, the first of seven protest suicides by Buddhists in 1963. Paramilitary forces commanded by Ngo Dinh Nhu, Diem's brother and chief adviser, raid Buddhist temples in several major cities on August 21 as Diem imposes martial law. Kennedy administration loses confidence in ability of Diem to prevent Communist takeover in South Vietnam and secretly informs generals plotting to overthrow Diem that the U.S. would not oppose a coup. Group of military commanders led by General Duong Van Minh overthrow Diem on November 1, and Diem and Nhu are murdered on November 2 by officers participating in coup. Kennedy is assassinated on November 22 and Vice-President Lyndon B. Johnson becomes president. Lao Dong Party leadership decides in December to intensify military operations in South Vietnam by supplying new Chinese and Soviet weapons to the Viet Cong and by sending North Vietnamese cadre to the South. Strategic hamlet program declines. American military personnel in South Vietnam total 16,300 by the end of the year.

1964   General Nguyen Khanh overthrows ruling military committee in bloodless Saigon coup on January 30 (until February 1965 Khanh will remain central figure in period of continued South Vietnamese political turmoil). In February 1964 President Johnson authorizes raids against the North Vietnamese coast by South Vietnamese naval commando units operating under U.S. control. North Vietnamese undertake major expansion of Ho Chi Minh Trail network, building roads capable of bearing heavy truck traffic and extending trail into northeastern Cambodia (eventually a force of 50,000 North Vietnamese soldiers will guard and maintain the roads, supply depots, and anti-aircraft defenses of the trail). American pilots working for the CIA begin flying fighter-bomber missions over Laos in late May as Laotian fighting intensifies, and two U.S. navy jets flying reconnaissance missions over Laos are shot down in early June. General William Westmoreland succeeds Harkins as commander of MACV on June 20. Fighting in South Vietnam intensifies in July as Viet Cong increase attacks against government outposts.

U.S. destroyer *Maddox* is attacked by North Vietnamese torpedo boats in the Gulf of Tonkin on August 2 while on an electronic intelligence-gathering mission. On the night of August 4 the *Maddox* and another destroyer, *C. Turner Joy*, report a second attack by North Vietnamese torpedo boats (evidence indicates that reports of August 4 attack were probably the result of false radar contacts caused by tropical weather conditions). Johnson responds to reports of second attack by ordering first U.S. airstrikes against North Vietnam, and on August 5 navy aircraft attack five military targets. Administration submits Tonkin Gulf Resolution to Congress; it authorizes the president to "take all necessary measures to repel any armed attack against the forces of the United States and to prevent further aggression" in Southeast Asia. Resolution is passed by the House of Representatives, 416–0, and the Senate, 88–2, on August 7.

Rioting breaks out in Saigon and other cities, August 21–29, in response to unsuccessful attempt by Khanh to assume the presidency. Viet Cong kill five Americans in mortar attack on Bien Hoa airbase, November 1; U.S. does not respond with airstrikes against North Vietnam. Johnson is elected president on November 3. U.S. air force and navy aircraft begin bombing northern Laos on November 14 (raids will be publicly described as "armed reconnaissance"). North Vietnamese infantry regiments begin moving into South Vietnam. American military personnel in South Vietnam total 23,300 by the end of the year; more than 260 Americans have died in combat since the conflict began.

1965   South Vietnamese army loses 200 men killed in Viet Cong ambush near village of Binh Gia, 40 miles from Saigon, in early January. Viet Cong kill eight Americans in attack on U.S. bases at Pleiku on February 7. Johnson orders retaliatory airstrikes against North Vietnam, February 7–8. Viet Cong blow up barracks at Qui Nhon on February 10, killing 23 Americans; U.S. aircraft bomb North Vietnam on February 11. American aircraft begin intensive bombing of Viet Cong targets in South Vietnam on February 19 (raids are no longer required to be flown with South Vietnamese personnel onboard). General Khanh is removed from power on February 21 by military coup that leaves Phan Huy Quat, a civilian, serving as premier of South Vietnam.

U.S. begins sustained bombing of North Vietnam on March 2, using navy aircraft based on carriers in the South China Sea and air force planes based in Thailand and South Vietnam. First American ground combat units are deployed to South Vietnam on March 8 as marines land at Danang to protect its airbase against Viet Cong attack. U.S. begins sustained bombing of Ho Chi Minh Trail in Laos on April 3. Johnson authorizes marines to conduct offensive ground operations around Danang base on April 6. U.S. and South Vietnam begin naval interdiction operations off Vietnamese coast (patrols will significantly reduce maritime flow of supplies to Communist forces in South Vietnam). First national demonstration against U.S. intervention in Vietnam, held in Washington, D.C., on April 17, draws 20,000 protestors. American paratroopers begin guarding Bien Hoa airbase on May 5 as first U.S. army ground combat units are deployed to South Vietnam. North Vietnamese plan major offensive in Central Highlands with objective of capturing Pleiku and Qui Nhon and inflicting decisive defeat on South Vietnamese. Viet Cong defeat South Vietnamese forces in heavy fighting in Quang Ngai and Phouc Long provinces in late May and early June, inflicting over 1,200 casualties. Westmoreland warns his superiors that the South Vietnamese army is on the brink of collapse. Military government takes power in Saigon on June 19 with Air Vice-Marshal Nguyen Cao Ky serving as premier and General Nguyen Van Thieu as chief of state.

Johnson decides in late July to send up to 200,000 U.S. troops to South Vietnam to avert defeat of Saigon government, but does not order mobilization of the reserves or the national guard, forcing a major increase in monthly draft calls. Johnson also limits U.S. ground operations to South Vietnam, and will consistently reject proposals to invade North Vietnam or launch ground attacks against Communist supply routes and bases in Laos and Cambodia. U.S. aircraft continue bombing North Vietnam, concentrating on transportation targets in attempt to interdict flow of supplies into South Vietnam. Effectiveness of bombing campaign is limited by the increasing strength and complexity of North Vietnamese air defenses, which

are equipped with Soviet-made anti-aircraft artillery, surface-to-air missiles, jet fighters, and radar control systems,
and by changing series of restrictions on targets and tactics
imposed by Johnson administration in effort to avoid Soviet or Chinese intervention in the war.

Marines conduct first major American ground operation, attacking Viet Cong regiment massed near Chu Lai
airbase, August 18–24; 45 marines and more than 600 Viet
Cong are killed in the fighting. About 100,000 demonstrators protest American intervention in marchs and rallies held in cities and on campuses throughout the U.S.,
October 15–16. U.S. special forces begin secret cross-border reconnaissance missions into southern Laos (missions
continue until early 1971, and are also carried out in eastern
Cambodia, 1967–70). North Vietnamese begin Central
Highlands offensive with attack on Plei Me special forces
camp in Pleiku province on October 19. Westmoreland
sends American "airmobile" troops heavily equipped with
helicopters to Pleiku in late October, beginning first major
battle between American and North Vietnamese forces.
Heaviest fighting occurs in two separate engagements in
the Ia Drang Valley, November 14–18, in which 234 Americans and more than 1,000 North Vietnamese are killed.
Campaign ends when North Vietnamese retreat into Cambodia and Americans return to base camp at An Khe in
late November; U.S. victory increases confidence of American commanders that superior mobility and firepower of
U.S. troops will give them decisive advantage in battles
with North Vietnamese and main-force Viet Cong units.
Johnson decides to extend Christmas bombing halt begun
on December 24 in hopes of starting negotiations with
the North Vietnamese. Over 184,000 American military
personnel are in South Vietnam by the end of the year,
and more than 1,300 Americans are killed in combat during 1965.

1966   Buildup of U.S. forces continues, with American combat
troops deployed both to defend bases, installations, and
roads, and to begin conducting offensive operations aimed
at finding and destroying North Vietnamese and main-
force Viet Cong units (U.S. commanders do not have sufficient combat troops to hold permanently large amounts
of territory, and the majority of South Vietnamese forces
are deployed to defend towns and cities). During the year

most major U.S. army combat operations are conducted in the region between Saigon and the Cambodian border, especially Binh Long, Tay Ninh, and Hau Nghia provinces; in Kontum and Pleiku provinces in the Central Highlands; and in the northern coastal plains in Binh Dinh province. Most ground operations by U.S. marines are initially directed at securing populated areas around major bases at Phu Bai, Danang, and Chu Lai. U.S. resumes bombing of North Vietnam on January 31.

Ky government dismisses General Nguyen Chanh Thi, South Vietnamese commander in I Corps, on March 10, leading to rebellion against Saigon regime in northern cities of South Vietnam. Forces loyal to Ky retake Danang, May 15–24, and Hue, June 15–23.

U.S. aircraft bomb targets close to Hanoi and Haiphong for the first time on June 29, beginning campaign directed at petroleum and oil storage sites (Johnson continues to forbid bombing of Haiphong harbor or central Hanoi). Campaign against oil targets continues until September 4 and succeeds in destroying most major storage sites, but fails to create significant fuel shortage because of widespread dispersion of oil storage undertaken by North Vietnamese since 1965; focus of bombing shifts back to transportation targets.

North Vietnamese army begins moving in strength across the Demilitarized Zone (DMZ) into northern Quang Tri province in early July. Marines deploy along southern boundary of the DMZ, where they fight North Vietnamese in series of infantry engagements and begin constructing series of fortified combat bases and outposts. U.S. incursion into War Zone C, major Viet Cong base area in Tay Ninh province, results in heavy fighting, November 3–15, in which 155 Americans and as many as 1,000 Viet Cong are killed. Determined Viet Cong resistance leads American commanders to plan further attacks on Communist base areas in hopes of forcing the Viet Cong and North Vietnamese into battle. (American efforts to wage successful war of attrition are made difficult by ability of Viet Cong and North Vietnamese to evade many offensive sweeps; to fight many engagements at close range and from dug-in positions, thereby reducing the effectiveness of American airstrikes and artillery fire; and to withdraw successfully their surviving forces from the battlefield after most engagements.) More than 385,000 American military personnel are in South Vietnam by the end of the year, and more than 5,000 Americans are killed in combat during 1966.

1967   American ground combat units begin operations in the Mekong delta. U.S. forces launch major operation in War Zone C on February 22; over 280 Americans and at least 2,000 Viet Cong and North Vietnamese are killed by April 1. Disruption caused by offensive contributes to increasing use of base areas inside Cambodia by Communist forces, who purchase large amounts of Cambodian rice and receive arms shipped through port of Kompong Som (Sihanoukville) with the collusion of the Cambodian government and army. American troops continue operations against North Vietnamese and Viet Cong units in the Central Highlands and in Binh Dinh, Quang Ngai, Quang Tin, and Quang Ngai provinces. North Vietnamese begin shelling U.S. outposts along the DMZ with long-range Soviet artillery.

Senator Robert F. Kennedy gives speech on March 2 calling for a halt in the bombing of North Vietnam and the opening of peace negotiations. U.S. aircraft begin bombing major North Vietnamese industrial sites and electric power plants in early March. Campaign continues until May, when priority is again given to interdiction targets. Johnson administration internally debates continued bombing of the North as Robert S. McNamara, the secretary of defense since 1961, loses confidence in American policy. Anti-war march in New York City on April 15 draws at least 125,000 people; speakers at rally include Dr. Martin Luther King Jr. and pediatrician Dr. Benjamin Spock.

U.S. marines attack North Vietnamese troops entrenched in hills near Khe Sanh combat base, April 24–May 11; 155 Americans and 900 North Vietnamese are killed before North Vietnamese withdraw into Laos (heavy fighting continues in northern Quang Tri province during the spring and summer).

Civil Operations and Revolutionary Development Support (CORDS) program is established in May to consolidate pacification efforts of the U.S. military, CIA, Agency for International Development, and the State Department.

Lao Dong Party leadership decides during summer to stage "General Offensive–General Uprising" in South Vietnam. North Vietnamese begin planning widespread attacks on towns and cities using Viet Cong forces with goal of inflicting major defeat on the South Vietnamese army and causing a widespread revolutionary uprising among the urban population.

Nguyen Van Thieu is elected president and Nguyen Cao Ky vice-president of South Vietnam on September 3, winning 35 per cent of the vote out of field of 11 electoral slates.

Giap initiates series of major battles along borders of South Vietnam as first phase of General Offensive–General Uprising with objective of drawing U.S. combat forces away from major South Vietnamese cities. North Vietnamese begin heavy shelling of Con Thien, marine outpost along the DMZ, on September 11; siege lasts until October 31 as U.S. forces respond with prolonged bombardment involving coordinated use of heavy artillery, naval gunfire, fighter-bombers, and B-52 heavy bombers.

March on Pentagon on October 22 draws 50,000 people.

Viet Cong lose 900 killed in unsuccessful attack on Loc Ninh in northern Binh Long province, October 29–November 3. U.S. and North Vietnamese fight series of engagements in Central Highlands near Dak To, November 3–December 1; almost 300 Americans and at least 1,000 North Vietnamese are killed before North Vietnamese units withdraw into Cambodia.

Johnson administration seeks to counter growing public and Congressional opposition to the war by stressing "progress" being made in Vietnam. In speech given in Washington on November 21, Westmoreland states that American forces have reached "an important point where the end begins to come into view" and that "the enemy's hopes are bankrupt." Resignation of McNamara, effective February 29, 1968, is announced by Johnson on November 29. Senator Eugene McCarthy announces on November 30 that he will oppose Johnson in 1968 Democratic presidential primaries and calls for a negotiated settlement in Vietnam. Over 485,000 American military personnel are in South Vietnam by the end of the year, and more than 9,300 Americans are killed in combat during 1967.

1968   North Vietnamese mass large number of troops around Khe Sanh combat base and its garrison of 6,000 U.S. marines. Westmoreland and Lieutenant General Frederick C.

Weyand, American field commander in III Corps, decide on January 10 to move significant number of American combat troops away from the Cambodian border and closer to Saigon to guard against possible attacks in the capital region. North Vietnamese bombard Khe Sanh with heavy rocket and mortar fire on January 21, beginning 77-day siege. U.S. forces respond with sustained bombing and shelling of North Vietnamese positions in surrounding area, using intelligence from aerial reconnaissance and from signals sent by hundreds of seismic and acoustic sensors (U.S. also uses recently developed sensors to target airstrikes against the Ho Chi Minh Trail in Laos).

North Vietnamese and Viet Cong open second phase of General Offensive–General Uprising with ground attacks on over 100 cities and towns throughout South Vietnam during the Tet holiday truce, when many South Vietnamese soldiers are home on leave. Communist forces attack Danang and six other cities in I and II Corps in early hours of January 30. U.S. and South Vietnamese commanders cancel remainder of Tet truce, but are still surprised by intensity and extent of main wave of Tet attacks, which begin in early hours of January 31. Viet Cong and North Vietnamese troops capture much of Hue; during their occupation, Viet Cong murder at least 2,800 residents. In the Saigon area Viet Cong attack several key installations, including the presidential palace, the government radio station, the U.S. embassy, the South Vietnamese Joint General Staff headquarters, Bien Hoa airbase, the U.S. army base at Long Binh, and Tan Son Nhut airbase, the site of MACV headquarters, where heavy fighting takes place between a large Viet Cong force and American base security troops, South Vietnamese paratroopers, and U.S. armored cavalry. Viet Cong in Saigon region fail to capture or hold any of their major objectives, and fail throughout the country to start popular uprisings or to cause South Vietnamese units to defect.

Lang Vei special forces camp, five miles from Khe Sanh, is overrun on February 7 as North Vietnamese use tanks in South Vietnam for the first time. By mid-February South Vietnamese and U.S. forces have retaken all of the cities attacked during Tet except for Saigon, where fighting continues in Cholon section, and Hue, where U.S. and South Vietnamese troops engage in house-to-house combat until city is recaptured on February 25. More than

1,700 Americans are killed in action during the Tet offensive, while South Vietnamese lose about twice as many men (20,000 South Vietnamese soldiers are killed in combat during 1968); Communist forces lose as many as 40,000 killed, most of them Viet Cong, including many veteran cadre.

Johnson asks Clark Clifford, who succeeds McNamara as secretary of defense on March 1, to conduct reassessment of U.S. policy in Vietnam after administration receives proposal from the military to send as many as 206,000 more troops to Vietnam by the end of 1968. Clifford becomes strong advocate for a major change in policy, arguing that a military victory in Vietnam is unachievable and that the U.S. must limit its commitment to South Vietnam. Johnson authorizes sending 13,500 more troops to Vietnam. McCarthy wins 42 per cent of the vote in the New Hampshire Democratic primary on March 12. Robert Kennedy announces on March 16 that he will seek the Democratic presidential nomination.

American infantry company murders between 200 and 500 unarmed South Vietnamese villagers at My Lai, hamlet in Quang Ngai province, on March 16. (U.S. army begins investigation of the atrocity in the spring of 1969, and the first press reports of the massacre appear in November 1969.)

North Vietnamese begin withdrawing some of their troops from the Khe Sanh area after suffering heavy casualties from sustained U.S. bombing and shelling. Johnson meets on March 26 with group of senior advisers, most of whom recommend reducing American involvement in Vietnam. In speech delivered on March 31, Johnson announces a partial halt in the bombing of North Vietnam in effort to start negotiations and declares that he will not seek reelection.

American forces begin major operation to relieve Khe Sanh on April 1. Bombing of North Vietnam is halted above the 20th parallel. North Vietnamese government announces on April 3 its willingness to meet with U.S. representatives. Assassination of Martin Luther King Jr. on April 4 is followed by widespread rioting in American cities and increase in racial tension among U.S. forces in Vietnam. Siege of Khe Sanh ends on April 8, though heavy fighting continues in region around base through June. U.S. begins major program to expand South Vietnamese armed forces and to provide them with modern equipment. North Vietnamese attack near Dong Ha begins series of engagements along eastern end of DMZ. Viet Cong launch two waves of attacks in Saigon area, May 5–13 and May 25–June 4, resulting in renewed fighting in Cholon and near Tan Son Nhut airbase in which South Vietnamese troops play a major role. Fighting is also intense in Quang Nam province, and over 100 towns and military bases in South Vietnam are hit by mortar and rocket attacks during May "mini-Tet" offensive. U.S. and North Vietnamese negotiators meet in Paris on May 13, but talks soon deadlock over North Vietnamese demand for an end to all U.S. bombing of the North. American combat deaths in May total more than 2,000, the highest loss of any month of the war.

Robert Kennedy is assassinated on June 5. General Creighton Abrams succeeds Westmoreland as commander of MACV on July 3. Marines abandon Khe Sanh base on July 5 in shift toward using more mobile tactics in defense of northern Quang Tri. North Vietnamese stage last wave of 1967–68 General Offensive in late August, launching unsuccessful ground attacks on city of Tay Ninh and the Duc Lap special forces camp in Quang Duc province. Heavy casualties suffered by Viet Cong during General Offensive, and its failure to bring a rapid end to the war, cause permanent decline in Viet Cong strength and force Communist commanders to send North Vietnamese replacements to serve with Viet Cong main-force units.

Police and protestors repeatedly clash in Chicago streets as Democratic National Convention meets, August 26–29, and nominates Vice-President Hubert H. Humphrey for president. U.S. and South Vietnamese troops continue combat operations designed to protect urban areas against further ground attack or rocket bombardment. Johnson announces complete halt in bombing of North Vietnam on October 31 as part of agreement to begin negotiations involving the U.S., North and South Vietnam, and the National Liberation Front. (Over 900 U.S. aircraft, most of them modern jets, are shot down over North Vietnam, 1965–68.) Republican candidate Richard M. Nixon wins presidential election on November 5. Negotiations in Paris deadlock over procedural issues. Over 536,000 American military personnel are in South Vietnam by the end of the year, and more than 14,500 Americans are killed in combat during 1968.

1969   First session of four-party peace talks is held in Paris on January 18. Nixon is inaugurated as president on January 20. U.S. marines conduct operation along Laotian border in western Quang Tri province, January 22–March 18, with aim of disrupting North Vietnamese supply system. (Capture of arms and food caches and protection of populated rural areas increasingly become major objectives of American operations during 1969 as less emphasis is placed on engaging large North Vietnamese and Viet Cong units in ground combat.) U.S. bombing of Ho Chi Minh Trail in Laos is increased as consequence of bombing halt over North Vietnam.

North Vietnamese and Viet Cong begin new offensive across South Vietnam on February 23; in effort to avoid high casualties suffered during 1967–68 General Offensive, Communist ground attacks on U.S. installations are increasingly carried out by small "sapper" units armed with explosive charges and trained in night infiltration tactics. More than 1,100 Americans are killed in action in first three weeks of the offensive, and heavy fighting continues for months in region between Saigon and the Cambodian border and in northern coastal plains. Nixon orders first in series of B-52 raids on Communist base areas in eastern Cambodia on March 18 (bombing is not disclosed to Congress or the American public). American troop strength in South Vietnam reaches peak level of 543,000 men in April; "Free World" forces in South Vietnam also include 50,000 troops from South Korea, 11,500 from Thailand, and more than 8,000 from Australia.

National Liberation Front delegation in Paris calls on May 8 for an unconditional U.S. withdrawal from Vietnam and the creation of a coalition government in Saigon; Nixon responds on May 14 by proposing the phased mutual withdrawal of American and North Vietnamese troops from South Vietnam. American troops conducting sweep through the A Shau Valley, a major North Vietnamese stronghold along the Laotian border 25 miles southwest of Hue, capture Hill 937 ("Hamburger Hill") on May 20 after ten-day battle in which at least 56 Americans and more than 500 North Vietnamese are killed. Engagement causes controversy in press and Congress over American tactics in Vietnam.

Nixon announces on June 8 that 25,000 American troops will be withdrawn from Vietnam as South Vietnamese armed forces assume greater role in the war (further withdrawals involving another 85,000 men will be announced on September 16 and December 15). National Liberation Front forms Provisional Revolutionary Government for South Vietnam on June 10. Nixon administration instructs Abrams in August to "hold down" U.S. casualties. Ho Chi Minh dies on September 2 after several years of poor health. Small group of senior officials, including Lao Dong Party general secretary Le Duan, premier Pham Van Dong, defense minister Vo Nguyen Giap, and party ideologist Truong Chinh, assume collective leadership of North Vietnam. Hmong forces drive North Vietnamese troops from the Plain of Jars in September as ground fighting in northern Laos intensifies.

Series of anti-war demonstrations held across the U.S. on October 15 draw large crowds, and 250,000 protestors attend rally in Washington on November 15. First draft lottery is held on December 1 as Selective Service moves to reduce number of draft deferments. U.S. forces in Vietnam suffer increasingly from declining morale, insubordination, racial tension, and drug use; breakdown in discipline is generally more severe among support troops in rear areas than in combat units. Control of Viet Cong "shadow government" over rural areas is reduced as aid administered through CORDS program increases size and effectiveness of village-based South Vietnamese paramilitary forces, and as U.S. and South Vietnamese forces achieve increasing success in capturing or killing Viet Cong political cadre. American military personnel serving in South Vietnam total 475,000 at the end of the year; more than 9,400 Americans are killed in action in 1969.

1970   U.S. air force uses B-52 bombers over northern Laos for the first time on February 17 as North Vietnamese overrun Hmong postions on the Plain of Jars. National security adviser Henry Kissinger holds first in series of secret negotiating sessions in Paris with Le Duc Tho, a senior member of the Lao Dong Party leadership, on February 21.

Prince Norodom Sihanouk is ousted as chief of state of Cambodia on March 18 in coup led by General Lon Nol, who also demands that all North Vietnamese and Viet Cong troops leave the country. South Vietnamese troops begin series of raids into Communist base areas in Cambodia on March 27. North Vietnamese begin attacking Cambodian army outposts in the border region on March 29. Hundreds of ethnic Vietnamese are murdered in Cambodia in April as Lon Nol regime incites anti-Vietnamese hatred. U.S. continues airstrikes against Communist forces in Cambodia and begins covertly sending weapons to the Cambodian army. Nixon announces on April 20 that an additional 150,000 U.S. troops will be withdrawn from Vietnam by the spring of 1971. After intense debate within the administration, Nixon approves "incursion" into North Vietnamese base areas inside Cambodia on April 26 and announces operation on April 30. American troops cross border on May 1. Four students are shot to death by National Guardsmen during demonstration at Kent State University in Ohio on May 4. As widespread protests continue across the U.S., Nixon announces on May 8 that all American troops will be withdrawn from Cambodia by June 30. U.S. and South Vietnamese forces capture large amounts of weapons, ammunition, and rice as North Vietnamese and Viet Cong troops retreat into Cambodia (U.S. troops are restricted from going further than 35 kilometers across the border). Demonstration by construction workers in support of Nixon draws 100,000 people in New York City on May 20. South Vietnamese troops continue ground operations in Cambodia after June 30 with American air support. By the end of July North Vietnamese and Viet Cong occupy most of eastern Cambodia and begin organizing Cambodian insurgents to fight the Lon Nol regime.

U.S. participation in ground combat in South Vietnam decreases as most remaining American combat units prepare to withdraw and South Vietnamese army assumes responsibility for defending border areas against North Vietnamese incursions. Land reform program instituted by Thieu increases support for government in rural areas. North Vietnamese work to reestablish supply system in Cambodia.

U.S. special forces raid camp at Son Tay in North Vietnam on November 21 in attempt to rescue 70 American prisoners of war, but discover that camp has been abandoned. Congress passes amendment to defense appropriations bill on December 22 forbidding deployment of U.S. troops or advisers in Laos and Cambodia. By the end of the year more than 334,000 U.S. military personnel remain in South Vietnam; more than 4,200 Americans are killed in action in 1970.

1971   South Vietnamese troops cross border into southern Laos west of Khe Sanh on February 8 in offensive designed to destroy North Vietnamese supplies and disrupt Ho Chi Minh Trail. U.S. provides extensive air support for operation, but recently passed legislation prevents U.S. advisers from accompanying South Vietnamese units on the ground. Advance is slowed by lack of coordination among South Vietnamese commanders. North Vietnamese begin series of counterattacks on February 18, using tanks, heavy artillery, and mass infantry assaults, and subjecting American supply helicopters to intense anti-aircraft fire. South Vietnamese enter town of Tchepone on March 6, then begin retreating from Laos on March 9. Operation ends on April 6 after South Vietnamese lose at least 1,700 men killed, many of them from elite airborne, marine, and ranger units. Encouraged by results of Laotian battle, North Vietnamese continue planning for major conventional offensive in South Vietnam.

The New York Times publishes on June 13 the first in series of excerpts from secret Defense Department study of U.S. involvement in Vietnam, prepared in 1967–68 on instructions from McNamara. Nixon administration obtains court order stopping publication of the "Pentagon Papers," but Supreme Court lifts injunction in 6–3 decision on June 30. (Attempt by Nixon administration to discredit Daniel Ellsberg, a former government official who gave the study to the press, results in illegal break-in in September 1971 conducted by operatives later involved in 1972 Watergate burglary.)

Thieu is relected president of South Vietnam on October 3, receiving 94 per cent of the vote after major opposition candidates withdraw from the race. Fighting in northern Laos continues as CIA hires increasing number of Thai soldiers to replace Hmong casualties. Cambodian army suffers series of defeats in engagements with North Vietnamese and Viet Cong troops, October–December. Nixon announces on November 12 that U.S. troops in Vietnam have ended offensive ground operations. More than 156,000 American military personnel remain in South Vietnam by the end of the year, and more than 1,300 Americans are killed in action in 1971.

1972   North Vietnamese launch massive invasion of South Vietnam ("Easter Offensive") on March 30, using hundreds of tanks, truck-drawn heavy artillery pieces, and surface-to-air missiles in cross-border attacks into Quang Tri, Binh Long, and Kontum provinces. Quang Tri offensive begins on March 30 and drives South Vietnamese from their bases along the DMZ by April 2. Binh Long offensive begins with capture of Loc Ninh, April 4–6. U.S. resumes bombing North Vietnam below the 20th parallel on April 6. North Vietnamese move south from Loc Ninh and surround An Loc on April 7. South Vietnamese hold defensive line along Cam Lo and Cau Viet rivers and halt offensive in Quang Tri on April 9. Offensive in Kontum province begins on April 12 with attacks on South Vietnamese bases at Tan Canh and Dak To. South Vietnamese repulse attack on An Loc on April 13 with intense U.S. air support. Nixon orders air attacks on Hanoi and Haiphong on April 16.

North Vietnamese resume offensive in Quang Tri on April 23 and overrun Tan Canh and Dak To on April 24. South Vietnamese troops abandon Quang Tri City on May 1 and retreat south of the My Canh river toward Hue on May 2. Major General Ngo Quang Truong assumes command of I Corps and organizes successful defense of Hue with heavy American air and naval gunfire support.

Nixon announces mining of North Vietnamese ports on May 8 while offering to withdraw all U.S. forces from Vietnam within four months after the signing of a cease-fire and the release of American prisoners. U.S. expands bombing of North Vietnam on May 10, attacking targets in the Hanoi-Haiphong area as well as rail lines and roads leading to the Chinese border; ability of American aircraft to destroy bridges and military targets in populated areas is greatly increased by use of new laser-guided bombs. (New air campaign operates under fewer political restrictions than the bombing carried out between 1965 and 1968.)

South Vietnamese repulse attacks on An Loc, May 11–14, and city of Kontum, May 14–30; air support controlled by American advisers includes helicopters firing new wire-guided anti-tank missiles and close-in B-52 strikes.

"Easter Offensive" ends in June after North Vietnamese lose as many as 100,000 men killed, wounded, or captured; on all three fronts, North Vietnamese operations suffer from poor coordination among artillery, tanks, and infantry, and from supply difficulties that prevent the quick exploitation of initial successes. General Frederick Weygand succeeds Abrams as commander of MACV. South Vietnamese begin counteroffensive north of Hue on June 28. Siege of An Loc is broken on July 11 as heavy fighting continues in Quang Tri province. South Vietnamese recapture Quang Tri City on September 15; counteroffensive in I Corps ends with North Vietnamese still holding much of the territory captured by them during the spring.

In meeting with Kissinger on October 8 Le Duc Tho drops previous North Vietnamese demand that a coalition government be formed in South Vietnam as part of any peace agreement; by October 12 negotiators have agreed on general terms of an agreement. Thieu strongly objects to proposed terms in series of meetings with Kissinger, October 18–23. Nixon halts bombing of North Vietnam above the 20th parallel on October 23. North Vietnamese make terms of tentative agreement public on October 26 and call for its signing by October 31. Kissinger holds press conference on October 26 during which he says "peace is at hand" while stating that many details in agreement remain to be worked out. Nixon wins reelection as president on November 7. Negotiations in Paris between Kissinger and Le Duc Tho over final agreement break down on December 13. Nixon orders renewed bombing of Hanoi and Haiphong. Bombing begins on December 18 with first B-52 raids of the war against Hanoi and continues, with 36-hour pause at Christmas, until December 29 as B-52s and other aircraft attack railroad yards, power plants, airfields, and military storage areas. U.S. loses 26 aircraft, including 15 B-52s, in raids, while more than 1,300 persons are killed in Hanoi during December bombing. Nixon halts bombing above 20th parallel on December 29 after North Vietnamese announce willingness to resume negotiations.

1973   Negotiations resume in Paris on January 8. Nixon halts all bombing of North Vietnam on January 15. Final agreement is initialed by Kissinger and Le Duc Tho on January 23 and formally signed in Paris by representatives of the

U.S., North Vietnam, South Vietnam, and the Provisional Revolutionary Government on January 27. Agreement calls for a cease-fire in place, the withdrawal of foreign troops from Vietnam, the release of prisoners of war, the establishment of a Council of National Reconciliation in South Vietnam, and the holding of elections under international supervision; under its terms, the North Vietnamese are not to reinforce their troops in South Vietnam or to seek reunification by other than peaceful means. Fighting continues after cease-fire goes into effect on January 28 as both sides attempt to seize control of disputed areas. (At the time of the cease-fire, Saigon government controls most of the population and the territory of South Vietnam, although the North Vietnamese occupy significant border areas in the northern provinces, in the Central Highlands, and along the Cambodian border north of Saigon.) Withdrawal of remaining 23,400 American troops in South Vietnam begins. Military draft is ended in the United States.

Cease-fire goes into effect in Laos on February 22 following the formation of a new coalition government. War in Cambodia between Lon Nol government and Communist insurgents (Khmer Rouge) continues. Thieu declares that he will not surrender any territory to the Communists, form a coalition government, negotiate with the Communists, or permit Communist political agitation. North Vietnamese continue to send reinforcements and new equipment into South Vietnam. General Van Tien Dung, who replaced Giap as commander of the North Vietnamese army after the failure of the 1972 spring offensive, orders major expansion of Communist supply system within South Vietnam.

Last U.S. troops are withdrawn from South Vietnam on March 29. North Vietnamese complete release of 566 military and 25 civilian American prisoners on April 1. Heavy U.S. bombing continues in Cambodia as Khmer Rouge advance on Phnom Penh. Congress passes legislation on June 30 prohibiting funding of combat operations in Cambodia, Laos, and North and South Vietnam after August 15. Khmer Rouge advance on Phnom Penh is halted in early August. Bombing of Cambodia ends on August 15 (American military aid to Lon Nol government continues; by the end of 1973 the Khmer Rouge control most of Cambodia but are unable to overrun government enclaves around the major cities). Fighting in South Vietnam increases as Lao Dong Party leadership decides that Thieu government can be overthrown only by "revolutionary violence."

1974   North Vietnamese launch series of local attacks in South Vietnam designed to protect new supply routes and to position their troops for general offensive planned for 1976. Inflation and cuts by Congress in American aid program cause increasing shortages of fuel, ammunition, and spare parts among South Vietnamese forces. Nixon resigns as president on August 9 to avoid impeachment and Vice-President Gerald Ford becomes president. North Vietnamese continue construction of new roads, fuel pipelines, and radio and telephone networks within South Vietnam. Dung reorganizes North Vietnamese army to increase coordination among infantry, artillery, and tank forces. Widespread fighting continues in South Vietnam (more than 50,000 South Vietnamese soldiers are killed in action in 1973 and 1974). North Vietnamese begin offensive in Phouc Long province on December 13.

1975   Khmer Rouge launch new offensive in Cambodia on January 1.
         North Vietnamese complete capture of Phouc Long province on January 6. Lack of American military response encourages Lao Dong Party leadership, who approve plans for a major offensive in the Central Highlands in 1975. Offensive begins on March 4 as North Vietnamese troops block roads around Ban Me Thuot in Darlac province. North Vietnamese assault Ban Me Thuot on March 10 and capture town on March 11. Thieu decides to withdraw troops from much of I and II Corps and on March 14 orders South Vietnamese forces to evacuate Kontum and Pleiku, move to the coast, and then recapture Ban Me Thuot. Evacuation of Central Highlands begins on March 16; retreating columns come under intense North Vietnamese attack (of the 60,000 troops who leave the Highlands, only 20,000 reach the coast at Tuy Hoa on March 27). Redeployment of elite airborne troops from Quang Tri to Saigon region weakens South Vietnamese forces in I Corps. North Vietnamese overrun Quang Tri province on March 19. Refugee flight and concern of soldiers for safety of their families undermine morale of South Viet-

namese troops in northern provinces. Hue is abandoned on March 25 as soldiers and refugees flee toward Danang in hope of being evacuated by sea or air. North Vietnamese capture Danang on March 30 and Nha Trang on April 1.

Khmer Rouge close Mekong River to supply convoys and begin intense rocket bombardment of Phnom Penh and its airport.

Dung redeploys North Vietnamese army in preparation for "Ho Chi Minh campaign" aimed at capture of Saigon. North Vietnamese attack on Xuan Loc on April 9 is repulsed by determined South Vietnamese resistance.

Khmer Rouge capture Phnom Penh on April 17 and forcibly evacuate its population into countryside as war in Cambodia ends.

Thieu resigns on April 21 and goes into exile. North Vietnamese capture Xuan Loc on April 22 and complete encirclement of Saigon on April 27. Duong Van Minh, leader of 1963 coup against Diem, becomes president of South Vietnam on April 28. U.S. evacuates several thousand Americans and South Vietnamese by helicopter from Saigon, April 29–30. North Vietnamese army enters Saigon on morning of April 30 as Minh orders South Vietnamese forces to surrender.

Pathet Lao troops enter Vientiane on August 23, and People's Democratic Republic of Laos is proclaimed on December 2. Communists establish "reeducation" camps in South Vietnam, where more than 200,000 persons are eventually sent to perform forced labor and undergo ideological indoctrination under harsh conditions.

1976   Socialist Republic of Vietnam is proclaimed in Hanoi on July 2 as North and South Vietnam are formally united.

1977   President Jimmy Carter pardons Vietnam-era draft resisters and evaders. Fighting begins along Vietnamese-Cambodian border in late April after Khmer Rouge stage major raid into Vietnam. Pathet Lao and Vietnamese troops attack Hmong villages inside Laos (over 300,000 people flee Laos after 1975). Refugees continue to leave Vietnam by boat (over 900,000 Vietnamese, many of them ethnic Chinese, become refugees between 1975 and 1988, in addition to the 140,000 who fled the country during the Communist victory in 1975).

1978   Vietnamese-Chinese relations worsen as Vietnam forms closer ties with the Soviet Union. Vietnamese army invades Cambodia on December 25.

1979   Vietnamese capture Phnom Penh on January 7 and install new regime. Khmer Rouge retreat into western Cambodia and begin guerrilla warfare against Vietnamese, using Chinese weapons supplied through Thailand. Chinese invade border region of northern Vietnam on February 17; fighting causes heavy casualties on both sides before Chinese withdraw on March 16. U.S. refuses to recognize new Cambodian government and tightens economic embargo imposed on Vietnam in 1975.

1982   Vietnam Veterans Memorial is dedicated in Washington, D.C., on November 13.

1986   Le Duan dies. Nguyen Van Linh becomes general secretary of the Communist Party and begins extensive program of economic reform.

1989   Vietnamese troops withdraw from Cambodia.

1994   President Bill Clinton lifts embargo on trade with Vietnam in response to increased Vietnamese cooperation in resolving cases of American servicemen missing in action.

1995   United States establishes full diplomatic relations with Vietnam on July 11.

———

More than 58,000 American military personnel died in Indochina between 1959 and 1975; of these deaths, more than 47,000 were the result of hostile action. Battle deaths by service were approximately 31,000 in the army, 13,000 in the marines, 1,700 in the air force, and 1,600 in the navy.

South Korea lost 4,400 men killed in action in Vietnam. Australia and New Zealand lost almost 500 dead. Thai losses in Vietnam and Laos are not known. The number of persons killed in the fighting in Laos is not known, although it is estimated that 30,000 Hmong died during the war. Cambodia lost at least 180,000 dead between

1970 and 1975, and at least one million Cambodians were executed, starved, or worked to death under the Khmer Rouge between 1975 and 1978; the number of Cambodians and Vietnamese killed in Cambodia since 1979 is not known. South Vietnam lost at least 220,000 military dead and at least 300,000 civilian dead during the war, and tens of thousands of Vietnamese refugees died at sea after 1975. It is estimated that at least 50,000 civilians were killed by American bombing in North Vietnam. In 1995 the Vietnamese government stated that 1,100,000 North Vietnamese and Viet Cong soldiers died between 1954 and 1975.

Biographical Notes

T. D. ALLMAN (October 16, 1944–   )   Born Timothy D. Allman in Tampa, Florida. Educated at Harvard University, graduating in 1966; worked as reporter for *Anchorage Daily News* and *Philadelphia Bulletin* while in college. Served as a Peace Corps volunteer in Nepal for two years beginning in 1966, then reported from Southeast Asia as a freelance journalist, 1968–70. Later worked as foreign correspondent for London *Guardian* and *Le Monde Diplomatique* (1971–75), and senior editor for Pacific News Service, San Francisco (1977–82), contributing editor of *Harper's* (1977–84), foreign correspondent for *Vanity Fair* (1987–95), and staff writer for *The New Yorker* (1995–97). Author of *Unmanifest Destiny* (1984) and *Miami: City of the Future* (1987).

STEWART ALSOP (May 17, 1914–May 26, 1974)   Born in Avon, Connecticut. Graduated from Yale University in 1936. After college worked as editor at Doubleday Doran & Company in New York. Volunteered for service in U.S. Army in World War II; rejected for medical reasons, joined British Army in 1942 and served as infantry officer in Italy. Volunteered for American Office of Strategic Services in 1944; parachuted into France after D-Day to join underground Maquis. From 1945 to 1957, wrote syndicated column "Matter of Fact" with brother Joseph Alsop. Became contributing editor of *The Saturday Evening Post* in 1962; later Washington editor. Contributed column to *Newsweek* beginning in 1968. Author of *Sub Rosa: The O.S.S. and American Espionage* (with Thomas Braden, 1946), *We Accuse! The Story of the Miscarriage of American Justice in the Case of J. Robert Oppenheimer* (with Joseph Alsop, 1954), *The Reporter's Trade* (with Joseph Alsop, 1958), *Nixon & Rockefeller: A Double Portrait* (1960), *The Center: People and Power in Political Washington* (1968), and *Stay of Execution: A Sort of Memoir* (1973). Died in Bethesda, Maryland.

MICHAEL J. ARLEN (December 9, 1930–   )   Born in London; educated at Harvard University. Worked as reporter for *Life* for four years beginning in 1952; contributor and television critic for *The New Yorker* from 1957 to 1982. His books include *The Living-Room War* (1969), *Exiles* (1970), *An American Verdict* (1973), *Passage to Ararat* (1975, winner of National Book Award), *The View from Highway 1: Essays on Television* (1976), *Thirty Seconds* (1980), *The Camera Age: Essays on Television* (1981), and *Say Goodbye to Sam* (1984).

PETER ARNETT (November 13, 1934–   )   Born in Riverton, New Zealand. Began career in 1951 as reporter for New Zealand newpapers *Southland Times* and *The Standard*. Moved to Sydney, Australia, in 1956, working briefly for *Sydney Sun* and *TV Preview*. After travel in Southeast Asia, took job in 1958 as reporter for *Bangkok World*; joined Associated Press in 1959 as stringer. Started paper *Vientiane World* in 1960. In 1961, hired as Associated Press Jakarta correspondent; expelled for anti-government stories. From 1962 until fall of Saigon in 1975, served as AP Vietnam correspondent, winning Pulitzer Prize in 1966. After war, continued to work for AP in New York; naturalized as U.S. citizen in 1979. Joined Cable News Network in 1981 as global correspondent, reporting from El Salvador, Iran, Lebanon, the Soviet Union, and Panama. Covered 1991 Gulf War from Baghdad. Memoir *Live from the Battlefield: From Vietnam to Baghdad, 35 Years in the World's War Zones* published in 1994.

KEYES BEECH (August 13, 1913–February 15, 1990) Born in Pulaski, Tennessee. Began career at St. Petersburg, Florida, *Evening Independent* as copyboy, 1931–36. In 1937 took job as reporter for *Akron Beacon Journal*, remaining until 1942, when he enlisted in the U.S. Marines. Served as combat correspondent until 1945; after the war, worked as Washington correspondent for *The Honolulu Star-Bulletin* (1945–47). From 1947 to 1977 was Far East correspondent for Chicago *Daily News*. Won Pulitzer Prize for Korean War reporting, 1951. Moved to Saigon in mid-1960s, remaining until 1975. Subsequently reported from Bangkok for the *Los Angeles Times*, retiring in 1983. Books include *The U.S. Marines on Iwo Jima* (1945, with Raymond Henri and other marine combat correspondents), *Uncommon Valor: Marine Divisions in Action* (1946), *Tokyo and Points East* (1954), and *Not without the Americans: A Personal History* (1971). Died in Washington, D.C.

HOMER BIGART (October 25, 1907–April 16, 1991) Born in Hawley, Pennsylvania. Educated at Carnegie Institute of Technology and New York University School of Journalism. While at NYU worked for New York *Herald Tribune* as copyboy; hired as a reporter in 1933. Traveled to Europe as war correspondent in 1942, moving to Pacific theater two years later. Went to Vietnam for *Tribune* in 1945, 1950, and 1953; won Pulitzer Prize in 1951 for coverage of Korean War. Left *Tribune* for *The New York Times* in 1955. Reported from the Middle East, and, in 1962, from Vietnam. Retired in 1972; died in Portsmouth, New Hampshire. Writings collected posthumously in *Forward Positions: The War Correspondence of Homer Bigart* (1992).

JEFFREY A. BLANKFORT (June 4, 1934–   ) Born in New York City; educated University of California at Los Angeles, graduating in 1957. Worked at *Los Angeles Examiner* while at UCLA. Began career as freelance photojournalist in mid-1960s, focusing on anti-Vietnam war protests in the U.S. and abroad, and domestic political movements; his photographs have appeared in *Newsweek, Esquire, Harper's, The Saturday Evening Post, Rolling Stone, Interview,* and *Ramparts,* among other publications. From 1988 to 1995, he edited *The Middle East Labor Bulletin*; currently teaching history at Richmond (California) High School.

PETER BRAESTRUP (June 8, 1929–August 10, 1997) Born in New York City. After graduation from Yale University in 1951 joined U.S. Marines in Korea;

discharged in 1953 following battle wound. Began career in journalism as staff writer for *Time* (1953–57). Later worked for the New York *Herald Tribune* as reporter (1957–59), for *The New York Times* as correspondent in Algiers, Bangkok, and Paris, and for *The Washington Post* as reporter and Saigon bureau chief (1968–73). Founded *Wilson Quarterly* in 1975; also worked as senior editor and director of communications for the Library of Congress (1989–97). Author of *Big Story: How the American Press and Television Reported and Interpreted the Crisis of Tet 1968 in Vietnam and Washington* (1977) and *Battle Lines: Report of the Twentieth Century Fund Task Force on the Military and the Media* (1985). Died in Rockport, Maine.

MALCOLM W. BROWNE (April 17, 1931–   ) Born Malcolm Wilde Browne in New York City; attended Swarthmore College and New York University, graduating in 1952. After college worked for four years as a chemist and technical writer. Drafted in 1956; began journalism career as reporter for *Pacific Stars and Stripes* in Korea. On return to U.S., hired as newsman and copy editor for Middletown (New York) *Daily Record*; moved to Baltimore bureau of Associated Press two years later, in 1960. Worked in Vietnam as chief AP Indochina correspondent (1961–65) and Saigon correspondent for the American Broadcasting Corporation (1965–66). Shared 1964 Pulitzer Prize for coverage of fall of Diem regime. After two years as a freelance correspondent and writer, joined staff of *The New York Times* in 1968, serving as correspondent in Buenos Aires, South Asia (1971–73), and Eastern Europe (1973–77). Since 1977 has been *Times* science correspondent and writer; edited *Discover* for three years beginning in 1981. His books include *The New Face of War* (1965) and memoir *Muddy Boots and Red Socks* (1993).

KEVIN BUCKLEY (December 31, 1940–   ) Born in New York City. Graduated in 1962 from Yale University, where he was managing editor of *Yale Daily News* and campus correspondent for New York *Herald Tribune*. Joined staff of *Newsweek* as religion writer in 1963; for next eleven years worked for *Newsweek* in Chicago, Boston, London, Saigon (bureau reporter 1968–69, bureau chief 1970–72), and Hong Kong. Later served as editor at *New Times* (1978), *Look* (1979), *Lear's* (1986–87), *Geo*, and *Playboy* (1991–   ); has taught at Hampshire College, Boston University, and Columbia School of Journalism. Author of *Panama: The Whole Story* (1991).

TOM BUCKLEY (January 2, 1930–   ) Born Thomas F.S. Buckley in Chatham, New York. Graduated from Columbia University in 1950, after which he served for two years in U.S. Army. Joined *The New York Times* in 1953, working as copy editor, rewrite man, and reporter (in Vietnam, 1966–68). Worked as staff writer for *The New York Times Magazine* from 1968 to 1973, and later as columnist and special writer. Since 1980 has been a freelance writer. Author of *Violent Neighbors: El Salvador, Central America, and the United States* (1984).

FOX BUTTERFIELD (July 8, 1939–) Born in Lancaster, Pennsylvania; educated at Harvard University (B.A. 1962, M.A. 1964; graduate study 1964–69). Joined *The New York Times* as Vietnam correspondent in 1969; also reported from Japan, Hong Kong, and China, and was a member of the reportorial team that wrote stories accompanying publication of the Pentagon Papers in 1971. Since 1984, has been chief of *Times* Boston bureau. Author of *China: Alive in the Bitter Sea* (1982) and *All God's Children: The Bosket Family and the American Tradition of Violence* (1985).

PHILIP CAPUTO (June 10, 1941–) Born in Chicago; graduated from Loyola University in 1964, after which he served as officer with U.S. Marines in Vietnam, 1965–66. Joined staff of the *Chicago Tribune* in 1968, working as foreign correspondent from 1972 until 1977, when he published memoir *A Rumor of War*. Has also written novels *Horn of Africa* (1980), *DelCorso's Gallery* (1983), *Indian Country* (1987), *Means of Escape* (1991), *Equation for Evil* (1996), and *Exiles: Three Short Novels* (1997).

GLORIA EMERSON (May 19, 1930–) Born in New York City. Began career in journalism in 1957, assigned to women's page of *The New York Times*; later worked in Paris and London bureaus. Covered war in Vietnam from 1970 to 1972; won George Polk Award for foreign reporting, 1971. Her books include *Winners & Losers: Battles, Retreats, Gains, Losses and Ruins from a Long War* (National Book Award, 1978), *Some American Men* (1985), and *Gaza: A Year in the Intifada* (1990).

BERNARD B. FALL (November 11, 1926–February 21, 1967) Born in Vienna, Austria. Served in French Underground and Fourth Moroccan Mountain Division during World War II; after the war worked as war crimes investigator and tracing officer for Nuremberg War Crimes Trials (1946–50), and as district manager for *Stars and Stripes* in Nuremberg (1950–51). Educated at universities of Paris and Munich (1948–50), the University of Maryland overseas program (1951), and at Syracuse University, from which he received his doctorate in 1955. Taught in American universities beginning in 1954, as Asian studies instructor at Cornell, assistant professor at American University, and professor of international relations at Howard (1956–67). Received George Polk Award in 1966. Author of *The Viet-Minh Regime* (1954), *Street Without Joy: Indochina at War, 1946–54* (1961), *Two Viet-Nams: A Political and Military History* (1963), *Viet-Nam Witness, 1953–66* (1966), *Hell in a Very Small Place* (1967), and editor of *Ho Chi Minh on Revolution: Selected Writings, 1920–1966* (1967). Killed by a booby-trap explosion on Highway 1, between Hue and Quang Tri, while covering operation by the U.S. Marines. Uncollected writings published posthumously as *Last Reflections on a War* (1967).

KARL FLEMING (August 30, 1927–) Born in Newport News, Virginia; grew up in church orphanage. Began career as police and court reporter for

Wilson, North Carolina, *Daily Times* and reporter for *Atlanta Constitution*. Joined *Newsweek* in 1960 as civil rights correspondent. In 1965 became Los Angeles bureau chief; seriously injured while reporting on Watts riots. Covered campaigns and political conventions for *Newsweek*. From 1978 to 1985 worked in television, as managing editor and on-air political editor for KNXT in Los Angeles; produced documentary *Watts Revisited* for CBS. From 1985 to 1987 was editor and publisher of *California Business*. Since 1988 has been president of Prime Time Communications, a media consulting firm. Author of *The First Time* (1975, with Anne Taylor Fleming).

HENRY F. GRAFF (August 11, 1921–   )   Born Henry Franklin Graff in New York City. Educated at the College of the City of New York (B.S.S. 1941) and Columbia University, from which he received a Ph.D. in history in 1949. Served in U.S. Army as Japanese linguist and cryptanalyst (1942–46). Taught history at Columbia (1946–91), becoming full professor in 1961. Author of *Bluejackets with Perry in Japan* (1952), *The Modern Researcher* (with Jacques Barzun, 1957), *The Tuesday Cabinet: Deliberation and Decision on Peace and War under Lyndon B. Johnson* (1970), *The Presidents: A Reference History* (1984), and several American history textbooks.

ZALIN GRANT (April 17, 1941–   )   Born Zalin B. Grant in Cheraw, South Carolina. Graduated from Clemson University in 1963; during college, worked as stringer for Associated Press. After two years of service in Saigon and Danang as U.S. Army intelligence officer and Vietnamese linguist, joined staff of *Time* magazine; reported on Vietnam from 1965 to 1967, and later from Washington and New York. Became Southeast Asia correspondent for *The New Republic* in 1968. Beginning in 1971, has been a freelance writer, living in Spain and France; has served as editorial director of Pythia Press since 1995. His books include *Survivors* (1975), *Over the Beach* (1986), *Facing the Phoenix* (1992), and *Flying Smart* (1995).

MEG GREENFIELD (December 27, 1930–   )   Born in Seattle, Washington; educated at Smith College (B.A. 1952) and, with a Fulbright scholarship, at Newnham College, Cambridge (1952–53). Joined staff of *The Reporter* in 1957, serving as Washington editor 1965–68; later worked for *The Washington Post* as editorial writer and editorial page editor (1968–   ). Began contributing columns to *Newsweek* in 1974. Received Pulitzer Prize for editorial writing in 1978.

DAVID HALBERSTAM (April 10, 1934–   )   Born in New York City; educated at Harvard University (B.A. 1955). After college took reporting job in West Point, Mississippi, with *West Point Daily Times Leader* (1955–56); later worked for Nashville *Tennessean* (1956–60), and as staff writer for *The New York Times* (1960–67), in Vietnam from 1962 to 1963. Shared Pulitzer Prize for reporting from Saigon and George Polk Award for foreign reporting, 1964. Left *Times* in 1967 to become contributing editor for *Harper's*. His books include *The*

Noblest Roman (novel, 1961), *The Making of a Quagmire* (1965), *One Very Hot Day* (novel, 1968), *The Unfinished Odyssey of Robert Kennedy* (1969), *Ho* (1971), *The Best and the Brightest* (1972; winner of Overseas Press Club Award), *The Powers That Be* (1979), *The Breaks of the Game* (1981), *The Amateurs* (1985), *The Reckoning* (1987), *Summer of '49* (1989), *The Next Century* (1992), *The Fifties* (1993), *October 1964* (1994), and *The Children* (1998).

MICHAEL HERR (April 13, 1940–   )   Born in Syracuse, New York; attended Syracuse University. Began career in journalism as an editor and freelance writer for *Holiday* magazine in the early 1960s. Went to Vietnam in November 1967 as freelance correspondent for *Esquire*; reports later included in *Dispatches* (1977). Other books include *The Big Room* (1984) and *Walter Winchell* (1990); also co-authored screenplays for *Apocalypse Now* (1979) and *Full Metal Jacket* (1987).

SEYMOUR M. HERSH (April 8, 1937–   )   Born in Chicago, Illinois; educated at University of Chicago. Began journalistic career as police reporter for City News Bureau of Chicago, 1959–60. Later United Press International correspondent in Pierre, South Dakota, 1962–63; Associated Press correspondent in Chicago and Washington, 1963–67, at the Pentagon beginning in 1966. Resigned AP position in 1967 after piece on biological warfare was drastically edited; briefly served as press secretary for Eugene McCarthy's New Hampshire primary campaign. Won 1970 Pulitzer Prize for reporting of My Lai massacre. Author of *Chemical and Biological Warfare: America's Hidden Arsenal* (1969), *My Lai 4: A Report on the Massacre and Its Aftermath* (1970), *The Price of Power: Kissinger in the Nixon White House* (1983), *The Target Is Destroyed: What Really Happened to Flight 007* (1986), *The Samson Option: Israel's Nuclear Arsenal and America's Foreign Policy* (1991), and *The Dark Side of Camelot* (1998).

ARNOLD R. ISAACS (February 6, 1941–   )   Born in New York City. Graduated from Harvard University in 1961. From 1962 to 1981 worked as reporter, Washington correspondent, foreign correspondent, and editor at *The Baltimore Sun*. Covered Vietnam for *Sun*, 1972–75; after war was based in Hong Kong for three years. Since 1981 has been a freelance journalist, author, and educator. His books include *Without Honor: Defeat in Vietnam and Cambodia* (1983) and *Vietnam Shadows: The War, Its Ghosts, and Its Legacy* (1997); co-authored *Pawns of War* (1987).

THOMAS A. JOHNSON (October 11, 1928–   )   Born in St. Augustine, Florida. Moved to New York City as a child; in 1954, graduated from Long Island University with a degree in English and journalism. Worked as social worker, Department of Welfare investigator, public relations man, and freelance writer before joining staff of *Newsday* in 1963. Joined *The New York Times* in 1966; served as national and local reporter, metropolitan desk assignment editor, and as foreign correspondent in Africa, Europe, the Caribbean, and Vietnam

(December 1967–March 1968). Taught at New York University from 1969–72 as adjunct professor of journalism. Retired from *Times* in 1981 to become president of Thomas A. Johnson Associates, a Manhattan public relations firm.

WARD S. JUST (September 5, 1935–   )   Born Ward Swift Just in Michigan City, Indiana; educated at Trinity College, Hartford, Connecticut. Began career as reporter for Waukegan (Illinois) *News-Sun* (1957–59); later worked for *Newsweek* (1959–65) and *The Washington Post* (1965–70), in Vietnam from December 1965 to June 1967. His nonfiction works include *To What End: Report from Vietnam* (1968), and *Military Men* (1970); his fiction *A Soldier of the Revolution* (1970), *The Congressman Who Loved Flaubert, and Other Washington Stories* (1973), *Stringer* (1974), *Nicholson at Large* (1975), *A Family Trust* (1978), *Honor, Power, Riches, Fame, and the Love of Women* (1979), *In the City of Fear* (1982), *The American Blues* (1984), *The American Ambassador* (1987), *Jack Gance* (1989), *Twenty-One: Selected Stories* (1990), *The Translator* (1991), *Ambition and Love* (1994), and *Echo House* (1997).

PETER R. KANN (December 13, 1942–   )   Born Peter Robert Kann in New York City. Began newspaper career in high school as copyboy for *The Princeton Packet*. Graduated from Harvard University, where he was political editor of *The Harvard Crimson*, in 1964. Joined *The Wall Street Journal* as staff reporter in 1964, working in Pittsburgh and Los Angeles bureaus. Covered Vietnam war as resident correspondent from 1967 to 1969; later served as Hong Kong–based Asia correspondent, 1969–76. Won Pulitzer Prize for 1971 coverage of India-Pakistan war. Named first publisher and editor of *The Asian Wall Street Journal* in 1976. In 1979 returned to United States as associate publisher of *The Wall Street Journal* and vice-president of Dow Jones & Company; appointed chief executive officer and chairman of Dow Jones in 1991.

STANLEY KARNOW (February 4, 1925–   )   Born in New York City. Served with U.S. Army Air Forces for three years beginning in 1943; later educated at Harvard, the Sorbonne, and the Ecole des Sciences Politiques. Began career in Paris as correspondent for *Time* (1950–57); worked subsequently as Time-Life bureau chief in North Africa (1958–59) and Hong Kong (1959–62), special correspondent for *London Observer* (1961–65) and *Time* (1962–63), and foreign correspondent for *The Saturday Evening Post* (1963–65). Joined staff of *The Washington Post* in 1965 as Far East correspondent, covering Vietnam, Southeast Asia, and China; was diplomatic correspondent for the *Post* in 1971 and 1972. Worked as NBC News correspondent from 1973 to 1975; later became associate editor of *The New Republic* (1973–75), King Features columnist (1975–88), and *Newsweek* columnist (1977–81). Was chief correspondent for PBS series *Vietnam: A Television History* (1983) and *The U.S. and the Philippines: In Our Image* (1989). Books include *Southeast Asia* (1963), *Mao and China: From Revolution to Revolution* (1972), *Vietnam: A History* (1983), *In Our Image: America's Empire in the Philippines* (1989, winner of the 1990 Pulitzer Prize for history), and *Paris in the Fifties* (1997).

DORIS KEARNS (January 4, 1943–) Born Doris Helen Kearns in Rockville Centre, New York. Educated at Colby College and Harvard University (Ph.D. 1968). Served as special assistant to President Lyndon Johnson, 1968. Appointed assistant professor at Harvard in 1969; associate professor of government beginning in 1972. Was special consultant to President Lyndon Johnson from 1969 to 1973. Married Richard Goodwin, 1975. Books include *Lyndon Johnson and the American Dream* (1976), *The Fitzgeralds and the Kennedys* (1986), *No Ordinary Time: Franklin and Eleanor Roosevelt—The Home Front in World War II* (1994, winner of 1995 Pulitzer Prize), and *Wait Till Next Time: A Memoir* (1997).

DONALD KIRK (May 7, 1938–) Born in New Brunswick, New Jersey; educated at Princeton (B.A. 1959), the Indian School of International Studies, New Delhi (1962–63), and the University of Chicago (M.A. 1965). Began career as a reporter for the *Chicago Sun-Times* (1960–61) and the *New York Post* (1961–64). Covered Vietnam as a freelance correspondent beginning in 1965, and later for *The Evening Star*, Washington, D.C. (1967–70), and the *Chicago Tribune* (1971–74). Received George Polk Award for foreign reporting, 1975. After war, reported from New York and the United Nations for the *Tribune* (1975–76), wrote for *Time* (1977–78), was special correspondent based in Tokyo for *The Observer*, London (1978–82), and special correspondent for *USA Today* (1982–90). Since 1991 has been a freelance writer; his books include *Wider War: The Struggle for Cambodia, Thailand, and Laos* (1971), *Tell It to the Dead: Memories of a War* (1975), *Korean Dynasty: Hyundai and Chung Ju Yung* (1994), and *Looted: The Philippines after the Bases* (1998).

JOSEPH KRAFT (September 4, 1924–January 10, 1986) Born in South Orange, New Jersey. Began journalism career at 14, covering high school sports for New York *World-Telegram*. Served as cryptographer in army during the Second World War, after which he studied at Columbia University (B.A. 1947) and Princeton (1948–51). Joined staff of *The Washington Post* in 1951 as editorial writer; later staff writer for *The New York Times* (1953–57), Washington correspondent for *Harper's* (1962–65), columnist for Field Newspapers (1965–80), and columnist for the Los Angeles Times Syndicate (1980–85). Won 1958 and 1972 Overseas Press Club Award for foreign reporting. His books include *The Struggle for Algeria* (1961), *The Grand Design: From Common Market to Atlantic Partnership* (1962), *Profiles in Power: A Washington Insight* (1963), and *The Chinese Difference* (1973).

LE KIM DINH (July 1, 1934–) Born in Hanoi; immigrated to South Vietnam after signing of Geneva Accords in 1954. After graduate education at Université de Saigon (1960), was drafted into South Vietnamese Army, serving until 1965. Worked as war correspondent for United Press International in Vietnam from 1965 to 1967, and later as reporter and assistant to *The New York Times* Saigon bureau chiefs (1968–75). After fall of Saigon joined staff of *Times* in New York City (1975–87). Moved to California in 1989; contributed articles to *The Orange County Register* and the *Los Angeles Times*. Currently a consultant and contributing editor for *CN* magazine, national monthly publication of Vietnamese-American community.

JOHN S. MCCAIN III (August 29, 1936–   ) Born in Panama Canal Zone; graduated from U.S. Naval Academy in 1958. Shot down over Hanoi in 1967 and held as prisoner of war for five and a half years. After attending National War College, served as director of Navy-Senate Liaison Office until retirement from service in 1981. A Republican from Arizona, he was elected to two terms as U.S. Representative (1982–86), and to U.S. Senate in 1986 and 1992. In 1993 was appointed chairman of the International Republican Institute; chairs Senate Commerce, Science, and Transportation Committee.

MARY MCCARTHY (June 21, 1912–October 25, 1989) Born in Seattle, Washington. Graduated Vassar College in 1933, then worked in various jobs in New York City: as book reviewer for *The Nation* and *The New Republic* (1933–36), editor at Covici Friede (1936–37), ghostwriter for H.V. Kaltenborn (1937), editor of *Partisan Review* (1937–38), and drama critic (1937–62). Taught literature at Bard College, Sarah Lawrence, and University of London. Her works of fiction include *The Company She Keeps* (1942), *The Oasis* (1949), *The Groves of Academe* (1952), *A Charmed Life* (1955), *The Group* (1963), *Birds of America* (1965), *Cannibals and Missionaries* (1979), *The Hounds of Summer and Other Stories* (1981); her nonfiction: *Cast a Cold Eye* (1950), *Sights and Spectacles, 1937–1956* (1956), *Venice Observed* (1956), *Memories of a Catholic Girlhood* (1957), *The Stones of Florence* (1959), *On the Contrary* (1961), *Mary McCarthy's Theatre Chronicles* (1963), *Vietnam* (1967), *Hanoi* (1968), *The Writing on the Wall and Other Literary Essays* (1970), *Medina* (1972), *The Mask of State: Watergate Portraits* (1974), *The Seventeenth Degree* (1974), *Ideas and the Novel* (1980), *Occasional Prose* (1985), and *How I Grew* (1987). Died in New York City.

NORMAN MAILER (January 31, 1923–   ) Born in Long Branch, New Jersey; educated at Harvard University (B.S. 1943) and the Sorbonne (1947–48). Served in U.S. Army from 1944 to 1946 as field artillery observer and infantry rifleman in Philippines and Japan; novel *The Naked and the Dead* (1948) based on wartime experiences. Subsequent novels include *Barbary Shore* (1951), *The Deer Park* (1955), *An American Dream* (1965), *Why Are We in Vietnam?* (1967), *A Transit to Narcissus* (1944, first published 1978), *The Executioner's Song* (1979, winner of Pulitzer Prize for fiction), *Ancient Evenings* (1983), *Tough Guys Don't Dance* (1984), *Harlot's Ghost* (1991), and *The Gospel According to the Son* (1997); nonfiction books include *The Armies of the Night* (1968, winner of National Book Award and Pulitzer Prize for general nonfiction), *Miami and the Siege of Chicago* (1969), *Of a Fire on the Moon* (1970), *The Prisoner of Sex* (1971) *King of the Hill: On the Fight of the Century* (1971), *St. George and the Godfather* (1972), *Marilyn: A Biography* (1973), *The Fight* (1975), and *Oswald's Tale: An American Mystery* (1995). Among collections of his works are *The White Negro: Superficial Reflections on the Hipster* (1957),

Advertisements for Myself (1959), *Cannibals and Christians* (1966), *The Short Fiction of Norman Mailer* (1967), and *Pieces and Pontifications* (1982). Candidate for New York City Democratic mayoral nomination in 1969.

JAMES A. MICHENER (February 3, 1907–October 16, 1997) Born in New York City; raised in Doylestown, Pennsylvania. Graduated from Swarthmore College in 1929; received a master's degree from the University of North Colorado in 1937. Taught at the George School, Newtown, Pennsylvania, and worked briefly as a textbook editor for Macmillan in New York before enlisting in the navy in 1941. Collection of stories, *Tales of the South Pacific* (1947, winner of 1948 Pulitzer Prize and adapted as musical *South Pacific*), became bestseller. Also published *The Fires of Spring* (1949), *Return to Paradise* (1951), *The Voice of Asia* (1951), *The Bridges at Toko-Ri* (1953), *Sayonara* (1954), *Floating World* (1955), *The Bridge at Andau* (1957), *Hawaii* (1959), *Caravans* (1963), *The Source* (1965), *Iberia* (1968), *Kent State* (1971), *Centennial* (1974), *Sports in America* (1976), *Chesapeake* (1978), *Space* (1982), *Poland* (1983), *Texas* (1985), *Legacy* (1987), *Alaska* (1988), *Caribbean* (1989), *Journey* (1989), *The Novel* (1991), *Mexico* (1992), *The World Is My Home: A Memoir* (1992), *Literary Reflections* (1993), *Recessional* (1994), *Miracle in Seville* (1995), and *This Noble Land* (1996).

DON MOSER (October 19, 1932–) Born Donald Bruce Moser in Cleveland, Ohio. Served in U.S. Army, 1953–55. Graduated from Ohio University in 1957; also attended Stanford and the University of Sydney. Worked for *Life* as reporter and assistant editor (1961–64), West Coast bureau chief (1964–65), Far East bureau chief (1966–69), and assistant managing editor (1970–72). After five years as a freelance writer (1972–77) became editor of *Smithsonian* (1977–). Author of *The Peninsula: A Story of the Olympic Country in Words and Photographs* (1962), *The Pied Piper of Tucson* (1968, with Jerry Cohen), *The Snake River Country* (1974), *Central American Jungles* (1975), *A Heart to the Hawks* (1975), and *China-Burma-India Theater* (1977).

DON OBERDORFER (May 28, 1931–) Born Donald Oberdorfer Jr. in Atlanta, Georgia. Graduated from Princeton University in 1952, after which he served for two years in U.S. Army in Korea. Began career in journalism as staff writer for *Charlotte Observer* (1955–61) and *The Saturday Evening Post* (1961–65). Reported from Vietnam beginning in 1965, first as staff writer for Knight and later for *The Washington Post*. Remained with *Post* until 1993, when he became journalist-in-residence at the Nitze School of Advanced International Studies, Johns Hopkins University. His books include *Tet!* (1971), *The Turn: From the Cold War to a New Era* (1991), *Princeton University: The First 250 Years* (1995), and *The Two Koreas: A Contemporary History* (1997).

JONATHAN RANDAL (February 14, 1933–) Born Jonathan C. Randal in Buffalo, New York. Graduated Harvard University in 1955, served for two years in U.S. Army, then worked in Paris for a year for United Press and Agence

France-Presse. Subsequently served as UPI correspondent in London (1958) and Geneva (1959–60), correspondent for *The Paris Herald* (1960–61), *Time* correspondent in Africa and the Middle East (1962–66), *The New York Times* correspondent in Vietnam (1966–67) and Eastern Europe (1967–69), and *The Washington Post* Paris correspondent (1969–75), with a long tour in Vietnam in 1972. Since 1975, has been *Washington Post* roving correspondent, principally in Middle East, Africa, and Balkans. Books include *Going All the Way: Christian Warlords, Israeli Adventurers and the War in Lebanon* (1983) and *After Such Knowledge, What Forgiveness: My Encounters with Kurdistan* (1997).

JOHN SAAR (June 4, 1939–   ) Born in London; educated at London Northwestern Polytechnic (1961–63), and served for two years in the British Army (1959–61). Began journalism career in England, working for Barnet Press in London (1957–59, 1961–63), *Farmers Weekly* (1963–64), and *Soldier Magazine* (1964–67). Moved to New York in 1967 as correspondent for *Life*; covered Vietnam for *Life* from 1968 to 1972. Later worked for *The Washington Post* as reporter (1972–75) and northeast Asia correspondent (1975–78), as a freelance writer (1978–81), as writer and senior editor at *People* (1981–92), and as senior editor at Time International and Time, Inc. (1992–98). Currently managing editor of *Cartoon News*.

SYDNEY H. SCHANBERG (January 17, 1934–   ) Born Sydney Hillel Schanberg in Clinton, Massachusetts. Graduated from Harvard University in 1955. Served in U.S. Army, 1956–58. Joined staff of *The New York Times* in 1959, becoming reporter in 1960; served as Albany, New York, bureau chief (1967–69), New Delhi bureau chief (1969–73), Southeast Asia correspondent (1973–75), metropolitan editor (1977–80), and columnist (1981–85). Became associate editor and columnist for New York *Newsday* in 1986. Won Pulitzer Prize for international reporting, 1976, Overseas Press Club Award in 1971 and 1975, and 1972 George Polk Award for foreign reporting. 1980 *New York Times Magazine* article "The Death and Life of Dith Pran" was basis for film *The Killing Fields* (1984); author of *The Killing Fields: The Facts behind the Film* (1984, with Dith Pran).

JONATHAN SCHELL (August 21, 1943–   ) Born in New York City. Graduated from Harvard University in 1965. Worked as writer for *The New Yorker* from 1967 to 1987, and as columnist for *Newsday* from 1990 to 1996. His books include: *The Village of Ben Suc* (1967), *The Military Half: An Account of the Destruction of Quang Ngai and Quang Tin* (1968), *The Time of Illusion* (1976), *The Fate of the Earth* (1982), *The Abolition* (1984), *History in Sherman Park* (1987), *Observing the Nixon Years* (1989), *Writing in Time* (1997), and *The Gift of Time* (1998).

ROBERT SHAPLEN (March 22, 1917–May 15, 1988) Born Robert Modell Shaplen in Philadelphia; educated at University of Wisconsin (B.A. 1937). After receiving master's in journalism from Columbia University (1938), worked as reporter for New York *Herald Tribune* (1937–43). Covered Pacific war for *Newsweek*, 1943–45; on return served as Far East bureau chief (1946–47). Left *Newsweek* to be Nieman Fellow at Harvard (1947–48), writer for *Fortune* (1948–50), and Asia correspondent for *Collier's* (1950–52). Joined staff of *The New Yorker* in 1952, where he worked until his death; from 1962 to 1978 he was magazine's Far East correspondent. His books include *A Corner of the World* (1949), *Free Love and Heavenly Sinners: The Story of the Great Henry Ward Beecher Scandal* (1954), *A Forest of Tigers* (novel, 1956), *Kreuger: Genius and Swindler* (1960), *The Lost Revolution* (1965), *Time out of Hand: Revolution and Reaction in Southeast Asia* (1969), *The Road from War: Vietnam 1965–1970* (1970), *A Turning Wheel* (1979), and *Bitter Victory* (1986).

NEIL SHEEHAN (October 27, 1936–   ) Born Cornelius Mahoney Sheehan in Holyoke, Massachusetts; graduated from Harvard University in 1958. Served as Saigon bureau chief for the Associated Press from 1962 to 1964. Joined *The New York Times* in 1964, working as reporter in New York, foreign correspondent in Indonesia (1965) and Vietnam (1965–66), Pentagon correspondent (1966–68), White House correspondent (1968–69) and special investigative reporter based in Washington (1969–72). Instrumental in 1971 publication of the Pentagon Papers. Has published books including *The Arnheiter Affair* (1972), *A Bright Shining Lie: John Paul Vann and America in Vietnam* (1988, National Book Award and Pulitzer Prize for nonfiction), and *After the War Was Over: Hanoi and Saigon* (1992).

JACK P. SMITH (April 25, 1945–   ) Born in Paris, grew up in London; moved to Washington, D.C., at age 12. Enlisted in the U.S. Army in 1964. Served in Vietnam from 1965 to 1966 with 1st Cavalry Division; wounded at Landing Zone Albany in the Ia Drang Valley, November 17, 1965. Left Army late in 1967 to study history at Carnegie-Mellon (B.A. 1971) and Oxford (B.A. 1974). Worked while at Carnegie-Mellon as news producer for WIIC-TV in Pittsburgh. Joined ABC in 1974, reporting from Paris from 1976 to 1980, and from Washington beginning in 1980; was principal correspondent for *This Week with David Brinkley* for nine years, beginning in 1985; currently contributor to ABC *World News Tonight* and *Nightline*.

BOB TAMARKIN (November 5, 1937–   ) Born Robert Allen Tamarkin in St. Louis, Missouri. Graduated from Washington University in 1961 and from the University of Missouri School of Journalism in 1963. Began career as business reporter for Fairchild Publications in Chicago (1963–66); later stock market columnist and financial writer for Chicago *Daily News* (1966–68), *Daily News* reporter in Saigon (1973–74) and Saigon bureau chief (1975), bureau chief in Bangkok (1975–76) and Nairobi (1976–77), editor and founder of *Generation* magazine (1968–71), senior editor at *Forbes* (1978–81), special writer for *The Wall Street Journal* (1983–84), writer for *Crain's Illinois Business*, host of "Inside Business," National Public Radio (1982–83), and managing editor of *Intermarket Magazine* (1987–   ). Author of *Young Executive Today* (1972), *The*

New Gatsbys: Fortunes and Misfortunes of Commodity Traders (1985), *The Merc: The Emergence of a Global Financial Powerhouse* (1993), and *Rumor Has It: A Curio of Lies, Hoaxes, and Hearsay* (1993).

WALLACE TERRY (April 21, 1938–) Born in Indianapolis, Indiana; graduated from Brown University in 1959, where he was reporter and editor-in-chief of *Brown Daily Herald*. Worked as civil rights reporter for *The Washington Post* from 1960 to 1963, then joined staff of *Time* as Washington correspondent. Went to Vietnam for *Time* in 1967 as deputy bureau chief; covered Tet offensive and Ashau Valley campaigns. Returned to U.S. in 1969, reporting again from Washington. Began academic career in 1974, teaching for eight years at Howard University, and also at the University of District of Columbia, Grinnell, Yale, Middle Tennessee State, Brown, the College of William and Mary, and the University of North Carolina. Has served as commentator and producer for CBS Radio, National Public Radio, and Mutual Radio Network, and as contributing editor of *Parade Magazine*. Author of *Bloods: An Oral History of the Vietnam War by Black Soldiers* (1984).

HUNTER S. THOMPSON (July 18, 1939–) Born Hunter Stockton Thompson in Louisville, Kentucky. Studied journalism at Columbia University. Served with the U.S. Air Force from 1956 to 1958; wrote for base magazine. Worked as Caribbean correspondent for *Time* and New York *Herald Tribune* (1959–60), South American correspondent for *The National Observer* (1961–63), West Coast correspondent for *The Nation* (1964–66), columnist for *Ramparts* (1967–68) and *Scanlan's Monthly* (1969–70), national affairs editor for *Rolling Stone* (1970–84), *High Times* global correspondent (1977–82), and media critic for the *San Francisco Examiner* (1985–90). Author of *Hell's Angels: A Strange and Terrible Saga* (1966), *Fear and Loathing in Las Vegas: A Savage Journey in the Heart of the American Dream* (1972), *Fear and Loathing on the Campaign Trail '72* (1973), *The Great Shark Hunt: Strange Tales from a Strange Time* (1979), *The Curse of Lono* (1983), *Generation of Swine: Tales of Shame and Degradation in the '80s* (1988), *Songs of the Doomed: More Notes on the Death of the American Dream* (1990), *Better than Sex: Confessions of a Campaign Junkie* (1993), and *The Proud Highway: Saga of a Desperate Southern Gentleman* (1997).

PAUL VOGLE (March 18, 1932–) Born in Anadarko, Oklahoma; educated at Sacred Heart Seminary, Detroit. Served in U.S. Army in Vietnam from 1955 to 1958 as Vietnamese language interpreter; later taught English at University of Hue. In 1961 joined editorial staff of *Saigon Daily News*. Worked as stringer for United Press International in Vietnam from 1968 until 1975. Remained with UPI after fall of South Vietnam on staff of bureaus in Bangkok and Hong Kong (1975–83), and Detroit (1983–91).

JOHN T. WHEELER (August 19, 1930–) Born John Tipton Wheeler in El Paso, Texas; graduated from University of Missouri School of Journalism in

1952. After college, served for five years in Strategic Air Command of U.S. Air Force as navigator-bombardier; later joined staff of *Santa Cruz Sentinel* as city hall reporter, and the Associated Press, working in New York and San Francisco. Reported for AP in Vietnam from 1965 to 1969, returning occasionally to Kuala Lumpur and New York; also spent a year in Cambodia, returning to the U.S. in 1971. Went into public relations in early 1970s, working for Booz, Allen & Hamilton and DuPont; retired to become full-time amateur triathlete.

TOM WOLFE (March 2, 1931–) Born Thomas Kennerly Wolfe Jr. in Richmond, Virginia; educated at Washington and Lee University and Yale, receiving a Ph.D. in American Studies in 1957. Began career in journalism as reporter for Springfield, Massachusetts, *Union* (1956–59); subsequently reporter and Latin American correspondent for *The Washington Post* (1959–62), city reporter for New York *Herald Tribune* (1962–66), contributing editor for *New York* (1968–76) and *Esquire* magazines (1977–), and contributing artist for *Harper's* (1978–81). Books include *The Kandy-Kolored Tangerine-Flake Streamline Baby* (1965), *The Electric Kool-Aid Acid Test* (1968), *The Pump House Gang* (1968), *Radical Chic & Mau-Mauing the Flak Catchers* (1970), *The Painted Word* (1975), *Mauve Gloves & Madmen, Clutter & Vine* (1976), *The Right Stuff* (1979), *In Our Time* (1980), *From Bauhaus to Our House* (1981), *The Purple Decades: A Reader* (1982), and *The Bonfire of the Vanities* (1987).

JOHN E. WOODRUFF (January 20, 1939–May 12, 1996) Born in Greenville, Michigan, and raised in Ann Arbor. Studied history at Williams College, graduating in 1960. After college, joined staff of *Williamstown News* as reporter; later worked for *Springfield Union*. Moved to *The Baltimore Sun* in 1965, covering police beat and city hall. Reported from Vietnam for *Sun*, 1969–70; subsequently served as bureau chief in Hong Kong (1970–73), Beijing (1982–87), and Tokyo (1988–93), and in Baltimore as deputy editorial page editor, city editor, and weekend editor. Served as Fellow at University of Michigan School of Journalism (1973–74), and later as Visiting Professor of Communication (1987–88). In 1989, published *China in Search of Its Future: Reform vs. Repression, 1982–1989.*

Note on the Texts

This volume collects newspaper and magazine articles and excerpts from books written between 1959 and 1977 and dealing with events connected with the Vietnam War in the period between July 1959 and May 1975. Excerpts from books have been taken from first editions; in some cases, these excerpts include material that had earlier appeared in magazines in different form. Newspaper and magazine articles have been taken from their original printings. Original wire copy for the three wire service articles included in this volume is not known to be extant; these articles have been taken from the most complete versions available.

The following is a list of the sources of the texts included in this volume, listed alphabetically by author (or, for anonymous items, by title of periodical). For untitled selections, a title is supplied and is enclosed in quotation marks. The texts listed here are reprinted without omission or alteration other than the silent correction of typographical errors.

T. D. Allman. Yesterday's Prisoners Lie Dead in Bloody Cambodian School-yard: *The Washington Post*, April 18, 1970; The Aftermath of a Massacre: Newsmen Rescue 7: *The Washington Post*, April 20, 1970. Copyright © 1970 T. D. Allman. Reprinted by permission of T. D. Allman.

Stewart Alsop. The American Class System: *Newsweek*, June 29, 1970. Copyright © 1970 by Newsweek, Inc. All rights reserved. Reprinted by permission.

Michael J. Arlen. A Day in the Life: *The New Yorker*, September 30, 1967. Copyright © 1967 by Michael J. Arlen. Reprinted by permission of Donadio & Olson, Inc.

Peter Arnett. Hill 875: Associated Press wire copy, November 22, 1967. Reprinted by permission of Associated Press.

Keyes Beech. We Clawed for Our Lives!: *Chicago Daily News*, May 1, 1975. Copyright © 1975 by The Chicago Sun-Times. Reprinted with special permission from the Chicago Sun-Times, Inc.

Homer Bigart. A "Very Real War" in Vietnam—and the Deep U.S. Commitment: *The New York Times*, February 25, 1962. Copyright © 1962 by The New York Times Company. Reprinted by permission.

Jeffrey Blankfort. Our Town: The War Comes to Beallsville, Ohio: *Ramparts*, July 1969. Copyright © by Jeffrey Blankfort 1969. Reprinted by permission of Jeffrey Blankfort.

Peter Braestrup. Quangtri: Anything But Easy: *The Washington Post*, July 9, 1972; Viet Soldier Serves Officer, Not Nation: *The Washington Post*, July 10, 1972. Copyright © 1972 The Washington Post. Reprinted by permission.

Malcolm W. Browne. Paddy War: Browne, *The New Face of War* (New York: Bobbs-Merrill, 1965), pp. 1–8; "He Was Sitting in the Center of a Column of Flame": *The New Face of War*, pp. 175–81. Reprinted with permission of Simon & Schuster. Copyright © 1965, 1968 by Malcolm W. Browne. Tenderness, Hatred and Grief Mark Saigon's Last Days: *The New York Times*, May 6, 1975. Copyright © 1975 by The New York Times Company. Reprinted by permission.

Kevin Buckley. A Small Contribution: *Newsweek*, October 14, 1968. Copyright © 1968, Newsweek, Inc. All rights reserved. Reprinted by permission.

Tom Buckley. Portrait of an Aging Despot: *Harper's*, April 1972. Copyright © 1972 by Tom Buckley. Reprinted by permission.

Fox Butterfield. Who Was This Enemy?: *The New York Times Magazine*, February 4, 1973. Copyright © 1973 by The New York Times Company. Reprinted by permission.

Philip Caputo. Running Again—the Last Retreat: *Chicago Tribune*, April 28, 1975. © Copyright Chicago Tribune Company. All rights reserved. Used with permission.

Gloria Emerson. Copters Return from Laos with the Dead: *The New York Times*, March 3, 1971; Spirit of Saigon's Army Shaken in Laos: *The New York Times*, March 28, 1971. Copyright © 1971 by The New York Times Company. Reprinted by permission.

Bernard B. Fall. Master of the Red Jab: *The Saturday Evening Post*, November 24, 1962. Reprinted with permission from *The Saturday Evening Post*. Vietnam Blitz: A Report on the Impersonal War: *The New Republic*, October 9, 1965; "Unrepentant, Unyielding": An Interview with Viet Cong Prisoners: *The New Republic*, February 4, 1967. Copyright © 1965, 1967, Dorothy Fall; reprinted with permission.

Karl Fleming. The Homecoming of Chris Mead: *Newsweek*, March 29, 1971. Copyright © 1971 by Newsweek, Inc. All rights reserved. Reprinted by permission.

Henry F. Graff. Teach-In on Vietnam By . . . the President, the Secretary of State, the Secretary of Defense and the Under Secretary of State: *The New York Times Magazine*, March 20, 1966. Copyright © 1966 by The New York Times Company. Reprinted by permission.

Zalin Grant. "We Lived for a Time Like Dogs": Grant, *Survivors* (New York: W. W. Norton, 1975), pp. 155–76. Copyright © 1975 by Claude Renee Boutillon. Reprinted by permission of W. W. Norton & Company, Inc.

Meg Greenfield. After the Washington Teach-In: *The Reporter*, June 3, 1965. Reprinted by permission of Meg Greenfield.

David Halberstam. "They Can Win a War if Someone Shows Them How": Halberstam, *The Making of a Quagmire* (New York: Random House, 1965), pp. 163–78. Copyright © by David Halberstam; reprinted with permission.

Michael Herr. Hell Sucks: Herr, *Dispatches* (New York: Alfred A. Knopf, 1977), pp. 70–85. Copyright © 1968, 1969, 1970, 1977 by Michael Herr. Reprinted by permission of Michael Herr.

Seymour M. Hersh. Lieutenant Accused of Murdering 109 Civilians: *St. Louis*

Post-Dispatch, November 13, 1969; Hamlet Attack Called "Point-Blank Murder": *St. Louis Post-Dispatch*, November 20, 1969; Ex-GI Tells of Killing Civilians at Pinkville: *St. Louis Post-Dispatch*, November 25, 1969. Reprinted with permission of the St. Louis Post-Dispatch, copyright © 1969.

Arnold R. Isaacs. War Lingers in Hamlets as Cease-Fire Hour Passes: *Baltimore Sun*, January 29, 1973. Courtesy of The Baltimore Sun and Arnold Isaacs.

Thomas A. Johnson. The U.S. Negro in Vietnam: *The New York Times*, April 29, 1968. Copyright © 1968 by The New York Times Company. Reprinted by permission.

Ward S. Just. Reconnaissance: Just, *To What End: Report from Vietnam*. (Boston: Houghton Mifflin, 1968), pp. 166–91. Copyright © by Ward Just. Reprinted by permission.

Peter R. Kann. A Long, Leisurely Drive Through Mekong Delta Tells Much of the War: *The Wall Street Journal*, November 10, 1969 Copyright © 1969 Dow Jones & Company, Inc. Reprinted by permission. All rights reserved.

Stanley Karnow. The Fall of the House of Ngo Dinh: *The Saturday Evening Post*, December 21, 1963. Reprinted by permission from *The Saturday Evening Post*.

Doris Kearns. From Who *Was* Lyndon Baines Johnson?: Who Was Lyndon Baines Johnson? (sections 3, 4, 6, 7, 8), *The Atlantic Monthly*, May 1976. Copyright © 1976 Doris Kearns; reprinted by permission of Doris Kearns Goodwin.

Donald Kirk. Who Wants To Be the Last American Killed in Vietnam?: *The New York Times Magazine*, September 19, 1971. Copyright © by The New York Times Company. Reprinted by permission; "I watched them saw him 3 days": *Chicago Tribune*, July 14, 1974. (Title appeared originally in quotation marks.) © Copyright Chicago Tribune Company. All rights reserved. Used by permission.

Joseph Kraft. Letter from Hanoi: *The New Yorker*, August 12, 1972. Copyright © 1972 The New Yorker Magazine, Inc. All rights reserved. Reprinted by permission.

Le Kim Dinh. For Those Who Flee, Life Is "Hell on Earth": *The New York Times*, April 2, 1975. Copyright © 1975 by The New York Times Company. Reprinted by permission.

John S. McCain III. How the POW's Fought Back: *U.S. News & World Report*, May 14, 1973. Copyright © 1973 by U.S. News & World Report. Reprinted by permission.

Mary McCarthy. Hanoi—March 1968: McCarthy, *Hanoi* (New York: Harcourt, Brace & World, 1968), pp. 1–24. Copyright © 1968 by Mary McCarthy, renewed 1996 by James West. Reprinted by permission of Harcourt, Inc.

Norman Mailer. From *The Armies of the Night*: Mailer, *The Armies of the Night* (New York: New American Library, 1968), pp. 116–31. Copyright © 1968 by Norman Mailer. Used by permission of Dutton Signet, a division of Penguin Putnam Inc.

Notes

In the notes below, the reference numbers denote page and line of this volume (the line count includes headings). No note is made for material included in standard desk-reference books such as Webster's *Collegiate, Biographical,* and *Geographical* dictionaries. Biblical references are keyed to the King James Version. Quotations from Shakespeare are keyed to *The Riverside Shakespeare,* ed. G. Blakemore Evans (Boston: Houghton, Mifflin, 1974). Footnotes and bracketed editorial notes within the text were in the originals. For historical background see Chronology in this volume. For weapons and military terms not identified in the notes, see Glossary in this volume. For further historical background and references to other studies, see Stanley Karnow, *Vietnam: A History* (revised edition; New York: Viking Penguin, 1991); Harry G. Summers Jr., *Vietnam War Almanac* (New York: Facts on File Publications, 1985); and *Encyclopedia of the Vietnam War,* ed. Stanley I. Kutler (New York: Macmillan Reference USA, 1996). For further background on Vietnam war journalism, see Clarence R. Wyatt, *Paper Soldiers: The American Press and the Vietnam War* (New York: W. W. Norton, 1993). For more detailed maps, see Harry G. Summers Jr., *Historical Atlas of the Vietnam War* (Boston: Houghton Mifflin, 1995).

1.3   *Death at Intermission Time*]   This story, which appeared in *Time* on July 20, 1959, was based on a dispatch filed from South Vietnam by Stanley Karnow.

1.16–17   1957 . . . Americans.]   Bombs were set off in Saigon on October 22, 1957, at buildings used by the Military Assistance Advisory Group and the United States Information Service, wounding 13 Americans.

1.35–36   Ovnand . . . Buis]   Ovnand and Buis were the first American servicemen to be killed in the Republic of Vietnam.

3.27–30   Thao . . . Diem]   Thao played a major role in the coups against Diem in November 1963, against Duong Van Minh in January 1964, and against Nguyen Khanh in February 1965. He was murdered in the summer of 1965 by South Vietnamese police officers allied with Nguyen Cao Ky. The Communists transferred his remains to a "patriots' cemetery" after their victory in 1975, and it is now believed that Thao served as a clandestine Communist agent after his apparent defection in 1954.

15.29   Frederick E. Nolting]   U.S. ambassador to South Vietnam, 1961–63.

18.31   a copy . . . Spock]   *Baby and Child Care* by Dr. Benjamin Spock, first published in 1946.

20.4–6   neutralist forces . . . civil war]   See Chronology, 1960–62.

25.28–29   a book of mine]   *Street Without Joy* (1961).

36.2   *The Fall . . . Ngo Dinh*]   Stanley Karnow used material from this article in writing "The End of Diem," chapter 8 in his book *Vietnam: A History* (1983, revised 1991), which includes information regarding American involvement in the overthrow of Diem unavailable to him in 1963.

46.38   tank-corps major]   Identified by Karnow in *Vietnam: A History* as Duong Huu Nghia. Karnow also writes in *Vietnam* that General Minh gave the order to kill Diem and Nhu to his bodyguard, Captain Nguyen Van Nhung, and that Nhung and Nghia both shot the Ngo brothers inside the armored vehicle.

48.12   Poulo Condore]   In Vietnamese, Con Son; an island 150 miles south of Saigon, used as a political prison by the French, the South Vietnamese government, and by the Communists after their victory in 1975.

50.6   battle of Ap Bac]   See Chronology, January 1963. Vann was the senior U.S. adviser with the South Vietnamese 7th Division, which had made the attack at Ap Bac.

52.1   Cao and Dam]   Colonel Huynh Van Cao, commander of the South Vietnamese 7th Division, 1959–62, and Colonel Bui Dinh Dam, commander of the 7th Division, 1962–63.

54.1   PIO's]   Public Information Officers.

64.30–31   Vann . . . Vietnam]   In his book *A Bright Shining Lie: John Paul Vann and America in Vietnam* (1988) Neil Sheehan writes that Vann was already planning to retire from the army in 1963 before he went to Vietnam in 1962, believing that his investigation by the army on statutory rape charges in 1959 would prevent him from ever being promoted to brigadier general.

66.5   *Capt. "Jerry" Shank*]   In a short profile that appeared with this article in *U.S. News & World Report*, the magazine's editors wrote that Edwin Gerald Shank Jr. was born on June 21, 1936, in Winamac, Indiana, and graduated from Notre Dame in 1959 with a B.S. degree in architecture. Shank joined the Air Force ROTC while in college, was called into active service in August 1959, and was assigned to duty in South Vietnam on October 15, 1963.

73.6   multi]   Multi-engined aircraft.

73.32   Hurlburt]   Hurlburt Field, near Fort Walton Beach, Florida.

76.10–11   national teach-in . . . Washington]   The event was held on May 15–16, 1965.

78.20   Dominican action] The United States sent 20,000 troops to the Dominican Republic after a coup and counter-coup split the ruling military junta in late April 1965. On May 6, 1965, the Organization of American States voted to establish an inter-American peace-keeping force in the Dominican Republic; U.S. troops became part of this force, which remained until after elections were held in 1966.

79.15   Carmine De Sapio] Leader of the New York City Democratic Party, 1949–61.

80.3   mote-and-beam] Cf. Matthew 7:3–5, Luke 6:41–42.

86.29–30   top of these pages] The photographs are reproduced on pp. 88–89 of this volume.

88.23–24   coups . . . overthows] See Chronology, 1964–65.

106.16–17   Dr. Strangelove missions] Several scenes in the film *Dr. Strangelove; or, How I Learned to Stop Worrying and Love the Bomb* (1963) take place on board a B-52 bomber.

108.14   Chulai operation] See Chronology, August 1965.

108.31   battle near Ankhé] Fought on September 18–19, 1965, between 224 paratroopers of the 101st Airborne Division and a force of about 600 Viet Cong main-force troops. More than 200 Viet Cong and 13 Americans were killed in the engagement.

109.4   Task Force Alfa] Task Force Alpha, a corps-level headquarters established at Nha Trang in August 1965 to control American military operations in the Central Highlands. It was renamed I Field Force Vietnam in March 1966.

109.14   Siegfried Line] Fortifications along the western German frontier in World War II, made with steel-reinforced concrete.

111.27   bombed . . . Embassy] A car bomb exploded outside the U.S. embassy in Saigon on March 30, 1965, killing 22 people; the bombing resulted in the construction of a new embassy building, which was attacked by the Viet Cong during the 1968 Tet Offensive.

112.39–40   executes VC . . . servicemen] Three alleged members of the Viet Cong political cadre were shot by South Vietnamese authorities in Danang on September 23, 1965. A Communist radio broadcast on September 26 announced that two U.S. soldiers captured in 1963 had been executed in reprisal.

113.26–27   newsreel . . . lighters,] On August 3, 1965, a CBS television news team headed by correspondent Morley Safer filmed U.S. marines using cigarette lighters to burn huts in the village of Cam Ne after receiving sniper fire from the village. The footage was broadcast on CBS on August 5.

114.10   torture in Algeria] During the Algerian War of Independence, 1954–62.

115.28   Hoa-Binh and Cao-Bang] For Hoa Binh, see Chronology, November 1951–February 1952. The French garrison retreating from the northeastern border outpost of Cao Bang was annihilated in October 1950.

116.23   redoubt of "Zone D"] A major Viet Cong base area north of Bien Hoa.

116.32–33   in 1951 . . . Tassigny] Lattre de Tassigny commanded the successful defense of the Red River Delta; see Chronology, January–June 1951.

117.4   Huks] A Communist-led guerrilla movement that staged an unsuccessful insurgency against the Philippine government, 1949–55.

118.5–6   1ST BATTALION . . . four days] The 1st Battalion, 7th Cavalry, made a helicopter assault into Landing Zone X-Ray in the Ia Drang Valley on the morning of November 14, 1965.

118.33   Charlie Company] Charlie Company, 2nd Battalion, 7th Cavalry, reached Landing Zone X-Ray on November 16, 1965.

120.8   Richards] This name, as well as the others used in this article, is a pseudonym.

121.34–37   The XO . . . crawl away] The body of the executive officer of Charlie Company was recovered by American troops on November 18, 1965.

132.16–17   about 150 . . . killed] 155 American soldiers were killed in the fighting at Landing Zone Albany.

133.11–12   Honolulu . . . Johnson] At their conference in Honolulu, held February 6–9, 1966, Johnson promised Premier Ky that the U.S. would increase economic aid to South Vietnam.

133.24–25   George W. Ball] Under Secretary of State, 1961–66.

134.6–7   peace offensive . . . January] Johnson halted the bombing of North Vietnam between December 24, 1965, and January 30, 1966.

136.21–22   T. S. Eliot . . . a bang."] Cf. "The Hollow Men" (1925).

139.36   Khrushchev threaten . . . Berlin] At their summit meeting in Vienna in June 1961.

140.2   time . . . missile crisis] October 1962.

140.29   test-ban treaty] The treaty, which was signed by the United States, the Soviet Union, and Great Britain, prohibited the testing of nuclear weapons in space, underwater, or in the atmosphere, but permitted continued underground testing. It went into effect on October 10, 1963.

141.3   Senator Morse] Senator Wayne Morse of Oregon, a Democrat, was one of two senators who voted against the Tonkin Gulf Resolution in August 1964.

141.30   bombing pause . . . May] Johnson suspended the bombing of North Vietnam from May 13 to May 17, 1965.

142.2   the Four Points] Set forth by North Vietnamese premier Pham Van Dong on April 8, 1965, the points called for an end to the bombing of North Vietnam and a complete U.S. withdrawal from South Vietnam, an end to U.S. military aid to South Vietnam, the acceptance of the political program of the National Liberation Front, and the peaceful reunification of Vietnam.

143.8–9   Vietcong . . . last year] The U.S. command claimed that 34,585 Viet Cong and North Vietnamese soldiers were killed in 1965.

143.16–37   'The Steaming . . . H.F.G.] This passage appeared as a sidebar in the original magazine article.

144.18–19   Senator Fulbright] J. William Fulbright, a Democrat from Arkansas, was chairman of the Foreign Relations Committee.

145.37   SEATO treaty] The Southeast Asia Treaty Organization was created under the terms of a treaty signed on September 8, 1954, by representatives of Australia, New Zealand, Pakistan, the Philippines, Thailand, France, Great Britain, and the United States. Members pledged to "act to meet the common danger" in the event of "aggression by means of armed attack" against territory covered by the treaty; under the terms of a separate protocol, Laos, Cambodia, and southern Vietnam were included in the treaty area. SEATO was dissolved in 1977.

146.35   enclave idea] Proposed strategy that would restrict the mission of U.S. ground forces in South Vietnam to defending populated coastal areas.

147.19–20   Churchill . . . streets] In a speech to the House of Commons on June 4, 1940.

147.30   Alamo . . . Houston] The Alamo was captured by the Mexicans on March 6, 1836; Texas forces under Sam Houston won a decisive victory at the Battle of San Jacinto on April 21, 1836.

151.38   101st Airborne Brigade] 101st Airborne Division.

154.35   Chris Verlumis] Chris C. Vurlumis.

157.1   A. J. Liebling] Writer for *The New Yorker* whose war reporting was collected in *The Road Back to Paris* (1944) and *Mollie & Other War Pieces* (1964).

168.8–9   Carpenter . . . overrun] The napalm bombing on June 8, 1966, temporarily halted the North Vietnamese attack, giving the American unit time to establish a secure perimeter. One American soldier was killed by the airstrike and another 11 were burned. Carpenter was awarded the Distinguished Service Cross for his actions during the engagement.

168.11–12   1,200 . . . 250 of their own] The U.S. command announced that 48 Americans and 531 North Vietnamese were killed during Operation Hawthorne.

185.26–27   Third Marine Amphibious Force] Corps-level headquarters in Danang that controlled marine operations in the northern provinces of South Vietnam.

189.11   gas] Nonlethal CS tear gas.

192.2–3   enterprising . . . lighters] See note 113.26–27 in this volume.

193.33   American . . . suicide] Norman Morrison, a 32-year-old Quaker who burned himself to death outside of the Pentagon on November 2, 1965.

194.25–26   *Et . . . chemin*] And if it had to be done over / I would follow the same path.

195.31   "Indonesia?"] In September 1965 the Indonesian army defeated a Communist coup attempt; by December 1965 at least 200,000 suspected Communists had been killed during the ensuing repression of the Indonesian Communist party.

198.35–36   Lord Russell] In 1966 the British philosopher Bertrand Russell had organized an International War Crimes Tribunal. The tribunal held a public meeting in Stockholm in May 1967 and issued a report condemning the U.S. for committing crimes against humanity in Vietnam.

211.29   COSVN] Central Office for South Vietnam.

212.8   Allen Dulles' book about intelligence] *The Craft of Intelligence* (1963). Dulles served as director of the CIA from 1953 until 1961.

236.23   106-mm. rifles] Recoilless rifles.

251.6–7   terminus of the March] The march, held on October 21, 1967, began at the Lincoln Memorial.

254.31   Macdougal Street] A street in the Greenwich Village section of New York City.

259.19–22   O to . . . waterfall—] From "Waking Early Sunday Morning," the first part of "Near the Ocean" (1967), by Robert Lowell.

259.27–32   Remember playing . . . ski-run] From "1958" (1967) by Robert Lowell.

267.14   Sunday] November 19, 1967.

268.2–3   machine gunner go down] Private First Class Carlos Lozada was posthumously awarded the Medal of Honor.

269.8–9   the chaplain . . . killed]   Major Charles Joseph Watters, a Roman Catholic priest, was killed by the bomb that fell within the American lines on November 19. For several hours before his death Watters moved about the battlefield under fire, carrying, aiding, and comforting wounded men. He was posthumously awarded the Medal of Honor.

269.31   gain the ridgeline]   The 173rd Airborne Brigade captured the crest on the morning of November 23, 1967, after losing 158 men killed and 402 wounded in the fighting on Hill 875.

277.9   Adolphe Menjou]   American film actor.

281.24–27   Jack Broughton . . . unacceptable]   In his book *Thud Ridge* (1969).

284.4   N—D—]   Nam Dinh.

284.7   Iron Triangle area]   The Hanoi–Haiphong–Thanh Hoa region of North Vietnam.

284.15–16   Harrison Salisbury! . . . *Times*]   In a story filed from Hanoi and printed in *The New York Times* on December 27, 1966, Harrison Salisbury reported that American bombing had caused extensive destruction of civilian housing in Nam Dinh, writing: "one can see that United States planes are dropping an enormous weight of explosives on purely civilian targets." Salisbury also reported the claim by Tran Thi Doan, the mayor of Nam Dinh, that the city was "essentially a cotton-and-silk textile town containing nothing of military significance." The Department of Defense responded to this story by stating that Nam Dinh contained a major railroad yard, a petroleum and oil storage depot, and a thermal power generating plant. Salisbury was also criticized by U.S. government officials for not acknowledging that some of the information in his story was taken from *Report on U.S. War Crimes in Nam-Dinh City*, a pamphlet published in North Vietnam in October 1966.

300.27   Spads]   See A-1 in Glossary.

302.12–13   General . . . Uprising]   See Chronology, 1967–68.

307.31–36   Manhard . . . heard from since]   Manhard was released in Hanoi on March 16, 1973.

310.22   Buddhist . . . 1966]   See Chronology, March–June 1966.

311.37   101st Airborne Brigade]   101st Airborne Division.

314.7   *On the Beach*]   Film (1959) about the aftermath of nuclear war, directed by Stanley Kramer.

315.14–16   American major . . . it."]   In his February 7, 1968, story about the fighting in Ben Tre, Associated Press correspondent Peter Arnett quoted an unnamed U.S. major as saying: "It became necessary to destroy the town to save it."

316.13–14   deuce-and-a-half] Two-and-a-half-ton truck.

318.38   2/5] Second Battalion, Fifth Marine Regiment.

319.7   Navy LCU's] Landing craft.

323.3   1/5] First Battalion, Fifth Marine Regiment.

323.20   mustang] An officer promoted from the ranks.

332.12   I.C.C.] International Control Commission, established under the Geneva Accords of 1954.

339.16–17   "Your leavy . . . are."] *Macbeth*, V, vi, 1–2.

352.6   Operation Junction City] The parachute assault was made in War Zone C on February 22, 1967.

352.19–20   Poitier . . . truckdriver] In the films *The Defiant Ones* (1958) and *Red Ball Express* (1952).

358.12   Clay's title] Muhammad Ali (Cassius Clay) was stripped of his world heavyweight boxing title in 1967 after he refused on religious grounds to be drafted into the armed forces.

362.2   *A Small Contribution*] This article appeared in *Newsweek* with a headnote that described it as a "report on a small contribution to Communist casualty figures."

363.18   sawed-off M-16] A version of the M-16 rifle manufactured with a shortened barrel and a telescoping stock, known as the CAR-15 or Colt Commando.

365.3   *"We Lived . . . Dogs"*] This excerpt from the book *Survivors* describes events that took place in a Viet Cong prison camp in western Quang Nam province.

365.5   *Anton . . .* Watkins] Anton, an army helicopter pilot, was captured on January 5, 1968. Watkins, an army infantryman, was captured on January 9, 1968.

365.16   Kushner, Williams] Captain Floyd William Kushner, an army doctor, was captured after his helicopter crashed in November 1967. Richard Williams, an army sergeant, was captured on January 8, 1968, after receiving a severe wound to his right hand.

366.1   Zawtocki] A marine captured during the 1968 Tet Offensive.

366.3–4   Strictland . . . Harker] Jim Strictland and David Harker, army riflemen captured on January 8, 1968, along with Sergeant Williams.

366.10   Russ Grissett] Member of a marine reconnaissance unit, captured early in 1966.

366.15   Garwood Mr. Dao] Robert Garwood, a marine private, was captured near Danang on September 28, 1965, and defected to the Viet Cong during 1967. Garwood chose to remain in North Vietnam after the signing of the 1973 cease-fire agreement, but returned to the United States in 1979. He was found guilty of collaboration by a court-martial in 1981 and dishonorably discharged from the marines. In 1968 the Viet Cong gave Garwood the name Huynh Chien Dao, "Brave Liberation Fighter."

366.18　*Daly*]　James Daly, an army rifleman captured with Watkins on January 9, 1968.

366.25　Davis]　Tom Davis, an army mortarman captured on March 12, 1968.

368.27　Mr. Ho]　Viet Cong political cadre who came to the camp in the summer of 1968 to indoctrinate the prisoners.

370.6　Denny]　Dennis Hammond, a marine captured during the 1968 Tet Offensive.

372.15　*McMillan*]　Ike McMillan, an army mortarman captured along with Davis on March 12, 1968.

373.24　Cannon]　Francis Cannon, an army rifleman captured on January 8, 1968, along with Strictland, Harker, and Williams.

374.28–30　Sherman's . . . escape attempt]　Robert Sherman, a marine captured in 1967 who was confined to wooden stocks for almost two months after a failed escape attempt in the spring of 1968.

379.37–380.2　Port . . . ground attack]　Port was posthumously awarded the Medal of Honor for his actions on January 12, 1968.

386.10–11　*Miller . . . Laird*]　Miller, a Republican, served in Congress from 1967 until 1993. Melvin Laird was Secretary of Defense during the first Nixon administration, 1969–73.

397.21–22　case . . . Kennedy]　Senator Edward M. Kennedy was the driver in an automobile accident on Chappaquiddick Island, Massachusetts, on the night of July 18–19, 1969, in which Mary Jo Kopechne, his passenger, died. Kennedy pleaded guilty on July 25, 1969, to leaving the scene of an accident and received a suspended sentence. A judicial inquest in 1970 found probable cause that negligence by Kennedy contributed to the accident, but no further charges were brought against him.

398.34　Hamburger Hill]　See Chronology, May 1969.

402.37–38　Nixon's troop-withdrawal]　See Chronology, June 1969.

403.14–15　"Saigon tea"]　Cold tea or soda which customers in a bar had to purchase in order to talk with a hostess.

409.28　Popular . . . Force]　People's Self Defense Force.

410.9–10　U.S.-controlled . . . (PRU)]　The Provincial Reconnaissance Units were organized and directed by the Central Intelligence Agency.

413.23   murder . . . Green Berets]   The army announced on August 6, 1969, that Colonel Robert Rheault, the former commander of the Fifth Special Forces Group, and seven men who had served under his command had been charged with the murder on June 20, 1969, of a Vietnamese intelligence agent whom they suspected of working for the Communists as well as the United States. The charges were dismissed on September 29, 1969, after the CIA refused to release documents pertaining to the case.

416.7–8   men who . . . Calley]   See page 422.13–22 in this volume.

420.37   copyright story]   The story was written by Joe Eszterhas, a reporter for the *Plain Dealer*. Haeberle later sold the photographs to *Life* for $19,550; they appeared in the magazine on December 5, 1969.

421.30   helicopter pilot]   Hugh Thompson Jr., an observation helicopter pilot with the 123rd Aviation Battalion.

421.34   pilot was killed]   Glenn Andreotta, the crew chief on Thompson's helicopter, was killed in action on April 8, 1968. Thompson reported what he had witnessed at My Lai to his superior officers on March 16 and to Colonel Oran Henderson, commander of the 11th Brigade, on March 18, 1968; he later testified at Calley's court-martial, as did his door gunner, Lawrence Colburn. In 1998 Thompson, Colburn, and Andreotta were awarded the Soldier's Medal by the U.S. army for having saved the lives of at least ten villagers at My Lai.

423.18–24   Medina . . . Calley]   Medina was court-martialed for murder and acquitted on September 22, 1971. Mitchell was court-martialed for assault with intent to commit murder and was acquitted on November 20, 1970. Calley was convicted of premeditated murder on March 29, 1971, and sentenced to life imprisonment. On April 1, 1971, President Nixon ordered that Calley be released from the stockade and placed under house arrest at Fort Benning, Georgia, while his conviction was appealed. Calley's sentence was reduced on administrative appeal to 20 years imprisonment in August 1971 and to ten years in April 1974; he was paroled on November 9, 1974. Ten other soldiers from Charlie Company were charged for crimes committed at My Lai; one was acquitted at court-martial and the charges against the other nine were dismissed. Colonel Oran Henderson, the former commander of the 11th Brigade, was court-martialed for his role in concealing the massacre and acquitted on December 17, 1971. Similar charges brought against 13 other officers, including Major General Samuel Koster, the former commander of the Americal Division, were dismissed.

424.6   17 M-16 . . . clip]   To reduce the risk of misfeeds, American soldiers often loaded only 17 or 18 rounds into a 20-round M-16 magazine.

430.11–12   catastrophe . . . March 18]   See Chronology, March–April 1970.

431.21   Thursday] April 16, 1970.

435.3   *Kent State . . . . Why*] In his afterword to *Kent State*, Michener
described the book as a collaboration with a team of researchers that included
Andrew Jones, John Hubbell, Leslie Laird, Nathan Adams, Eugene Methvin,
Mari Yoriko Sabusawa, Linda Peterson, Ben Post, Jeff Sallot, Larry Rose, Scott
Mueller, John P. Hayes, Howard Ruffner, and John Filo.

435.13   confusion on campus] The ROTC building on the Kent State
campus was destroyed by arson on the evening of Saturday, May 2, 1970, as
a large crowd of student demonstrators watched. Units of the Ohio National
Guard arrived on campus later that night, and on Sunday night, May 3, student demonstrators and Guardsmen clashed during rioting on campus and in
the town of Kent.

435.21   Satrom] LeRoy Satrom, the mayor of Kent, Ohio.

439.34   Eszterhas and Roberts] Joe Eszterhas and Michael D. Roberts,
in *13 Seconds: Confrontation at Kent State* (1970).

446.21–22   Alewitz . . . later] Alewitz, a member of the Trotskyist
Young Socialist Alliance, had been tear-gassed earlier in the confrontation and
was running toward Johnson Hall so that he could wash the irritants from his
eyes. After seeing the Guard he retreated to the fence and then passed through
a small hole in it.

450.40   the Guard] In a report issued on October 16, 1970, a special state
grand jury stated that the Guardsmen had fired their weapons "in the honest
and sincere belief that they would suffer bodily injury had they not done so"
and therefore were not subject to criminal prosecution.

451.2–4   Walker . . . Filo] Walker and Filo were Kent State students who
photographed the events of May 4. Filo was awarded the Pulitzer Prize for
Spot News Photography for his photograph of 14-year-old Mary Vecchio
kneeling beside the body of Jeffrey Miller.

459.14   'bums'] During a visit to the Pentagon on May 1, 1970, Nixon
had praised American troops in Vietnam and then said: "You know, you see
these bums, you know, blowing up the campuses."

463.4   Supreme Court ruling] *Welsh* v. *United States*.

464.19   Secretary Laird] See note 386.10–11.

464.39   Life . . . last year] The photographs appeared in *Life* on June
27, 1969.

468.4   Nixon's . . . cease-fire] In a televised address on October 7, 1970,
Nixon proposed an internationally supervised "cease-fire in place" throughout
Indochina and the convening of an Indochina peace conference.

477.37–38   Robert McNamara]   Secretary of Defense from January 1961 to February 1968.

484.21   Fulbright]   See note 144.18–19.

485.26   Galbraiths]   Galbraith, a professor of economics at Harvard, had served as U.S. ambassador to India, 1961–63.

485.27–28   Burnet Cave]   Near Burnet, Texas, about 30 miles from Johnson's childhood home.

488.33   first bombing pause]   May 13–17, 1965.

488.38   Senator Morse]   See note 141.3

489.1   Clark . . . Church]   Democratic senators Joseph Clark of Pennsylvania, Mike Mansfield of Montana, and Frank Church of Idaho.

489.2   Dobrynin]   Anatoli Dobrynin, the Soviet ambassador to the United States.

489.4   Rusk . . . Clifford]   Dean Rusk served as Secretary of State, 1961–69. Clark Clifford served as an unofficial presidential adviser before becoming Secretary of Defense in 1968.

489.7   ordered a pause]   From December 24, 1965, until January 30, 1966.

490.26   Henry Fowler]   Secretary of the Treasury, 1965–68.

491.6   Geneva Accords]   See Chronology, 1954.]

491.33   elections . . . 1967?]   The presidential and senate elections held on September 3, 1967, in which 83 percent of the registered voters were reported to have voted.

498.32   Continental Air Services]   Charter airline that flew missions on contract for the CIA and the Agency for International Development.

502.38   agency that preceded]   United States Operations Mission.

505.6–8   Vang Pao . . . country]   Vang Pao was evacuated from Laos on May 14, 1975, and later became an American citizen.

507.39   Phou Pha Thi]   Mountain, over 5,500 feet high, in northeastern Laos, 160 miles west of Hanoi. In late 1967 the U.S. air force built a secret radar installation near the summit that was used to guide aircraft bombing North Vietnam in bad weather and at night. The installation, which was supplied by helicopter and guarded by Hmong soldiers, was overrun by the North Vietnamese on March 11, 1968; 11 air force technicians were killed during the attack.

511.16   Hotel 2]   A South Vietnamese artillery base.

513.32   Wednesday]   March 24, 1971.

514.31   Brigade A]   Possibly a mistranslation of Battery A.

520.13   amphibious "duck"]   An amphibious truck equipped with a propeller and a rudder.

525.38–40   brigade commander . . . defoliant]   Brigadier General John Donaldson was accused in June 1971 of murdering six Vietnamese civilians in 1968–69; the charges were dropped in December 1971. In October 1970 *Time* magazine reported that units of the Americal Division were continuing to disperse Agent Orange despite an April 15, 1970, order suspending its use in Vietnam.

526.2   attack . . . firebase]   Fire Base Mary Ann was attacked on the night of March 27–28, 1971, by North Vietnamese sappers who infiltrated through the perimeter without being detected and then killed 30 American soldiers before withdrawing.

547.27   mercenaries . . . Asia]   American aid paid for the deployment of Thai and South Korean troops in South Vietnam.

548.10   Hué . . . hundreds]   At least 2,800 people were murdered by the Viet Cong in Hue during the Tet Offensive in 1968.

549.2   Tansonhut]   The headquarters of the South Vietnamese Joint General Staff were at Tan Son Nhut air base.

550.37   prize money]   Eddie Adams was awarded the Pulitzer Prize for Spot News Photography for his photograph of General Loan shooting the Viet Cong suspect.

563.5   Pentagon Papers]   See Chronology, June 1971.

569.4   "Guernica"-like]   Painting (1937) by Pablo Picasso, inspired by bombing of the town of Guernica during the Spanish Civil War.

574.21–22   book . . . voyage]   *History of a Voyage to the China Sea.*

580.28–29   Sûreté headquarters]   French police headquarters and prison.

594.12   pro-Kuomintang]   Supporters of the Chinese Nationalists.

596.9   "Hansel and Gretel"]   Three-act opera (1893) by Engelbert Humperdinck, with libretto by Adelheid Wette.

598.27   first coup]   The coup attempt, staged by disaffected army officers on November 11–12, 1960, failed.

599.26   Pham Xuan An]   An worked for the Reuters news agency before becoming a staff correspondent for *Time* magazine. He remained in Vietnam in 1975, and later revealed that he had served as a Viet Cong intelligence officer from 1960 onward.

607.7–8   "Freedom's . . . lose]   From "Me and Bobby McGee" by Kris Kristofferson, recorded by Janis Joplin for her album *Pearl* (1971).

608.36   tac air]   Tactical air support by fighter-bombers.

611.30   fire . . . Bastogne]   The fire base had been built by the U.S. 101st
Airborne Division and named after the Belgian town defended by the division
during the Battle of the Bulge in December 1944.

616.32   draftee division]   Conscripts served in the 11 regular infantry divisions of the South Vietnamese army, but not in the all-volunteer airborne and
marine divisions.

618.3   Carmine De Sapio]   See note 79.15.

620.30–31   end of May]   End of March.

621.34   Ky, Big Minh]   Both Vice-President Nguyen Cao Ky and Duong
Van Minh, the general who led the 1963 coup against Diem, were presidential
candidates in 1971 before they withdrew from the race and charged Thieu with
rigging the election. (Minh was called "Big Minh" by some Americans because of his six-foot height.)

632.31–32   use anti-personnel bombs]   Anti-personnel cluster bombs were
used by American aircraft over North Vietnam to attack anti-aircraft artillery
batteries and surface-to-air missile sites.

638.6   *Pravda*]   Official newspaper of the Soviet Communist Party.

641.3–4   "J'ai . . . Paris]   I have two loves / My country and Paris.

641.10   Yevtushenko]   Russian poet Yevgeny Yevtushenko.

642.13–14   Aeroflot]   Soviet airline.

643.8   *Izvestia*]   Official newspaper of the Soviet government.

645.29   San Diego]   The 1972 Republican National Convention was originally scheduled to be held in San Diego, but was moved to Miami for security
reasons.

645.30–31   Five weeks . . . McGovern]   The 1972 Democratic National
Convention was held in Miami, July 10–14, and nominated Senator George
McGovern for president.

650.17   Pete McCloskey]   Republican congressman from California who
had received 20 percent of the vote running as an anti-war candidate against
Nixon in the 1972 New Hampshire presidential primary.

652.7   Ron Kovic]   Later author of the memoir *Born on the Fourth of July*
(1976).

652.23–653.2   last year . . . fence]   On April 23, 1971, members of the Vietnam Veterans Against the War threw their medals over a fence onto the steps
of the Capitol.

671.24   name . . . birth]   The only information a prisoner of war is
obliged to give under the Geneva Convention.

672.20   father . . . admiral]   John S. McCain Jr., who served as commander of U.S. forces in the Pacific, 1968–72.

674.10–11   Vietnamese Workers Party]   Official name of the Vietnamese Communist Party.

676.6–9   Day . . . recaptured]   After his release in 1973 Day was awarded the Medal of Honor for his escape attempt and his determined resistance to interrogation.

677.34   Ernie . . . civilian pilot]   Brace flew for Air America, the CIA-owned airline that provided logistical support for anti-Communist forces in Laos.

679.13   Code of Conduct]   The Code of Conduct for Members of the Armed Forces of the United States, first issued in 1955.

679.19   Alvarez]   Everett Alvarez, a navy pilot shot down over North Vietnam on August 5, 1964.

683.37   Fort Hood Three]   Three soldiers who were court-martialed for refusing to go to Vietnam after completing basic training at Fort Hood, Texas, in June 1966. They each served two years in prison.

684.29–30   Capt. Dick Stratton]   Stratton, a naval officer, held the rank of commander when he was shot down on January 5, 1967.

685.6   press conference]   Held on March 6, 1967. A photograph of Stratton bowing at the conference appeared in *Life* on April 7, 1967.

690.23   Capt. Jeremiah Denton]   A naval officer.

693.1–2   Senator Brooke]   Edward W. Brooke, a Republican from Massachusetts.

693.6   Ramsey Clark]   Clark had served as Attorney General in the Johnson administration, 1967–69. He visited North Vietnam in July 1972.

695.11   China . . . Russia]   Nixon visited China in February 1972 and signed agreements on strategic arms during his visit to the Soviet Union in May 1972.

697.27   Kissinger . . . Hanoi]   In February 1973.

700.5   Monday]   August 6, 1973.

707.6–7   Hac . . . Panthers).]   An elite company of the 1st Division.

713.4–6   *Cambodia . . . Revolution'*]   This story appeared in *The New York Times* with a headnote that read: "The writer of the following dispatch remained in Cambodia after the American evacuation and was among the foreigners who arrived in Thailand last Saturday. His dispatches were withheld, under an agreement among all the confined correspondents, until the remaining foreigners were transported to safety yesterday."

719.23–29   Long Boret . . . executed]   Long Boret, Sisowath Sirik Matak, and Lon Non were executed by the Khmer Rouge.

720.21   Congress . . . aid]   President Gerald Ford requested $222 million in supplemental military aid for Cambodia on January 28, 1975, but Congress did not approve any additional funds.

725.38   Dith Pran]   Pran was forced to leave the French embassy compound on April 20, 1975, and was sent by the Khmer Rouge to the countryside, where he pretended to be a former Phnom Penh taxi driver. He escaped across the border into Thailand on October 3, 1979, and immigrated to the United States. Sydney Schanberg wrote about his experiences in an article, "The Death and Life of Dith Pran," published in *The New York Times Magazine* on January 20, 1980, which became the basis for the film *The Killing Fields* (1984).

740.4   Tuesday]   April 29, 1975.

744.35   Graham Martin]   U.S. ambassador to South Vietnam, 1973–75.

746.19   H. G. Summers]   Harry G. Summers Jr., later the author of *On Strategy: A Critical Analysis of the Vietnam War* (1982).

752.36   Thomas Polgar]   CIA station chief in Saigon, 1973–75.

Glossary of Military Terms

Notes on U.S. military organization appear at the end of the Glossary.

A-1] Single piston-engined fighter-bomber used by both the navy and the air force. The "Skyraider" had a maximum speed of 325 mph, was armed with four rapid-firing 20 mm. cannon, and could carry up to 8,000 pounds of bombs or air-to-ground rockets. It was manufactured in both single-seat (A-1H) and two-seat (A-1E) models, and was sometimes called a "Spad," after the World War I French biplane.

A-4] Single-seat, carrier-based jet fighter-bomber. The "Skyhawk" had a maximum speed of 670 mph, was armed with two rapid-firing 20 mm. cannon, and could carry up to 8,200 pounds of bombs.

A-6] Carrier-based jet attack aircraft. The "Intruder" had a crew of two, a cruising speed of 480 mph, and could carry up to 15,000 pounds of bombs. It was equipped with an electronic navigation and bombing system and was often used to attack targets at night or in bad weather.

AC-47] Gunship version of the C-47 transport aircraft, known as "Spooky" and "Puff." It had a crew of seven, a cruising speed of 150 mph, and was armed with three six-barreled machine guns firing bullets 7.62 mm. in diameter; each "minigun" could fire up to 6,000 rounds per minute (the aircraft carried 24,000 rounds of ammunition, as well as dozens of parachute flares for illuminating targets at night).

AD-6] Alternate designation for the A-1 Skyraider.

Air America] Charter airline covertly owned by the Central Intelligence Agency that operated in Southeast Asia from 1959 until 1976. It was especially active in providing logistical support to American-backed forces in Laos.

AK-47] Soviet rifle, also manufactured in Communist China, that fired a 7.62 mm. bullet and was capable of both semiautomatic and full automatic fire. It was fed from a 30-round magazine, had an effective range of 330 yards, and weighed 10.5 pounds when loaded. The AK-47 was increasingly used by Viet Cong main-force units after 1965 and was the standard-issue rifle of the North Vietnamese army; it proved to be a highly reliable weapon under combat conditions.

Americal] American infantry division formed in Vietnam in September 1967 and deactivated in November 1971. It was named after the Americal (from "Americans in New Caledonia") Division formed in the Southwest Pacific in 1942.

ARVN] Army of the Republic of Vietnam; the South Vietnamese army.

B-26]   Twin piston-engined medium bomber. The "Invader" had a crew of three, a cruising speed of 284 mph, was armed with six .50 caliber machine guns, and could carry up to 6,000 pounds of bombs. (Until 1948, this aircraft was designated as the A-26.)

B-40]   Soviet rocket-propelled grenade, also manufactured in Communist China. The grenade had a diameter of 82 mm. and an effective range of 150 yards; it was fired from a shoulder-carried tube launcher, and contained a shaped charge that could penetrate armor plate.

B-52]   Eight-engined jet heavy bomber. It had a crew of six, a cruising speed of 520 mph, and was armed with four .50 caliber machine guns mounted in the tail. The B-52F, used in Southeast Asia in 1965–66, could carry up to 38,000 pounds of bombs; the B-52D, used in 1966–73, up to 60,000 pounds; the B-52G, used along with the B-52D in 1972, up to 20,000 pounds. B-52 crews usually bombed from an altitude of 30,000 feet after using electronic equipment to locate their target.

B-57]   Twin-engined jet bomber. The B-57 had a crew of two, a cruising speed of 476 mph, was armed with four rapid-firing 20 mm. cannon, and could carry up to 6,000 pounds of bombs.

BAR]   Browning automatic rifle, used by American infantry during World War II as a light machine gun. It fired a .30 caliber bullet, was fed from a 20-round magazine, had an effective range of over 600 yards, and weighed 19 pounds.

C-123]   Twin piston-engined transport aircraft designed for use on short runways.

C-130]   Four-engined turboprop transport aircraft.

Carbine]   A short rifle. The American M-1 carbine, first used in World War II, was a semiautomatic weapon with a 15- or 30-round magazine; it fired a .30 caliber bullet, had an effective range of 300 yards, and weighed six pounds. Another model, the M-2, was capable of both semiautomatic and full automatic fire.

CH-53]   Transport helicopter capable of carrying up to 38 troops.

Chinook]   Twin-rotor transport helicopter that could carry 33 troops or up to 16,000 pounds of cargo.

Claymore]   American anti-personnel mine detonated from a remote position by sending an electric signal to the weapon. It fired 700 steel balls in a fan-shaped pattern with an 80° arc and had a lethal range of 50 yards.

C-rations]   American canned field rations that could be eaten hot or cold.

CS]   Tear gas.

82 mm. mortar]   Soviet mortar, also manufactured in Communist China. It fired a 6.7 pound shell 82 mm. in diameter and had a range of almost two miles (3,300 yards).

F-4]   Jet fighter and fighter-bomber used by both the navy (F-4B) and the air force (F-4C, F-4D). The "Phantom" had a crew of two, a maximum speed of 816 mph at sea level, and could carry up to 16,000 pounds of bombs. When used as an escort fighter it could carry up to four heat-seeking and four radar-guided air-to-air missiles; in 1967 air force F-4s also began carrying a rapid-firing 20 mm. cannon mounted in an external pod.

F-8]   Single-seat navy jet fighter. The "Crusader" had a maximum speed of 748 mph at sea level, was armed with four rapid-firing 20 mm. cannon and up to four heat-seeking air-to-air missiles, and could carry up to 4,000 pounds of bombs or rockets.

F-105]   Single-seat air force jet fighter-bomber. The "Thud" had a maximum speed of 839 mph at sea level, was armed with a rapid-firing 20 mm. cannon, and usually carried 6,000 pounds of bombs on missions against North Vietnam. A two-seat version was used as a "Wild Weasel" aircraft to locate and attack surface-to-air missile sites.

F-111A]   Air force jet bomber. The F-111A had a crew of two, a cruising speed of 665 mph, and could carry up to 20,000 pounds of bombs.

FAC]   Forward Air Controller. FACs directed airstrikes either from the ground or from a light airplane flying over the battlefield.

.50 caliber]   American heavy machine gun that was mounted on armored personnel carriers, tanks, and other vehicles. It fired a .50 caliber bullet and had an effective range of over 2,000 yards.

4.2-inch mortar]   U.S. mortar that fired a 24-pound shell 4.2 inches in diameter, with a maximum range of over 2.5 miles (4,500 yards).

Grease gun]   American M-3 submachine gun. It fired a .45 caliber bullet, had a 30-round magazine, an effective range of 100 yards, and weighed 10 pounds.

Howitzer]   An artillery gun capable of having its barrel elevated past 45°.

Huey]   Popular name for the UH-1 Iroquois, the most widely used helicopter of the Vietnam War. The Huey could carry 8–12 troops or 3,000 pounds of supplies into assault landing zones and was also used for medical evacuation missions; gunship versions carried a variety of weapons, including multi-barreled 7.62 mm. machine guns, multi-tubed launchers for firing 2.75-inch diameter rockets, and 40 mm. automatic grenade launchers.

Intruder]   See A-6.

L-19]   See O-1.

M-1 rifle]   Standard U.S. infantry rifle of World War II. A semiautomatic weapon, it fired a .30 caliber bullet, held eight rounds in its magazine, had an effective range of 550 yards, and weighed over nine pounds.

M-16]   American rifle firing a 5.56 mm. bullet and capable of both semiautomatic and full automatic fire. It was fed by a 20-round magazine, had an effective range of 430 yards, and weighed seven pounds. The M-16 frequently jammed under combat conditions in 1965–67, but modifications to its design, the widespread issue of cleaning kits, and improved training significantly reduced problems with the weapon after 1968.

M-48]   American tank. It weighed 52 tons, had a four-man crew, a maximum speed of 30 mph, armor with a maximum thickness of 120 mm., and was armed with a 90 mm. gun.

M-60]   American light machine gun, known as "The Pig," issued to the weapons squad of infantry platoons and usually operated by a two-man team, although it could be fired by one man. It fired a 7.62 mm. bullet, was fed by a metal belt, weighed 23 pounds, and had an effective range of 1,100 yards when used with its bipod mount. The M-60 was also used by door gunners on Huey helicopters and was often mounted on M-113 armored personnel carriers.

M-79]   Single-shot grenade launcher that fired a projectile 40 mm. in diameter. It weighed six and a half pounds and had a maximum range of 400 yards.

M-113]   Armored personnel carrier capable of transporting 11 troops. It weighed 12 tons, had a maximum speed of 40 mph, and was often armed with three machine guns. Although its armor gave protection against bullets and shell fragments, the M-113 proved vulnerable to rocket-propelled grenades and large land mines.

MACV]   Military Assistance Command Vietnam; the headquarters that commanded American forces in South Vietnam, 1962–73.

MATS]   Military Air Transport Service.

MiG]   Soviet single-seat jet fighter used for air defense by the North Vietnamese. The MiG-17 had a maximum speed of 661 mph at sea level and was armed with one 37 mm. and two 23 mm. rapid-firing cannon, while the MiG-21 had a maximum speed of 684 mph at sea level and was armed with one 30 mm. cannon and two heat-seeking air-to-air missiles; both aircraft were highly maneuverable in aerial combat.

NVA]   North Vietnamese Army.

O-1]   Single piston-engined observation plane. The O-1 had two seats, a maximum speed of 118 mph, and carried four rockets for marking targets with smoke.

105]   American howitzer that fired a 33-pound shell 105 mm. in diameter, with a maximum range of almost seven miles (12,200 yards).

122-millimeter rockets]   Soviet rocket with a 41-pound warhead 122 mm. in diameter and a maximum range of almost seven miles (12,000 yards). The rocket, launching tube, and tripod mount could be carried to its firing position and set up by a six-man crew.

130-mm]   Soviet artillery gun that fired a 74-pound shell 130 mm. in diameter, with a maximum range of almost 17 miles (29,700 yards).

155]   American howitzer that fired a 95-pound shell 155 mm. in diameter, with a maximum range of over nine miles (16,000 yards).

175]   American artillery gun that fired a 175-pound shell 175 mm. in diameter, with a range of over 20 miles (35,600 yards).

People's Self Defense Force]   South Vietnamese hamlet-based militia.

Popular Forces]   South Vietnamese village-based militia.

Regional Forces]   South Vietnamese provincial militia.

SAC]   Strategic Air Command.

SAM]   Surface-to-air missile. The Soviet SA-2 used by the North Vietnamese was a two-stage missile with a range of 25 miles and a 288-pound warhead; it could accelerate to a maximum speed of Mach 3 and was guided by a radio beam linked to a tracking radar.

Shrike]   Air-to-ground missile with a 145-pound warhead and a range of 10 miles, designed to home in on enemy radar sites.

60 mm. mortar]   U.S. mortar firing 60 mm. shell weighing 3.1 pounds, with a maximum range of over one mile (1,985 yards). The Viet Cong and North Vietnamese used a similar weapon manufactured in China with a shorter range (1,670 yards).

Skycrane]   Transport helicopter capable of carrying over 20,000 pounds of cargo in an underslung load.

Skyhawk]   See A-4.

Skyraider]   See A-1.

Swedish K]   Name for the Swedish Carl Gustav M-45 submachine gun ("kulspruta" is Swedish for "machine gun"). It fired a 9 mm. bullet, had a 36-round magazine, weighed over nine pounds, and had an effective range of over 100 yards.

T-28]   Single piston-engined fighter-bomber. The T-28 had a crew of two, a maximum speed of 346 mph, was armed with two .50 caliber machine guns, and could carry 1,800 pounds of bombs.

TAC]   Tactical Air Command.

Thompson submachine gun]   American submachine gun used in World War II. It fired a .45 caliber bullet, had a 20-round magazine, an effective range of 100 yards, and weighed 12 pounds.

U.S. ARMY AND MARINE ORGANIZATION

Platoon]   Unit of about 40 men at full strength, commanded by a second lieutenant.

Company]   Unit made up of three rifle platoons and one weapons platoon, and other troops, usually commanded by a captain. The equivalent unit in the air and armored cavalry is a troop.

Battalion]   Unit usually made up of four rifle companies, one support company, and a headquarters company, usually commanded by a lieutenant colonel. The equivalent unit in the cavalry is a squadron.

Regiment]   In the marines and the armored cavalry, a formation made up of three battalions or squadrons plus supporting troops, commanded by a colonel. During the Vietnam War army infantry battalions were identified by the names of their historic regimental affiliations, but were operationally organized into brigades.

Brigade]   Formation made up of between two and four battalions plus supporting troops, commanded by either a colonel or a brigadier general.

Division]   Formation made up of three brigades (in the marines, three regiments) plus supporting troops. American divisions in Vietnam had between 15,000 and 22,000 men and were commanded by a major general. By 1969 the U.S. had seven army and two marine divisions in Vietnam, along with four separate brigades and an armored cavalry regiment.

Index

A Shau Valley, South Vietnam, 309, 615
Abernathy, Rev. Ralph D., 359
Abrams, Gen. Creighton W., 617
Acheson, Dean, 476
Adams, Eddie, 547
Adda River (Italy), 341
Aden, 115
Adinolfi, 1st Lt. Jack, 201–2
Agency for International Development (AID), U.S., 312, 404, 497–99, 502–3, 505
Agricultural Adjustment Act, 148
Air America, 495, 498, 707
Airborne Division, South Vietnamese, 512, 619, 622, 625
Akron, Ohio, 451
Aladonia, Ohio, 392
Alewitz, Mike, 446
Alexandria, Virginia, 541
Algeria, 114–15
Algerian rifle battalions, 199
Alleg, Henri, 114
Allman, T.D., *428–34*
Alsop, Joseph, 109
Alsop, Stewart, *463–66*
Altekoester, Alois, 310
Alvarez, Everett, 679–80
Americal Division (Twenty-third Infantry), U.S., 413, 417, 525–26
American Chamber of Commerce, Saigon, 596
American Code of the Fighting Man, 112
American Friends Service Committee, 80
American Legion, 393
An Cuu, South Vietnam, 317
An Giang Province, South Vietnam, 401, 403–5
An Khe, South Vietnam, 108
An Loc, South Vietnam, 612, 613, 620, 622–23, 627
An Quang Pagoda (Saigon), 31, 546
Anatomy of Courage, The (Moran), 295

Anderson, Marian, 259
Angola, 115
Annam, 573, 575, 581
Anson, Robert, 429–31
Anton, Frank, 365–67, 370–71, 374, 376, 378, 382–84
Ap Bac, South Vietnam, 50, 53, 55
Appalachia, 106, 386, 391
Aristotle, 641
Arlen, Michael J., *235–50*
Armed Forces Radio Network, 606, 668
Armstrong Mills, Ohio, 392
Army of the Republic of Vietnam (ARVN), 60, 62, 86, 99, 108, 114–15, 188, 199, 204, 215, 320, 324–25, 349, 356, 410–11, 512–13, 519, 523–24, 528–30, 558, 565, 567, 607–9, 610–12, 613, 618, 620–21, 623, 626, 654, 667, 669, 710, 738
Arnett, Peter, *267–69*
Associated Press, 547, 735–36, 742, 744
At Ease (Eisenhower), 229
Atlanta, Georgia, 458
Atlantic Monthly, 494
Atterberry, Ed, 685–86
Aurora, Ohio, 458
Auschwitz, 345
Austin, Bill, 741–42

Bach Duc Hach, 103
Bach Thanh, 103
Baker, Col. Basil Lee, 59
Baker, Josephine, 640
Baldwin, Hanson, 137
Baltimore Sun, 500, 504, 508, 669
Ball, George W., 133–36, 138
Baltimore, Maryland, 363
Ban Co (district of Saigon), South Vietnam, 588–89
Ban Son, Laos, 495, 508
Bangkok, 214, 333
Bao Dai, Emperor, 170–72, 581, 583, 641
Bao Quoc Pagoda (Hue), 303
Barnesville, Ohio, 390

Library of Congress Cataloging-in-Publication Data

Reporting Vietnam : American journalism, 1959–1975.
    p. cm.
  Originally published as 2 vol. set: 1998.
  Includes bibliographical references and index.
  ISBN 1–883011–90–6 (pbk.)
    1. Vietnamese Conflict, 1961–1975—Press coverage—United States.
2. Journalism—United States—History—20th century.

DS559.46 .R46 2000
959.704'38—dc21

                                    99-059744

REPORTING VIETNAM